SHAWNEE HE
Selected Lineage

Shawnee Heritage II

Selected Lineages of Notable Shawnee

by
Don Greene

by Don Greene

Shawnee Heritage II

Selected Lineages of Notable Shawnee

by Don Greene

Author's Foreword

First and foremost, I want to say what a pleasure and honor it is to be able to bring this work to the people of Shawnee ancestry. From my humble and somewhat naive earliest attempts this research has grown to an apparent lifetime vision of finding all people of Shawnee blood from before the coming of the whites until the Removal.

This has proven to be quite an undertaking, more suitable for a literal host of researchers, than to one rapidly aging person. I've seen my modest list of names grow to over 30,000 entries as families expand and individuals are added and I have more than that to add in the future.

Secondly I have to defend my seemingly stiff-necked attitude towards footnotes, bibliographies and such. All this work comes, with few exceptions, from easily accessible public sources; books, lists, rolls, treaties, military and trade records, histories of many States, Counties, municipalities, areas, groups and individuals, including sources appearing daily on the Internet. The combination of information, conclusions and format presented here is solely mine however. Dedicating four or five hours in the pre-dawn hours to this work each day, I have chosen to bypass such steps that would basically only serve to eat up my limited time and let nitpickers back-track my process, while doing nothing to further my Great Work. I have attempted to include a list of important sources but you may find it less minutely detailed than you would like.

Along that line, let me give a synopsis of how I basically work. I call it a conjunctive approach in that I try to use every possible source of information available to me before making a definitive conclusion. This includes reading and re-reading Tribal histories, genealogical records of hordes of Shawnee, Native and non-Native families, Colonial histories, military records, trade records, State, County and municipal histories and family histories and stories from all everywhere and anywhere. You never know when a clue will arise that may open the door to a wealth of information, so I take in a huge gamut of material.

While absorbing all this information I watch for; first the obvious connections, as in who begat whom, secondly the obscured connections where names or dates are slightly different or the lines seem to twist or disappear and thirdly for the implied connections to the Shawnee, as in references to northern, eastern, western or southern Natives, or simply to a person that isn't the same as most of the ones in that particular material, so when I connect some such folks with the Shawnee, I begin to look at any others described in those terms.

Then, being the old hillbilly that I am, everything has to pass the common sense muster. In the simplest terms, does it make any sense when written out? I can't swallow the ideas that fifty year old women had babies or that fifteen year old boys fathered children anymore than the idea that one hundred year old men charged off into battle, so I am always resolving those types of conundrums.

In addition, I constantly on the lookout for the answers to those basic journalistic questions, who, where, when and why. Who was the person I am researching? Where did they live? When did they live there? Why did they have Shawnee blood?

Then of course comes one of the hardest part of this work, sorting out the wheat from the chaff of family stories and lore. Just because a person was called "Chief" by his family and neighbors, doesn't necessarily mean he was an actual Chief, nor does the fact that a many times removed Grandma wore her hair in braids mean she was a Native American. Likewise simply being dark-skinned, dark eyed or black-haired doesn't mean you are a Native either. You might just be a dark-skinned, black-haired descendant of Europeans for Heaven's sake! Any of this could be either a clue or a red herring.

I shouldn't even have to tell you that everyone can't be descended from a noted historical Native American, anymore than we can all be descended from a President or King – but just surfing the Internet you would think we all are.

I hope that those of you that have followed my work over the years understand that this work is always in flux, it changes when new or better information comes to hand or some new connection or relationship becomes obvious. I have found many people over the years that I at first called white only to discover later were actually a Shawnee-Metis and therefore had to go back and adjust their blood percent to reflect that knowledge. Likewise I have found some folks that I took for full-blood that also ended up being of some mixture and so had to adjust my listings to reflect that. I find it thrilling to discover who these folks actually were and hope the readers don't have any problems in finding out that you have more, or in some cases, less Shawnee ancestors than you thought.

I do this Great Work for all those of Shawnee blood in an effort to broaden our understanding of our great people and their history. If those of non-Shawnee ancestry don't like what I have done, they need not read it. It is not for them anyway. I want everyone to understand that I do not work with what I call "political" status, i.e. whether a person is designated as a Native of some sort by a government mandated, encouraged or recognized roster, list or census. I only look at the bloodline, it makes little difference to me what any government, white or Native, says a person is, political status can't change your blood. If the more anal retentive among the readers are dissatisfied with the presentation then I whole-heartedly encourage them to do the research, do the comparison of all data and reach their own conclusions for themselves.

If you are of our blood, you will likely be content with the presentation the way it is. If you are not of the blood, all the time-consuming footnotes, lists of sources, references and bibliographies in the world would probably not make you accept or appreciate it any more.

So this is for us who share the blood of the old ones, the true ancients, for those like us, those descended from the great pre-Columbian culture that spanned the bulk of what is now the United States, those people that lost that same territory to the aggression of the Europeans.

I believe it is vital for those who are of Shawnee blood to know who we were, who we became and the ways we have survived; with some forced into the zoo-like life of the reservations, with others disappearing into the fabric of other tribes and with some fading from easy view into American culture only to reappear as mountaineers, hillbillies, "holler and ridge" people, generally any isolated or nearly isolated groups near the bottom of the socio-economic ladder throughout the eastern portion of the nation but with a few nearly astounding exceptions that have risen to zenith heights among the whites.

The reader will begin to notice in this second volume that there are at least two lines of Shawnee History running through the years since the whites arrived; one more or less in the drainage of the Ohio River and the other further to the south on both sides of the Appalachian mountains. It is apparent that the two concurrent lines intersected and interacted with one another, at least it is to me, but those intersections and interactions are very poorly reflected in histories of the United States, in the wars against the natives and even in histories of the Shawnee in general. The misunderstandings and misconceptions beginning four hundred years ago are still accepted as being true with little question by anyone. I hope that in some way my Great Work can move towards correcting that blindness and all the people of Shawnee descent, from the Ohio valley, from the full extent of the Appalachians and from the south can recognize one another as being of Shawnee heritage and ancestry.

One aspect that has become obvious is the constant occurrence of what can only be called "political marriages", where the union appeared to tie two of the Historic Tribes or at least two major families together. I see it happening again and again through the years in question even though it is scarcely mentioned in most if not all histories of the Shawnee.

Another marriage related happening is the repeated marriages among the Shawnee-Metis, most living as cultural whites. In some families it amounts to hundreds of marriages, which of course distresses some of our modern folks to no end, all of those cousins marrying one another. I have come to feel that there are likely several factors involved in this situation. It may have begun as an attempt to keep "the blood" within the family but it may also involve their position in society, a socio-economic sort of thing, with those in similar circumstances marrying among themselves. Then also, it may involve what denomination of white religion they had chosen to be members of, marrying within a certain circle. More than likely all of these and some other factors as well are involved. Another repeated occurrence worth mentioning is that of whites who had been adopted by the Shawnee marrying one another after returning to the whites.

I hope with this second volume to begin to establish my thoughts on the status of the Native inhabitants of what would become the United States of America. My conclusions may vary greatly from some accepted versions of history but these conclusions are simply a matter of research, observation and correlation, based on using common sense without allowing restraints of one sort or the other to inhibit my thinking.

If a person looks at the many known facts, eliminates the fantasies of some smaller tribes and/or former enemies of the Shawnee and bases their judgment on facts and extrapolated knowledge, then it becomes clear that the predominant culture in pre-Columbian times had to be the forerunners of the five historic Shawnee Tribes, as well as the mother culture of the so-called Algonquin-speaking tribes in what is now the United States.

My personal "shorthand" can seem confusing at first but once you understand it can be followed easily. A name or term followed by a slash, "/", then a number i.e. John Smith/74 simply means that John Smith was born in 1774 and Fallen Timber/94 means the battle of Fallen Timber in 1794. I try to always list dates from the 1600's or 1800's in full but had usually dropped the "17" prefix of the dates from the 1700's due to the huge number of dates from that century. I am in the process of filling in all my shorthand notes but bear with me if I miss some along the line.

1. Each listing starts with a surname, usually their actual surname but in many cases the name of their originating ancestor, simply assigned to them by me as a surname and used to simplify the process of identifying who is descended from whom, i.e. my use of Cornstalk or Longtail as a surname.
2. This will be followed by their given or first name then by any other names this person was known by, as in "Smith, John aka White Buffalo" or such. my best estimate of their dates of birth and death and the places of both if possible.
3. Next will be a list such as "3/4th Chalakatha-Thawikila-Creek-Metis". This decodes to show that this person was three-quarters Chalakatha & Thawikila, i.e. three-fourth Shawnee, with the remaining fourth being composed of Creek & white blood. I use the term "Metis" to show that a person has some white blood since it is a French term used widely since the colonial days to indicate that a person was of mixed native & white blood, so Metis simply means a person has some white in them, however large or small it may be. If the reader wants to decipher the non-Shawnee percents they simply need to follow the family bloodline back through the ancestors to where the non-Shawnee blood, white, black or other native entered the line.
4. Their names and blood information will be followed by my best estimate of their dates of birth and death and the places of both if possible.
5. Whenever known I next list their parents, sometimes followed by siblings if pertinent or of interest or a grandparent or other ancestor if I feel it helps recognize the bloodline more clearly.
6. Next I list actions of the person, known councils, treaties etc. that their name appears on and wars, battles, raids etc. they are known to have been in or are felt to have taken part in. Along this line, I have codified some of the military actions of the Shawnee into two major groups, the Cornstalk War running from about 1755 until his assassination in 1777, portions of which were called the Shawnee War, the French-Indian War, the Pontiac War and Dunmore's War and the Blue Jacket War lasting from 1777 until 1794, including the American Revolution and what is known to most whites as Little Turtle's War despite the Shawnee being the principle war chiefs and warriors of that series of actions. The first was obviously headed by Cornstalk/1710-1777, who, despite being neglected generally by history, was the foremost opponent of the British expansion during that time period. The second was led in the most part by

Blue Jacket/1735-1808, though others played important roles in both at different times.

7   Then a spouse or spouses will be listed, followed by the known children that lived to adulthood. I call men and women that had children together husband and wife and their unions marriages even if there are no documents or papers that "officially" join them as spouses. It is just simpler for me to handle it in that fashion. I decided to usually forego adding children that died as infants or children simply because of the limits of my time and patience. It is generally unnecessary to know their names for they have no impact on the bloodline. If I feel there is an exception, like being a namesake for a grandparent, I will list them, usually with whatever the exceptional situation was, like the circumstances of their death or such.

8   At the end of some listings you may find a "See such and such" note, usually for a wife. That simply means that this name is more fully detailed under that name, usually the maiden name of a woman but perhapsit is a name that they are better known by.

In this second volume, I have taken the liberty and opportunity to use a series of appendixes to give the reader some background information on the Shawnee so that they can better understand my thinking and conclusions.

A Note on the Appendices:

Appendix 1 is Noel Schutz's Guide to Pronunciation of the Shawnee language.

Appendix 2 is a Timeline of my own construction in which I try to both follow the thread of history and juxtaposition the Shawnee within that framework. In it are many notes on the Pre-Columbian presence of Europeans in this continent, that I hope to expand upon in a later volume, as well as dates of important happenings in the Old World that I feel may have an impact on the people of this continent, like the Black Death or the rise and fall of certain societies.

Appendix 3 is a long list of names that you will find applied to the Shawnee and often used instead of Shawnee by various sources.

Appendix 4 gives you will find some lists of the Shawnee Clans as recorded at various times and for comparison the clans of some other tribes closely connected to the Shawnee.

In Appendix 5 I have listed many of the known Shawnee villages and villages of many States where Shawnee lived that I have found.

Appendix 6 is my attempt to gather together some or most of the sources that I have used in developing this work. These are the names of the authors and the titles of some of the collected works but not the titles of individual books and such.

Finally, after the appendices, there is my brief and humble biography.

In closing I want to mention just quickly this information can change. All it takes is a single discovery or epiphany and I find myself tippity-typing my little heart out, changing the listings of hundreds of folks. It has become a joke between Patty and me that the more concrete the format I put this in, the website or a book, the more likely it is that some part of it will almost instantly change. It drives me crazy but I hope the readers can understand that I change it because of my desire for accuracy. So please don't lose you mind if Grandma's percent of Shawnee blood changes a little. It is only a reflection of the latest information I have uncovered.

Don Greene
October 7, 2008

CONTENTS

Author's Forward.. 3
Chapter One   Rippling Stream/1415, Dashing Stream/1474, Running Stream/1500, Scent Flower Stream/1525, ahunsonacock-Chief Powhatan/1545, Opechan Stream/1556............... 10

Chapter Two   Straight Tail-Meaurroway/1630, Cornstalk(4)-Hokolesqua

Stream/1630, Martin Chartier/1655, Cakundawanna Straight Tail/1662, Opessa Straight Tail/1664, Fireheart-Skootekitehi-Thomas Greenwood/1641... 40

Chapter Three Paxinosa/1670, Kakawatchekee/1670, Kishacoquillas/1670, Neucheconner/1670, Tamenebuck Cornstalk/1670, Rising Sun/1685………………………….. 89

Chapter Four Cornstalk(5)-Okowellos Cornstalk/1674..................... 105

Chapter Five Savannah Tom Carpenter-Moytoy (1)/1680…………….. 133

Chapter Six Standing Turkey Cornstalk-Old Hop/1688……………. 154

Chapter Seven Peter Chartier/1690, Loyparcoweh Straight Tail/1705….. 183

Chapter Eight John Forked Tail Watts/170…………………………... 203

Chapter Nine Cornstalk (6)-Keightughqua Cornstalk/1710…………….. 235

Chapter Ten Nonhelema Cornstalk/1718 and the other Grenadier Squaws…………………………………………………….. 268

Chapter Eleven Black Fish/172, Moluntha/1710, Blue Jacket-Whirlpool Straight Tail/173, Black Hoof/173, Puckenshinwa Rising Sun/1735…………………………………………………….. 304

Chapter Twelve Tecumseh Rising Sun/1768, Lalawethika Rising Sun-the Prophet/1774…………………………………………….. 366

Chapter Thirteen Flying Cloud/1735, Black Bob/1775, the Last Chief ……. 400

APPENDIX 1: Guide to Pronoucing Shawnee……………………….. 407
APPENDIX 2: Timelane………………………………………….402
APPENDIX 3: Names for the Ancient and Historic Shawnee Tribe……….. 462
APPENDIX 4: Clans……………………………………………………….
APPENDIX 5: Villages……………………………………………………
APPENDIX 6: Sources……………………………………………………..
About the Author………………………………………………………...

CHAPTER ONE

Rippling Stream/1415

Dashing Stream/1474

Running Stream/1500

Scent Flower Stream/1525

Powhatan-Wahunsonacock/1545

Opechan/1556

Rippling Stream/1415

Stream, Rippling aka Murmuring Ripple – Chalaka born 1415 corner of VA-TN-NC-died 1495 VA – a **Chalaka Chief** from western VA, Water Clan, due to his age earlier marriages are obvious but unknown, husband about 1470 VA of **Daughter of Shawano Chief**/1455-(likely a political marriage to consolidate two of the major Shawnee Tribes in the East), other marriages obvious but unknown, father of Dashing Stream/1474-Chalaka-Shawano.

WIFE OF RIPPLING STREAM - 1470 - VA

Steam, Wife of Rippling aka **Daughter of Shawano Chief** – Shawano born about 1455 central VA-died after 1474 VA, daughter of a **Shawano Chief**, wife about 1470 VA of **Rippling Stream**/1415-Chalaka (likely a political marriage to consolidate the two major Shawnee Tribes), mother of Dashing Stream/1474-Chalaka-Shawano.

SON OF RIPPLING STREAM/1415 & DAUGHTER OF SHAWANO CHIEF/1455
Dashing Stream/1474

Stream, Dashing – Chalaka-Shawano born 1474 Lancer River VA-died 1526 VA – son of **Rippling Stream-Murmuring Ripple**/1415 & **Daughter of Shawano Chief**/1455, Water Clan, his marriage was yet another political move to bond the Chalaiwa & Shawano, husband about 1494 VA of **Scent Flower (1)**/1480-Shawano, father of Running Stream/1500 & Scent Flower Stream/1525-both Shawano-Chalaka.

WIFE 1494 VA OF DASHING STREAM

Scent Flower (1) – Shawano born 1480 VA-died after 1525 – parents unknown but likely a daughter of a **Shawano Chief** from central VA, Corn Clan Shawano, wife 1494 VA of **Dashing Stream**/1474, mother of Running Stream/1500 & Scent Flower Stream-Scent Flower (2)/1525both Shawano-Chalaka.

SON OF DASHING STREAM/1474
& SCENT FLOWER/1480
Running Stream/1500

Stream, Running – Shawano-Chalaka born 1500 VA-died 1558 VA – son of **Dashing Stream**/1474 & **Scent Flower (1)**/1480, Water Clan, relatively early death may be the result of a conflict with the whites or from a disease contracted from them, husband 1st about 1520 of **Unknown Woman**, husband 2nd 1530 VA of **Morning Flower**/1515-Shawano, children with **Unknown Woman** unknown, , father **with Flower** of Katataugh Stream/1552, Opitchapam Stream/1554 & Opechan Stream/1556-all Shawano-Chalaka (who all three went on to become Chiefs of the Pamukey on the coast).

Shawnee Heritage II

WIFE OF RUNNING STREAM

Stream, Morning Flower – Shawano born 1515 central VA-died after 1560 VA – parents unknown, Corn Clan Shawano, wife 1st 1530 at junction of the Dan & Staunton Rivers VA of **Running Stream**/1500Shawano-Chalaka, 2nd 1558 VA of **Ensenore Powhatan-Chief Morning (2)**-Powhatan born 1520-died after 1559-(son of **Chief Morning**Powhatan), mother **with Running Stream** of Katataugh Stream/1552, Opitchapam Stream/1554 & Opechan Stream/1556-all ShawanoChalaka, no known children **with Ensenore** but he becomes the adopted father of Katataugh/1552, Opitchapam/1554 & Opechan/1556.

CHILDREN OF RUNNING STREAM/1500 & MORNING FLOWER/1515

SON

Stream, Katataugh aka Katataugh Shawano – Shawano-Chalaka born 1552 VA-died after 1618 VA – son of **Running Stream**/1500 & **Morning Flower**/1517, Water Clan, brother of **Opechan**/1556 & **Opitchapam**/1554, adopted son 1560 of **Chief Morning (2)-Ensenore Powhatan**/1520, a **Chief of a Pamukey** village by 1600, husband by 1580 coast of VA of **Pamukey Woman**, children unknown.

SON

Stream, Opitchapam (1) aka Opitchapan-Opitchapam Shawano – Shawano-Chalaka born 1554 VA-died after 1618 – son of **Running Stream**/1500 & **Morning Flower**/1517, Water Clan, brother of **Opechan**/1556 & **Katataugh**/1552, adopted son 1560 of **Ensenore Powhatan-Chief Morning (2)**/1520, a **Chief of a Pamukey** village by 1600 at Cinquoateck VA, husband by 1580 coast of VA of **Pamukey Woman**, children unknown.

DAUGHTER OF DASHING STREAM/1474

& SCENT FLOWER/1480

Scent Flower Stream/1525

Stream, Scent Flower (2) – Shawano-Chalaka born 1525 VA-died 1600 VA – daughter of **Dashing Stream**/1474 & **Scent Flower (1)**/1480, Water-Corn Clan, sister of **Running Stream**/1500, aunt of **Opechan**/1556, wife 1st 1540 VA of **Ensenore Powhatan**/1520-(son of **Chief Morning**-Powhatan), (remarried when Ensenore married her sister-in-law **Morning Flower**) 2nd 1558 central VA of **Shawano Chief**/1520, 3rd 1571 VA of **Don Luis Velasco**/1530-Powhatan, mother **with Ensenore** of Wahunsonacock (**Chief Powhatan**) Powhatan/1545, Mangopeesomon Powhatan/1547, Wowincho Powhatan/1549, Itoyatin Powhatan/1551, Apachano Powhatan/1553, Kekataugh Powhatan/1555, Winsonocock Powhatan/1557-all ½ ShawanoChalaka-Powhatan, **with Shawano Chief** of Opachisco Shawano/1558, Ioutegaoan Shawano/1560, Powtianan Shawano/1562, Kecatough Shawano/1564, Opitchapan Shawano/1566, **Amopotoiske Shawano**/1568-(wife 1582 of **Chief Powhatan**/1545), Wahunsonacock Shawano/1569-all Shawano-Chalaka, **with Velasco** of Oppechancino Velasco/1571, Wereowance Velasco/1572, Cleopatra Velasco/1573, Winsonocock Velasco/1574-all ½ Shawano-Chalaka-Powhatan

HUSBANDS OF SCENT FLOWER STREAM/1525

1ST HUSBAND 1540 - COAST OF VA

Powhatan, Ensenore aka **Chief Morning (2)-Great Powhatan** – Powhatan born 1516 VA-died 1570 Jamestown VA – son of **Chief Morning** & **Powhatan Woman**, husband 1540 of **Scent Flower Stream**/1525, 2nd 1558 of her sister in law **Morning Flower (Stream)**/1517, father **with Scent Flower** of Wahunsonacock (**Chief Powhatan**) Powhatan/1545, Mangopeesomon Powhatan/1547, Wowincho Powhatan/1549, Itoyatin Powhatan/1551, Apachano Powhatan/1553, Kekataugh Powhatan/1555, Winsonocock Powhatan/1557-all ½ Shawano-Chalaka-Powhatan, **adopted father** with Morning Flower of **Kataraugh Stream**/1552, **Opitchapam Stream**/1554 & **Opechan Stream**/1556-that all become **Chiefs of the Pamukey**.

2ND HUSBAND 1558 - SOUTH-CENTRAL VA

Shawano Chief – Shawano born about 1520 central VA-**killed** 1568 VA – a **Shawano Chief** from the central VA area, early marriages & children unknown, husband 1539 VA of **Shawano Woman**/1524, husband 1558 VA of **Scent Flower Stream**/1525, father **with Shawano** of Bear Clan Chief/1540-(father of **Amoputuskee**/1576-wife 1590 of **Chief Powhatan**/1545), father **with Scent Flower** of Opachisco Shawano/1558, Ioutegaoan Shawano/1560, Powtianan Shawano/1562, Kecatough Shawano/1564, Opitchapan Shawano/1566, daughter**Amopotoiske Shawano**/1568-(wife of Chief Powhatan/1545), Wahunsonacock Shawano/1569-all Shawano-Chalaka.

3RD HUSBAND 1568 - COAST OF VA

Velasco, Don Luis – Powhatan born about 1530 VA-died after 1574 - parents unknown but related to the family of **Ensenore PowhatanChief Morning**, taken to Europe by Spanish, converted to Catholicism, returned to VA, father **with Scent Flower** of Oppechancino Velasco/1571, Wereowance Velasco/1573, Cleopatra Velasco/1572, Winsonocock Velasco/1574-all ½ Shawano-Chalaka-Powhatan.

CHILDREN OF SCENT FLOWER STREAM/1525 WITH ENSENORE POWHATAN/1520

SON

Chief Powhatan/1545
(see end of this list of children of Scent Flower for extensive listing of Chief Powhatan's Lineage)

SON

Powhatan, Mangopeesomon – ½ Shawano-Chalaka-Powhatan born 1547 near Jamestown colony VA-**killed** 1618 VA – son of **Scent Flower (2)**/1525 & **Chief Morning (2)-Ensenore**/1516-Powhatan, brother of **Chief Powhatan**/1545, a **Powhatan Chief**, killed in battle, husband 1566 VA of **Chalakatha Woman**/1551, father of Daughter of Mangopeesmon/1579-3/4th Chalakatha-Shawano-Chalaka-Powhatan(wife 1593 of her uncle **Chief Powhatan**)

SON

Powhatan, Wowincho – ½ Shawano-Chalaka-Powhatan born 1549 Powhatan village VA-died after 1580 VA - son of **Scent Flower (2)**/1525 & **Chief Morning (2)-Ensenore**/1516-Powhatan, brother of **Chief Powhatan**/1545, a **Powhatan Chief**, husband 1560 VA of **Powhatan Woman**/1546, father of Daughter of Wowincho/1580-1/4th Shawano-Chalaka-Powhatan (=wife 1595 of her uncle **Chief Powhatan**)

SON

Powhatan, Itoyatin – ½ Shawano-Chalaka-Powhatan born 1551Powhatan village VA-died 1620 Tsenacoma VA - son of **Scent Flower (2)**/1525 & **Chief Morning (2)-Ensenore**/1516-Powhatan, brother of **Chief Powhatan**/1545, a **Powhatan Chief**, husband 1570 VA of **Shawano Woman**/1555, father of Daughter of Itoyatin/1570-3/4th Shawano-Chalaka-Powhatan-(= wife 1585 of her uncle **Chief Powhatan**)

DAUGHTER

Powhatan, Apachano – ½ Shawano-Chalaka-Powhatan born 1553 near Jamestown colony VA-died before 1618 VA, daughter of **Scent Flower (2)**/1525 & **Chief Morning (2)-Ensenore**/1516-Powhatan, sister of **Chief Powhatan**/1545, wife 1575 VA of adopted brother **Opechan**/1556, mother of Daughter of Opechan/1578-3/4th Shawano-Chalaka-Powhatan -(wife 1591 of her uncle **Chief Powhatan**)

SON

Powhatan, Kekataugh - ½ Shawano-Chalaka-Powhatan born 1557 Powhatan village VA-**killed** 1622 VA – son of **Scent Flower (2)**/1525 &

Chief Morning (2)-Ensenore/1516-Powhatan, brother of **Chief Powhatan**/1545, a **Powhatan Chief**, killed in battle, husband 1576 VA of **Powhatan Woman**/1561, children unknown

SON

Powhatan, Winsonocock – ½ Shawano-Chalaka-Powhatan born 1559 Werewocomoco VA-**killed** 1618 King William Co VA – son of **Scent Flower (2)**/1525 & **Chief Morning (2)-Ensenore**/1516-Powhatan, brother of **Chief Powhatan**/1545, a **Powhatan Chief**, killed in battle, husband 1579 VA of **Powhatan Woman**/1565, children unknown

CHILDREN OF SCENT FLOWER STREAM WITH SHAWANO CHIEF/1520

SON

Shawano, Opachisco – Shawano-Chalaka born 1558 VA-**killed** by whites 1608 VA – son of **Scent Flower (2)**/1525 & **Shawano Chief**, halfbrother of **Chief Powhatan**/1545, killed in battle, wife & children unknown

SON

Shawano, Ioutegaoan – Shawano-Chalaka born 1560 VA-**killed** 1608 VA – son of **Scent Flower (2)**/1525 & **Shawano Chief**, half-brother of **Chief Powhatan**/1545, killed by whites, wife & children unknown

SON

Shawano, Powtianan – Shawano-Chalaka born 1562 Werewocomoco VA-**killed** 1618 VA – son of **Scent Flower (2)**/1525 & **Shawano Chief**, half-brother of **Chief Powhatan**/1545, a **Werewocomoco Chief** by 1590, killed by whites, husband about 1584 coast of VA of **Werewocomoco Woman**/1569, children unknown

SON

Shawano, Kecatough – Shawano-Chalaka born 1564 Cinquoateck VA died after 1608 VA – son of **Scent Flower (2)**/1525 & **Shawano Chief**, half-brother of **Chief Powhatan**/1545, a **Chief at Cinquoateck**

VA before 1600, husband about 1586 coast of VA of **Cinquoateck Woman**/1570, children unknown

SON

Shawano, Opitchapan – Shawano-Chalaka born 1566 Mattaponi VA died after 1608 VA – son of **Scent Flower (2)**/1525 & **Shawano Chief**, half-brother of **Chief Powhatan**/1545, a **Chief at Mattaponi** VA by 1600, husband about 1588 coast of VA of **Mattaponi Woman**/1572, children unknown

DAUGHTER

Shawano, **Amopotoiske** - Shawano born 1568 VA-died after 1583 - daughter of **Scent Flower (2)**/1525 & **Shawano Chief**/1520, aunt of **Amopotuskee**/1576, wife 1582 VA of her half-brother (same mother) **Chief Powhatan**/1545, mother of Pochins Powhatan/1583 – 3/4th Shawano-Chalaka-Powhatan

SON

Shawano, Wahunsonacock – Shawano-Chalaka born 1569 Powhatan VA-**killed** 1618 VA – son of **Scent Flower (2)**/1525 & **Shawano Chief**, half-brother of **Chief Powhatan**/1545, a **Powhatan Chief** by 1600, killed by whites, husband about 1589 of **Powhatan Woman**/1563, children unknown

CHILDREN OF SCENT FLOWER STREAM WITH DON LUIS VELASCO/1530

SON

Velasco, Oppechancino – ½ Shawano-Chalaka-Powhatan born 1569 VA-died 1644 Barbados – son of **Scent Flower (2)**/1525 & **Don Luis Velasco**/1530, half-brother of **Chief Powhatan**/1545, wife & children unknown

SON

Velasco, Wereowance - ½ Shawano-Chalaka-Powhatan born 1570 VA killed 1618 VA – son of **Scent Flower (2)/1525** & **Don Luis Velasco/1530**, half-brother of **Chief Powhatan/1545**, killed by whites, husband about 1592 coast of VA of **Powhatan Woman/1576**, children unknown

DAUGHTER

Velasco, Cleopatra - ½ Shawano-Chalaka-Powhatan born 1572 VA-died after 1600 – daughter of **Scent Flower (2)/1525** & **Don Luis Velasco/1530**, half-sister of **Chief Powhatan/1545**, husband & children unknown

SON

Velasco, Winsonocock - ½ Shawano-Chalaka-Powhatan born 1574 VA killed 1618 VA – son of **Scent Flower (2)/1525** & **Don Luis Velasco/1530**, half-brother of **Chief Powhatan/1545**, killed by whites, husband about 1594 coast of VA of **Powhatan Woman/1579**, children unknown

1ST SON OF SCENT FLOWER STREAM/1525 & ENSENORE POWHATAN/1516 Powhatan-Wahunsonacock/1545

Powhatan, Chief aka **Wahunsonacock Powhatan** – ½ ShawanoChalaka-Powhatan born 1545 on James River VA-**killed** 1618 VA - son of **Scent Flower (2)/1525** & **Chief Morning (2)-Ensenore/1516**Powhatan, brother of **Mangopeesomon/1547**, **Wowincho/1549**, **Itoyatin/1551**, sister **Apachano/1553**, adoptive brother 1560 of **Katataugh/1552**, **Opitchapam/1554** & **Opechan/1556**-all Shawano-Chalaka that become **Chiefs of the Pamukey**, leader of 1st AngloPowhatan War/1607 (so many marriages are simply for political purposes with each wife coming from a different village or band within the nearby area with which Chief Powhatan needed to tighten his relationship; he did so by becoming part of their family through marriage to a girl from within the village or group, including marriages to his own nieces, to keep his own brothers aligned with him; the repetition of some of the names could mean that they are more like titles than names and many of the names of the wives are probably more likely names of their bands or villages & might better be written "Woman of Ponnoiske", etc.), husband 1st 1564 VA of **Ponnoiske**/1551-Quiquocohannock, 2nd 1570 VA of **Ottermiske**/1556, 3rd 1571 VA of **Appomosiscut**/1557, 4th 1572 VA of **Appimmonoiske**/1558-Tauxenent, 5th 1574 VA of **Attossocomiske**/1560, 6th 1575 VA of **Oweroughwough**/1561, 7th 1576 VA of Nonoma Cornstalk/1562-Wind Clan Chalakatha, 8th 1578 VA of **Ottopomtacke**/1564, 9th 1579 VA of **Ortoughnoiske**/1565, 10th 1581 VA of **Uttopomtacke**/1566Uttamussamacoma, 11th 1582 VA of his half-sister (same mother) Amopotoiske Bear Clan/**1567-Shawano**, 12th 1583 VA of **Artoughnoiske**/1569, 13th 1584 VA of **Wahunseeacawh**/1570Secacawoni, 14th 1585 VA of his niece a Daughter of (his brother) Itoyatin Powhatan/1570-3/4th Shawano-Chalaka-Powhatan, 15th 1586 VA of **Matatiske**/1571-Winganuske, 16th 1587 VA of **Itoyah Opirhapan**/1573-Sasawpen, 17th 1588 VA of **Ashetoiske**/1574, 18th 1589 VA of **Nonoma Winganuske**/1574, 19th 1590 VA of Amopotuskee Bear Clan/**1576-Shawano-**(niece of Amopotoiske/1568-daughter of her half-brother Bear Clan Chief/**1540**), 20th 1591 VA of **Queen Winganuske**/1576, 21st 1592 VA of his niece a Daughter of (his sister & his adopted brother) Opechan Stream/1578-3/4th Shawano-ChalakaPowhatan, 22nd 1593 VA of his niece a Daughter of (his brother) Mangopeesomon Powhatan/1579-3/4th Chalakatha-Shawano-Chalaka-Powhatan, 23rd 1594 VA of **Oholase**/1580-Quiquoghcohannock, 24th 1595 VA of his niece a Daughter of (his brother) Wowincho Powhatan/1580-1/4th Shawano-Chalaka-Powhatan , father **with Ponnoiske** of Nanatahoack Powhatan/1566, Mehta Powhatan/1568, Tahacoope Quiquocohannock Powhatan (1)/1570, **with Ottermiske** of Tomoco Powhatan/1571, **with Appomosiscut** of Mantequos Powhatan/1572, **with Appimmoiske** of Taux Powhatan/1573, **with Attossocomiske** of Parahunt Powhatan/1575, **with Oweroughwaugh** of Namontack Powhatan/1576-all ¼th Shawano-Chalaka-Powhatan, with Nonoma Cornstalk **(1)**/1577-3/4th Chalakatha-Shawano-

ChalakaPowhatan, **with Ottopomtacke** of Quimca
Powhatan/1579,**with Ortoughnoiske** of Pochins Powhatan/1580, **with Uttopomtacke** of
Parahunt Powhatan/1581-all ¼th Shawano-Chalaka-Powhatan, with
Amopotoiske Bear Clan of Pochins Powhatan/1583-3/4th
ShawanoChalaka-Powhatan, **with Artoughnoiske** of Secotin
Powhatan/1584, **with Wahunseeacawh** of Opachankeno
Powhatan/1585-both ¼th Shawano-Chalaka-Powhatan, with **Daughter of Itoyatin** of Nataquous
Powhatan/1586 & Mehtafe Powhata/1588-1/2 Shawano-
ChalakaPowhatan, **with Matatiske** of Matachanna Powhatan/1587, Parahunt
Powhatan/1589, Mantaquos Powhatan/1591, Taux Powhatan/1593,
Pochins Powhatan/1595, Tahacope Powhatan/1597, Cleopatra
Powhatan/1599, Namontack Powhatan/1601-all ¼th Shawano-Chalaka-
Powhatan, **with Opirhapan** of Pamouic Powhatan/1588 & Nantquos
Powhatan/1590-1/4th Shawano-Chalaka-Powhatan, **with Ashetoiske** of
Matachanna Powhatan/1589, **with Nonoma Winganuske** of Tatacoope
Powhatan/1589, Pochin Powhatan/1591, Matachanna Powhatan/1593,
Mantaquos Powhatan/1594, Matoaka-Pocahontas Powhatan/1595,
Pochins Powhatan/1599-all ¼th Shawano-Chalaka-Powhatan, **with Amopotuskee Bear Clan** of Tatacoope the Shawano/1590, Taux the
Shawano/1592, Pochins the Shawano/1594, Nantaquas the
Shawano/1596, Parahunt the Shawano/1598, Cleopatra the
Shawano/1602-3/4th Shawano-Chalaka-Powhatan, **with Queen Winganuske** of Secotin Powhatan/1592, Pamouic Powhatan/1594,
Cleopatra Powhatan/1596, Nantaquas Powhatan/1598-all ¼th
Shawano-Chalaka-Powhatan, with **Daughter of Opechan** of
Powcanoe Powhatan/1591 & Nataquos Powhatan/1593-both 5/8th
Shawano-Chalaka-Powhatan, with **Daughter of Mangopeesomon** of
Mahtafe Powhatan/1594-1/2 Chalakatha-Shawano-Chalaka-Powhatan,
with Oholase of Tahacoope Quiquoghcohannock Powhatan/1595-1/4th
Shawano-Chalaka-Powhatan, with **Daughter of Wowincho** of
Namontack Powhatan/1596, Quimeca Powhatan/1598, Tomoco
Powhatan/1600-all 7/16th Shawano-Chalaka-Powhatan

WIVES OF CHIEF POWHATAN/1545

WIFE 1564 - VA

Ponnoiske - Quiquocohannock born 1551 Surry Co VA-died after 1600, wife 1564 VA of **Chief Powhatan**/1545, mother of Nanatahoack Powhatan/1566, Mehta Powhatan/1568, Tahacoope Quiquocohannock Powhatan (1)/1570

WIFE 1570 - VA

Ottermiske – Ottachugh born 1556 Lancaster Co VA-died after 1591, wife 1570 VA of **Chief Powhatan**/1545, mother Tomoco Powhatan/1571

WIFE 1571 - VA

Appomosiscut – Pamukey born 1557 King William Co VA-died after 1600, wife 1571 VA of **Chief Powhatan**/1545, mother Mantequos Powhatan/1572

WIFE 1572 - VA

Appimmonoiske – Tauxenent born about 1558 Fairfax Co VA-died after 1573 – wife 1572 of **Chief Powhatan**/1545, mother Taux Powhatan/1573

WIFE 1574 - VA

Attossocomiske – Sockobeck born 1560 King George Co VA-died after 1575, wife 1574 VA of **Chief Powhatan**/1545, mother Parahunt Powhatan/1575

WIFE 1575 - VA

Oweroughwough – Werawahon born about 1561 New Kent Co VA died after 1576, wife 1575 VA of **Chief Powhatan**/1545, mother Namontack Powhatan/1576

WIFE 1576 - CENTRAL VA

Cornstalk, Nonoma (1) aka Daughter of Cornstalk-Nonoma Wind Clan (1) - Chalakatha born 1562 central VA-died after 1580 - daughter of **Chief Cornstalk (1)**/1537-Wind Clan Chalakatha & **Chalakatha**

Woman/1540, Wind Clan, wife 1576 VA of **Chief Powhatan**/1545, mother of **Cornstalk (2)-Cornstalk Powhatan**/1577-3/4th Chalakatha-Shawano-Chalaka-Powhatan

WIFE 1578 - VA

Ottopomtacke – Potomac born about 1564 Stafford Co VA-died after 1579, wife 1578 VA of **Chief Powhatan**/1545, mother Quimca Powhatan/1579

WIFE 1579 - VA

Ortoughnoiske – born about 1565 VA-died after 1580, wife 1579 VA of **Chief Powhatan**/1545, mother Pochins Powhatan/1580

WIFE 1581 - VA

Uttopomtacke – Uttamussamacoma born 1566 Uttamussamacoma Westmoreland Co VA-died after 1581, wife 1581 VA of **Chief Powhatan**/1545, mother Parahunt Powhatan/1581

WIFE 1582 - CENTRAL VA

Shawano, Amopotoiske - Shawano born 1568 VA-died after 1583 - daughter of **Scent Flower (2)**/1525 & **Shawano Chief**/1520, aunt of **Amopotuskee**/1576-(half-sister of her father Bear Clan Chief/1540), wife 1582 VA of her half-brother (same mother) **Chief Powhatan**/1545, mother of Pochins Powhatan/1583 – 3/4th Shawano-Chalaka-Powhatan

WIFE 1583 - VA

Artoughnoiske – born about 1569 VA-died after 1584, wife 1583 VA of **Chief Powhatan**/1545, mother of Secotin Powhatan/1584

WIFE 1584 - VA

Wahunseeacawh – Secacawoni born about 1570 Secacawoni Northumberland Co VA-died after 1585, wife 1584 VA of **Chief Powhatan**/1545, mother Opachankeno Powhatan/1585

WIFE 1585 - VA

Itoyatin, Daughter of aka Nonoma Itoyatin – 3/4th Shawano-Chalaiwa-

Powhatan born 1570 VA-died after 1586 – daughter of **Itoyatin Powhatan**/1551 & **Shawano Woman**/1555, wife 1585 VA of her uncle **Chief Powhatan**/1545, mother of Nataquous Powhatan/1586 & Mehtafe Powhata/1588

WIFE 1586 - VA

Winganuske, Matatiske – Winganuske born 1571 VA-died after 1603, daughter of **Chief Winganuske**, sister of **Nonoma**/1574 & **Queen**/1576, wife 1586 VA of **Chief Powhatan**/1545, mother of Matachanna Powhatan/1587, Parahunt Powhatan/1589, Mantaquos Powhatan/1591, Taux Powhatan/1593, Pochins Powhatan/1595, Tahacope Powhatan/1597, Cleopatra Powhatan/1599, Namontack Powhatan/1601

WIFE 1587 - VA

Opirhapan, Itoyah – Sasawpen born about 1572 Sasawpen VA-died after 1590, wife 1587 VA of **Chief Powhatan**/1545, mother of Pamouic Powhatan/1588 & Nantquos Powhatan/1590

WIFE 1588 - VA

Ashetoiske – born about 1574 VA-died after 1589, wife 1588 VA **of Chief Powhatan**/1545, mother of Matachanna Powhatan/1589

WIFE 1589 - VA

Winganuske, Nonoma aka Daughter of Winganuske – born about 1774 VA-died after 1600, daughter of **Chief Winganuske**, sister of **Matatiske**/1571 & **Queen**/1576, wife 1589 VA of **Chief Powhatan**/1545, mother of Tatacoope Powhatan/1589, Pochin Powhatan/1591, Matachanna Powhatan/1593, Mantaquos Powhatan/1594, Matoaka-**Pocahontas** Powhatan/1595, Pochins Powhatan/1599

WIFE 1590 - CENTRAL VA

Shawano, Amopotuskee – Bear Clan Shawano born 1576 Shenandoah valley VA-died after 1604, daughter of **Bear Clan Chief**/1540-Shawano, niece of **Amopotoiske**/1567-(half-sister of her father), wife 1590 VA of

Chief Powhatan/1545, mother of Tatacoope the Shawano/1590, Taux the Shawano/1592, Pochins the Shawano/1594, Nantaquas the Shawano/1596, Parahunt the Shawano/1598, Cleopatra the Shawano/1602

WIFE 1591 - VA

Winganuske, Queen – born about 1576 VA-died after 1622 VA, daughter of **Chief Winganuske**, sister of **Matatiske**/1571 & **Nonoma**/1574, wife 1591 VA of **Chief Powhatan**/1545, mother of Secotin Powhatan/1592, Pamouic Powhatan/1594, Cleopatra Powhatan/1596, Nantaquas Powhatan/1598

WIFE 1592 - VA

Opechan, Daughter of aka Nonoma Opechan – 3/4th ShawanoChalaiwa-Powhatan born 1576-died after 1596 – daughter of **Opechan**/1556 & **Apachano Powhatan**/1553, 21st 1590 VA wife of her uncle **Chief Powhatan**/1545, mother of Powcanoe Powhatan/1591 & Nataquos Powhatan/1593

WIFE 1593 - VA

Mangopeesomon, Daughter of aka Nonoma Mangopeesomon - 3/4th Chalakatha-Shawano-Chalaka-Powhatan born 1579 VA-died after 1592 – daughter of **Mangopeesomon Powhatan**/1547 & **Chalakatha Woman**/1551, wife 1593 VA of her uncle **Chief Powhatan**/1545, mother of Mahtafe Powhatan/1594

WIFE 1594 - VA

Oholase - Quiquocohannock born about 1580 Quiquocohannock Surry Co VA-died after 1595, wife 1594 VA of **Chief Powhatan**/1545, mother of Tahacoope Quiquoghcohannock Powhatan/1595

WIFE 1595 - VA

Wowincho, Daughter of aka Nonoma Wowincho – 1/4th Shawano-Chalaka-Powhatan born 1580 VA-died after 1606 – daughter of **Wowincho Powhatan**/1547 & **Powhatan Woman**/1551, wife 1595 VA of her uncle **Chief Powhatan**/1545, mother of Namontack Powhatan/1596, Quimeca Powhatan/1598, Tomoco Powhatan/1600

CHILDREN OF CHIEF POWHATAN/1545
BY PONNOISKE/1551-QUIQUOCOHANNNOCK

SON

Powhatan, Nanatahoack – 1/4th Shawano-Chalaka-Powhatan born 1566 VA-died after 1586 – son of **Chief Powhatan**/1545 & **Ponnoiske**/1551Quiquoghcohannock, wife & children unknown

SON

Powhatan, Mehta – 1/4th Shawano-Chalaka-Powhatan born 1568 VAdied after 1588 – son of **Chief Powhatan**/1545 & **Ponnoiske**/1551Quiquoghcohannock, wife & children unknown

SON
Powhatan, Tahacoope Quiquocohannock – 1/4th Shawano-ChalakaQuiquoghcohannock-Powhatan born 1570 VA-died after 1590 – son of **Chief Powhatan**/1545 & **Ponnoiske**/1551-Quigoughcohannock, wife & children unknown

CHILDREN OF CHIEF POWHATAN/1545
BY OTTERMISKE/1556

SON

Powhatan, Tomoco – 1/4th Shawano-Chalaka-Powhatan born 1571 VAdied after 1600 – son of **Chief Powhatan**/1545 & **Ottermiske**/1556, wife & children unknown

CHILDREN OF CHIEF POWHATAN/1545
BY APPOMOSISCUT/1557

SON

Powhatan, Mantequos (1) - 1/4th Shawano-Chalaka-Powhatan born 1572 VA-died after 1600 – son of **Chief Powhatan**/1545 & **Appomosiscut**/1557, wife & children unknown

CHILDREN OF CHIEF POWHATAN/1545 BY APPIMMONOISKE/1558-TAUXENENT

SON

Powhatan, Taux (1) - 1/4th Shawano-Chalaka-Tauxenent-Powhatan born 1573 VA-died after 1600 – son of **Chief Powhatan**/1545 & **Appimmoiske**/1558-Tauxenent, wife & children unknown

CHILDREN OF CHIEF POWHATAN/1545 BY ATTOSSOCOMISKE/1560

SON

Powhatan, Parahunt (1) - 1/4th Shawano-Chalaka-Powhatan born 1575 VA-died after 1600 – son of **Chief Powhatan**/1545 & **Attossocomiske**/1560, wife & children unknown

CHILDREN OF CHIEF POWHATAN/1545 BY OWEROUGHWOUGH/1561

SON

Powhatan, Namontack (1) – 1/4th Shawano-Chalaka-Powhatan born 1576 VA-died after 1600 – son of **Chief Powhatan**/1545 & **Oweroughwough**/1561, wife & children unknown

CHILDREN OF CHIEF POWHATAN/1545

BY NONOMA CORNSTALK/1562-CHALAKATHA

SON

Powhatan, Cornstalk Wind Clan aka **Cornstalk (2)** – 3/4th ChalakathaShawano-Chalaka-Powhatan born 1577 VA-died after 1635 – son of **Chief Powhatan**/1545 & **Nonoma Cornstalk**/1562-Chalakatha, Wind Clan Chalakatha, husband of **Chalakatha Woman**/1581, father of Cornstalk Wind Clan (2)-Cornstalk (3)/1598-7/8th ChalakathaShawano-Chalaka-Powhatan

CHILDREN OF CHIEF POWHATAN/1545
BY OTTOPOMTACKE/1564

SON

Powhatan, Quimca -1/4th Shawano-Chalaka-Powhatan born 1579 VA died after 1600 – son of **Chief Powhatan**/1545 & **Otterpomtacke**/1564, wife & children unknown

CHILDREN OF CHIEF POWHATAN/1545
BY ORTOUGHNOISKE/1565

SON

Powhatan, Pochins (1) - 1/4th Shawano-Chalaka-Powhatan born 1580 VA-died after 1600 - son of **Chief Powhatan**/1545 & **Ortoughnoiske**/1565, wife & children unknown

CHILDREN OF CHIEF POWHATAN/1545
BY UTTOPOMTACKE/1566-UTTAMSSAMACOMA

SON

Powhatan, Parahunt (2) - 1/4th Shawano-Chalaka-Powhatan born 1581

VA-died after 1600 – son of **Chief Powhatan**/1545 & **Uttopomtacke**/1566, wife & children unknown

CHILDREN OF CHIEF POWHATAN/1545
BY AMOPOTOISKE BEAR CLAN/1567-SHAWANO
SON

Powhatan, Pochins (2) – 3/4th Shawano-Chalaka-Powhatan born 1583 VA-died after 1603 – son of **Chief Powhatan**/1545 & **Amopotpiske Bear Clan**/1567-Shawano, Bear Clan Shawano, wife & children unknown

CHILDREN OF CHIEF POWHATAN/1545
BY ARTOUGHNOISKE/1569
SON

Powhatan, Secotin (1) - 1/4th Shawano-Chalaka-Powhatan born 1584 VA-died after 1604 – son of **Chief Powhatan**/1545 & **Artoughnoiske**/1569, wife & children unknown

BY WAHUNUNSEEACAWH/1570-SECACAWONI
SON

Powhatan, Opachankeno - 1/4th Shawano-Chalaka-Powhatan born 1584 VA-died after 1604 – son of **Chief Powhatan**/1545 & **Wahunseeacawh**/1570, namesake of adopted brother **Opechan Stream-Opechanako**/1556, wife & children unknown

BY DAUGHTER OF ITOYATIN POWHATAN/1570
DAUGHTER

Powhatan, Nataquous (1) – ½ Shawano-Chalaka-Powhatan born 1586 VA-killed 1607 VA – daughter of **Chief Powhatan**/1545 & **Nonoma-**

Daughter of Itoyatin Powhatan/1570, husband & children unknown

SON

Powhatan, Mehtafe Powhatan/1588-1/2 Shawano-Chalaka-Powhatan born 1588 VA-died after 1606 – son of **Chief Powhatan**/1545 & **Nonoma-Daughter of Itoyatin**/1570, wife & children unknown

BY MATATISKE WINGANUSKE/1571

DAUGHTER

Powhatan, Matachanna (1) – 1/4th Shawano-Chalaka-Powhatan born 1587 VA-died after 1601 – daughter of **Chief Powhatan**/1545 & **Matatiske**/1571-Winganuske, husband & children unknown

SON

Powhatan, Parahunt (3) – 1/4th Shawano-Chalaka-Powhatan born 1589 VA-**killed** 1607 VA – son of **Chief Powhatan**/1545 & **Matatiske**/1571-Winganuske, killed by whites, wife & children unknown

SON

Powhatan, Mantequos (2) – 1/4th Shawano-Chalaka-Powhatan born 1591 VA-**killed** 1607 VA – son of **Chief Powhatan**/1545 & **Matatiske**/1571-Winganuske, killed by whites, died unmarried

SON

Powhatan, Taux (2) – 1/4th Shawano-Chalaka-Powhatan born 1593 VAdied after 1618 – son of **Chief Powhatan**/1545 & **Matatiske**/1571Winganuske, wife & children unknown

SON

Powhatan, Pochins (3) – 1/4th Shawano-Chalaka-Powhatan born 1597 VA-died after 1618 – son of **Chief Powhatan**/1545 & **Matatiske**/1571Winganuske, wife & children unknown

SON

Powhatan, Tahacope – 1/4th Shawano-Chalaka-Powhatan born 1599

VA-died after 1618 – son of **Chief Powhatan**/1545 & **Matatiske Winganuske**/1571, wife & children unknown

DAUGHTER

Powhatan, Cleopatra (2) – 1/4th Shawano-Chalaka-Powhatan born 1599 VA-died after 1615 – daughter of **Chief Powhatan**/1545 & **Matatiske**/1571-Winganuske, husband & children unknown

SON

Powhatan, Namontack (3) – 1/4th Shawano-Chalaka-Powhatan born 1603 VA-died after 1622 – son of **Chief Powhatan**/1545 & **Matatiske**/1571-Winganuske, wife & children unknown

BY ITOYAH OPIRHAPAN/1573-SASAWPEN

SON

Powhatan, Pamouic (1) – 1/4th Shawano-Chalaka-Powhatan born 1588 VA-**killed** 1607 VA – son of **Chief Powhatan**/1545 & **Itoyah Opirhapan**/1573, killed by whites, died unmarried

DAUGHTER

Powhatan, Nantquous – 1/4th Shawano-Chalaka-Powhatan born 1590 VA-died after 1605 – daughter of **Chief Powhatan**/1545 & **Itoyah Opirhapan**/1573, husband & children unknown

BY ASHETOISKE/1574

DAUGHTER

Powhatan, Matachanna (2) – 1/4th Shawano-Chalaka-Powhatan born 1589 VA-died after 1603 – daughter of **Chief Powhatan**/1545 & **Ashetoiske**/1574, husband & children unknown

BY NONOMA-DAUGHTER OF WINGANUSKE/1574

SON

Powhatan, Tatacoope – 1/4th Shawano-Chalaka-Powhatan born 1589 VA-**killed** 1607 VA – son of **Chief Powhatan**/1545 & **Nonoma**/1574Winganuske, killed by whites, died unmarried

SON

Powhatan, Pochin – 1/4th Shawano-Chalaka-Powhatan born 1589 VAdied after 1607 – son of **Chief Powhatan**/1545 & **Nonoma**/1574Winganuske, wife & children unknown

DAUGHTER

Powhatan, Matachanna (3) – 1/4th Shawano-Chalaka-Powhatan born 1593 VA-died after 1613 – daughter of **Chief Powhatan**/1545 & **Nonoma**/1574-Winganuske, well known for "frolicking" with the white men of the fort-colony along with her sister **Matoaka**/1595, husband & children unknown

SON

Powhatan, Mantequos – 1/4th Shawano-Chalaka-Powhatan born 1594 VA-died after 1614 VA – son of **Chief Powhatan**/1545 & **Nonoma**/1574-Winganuske, wife & children unknown

DAUGHTER

Powhatan, Matoaka aka **Pocahontas-Little Frolic**-Little Wanton-Lady Rebecca Rolfe – 1/4th Shawano-Chalaka-Powhatan born 1595 VA-died after 1613 – daughter of **Chief Powhatan**/1545 & **Nonoma Winganuske**/1574, well know for "frolicking" with the white men of the fort-colony along with her sister **Matachanna**/1593, wife 1st 1610 VA of **Kokum**/1590-Powhatan, 2nd 1614 VA of **John Rolfe**/1585-white, any children/1610-1614 **with Kokum** unknown, mother **with Rolfe** of Thomas Rolfe/1615-1/8th Shawano-Chalaka-Powhatan-Metis

SON

Powhatan, Pochins (4) – 1/4th Shawano-Chalaka-Powhatan born 1599 VA-died after 1618 – son of **Chief Powhatan**/1545 & **Nonoma**/1574-Winganuske, wife & children unknown

BY AMOPOTUSKEE - BEAR CLAN/1576 - SHAWANO

SON

Powhatan, Tatacoope the Shawano – 3/4th Shawano-Chalaka-Powhatan born 1590 VA-died after 1610 – son of **Chief Powhatan**/1545 & **Amopotuskee Bear Clan**/1576-Shawano, Bear Clan Shawano, wife & children unknown

SON

Powhatan, Taux the Shawano – 3/4th Shawano-Chalaka-Powhatan born 1592 VA-died after 1610 – son of **Chief Powhatan**/1545 & **Amopotuskee Bear Clan**/1576-Shawano, Bear Clan Shawano, wife & children unknown

SON

Powhatan, Pochins the Shawano – 3/4th Shawano-Chalaka-Powhatan born 1594 VA-died after 1614 – son of **Chief Powhatan**/1545 & **Amopotuskee Bear Clan**/1576-Shawano, Bear Clan Shawano, wife & children unknown

DAUGHTER

Powhatan, Nantaquas the Shawano – 3/4th Shawano-Chalaka-Powhatan born 1596 VA-died after 1614 – daughter of **Chief Powhatan**/1545 & **Amopotuskee Bear Clan**/1576-Shawano, Bear Clan Shawano, husband & children unknown

SON

Powhatan, Parahunt the Shawano – 3/4th Shawano-Chalaka-Powhatan born 1598 VA-**killed** 1618 VA – son of **Chief Powhatan**/1545 & **Amopotuskee Bear Clan**/1576-Shawano, Bear Clan Shawano, killed by the whites, died unmarried

DAUGHTER

Powhatan, Cleopatra (3) aka **Cleopatra the Shawano** – 3/4th ShawanoChalaka-Powhatan born 1602 near Jamestown colony VA-died 1680 VA – daughter of **Chief Powhatan**/1545 & **Amopotuskee Bear Clan**/1585Shawano, wife 1618 VA of her adopted uncle **Opechan**/1556-Shawano-(adopted Pamukey), mother of Nicketti Opechan/1624 & Hokolesqua Opechan-Cornstalk (4)/1628-both 7/8th Shawano-Chalaka-Powhatan

BY QUEEN WINGANUSKE/1576

SON

Powhatan, Secotin (2) – 1/4th Shawano-Chalaka-Powhatan born 1592 VA-died after 1613 – son of **Chief Powhatan**/1545 & **Queen Winanuske**/1576, wife & children unknown

SON

Powhatan, Pamouic (2) – 1/4th Shawano-Chalaka-Powhatan born 1594 VA-died after 1613 – son of **Chief Powhatan**/1545 & **Queen Winanuske**/1576, wife & children unknown

DAUGHTER

Powhatan, Cleopatra (1) – 1/4th Shawano-Chalaka-Powhatan born 1596 VA-died after 1613 – daughter of **Chief Powhatan**/1545 & **Queen Winanuske**/1576, husband & children unknown

DAUGHTER

Powhatan, Nantaquas – 1/4th Shawano-Chalaka-Powhatan born 1598 VA-died after 1614 – daughter of **Chief Powhatan**/1545 & **Queen Winganuske**/1576, husband & children unknown

BY DAUGHTER OF OPECHAN STREAM/1578

SON

Powhatan, Powcanoe – 5/8th Shawano-Chalaka-Powhatan born 1591 VA-**killed** 1618 VA – son of **Chief Powhatan**/1545 & **Daughter of Opechan**/1576, killed by whites, apparently died unmarried

DAUGHTER

Powhatan, Nataquous (2) - 5/8th Shawano-Chalaka-Powhatan born 1593 VA-died after 1607 – daughter of **Chief Powhatan**/1545 & **Daughter of Opechan**/578, husband & children unknown

BY DAUGHTER OF MANGOPEESOMON POWHATAN/1579

SON

Powhatan, Mahtafe - 1/2 Chalakatha-Shawano-Chalaka-Powhatan born 1594 VA-**killed** 1618 VA – son of **Chief Powhatan**/1545 & his niece **Daughter of Mangopeesomon Powhatan**/1579, killed in battle, wife & children unknown

CHILDREN OF CHIEF POWHATAN/1545 BY OHOLASE/1580-QUIQUOGHCOHANNOCK

SON

Powhatan, Tahacoope Quiquoghcohannock - 1/4th Shawano-ChalakaQuiquoghcohannock-Powhatan born 1595 VA-died after 1613 – son of **Chief Powhatan**/1545 & **Oholase**/1580-Quigoughcohannock, wife & children unknown

BY DAUGHTER OF WOWICHO POWHATAN/1580

SON

Powhatan, Namontack (2) - 7/16th Shawano-Chalaka-Powhatan born 1596 VA-died after 1616 – son of **Chief Powhatan**/1545 & **Daughter of Wowincho**/1580, wife & children unknown

SON

Powhatan, Quimeca (2) - 7/16th Shawano-Chalaka-Powhatan born 1598 VA-**killed** 1618 VA – son of **Chief Powhatan**/1545 & **Daughter of Wowincho**/1580, killed in battle, died unmarried

SON

Powhatan, Tomoco - 7/16th Shawano-Chalaka-Powhatan born 1600 VA died after 1618 – son of **Chief Powhatan**/1545 & **Daughter of Wowincho**/1580, wife & children unknown

NIECES OF CHIEF POWHATAN

DAUGHTER OF MANGOPESOMON POWHATAN & CHALAKATHA WOMAN

Powhatan, Daughter of Mangopeesomon aka Nonoma Mangopeesomon - 3/4th Chalakatha-Shawano-Chalaka-Powhatan born 1579 VA-died after 1592 – daughter of **Mangopeesomon Powhatan**/1547 & **Chalakatha Woman**/1551, wife 1593 VA of her uncle **Chief Powhatan**/1545, mother of Mahtafe Powhatan/1594-1/2 Chalakatha-Shawano-Chalaka-Powhatan

DAUGHTER OF WOWICHO POWHATAN & POWHATAN WOMAN

Powhatan, Daughter of Wowincho aka Nonoma Wowincho – 1/4th Shawano-Chalaka-Powhatan born 1580 VA-died after 1606 – daughter of **Wowincho Powhatan**/1547 & **Powhatan Woman**/1551, wife 1595 VA of her uncle **Chief Powhatan**/1545, mother of Namontack Powhatan/1596, Quimeca Powhatan/1598, Tomoco Powhatan/1600-all 7/16th Shawano-Chalaka-Powhatan

DAUGHTER OF ITOYATIN POWHATAN & SHAWANO WOMAN

Powhatan, Daughter of Itoyatin aka Nonoma Itoyatin – 3/4th Shawano-Chalaka-Powhatan born 1570 VA-died after 1586 – daughter of **Itoyatin Powhatan**/1551 & **Shawano Woman**/1555, wife 1585 VA of her uncle **Chief Powhatan**/1545, mother of Nataquous Powhatan/1586 & Mehtafe Powhatan/1588-1/2 Shawano-Chalaka-Powhatan

DAUGHTER OF APACHANO POWHATAN & OPECHAN STREAM

Opechan, Daughter of aka Nonoma Opechan – 3/4th Shawano-ChalakaPowhatan born 1576-died after 1596 – daughter of **Opechan**/1556 & **Apachano Powhatan**/1553, 21st 1590 VA wife of her uncle **Chief Powhatan**/1545, mother of Powcanoe Powhatan/1591 & Nataquous Powhatan/1593-both 5/8th Shawano-Chalaka-Powhatan

THE BEST KNOWN SON OF RUNNING STREAM/1500 &

MORNING FLOWER/1517 Opechan Stream/1556

Stream, Opechan aka **Opechanancanough**-Mangopeoman-Opechanako-White Heart-His Soul is White-Opechan Shawano – Shawano-Chalaka born about 1556 VA-died 1644 VA – son of **Running Stream**/1500 & **Morning Flower**/1517, Water Clan, brother of **Opitchapam**/1550 & **Katataugh**/1552, adopted brother 1560 VA of **Chief Powhatan**/1545-(when his mother **Morning Flower** marries **Ensenore Powhatan**-the husband of his sister **Scent Flower** & father of **Chief Powhatan**), before 1600 was **Chief of the Pamukey** villages, succeeded **Powhatan** as **Chief of the Powhatan** 1618, leader of 2nd Anglo-Powhatan War/1622 & 3rd Anglo-Powhatan War/1644, husband 1st 1575 VA of his adopted sister & 1st cousin **Apachano Powhatan**/1553-(sister of Chief Powhatan/1545), 2nd by 1600 coast of VA of **Pamukey Woman**, 1618 VA of **Cleopatra Powhatan**/1604(daughter of Chief Powhatan/1545), father **with Apachano** of Daughter/1576, Mangopeesomon Opechan/1580-both 3/4th ShawanoChalaka-Powhatan, **with Cleopatra** of Nicketti Opechan/1624 & Hokolesqua Opechan-Cornstalk (4)/1628-both 7/8th Shawano-ChalakaPowhatan

WIVES OF OPECHAN/1556

WIFE - 1575 VA

Powhatan, Apachano – ½ Shawano-Chalaka-Powhatan born 1553 near

Jamestown colony VA-died before 1618 VA, daughter of **Scent Flower (2)**/1525 & **Chief Morning (2)-Ensenore**/1516-Powhatan, Water-Corn Clan, sister of **Chief Powhatan**/1545, wife 1575 VA of her adopted brother **Opechan Stream**/1556, mother of Nonoma-Daughter of Opechan/1578-(wife 1591 of **Chief Powhatan**) & Mangopeesomon Opechan/1580-both 3/4th Shawano-Chalaka-Powhatan

WIFE BEFORE 1600 - VA

Pamukey Woman - born about 1580 coast of VA-died about 1622 VA, wife before 1600 coast of VA of **Opechan Stream**/1556, children unknown

WIFE 1618 COAST OF VA

Powhatan, Cleopatra (3) aka **Cleopatra the Shawano**-Cleopatra the Algonquin-(a modern reference) – 3/4th Shawano-Chalaka-Powhatan born 1602 near Jamestown colony VA-died 1680 VA – daughter of **Chief Powhatan**/1545 & **Amopotuskee Bear Clan**/1585-Shawano, Water-Corn-Bear Clan, wife 1618 VA of her adopted uncle **Opechan Stream**/1556-Shawano-(adopted Pamukey), mother of Nicketti Opechan/1624 & Hokolesqua Opechan-Cornstalk (4)/1628-both 7/8th Shawano-Chalaka-Powhatan

CHILDREN OF OPECHAN/1556
WITH APACHANO POWHATAN/1553

DAUGHTER

Opechan, Nonoma aka Daughter of Opechan – 3/4th Shawano-ChalakaPowhatan born 1576-died after 1596 – daughter of **Opechan Stream**/1556 & **Apachano Powhatan**/1553, Water-Corn Clan, wife 1590 coast of VA of her uncle **Chief Powhatan**/1545, mother of Powcanoe Powhatan/1591 & Nataquous Powhatan/1593-both 5/8th Shawano-Chalaka-Powhatan

SON

Opechan, Mangopeesomon - 3/4th Shawano-Chalaka-Powhatan born

1580 VA-**killed** by whites 1608 VA – son of **Opechan Stream**/1556 & **Apachano Powhatan**/1553, wife & children unknown

WITH CLEOPATRA THE SHAWANO POWHATAN/1603

DAUGHTER
NICKETTI OPECHAN/1624

Opechan, Nicketti aka Sweeps Dew from the Flowers-Beautiful Flower-Nicketti Stream – 7/8th Shawano-Chalaka-Powhatan born 1624 near Jamestown colony VA-died after 1680 VA – daughter of **Opechan Stream**/1556 & **Cleopatra Powhatan**/1602, Water-Corn-**Bear** Clan, wife about 1640 near Jamestown colony VA of **Capt. John Rice Hughes**/1610-white, mother of Mary Hughes/1650, Elizabeth Hughes/1654-both 7/16th Shawano-Chalaka-Powhatan-Metis

SON
HOKOLESQUA-CORNSTALK/1628

Opechan, Cornstalk aka Cornstalk (4)-Hokolesqua Opechan-**Hokolesqua Cornstalk**- – 7/8th Shawano-Chalaka-Powhatan born 1628 southwest VA-died 1696 west PA – son of **Opechan Stream/**1556 & **Cleopatra Powhatan**/1602, Water-Corn-**Bear** Clan, half-uncle (through his mother) of **Pride Cornstalk**/1617- **Wind Clan**-(wife of Thomas Pashmere Carpenter), **Nepikeweewa Cornstalk**/1625 **Wind Clan**-(wife of John Spemcia Helene-Big Man Greenwood), half-great-uncle of **Locha Greenwood**/1643-(wife of Trader Tom Carpenter) & **Mikona Carpenter**/1644-(wife of Tom Skootekitehi Greenwood), some connection/relation with **Straight Tail-Meaurroway**-Pekowi, **PheasantKakawatchekee**-Pekowi, entered Chalakatha leadership lineage with marriage to Nonoma Cornstalk-daughter of Cornstalk (3), name switch of children to Cornstalk may indicate a matrilineal custom during his lifetime, living in corner of VA-KY-TN 1648, living in PA before 1674, husband 1st 1648 VA of Nonoma Cornstalk/1630-Wind Clan, 2nd 1662 Running Water TN of **Pashmere Carpenter (1)**/1637-Wind Clan, children **with Nonoma Cornstalk** unknown but apparently died childless, father **with Carpenter** of Okowellos-Cornstalk (5)/1674

& Tamenebuck-Corn Blade Cornstalk/1680-11/16th Shawano-ChalakaChalakatha-Powhatan-Metis

GRANDCHILDREN OF OPECHAN/1556
BY NONOMA OPECHAN/1576 & CHIEF POWHATAN/1545

GRANDSON

Powhatan, Powcanoe – 5/8th Shawano-Chalaka-Powhatan born 1591 VA-**killed** 1618 VA – son of **Chief Powhatan**/1545 & **Nonoma Opechan**/1576, killed in battle with the whites, apparently died unmarried

GRANDDAUGHTER

Powhatan, Nataquous - 5/8th Shawano-Chalaka-Powhatan born 1593 VA-died after 1607 (VA?) – daughter of **Chief Powhatan**/1545 & **Nonoma Opechan**/1576, husband & children unknown

BY NICKETTI OPECHAN/1524 & CAPT. JOHN RICE HUGHES/1610

GRANDDAUGHTER

Hughes, Mary (1) – 7/16th Shawano-Chalaka-Powhatan-Metis born 1650-died after 1670 – daughter of **Nicketti Opechan**/1624 & **Capt. John Rice Hughes**/1610-white, possible wife 1665 VA of **Nathaniel Davis**/1645, children unclear

GRANDDAUGHTER

Hughes, Elizabeth (1) – 7/16th Shawano-Chalaka-Powhatan-Metis born about 1654 Jamestown VA-died after 1700 (VA-TN?) – daughter of **Nicketti Opechan**/1624 & **Capt. John Rice Hughes**/1610, Bear Clan, wife 1675 Hanover Co VA of **Nathaniel Davis**/1645-white, mother of Nathaniel Davis/1676, James Davis/1678, Phillip Davis/1680, Samuel Davis/1683, Mary Elizabeth Davis/1685-all 7/32nd Shawano-Chalaka-

BY HOKOLESQUA CORNSTALK (OPECHAN)/1628 & PASHMERE CARPENTER/1637

GRANDSON
OKOWELLOS CORNSTALK

Cornstalk, Okowellos aka Akowellos-Hokowellos-Hakowellos-Stalk of Plant-Cornstalk (5) - 11/16th Chalakatha-Shawano-Chalaka-PowhatanMetis born 1674 PA-died 1758 in epidemic OH – son of **Hokolesqua Cornstalk**/1630 & **Pashmere Carpenter (1)**/1637, Bear-Wind Clan, living in TN before 1704, a **Chalakatha Chief** in OH by 1707, in PA by 1723-(called **King of the Upper Shawnee** in PA 1723), in AL by 1725(called **Chief of the Shawnee on the Savannah River** AL 1725), in PA by 1730-(called a **major Chalakatha Chief** in PA 1731), returned to AL by 1755-(called **Chief of the Shawnee in AL** 1755), returned to OH by 1758-(called **Head Chief of Chalakatha in OH** 1758), over 6' tall, associated at times with **Straight Tail**-Pekowi, **Opessa**-Pekowi, **Poxinosa**-Pekowi, **Kakawatchekee-Pheasant**-Pekowi & **White Fish**Pekowi, all major Chiefs of his time, also some connection with family of **Standing Turkey-Old Hop**/1688-Chalakatha, uncle of **Red Shoes (1) Marchand**/1720-son of his sister in law **Sehoy (1)**/1704, husband 1st
1695 PA of **Katee Mekoche**/1680, 2nd 1713 PA of **Daughter of Sassoon**/1698-Delaware, 3rd 1725 AL of **Sister of Sehoy**/1709-Creek, father **with Katee** of unknown daughters/1695-03, daughter Wakuta/1704-(wife of Thomas Greenwood), child/06, child/08, son Keightughqua Cornstalk (6)/1710, Sawelaha-Eliza/1712-(wife of James Francis & Old Belt), son Keeweeton/1714, daughter **Cawechile**/1716(wife of Cold Water), daughter **Nonhelema**/1718, son **Nimwha**/1720, son **Red Hawk**/1722, son **Silverheels** Hokolesqua/1724-all 27/32tnd Chalakatha-Mekoche-Shawano-Chalaka-Powhatan-Metis, **with Daughter of Sassoon** of son Wakeeampea/1714, Ewikunwee/1716, Naythakiena/1718, **Bukangolas**/1720-all 11/32nd Chalakatha-ShawanoChalaka-Powhatan-Delaware-Metis, **with Sister of Sehoy** of daughters

Elizabeth/1726 & Catherine-Kitty Hokolesqua/1728-both 11/32nd Chalakatha-Shawano-Chalaka-Powhatan-Creek-Metis

GRANDSON
TAMING BUCK-CORN BLADE

Cornstalk, Tamenebuck aka Corn Blade-Tamininipakwa-Tamininipaquah-Taming Buck-Tammany Buck-Domini Buck – 11/16th Chalakatha-Shawano-Chalaka-Powhatan-Metis born about 1680 PA died about 1758 OH (epidemic?) - son of **Hokolesqua Cornstalk**/1630 & **Pashmere Carpenter (1)**/1637, Bear-Wind Clan, a major **Pekowi Chief** in PA by 1744, joined the French with **Peter Chartier** & **Neucheconner** 1744, moved to the mouth of the Sciota in OH 1745 & perhaps on to Winchester KY area 1746, returned to PA & British 1747, Council Lancaster PA 1748-apology to the British rejected, rejoined the French supporting faction before 1752, Council Logstown 1752, Ft. Pitt Nov. 1753, Cornstalk War/1755-58, husband about 1700 PA of **Daughter of Straight Tail**/1680, father of Corn Cob Cornstalk/1710-27/32nd Chalakatha-Pekowi-Shawano-Chalaka-Powhatan-Metis

CHAPTER TWO

Straight Tail-Meaurroway/1630
Hokolesqua-Cornstalk (4)/1630
Martin Chartier/1655
Cakundawanna Straight Tail/1662
Opessa Straight Tail/1664

Thomas Fireheart-Skootekitehi Greenwood/1641

Straight Tail-Meaurroway/1630

Straight Tail aka **Meaurroway** - Pekowi born about 1630 OH-died 1709 PA - **parents unknown**, Turtle Clan, 1670 a **Pekowi Chief** in OH, 1677 band moved from OH-mid-Ohio valley to IN-IL-Miami & Illinois River valleys near Miami & Illinois, about 1680 some of the band begin to move to the corner of TN-KY-VA-NC to join the Chalakatha-MekocheKishpoko already there while some follow the Ohio River into PA, by
1689 the bulk of the band from IL-IN joins **Chalakatha, Mekoche, Kishpoko** in east TN-west NC-east KY-southwest VA, by 1690 some of the band was living in PA having went there instead of going south, by 1693 most of band from NC-TN-VA-KY living in Cecil Co MD, by 1697 most of the band living in Lancaster Co PA-Susquehanna valley, some connection with **Paxinosa, Kakawatchekee, Kishacoquillas** & **Neucheconner**-all apparently from his band, 1697 succeeded by his son **Opessa** as **Pekowi Chief** in Pequea PA, 1709 succeeded by **PheasantKakawatchekee** as **Pekowi Chief** in Pechoquealin PA, husband 1650
OH of **Pekowi Woman**/1635, father of son Wolf/1654, children/1656-58, daughter Sewatha/1660, sons Cakundawanna-Sevana/1662, Opessa/1664, daughter Snow White/1666, son John White/1670, children/1672-78, Daughter/1680-all Pekowi

CHILDREN OF STRAIGHT TAIL-MEAURROWAY/1630

SON

Straight Tail, Wolf - Pekowi born about 1654-died after 1685 – son of **Straight Tail -Meaurroway**/1630 & **Pekowi Woman**/1735, turned over to the priests at Montreal 1668 for education, meets Martin Chartier/1655, on **LaSalle's** 1st expedition 1669, 1646 on **Louis Joliet's** 1st expedition 1669, on **Louis Joliet's** 2nd expedition 1672, with **LaSalle** at build Ft. Crevecoeur on the Illinois River 1679, with the Shawnee at Ft. St. Louis 1683, living with **Straight Tail** band in IL territory 1685, wife & children unknown

DAUGHTER

Straight Tail, Sewatha aka Seaworth-Francoise Daudo – Pekowi born about 1660 OH-died after 1700 PA - daughter of **Straight Tail Meaurroway**/1630 & **Pekowi Woman**/1635, Turtle Clan, 1677 moved with band from OH-mid-Ohio valley to IN-IL-Miami & Illinois River valleys near Miami & Illinois, 1689 band from IL-IN joins **Chalakatha, Mekoche** & **Kishpoko** in corner of east TN-west NC-east KY-southwest VA, by 1693 most of band was living in Cecil Co MD, by 1697 was living in Lancaster Co PA-Susquehanna valley, wife 1676 IL of **Martin Chartier**/1655-adopted French, mother of Madeleine Chartier/1678, Charles Chartier-Charleville/1680 IL, children/1682-84, Jean Chartier-Charleville/1686 IL, Mary Chartier/1688 IL-TN, Peter Chartier/1790TN, Jacquette Chartier/1692 MD & likely other unrecorded children-all 1/2 Pekowi-Metis

SON

Straight Tail, Cakundawanna aka Sevana-Savanna-Savannah - born about 1662 OH-died after 1722 PA - son of **Straight Tail**/1630 & **Pekowi Woman**/1635, 1677 moved with band to IN, 1680 moved to IL, 1689 moved with band to TN-NC-KY-VA, by 1693 moved to Old Savannah Town GA, 1700 moved to PA before of death of his father **Straight Tail**, 1711 succeeded his brother **Opessa** as **Pekowi Chief** in Pequea PA, 1714 Council Philadelphia with **Conestoga Chiefs**, replaced as **Pekowi Chief** 1723 by brother **Opessa**, husband 1st about 1682 IL of **Pekowi Woman**/1665, 2nd before 1711 PA of **Mohawk Woman**/1695- (sister of wife of **Rising Sun**), children unknown

SON

Straight Tail, Opessa aka Opethatha-Wapatha-Wopatha-HopeshaOppaymolleh – Pekowi born 1664 OH-died latter 1760 OH - son of **Straight Tail-Meaurroway**/1630 & **Pekowi Woman**/1635, Turtle Clan, moved 1677 with band to IN, moved 1680 to IL, 1689 moved with band to TN-NC-KY-VA, by 1693 living in Cecil Co MD, about 1693 a **Pekowi Chief** under his father in Cecil Co MD, 1697 moved to Lancaster Co PA with band, 1697 succeeded **Straight Tail** as **Pekowi Chief** in Pequea PA, signed Treaty 1701 with **William Penn** with **Lemoytungh** & **Pemoyajagh**, 1706 Council Philadelphia, 1707 Conference at Pequea Lancaster Co PA with **Governor John Evans**, 1710 Conference at Conestoga PA with **John French & Henry Worley**, resigned 1711 to move to Sassoonan's Delaware village-Shamokin PA, succeeded 1711 as **Pekowi Chief** at Pequea PA by his brother **Cakundawanna**, 1715 Conference Philadelphia with **Sassoonan**, 1722 moved to Old Town MD-upper Potomac & replaced his brother Cakundawanna as **Pekowi Chief** again by 1723, by 1734 moved to AL with band, by 1738 returned to western MD/southeast PA, Aug. 1749 Council Philadelphia, 1750 moved to OH, 1752 succeeded **Pheasant-Kakawatchekee** as **Head Pekowi Chief** on the Ohio River, May 1756 Council Tioga Point, Aug. 1760 Council Ft. Pitt, brother in law (through sister Snow White) of **Peter Chartier**, connected with **Poxinosa**-Pekowi, **White Fish (1)**Pekowi & **Okowellos Cornstalk**-Chalakatha (Head Chiefs of bands), great-grandfather of **Tecumseh**, husband 1st by 1684 IN of **Margaret Pekowi**/1670, 2nd 1711 PA of **Polly-Daughter of Sassoonan**/1695Delaware, father **with Margaret** of children/1685-94, daughter Snow White/1695, sons Tecoomteh/1698, Wawwaythi/1700, Loyparkoweh/1702 & Lawaquaqua-Pride Opessa/1710-all Pekowi, children **with Polly** unknown

DAUGHTER

Straight Tail, Snow White aka Sarah White-Daughter of Straight Tail – Pekowi born about 1666 OH-died after 1685-(possibly by 1695 when her namesake Snow White Opessa is born) – daughter of **Straight Tail**/1630 & **Pekowi Woman**/1635, Turtle Clan, husband & children unknown

SON

White, John aka John White Straight Tail - Pekowi born about 1670 OH died after 1715 PA – son of **Straight Tail-Meaurroway**/1630 & **Pekowi Woman**/1635, Turtle Clan, a **Pekowi Chief** in PA by 1715, husband about 1690 of **Pekowi Woman**/1675, 2nd of a **White Woman**, father **with Pekowi** of John White (2)/1700 & other children, any children **with White Woman** unknown, grandfather of White Thunder/1730

DAUGHTER

Straight Tail, Daughter of - Pekowi born about 1680 IL-died after 1720 PA – daughter of **Straight Tail-Meaurroway**/1630 & **Pekowi Woman**/1635, Turtle Clan, wife about 1700 PA of **Tamenebuck-Corn Blade Cornstalk**/1680, mother of Corn Cob Cornstalk/1710-27/32nd Chalakatha-Pekowi-Shawano-Chalaka-Powhatan-Metis

GRANDCHILDREN OF MEAURROWAY-STRAIGHT TAIL

By SEWATHA/1660 & MARTIN CHARTIER/1655

GRANDDAUGHTER

Chartier, Madeleine - 1/2 Pekowi-Metis born about 1678 IL-died after 1700 - daughter of **Martin Chartier**/1655-adopted-French & **Sewatha Straight Tail**/1660, namesake of deceased grandmother **Madeleine Ranger**, Turtle Clan, sister of **Peter Chartier**/1690, granddaughter of **Meaurroway-Straight Tail**/1630, by 1689 living with father on the Cumberland River TN, 1690 in east TN, by 1701 living in Lancaster Co PA with father, husband & children unknown

GRANDSON

Chartier, Charles aka Charles Charleville - 1/2 Pekowi-Metis born about 1680 IL-died after 1714 - son of **Martin Chartier**/1655-adoptedFrench & **Sewatha Straight Tail**/1660, Turtle Clan, grandson of **Meaurroway-Straight Tail**/1630, by 1689 living with father on the

Cumberland River TN, 1690 in east TN-NC, by 1700 living in Lancaster Co PA with father, by 1710 returned to the south & established a trading post with his brother Jean at French Lick on the Cumberland River TN-the site of Nashville, wife & children unknown

GRANDSON

Chartier, Jean aka Jean Charleville-Jean de Charleville-Jean du Charleville - 1/2 Pekowi-Metis born about 1686 IL-died 1780 TN - son of **Martin Chartier**/1655-adopted-French & **Sewatha Straight Tail**/1660, Turtle Clan, grandson of **Meaurroway-Straight Tail**/1630, by 1689 living with father on the Cumberland River TN, 1690 in east TN-NC, by 1700 living in Lancaster Co PA with father, by 1710 returned to the south & established a trading post with his brother Charles at French Lick on the Cumberland River TN-the site of Nashville, 1714 he took bateau load of furs New Orleans to trade, wife & children unknown

GRANDDAUGHTER

Chartier, Mary (1) aka Maria Chartier - 1/2 Pekowi-Metis born about 1688 IL-**killed** 1732 PA - daughter of **Martin Chartier**/1655-adopted-French & **Sewatha Straight Tail**/1660, Turtle Clan, sister of **Peter Chartier**/1690, namesake of her **half-aunt Marie Anne Chartier, killed in Native attack with 7 of 12 children**, wife by 1705 PA of **Jean DeBert**John Burt/1685-white, mother of 11 children-5 that survived 1732- Wilhelm DeBert (husband of Rechler & Weigner)/1711, Daughter (wife of George Heurtzinger)/1713, Daughter (wife of John Geuert)/1715, Michael DeBert/1717 & Charles Christopher Dibert/1719- all 1/4th Pekowi-Metis

GRANDSON

Chartier, Peter aka **Wocunuckshenah-Pale Brother** - 1/2 Pekowi-Metis born about 1690 TN-died about 1759 on the Wabash IN (possibly in epidemic) - son of **Martin Chartier**/1655-adopted-French & **Sewatha Straight Tail**/1660, namesake of his uncle **Pierre Chartier**/1646, before 1697 moved with Opessa Band to Lancaster Co PA, 1707 living on

Pequea Creek Lancaster Co PA, 1718 living in Dekanoagah Lancaster Co PA-obtained title to 300 acres on the Susquehanna River where his father had died, 1732 witnessed a letter from **Neucheconner** & other Shawnee Chiefs to the Governor of PA , 1732 attended Council Philadelphia with **Opakethwa, Opakeita** & **Kwassenung Pheasant**, 1734 founded Chartier's Town Alleghany Co PA, 1737 a **Pekowi Chief in PA**, 1738 signed **Petition to PA** with **Pride Opessa, Tecomteh Opessa** & **George Miranda**, 1744 left the British of PA with about 400 Pekowi & Kishpoko-including **Neucheconner** & **Tamenebuck,** to join the French of OH , (**Kakawatchekee** & **Kishacoquillas** refused to join them), moved southwest to the mouth of the Sciota River-Lower Shawnee Town with sons, 1745 moved on to near Winchester KY(**Neucheconner** & **Tamenebuck** return to PA), 1746 moved to the French Lick-Nashville TN, 1747 moved to the Coosa River AL, 1748 allegedly seen with some of his band in IL & Detroit when the French doubted his control of the band-(it was one of his sons **Francois Pale Croucher Chartier** or **Rene Pale Stalker Chartier** that was seen), 1749 met Col. **Celeron De Blainville** at the forks of the Ohio (Pittsburgh), 1752 returned to KY, active in opposition to the British on the frontier in the French-Indian War/1754-59, 1754 present with his Shawnee warriors at the murder of Capt. **Jumonville** & responsible for the French victory of **George Washington** at Ft. Necessity, 1758 in OH with band, last seen in a village on the Wabash, husband about 1710 PA of his 1st cousin **Snow White Opessa**/1695-Pekowi, father of Francois Pale Croucher Chartier/1712, children/1714-18, Rene Pale Stalker Chartier/1720, Anna Chartier/1730 & other children/1732-36-all 3/4th Pekowi-Metis

GRANDDAUGHTER

Chartier, Jacquette – ½ Pekowi-Metis born about 1692 MD-died after 1712 (PA-OH?) – daughter of **Martin Chartier**/1655 & **Sewatha Straight Tail**/1660, Turtle Clan, namesake of her deceased **great-aunt Jacquette Chartier**/1649, husband & children unknown

By CAKUNDAWANNA/1662
UNKNOWN

By OPESSA/1664
& MARGARET PEKOWI/1670

GRANDDAUGHTER

Opessa, Snow White aka **Blanceneige-Wapakonee**-Daughter of Opessa-Snow in the Face-Wife of Peter Chartier – Pekowi born about 1695 Cecil Co MD-died about 1737 PA - daughter of **Opessa**/1664 & **Margaret Pekowi**/1670, Turtle Clan, namesake of her aunt **Snow White Straight Tail**, wife 1710 PA of **Peter Chartier**/1690, mother of children/1714-18, Rene Pale Stalker Chartier/1720, children/1722-28, Anna Chartier/1730 & other children/1732-36-all 3/4th Pekowi-Metis

GRANDSON

Opessa, Tecoomteh aka Tecomteh – Pekowi born about 1698 Lancaster Co PA-died after 1738 PA - son of **Opessa**/1664 **Margaret Pekowi**/1670, Turtle Clan, in west PA 1711-23 with father **Opessa**, returned to north MD/east PA area with **Opessa** 1723, living on the Alleghany River by 1727, unclear whether he moved to AL 1734 with **Opessa**, 1738 called the 1st warrior of the band, 1738 signed Petition to PA to stop the sell of liquor to Natives with brother **Pride Opessa**, brother in law **Peter Chartier**/1690, **George Miranda**/1700 & 94 other Natives, wife & children unknown

GRANDSON

Opessa, Waywayti aka Wawwaythi-Waywaythee-Wauwaythee-Weyweyti-Wauweythi – Pekowi born about 1700 PA-died after 1750 (AL?) – son of **Opessa**/1664 **Margaret Pekowi**/1670, grandson of **Meaurroway-Straight Tail**/1630, Turtle Clan, in west PA 1711-23 with father **Opessa**, returned to north MD/east PA area with **Opessa** 1723, living on the Alleghany River by 1727, moved to AL 1734 with **Opessa**, didn't return to MD 1738, husband 1st 1720 PA of **Elizabeth**-Aunt of Metheotashe/1704, 2nd 1739 AL of her sister **Nancy**-Mother of Metheotashe/1706, (he & his brother were married to sisters & switched wives in 1738) children/1720-38 **with 1st Wife** unknown but **stepfather** 1739 AL of Middle Daughter of Loyoarkoweh-Nancy/1734,

Younger Daughter of Loyparkoweh-Sarah/1736 & MetheotasheMary/1738

GRANDSON

Opessa, Loyparkaweh aka Loapeckeway-Lawpakaway – Pekowi born about 1702 PA-died after 1760 OH - son of **Opessa**/1664 **MargaretPekowi**/1670, grandson of **Meaurroway-Straight Tail**/1630, Turtle
Clan, in west PA 1711-23 with father **Opessa**, returned to north MD/east PA area with **Opessa** 1723, living on the Alleghany River by 1727, a **Pekowi Chief** in PA by 1732, in 1732-1733-1734 signed letters to the Governor of PA as one of the Chiefs on the Alleghany complaining about the sale of rum to the natives, moved to AL with **Opessa** 1734, left his 1st wife & children in AL with relatives/clan members, returned to PA by 1738, sent letter to the Governor of PA 1738 with **Neucheconner** & **Coycacolenne** protesting the sale of rum, then called a young Chief guided by vice regent **Neucheconner**, between 1738 & 1744 lived at Chartier's Town-Alleghany Co PA & Logstown-Alleghany Co PA, apparently moved to OH with **Peter Chartier** & **Neucheconner** in 1744 for he is living in Lower Shawnee Town OH in 1752 when he sent a letter with 3 other Shawnee Chiefs there to the Governor of PA reporting that they were still loyal to the British though most of their neighbors had gone over to the French, attended Council Philadelphia 1753 after **Opessa** moved to OH, apparently opposed the Shawnee participation in French-Indian War/1754-60, a minor **Pekowi Chief in OH** after death of **Opessa**, husband 1st 1720 MD of **Nancy**-Mother of Metheotashe/1706, 2nd 1739 PA of **Elizabeth**-Aunt of Metheotashe/1704, (he & his brother were married to sisters & switched wives in 1738) , father **with Nancy** of TecumsapahMargaret/1725, Older Daughter-Sarah/1727, Watmeme-Polly/1730, Middle Daughter-Nancy/1734, Younger Daughter-Sarah/1736 & Metheotashe-Mary/1738-all Pekowi, any children **with Elizabeth** unknown

GRANDSON

Opessa, Pride aka **Lawaquaqua**-Lawachkamikee-Lawakwakwaltawachcomequ about 1710 MD-died 1753 SC - son of

Opessa/1664 **Margaret Pekowi**/1670, Turtle Clan, 1711 taken to Sassoonan's village with Opessa, 1722 returned to Opessa's Town MD with **Opessa**, remained in north 1734 when **Opessa** took band to AL, 1738 signed
Petition to PA with **Peter Chartier, George Miranda**, brother **Tecoomteh** & 94 Natives to stop the sell of liquor to Natives, by 1738 a **Pekowi Chief** in west MD/central PA, raiding PA/1740, 1744 joined **Peter Chartier, Big Hominy** & others in moving to Lower Shawnee Town OH to support the French, 1748 Conference Logstown with **Conrad Weiser, Big Hominy & Kakawatchekee**, 1753 captured on trip to the south to locate Pekowi relatives on the Savannah River & died in SC prison, husband 1st 1730 east PA of **Sarah Rising Sun**/1715Kishpoko, 2nd by 1739 east PA of (widow) **Sister of Moluntha**/1710, father **with Rising Sun** of Lawagqua-Elder Brother of Blue Jacket/1733, **Blue Jacket**- Whirlpool-Weyapiersenwha/1735, Wabete-Elk-Younger Brother of Blue Jacket/1737 & Sally Opessa-sister of Blue Jacket/1739all Kishpoko-Pekowi, **with Sister of Moluntha** of Red Pole/1740Mekoche-Pekowi, step-father of **Black Fish**/1725, Kwatooka/1727, Nakanapaseka/1729-all Chalakatha-Mekoche

BY SNOW WHITE STRAIGHT TAIL/1666 & UNKNOWN HUSBAND

UNKNOWN

BY JOHN WHITE (STRAIGHT TAIL)/1670 & PEKOWI WOMAN/1675

GRANDSON

White, John (2) – Pekowi born about 1700 PA-died after 1730 likely PA – son of **John White**/1670 & **Pekowi Woman**/1675, Turtle Clan, husband about 1720 PA of **Pekowi Woman**/1705, father of White Thunder/1730 & other children, was grandfather of **Peter White**/1778 & **Sarah White**/1784

BY JOHN WHITE (STRAIGHT TAIL)/1670

& WHITE WOMAN

UNKNOWN

BY DAUGHTER OF STRAIGHT TAIL/1680
& TAMENEBUCK-CORN BLADE CORNSTALK/1680

GRANDSON

Cornstalk, Corn Cob aka Charlowe-Charlot Kaske-Casquie-Chariot Kaske-Charlokaskee – 27/32nd Chalakatha-Pekowi-Shawano-Chalaka-Powhatan-Metis born about 1710 PA-died after 1768 OH – son of **Tamenebuck-Corn Blade Cornstalk**/1680 & **Daughter of Straight Tail**/1680, Bear Clan, raiding PA/1740, 1744 left the British of PA with about 400 Pekowi, Chalakatha & Kishpoko lead by Peter Chartier to join the French of OH , 1745 moved southwest to the mouth of the Sciota River-Lower Shawnee Town , 1746 moved on to near Winchester KY, a **Chalakatha Chief** in OH by 1755, Cornstalk War/1755-68, 1763 a major Chief in the IL-IN territory, 1764 traveled to New Orleans for Council with French Governor Jen Jacques Blaise d'Abbadie to solicit French support for Pontiac War, 1765 moved beyond the Mississippi with French & French-Metis refugees of the Pontiac War, erroneously said to have a German father by the British, 1768 traveled with **Rene-Pale Stalker Chartier** to Detroit, husband 1st about 1740 PA of **Chalakatha Woman**/1725, 2nd 1763 OH of **White Woman**/1748, father with **Chalakatha** of several children/1740-64, **with White Woman** of three known children/1764-68

Hokolesqua-Cornstalk (4)/1630

Cornstalk (4) aka **Hokolesqua** Cornstalk-Hokolesqua OpechanCornstalk Opechan-Hokolesqua Stream– 7/8th Shawano-Chalaka-
Powhatan born 1628 southwest VA-died 1696 west PA – son of **Opechan Stream**/1556 & **Cleopatra Powhatan**/1602, Bear Clan, halfuncle (through his mother) of **Pride Cornstalk**/1617-wife of Thomas Pashmere Carpenter, **Nepikeweewa Cornstalk**/1625-wife of John Spemcia Helene-Big Man Greenwood, half-great-uncle of **Locha**

Greenwood/1643-wife of Trader Tom Carpenter & **Mikona Carpenter**/1644-wife of Tom Skootekitehi Greenwood, some connection/relation with **Straight Tail**-Pekowi & **Pheasant**-Pekowi a, entered Chalakatha leadership lineage with marriage to Nonoma, living in corner of VA-KY-TN 1648, living in PA before 1674, husband 1st 1648 VA of his niece **Nonoma Cornstalk**/1630, 2nd 1664 Running Water TN of **Pashmere Carpenter (1)**/1637, father **with Nonoma** of unknown children/1648-58, Big Turkey/1660, Little Turkey/1662, Nancy Turkey/1664 & Sister Turkey/1666-all 31/32nd Chalakatha-ShawanoChalaka-Powhatan, father **with Carpenter** of **Okowellos-Cornstalk (5)**/1674 & Tamenebuck-Corn Blade Cornstalk/1680-11/16th Chalakatha-Shawano-Chalaka-Powhatan-Metis

WIVES OF HOKOLESQUA-CORNSTALK (4)/1630

WIFE 1648 - VA

Cornstalk, Nonoma (2) aka Daughter of Cornstalk (2)-Nonoma Wind Clan (2) - 15/16th Chalakatha-Shawano-Chalaka-Powhatan born 1630 Shawnee Nation-southwestern VA-died 1679 Running Water TN – daughter of **Cornstalk (3)**/1598-Wind Clan & **Chalakatha Woman**/1602-Turkey Clan, Wind-Turkey Clan, sister of **Pride**/1617 & **Nepikeweewa**/1625, wife 1648 VA of **Hokolesqua Opechan-Cornstalk (4)**/1628, mother of unknown children/1648-58, Big Turkey/1660, Little Turkey/1662, Nancy Turkey/1664 & Daughter/1666-all 31/32nd Chalakatha-Shawano-Chalaka-Powhatan

WIFE 1662 - RUNNING WATER TN

Carpenter, Pashmere (1) – ½ Chalakatha-Metis born 1637 VA-died 1681 PA – daughter of **Pride Cornstalk**/1617 & **Thomas Pashmere Carpenter**/1607-white, Wind Clan, taught to cipher, read & write English by her father, wife 1662 Running Water TN of **Hokolesqua Opechan-Cornstalk (4)**/1628, mother of Okowellos HokolesquaCornstalk (5)/1674 & Tamenebuck Corn Blade Cornstalk/1680-11/16th Chalakatha-Shawano-Chalaka-Powhatan-Metis

CHILDREN OF HOKOLESQUA CORNSTALK (4)/1630

BY NONOMA CORNSTALK (2)/1630

SON

Cornstalk, Big Turkey – 31/32nd Chalakatha-Shawano-ChalakaPowhatan born about 1660 northwest TN/southwest VA- **killed** 1694 southwest VA – son of **Cornstalk (4)-Hokolesqua**/1628 & **Nonoma (2)Daughter of Cornstalk**/1630,Bear Clan, **killed** with wife by Catawba raiders 1694, husband about 1679 VA-TN of **Chalakatha Woman**/1664, father of son Raven Moytoy-Turkey/1680, daughters Quatsis HopTurkey/1682, Aganunitsi-Wild Potato Hop-Turkey/1684, SwanWapehti Hop-Turkey/1686, son Standing Turkey-Old Hop/1688, daughters April-Tkikami Hop-Turkey/1690, Oolootah-Ulutse HopTurkey/1692 & Ghigoneli Hop-Turkey/1694-all 63/64th ChalakathaShawano-Chalaka-Powhatan

SON

Cornstalk, Little Turkey – 31/32nd Chalakatha-Shawano-ChalakaPowhatan born about 1662 VA-**killed** 1698 southwest VA- son of
Cornstalk (4)-Hokolesqua/1628 & **Nonoma (2)-Daughter of Cornstalk**/1630, Bear Clan, husband about 1682 VA of **Chalakatha Woman**/1666, father of Katie Turkey/1684-63/64th ChalakathaShawano-Chalaka-Powhatan

DAUGHTER

Cornstalk, Nancy Turkey– 31/32nd Chalakatha-Shawano-Chalaka-Powhatan born 1664 Running Water TN-died 1732 ENG – daughter of **Cornstalk (4)-Hokolesqua**/1628 & **Nonoma-Daughter of Cornstalk**/1630, known to be an aunt of **Standing Turkey-Old Hop** & his siblings, wife 1678 Running Water TN of **Trader Tom Carpenter (2)Moytoy (2)**/1660, mother of sons White Owl Raven-Moytoy (4)/1678,
Savannah Tom Carpenter(1)-Moytoy (3)/1680 & daughter Pashmere

Carpenter (2)/1681-all 23/32nd Chalakatha-Shawano-ChalakaPowhatan-Metis & **adopted mother** of her nieces (daughters of her brother) Quatsis Turkey/1682, Swan-Wapehti Turkey/1686, AprilTkikami Turkey/1690 & **adopted mother** of her nephews (sons of her brother) Raven (of Hiwassee) Turkey/1680, Standing Turkey-Old Hop/1688-all 63/64th Chalakatha-Shawano-Chalaka-Powhatan & 1698 of **adopted mother** of her nephew (son of her sister) Oshasqua-Muskrat (2)-Moytoy (5)/1686-63/64th Pekowi-Chalakatha-Shawano-ChalakaPowhatan

DAUGHTER

Cornstalk, Sister Turkey aka Daughter of Hokolesqua-Daughter of Cornstalk (4) - 31/32nd Chalakatha-Shawano-Chalaka-Powhatan born 1666 Running Water TN-**killed** 1698 southwest VA – daughter of **Cornstalk (4)-Hokolesqua**/1628 & **Nonoma-Daughter of Cornstalk**/1630, Bear Clan, known to be an aunt of the **Turkey-Hop children**, wife 1682 TN of **Muskrat-Oshasqua (1)**/1660-Pekowi, mother of Muskrat's Sister/1684 & Muskrat-Oshasqua (2)-Moytoy (5)/1686both 63/64th Pekowi-Chalakatha-Shawano-Chalaka-Powhatan

BY PASHMERE CARPENTER/1637

SON

Cornstalk (5) aka **Okowellos** Cornstalk-Okowellos HokolesquaAkowellos-Hokowellos-Hakowellos-Stalk of Plant - 11/16th Chalakatha-Shawano-Chalaka-Powhatan-Metis born 1674 PA-died 1758 in epidemic OH – son of **Hokolesqua Opechan-Cornstalk (4)/1630 & Pashmere Carpenter (1)/1637**, Bear Clan, taught to cipher, read, speak & write some English by his mother, in TN before 1704, a **Chalakatha Chief** in OH by 1707, a **Chalakatha Chief** in WV on the Greenbrier River 1710, in PA by 1723-**King of the Upper Shawnee** in PA 1723, in AL by 1725-**Chief of the Shawnee on the Savannah River** AL 1725, in PA by 1730-a **major Chalakatha Chief** in PA 1731, returned to AL by 1755-**Chief of the Shawnee in AL** 1755, returned to OH by 1758-**Head Chief of Chalakatha in OH** 1758, over 6' tall, associated at times with

Straight Tail-Pekowi, **Opessa**-Pekowi, **Poxinosa**-Pekowi, **Pheasant**Pekowi & **White Fish**-Pekowi-all major Chiefs of his time, taught most of his children to cipher, read & speak some English, husband 1st 1695
PA of **Katee Mekoche**/1680, 2nd 1713 PA of **Daughter of Sassoonan/**1695-Delaware, 3rd 1725 AL of **Sister of Sehoy**/1709-Wind Clan Creek, father **with Katee** of unknown daughters/1695-1703, daughter Wakuta/1704-(wife of **Thomas Greenwood**), child/1706, child/1708, son Keightughqua **Cornstalk (6)**/1710, Sawelaha-Eliza/1712-(wife of a **Chalakatha Man, James Francis & Old Belt**), son Keeweeton/1714, daughter **Cawechile**/1716-(wife of **Cold Water**), daughter **Nonhelema**/1718, son **Nimwha**/1720, son **Red Hawk**/1722, son **Silverheels**/1724-all 27/32tnd Chalakatha-Mekoche-ShawanoChalaka-Powhatan-Metis, **with Daughter of Sassoonan** of son Wakeeampea/1714, Ewikunwee/1716, Naythakiena/1718, **Bukangolas/**1720-all 11/32nd Chalakatha-Shawano-Chalaka-Powhatan-Delaware-Metis, **with Sister of Sehoy** of daughters Elizabeth/1726 & Catherine-Kitty Cornstalk/1728-both 11/32nd Chalakatha-Shawano-Chalaka-Creek-Metis

SON

Cornstalk, Tamenebuck aka **Corn Blade**-Taming Buck-Tamininipakwa-Tamininipaquah-Tammony Buck-Domini Buck-TameeneebookTamenebuck Hokolesqua – 11/16th Chalakatha-Shawano-ChalakaPowhatan-Metis born about 1680 PA-died about 1758 OH (epidemic?) - son of **Hokolesqua Opechan-Cornstalk (4)**/1630 & **Pashmere Carpenter**/1637, Bear Clan, a major **Pekowi Chief** (via marriage) by
1744 in PA, 1744 deserted to the French with **Peter Chartier & Neucheconner**, 1745-46 moved at least to the mouth of the Sciota in OH-perhaps to Winchester KY area, 1747 returned to PA & British, Council Lancaster PA 1748-apology to the British was rejected, by 1752 joined the French supporting faction, Council Logstown 1752, Ft. Pitt Nov. 1753, husband about 1700 PA of **Daughter of Straight Tail**/1680Pekowi, father of Corn Cob Cornstalk/1710-27/32nd ChalakathaPekowi-Shawano-Chalaka-Powhatan-Metis

GRANDCHILDREN OF HOKOLESQUA CORNSTALK (4)/1630

BY BIG TURKEY CORNSTALK/1660

GRANDSON

Turkey, Raven aka **Raven Moytoy**-Raven of Hiwassee-CollanahCorani-Corane-Raven Hop-Raven Cornstalk – 63/64th ChalakathaShawano-Chalaka-Powhatan born 1680 Upper Hiwassee VA-died 1756 Chewohe TN – son of **Big Turkey Cornstalk**/1660 & **Chalakatha Woman**/1664, parents killed 1694 VA by Catawba raiders, adopted son 1694 TN of **Trader Tom Carpenter (2)-Moytoy (2)**/1660 & his aunt **Nancy Turkey Cornstalk**/1664, took the surname Moytoy from his adopted father **Trader Tom aka Moytoy (2)**, could cipher, read & speak some English, Treaty 1684 with SC, delegation to ENG 1730, husband 1st 1700 Upper Hiwassee TN of his adopted sister **Pashmere Carpenter (2)**/1681, 2nd 1718 of **Ahneewakee Muskrat**/1704, 3rd 1729 TN of **Cherokee Woman**/1714, father with Pashmere of Amoyah Pigeon Moytoy (1)/1715-27/64th Chalakatha-Shawano-Chalaka-PowhatanMetis, **with Ahneewakee** of Bushyhead Chiesatebe Moytoy/1718, Savanooka Moytoy/1720, Goohsohly Moytoy/1722, Elizabeth-Raven's Sister Moytoy/1724, Nancy Augustus Moytoy/1726 & Amahetai Muskrat (3)-Moytoy (7)/1728-all 63/64th Chalakatha-Pekowi-ShawanoChalaka-Powhatan, children **with Cherokee** unknown

GRANDDAUGHTER

Turkey, Quatsis aka Quatsis Hop-Quatsis Aniwadi-Quatsis Cornstalk – 63/64th Chalakatha-Shawano-Chalaka-Powhatan born 1682 Great Tellico TN-died 1758 Tellico Plains TN – daughter of **Big Turkey Cornstalk**/1660 & **Chalakatha Woman**/1664, parents killed 1694 VA by Catawba raiders, adopted daughter 1694 TN of **Trader Tom Carpenter (2)-Moytoy (2)**/1660 & her aunt **Nancy Turkey**/1664, could cipher, read & speak some English, known as aunt of **Savanooka**/1720 & **Goohsohly**/1722-(sons of **Ahneewakee Muskrat** & her brother **Raven Moytoy**), Red Paint Clan Cherokee, her sister **Oolootah** lived

with her from 1699-1705, wife 1st 1697 Great Tellico TN of **John Beamer**/1676-ENG, 2nd 1705 Settico TN of **Tsula Fox-Smallpox Conjurer**/1670-Cherokee (husband 1741 of her sister **Aganunitsi**), 3rd 1709 Chota TN of **William Webber**/1680-ENG, mother **with Beamer** of Ooloosta Beamer/1698, John Beamer Jr/1700, Peggy Beamer/1702 & Nionee Beamer/1704-all 31.64th Chalakatha-Shawano-ChalakaPowhatan-Metis, **with Fox-Conjurer** of Rising Fawn (1)-Rising Fawn
Fox/1706 & Quatsis Fox/1708-both 31/64th Chalakatha-ShawanoChalaka-Powhatan-Cherokee, **with Webber** of Catherine Webber/1710
& William Webber (2)/1712-both 31/64th Chalakatha-ShawanoChalaka-Powhatan-Metis

GRANDDAUGHTER

Turkey, Aganunitsi aka **Wild Potato**-Aganunitsi Hop-Elder Sister of Old Hop-Elder Sister of Standing Turkey- Aganunitsi Rainmaker-Wife of Young Rainmaker-Anigatagewi Woman-Wife of Smallpox ConjurerWife of Tsula Fox-Wild Potato Woman-Blind Savannah Woman - 63/64th Chalakatha-Shawano-Chalaka-Powhatan born 1684 Upper
Hiwassee VA-died after 1741 TN - daughter of **Big Turkey**/1660 & **Chalakatha Woman**/1664, parents killed 1694 VA by Catawba raiders, adopted daughter 1694 TN of **Rainmaker (1)**/1640 & **Quatsey (1)**/1650both Cherokee, Blind Savannah Clan Cherokee, wife 1st 1700 TN of her adopted brother **Young Rainmaker**/1685-Cherokee, 2nd 1741 TN of **Tsula Fox-Smallpox Conjurer**/1670-Cherokee, mother **with Rainmaker** of son **Oconastota** Rainmaker/1702, child/1704, son Cloggoittah Rainmaker/1706, daughter **Ooloosta** Rainmaker/1708, sons **Kitegista** Rainmkaer/1710, Tathtowe Rainmaker/1712, Wallenaeoa-Gray Eagle Rainmaker/1714, Oukahoukah Rainmaker/1716, Kallannah Rainmaker/1718-all 31/64th Chalakatha-Shawano-Chalaka-Powhatan -Cherokee, children **with Smallpox Conjurer** unlikely due to her age

GRANDDAUGHTER

Turkey, Swan aka Wapehti-Swan Hop – 63/64th Chalakatha-ShawanoChalaka-Powhatan born 1686 Upper Hiwassee TN-died 1754 Chota TN – daughter of **Big Turkey Cornstalk**/1660 & **Chalakatha Woman**/1664, parents killed 1694 VA by Catawba raiders, adopted daughter 1694 TN of **Trader Tom Carpenter (2)-Moytoy (2)**/1660 & her aunt **Nancy Turkey Cornstalk**/1664, could cipher, read & speak some English, wife
1703 Running Water TN of her adopted brother **Oshasqua-Muskrat (2)**/1686, mother of daughters Ahneewakee Muskrat/1704, children/1706-14, Ounacona Muskrat/1716, Tame Deer Muskrat/1720 & son Bad Water Muskrat-Moytoy (6)/1722-all 63/64th ChalakathaPekowi-Shawano-Chalaka-Powhatan, adopted mother 1708 TN-VA of
John Fork Tail Watts/1704-nephew of Oshasqua-Muskrat/1686- 55/64th Chalakatha-Pekowi-Shawano-Chalaka-Powhatan-Metis

GRANDSON

Turkey, Standing (1) aka **Old Hop**-Kanagatoga-Standing Turkey Cornstalk-Uka-Fire King-Kanetekoka-Conarcorturer-Connecorte - 63/64th Chalakatha-Shawano-Chalaka-Powhatan born 1688 Chota TN (some records indicate Upper Hiwassee VA-where older siblings were born or further north-Ohio valley or further west in TN)-died 1761 Chota TN – son of **Big Turkey Cornstalk**/1660 & **Chalakatha Woman**/1664, parents killed 1694 VA by Catawba raiders, adopted son 1694 TN of **Trader Tom Carpenter (2)-Moytoy (2)**/1660 & his aunt **Nancy Turkey Cornstalk/**1664, commonly known as **Old Hop** or simply Hopper (perhaps a nickname that reflects back to the Norse term "hop" i.e. a small fortified place) , could cipher, read & speak some English, Wolf Clan Cherokee, removed British appointed (**Carpenter-Moytoy & Rainmaker**) leaders & united 4 (of 7) Cherokee clans at Chota 1751, leader of pro- French faction in French-Indian War/1754- 61, sent warriors to support the Shawnee at Braddock/1755, **Principal Chief** of the Cherokee **1751-61**, passed actual
power/authority to his nephews **Oconastota Rainmaker** & **Kitegista Rainmaker** upon his death in 1761 even though his son **Young Standing Turkey-Little Turkey** succeeded him as titular Chief, husband by 1708 Chota TN of **Sugi Rainmaker**/1690-Wolf Clan

Cherokee, known father of sons Little Turkey-Young Standing Turkey/1709, Young Turkey-Young Hop/1715 & daughter Grasshopper Turkey/1725-all 31/64th Chalakatha-Shawano-ChalakaPowhatan -Cherokee, adopted father 1723 TN of his nephews **John French**/1710 & **Capt. French**/1712-both 31/64th Chalakatha-ShawanoChalaka-Powhatan-Black-Metis-(sons of his sister Ghigoneli/1694)

GRANDDAUGHTER

Turkey, April-**Tkikami** aka Tkikami Hop-April Hop-Middle Sister of Old Hop-Middle Sister of Standing Turkey-Wife of Tsula Fox-Wife of Smallpox Conjurer-Wife of Richard Barnes - 63/64th ChalakathaShawano-Chalaka-Powhatan born 1690 Chota TN-died 1744 Upper
Hiwassee TN – daughter of **Big Turkey Cornstalk**/1660 & **Chalakatha Woman**/1664, parents killed 1694 VA by Catawba raiders, adopted daughter 1694 TN of **Trader Tom Carpenter (2)-Moytoy (2)**/1660 & her aunt **Nancy Turkey Cornstalk**/1664, could cipher, read & speak some English, wife 1st 1704 Chota TN of **Tsula Fox-Smallpox Conjurer**/1670, 2nd 1718 Chota TN of **Richard Barnes**/1695-white, children/1705-17 **with Fox-Conjurer** unknown, mother **with Barnes** of Mary Barnes/1720 & Charity Barnes/1726-both 31/64th ChalakathaShawano-Chalaka-Powhatan -Metis

GRANDDAUGHTER

Turkey, Oolootah aka Oolootah Hop-Ulutse-Oolootsee-Oolootah Rainmaker-Wife of John Bowles – 63/64th Chalakatha-ShawanoChalaka-Powhatan born 1692 Chota TN-died after 1756 TN - daughter of **Big Turkey**/1660 & **Chalakatha Woman**/1664, parents killed 1694
VA by Catawba raiders, adopted daughter 1694 TN of **Rainmaker (1)**/1640 & **Quatsey (1)**/1650-both Cherokee, Blue Holly Clan Cherokee, lived with sister **Quatsis Hop-Beamer** from 1699-1705, wife 1st 1705 Chota TN of **Blue Holly Cherokee**/1685-(also husband 1707 of her sister **Ghigoneli**), 2nd by 1722 Settico TN of **John Bowles**/1688SCO, children/1706-21 **with Blue Holly** unknown, mother **with**

Bowles of Ghigoneli Bowles/1723-1/2 Chalakatha-Shawano-Chalaka-Powhatan-Metis

GRANDDAUGHTER

Turkey, Ghigoneli aka Ghigoneli Hop-Younger Sister of Old Hop-Ghigoneli Rainmaker - 63/64th Chalakatha-Shawano-ChalakaPowhatan born 1694 Chota TN-died 1724 Chota TN – daughter of **Big Turkey**/1660 & **Chalakatha Woman**/1664, parents killed 1694 VA by Catawba raiders, adopted daughter 1694 TN of **Rainmaker (1)**/1640 & **Quatsey (1)**/1650-both Cherokee, Blue Holly Clan Cherokee, wife 1st 1707 TN of **Blue Holly Cherokee**/1685-(also husband 1705 of her sister Oolootha/1692), 2nd by 1710 TN of **French-Canadian Mulatto**/1690-(or a Melungeon?), 3rd 1720 TN of **May Apple**/1690-Kishpoko, any children/1707-10 **with Blue Holly** unknown, mother **with Mulatto** of John French (French John)/1710 & Capt. French (Cappee)/1712-both 31/64th Chalakatha-Shawano-Chalaka-Powhatan-Black-Metis, **with May Apple** of Ninihica Mayapple/1721 & Laskigitchi Mayapple/1723both 63/64th Chalakatha-Kishpoko-Shawano-Chalaka-Powhatan

BY LITTLE TURKEY CORNSTALK/1662

GRANDDAUGHTER

Turkey, Katie – 63/64th Chalakatha-Shawano-Chalaka-Powhatan born 1684 Nickajack TN-died 1738 Great Tellico TN – daughter of **Little Turkey Cornstalk**/1662 & **Chalakatha Woman**/1666, Turkey Clan, known as a niece of **Big Turkey**/1660 & **Nancy Turkey**/1664, wife 1698 Nickajack TN of **Thomas Caesar-Skiagunsta Greenwood**/1680, could read, speak & cipher some English, mother of Thomas Sutichettchee Greenwood/1698, John Cheesquatalone Greenwood/1700, children/1701-11, daughters Quatsis Atawaya Greenwood/1712, Sedano Greenwood/1715, childen/1716-19, daughter Nancy Greenwood/1720, son Big Turkey Greenwood/1722, children/1723-28 & daughter Ankee Greenwood/1729-all 51/64th Chalakatha-ThawikilaKishpoko-Shawano-Chalaka-Powhatan-Black-Metis

BY NANCY TURKEY CORNSTALK/1664

GRANDSON

Carpenter, White Owl (1) aka White Owl Raven- White Owl (1)**Caulanna**-Collanah-**Moytoy (4)** – 23/32nd Chalakatha-ShawanoChalaka-Powhatan-Metis born 1678 Running Water TN-**killed 1741 TN in battle** – son of **Trader Tom Carpenter (2)-Moytoy (2)**/1660 & **Nancy Turkey Cornstalk**/1664, Long Hair Clan Cherokee, could cipher, read & speak some English, delegation to ENG 1730, leader of the 7 Cherokee Clans, killed in same battle as **Young Rainmaker**, husband 1st about 1698 (TN?) of **Unknown (Shawnee?) Woman**, 2nd 1711 TN of **Nancy Rainmaker**/1683-Cherokee, children/1698-1711 **with Unknown Woman** not known, father **with Nancy Rainmaker** of Killancea-Buck Carpenter/1712, Killaqua Carpenter/1714, Betsy-Eliza-Quatie Ooloocha Carpenter/1716, Tame Doe-Cati-Catherine Carpenter/1718, All Bones-Flying Squirrel Carpenter/1720, Oousta Carpenter/1722 & Bushy Head Carpenter/1724-all 1/4th Chalakatha-Shawano-ChalakaPowhatan-Cherokee-Metis, **adopted father** 1710 with marriage to his brother's widow of Great Eagle Carpenter/1702, Elizabeth Tassel Carpenter/1704, Attakullakulla Carpenter/1706, (Old) Corn Tassel Carpenter/1708 & Susan Moytoy Carpenter/1710, adopted father 1715 of **Amoyah Pigeon Moytoy**/1715 (son of his sister **Pashmere Carpenter (2)**/1681)

GRANDSON

Carpenter, Savannah Tom (1) aka Thomas Carpenter (4)-Corn Planter (4)-**Moytoy (3)** – 23/32nd Chalakatha-Shawano-Chalaka-PowhatanMetis born 1680 Chota TN-died 1710 Oconee SC - son of **Nancy Turkey Cornstalk**/1664 & **Trader Tom Carpenter (2)-Moytoy (2)**/1660, from Chota & Running Water TN, associated with adopted brother (1st cousin) **Standing Turkey-Old Hop** & **Young Rainmaker**, taught to speak, cipher, read & write English by his father, husband 1st 1697 Upper Hiwassee VA of **Susan-Quatsey (2) Rainmaker**/1682-Cherokee, 2nd 1698 of her sister **Nancy Rainmaker**/1683-Cherokee, father **with Susan-Quatsey** of Savannah Tom Carpenter (2)-Corn Planter (5)/1698, **with Nancy** of Great Eagle Carpenter/1702, Elizabeth Tassel Carpenter/1704, Attakullakulla Carpenter/1706, Corn Tassel

Shawnee Heritage II

Carpenter/1708 & Susan Moytoy Carpenter/1710-all 23/64th Chalakatha-Shawano-Chalaka-Powhatan-Cherokee-Metis

GRANDDAUGHTER

Carpenter, Pashmere (2) – 23/32nd Chalakatha-Shawano-ChalakaPowhatan-Metis born 1681 Chota TN-died 1715 Upper Hiwassee VA – daughter of **Trader Tom Carpenter (2)-Moytoy (2)**/1660 & **Nancy Turkey Cornstalk**/1664, could cipher, read & speak some English, wife
1705 Upper Hiwassee VA of her adopted brother **Raven of Hiwassee Hop-Raven Moytoy**/1683, mother of Amoyah Pigeon Moytoy/1715-27/64th Chalakatha-Shawano-Chalaka-Powhatan-Metis

BY SISTER TURKEY/1666

GRANDDAUGHTER

Muskrat, Daughter of Muskrat (1) aka Muskrat's Sister-Sister of Muskrat (2) –Sister of Oshasqua-Granddaughter of Hokolesqua – 63/64th Pekowi-Chalakatha-Shawano-Chalaka-Powhatan born 1784 VA-**killed** 1708 by Catawba – daughter of **Muskrat-Oshasqua (1)**/1660 & **Sister Turkey-Daughter of Hokolesqua**/1666, sister of OshasquaMuskrat-Moytoy (5), parents but killed by southern raiders 1698, Turtle Clan, wife 1700 of **Thomas Tassel Watts**/1683-3/4th Chalakatha-Metis, mother of John Forked Tail Watts/1704-55/64th Chalakatha-PekowiShawano-Chalaka-Powhatan-Metis

GRANDSON

Muskrat (2) aka Oshasqua (2)-**Moytoy (5)**-Ossaghqua-OshkesquaHotthashkwa - 63/64th Pekowi-Chalakatha-Shawano-ChalakaPowhatan born 1686 Hiwassee TN-died 1754 Hiwassee TN – son of
Muskrat-Oshasqua (1)/1660 & **Sister Turkey-Daughter of Hokolesqua**/1666, parents killed 1698 VA-TN by Catawba, Turtle Clan Pekowi, from the Straight Tail band, adopted son 1698 of **Trader Tom Carpenter (2)-Moytoy (2)**/1660 & aunt **Nancy Turkey Cornstalk**/1664,

taught to read, speak & cipher some English by Carpenter, husband 1704 of adopted sister **Swan-Wapehti Hop**/1686, father of daughters Ahneewakee Muskrat/1704, Ounacona Muskrat/1716, Tame Deer Muskrat/1720, sons Oshasqua-Muskrat (3)/1718 & Bad Water MuskratMoytoy (6)/1722 & other unknown children/1705-31-all 63/64th Chalakatha-Pekowi-Shawano-Chalaka-Powhatan, adopted father 1708 of nephew **John Forked Tail Watts**/1704-55/64th Chalakatha-PekowiShawano-Chalaka-Powhatan-Metis

BY OKOWELLOS-CORNSTALK (5)/1674 WITH KATEE MEKOCHE/1680

GRANDDAUGHTER

Cornstalk, Wakuta – 27/32nd Chalakatha-Mekoche-Shawano-Chalaka-Powhatan-Metis born 1704 Running Water TN-died 1758 Running Water TN – daughter of **Okowellos**/1674 & **Katee Mekoche**/1680, Bear Clan, taught to read, speak & cipher some English by her father, wife 1718 Nickajack TN of **Thomas Sutichettchee Greenwood**/1698, mother of sons David Swallow-tail Greenwood/1718, Joseph Tallichama Greenwood/1720, Robert Tallitaha Greenwood/1722 & daughters Puki-Pequea Greenwood/1724 & Cheekee Greenwood/1728-all 13/16th Chalakatha-Thawikila-KishpokoMekoche-Shawano-Chalaka-Powhatan-Black-Metis

GRANDSON

Cornstalk (6) aka **Keightughqua Cornstalk**-Hokolesqua Cornstalk (3)Okowellos Cornstalk (2)-Stalk of Corn-Stalk of Plant-Hokolesqua (3)-Hokoleshka (3)-Okowellos (2)-Akulusska-Wneypuechsika-Waynaypooechseeka-Stout Man-Strong Man-Simaquan-Seemakwan – 27/32nd Chalakatha-Mekoche-Shawano-Chalaka-Powhatan-Metis born 1710 WV-**murdered** 1777 Point Pleasant WV - son of **Okowellos-Cornstalk (5)**/1674 & **Katee Mekoche**/1680, Bear Clan, taught to cipher, read, speak & write English by his father, went to AL with father by 1725, in PA by 1730-(married 1st 1730 PA), in TN by 1734(married 2nd in Running Water TN 1734), a **Chalakatha Chief** in PA by 1740, raiding PA/1740, (married 3rd in PA 1741), in OH about 1745, a **major**

Chalakatha chief in OH by 1749, Council near site of Ft. Pitt Nov. 1753, lead Chief & force in **Cornstalk War/1755-77 (**Cornstalk War = leading Shawnee Chief in French-Indian War/1754-63, leading Shawnee Chief at Braddock/1755, raiding New-Shenandoah valleys/1755-56, raiding PA/1755-56, negotiated Treaty 1757 at mouth of Big Sandy River with **Thomas Lewis & William Preston**, led raiding Ohio-New River valleys.1758, Council Ft. Pitt June 1762, **Head Shawnee Chief** in Pontiac War/1762-66, led Shawnee at Bushy Run/1763, led raiding of New-Greenbrier-Jackson River valleys/1763, Council with **Col. Bouquet** Oct. 1764, hostage of Col. Bouquet winter 1764-65 with brothers **Wakeeampea, Ewikunwee, Naythakeina & Red Hawk**, negotiated Treaty Spring 1765 with **Col. Bouquet** Oct. 1764, hostage of Col. Bouquet winter 1764-65 with brothers **Wakeeampea, Ewikunwee, Naythakeina & Red Hawk**, negotiated Treaty Spring 1765 with **Col. Bouquet**, raiding Ohio-New-Big Sandy-Little Kanawha valleys/1772, traveled & sent emissaries 1774 to Shawnee & related Tribes in **VA-NC-SC-GA-AL-TN-KY-MO-IL-MI-IN-OH-PA-MD-NY** enlisting support for upcoming Dunmore's War 1774, sought support of **nephew Dragging Canoe**, Point Pleasant/1774, **Head Chief of Northern Confederacy** at Point Pleasant/1774, negotiated Treaty Camp Charlotte 1774 with **Lord Dunmore**, Point Pleasant/1775, Council Ft. Pitt 1775 with **Nimwha, Silver Heels, Wryneck & Blue Jacket**, Council Ft. Pitt-George Morgan 1776 with **Nimwha, Ellinipsico, sister Cawechile, Capt. Johnny, Blue Jacket & Black Caesar**, Council 1776 with **White Eyes-Delaware, John Montour-Seneca-Metis, Wyandot Half-King & William Wilson**, Council Ft. Pitt 1777**)**, in AL 1754-55, returned to OH in 1755, in AL for a while 1757-58-(mentioned as **a Chief of the Shawnee among the Creeks**), returned to OH in 1758 (death of his father in epidemic), associated with **John Swift, Dragging Canoe, Double Head, Red Bird, John Watts & Nathaniel Gist** in silvermines-counterfeiting 1755-69 furnishing silver to Shawnee & Confederacy, **Head Chief of Chalakatha & All Shawnee** 1758-77, **Head Chief of 20 tribe Northern Confederacy** 1760-74-(most of the prewhite, west of Appalachians Shawnee confederacy), last home was at Cornstalk's village on Sippio Creek of Scioto River OH from early 1770's, **murdered** by whites at Ft. Randolph-Point Pleasant/1777 with brother **Red Hawk**, son **Ellinipsico** & son in law/adopted son **Petella**, taught most of his children to cipher read & write in English, at least to some degree, husband 1st 1730 PA of **Helizikinopo Snake**/1715Mekoche, 2nd 1734 Running Water TN of **Ounaconoa Muskrat**/171663/64th Chalakatha-Pekowi-Shawano-Chalaka-Powhatan, 3rd 1741 PA of **Julia Mulatto**/1720-adopted-Mulatto, (at least) 4th 1763 OH of **Catherine Vanderpoole See**/1725-adopted-white, (other wives/173077 possible including a Creek/Shawnee-Creek about 1757), father **with Helizikinopo** of Walker-Pomeatha/1730, Wolf/1732, Catherine (Petella)/1734, Chenusaw/1736, Newa/1738, Greenbrier (Kennison)/1740, Aracoma (Baker)/1742, Elizabeth (Swift-Petella)/1744,Young Cornstalk/1746, Ellinipsico/1748, Blue Sky-Mary (Adkins)/1750, Esther (Soward)/1751, Oceana/1752-all 29/32nd Chalakatha-Mekoche-Shawano-Chalaka-Powhatan-Metis, **with Ounaconoa** of Black Beard/1736, Black Wolf/1740, John Wolf (Cornstalk)/1750, Peter Cornstalk/1755 & Susannah Cornstalk/1757-all 29/32nd Chalakatha-Mekoche-Pekowi-Shawano-Chalaka-PowhatanMetis, **with Julia** of Sun Fish/1742, Elijah Cornstalk/1744, Abraham Cornstalk "Ailstock"/1748, Absalom Cornstalk "Ailstock"/1750 & Michael Cornstalk "Ailstock"/1752-all 27/64th Chalakatha-Mekoche-Shawano-Chalaka-Powhatan-Black-Metis, **with Catherine** of Mary (Cornstalk) See/1764-27/64th Chalakatha-Mekoche-Shawano-ChalakaPowhatan-Metis, **adopted father** about 1740 PA of **Petella**/1730-white, 1763 OH of **Elizabeth See**/1754 & **John See**/1759-white, (unknown children with all wives likely & a **Creek Wife** about 1758 also likely)

GRANDDAUGHTER

Cornstalk, Sawelaha aka Eliza Cornstalk-Wife of James Francis-Wife of Old Belt-Grenadier Squaw – 27/32nd Chalakatha-Mekoche-ShawanoChalaka-Powhatan-Metis born 1712 WV-died after 1745 likely OH - daughter of **Okowellos**/1674 & **Katee Mekoche**/1680, Bear Clan, taught to cipher, read & speak some English by her father, wife 1st 1730 PA of **Chalakatha Man**/1710, 2nd 1739 PA of **James Francis**/1700British Colonial Military, 3rd after 1745 OH of **Old Belt**/1700-Seneca, mother **with Chalakatha** of Aroas-Silverheels (2)/1732 &

Counasona/1735-both 59/64th Chalakatha-Mekoche-Shawano-ChalakaPowhatan-Metis -(later adopted Seneca), **with Francis** of David Francis/1740 & John Francis (1)/1745-both 27/64th ChalakathaMekoche-Shawano-Chalaka-Powhatan-Metis, any children **with Belt** unknown

GRANDSON

Cornstalk, Keeweeton aka Keeweeton Okowellos-KeewetonKeywayton-Kaywayton-Quiouiton-Quiwetahn-Keywetahn-KiwitahnBrother of Cornstalk – 27/32nd Chalakatha-Mekoche-Shawano-Chalaka-Powhatan-Metis born 1714 WV-died before 1804 OH - son of **Okowellos**/1674 & **Katee Mekoche**/1680, moved to AL with father 1725, returned to PA by 1730, may have returned to AL for a short while in 1755, Bear Clan, over 6' tall, taught to cipher, read & speak some English by his father, raiding PA/1740, Cornstalk War /1755-77, a **Chalakatha Chief** in OH by 1763, **an emissary to the Shawnee for Cornstalk** 1774, Blue Jacket War/1777-80, husband 1734 PA of **Chalakatha Woman**/1718, children unknown

GRANDDAUGHTER

Cornstalk, Cawechile aka Younger Daughter of-Wife of Cold Water – 27/32nd Chalakatha-Mekoche-Shawano-Chalaka-Powhatan-Metis born 1716 WV-died after 1807 OH - daughter of **Okowellos**/1674 & **Katee Mekoche**/1680, a Chalakatha, Bear Clan, taught to cipher, read & speak English by her father, in later years the **Chief of the Women's Council**, speaker for the women & children, about 6' tall, Council Ft. Pitt 1776 with **Cornstalk, Nimwha, Ellinipsico, Blue Jacket, Capt. Johnny & Caesar** with George Morgan, Council Ft. Finney 1786 with **Moluntha, Capt. Johnny, Red Pole, Black Snake, Nianimissico (?), Wapachcawela (?), Nihipeewa & Nihinessiko**, wife 1st about 1735 PA of **Cold Water-Wepenipe**/1715– Chalakatha, 2nd 1753 OH of **ElkWabete**/1715-Mekoche, mother **with Cold Water** of children/1736-39, Young Cold Water/1740, Lacumtequa Cold Water/1744 & other children-all 1759/64th Mekoche-Chalakatha-Shawano-ChalakaPowhatan-Metis, any children **with Elk-Wabete** unknown

GRANDDAUGHTER

Cornstalk, Nonhelema aka Grenadier Squaw-Shawnee Warrior Woman-Nonhelema Okowellos-Nonhelema Hokolesqua - 27/32nd Chalakatha-Mekoche-Shawano-Chalaka-Powhatan-Metis born 1718 Greenbrier River WV-died after 1786 OH - daughter of **Okowellos**/1674 & **Katee Mekoche**/1680, about 6'6" tall, well built & attractive, often referred to as a giant, moved to AL by 1725 with Okowellos' band-returned to PA by 1730, a **Chalakatha village Head woman** in OH by 1750, read & spoke some English, an occasional warrior in Cornstalk War /1755-74, Head Woman of Nonhelema's village on Sippio Creek of Sciota River OH before 1773, **an emissary to the Shawnee for Cornstalk** 1774, the **only woman warrior** Point Pleasant/1774, Grand Council 1782, Council Miami Jan. 1786, had the fingers cut off of her right hand to the 1st knuckle by whites following **murder of Moluntha** during Benjamin Logan's attack on Moluntha's village 1786, moved to Apple Creek MO area following death of Moluntha-returned to OH home to die, wife 1st 1734 PA of **Savannah King-Wahootasika**/1710-Chalakatha-widowed 1754, 2nd 1754 OH of 1st cousin **Moluntha**/1708-Mekoche, unmarried partner (she never really left Moluntha) 3rd 1762 OH with **Richard Butler**/1742-white-(adopted Seneca), mother **with Savannah King-Wahootasika** of Elder Daughter/1735, Mellana/1748, twin daughters Wynema & Waheeta/1750--all 59/64th Chalakatha-Mekoche-Shawano-Chalaka-Powhatan-Metis, **with Moluntha** of Chieska/1755, Younger Daughter/1757 & Big Capt. Johnny/1759-all 59/64th MekocheChalakatha-Shawano-Chalaka-Powhatan-Metis, **with Richard Butler** of Capt. Butler/1763-27/64th Chalakatha-Mekoche-Shawano-Chalaka-Powhatan-Metis, adoptive mother of niece **Fanny Butler**/1755- (daughter of her half-sister **Elizabeth Cornstalk**/1726 & **John Sugantah-Lodging Pole Butler**/1730-white-adopted Seneca), often confused in white histories with her sisters & nieces

GRANDSON

Cornstalk, Nimwha aka Nimwha Okowellos –27/32nd ChalakathaMekoche-Shawano-Chalaka-Powhatan-Metis born 1720 WV-died after

1786 likely OH - son of **Okowellos**/1674 & **Katee Mekoche**/1680, to AL with father 1725-returned to PA by 1730, Bear Clan, taught to cipher, read & speak some English by his father, a **Chief of the Shawnee among the Delaware** 1750, Cornstalk War /1755-77, Council Muskingum Nov. 1764, Council Logstown 1765, Council Ft. Pitt 1765, **an emissary to the Delaware for Cornstalk** 1774, Blue Jacket War/1777-86, Treaty Camp Charlotte 1774, hostage of whites winter 1774-75, Council Ft. Pitt 1775 with **Corn Stalk, Silver Heels, Wryneck & Blue Jacket**, Council Ft. Pitt 1776, **succeeded Red Hawk as Chief of Shawnee among the Delaware 1777**, Council Ft. Pitt 1785, Council Ft. Pitt 1786, Treat 1786, husband 1739 PA of **Delaware Woman**/1723, children unknown

GRANDSON

Cornstalk, Red Hawk aka **Miskapelathee**-Misquapolathe-Red Hawk Okowellos –27/32nd Chalakatha-Mekoche-Shawano-ChalakaPowhatan-Metis born 1722 WV-died 1777 Point Pleasant WV - son of **Okowellos**/1674 & **Katee Mekoche**/1680, Bear Clan, taught to cipher, read & speak English by his father, a **Mekoche Chief** by 1759, Cornstalk War /1755-77, Council Ft. Pitt Aug. 1759, Council Ft. Pitt Aug.-Sept. 1762, Council Lancaster Aug. 1762, hostage of **Bouquet** winter of 1764-65 with **Cornstalk, Wakeeampea, Ewikunwee & Naythakeina**, often represented Cornstalk at Councils/1760-74, Treaty 1765, **Chief of Shawnee among the Delaware** about 1764, **an emissary/carried wampum to Dragging Canoe for Cornstalk** before Point Pleasant 1774, Camp Charlotte 1774, **murdered at Ft. Randolph**/Point Pleasant WV 1777 with **Cornstalk,** nephew **Ellinipsico** & adopted nephew **Petella**, husband 1st 1742 PA of a **Mekoche Woman**/1726 & 2nd about 1754 OH of a **Delaware Woman**/1738, children unknown

GRANDSON

Cornstalk, Silverheels (1) aka Halowas-Silverheels Okowellos (1) – 27/32nd Chalakatha-Mekoche-Shawano-Chalaka-Powhatan-Metis born 1724 PA-died 1804 OH - son of **Okowellos**/1674 & **Katee Mekoche**1680, Bear Clan, taught to cipher, read & speak English by his father, Cornstalk War /1755-77, a **Chalakatha Chief, an emissary to the Shawnee for Cornstalk** 1774, Blue Jacket War /1777-94,

Boonesboro/78, Council Camp Charlotte 1774, Council Ft. Woods 1775, Council Ft. Pitt 1775 with **Cornstalk, Nimwha, Wryneck & Blue Jacket**, over 6' tall, husband about 1745 OH of **Chalakatha Woman**/1730, father of Silverheels (4)-Young Halowas (2)/1760, Daughter/1770, Sarah Silverheels/1775 & other unknown children/1744-74-all 59/64th Chalakatha-Mekoche-Shawano-Chalaka-Powhatan-Metis

WITH DAUGHTER OF SASSOONAN/1697

GRANDSON

Cornstalk, Wakeeampea aka Wakeeampea Okowellos – 11/32nd Chalakatha-Shawano-Chalaka-Powhatan-Delaware-Metis born 1714 PA-died after 1765 likely OH - son of **Okowellos**/1674 & **Daughter of Sassoonan**/1697, Bear-Turkey Clan, taught to cipher, read & speak some English by his father, raiding PA/1740, Cornstalk War /1755-65, a **Delaware Chief** in Ohio valley by 1750, hostage of **Col. Bouquet** 1765 with **Cornstalk, Ewikunwee, Naythakeina & Red Hawk**, husband by 1734 PA of **Delaware Woman**/1719, children unknown

GRANDSON

Cornstalk, Ewikunwee aka Hewikunwee-Ewikunwee Okowellos – 11/32nd Chalakatha-Shawano-Chalaka-Powhatan-Delaware-Metis born 1716 PA-died after 1765 OH - son of **Okowellos**/1674 & **Daughter of Sassoonan**/1697, Bear-Turkey Clan, taught to cipher, read & speak some English by his father, raiding PA/1740, Cornstalk War /1755-65, a **Chief of the Shawnee among the Delaware** in the Ohio valley by 1755, hostage of **Col. Bouquet** winter of 1764-65 with **Wakeeampea, Cornstalk, Naythakeina & Red Hawk**, husband about 1736 PA of a **Delaware Woman**/1719, children unknown

GRANDSON

Cornstalk, Naythakeina aka Neightthakeina-Naythakeina Okowellos – 11/32nd Chalakatha-Shawano-Chalaka-Powhatan-Delaware-Metis born 1718 PA-died after 1765 - son of **Okowellos**/1674 & **Daughter of Sassoonan**/1697, Bear-Turkey Clan, taught to cipher, read & speak some English by his father, raiding PA/1740, a **Chief of the Shawnee among the Delaware** 1745, Cornstalk War /1755-65, hostage of **Col.**

Bouquet 1765 with **Wakeeampea, Cornstalk, Ewikunwee & Red Hawk**, husband 1738 PA of **Delaware Woman**/1722, children unknown

GRANDSON

Cornstalk, Bukangolas aka Bukangolas Hokolesqua-Bukangolas Okowellos-Bukangolas-Bukanghelas-Pukangolas-Breaks to PiecesBuckongahlas-Beloved Leader-He Who Fulfills – 11/32nd ChalakathaShawano-Chalaka-Powhatan-Delaware-Metis born 1720 PA-died 1804 OH - son of **Okowellos**/1674 & **Daughter of Sassoonan**/1697, BearTurkey Clan, went to AL with father 1725, returned to PA by 1731, taught to cipher, read & speak some English by his father, in OH before 1758, raiding PA/1740, Cornstalk War /1755-77, Council 1763, a **Major Delaware Chief** by mid-1760's, an **emissary to the Delaware for Cornstalk** 1774, scarred on left cheek-left ear cut off in battle by sword blow before 1778, Blue Jacket War /1777-94, Council Detroit Nov. 1781, Grand Council 1782, Treaty 1785, Council Miami Jan. 1786 & Aug. 1786, Grand Council 1792, Treaty Greenville 1795, Council Swan Creek OH 1795 with **Capt. Johnny, Black Beard & George Ironside**, Treaty 1803 & 1804, **refused Tecumseh** in early ventures, husband 1740 PA of **Delaware Woman**/1725, father of many 11/64th Chalakatha-ShawanoChalaka-Powhatan-Delaware-Metis children/1740-70

WITH SISTER OF SEHOY/1709

GRANDAUGHTER

Cornstalk, Elizabeth aka Elizabeth Okowellos-Sister of Cornstalk-Grenadier Squaw – 11/32nd Chalakatha-Shawano-Chalaka-PowhatanCreek-Metis born 1726 Shawnee village AL-died after 1817 OH- daughter of **Okowellos**/1674 & **Sister of Sehoy**/1709-Creek, in PA by 1730 with father, taught to cipher, read & speak English by her father, appears to have not returned to AL 1755-58, Bear-Wind Clan, a Christian Chalakatha, about 6' tall i.e. a Grenadier Squaw & attractive, often a translator-messenger for the whites, wife 1st about 1744 PA of **Chalakatha Man**/1724, 2nd about 1754 OH of **Capt. John Butler**Lodging Pole/1730-white-(adopted Seneca), 3rd 1760 OH of **Mekoche Man**/1720, children/1744-54 & 1760/71 **with Chalakatha &**

Mekoche husbands unknown, mother **with John Butler** of Fanny Butler/1755 & Tommy Butler/1760-both 11/64th Chalakatha-Shawano-ChalakaPowhatan-Creek-Metis, often confused in white histories with her sisters & nieces

GRANDAUGHTER

Cornstalk, Catherine (1) aka Kitty-Catherine Kitty Okowellos-Catherine Kitty Cornstalk (1)-Sister of Cornstalk-Grenadier Squaw – 11/32nd Chalakatha-Shawano-Chalaka-Powhatan-Creek-Metis born 1728 Shawnee village AL-died after 1797 likely OH - daughter of **Okowellos**/1674 & **Sister of Sehoy**/1709-Creek, Bear-Wind Clan, a Christian Chalakatha, about 6' tall i.e. a Grenadier Squaw & attractive, taught to cipher, read & speak English by her father, often a translatormessenger for the whites, wife 1st 1745 OH of **Wrynek-Aquilsa**/1725Pekowi, partner 2nd 1764 of **William Butler**/1744-white (adoptedSeneca), children/1745-65 **with Wrynek-Aquilsa** unknown, mother **with Butler** of Polly Butler/1765-11/64th Chalakatha-ShawanoChalaka-Powhatan-Creek-Metis, often confused in white histories with her sisters & nieces

BY TAMENEBUCK-CORN BLADE CORNSTALK/1680
WITH DAUGHTER OF STRAIGHT TAIL/1680

GRANDSON

Cornstalk, Corn Cob – 27/32nd Chalakatha-Pekowi-Shawano-Chalaka-Powhatan-Metis born about 1710 PA-died after 1768 OH-IL – son of **Tamenebuck-Corn Blade**/1680 & **Daughter of Straight Tail**/1680, Bear Clan, raiding PA/1740, Cornstalk War/1755-68, a **Chalakatha Chief** in OH by 1755, traveled with **Rene-Pale Stalker Chartier** to Detroit 1768, husband 1st about 1740 PA of **Chalakatha Woman**/1725, 2nd 1763 OH of **Adopted-White Woman**/1750, father **with Chalakatha** of several children/1740-64, **with White Woman** of three known children/1764-68

Martin Chartier/1655

Chartier, Martin - adopted-French born 1655 FRA-died 1718 PA – son of **Rene Chartier/1621** & **Madeleine Ranger**/1625, arrived in Quebec 1667 with father **Rene Chartier**/1621, brother **Pierre Chartier**/1646 & a sister **Jeanne-Renee Chartier**/1652 & **Robert Cavellier de LaSalle**/1643, 1668 meets **Wolf**/1654 a Shawnee boy turned over to the priests at Montreal that becomes his constant companion, 1669 his father Rene/1621 remarries to Marguerite Delorme, 1669 with **his brother Pierre**/1646 on **LaSalle's** 1st expedition, 1669 with his brother Pierre/1646 on **Louis Joliet's** 1st expedition, 1672 with **his brother Pierre**/1646 on **Louis Joliet**'s 2nd expedition, 1674 he was living **with the Shawnee** in IL on the Wabash, by 1675 he had taken **Sewatha** as his Shawnee wife, 1679 **with Wolf**/1654 went with **LaSalle** to build Ft. Crevecoeur on the Illinois River, by 1680 he had at least a daughter & a son **by Sewatha**, 1683 trading with the Shawnee at Ft. St. Louis with **his brother Pierre**/1646, 1684 in the company of a Ms. **Francoise Daudolikely Sewatha** in Lachine, 1684 **his brother Pierre Chartier**/1646 is killed in the massacre at Ft. St. Louis, 1685 he was living with **Straight Tail** band in IL territory, 1687 arrested in Montreal, 1689 **his father Rene Chartier**/1621, half-sister **Marie Anne Chartier**/1671, **halfbrothers Francois Chartier**/1672 & **Rene Chartier**/1674 are killed in the massacre at Lachine, **half-sister Jeanne Chartier**/1675 survives, 1689 known to be a fur-trader on Cumberland River TN, 1690 stopped in a Shawnee village in east TN, 1691 reunited on the Potomac with companions from Ft. St. Louis; **Jacques & Ann LeTort, Pierre, Michael & Louis Bisaillon, Nicholas Godin** & **Jean or Joseph Dubois**, 1692 on the Potomac in MD with the Shawnee, then in Baltimore Co MD, then jailed in Ste. Marie & Ann Arundel Counties MD as a French spy but escaped, 1693 went with **a group of Shawnee** leaving VA to OH, 1700 living on Conestoga Creek in Lancaster Co PA, husband 1676 IL of **Sewatha Straight Tail**/1660, father of Madeleine Chartier/1678,
Charles Chartier-Charleville/1680 IL, children/1682-84, Jean Chartier-

Charleville/1686 IL, Mary Chartier/1688 IL-TN, Peter Chartier/1790TN, Jacquette Chartier/1692 MD & likely other unrecorded children-all 1/2 Pekowi-Metis

WIFE OF MARTIN CHARTIER

Straight Tail, Sewatha aka Seaworth – Pekowi born about 1660 OH-died after 1700 PA - daughter of **Straight Tail -Meaurroway**/1630 & **Pekowi Woman/**1635, Turtle Clan, 1677 moved with band from OHmid-Ohio valley to IN-IL-Miami & Illinois River valleys near Miami & Illinois, 1689 band from IL-IN joins **Chalakatha, Mekoche & Kishpoko** in corner of east TN-west NC-east KY-southwest VA, by 1693 most of band was living in Cecil Co MD, by 1697 was living in Lancaster Co PA-Susquehanna valley, wife by 1676 IL of **Martin Chartier**/1655adopted French, mother of Madeleine Chartier/1678, Charles ChartierCharleville/1680 IL, children/1682-84, Jean Chartier-Charleville/1686
IL, Mary Chartier/1688 IL-TN, Peter Chartier/1790-TN, Jacquette Chartier/1692 MD & likely other unrecorded children-all 1/2 Pekowi-Metis

CHILDREN OF MARTIN CHARTIER & SEWATHA STRAIGHT TAIL

DAUGHTER

Chartier, Madeleine - 1/2 Pekowi-Metis born about 1678 IL-died after 1700 - daughter of **Martin Chartier**/1655-adopted-French & **Sewatha Straight Tail**/1660, namesake of deceased grandmother Madeleine Ranger, Turtle Clan, sister of **Peter Chartier**, granddaughter of **Meaurroway-Straight Tail**/1630, by 1689 living with father on the Cumberland River TN, 1690 in east TN, by 1701 living in Lancaster Co PA with father, husband & children unknown

SON

Chartier, Charles aka Charles Charleville - 1/2 Pekowi-Metis born about 1680 IL-died after 1714 - son of **Martin Chartier**/1655-adoptedFrench & **Sewatha Straight Tail**/1660, Turtle Clan, grandson of **Meaurroway-Straight Tail**/1630, by 1689 living with father on the Cumberland River TN, 1690 in east TN-NC, by 1700 living in Lancaster Co PA with father, by 1710 established a trading post with his brother Jean at French Lick on the Cumberland River TN-the site of Nashville, wife & children unknown

SON

Chartier, Jean aka Jean Charleville-Jean de Charleville-Jean du Charleville - 1/2 Pekowi-Metis born about 1686 IL-died 1780 TN - son of **Martin Chartier**/1655-adopted-French & **Sewatha Straight Tail**/1660, Turtle Clan, grandson of **Meaurroway-Straight Tail**/1630, by 1689 living with father on the Cumberland River TN, 1690 in east TN-NC, by 1700 living in Lancaster Co PA with father, by 1710 established a trading post with his brother Charles at French Lick on the Cumberland River TN-the site of Nashville, 1714 he took bateau load of furs New Orleans to trade, wife & children unknown

DAUGHTER

Chartier, Mary (1) aka Maria Chartier - 1/2 Pekowi-Metis born about 1688 IL-**killed** 1732 Bedford Co PA - daughter of **Martin Chartier**/1655adopted-French & **Sewatha Straight Tail**/1660,Turtle Clan, sister of **Peter Chartier**/1690, **killed in Native attack with 7 of 12 children**, wife by 1705 PA of **Jean DeBert**-John Burt/1685-white, mother of 12 children-5 that survived 1732- Wilhelm DeBert (husband of Rechler & Weigner)/1711, Daughter (wife of George Heurtzinger)/1713,
Daughter (wife of John Geuert)/1715, Michael DeBert/1717 & Charles Christopher Dibert/1719- all 1/4th Pekowi-Metis

SON

Chartier, Peter aka **Wocunuckshenah-Pale Brother** - 1/2 Pekowi-Metis born about 1690 TN-died about 1759 OH (possibly in epidemic) - son of **Martin Chartier**/1655 & **Sewatha Straight Tail**/1660, Turtle Clan, grandson of **Straight Tail-Meaurroway**/1630, before 1697 moved with

Opessa Band to Lancaster Co PA, 1707 living on Pequea Creek Lancaster Co PA, 1718 living in Dekanoagah Lancaster Co PA-obtained title to 300 acres on the Susquehanna River where his father had died, 1732 witnessed a letter from **Neucheconner** & other Shawnee Chiefs to the Governor of PA , 1732 attended Council Philadelphia with **Opakethwa, Opakeita** & **Kwassenung Pheasant**, 1734 founded Chartier's Town Alleghany Co PA, 1737 a **Pekowi Chief in PA**, 1738 signed **Petition to PA** with **Pride Opessa**, **Tecomteh Opessa** & **George Miranda**, 1744 left the British of PA with about 400 Pekowi, Chalakatha & Kishpoko-including **Neucheconner** & **Tamenebuck,** to join the French of OH , (**Kakawatchekee** & **Kishacoquillas** refused to join them) moved southwest to the mouth of the Sciota River-Lower Shawnee Town with sons, 1745 moved on to near Winchester KY- (**Neucheconner** & **Tamenebuck** return to PA), 1746 moved on to French Lick-Nashville TN, 1747 moved to the Coosa River AL, 1748 allegedly seen with some of his band in IL & Detroit when the French doubted his control of the band-(it may have been one of his sons **Francois Chartier** or **Rene-Pale Stalker Chartier** that were seen), 1752 returned to KY, active in opposition to the British on the frontier in the French-Indian War/1754-59, 1758 in OH with band, died either just after the band moved to OH, husband about 1710 PA of his 1st cousin **Snow White Opessa**/1695-Pekowi, father of children/1714-18, Rene Pale Stalker Chartier/1720, children/1722-28, Anna Chartier/1730 & other children/1732-36-all 3/4th Pekowi-Metis

DAUGHTER

Chartier, Jacquette – ½ Pekowi-Metis born about 1692 (PA?)-died after 1712 – daughter of **Martin Chartier**/1655 & **Sewatha Straight Tail**/1660, Turtle Clan, husband & children unknown

GRANDCHILDREN OF MARTIN CHARTIER & SEWATHA STRAIGHT TAIL

BY MARY CHARTIER/1688 & JEAN DEBURT/1685

GRANDSON

DeBert, Wilhelm - 1/4th Pekowi-Metis born 1711 PA-died after 1742 – son of **Mary Chartier**/1687 & **John DeBert**/1685, survived the massacre of 1732, Turtle Clan, husband 1st of **Miss Rechler**, 2nd of **Miss Weigner**, father **with**
Rechler of John Dubert, Rosina Dubert, Catherine Dubert, **with**
Weigner of Michael Dubert, William Dubert, George Dubert, Henry Dubert, Elizabeth Dubert-all 1/8th Pekowi-Metis

GRANDAUGHTER

DeBert, Older Daughter of John – 1/4th Pekowi-Metis born 1713 PAdied after 1733 (VA?) – daughter of **Mary Chartier**/1687 & **John DeBert**/1685, survived the massacre of 1732, Turtle Clan, wife after 1732 of **George Heurtzinger**, children unknown

GRANDAUGHTER

DeBert, Younger Daughter of John - 1/4th Pekowi-Metis born 1715 PAdied after 1733 (VA?) – daughter of **Mary Chartier**/1687 & **John DeBert**/1685, survived the massacre of 1732, Turtle Clan, wife after 1732 of **John Geuert**, children unknown

GRANDSON

DeBert, Michael - 1/4th Pekowi-Metis born 1717 PA-died after 1733 – son of **Mary Chartier**/1687 & **John DeBert**/1685, survived the massacre of 1732, Turtle Clan, husband of **Unknown Woman**, father of Henry Dubert (husband of Miss Kriner), Andrew Dubert (husband of Miss Luckenbill), Michael Dubert (husband of Miss Luckenbill), Christian Dubert (husband of Miss Miller), Catherine Dubert (wife of John Howard), Elizabeth Dubert (wife of John Repp), John Dubert/1799-all 1/8th Pekowi-Metis

GRANDSON

Dibert, Charles Christopher aka Deburt-Debert-Debolt - 1/4th PekowiMetis born 1719 PA-**killed** 1757 Bedford Co PA in Native attack - son of **Mary Chartier**/1687 & **John Deburt**/1685-white, Turtle Clan, grandson of **Martin Chartier** & **Sewatha Straight Tail**, nephew of **Peter Chartier**/1690, husband 1st (legally) 1738 VA of his 1st cousin **Elizabeth Dubert**/1720, 2nd after 1740 Bedford Co PA of household servant **Eve Shawnee**/1722-Pekowi-(of Opessa Band), father **with Dubert** of Michael Dibert/1738, Margaret Dibert/1743, John Dibert/1746, Sophia Dibert/1748, Fredrick Dibert/1750-all 1/8th Pekowi-Metis, **with Eve** of Adam Dibert/1741, George Debolt/1745, Charles Christopher Dibert Jr/1747, Mary Debolt/1751- all 5/8th Pekowi-Metis

GRANDCHILDREN OF MARTIN CHARTIER & SEWATHA STRAIGHT TAIL

BY PETER CHARTIER/1690 & SNOW WHITE OPESSA/1695

GRANDSON

Chartier, Francois aka **Pale Croucher**-Chartier's Son - 3/4th Pekowi-Metis born about 1712 PA-died after 1752 OH - son of **Peter Chartier**/1690 & **Snow White Opessa**/1695-Pekowi, Turtle Clan, 1744 moved with father from PA-MD to Lower Shawnee Town OH to support the French, 1746 returned to PA with **Neucheconner**, by 1752 had moved to OH with **Neucheconner** & others-living on the Miami River, husband about 1734 PA of **Younger Daughter of Poxinosa**/1720Pekowi, father of Nancy Chartier Nadachine Chartier/1735-7/8th Pekowi-Metis

GRANDSON

Chartier, Rene aka **Pale Stalker**-Chartier's Son - 3/4th Pekowi-Metis born about 1720 PA-died after 1775 (OH?) - son of **Peter Chartier**/1690 & **Snow White Opessa**/1695-Pekowi, Turtle Clan, a Pekowi warrior, 1744 moved with father from PA-MD to Lower Shawnee Town OH to support the French, 1745 with father near site of Winchester KY, 1748 in IL & Detroit, 1752 in KY with his father, Cornstalk War/1755-75, 1759 living in OH, 1768 traveled with **Corn Cob Cornstalk** to Detroit, husband about 1740 OH-KY of **Pekowi Woman**/1725, father of

Elizabeth Chartier/1760, Mary Chartier/1770 & other unrecorded 7/8th Pekowi-Metis children

GRANDAUGHTER

Chartier, Anna aka Anne - 3/4th Pekowi-Metis born about 1730 PA-died after 1779 (PA?) - daughter of **Peter Chartier**/1690 & **Snow White Opessa**/1695, Turtle Clan, namesake of **Anne LeTort**, wife about 1750 PA of **David Troxell**/1730, mother of child/52, Solomon Troxell/1754, George Troxell/1756, **Jacob-Big Jake Troxell**/1758, John Troxell/1760, Fredrick Troxell/1762, twins Mary & Elizabeth Troxell/1764, **Peter Jacob-Little Jake Troxell**/1766, Abraham Troxell/1768, David Troxell Jr/1770 & Catherine Troxell/1772-all 3/8th Pekowi-Metis

Cakundawanna Straight Tail/1670

Straight Tail, Cakundawanna aka **Sevana (Savannah)**- born about 1662 OH-died after 1722 PA - son of **Straight Tail**/1630 & **Pekowi Woman**/1635, Turtle Clan, 1677 moved with band to IN, 1680 moved to IL, 1689 moved with band to TN-NC-KY-VA, 1693 moved to Old Savannah Town GA, 1700 moved to PA about time of death of **Straight Tail**, 1711 succeeded his brother **Opessa** as **Pekowi Chief** in Pequea PA, 1714 Council Philadelphia **with Conestoga Chiefs**, 1723 replaced as Pekowi Chief at Opessa's Town-Oldtown MD, apparently lived with the Mohawk after 1723, husband 1st about 1682 IL of **Pekowi Woman**/1665, 2nd before 1711 of **Mohawk Woman**/1695-(sister of wife of Rising Sun), children unknown

Opessa Straight Tail/1664

Straight Tail, Opessa aka Opethatha-Wapatha-Wopatha-HopeshaOppaymolleh – Pekowi born 1670 OH-died latter 1760 OH - son of

Straight Tail-Meaurroway/1630 & **Pekowi Woman**/1635, Turtle Clan, 1677 moved with band to IN, 1680 moved to IL, 1689 moved with band to TN-NC-KY-VA, by 1693 living in Cecil Co MD, 1697 moved to Lancaster Co PA with band, 1697 succeeded **Straight Tail** as **Pekowi Chief** in Pequea PA, 1701 signed Treaty with **William Penn** with **Lemoytungh** & **Pemoyajagh**, 1706 Council Philadelphia, 1707 Conference at Pequea Lancaster Co PA with **Governor John Evans**, 1710 Conference at Conestoga PA with **John French** & **Henry Worley**, resigned 1711 to move to Sassoonan's Delaware village, succeeded 1711 as **Pekowi Chief** at Pequea PA by his brother **Cakundawanna**/1670, 1715 Conference Philadelphia with **Sassoonan**, 1722 moved to Old Town MD-upper Potomac & **Pekowi Chief** again by 1723, by 1734 moved to AL with band, by 1738 returned to western MD/southeast PA, Aug. 1749 Council Philadelphia, 1750 moved to OH, 1752 succeeded **Pheasant-Kakawatchekee** as **Head Pekowi Chief** in OH, May 1756 Council Tioga Point, Aug. 1760 Council Ft. Pitt, brother in law (through Sister) of **Peter Chartier**/1690, connected with **Poxinosa**Pekowi, **White Fish (1)**-Pekowi & **Okowellos Cornstalk**-Chalakatha (Head Chiefs of bands), great-grandfather of **Tecumseh**/1768, husband 1st by 1695 MD of **Margaret Pekowi**/1670, 2nd 1711 PA of **PollyDaughter of Sassoonan**/1695-Delaware, father **with Margaret** of Snow White/1695, Tecoomteh/1698, Waywayti/1700, Loyparkoweh/1702 & Lawaquaqua-Pride Opessa/1710-all Pekowi, children **with Polly** unknown

1st WIFE 1695 - MD

Pekowi, Margaret – Pekowi born 1670-died 1710 MD – **parents unknown**, wife 1695 MD of **Opessa**/1664, mother of Snow White/1695, Tecoomteh/1698, Waywayti/1700, Loyparkoweh/1705 & Lawaquaqua-Pride Opessa/1710-all Pekowi

2nd WIFE 1711 - PA

DAUGHTER OF SASSOONAN/1695 - DELAWARE

Sassoonan, Polly aka Daughter of Sassoonan-Delaware Wife of Opessa

– adopted-Delaware born 1695 PA-died after 1760 OH, daughter of **Sassoonan-Alumapee**/1675, granddaughter of **Tamenend**/1640, sister of **Wife of Okowelos**/1697, **Shingas**/1700, **King Beaver**/1705 & **Pisquetomen**/1710-all noted Delaware, marriage represents an attempt to cement Shawnee-Delaware relations in PA, Turkey Clan, children unknown

CHILDREN OF OPESSA

DAUGHTER

Opessa, Snow White aka **Blanceneige-Wapakonee**-Daughter of Opessa-Wife of Peter Chartier – Pekowi born about 1695 Cecil Co MDdied after 1744 OH-PA - daughter of **Opessa**/1664 & **Margaret Pekowi**/1670, namesake of her aunt **Snow White Straight Tail**, Turtle Clan, wife 1710 PA of **Peter Chartier**/1690, mother of Francois Pale Croucher Chartier/1712, Rene Pale Stalker Chartier/1725, Anna Chartier/1730 & other children/1713-40-all 3/4th Pekowi-Metis

SON

Opessa, Tecoomteh aka Tecomteh – Pekowi born about 1698 Lancaster Co PA-died after 1738 PA - son of **Opessa**/1664 & **Margaret Pekowi**/1670, Turtle Clan, in west PA 1711-23 with father **Opessa**, returned to north MD/east PA area with **Opessa** 1723, living on the Alleghany River by 1727, unclear if he moved to AL with **Opessa** 1734, 1738 called the 1st warrior of the band, 1738 signed Petition to PA to stop the sell of liquor to Natives with brother **Pride**/1710, brother in law **Peter Chartier**/1690, **George Miranda**/1700 & 94 other Natives, wife & children unknown

SON

Opessa, Waywayti aka Wawwaythi-Waywaythee-Wauwaythee-Weyweyti-Wauweythi – Pekowi born about 1700 PA-died after 1750 (AL?) – son of **Opessa**/1664 **Margaret Pekowi**/1670, grandson of **Meaurroway-Straight Tail**/1630, Turtle Clan, in west PA 1711-23 with father **Opessa**, returned to north MD/east PA area with **Opessa** 1723, living on the Alleghany River by 1727, moved to AL 1734 with **Opessa**, husband 1st 1720 PA of **Elizabeth Pekowi**/1704, 2nd 1739 AL of her sister **Nancy Pekowi**/1706, children/1720-38 **with Elizabeth** unknown but **stepfather** of Middle Daughter of Loyoarkoweh-Nancy/1734, Younger Daughter of Loyparkoweh-Sarah/1736 & MetheotasheMary/1738

SON

Opessa, Loyparkaweh aka Loapeckeway-Lawpakaway – Pekowi born about 1702 PA-died after 1760 OH - son of **Opessa**/1664 & **Margaret Pekowi**/1670, grandson of **Meaurroway-Straight Tail**, Turtle Clan, in west PA 1711-23 with father **Opessa**, returned to north MD/east PA area with **Opessa** 1723, living on the Alleghany River by 1727, a **Pekowi Chief** in PA by 1732, in 1732-1733-1734 signed letters to the Governor of PA as one of the Chiefs on the Alleghany complaining about the sale of rum to the natives, moved to AL 1734 with **Opessa**, left a wife & children in AL with relatives/clan members, returned to PA by 1738 sent letter to the Governor with **Neucheconner** & **Coycacolenne** protesting the sale of rum, then called a young Chief guided by vice regent **Neucheconner**, between 1738 & 1744 lived at Chartier's Town-Alleghany Co PA & Logstown-Alleghany Co PA, apparently moved to OH with **Peter Chartier & Neucheconner** in 174445 for he is living in Lower Shawnee Town OH in 1752 when he sent a letter with 3 other Shawnee Chiefs there to the Governor of PA reporting that they were still loyal to the British though most of their neighbors had gone over to the French, attended Council Philadelphia 1753 after **Opessa** moved to OH, apparently opposed the Shawnee participation in French-Indian War/1754-60, a minor **Pekowi Chief in OH** after death of **Opessa**, husband 1st 1720 MD of **Nancy Pekowi**/1706, 2nd 1738 PA of her sister **Elizabeth Pekowi**/1704, father **with Nancy** of Tecumsapah-Margaret/1724, Sewatha-Sarah/1727, Watmeme-Polly/1730, Middle Daughter-Nancy/1734, Younger Daughter-Sarah/1736 & Metheotashe-Mary/1738-all Pekowi, children **with Elizabeth** unknown

SON

Opessa, Pride aka **Lawaquaqua**-Lawachkamikee-Lawakwakwaltawachcomequ about 1710 MD-died 1753 SC - son of

Opessa/1664 **Pekowi Woman**/1670, Turtle Clan, 1711 taken to Sassoonan's village with Opessa, 1722 returned to Opessa's Town MD with **Opessa**, 1732 remained in north 1734 when **Opessa** took band to AL, 1738 signed Petition to PA with **Peter Chartier, George Miranda**, brother
Tecoomteh & 94 Natives to stop the sell of liquor to Natives, by 1738 a **Pekowi Chief** in west MD/central PA, raiding PA/40, 1744 joined **Peter Chartier, Big Hominy** & others in moving to Lower Shawnee Town OH to support the French, 1748 Conference Logstown with **Conrad Weiser, Big Hominy** & **Kakawatchekee**, 1753 captured on trip to the south to locate Pekowi relatives on the Savannah River & died in SC prison, husband 1st 1730 east PA of **Sarah Rising Sun**/1715Kishpoko, 2nd by 1739 east PA of (widow) **Sister of Moluntha**/1710, father with **Rising Sun** of Lawagqua-Elder Brother of Blue Jacket/1733, **Blue Jacket**- Weyapiersenwha-Whirlpool /1735, Wabete-Elk-Younger Brother of Blue Jacket/1737 & Sally Opessa-sister of Blue Jacket/1739all Kishpoko-Pekowi, with **Sister of Moluntha** of Red Pole/1740Mekoche-Pekowi, step-father of **Black Fish**/1725, Kwatooka/1727, Nakanapaseka/1729-all Chalakatha-Mekoche

GRANDCHILDREN OF OPESSA

BY SNOW WHITE/1694 & PETER CHARTIER/1690

GRANDSON

Chartier, Francois aka **Pale Croucher**-Chartier's Son - 3/4th Pekowi-Metis born about 1712 PA-died after 1744 PA-OH - son of **Peter Chartier**/1690 & **Snow White Opessa**/1695-Pekowi, Turtle Clan, moved with father from PA-MD to Lower Shawnee Town OH to support the French, 1746 returned to PA with **Neucheconner**, husband about 1734 PA of **Younger Daughter of Poxinosa**/1720-Pekowi, father of Nancy Nadachine Chartier/1735-7/8th Pekowi-Metis

GRANDSON

Chartier, Rene aka **Pale Stalker**-Chartier's Son - 3/4th Pekowi-Metis born about 1725 PA-died after 1775 (OH?) - son of **Peter Chartier**/1690 & **Snow White Opessa**/1695-Pekowi, Turtle Clan, a Pekowi warrior, 1744 moved with father from PA-MD to Lower Shawnee Town OH to support the French, 1745 with father near site of Winchester KY, 1748 with father in IL & Detroit-when French, 1749 in AL with father, Cornstalk War/1755-75, 1759 living in OH1768 traveled with **Corn Cob Cornstalk** to Detroit, husband about 1745 OH-KY of **Pekowi Woman**/1730, father of Elizabeth Chartier/1760, Mary Chartier/1770 & other unrecorded 7/8th Pekowi-Metis children/1746-74

GRANDDAUGHTER

Chartier, Anna - 3/4th Pekowi-Metis born about 1730 PA-died after 1779 (PA?) - daughter of **Peter Chartier**/1690 & **Snow White Opessa**/1695, Turtle Clan, wife about 1750 PA of **David Troxell**/1730-white, mother of child/52, Solomon Troxell/1754, George Troxell/1756, **Jacob-Big Jake Troxell**/1758, John Troxell/1760, Fredrick Troxell/1762, twins Mary & Elizabeth Troxell/1764, **Peter Jacob-Little Jake Troxell**/1766, Abraham Troxell/1768, David Troxell Jr/1770 & Catherine Troxell/1772-all 3/8th Pekowi-Metis

BY WAYWAYTI/1700
& ELIZABETH PEKOWI/1704

UNKNOWN

BY WAYWAYTI/1700
& NANCY PEKOWI/1706

UNKNOWN

BY LOYPARCOWAH/1702
& & NANCY PEKOWI/1706

GRANDDAUGHTER

Opessa, Tecumsapah aka Margaret – Pekowi born about 1724 PA-died after 1769 PA - daughter of **Loyparkoweh Opessa**/1702 & **Nancy Pekowi**/1706, Turtle Clan, namesake of father's mother **Margaret Pekowi**/1670, aunt of **Tecumseh**, moved to AL 1735 with **Opessa** & her father, returned to PA by 1738 with her father, remained in PA 1744 when **Peter Chartier** led Shawnee to OH to join the French, wife 1738 PA of **Thomas McKee**/1695-adopted-Irish, step-mother of Thomas McKee- Pelewiechen /1720-Irish adopted- by Delaware & **Col. Alexander McKee-Wapimescheu** /1725-Irish adopted by Shawnee, mother of Alexander McKee/1738, Nancy McKee/1740, Hugh McKee/1742, Catherine McKee/1744, Thomas McKee/1750, John McKee/1754, James McKee/1755-all 1/2 Pekowi-Metis

GRANDDAUGHTER

Opessa, Sarah aka Older Daughter of Loyparkaweh-Mother of Tecumpolas-Older Sister of Metheotashe – Pekowi born 1727 MD-died after 1750 (OH?) - daughter of **Loyparkoweh Opessa**/1702 & **Nancy Pekowi**/1706, Turtle Clan, namesake of mother's mother **Sarah Pekowi**, aunt of **Tecumseh**, moved to AL 1735 with **Opessa** & her father, returned to PA by 1738 with her father, moved 1744 to OH with **Peter Chartier**, 1750 with Pekowi in the west WV/east OH-Ohio valley, wife by 1742 (MD?) of **Pekowi Man**/1722, mother of TecumpolasMargaret Opessa/1742, grandmother of Jane Collins/1768

GRANDDAUGHTER

Opessa, Watmeme aka Polly – Pekowi born 1730 PA-died 1797 MO – daughter of **Loyparkoweh Opessa**/1702 & **Nancy Pekowi**/1706, Turtle Clan, namesake of father's step-mother **Polly-Daughter of Sassoonan**/1695, wife 1745 OH of **Black Fish**/1725, moved to AL 1735 with **Opessa** & her father, returned to PA by 1738 with her father, moved 1744 to OH with **Peter Chartier**, moved to MO 1779 with adopted son Stephen Ruddle after death of Black Fish, Ruddle returned to whites upon her death/1797, mother **with Black Fish** of sons Chinwa/1746, Black Fish (2)/1748, daughter Pimegeezhigoqua/1752, son Black Fish (3)/1754, daughters Chelatha/1756, Lamatashe/1758 & Parlie/1760-all Chalakatha-Mekoche-Pekowi, adopted mother & mother in law of **Capt. Joseph Dusquene**/1755, **Lewis Rogers**/1750 &

Henry Rogers/1755, adopted mother 1774 of **William Jackson aka Fish**/1770 & **Stephen Ruddle**/1768

GRANDDAUGHTER

Opessa, Nancy aka Middle Daughter of Loyparkaweh-Wife of Daniel McQueen-Middle Sister of Metheotashe – Pekowi born 1734 PA-died after 1755 (AL?) - daughter of **Loyparkoweh Opessa**/1702 & **Nancy Pekowi**/1706, Turtle Clan, namesake of her mother **Nancy**/1710, moved to AL 1735 with **Opessa** & her father, raised in AL by her mother & uncle/stepfather **Wawwaythi**, a Pekowi from Souvanogee (Shawnee) village AL, wife by 1754 AL of **Daniel McQueen**/1736-1/2 Creek-Metis, mother of Elder Daughter aka Mother of **Seekaboo**-Niece of Metheotashe/1755, Younger Daughter-Sarah/1758-(wife 1st of Thawikila Man/1755, 2nd of Robert McQueen/1747) & Joseph McQueen/1760-all 1/2 Pekowi-Creek-Metis, grandmother of **Seekaboo**/1770-3/4th Kishpoko-Pekowi-Creek-Metis

GRANDDAUGHTER

Opessa, Sarah aka Younger Daughter of Loyparkoweh-Wife of Isadore Chesne – Pekowi born about 1736 AL-died after 1756 OH – daughter of **Loyparkoweh Opessa**/1702 & **Nancy Pekowi**/1706, Turtle Clan, namesake of father's sister **Sarah-Snow White Opessa**/1695 & father's aunt **Snow White Straight Tail-Sarah White**/1666, raised in AL by her mother & uncle/stepfather **Wawwaythi**, went north 1752 with members of the **Peter Chartier** band, wife 1754 OH of **Isadore Chesne**/1735-Wyandot-Metis, mother of Mary Shane/1754 & Capt. Joseph Dusquene/1756-1/2 Pekowi-Wyandot-Metis-(adoptedChippewa)

GRANDDAUGHTER

Opessa, Metheotashe aka Mary-Meetheeotashe-Methotasa-Turtle Laying Eggs – Pekowi born 1738 AL-died 1789 MO - daughter of **Loyparcoweh Opessa**/1702 & **Nancy Pekowi**/1706, Turtle Clan, namesake of her father's 1st cousin **Mary Chartier**/1688 who had just been murdered, raised in AL by her mother & uncle/stepfather **Wawwaythi**, a Pekowi from Souvanogee (Shawnee) village AL, 1st cousin of **Blue Jacket** & his siblings-(fathers were brothers), moved from AL to KY, 1760 moved from KY to OH, widowed 1774, lived with relatives in the **Black Fish** family/1774-79, moved 1779 to Apple Creek village MO **with Menewaulakoose**/1764 & **Vocemassussia**/1771, wife 1st 1755 AL of **Puckenshinwa Rising Sun**/1735-(widowed 1774), 2nd 1775 OH of **Young Hard Striker-Pucksinwa Pheasant**/1738-(widowed the same year), mother **with Puckenshinwa** of son **Cheeseekau**/1756 AL, daughter **Tecumapease**/1758 AL, sons Sauwaseekou/1760 KY, (daughter/1762?), Nahaaseema/1764 OH, daughter Menewaulakoose/1766 OH, sons **Tecumseh**/1768 OH, Kumshaka/1770 OH, daughter Vocemassussia/1772 OH & son **Lalawethika**-Tenskawatawa-Shawnee Prophet/1774 OH -all 3/4th Kishpoko-Pekowi-Creek-Metis, no known child **with Young Hard Striker**/1738, aunt of **Tecumoplas-Margaret Collins**/1742 & greataunt of **Jane Collins**/1768, 1759 adopted mother 1760 OH of **Joshua Renicks**/1746, 1768 OH of **John Sparks**/1760 & **Richard SparksShawtunte**/1765, 1772 OH of **Stephen Ruddell-Big Fish**/1767 & **Abraham Ruddell-Black Hawk**/1764, all adopted children went to other families in extended family upon death 1774 of Puckenshinwa

BY LOYPARCOWAH/1702 & ELIZABETH PEKOWI/1704

UNKNOWN

BY PRIDE-LAWAQUAQUA/1710 & SARAH RISING SUN/1715

GRANDSON

Opessa, Lawagqua aka Lawoughqua-Lawagkwa-**Elder Brother of Blue Jacket** – Pekowi-Kishpoko born 1733 PA-died after 1774 OH – son of **Pride Opessa**/1710-Pekowi & **Sarah Rising Sun**/1715-Kishpoko, Turtle Clan, trading with Ohio Fur Co. in PA **with Blue Jacket** & **Wabete** by early 1750's, Cornstalk War/1755-74, 1765 Council Logstown PA, 1765 a **Pekowi Chief** in OH, 1765 returned captives to Ft. Pitt, husband about 1753 OH of **Pekowi Woman**/1737, father of Resting

Fish-Masemo/1760 & Resting Snake-Monetoshe/1770-both PekowiKishpoko

GRANDSON

Blue Jacket aka Weyapiersenwha-**Whirlpool**-Sepettekenathe-Big Rabbit – Pekowi-Kishpoko born 1735 PA-died 1809 OH - son of **Pride Opessa**/1710-Pekowi & **Sarah Rising Sun**/1715-Kishpoko, Turtle Clan, grandson of **Opessa**/1664, by 1755 trading with Ohio Fur Co. in PA **with brothers Lawagqua**/1733 & **Wabete-Elk**/1737, **Pekowi by birth** but reverted to mother's **Kishpoko** family with his mother upon death of Pride, Cornstalk War/1755-77, lead Chief in **Blue Jacket War/1777**94 (Blue Jacket War = allied with British-Revolution/1776-83, Vincennes/1778, Point Pleasant/1778, Boonesboro/1778, Martin & Ruddle Stations KY/1780, Lochery/1781, Blue Licks/1782, Crawford/1782, Ft. Finney/1786, raiding KY-TN/1786, raiding Ohio River valley/1788-92, Harmer/1790, Dunlap Station/1791, St. Clair/1791, Ft. Recovery/1794, defeated by Anthony Wayne & American Army at Fallen Timbers 1794), a **Pekowi Chief** in OH by 1772, by 1773 established Blue Jacket Town on Deer Creek of Sciota River OH, 1774 Treaty Camp Charlotte, 1775 Council Ft. Pitt **with Cornstalk**/1710, **Silverheels**/1730, **Nimwha**/1726 & **Wryneck**/1725, 1776 Treaty Ft. Pitt, Grand Council 1782, 1785 **succeeded Black Snake as Head War Chief** , Jan. 1786 Council Miami, 1786 attended Treaty Ft. Finney, 1786 leader of an opposing faction when **Capt. Johnny** succeeded **Moluntha** as Head of Chalakatha-Mekoche led faction (split = 3 groups-Black Hoof in OH, **Capt. Johnny** in MO & Blue Jacket in OH), Grand Council 1791, Grand Council Sept. 1792, 1794 **succeeded Little Turtle**-Miami as **leader of United Tribes with Turkey Foot (1)**/1750-adopted-Ottawa, 1794 stepped down as Head War Chief following defeat at Fallen Timbers, 1795 Treaty Greenville, never openly opposed whites after 1795, Grand Council 1805, Treaty 1805, **refused Tecumseh** in early ventures but was supportive later, stephalfbrother (by marriage 1739 of Pride Opessa/1710 to Mother of Black Fish/1710) of **Black Fish**/1725, 1st cousin of Metheotashe/1740-(fathers were brothers), **double-uncle of Tecumseh**/1768 (1st cousin of **Metheotashe** & brother-in-law of **Puckenshinwa**), husband 1st 1755

OH-KY of **Older Sister of Puckenshinwa**/1739-1/2 Kishpoko-CreekMetis, 2nd 1762 OH of **Margaret Moore**/1746-adopted-white, 3rd 1765
OH of **Clear Water Baby**/1750-1/2 Pekowi-Metis, father **with Sister of Puckenshinwa** of Young Whirlpool-Young Blue Jacket (1)/1756, Spybeech Blue Jacket/1758, Wayweleapee Blue Jacket/1760 & George Blue Jacket (1)/1762-all 3/4th Pekowi-Kishpoko-Creek-Metis, **with Moore** of Joseph Moore-Blue Jacket/1763 & Nancy Moore-Stewert/1765-(born after Margaret's return to the whites)-both 1/2 Pekowi-Kishpoko-Metis, **with Baby** of James Blue Jacket/1766, Young Blue Jacket (2)/1770, Marie Louise Blue Jacket/1774, Sally Blue Jacket/1776, Nancy Blue Jacket/1778, George Blue Jacket/1780-all 3/4th Pekowi-Kishpoko-Metis

GRANDSON

Opessa, Wabete aka **Elk-Younger Son-Younger Brother of Blue Jacket** – Pekowi-Kishpoko born 1737 OH-died after 1774 OH - son of **Pride Opessa**/1710-Pekowi & **Sarah Rising Sun**/1715-Kishpoko, Turtle Clan, a Pekowi-Kishpoko warrior, younger brother of **Blue Jacket**/1735, by 1755 trading with OH Fur Co. in PA in early with brothers **Lawagqua & Blue Jacket**, Cornstalk War/1755-74, father in law of **Blue Pocket Swearingen**/1763-adopted-white, husband 1757 OH of **Kishpoko Woman**/1742, 2nd 1766 OH of **Ms. Baby**/1752-1/2 Pekowi-Metis, children/1757-66 **with Kishpoko** unknown, father **with Baby** of SwanWapehti Opessa/1768-3/4th Pekowi-Metis - (some children may have been called Blue Jacket's)

GRANDDAUGHTER

Opessa, Sarah aka Sally Bluejacket-**Sister of Blue Jacket** – Pekowi-Kishpoko born 1739 OH-died after 1825 OH - daughter of **Pride Opessa**/1710-Pekowi & **Sarah Rising Sun**/1715-Kishpoko, namesake of father's sister **Sarah-Snow White Opessa**/1695 & father's aunt **Snow White Straight Tail-Sarah White**/1666, Turtle Clan, sister of Lawagqua/1733, **Blue Jacket**/1735 & Wabete Opessa/1737, half-sister of **Red Pole**/1740-Mekoche, 1st cousin of **Metheotashe**/1738-(fathers were brothers) & step-half-sister **Black Fish**/1725-(by marriage of Pride/1710 to Mother of Black Fish/1710), aunt of **Tecumseh**/1768,

Bright Horn/1772, **Billy Caldwell**/1776, never known to have married

BY PRIDE/1710
& SISTER OF MOLUNTHA/1710
GRANDSON

Red Pole aka **Mesquakinoe**-Mesquakunigou-Meskwakeeno – PekowiMekoche (Thawikila by marriage) born about 1740 (PA?)-died 1797 PA
- son of **Pride Opessa**/1710-Pekowi & **Sister of Moluntha**/1710Mekoche, Turtle Clan, a **Pekowi** by birth but reverted to mother's division-**Mekoche** with death of Pride 1753, then raised by mother's 3rd husband **Mekoche Chief**/1710, grandson of **Opessa**/1664, half-brother of **Blue Jacket**/1735 (through Pride/1710) & half brother of **Black Fish**/1725 (through Mother/1710), Cornstalk War/1758-77, a **Mekoche Chief** in OH by 1778, Blue Jacket War/1777-82, May 1782 Council Detroit, 1786 attended Treaty Ft. Finney, Sept. 1792 Council, Dec. 1792 Council, 1792 delegation to **Thomas McKee**, 1792-94 led delegation of 7 **Shawnee** & **George Ash** to the Shawnee in TN-AL-GA, the Chickamauga (their leader **Cheeseekau**-brother of **Tecumseh** had just been killed near Nashville), the Cherokee in TN & Creek in AL & GA, Treaty Greenville 1795, a **Thawikila Chief** (by marriage?) before 1797, cousin of **Metheotashe**/1740 (through his uncle Loyparkoweh) & uncle of **Tecumseh**/1768, died returning from Council in Philadelphia 1797, husband about 1760 OH of **Thawikila Woman**/1745, children unknown

Thomas Fireheart-Skootekitehi
Thomas Fireheart-Skootekitehi

Greenwood/1641

Greenwood, Thomas Skootekitehi aka Fireheart-Papapanawe-Lightning Fire - 15/32nd Chalakatha-Shawano-Chalaka-Powhatan-Metis born 1641 Shawnee Nation-western VA-died 1704 Running Water TN – son of **Spemcia Elene-Big Man John Greenwood**/1619-adopted white & **Nepikeweewa Cornstalk**/1625, Wind Clan, husband 1659 VA of **Mikona Carpenter**/1644, father of Joseph Gorhaleke-Winter Fever Greenwood/1660, Richard-Gohoma Greenwood/1662, Martin-Owasta Greenwood/1664, David-Calunna-Raven Greenwood/1666, Killer-Nellawgitchi Greenwood/1668 & Hawk-Sinnawa-Tlanuwa Greenwood/1670-all 15/32nd Chalakatha-Shawano-Chalaka-PowhatanMetis

SISTER

Greenwood, Locha – 15/32nd Chalakatha-Shawano-Chalaka-PowhatanMetis born 1643 Shawnee Nation-southwest VA-died 1692 Great Tellico TN – daughter of **John Spemcia Big Man Greenwood**/1691-white & **Nepikeweewa Cornstalk**/1635, Wind Clan, a cousin of **Big Turkey**/1660 & **Nancy Turkey**/1664-(mother's were sisters), wife by 1658 Shawnee Nation-western VA of **Trader Tom Carpenter (1)Moytoy I**/1635, mother of Trader Tom Carpenter (2)-Moytoy (2)/1660-15/32nd Chalakatha-Shawano-Chalaka-Powhatan-Metis

WIFE 1659 - VA

Carpenter, Mikona – 15/32nd Chalakatha-Shawano-Chalaka-Powhatan-Metis born 1644 Shawnee Nation-southwest VA-died 1695 Running Water TN – daughter of **Pride Cornstalk**/1617-Wind Clan & **Thomas Pashmere Carpenter**/1607-white, Wind Clan, could cipher, read & write English, a cousin of **Big Turkey**/1660 & **Nancy Turkey**/1664(mother's were sisters), wife 1659 Shawnee Nation-southwestern VA of
Thomas –Fireheart-Skootekitehi Greenwood/1641, mother of Joseph-Gorhaleke-Winter Fever Greenwood/1660, Richard-Gohoma Greenwood/1662, Martin-Owasta Greenwood/1664, David-Calunna-

Raven Greenwood/1666, Killer-Nellawgitchi Greenwood/1668 & Hawk-Sinnawa-Tlanuwa Greenwood/1670-all 15/32nd ChalakathaShawano-Chalaka-Powhatan-Metis

CHILDREN OF THOMAS FIREHEART-SKOOTEKITEHI GREENWOOD/1641 & MIKONA CARPENTER/1644

SON

Greenwood, Joseph **Gorhaleke** aka Winter Fever – 15/32nd Chalakatha-Shawano-Chalaka-Powhatan-Metis born 1660 Running Water TN-died 1727 Toxaway TN – son of **Thomas Fireheart-Skootekitehi Greenwood**/1641 & **Mikona Carpenter**/1644, Wind Clan, Treaty 1684 with SC, from the Lower Towns, husband 1679 Running Water TN of **Quaghcunnega Rainbow**/1662-1/2 Thawikila-Kishpoko-Black , father of Thomas Caesar-Skiagunsta Greenwood/1680 & Joseph Greenwood/1682-both 31/64th Chalakatha-Thawikila-KishpokoShawano-Chalaka-Powhatan-Black-Metis

SON

Greenwood, Richard Gohoma – 15/32nd Chalakatha-ShawanoChalaiwa-Powhatan-Metis born 1662 Running Water TN-died 1729 Keowee TN – son of **Thomas Fireheart-Skootekitehi Greenwood**/1641 & **Mikona Carpenter**/1644, Wind Clan, Treaty 1684 with SC, wife & children unknown

SON

Greenwood, Martin Owasta – 15/32nd Chalakatha-Shawano-ChalakaPowhatan-Metis born 1664 Running Water TN-died 1731 Toxawa TN – son of **Thomas Skootekitehi Greenwood**/1641 & **Mikona Carpenter**/1644, Wind Clan, Treaty 1684 with SC, wife & children unknown

SON

Greenwood, David **Calunna**-Raven – 15/32nd Chalakatha-Shawano-

Chalaka-Powhatan-Metis born 1666 Running Water TN-died 1726 Toxawa TN – son of **Thomas Fireheart-Skootekitehi Greenwood**/1641 & **Mikona Carpenter**/1644, Wind Clan, Treaty 1684 with SC, wife & children unknown

SON

Greenwood, Killer **Nellawgitchi** aka Nettawagetchee-Nottawago Killer – 15/32nd Chalakatha-Shawano-Chalaka-Powhatan-Metis born 1668 Running Water TN-died 1730 Toxawa TN – son of **Thomas FireheartSkootekitehi Greenwood** /1641 & **Mikona Carpenter**/1644, Wind
Clan, Treaty 1684 with SC, wife & children unknown

SON

Greenwood, Hawk **Sinnawa** aka Tlanuwa – 15/32nd ChalakathaShawano-Chalaka--Powhatan-Metis born 1670 Running Water TN-died
1733 Toxawa TN – son of **Thomas Fireheart-Skootekitehi Greenwood**/1641 & **Mikona Carpenter**/1644, Wind Clan, Treaty 1684 with SC, husband 1690 TN of **Cherokee Woman**/1675, father of John Sinnawa Greenwood/1695-15/64th Chalakatha-Shawano-ChalakaPowhatan-Cherokee-Metis

GRANDCHILDREN

BY JOSEPH GORHELEKE/1660 & QUAGHCUNNEGA RAINBOW/1662

GRANDSON

Greenwood, Thomas **Caesar Skiagunsta** aka Capt. Caesar-Three Nosed Warrior-Triple-nose Warrior-Old Caesar-Blind Warrior-Old Warrior-Breed Slave-Catcher – 31/64th Chalakatha-Thawikila-KishpokoShawano-Chalaka-Powhatan-Black-Metis born 1680 Nickajack TN-died

1775 Great Tellico TN – son of **Joseph Gorhaleke Greenwood**/1660 & **Quaghcunnega Rainbow**/1662, Wind Clan, advisor to **Young Rainmaker**/1680-Cherokee & then to **Old Hop**/1688, a **Headman of Chatuga** in Great Tellico faction, delegate to ENG 1730, **pro-British** faction-**with George Washington** & **Colonial Army** in French-Indian War/54-63, from the Overhills & Chatuga TN, on Council 1741 of **Bad Water Muskrat-Moytoy (6)**/1722, Treaty Sycamore Shoals 1775, husband 1700 Nickajack TN of **Katie Turkey Cornstalk**/1684, father of Thomas Sutichettchee Greenwood/1698, John Cheesquatalone Greenwood/1700, children/1702-10, daughters Quatsis Atawaya Greenwood/1712, Sedano Greenwood/1715, son Big Turkey Greeenwood/1718, daughter Nancy Greenwood/1720 & daughter Ankee Greenwood/1729-all 23/32nd Chalakatha-Thawikila-KishpokoShawano-Chalaka-Powhatan-Black-Metis

GRANDSON

Greenwood, Joseph (2) aka **Gorhaleke (2)** –Winter Fever (2) – 31/64th Chalakatha-Thawikila-Kishpoko-Shawano-Chalaka-Powhatan-BlackMetis born 1682- Running Water TN-died after 1730 Great Tellico TN – son of **Joseph Gorhaleke Greenwood**/1660 & **Quaghcunnega Rainbow**/1662, Wind Clan, wife & children unknown

BY HAWK SINNAWA/1670 & CHEROKEE WOMAN/1675

GRANDSON

Greenwood, John **Sinnawa** aka Hawkhead-Chuchia-Johnny Sinawaska – 15/64th Chalakatha-Shawano-Chalaka-Powhatan-Cherokee-Metis born 1695 Running Water TN-died after 1753 Tuskasegee AL – son of **Hawk Sinnawa Greenwood**/1670 & **Cherokee Woman**/1675, Wind Clan, a **Headman from Tuskasegee**, wife & children unknown

CHAPTER THREE

Paxinosa/1670,

Kakawatchekee-Pheasant/1670, Kishacoquillas/1670,

Neucheconner/1670

Tamenebuck Cornstalk/1670

Rising Sun/1685

Paxinosa/1670

Poxinosa aka Paxinosa-Pakshinotha-Pakshinosha-From Another PlaceBukshenoatha-Bukshinosa - Pekowi born about 1670 OH-died 1760 OH - **parents unknown**, apparently part of the **Straight Tail** band that followed the Ohio River into PA beginning about 1680, moved from OH to PA by 1690, 1690 Council with N.Y. Gov. Donegon, 1701 Treaty with William Penn, 1701 a **Pekowi Chief** in PA, lived most of adult life in Wyoming valley-Luzerne Co PA, 1744 succeeded his relative **Pheasant-Kakawatchekee**/1680 as **Chief of Pekowi** in Wyoming valley PA, 1749 joined with **Six Nations** in Treaty Philadelphia selling most of land between the Susquehanna & the Delaware-most of 10 current counties, 1752 Treaty , 1754 tried to get

Christian Indians at Gnadenhutten to remove to a safer place, 1755 Grand Council Philadelphia with **Scarouady**, 1756 Council Tioga Point with **Canachquasy**, 1756 moved from Shawnee Flats-Luzerne Co PA to Tioga Bradford Co PA at the insistence of the hostile Tribes, 1757 protected the Moravians at Bethlehem with **Teedyuskung**, 1757 Council with William Johnson at Ft. Johnson **with Hamightaghlawatawa**-Nanticoke, **Mammatisicas**-Mohawk, & **Peter Ooligasha Spelman**-adopted German, 1757 Council Easton with **Teedyuskung**, 1757 living at Osteningo NY, 1758 returned to OH, 1760 Council Ft. Pitt with **General Monckton**, associated with **Shikellimus**Seneca & **Teedyuskung**-Delaware, **Opessa, Okowellos** & **White Fish**all Shawnee, moved from PA to OH about 1758, husband 1st about 1690 PA of **Pekowi Woman**/1675, 2nd about 1715 PA of **Elizabeth Nutimaes**/1700-Pekowi, children/1690-1715 **with Pekowi** unknown, father **with Elizabeth** of Teatapercaum/1716, Elder Daughter/1718, Awanoos/1719, Younger Daughter/1720 & Kolapeka/1722 & 3 other children-all Pekowi

1st WIFE 1690 - PA
PEKOWI WOMAN/1675

CHILDREN/1690-1715 UNKNOWN

2nd WIFE 1716 - PA

Nutimaes, Elizabeth – Pekowi born about 1700 PA-died after 1754 – daughter of **Pekowi Woman**/1680 & **Pekowi Man**/1675-(both of **Kakawatchekee-Pheasant** band), adopted daughter by 1705 PA of **Nutimaes**/1670-Delaware-(by marriage of her mother/1680 to Nutimaes), a Christian Pekowi, half-sister of **Ben Nutimaes**/1705-(same Pekowi mother), 2nd wife about 1715 PA of **Poxinosa**/1670, mother of Teatapercaum/1716, Elder Daughter/1718, Awanoos/1719, Younger Daughter/1720 & Kolapeka/1722 & 3 other children-all Pekowi

BROTHER IN LAW OF PAXINOSA

(HALF-BROTHER OF ELIZABETH)

Nutimaes, Ben - 1/2 Pekowi-Delaware born about 1705 PA-died after 1760 - son of **Pekowi Woman**/1680-(the mother of Elizabeth/1700) & **Nutimaes**/1670-Delaware, half-brother of **Elizabeth Nutimaes**/1700, associated with brother-in-law **Poxinosa**/1670-Pekowi, wife & children unknown

CHILDREN OF PAXINOSA/1670 & ELIZABETH NUTIMAES/1700

SON

Poxinosa, Teatapercaum – Pekowi born about 1716 PA-died after 1766 (OH?) - son of **Poxinosa**/1670 & **Elizabeth Nutimaes**/1700, little or no part in Cornstalk War/1755-66, moved to OH 1758 with father, wife & children unknown

DAUGHTER

Poxinosa, Elder Daughter of aka Wife of Peter Spelman – Pekowi born about 1718 PA-died after 1758 - daughter of **Poxinosa**/1670 & **Elizabeth Nutimaes**/1700-Pekowi, moved to OH about 1758, wife about 1733 PA of **Peter Ooligasha Spelman**/1705-adopted German, mother of Sabra Spelman/1735-1/2 Pekowi-Metis

SON

Poxinosa, Awanoos – Pekowi born about 1719 PA-died about 1758 OH in epidemic - son of **Poxinosa**/1670 & **Elizabeth Nutimaes**/1700Pekowi, a Pekowi warrior, little or no part in Cornstalk War/55-58 or
French-Indian War/1754-58, wife & children unknown

DAUGHTER

Poxinosa, Younger Daughter of aka Wife of Francois Chartier – Pekowi born about 1720 PA-died after 1740 - daughter of **Elizabeth Nutimaes**/1700 & **Poxinosa**/1670, a Pekowi, associated with the Delaware & may have often lived among them, wife 1734 PA of

Francois Chartier/1712, mother of Nancy Nadachine Chartier/17347/8th Pekowi-Metis

SON

Poxinosa, Kolapeka aka Kolapechka-Kolapecha-Copelin – Pekowi born about 1722 PA-died after 1758 (OH?) - youngest son of **Poxinosa**/1670 & **Elizabeth Nutimaes**/1700, a Pekowi warrior, little or no part in Cornstalk War/1755-58, wife & children unknown

GRANDCHILDREN OF POXINOSA/1670 & ELIZABETH NUTIMAES/1700

BY ELDER DAUGHTER/1718 & PETER SPELMEN/1705

GRANDDAUGHTER

Spelman, Sabra - 1/2 Pekowi-Metis born about 1735 PA-died after 1758 - daughter of **Elder Daughter of Poxinosa**/1718-Pekowi & **Peter Spelman** aka **Ooligasha-Owligascho**/1705-adopted German, a Pekowi woman, husband & children unknown

BY YOUNGER DAUGHTER/1720 & FRANCOIS CHARTIER/1712

GRANDDAUGHTER

Chartier, Nancy Nadachine – 7/8th Pekowi-Metis born about 1735 PAdied about 1787 NC - daughter of **Francois Chartier**/1712 & **Younger Daughter of Poxinosa**/1721-Pekowi, Turtle Clan, wife about 1750 of **John Three Rivers Yaunts**/1718-1/4th Pekowi-Delaware-Metis, mother of John Yaunts Jr/1751-9/16th Pekowi-Delaware-Metis

Kakawatchekee-Pheasant/1670

Pheasant (1) aka **Kakawatchekee**-Kawcowatchety-Kawawachekee-Cawcawatchety-Cockawatchy-Cochawitchakee-White Pheasant – Pekowi born about 1670 OH-died about 1755 PA – **parents unknown**, 1677 family moved with the band from OH-mid-Ohio valley to IN-ILMiami & Illinois River valleys near Miami & Illinois, 1679 band from ILIN returns to OH, apparently part of the **Straight Tail** band that followed the Ohio River into PA beginning about 1680, 1694 Kakawatchekee-Pheasant's **Pekowi** band from the Ohio valley join **Mekoche** already in northeast **PA**-Lehigh River valley among Delaware, Mohican & Mohawk, 1709 **succeeded Straight Tail as Pekowi Chief** at Pechoquealin PA, 1728 Council at Conestoga PA with **Capt. Civility**, 1728 moved with most of band to Wyoming valley Luzerne Co PA, about 1734 moved to AL with band, by 1738 returned to western MD/southeast PA, 1739 Conference Philadelphia with **Neucheconner, Tamenebuck & Kishacoquillas**, 1743 band moved to Logstown-west PA-Ohio valley, 1744 refused to desert to the French with **Peter Chartier**, 1744 succeeded as **Pekowi Chief** in Wyoming valley PA by relative **Poxinosa**, 1747 signed letter to Governor of PA on behalf of Miami of the Ohio valley with **Neucheconner, Scarouady & Tanacharisson**, 1748 Council Logstown with **George Croghan**, 1748 Council Logstown with **Neucheconner, Tanacharisson & Scarouady**, 1748 Conference Logstown with **Conrad Weiser, Big Hominy & Pride Opessa**, 1750 visited by **George Croghan & Andrew Montour**, 1752 succeeded as **Pekowi Chief** in Ohio valley by **Opessa**, husband 1st 1690 OH of **PekowiWoman**/1675, 2nd before 1730 PA of **White Woman**/1700 aka **Mother of Hard Man**, children/1700-30 **with Pekowi** unknown, father **with White Woman** of Hard Man/1730 & other 1/2 Pekowi-Metis children

SIBLING OF KAKAWATCHEKEE

SISTER

Pheasant, Sister of aka **Sister of Kakawatchekee** – Pekowi born about 1690 MD-died after 1740 - sister of **Kakawatchekee-Pheasant**/1670, wife about 1710 (PA) of **Kishpoko Man**/1685, mother of PucksinwaHard Striker/1716, Young Pheasant/1724, Pucksinekau/1734,

Catherine-Sister of Pucksinekau-wife of William Galloway Ice/1738-(sons all called Nephews of Pheasant-Kakawatchekee)

WIVES OF KAKAWATCHEKEE

WIFE 1690 OH
PEKOWI WOMAN/1675

CHILDREN UNKNOWN

WIFE BY 1730 PA
WHITE WOMAN/1700

Pheasant, Wife of aka Wife of Kakawatchekee(1)-Mother of Hard Man – adopted-white born about 1700-died after 1730 – adopted by 1730 PA, wife by 1730 PA of **Pheasant-Kakawatchekee (1)**/1670, mother of Hard Man/1730-1/2 Pekowi-Metis

CHILDREN OF KAKAWATCHEKEE
BY PEKOWI WOMAN/1675

SON

Pheasant, Kwassenung – Pekowi born about 1692 (PA?)-died 1732 of smallpox Philadelphia PA at council – son of **Pheasant-Kakawatchekee**/1670 & **Pekowi Woman**/1675, attended Council Philadelphia 1732 with **Peter Chartier, Opakethwa** & **Opakeita**, died of smallpox while there, wife about 1712 & children unknown

BY ADOPTED WHITE WOMAN/1700

SON

Pheasant, Hard Man aka **Kishanositee**-Guschanatsi-GieschantsiBittamaugh-Trapped Raccoon - 1/2 Pekowi-Metis born about 1730-died after 1779 - son of **Pheasant(1)-Kakawatchekee (1)**/1670 & **Adopted White Woman**/1700, Cornstalk War/1755-74, a

Shawnee Heritage II

Pekowi Chief by 1764, Council with **Col. Bouquet** 1764, living on Deer Creek of Sciota River OH 1773, removed as war chief 1774, a **Pekowi sachem** 1776, Treaty Ft. Pitt 1776, moved to MO 1779, 1st cousin (through father) of **Pheasant-Kakawatchekee (2)**/1730, **Pucksinekau**/1735 & **Hard StrikerPucksinwa**/1740, husband 1750 OH of **Eve Ice**/1735, father of several 1/4th Pekowi-Metis children/1750-80 (children or grandchildren took the surname Hardman then Herdman)

NEPHEWS & NIECES

BY SISTER/1690

NEPHEW

Pheasant, Hard Striker aka **Pucksinwa** – Kishpoko-Pekowi born 1716 PA-**killed** 1775 siege of Point Pleasant WV - son of **Sister of Kakawatchekee**-Pheasant/1690-Pekowi & **Kishpoko Man**, Cornstalk War/1755-75, a **Kishpoko Chief** by 1750, nephew of **PheasantKakawatchekee**, 1st cousin of **Hard Man**, Council Philadelphia 1750, Council Quebec & Montreal 1750, Council Muskingum 1750, killed at siege of Point Pleasant/1775, husband about 1736 PA of **Pekowi Woman**/1720, father **with Pekowi** of Young Hard Striker/1738 & other children/1740-56

NEPHEW

Pheasant, Young aka Pheasant (2)-Kakawatchekee (2)-Kakawatchekee's Nephew-Pheasant's Nephew – Kishpoko-Pekowi born about 1724-died after 1765 - son of **Sister of Kakawatchekee**/1690 & **Kishpoko Man**, guide 1762 **with Joe Nichols for George Washington** on OhioKanawha Rivers, husband 1745 (WV-OH) of **Christina Ice**/1728, father of Pheasant (3)-Kakawatchekee-Cawacawachi-Kawkawatchi/1748-1/2 Kishpoko-Pekowi-Metis

NEPHEW

Pheasant, Pucksinekau aka Hard Striker –(began being called Hard Striker in 1775 after his brother was killed) – Kishpoko-Pekowi born about 1734-died about 1823 - son of **Sister of Kakawatchekee**/1690 &

Kishpoko Man, Cornstalk War/1755-77, Blue Jacket War/1777-94, husband about 1754 of **Mary Ice**/1738-adopted white, father of Young Pucksinekau/1754, Red Hair/1756 & other 1/2 Kishpoko-Pekowi-Metis children

NIECE

Pheasant, Catherine aka Sister of Pucksinekau-wife of William Galloway – Kishpoko-Pekowi born about 1738-died after 1765 - daughter of **Sister of Pheasant-Kakawatchekee**/1690 & **Kishpoko Man**/1690, niece of Principal Chief **Pheasant-Kakawatchekee**, 1st wife about 1755 OH of **William-Indian Billy Ice**/1730-adopted white, mother of Christina Ice/1752, Elizabeth Ice/1754, Eve Ice/1756, John Ice/1758, Lewis Ice/1760, Thomas Ice/1762-all 1/2 Kishpoko-PekowiMetis

Kishacoquillas/1670

Kiskoquallah aka Kishacoquillas-Keekokwallah-KashhawaghquillasKissakochquilla-Kishequochkies-Kishiquoquiillis-possilby Snakes Have Left Their Dens – Pekowi born about 1670 (IN-IL?)-died 1754 PA – **parents unknown**, 1689 Pekowi band from IL-IN joins **Chalakatha, Mekoche** & **Kishpoko** in east TN-west NC-east KY-southwest VA, by 1693 most of band from NC-TN-VA-KY was living in Cecil Co MD, by 1697 band was living in Lancaster Co PA-Susquehanna valley, a **Pekowi Chief** in Mifflin Co PA before 1731, living on the Juniata River PA in 1731, Council Philadelphia 1739 with **Kakawatchekee, Neucheconner, Tamenebuck** & other Shawnee chiefs, as a **Pekowi Chief** he opposed the raiding of PA/1740, a loyal friend of the British throughout his life, refused to desert to the French with **Peter Chartier** in 1744, husband about 1690 PA of **Pekowi Woman**/1674, children unknown but known to have sons that survived him

Neucheconner/1670

Newchekonno aka Neucheconner-Neuconneh-NuchekonnerNoocheekonno – Pekowi born about 1670 OH-died after 1753 OH - **parents unknown**, apparently part of the **Straight Tail** band that followed the Ohio River into PA beginning about 1680, living in PA by 1700, a **Pekowi Chief** in PA under **Opessa** about 1710, called viceregent under **Loyparcoweh Opessa** in 1732 but was actually the more influential of the two, 1732 signed a letter to the Governor of PA opposing the sale of rum with several other Chiefs, 1737 living on Allegheny River PA, 1737 listed as "King" of the French Town on the Alleghany River, 1737 signed a letter to the Governor of PA requesting ammunition & supplies to fight their enemies as **one of the Chiefs of the Shawnee at Alleghany**, 1738 signed a letter to the Governor of PA with **Loyparcoweh** & **Coycacolenne** opposing the sale of rum, 1738 signed a letter to the Governor of PA as the **King of the Alleghany Shawnee** reporting that the Mekoche had passed through Chartier's Town carrying scalps taken in VA, 1738 sent a letter to the governor of VA as the **King of the Shawnee at Alleghany** reporting that the Catawba had raided & killed several of his people, Council Philadelphia 1739 with **Kakawatchekee, Kishacoquillas, Tamenebuck** & others, 1743 sent a message to a council at Shamokin referring to **Kakawatchekee** as the older & greater Chief, 1744 deserted to the French with **Peter Chartier**, 1745 living in Lower Shawnee Town OH, 1746 returned to PA, 1747 signed a letter to the Governor of PA with **Kakawatchekee, Tamenebuck, Tanacharisson, Scarouady** & others on behalf of the Miami, 1748 asked PA to forgive him for deserting, 1752 living at the mouth of the Miami in OH when seen by **Andrew Montour** & **William Trent**, 1753 attended the Treaty of Carlisle PA, husband about 1690 PA of **Pekowi Woman**/1675, children unknown

Tamenebuck Cornstalk/1680

Cornstalk, Tamenebuck aka **Corn Blade**-Taming Buck-Tamininipakwa-Tamininipaquah-Tammony Buck-Domini Buck-TameeneebookTamenebuck Hokolesqua – 11/16th Chalakatha-Shawano-ChalakaPowhatan-Metis born about 1680 PA-died about 1758 OH (epidemic?) - son of **Hokolesqua Opechan-Cornstalk (4)**/1630 &

Pashmere Carpenter/1637, Bear Clan, a major **Pekowi Chief** (via marriage) by
1744 in PA, 1744 deserted to the French with **Peter Chartier** & **Neucheconner**, 1745-46 moved at least to the mouth of the Sciota in OH-perhaps to Winchester KY area, 1747 returned to PA & British, Council Lancaster PA 1748-apology to the British was rejected, by 1752 joined the French supporting faction, Council Logstown 1752, Ft. Pitt Nov. 1753, husband about 1700 PA of **Daughter of Straight Tail**/1680Pekowi, father of Corn Cob Cornstalk/1710-27/32nd ChalakathaPekowi-Shawano-Chalaka-Powhatan-Metis

WIFE OF TAMENEBUCK 1700 – PA

Straight Tail, Daughter of - Pekowi born about 1680-died after 1720 – name unknown, daughter of **Straight Tail-Meaurroway**/1630 & **Pekowi Woman**/1635, Turtle Clan, wife about 1700 PA of **Tamenebuck-Corn Blade Cornstalk**/1680, mother of Corn Cob Cornstalk/1710-27/32nd Chalakatha-Pekowi-Shawano-Chalaka-Powhatan-Metis

CHILD OF TAMENEBUCK

SON

Cornstalk, Corn Cob – 27/32nd Chalakatha-Pekowi-Shawano-Chalaka-Powhatan-Metis born about 1710 PA-died after 1768 OH-IL – son of **Tamenebuck-Corn Blade**/1680 & **Daughter of Straight Tail**/1680, Bear Clan, raiding PA/1740, Cornstalk War/1755-68, a **Chalakatha Chief** in OH by 1755, traveled with **Rene-Pale Stalker Chartier** to Detroit 1768, husband 1st about 1740 PA of **Chalakatha Woman**/1725, 2nd 1763 OH of **Adopted-White Woman**/1750, father with **Chalakatha** of several children/1740-64, **with White Woman** of three known children/1764-68

Rising Sun/1685

Rising Sun, Chief – Kishpoko born about 1685 Tuckabatchee AL-died after 1744 (OH?) – moved with Band from AL to Lehigh valley of PA by 1705, lived near/among the **Kakawatchekee-Pheasant** Pekowi Band & the **Opessa** Pekowi Band & near/among the Mohawk community, a minor **Kishpoko Chief** in PA-MD by 1715, some of family including Young Rising Sun-Father of Puckenshinwa moved back to AL about 1730, among the Shawnee that went to OH 1744 with **Peter Chartier**, husband 1st about 1705 PA of **Kishpoko Woman**/1690, 2nd about 1730 PA of **Mohawk Woman**/1698-(sister of wife of **Cakundawanna Straight Tail**), father **with Kishpoko** of Young Rising Sun/1710-(father of Puckenshinwa), Sarah Rising Sun/1715-(mother of Blue Jacket)-both Kishpoko, children **with Mohawk** unknown

WIVES OF RISING SUN/1685

1ST WIFE 1705 PA

Kishpoko Woman born about 1790 AL-died by 1730 PA, parents unknown, wife 1705 PA of **Rising Sun**/1685, mother of Young Rising Sun/1710-(father of Puckenshinwa), Sarah Rising Sun/1715-(mother of Blue Jacket)-both Kishpoko

2ND WIFE 1730 PA

Mohawk Woman born about 1698 PA-died after 1730, **parents** 1730 PA of **Rising Sun**/1685, children unknown **unknown**, sister of wife of **Cakundawanna Straight Tail**, wife about

CHILDREN OF RISING SUN/1685

SON

Rising Sun, Young aka Father of Puckenshinwa – Kishpoko born about 1710 Lehigh valley PA-died after 1745 (OH?) – son of **Rising Sun**/1685 & **Kishpoko Woman**/1690, moved to Tallapoosa River AL about 1730 with Band & family, appears to have returned north (to OH?) about 1745, married about 1735 AL **Older Daughter of James McQueen**/1720, father of **Puckenshinwa**/1735, child/1737, Older Daughter/1739-(1st wife of **Blue Jacket**), Mary Rising Sun/1744-(wife of **David Francis**) -all 1/2 Kishpoko-Creek-Metis

DAUGHTER

Rising Sun, Sarah aka Rising Sun-Daughter of Rising Sun – Kishpoko born 1715 PA-died after 1765 OH - daughter of **Rising Sun**/1685 & **Kishpoko Woman**/1690, lived in a mixed Pekowi-Kishpoko-Mohawk community in PA, wife 1st 1730 PA of **Pride Opessa**/1710-Pekowi, widowed 1753, wife 2nd 1753 OH of **Kishpoko Man**/1710-(from the same mixed Pekowi-Kishpoko-Mohawk community that had moved to OH), widowed 1758, wife 3rd 1758 OH of **Mohawk Man**/1715-(from the same mixed Pekowi-Kishpoko-Mohawk community that had moved to OH), widowed by 1765, mother **with Pride** of Lawagqua-Elder Son/1733, Blue Jacket-Whirlpool/1735, Wabete-Elk-Younger Son/1737 & SarahOpessa/1739-all Pekowi-Kishpoko, **with Kishpoko** of No Worries-Mary Louise Sanschagrin/1754 & Yellow Britches-Edna Rising Sun/1756-Kishpoko, mother **with Mohawk** of Sarah Rising Sun/17591/2 Kishpoko-Mohawk

GRANDCHILDREN OF RISING SUN/1685 BY YOUNG RISING SUN/1710 & OLDER DAUGHTER OF JAMES MCQUEEN/1720

GRANDSON

Rising Sun, Puckenshinwa aka Pookaynsheenwah-PukenshinwaPuckinshinoawa-Alights from Flying-Alight From Flying-Something
Coming Downward - 1/2 Kishpoko-Creek-Metis born 1735 Tuckabatchee AL-**killed** 1774 Point Pleasant WV - son of **Young Rising Sun**/1710 & **Older Daughter of James McQueen**/1720, grandson of **Rising Sun (1)**/1685 & of **James McQueen**/1700-white, nephew of **Sarah Rising Sun**/1715-mother of Blue Jacket, father returned to AL from the Lehigh valley PA about 1730, a Kishpoko from AL, moved to KY 1759-to OH 1760, French-Indian War in south/1754-58, Cornstalk War/1759-74, Grand Council June 1762, Sept. 1762, 1763, Council Bouquet Oct. 1764, **Head Chief of Kishpoko in OH** by 1770, **killed** in battle at Point Pleasant 1774, brother of **Older Sister**/1739-(1st wife of **Blue Jacket**) & **Younger Sister**/1745-(wife of **David Mumagechee**

Francis), husband 1755 AL of **Metheotashe Opessa**/1740-Pekowi, father of son **Cheeseekau**/1756 AL, daughter **Tecumapease**/1758 AL, sons Sauwaseekou/1760 KY, (daughter Rising Star/1762 OH?), Nahaaseema/1764 OH, daughter Menewaulakoose/1766 OH, sons **Tecumseh**/1768 OH, Kumshaka/1770 OH, daughter Vocemassussia/1772 OH & son **Lalawethika**-Tenskawatawa-Shawnee Prophet/1774 OH -all 3/4th Kishpoko-Pekowi-Creek-Metis, adopted father 1760 OH of **Joshua Renicks**/1746, 1768 OH of **John Sparks**/1760 & **Richard Sparks**/1757, 1772 OH of **Stephen Ruddell**/1767

GRANDDAUGHTER

Rising Sun, Older Daughter of Young aka Older Sister of Puckenshinwa-wife of Blue Jacket-wife of Isadore Chesne-wife of Big Swamp - 1/2 Kishpoko-Creek-Metis born 1739 AL-died about 1774 OH - daughter of **Young Rising Sun**/1710 & **Daughter of James McQueen**/1720, appears to have returned north (OH?) about 1745 with their father, 1st wife 1st 1755 OH of 1st cousin **Blue Jacket-Whirlpool Straight Tail**/1735-Kishpoko-Pekowi, remarried when Blue Jacket married Margaret Moore-white, 2nd 1762 OH of **Isadore Chesne**/1735Wyandot-Metis, 3rd 1769 OH of **Big Swamp**/1730, mother **with Blue Jacket** of Young Whirlpool-Young Blue Jacket/1756, Spybeech/1758, Wayweleapee/1760 & George Bluejacket (1)/1762-all 3/4th KishpokoPekowi-Creek-Metis, **with Chesne** of Anthony Shane-Chesne/1763 & Joseph Shane-Chesne/1765-both 1/4th Kishpoko-Creek-Wyandot-Metis, **with Big Swamp** of Thick Water/1770-3/4th Kishpoko-Creek-Metis

GRANDDAUGHTER

Rising Sun, Mary aka Younger Daughter of Young Rising Sun-Younger Sister of Puckenshinwa-wife of David Francis - 1/2 Kishpoko-Creek-Metis born 1745 AL-died after 1805 - daughter of **Young Rising Sun**/1710 & **Older Daughter of James McQueen**/1720, remained in the south when their father returned to the north, aunt of **Tecumseh**, wife 1759 AL of **David Mumagechee Francis**/1740, mother of John Francis/1760, Josiah Francis/1765, Joseph Francis/1770 & Susan

Francis/1775-all 29/64th Kishpoko-Chalakatha-Mekoche-ShawanoChalaka-Powhatan-Metis

BY SARAH RISING SUN/1715 & PRIDE STRAIGHT TAIL/1710

GRANDSON

Opessa, Lawagqua aka Lawoughqua-Lawagkwa-**Elder Brother of Blue Jacket** – Pekowi-Kishpoko born 1733 PA-died after 1774 OH?– son of **Pride Opessa**/1710-Pekowi & **Sarah Rising Sun**/1715-Kishpoko, Turtle Clan, trading with Ohio Fur Co. in PA **with Blue Jacket & Wabete** by early 1750's, Cornstalk War/1755-74, 1765 Council Logstown PA, 1765 a **Pekowi Chief** in OH, 1765 returned captives to Ft. Pitt, husband about 1753 OH of **Pekowi Woman**/1737, father of Resting Fish-Masemo/1760 & Resting Snake-Monetoshe/1770-both PekowiKishpoko

GRANDSON

Blue Jacket aka Weyapiersenwha-**Whirlpool**-Sepettekenathe-Big Rabbit – Pekowi-Kishpoko born 1735 PA-died 1809 OH - son of **Pride Opessa**/1710-Pekowi & **Sarah Rising Sun**/1715-Kishpoko, Turtle Clan, grandson of **Opessa**, by 1755 trading with Ohio Fur Co. in PA **with brothers Lawagqua & Wabete-Elk, Pekowi by birth** but reverted to mother's **Kishpoko** family with his mother upon death of his father, Cornstalk War/1755-77, a **Pekowi Chief** in OH by 1772, by 1773 established Blue Jacket Town on Deer Creek of Sciota River OH, 1774 Treaty Camp Charlotte, 1775 Council Ft. Pitt **with Cornstalk, Silverheels, Nimwha & Wryneck**, 1776 Treaty Ft. Pitt, lead Chief in **Blue Jacket War/1777-94** (Blue Jacket War = allied **with British**Revolution/1776-83, Vincennes/1778, Point Pleasant/1778, Boonesboro/1778, Martin & Ruddle Stations KY/1780, Lochery/1781, Blue Licks/1782, Crawford/1782, Ft. Finney/1786, raiding KYTN/1786, raiding Ohio River valley/1788-92, Harmer/1790, Dunlap Station/1791, St. Clair/1791, Ft. Recovery/1794, defeated by Anthony Wayne & American Army at Fallen Timbers 1794), **Grand Council 1782,**

1785 **succeeded Black Snake as Head War Chief**, Jan. 1786 Council Miami, 1786 attended Treaty Ft. Finney, 1786 leader of an opposing faction when **Capt. Johnny** succeeded **Moluntha** as Head of Chalakatha-Mekoche led faction (split = 3 groups-**Black Hoof** in OH, **Capt. Johnny** in MO & **Blue Jacket** in OH), Grand Council 1791, Grand Council Sept. 1792, 1794 **succeeded Little Turtle**-Miami as **leader of United Tribes with Turkey Foot (1)**/1750-adopted-Ottawa, 1794 stepped down as **Head War Chief** following defeat at Fallen Timbers but due to hs influence & prestige laid claim to a position as **Civil Chief**, 1795 Treaty Greenville, never openly opposed whites after 1795, Grand Council 1805, Treaty 1805, **refused Tecumseh** in early ventures but was supportive later, step-half-brother (by marriage 1739 of Pride Opessa to Mother of Black Fish) of **Black Fish**, 1st cousin of Metheotashe-(fathers were brothers), **double-uncle of Tecumseh**-(1st cousin of **Metheotashe** & brother-in-law of **Puckenshinwa**), husband 1st 1755 OH-KY of **Older Sister of Puckenshinwa**/1739-1/2 KishpokoCreek-Metis, 2nd 1762 OH of **Margaret Moore**/1746-adopted-white, 3rd 1765 OH of **Clear Water Baby**/1750-1/2 Pekowi-Metis, father **with Sister of Puckenshinwa** of Young Whirlpool-Young Blue Jacket (1)/1756, Spybeech Bluejacket/1758, Wayweleapee Bluejacket/1760 & George Bluejacket (1)/1762-all 3/4th Pekowi-Kishpoko-Creek-Metis, **with Moore** of Joseph Moore-Bluejacket/1763 & Nancy Moore-Stewert/1765-(born after Margaret's return to the whites)-both 1/2 Pekowi-Kishpoko-Metis, **with Baby** of James Bluejacket/1766, Young Blue Jacket (2)/1770, Marie Louise Bluejacket/1774, Sally Bluejacket/1776, Nancy Bluejacket/1778, George Bluejacket/1780-all 3/4th Pekowi-Kishpoko-Metis

GRANDSON

Opessa, Wabete aka **Elk**-Younger Son-**Younger Brother of Blue Jacket** – Pekowi-Kishpoko born 1737 OH-died after 1774 OH - son of **Pride Opessa**/1710-Pekowi & **Sarah Rising Sun**/1715-Kishpoko, Turtle Clan, a Pekowi-Kishpoko warrior, younger brother of **Blue Jacket**/1735, by 1755 trading with OH Fur Co. in PA in early with brothers **Lawagqua** & **Blue Jacket**, Cornstalk War/1755-74, father in law of **Marmaduke Blue Pocket Swearingen**/1763-adopted-white, husband 1757 OH of

Kishpoko Woman/1742, 2nd 1766 OH of **Ms. Baby**/1752-1/2 PekowiMetis, children/1757-66 **with Kishpoko** unknown, father **with Baby** of Swan-Wapehti Opessa/1768-3/4th Pekowi-Metis - (some children may have been called Blue Jacket's)

GRANDDAUGHTER

Opessa, Sarah aka Sally Bluejacket-**Sister of Blue Jacket** – PekowiKishpoko born 1739 OH-died after 1825 OH - daughter of **Pride Opessa**/1710-Pekowi & **Sarah Rising Sun**/1715-Kishpoko, Turtle Clan, namesake of father's sister **Sarah-Snow White Opessa**/1695 & father's aunt **Snow White Straight Tail-Sarah White**/1666, sister of Lawagqua/1733, **Blue Jacket**/1735 & Wabete Opessa/1737, half-sister of **Red Pole**/1740-Mekoche, 1st cousin of **Metheotashe**-(fathers were brothers) & step-half-sister **Black Fish**-(by marriage of Pride Opessa to Mother of Black Fish), aunt of **Tecumseh, Bright Horn, Billy Caldwell**, never known to have married

BY SARAH RISING SUN/1715 & KISHPOKO MAN/1710

GRANDDAUGHTER

Rising Sun, No Worries aka **Marie Louise Sanschagrin**-1st Half-sister of Blue Jacket-2nd wife of **Col. Matthew Elliott**-adopted white – Kishpoko born 1754 OH-died 1826 - daughter of **Sarah Rising Sun**/1715 & **Kishpoko Man**/1710, sister of **Yellow Britches-Edna**/1756, half-sister of **Blue Jacket**/1735 & siblings, half-sister of **Sarah Rising Sun**/1759, 2nd wife 1769 PA of **Col. Matthew Elliott**/1730-adopted Irish, mother of Isabella Elliott/1770, Matthew Elliott Jr/1772, William Elliott/1775, Alexander Elliott/1780-all 1/2 Kishpoko-Metis, likely other unknown children

GRANDDAUGHTER

Rising Sun, Yellow Britches aka Edna-Daughter of Rising Sun-2nd Halfsister of Blue Jacket- 2nd wife of **Col. Alexander McKee**-adopted white – Kishpoko born 1756 OH-died after 1793 OH – daughter of **Sarah Rising**

Sun /1715 & **Kishpoko Man**/1710, sister of **No Worries-Marie Louis Sanschagrin**/1754, half-sister of **Blue Jacket**/1735 & siblings, half-sister of **Sarah Rising Sun**/1759, 2nd wife 1769 PA of **Col. Alexander McKee**/1725-adopted-Irish, mother of Thomas McKee/1770, Elizabeth McKee/1772, Alexander McKee/1775, Catherine McKee/1780 & at least 2 other children by 1780-all 1/2 Kishpoko-Metis

BY SARAH RISING SUN/1715 & MOHAWK MAN/1715

GRANDDAUGHTER

Rising Sun, Sarah aka 3rd Half-sister of Blue Jacket-wife of Brother of Mink-wife of William Caldwell-**Sarah Caldwell**-wife of James Colwellwife of William Vance - 1/2 Kishpoko-Mohawk born 1759 OH- died after 1796 Gallia Co. OH - daughter of **Sarah Rising Sun** /1715Kishpoko & **Mohawk Man**/1710, half-sister of **No Worries-Marie Louise Sanschagrin**/1754 & **Yellow Britches-Edna**/1756, half-sister of **Blue Jacket**/1735, wife 1st 1772 OH of **Brother of Mink**/1750- Mekoche,widowed 1774, 2nd 1776 OH of **William Caldwell**/1750-white, seperated 1778, 3rd 1779 WV of **James Colwell**/1757-white, 4th 1789 WV of **William Vance**/1755-1/4th Pekowi-Metis, abandoned **Bright Horn** 1776 when she married **William Caldwell**, abandoned **Billy Caldwell** 1779 & moved to WV, went by name of **Sarah Caldwell** in marriages to **Colwell & Vance**, mother **with Brother of Mink** of Bright Horn/1772- 3/4th Mekoche-Kishpoko-Mohawk, **with Caldwell** of Billy Caldwell/1777-1/4th Kishpoko-Mohawk-Metis, **with Colwell** of James Colwell/1780, Jacob Colwell/1782, Sarah Colwell/1784 & Martha Patsy Colwell/1786 & **with Vance** of Thomas Vance/1790 & Christina Vance/1796-all 3/8th Kishpoko-Pekowi-Mohawk-Metis

CHAPTER FOUR

Okowellos Cornstalk/1674

Okowellos Cornstalk/1674

Cornstalk (5) aka **Okowellos** Cornstalk-Okowellos Hokolesqua-Akowellos-Hokowellos-Hakowellos-Stalk of Plant - 11/16th Chalakatha-Shawano-Chalaka-Powhatan-Metis born 1674 PA-died 1758 in epidemic OH – son of **Hokolesqua Opechan-Cornstalk (4)/1630** & **Pashmere Carpenter (1)/1637**, Bear Clan, taught to cipher, read, speak & write some English by his mother, in TN before 1704, a **Chalakatha Chief** in OH by 1707, a **Chalakatha Chief** in WV on the Greenbrier River 1710, in PA by 1723-**King of the Upper Shawnee** in PA 1723, in AL by 1725-**Chief of the Shawnee on the Savannah River** AL 1725, in PA by 1730-a **major Chalakatha Chief** in PA 1731, returned to AL by 1755-**Chief of the Shawnee in AL** 1755, returned to OH by 1758-**Head Chief of Chalakatha in OH** 1758, over 6' tall, associated at times with **Straight Tail**-Pekowi, **Opessa**-Pekowi, **Poxinosa**-Pekowi, **Pheasant**Pekowi & **White Fish**-Pekowi-all major Chiefs of his time, taught most of his children to cipher, read & speak some English, husband 1st 1695 PA of **Katee Mekoche/1680**, 2nd 1713 PA of **Daughter of Sassoonan/1697**-Delaware, 3rd 1725 AL of **Sister of Sehoy/1709**-Wind Clan Creek, father with Katee of unknown daughters/1695-1703, daughter Wakuta/1704-(wife of **Thomas Greenwood**), child/1706, child/1708, son Keightughqua **Cornstalk (6)/1710**, Sawelaha-Eliza/1712-(wife of a **Chalakatha Man, James Francis & Old Belt**), son Keeweeton/1714, daughter **Cawechile**/1716-(wife of **Cold Water**), daughter **Nonhelema**/1718, son **Nimwha**/1720, son **Red Hawk**/1722, son **Silverheels**/1724-all 27/32tnd Chalakatha-Mekoche-

ShawanoChalaka-Powhatan-Metis, **with Daughter of Sassoonan** of son Wakeeampea/1714, Ewikunwee/1716, Naythakiena/1718, **Bukangolas/**1720-all 11/32nd Chalakatha-Shawano-Chalaka-Powhatan-Delaware-Metis, **with Sister of Sehoy** of daughters Elizabeth/1726 & Catherine-Kitty Cornstalk/1728-both 11/32nd Chalakatha-ShawanoChalaka-Creek-Metis

WIVES OF OKOWELLOS

WIFE 1695 - PA
KATEE MEKOCHE/1680

Mekoche, Katee aka Katee Cornstalk-Katee Okowellos – Mekoche born 1680 OH-died about 1744 Logan Co OH – **parents unknown**, aunt of **Moluntha**-(son of her brother), band moves to PA 1683, wife 1695 PA of **Okowellos Cornstalk**/1674, mother of unknown daughters/1695-1703, daughter Wakuta/1704, child/1706, child/1708, son Cornstalk (6)/1710, Sawelaha-Eliza/1712, son Keeweeton/1714, daughter Cawechile/1716, daughter Nonhelema/1718, son Nimwha/1720, son Red Hawk/1722, son Silverheels/1724-all 27/32tnd ChalakathaMekoche-Shawano-Chalaka-Powhatan-Metis

WIFE 1713 PA
DAUGHTER OF SASSOONAN/1697-DELAWARE

Sassoonan, Daughter of aka Delaware Wife of Okowellos – adoptedDelaware born 1697 PA-died about 1725 PA, daughter of **Sassoonan**Alumapee/1675, granddaughter of **Tamenend**/1640, sister of **Polly**wife of Opessa/1695, **Shingas**/1700, **King Beaver**/1705 & **Pisquetomen**/1710-all noted Delaware, marriage represents an attempt to cement Shawnee-Delaware relations in PA, Turkey Clan, 2nd wife 1713 OH of **Okowellos Cornstalk**/1674, mother of Wakeeampea/1714, Ewikunwee/1716, Naythakiena/1718, Bukangelos/1720 & possibly others-all 11/32nd Chalakatha-Shawano-Chalaka-Powhatan-DelawareMetis

WIFE 1725 AL
SISTER OF SEHOY/1709-KOASATI CREEK

Sehoy, Sister of aka Creek Wife of Okowellos – Koasati **Wind** Clan Creek born about 1709 AL-died after 1758 likely OH – **parents unknown**, sister of **Sehoy (1)**/1704, aunt of **Red Shoes (1)**/1720 & **Sehoy (2)**/1722, Wind Clan, marriage represents an attempt to cement Shawnee-Creek relations, 3rd wife 1725 Shawnee village AL of **Okowellos Cornstalk**/1674, mother of Elizabeth Cornstalk/1726, Catherine Kitty Cornstalk/1728 & other children/1730-45- 11/32nd Chalakatha-Shawano-Chalaka-Creek-Metis

CHILDREN OF OKOWELLOS/1674
WITH KATEE MEKOCHE/1680

DAUGHTER

Cornstalk, Wakuta – 27/32nd Chalakatha-Mekoche-Shawano-Chalaka-Powhatan-Metis born 1704 Running Water TN-died 1758 Running Water TN – daughter of **Okowellos**/1674 & **Katee Mekoche**/1680, Bear Clan, taught to cipher, read & speak some English by her father, wife 1718 Nickajack TN of **Thomas Sutichettchee Greenwood**/1698, mother of sons David Swallow-tail Greenwood/1718, Joseph Tallichama Greenwood/1720, Robert Tallitaha Greenwood/1722 & daughters Puki-Pequea Greenwood/1724 & Cheekee Greenwood/1728- all 13/16th Chalakatha-Thawikila-Kishpoko-Mekoche-Shawano-Chalaka-Powhatan-Black-Metis

SON

Cornstalk, Keightughqua aka **Cornstalk (6)** -Strong Man-Hokolesqua Cornstalk (3)-Okowellos Cornstalk (2)-Stalk of Corn-Stalk of PlantHokolesqua (3)-Hokoleshka (3)-Okowellos (2)-AkulusskaWneypuechsika-Waynaypooechseeka-Stout Man-SimaquanSeemakwan – 27/32nd Chalakatha-Mekoche-Shawano-ChalakaPowhatan-Metis born 1710 WV-**murdered** 1777 Point Pleasant WV - son of **Okowellos-Cornstalk (5)**/1674 & **Katee Mekoche**/1680,

Bear Clan, taught to cipher, read & speak some English by his father, went to AL with father by 1725, in PA by 1730-(married 1st 1730 PA), in TN by 1734(married 2nd in Running Water TN 1734), a **Chalakatha Chief** in PA by 1740, raiding PA/1740, (married 3rd in PA 1741), moved to OH with **Peter Chartier** 1744, a **major Chalakatha chief** in OH by 1749, Council near site of Ft. Pitt Nov. 1753, lead Chief & force in **Cornstalk War**/1755-77 (Cornstalk War = leading Shawnee Chief in French-Indian War/1754-63, leading Shawnee Chief at Braddock/1755, raiding NewShenandoah valleys/1755-56, raiding PA/1755-56, negotiated Treaty 1757 at mouth of Big Sandy River with **Thomas Lewis** & **William Preston**, led raiding Ohio-New River valleys.1758, Council Ft. Pitt June 1762, **Head Shawnee Chief** in Pontiac War/1762-66, led Shawnee at Bushy Run/1763, led raiding of New-Greenbrier-Jackson River valleys/1763, Council with **Col. Bouquet** Oct. 1764, hostage of Col. Bouquet winter 1764-65 with brothers **Wakeeampea, Ewikunwee, Naythakeina & Red Hawk**, negotiated Treaty Spring 1765 with **Col. Bouquet** Oct. 1764, hostage of Col. Bouquet winter 1764-65 with brothers **Wakeeampea, Ewikunwee, Naythakeina & Red Hawk**, negotiated Treaty Spring 1765 with **Col. Bouquet**, raiding Ohio-NewBig Sandy-Little Kanawha valleys/1772, traveled & sent emissaries 1774 to Shawnee & related Tribes in **VA-NC-SC-GA-AL-TN-KY-MOIL-MI-IN-OH-PA-MD-NY** enlisting support for upcoming Dunmore's War 1774, sought support of **nephew Dragging Canoe**, Point Pleasant/1774, **Head Chief of Northern Confederacy** at Point Pleasant/1774, negotiated Treaty Camp Charlotte 1774 with **Lord Dunmore**, Point Pleasant/1775, Council Ft. Pitt 1775 with **Nimwha, Silver Heels, Wryneck & Blue Jacket**, Council Ft. Pitt-George Morgan 1776 with **Nimwha, Ellinipsico**, sister **Cawechile, Capt. Johnny, Blue Jacket & Black Caesar**, Council 1776 with **White Eyes**-Delaware, **John Montour**-Seneca-Metis, **Wyandot Half-King & William Wilson**, Council Ft. Pitt 1777), in AL 1754-55, returned to OH in 1755, in AL for a while 1757-58-(mentioned as **a Chief of the Shawnee among the Creeks**), returned to OH in 1758 (death of his father in epidemic), associated with **John Swift, Dragging Canoe, Double Head, Red Bird, John Watts & Nathaniel Gist** in silver-mines-counterfeiting 1755-69 furnishing silver to Shawnee & Confederacy, **Head Chief of**

Chalakatha & All Shawnee 1758-77, **Head Chief of 20 tribe Northern Confederacy** 1760-74-(most of the pre-white, west of Appalachians Shawnee confederacy), last home was at Cornstalk's village on Sippio Creek of Scioto River OH from early 1770's, **murdered** by whites at Ft. Randolph-Point Pleasant/1777 with brother **Red Hawk**, son **Ellinipsico** & son in law/adopted son **Petella**, taught most of his children to cipher read & write in English, at least to some degree, husband 1st 1730 PA of **Helizikinopo Snake**/1715, 2nd 1734 Running Water TN of **Ounaconoa Muskrat**/1716, 3rd 1741 PA of **Julia Mulatto**/1720-adopted-Mulatto, (at least) 4th 1763 OH of **Catherine Vanderpoole See**/1725-adopted-white, (other wives/1730-77 possible including a Creek/Shawnee or Creek about 1757), father **with Helizikinopo** of Walker-Pomeatha/1730, Wolf/1732, Catherine Katee/1734, Chenusaw/1736, Newa/1738, Greenbrier/1740, Aracoma/1742, Elizabeth/1744,Young Cornstalk/1746, Ellinipsico/1748, Blue Sky-Mary/1750, Esther/1752, Oceana/1754-all 29/32nd Chalakatha-Mekoche-Shawano-Chalaka-Powhatan-Metis, **with Ounaconoa** of Black Beard/1736, Black Wolf/1740, John Wolf (Cornstalk)/1750, Peter Cornstalk/1755 & Susannah Cornstalk/1757-all 29/32nd Chalakatha-Mekoche-PekowiShawano-Chalaka-Powhatan-Metis, **with Julia** of Sun Fish/1742, Elijah Cornstalk/1744, Abraham Cornstalk "Ailstock"/1748, Absalom Cornstalk "Ailstock"/1750 & Michael Cornstalk "Ailstock"/1752-all 27/64th Chalakatha-Mekoche-Shawano-Chalaka-Powhatan-Black-Metis, **with Catherine** of Mary (Cornstalk) See/1764-27/64th ChalakathaMekoche-Shawano-Chalaka-Powhatan-Metis, **adopted father** about 1740 PA of **Petella**/1730-white, 1763 OH of **Elizabeth See**/1754 & **John See**/1759-white, (unknown children with all wives likely & a **Creek Wife** about 1758 also likely)

DAUGHTER

Cornstalk, Sawelaha aka Eliza Cornstalk-Wife of James Francis-Wife of Old Belt-Grenadier Squaw – 27/32nd Chalakatha-Mekoche-ShawanoChalaka-Powhatan-Metis born 1712 WV-died after 1745 (PA?) - daughter of **Okowellos**/1674 & **Katee Mekoche**/1680, Bear Clan, taught to cipher, read & speak some English by her father, didn't move to OH with **Peter Chartier** 1744, wife 1st 1730 PA of **Chalakatha Man**/1710, 2nd 1739 PA of **James Francis**/1700-British Colonial Military, 3rd about 1745 OH of **Old Belt**/1700-Seneca, mother **with Chalakatha** of Aroas-Silverheels/1732 & Counasona/1735-both 59/64th Chalakatha-Mekoche-Shawano-Chalaka-Powhatan-Metis -(later adopted Seneca), **with Francis** of David Francis/1740 & John Francis/1745-both 27/64th Chalakatha-Mekoche-Shawano-Chalaka-Powhatan-Metis, any children **with Belt** unknown

SON

Cornstalk, Keeweeton aka Keeweeton Okowellos-KeewetonKeywayton-Quiouiton-Quiwetahn-Keywetahn-Kiwitahn-Brother of Cornstalk – 27/32nd Chalakatha-Mekoche-Shawano-Chalaka-Powhatan-Metis born 1714 WV-died about 1804 OH - son of **Okowellos**/1674 & **Katee Mekoche**/1680, moved to AL with father 1725, returned to PA by 1730, moved to OH with **Peter Chartier** 1744, may have returned to AL for a short while in 1755, Bear Clan, over 6' tall, taught to cipher, read & speak some English by his father, raiding PA/1740, Cornstalk War /1755-77, a **Chalakatha Chief** in OH by 1763, **an emissary to the Shawnee for Cornstalk** 1774, Blue Jacket War/1777-80, husband 1734 PA of **Chalakatha Woman**/18, children unknown

DAUGHTER

Cornstalk, Cawechile aka Younger Daughter of-Wife of Cold Water – 27/32nd Chalakatha-Mekoche-Shawano-Chalaka-Powhatan-Metis born 1716 WV-died after 1807 OH - daughter of **Okowellos**/1674 & **Katee Mekoche**/1680, a Chalakatha, Bear Clan, taught to cipher, read & speak some English by her father, didn't move to OH with **Peter Chartier** 1744, in later years the **Chief of the Women's Council**, speaker for the women & children, about 6' tall, Council Ft. Pitt 1776 with **Cornstalk, Nimwha, Ellinipsico, Blue Jacket, Capt. Johnny & Caesar** with George Morgan, Council Ft. Finney 1786 with **Moluntha, Capt. Johnny, Red Pole, Black Snake, Nianimissico (?), Wapachcawela (?), Nihipeewa & Nihinessiko**, wife 1st about 1735 PA of **Cold Water** aka **Wepenipe**/1715–Chalakatha, 2nd 1753 OH of **ElkWabete**/1715-Mekoche-(brother of Moluntha), mother **with Cold Water** of children/1736-39, Young Cold Water/1740, Lacumtequa Cold

Water/1744 & other children-all 1759/64th Mekoche-ChalakathaShawano-Chalaka-Powhatan-Metis, any children **with Elk-Wabete** unknown

DAUGHTER

Cornstalk, Nonhelema aka Grenadier Squaw-Warrior Woman of the Shawnee-Nonhelema Okowellos - 27/32nd Chalakatha-MekocheShawano-Chalaka-Powhatan-Metis born 1718 WV-died after 1786 OH - daughter of **Okowellos**/1674 & **Katee Mekoche**/1680, Bear Clan, about
6'6" tall-well built & attractive, taught to cipher, read & speak some English by her father, moved to AL by 1725 with Okowellos' bandreturned to PA by 1730, moved to OH with **Peter Chartier** 1744, a **village Head woman** by 1750, an occasional warrior in Cornstalk War /1755-74, Head Woman of Nonhelema's village on Sippio Creek of Sciota River OH before 1773, **an emissary to the Shawnee for Cornstalk** 1774, the **only woman warrior** Point Pleasant/1774, Grand Council 1782, Council Miami Jan. 1786, had the fingers cut off of her right hand to the 1st knuckle by whites following **murder of Moluntha** during Benjamin Logan's attack on Moluntha's village 1786, moved to Apple Creek MO area following death of Moluntha, returned to OH home a few years later to die, wife 1st 1734 PA of
WahootasikaSavannah King/1710-Chalakatha-widowed 1754, 2nd 1754 OH of 1st cousin **Moluntha**/1710-Mekoche, partner 3rd 1762 OH with **Richard Butler**/1742-white-(adopted Seneca), mother **with Wahootasika** of
Elder Daughter/1735, Mellana/1748, twin daughters Wynema & Waheeta/1750--all 59/64th Chalakatha-Mekoche-Shawano-ChalakaPowhatan-Metis, **with Moluntha** of Chieska/1755, Younger Daughter/1757 & Big Capt. Johnny/1759-all 59/64th MekocheChalakatha-Shawano-Chalaka-Powhatan-Metis, **with Richard Butler** of
Capt. Butler/1763-27/64th Chalakatha-Mekoche-Shawano-ChalakaPowhatan-Metis, adoptive mother of her niece **Fanny Butler**/1755, often confused in white histories with her sisters & nieces

SON

Cornstalk, Nimwha aka Nimwha Okowellos –27/32nd ChalakathaMekoche-Shawano-Chalaka-Powhatan-Metis born 1720 WV-died after 1786 likely OH - son of **Okowellos**/1674 & **Katee Mekoche**/1680, to AL with father 1725-returned to PA by 1730, Bear Clan, taught to cipher, read & speak some English by his father, moved to OH with **Peter Chartier** 1744, a **Chief of the Shawnee among the Delaware** 1750, Cornstalk War /1755-77, Council Muskingum Nov. 1764, Council Logstown 1765, Council Ft. Pitt 1765, **an emissary to the Delaware for Cornstalk** 1774, Blue Jacket War/1777-86, Treaty Camp Charlotte 1774, hostage of whites winter 1774-75, Council Ft. Pitt 1775 with **Corn Stalk, Silver Heels, Wryneck & Blue Jacket**, Council Ft. Pitt 1776, **succeeded Red Hawk as Chief of Shawnee among the Delaware 1777**, Council Ft. Pitt 1785, Council Ft. Pitt 1786, Treaty 1786, husband 1739 PA of **Delaware Woman**/1723, children unknown

SON

Cornstalk, Red Hawk aka **Miskapelathee**-Misquapolathe-Red Hawk Okowellos –27/32nd Chalakatha-Mekoche-Shawano-ChalakaPowhatan-Metis born 1722 WV-died 1777 Point Pleasant WV - son of **Okowellos**/1674 & **Katee Mekoche**/1680, Bear Clan, taught to cipher, read & speak some English by his father, moved to OH with **Peter Chartier** 1744, a **Mekoche Chief** by 1759, Cornstalk War /1755-77, Council Ft. Pitt Aug. 1759, Council Ft. Pitt Aug.-Sept. 1762, Council Lancaster Aug. 1762, hostage of **Bouquet** winter of 1764-65 with **Cornstalk, Wakeeampea, Ewikunwee & Naythakeina**, often represented Cornstalk at Councils/1760-74, Treaty 1765, **Chief of Shawnee among the Delaware about 1764, an emissary/carried wampum to Dragging Canoe for Cornstalk** before Point Pleasant 1774, Camp Charlotte 1774, **murdered at Ft. Randolph**/Point Pleasant WV 1777 with **Cornstalk**, nephew **Ellinipsico** & adopted nephew **Petella**, husband 1st 1742 PA of a **Mekoche Woman**/1726 & 2nd about 1754 OH of a **Delaware Woman**/1738, children unknown

SON

Cornstalk, Silverheels (1) aka Halowas-Silverheels Okowellos (1) – 27/32nd Chalakatha-Mekoche-Shawano-Chalaka-Powhatan-Metis born

1724 PA-died 1804 OH - son of **Okowellos**/1674 & **Katee Mekoche**-1680, Bear Clan, taught to cipher, read & speak some English by his father, moved to OH with **Peter Chartier** 1744, Cornstalk War /1755-77, a **Chalakatha Chief, an emissary to the Shawnee for Cornstalk** 1774, Blue Jacket War /1777-94, Boonesboro/78, Council Camp Charlotte 1774, Council Ft. Woods 1775, Council Ft. Pitt 1775 with **Cornstalk, Nimwha, Wryneck & Blue Jacket**, over 6' tall, husband about 1745 OH of **Chalakatha Woman**/1730, father of Silverheels (4)-Young Halowas (2)/1760, Daughter/1770, Sarah Silverheels/1775 & other unknown children/1744-74-all 59/64th Chalakatha-Mekoche-Shawano-ChalakaPowhatan-Metis

WITH DAUGHTER OF SASSOONAN/1697

SON

Cornstalk, Wakeeampea aka Wakeeampea Okowellos – 11/32nd Chalakatha-Shawano-Chalaka-Powhatan-Delaware-Metis born 1714 PA-died after 1765 likely OH - son of **Okowellos**/1674 & **Daughter of Sassoonan**/1697, Bear-Turkey Clan, taught to cipher, read & speak some English by his father, raiding PA/1740, likely moved to OH with **Peter Chartier** 1744, Cornstalk War /1755-65, a **Delaware Chief** in Ohio valley by 1750, hostage of **Col. Bouquet** 1765 with **Cornstalk, Ewikunwee, Naythakeina & Red Hawk**, husband by 1734 PA of **Delaware Woman**/1719, children unknown

SON

Cornstalk, Ewikunwee aka Hewikunwee-Ewikunwee Okowellos – 11/32nd Chalakatha-Shawano-Chalaka-Powhatan-Delaware-Metis born 1716 PA-died after 1765 OH - son of **Okowellos**/1674 & **Daughter of Sassoonan**/1697, Bear-Turkey Clan, taught to cipher, read & speak some English by his father, raiding PA/1740, likely moved to OH with **Peter Chartier** 1744, Cornstalk War /1755-65, a **Chief of the Shawnee among the Delaware** in Ohio valley by 1755, hostage of **Col. Bouquet** winter of 1764-65 with **Wakeeampea, Cornstalk, Naythakeina & Red Hawk**, husband about 1736 PA of a **Delaware Woman**/1719, children unknown

SON

Cornstalk, Naythakeina aka Neightthakeina-Naythakeina Okowellos – 11/32nd Chalakatha-Shawano-Chalaka-Powhatan-Delaware-Metis born 1718 PA-died after 1765 - son of **Okowellos**/1674 & **Daughter of Sassoonan**/1697, Bear-Turkey Clan, taught to cipher, read & speak some English by his father, raiding PA/1740, likely moved to OH with **Peter Chartier** 1744, a **Chief of the Shawnee among the Delaware** 1745, Cornstalk War /1755-65, hostage of **Col. Bouquet** 1765 with **Wakeeampea, Cornstalk, Ewikunwee** & **Red Hawk**, husband 1738 PA of **Delaware Woman**/1722, children unknown

SON

Cornstalk, Bukangolas aka Bukangolas Hokolesqua-Bukangolas Okowellos-Bukangolas-Bukanghelas-Pukangolas-Breaks to PiecesBuckongahlas-Beloved Leader-He Who Fulfills – 11/32nd ChalakathaShawano-Chalaka-Powhatan-Delaware-Metis born 1720 PA-died 1804
OH - son of **Okowellos**/1674 & **Daughter of Sassoonan**/1697, BearTurkey Clan, went to AL with father 1725, returned to PA by 1731, taught to cipher, read & speak some English by his father, raiding PA/1740, moved to OH with **Peter Chartier** 1744, Cornstalk War /175577, Council 1763, a **Major Delaware Chief** by mid-1760's, an **emissary to the Delaware for Cornstalk** 1774, scarred on left cheek-left ear cut off in battle by sword blow before 1778, Blue Jacket War /1777-94, Council
Detroit Nov. 1781, Grand Council 1782, Treaty 1785, Council Miami Jan. 1786 & Aug. 1786, Grand Council 1792, Treaty Greenville 1795, Council Swan Creek OH 1795 with **Capt. Johnny, Black Beard & George Ironside**, Treaty 1803 & 1804, **refused Tecumseh** in early ventures, husband 1740 PA of **Delaware Woman**/1725, father of many 11/64th Chalakatha-Shawano-Chalaka-Powhatan-Delaware-Metis children/1740-70

WITH SISTER OF SEHOY/1709

DAUGHTER

Cornstalk, Elizabeth aka Elizabeth Okowellos-Sister of Cornstalk-Grenadier Squaw - 11/32nd Chalakatha-Shawano-Chalaka-PowhatanCreek-Metis born 1726 Shawnee village AL-died after 1817 OH- daughter of **Okowellos**/1674 & **Sister of Sehoy**/1709-Creek, in PA by 1730 with father, taught to cipher, read & speak some English by her father, moved to OH with **Peter Chartier** 1744, appears to have not went to AL 1755-58, Bear-Wind Clan, a Christian Chalakatha, about 6' tall i.e. a Grenadier Squaw & attractive, often a translator/messenger for the whites, wife 1st about 1744 PA of **Chalakatha Man**/1724, 2nd about 1754 OH of **Capt. John Butler**-Lodging Pole/1730-white-(adopted Seneca), 3rd 1760 OH of **Mekoche Man**/1720, children/174454 & 1760/71 **with Chalakatha & Mekoche husbands** unknown, mother **with John Butler** of Fanny Butler/1755 & Tommy Butler/1760both 11/64th Chalakatha-Shawano-Chalaka-Powhatan-Creek-Metis, often confused in white histories with her sisters & nieces

DAUGHTER

Cornstalk, Catherine (1) aka Kitty-Catherine Kitty Okowellos-Catherine Kitty Cornstalk (1)-Sister of Cornstalk-Grenadier Squaw – 11/32nd Chalakatha-Shawano-Chalaka-Powhatan-Creek-Metis born 1728 Shawnee village AL-died after 1797 likely OH - daughter of **Okowellos**/1674 & **Sister of Sehoy**/1709-Creek, Bear-Wind Clan, a Christian Chalakatha, about 6' tall i.e. a Grenadier Squaw & attractive, taught to cipher, read & speak some English by her father, moved to OH with **Peter Chartier** 1744, often a translator/messenger for the whites, wife 1st 1745 OH of **Wrynek-Aquilsa**/1725-Pekowi, partner 2nd 1764 of **William Butler**/1744-white (adopted-Seneca), children/1745-65 **with Wrynek-Aquilsa** unknown, mother **with Butler** of Polly Butler/1765-11/64th Chalakatha-Shawano-Chalaka-Powhatan-Creek-Metis, often confused in white histories with her sisters & nieces

GRANDCHILDREN OF OKOWELLOS/1674 BY WAKUTA/1704

& THOMAS SUTICHETTCHEE GREENWOOD/1701

GRANDSON

Greenwood, David **Swallowtail Warrior** aka Little Yellow Bird-Second Yellow Bird – 13/16th Chalakatha-Thawikila-Kishpoko-MekocheShawano-Chalaka-Powhatan-Black-Metis born 1718 Nickajack TN**murdered** 1760 Ft. Prince George-Keowee TN – son of **Thomas Sutichettchee Greenwood**/1698 & **Wakuta Cornstalk**/1704, Wind Clan, head warrior of Estatoe, led the Lower Town warriors in an attack on Ft. Duquesne 1757, **pro-British** faction in French-Indian War but murdered 1760 with **John Yellow Bird Greenwood, Joseph Two tails Greenwood** & **Robert Two Killer Greenwood** while held captive by the British, husband 1738 Nickajack TN of **Blind Savannah Woman**/1723, children/1738-60 unknown

GRANDSON

Greenwood, Joseph **Tallichama** aka Two Tails – 13/16th Chalakatha-Thawikila-Kishpoko-Mekoche-Shawano-Chalaka-Powhatan-BlackMetis born 1720 Nickajack TN-**murdered** 1760 Ft. Prince GeorgeKeowee TN – son of **Thomas Sutichettchee Greenwood**/1698 & **Wakuta Cornstalk**/1704, Wind Clan, murdered 1760 with **John Yellow Bird Greenwood, David Swallow-tail Greenwood** & **Robert Two Killer Greenwood** while held captive by the British, ,husband 1740 Nickajack TN of **Blind Savannah Woman**/1725, children/1740-60 unknown

GRANDSON

Greenwood, Robert **Tallitaha** aka Two Killer – 13/16th ChalakathaThawikila-Kishpoko-Mekoche-Shawano-Chalaka-Powhatan-BlackMetis born 1722 Nickajack TN-**murdered** 1760 Ft. Prince GeorgeKeowee TN – son of **Thomas Sutichettchee Greenwood**/1698 & **Wakuta Cornstalk**/1704, Wind Clan, murdered 1760 with **John Yellow Bird Greenwood, Joseph Two-tails Greenwood** & **David Swallow-tail Greenwood** while held captive by the British, husband 1742 Nickajack TN of **Blind Savannah Woman**/1727, children/1742-60 unknown

GRANDDAUGHTER

Greenwood, Puki aka Pequea – 13/16th Chalakatha-ThawikilaKishpoko-Mekoche-Shawano-Chalaka-Powhatan-Black-Metis born 1724 Nickajack TN-died after 1770 OH – daughter of **Thomas Sutichettchee Greenwod**/1698 & **Wakuta Cornstalk**/1704, Wind Clan, 2nd wife 1742 Nickajack TN of **Amoyah Pigeon Moytoy**/1715, mother of Katie-Naky Moytoy-Pigeon/1745, Jane-Pugi Moytoy-Pigeon/1747 & Jenny-Sula Moytoy-Pigeon/1749-all 7/8th Chalakatha-ThawikilaKishpoko-Mekoche-Shawano-Chalaka-Powhatan-Black-Metis

GRANDDAUGHTER

Greenwood, Cheekee (1) – 13/16th Chalakatha-Thawikila-KishpokoMekoche-Shawano-Chalaka-Powhatan-Black-Metis born 1728 Nickajack TN –died 1780 Chota TN – daughter of **Thomas Sutichettchee Greenwood**/1698 & **Wakuta Cornstalk**/1704, Wind Clan, wife 1743 Chota TN of **Savanooka Moytoy**/1720-ChalakathaPekowi, mother of Savanooka Moytoy (2)/1750, Skootekitehi-Fire Heart Moytoy/1752-both 7/8th Chalakatha-Pekowi-Thawikila-KishpokoMekoche-Shawano-Chalaka-Powhatan-Black-Metis

BY CORNSTALK (6)/1710
WITH HELIZIKINOPO SNAKE/1715

GRANDSON

Cornstalk, Walker aka **Pomeatha**-Passes By-Pomeseh – 29/32nd Chalakatha-Mekoche-Shawano-Chalaka-Powhatan-Metis born 1730 PA-died before 1825 OH – oldest son of **Cornstalk (6)**/1710 & **Helizikinopo**/1715, Bear Clan, over 6' tall, taught to cipher, read & speak some English by his father, Cornstalk War/1755-77, a **Chalakatha Chief** in OH before 1774, **an emissary for Cornstalk** 1774, **hostage of Virginians** 1775-76, Blue Jacket War/1777-94, no part in War 1812, an **Elder Chalakatha Chief** at Wapakoneta 1817, Treaty 1814, 1817, 1818, husband 1st 1751 Great Tellico TN to **Oousta White Owl Carpenter**/1722, 2nd 1755 OH of **Chalakatha Woman**/1740, 3rd 1763 OH of **Margaret Peggy See**/1744-adopted-white, father **with Carpenter** of John Walker/1752-9/16th Chalakatha-Mekoche-Shawano-ChalakaPowhatan-Cherokee-Metis, **with Chalakatha** of Capt. Walker/1760 & others/1755-85-all 31/32nd Chalakatha-Mekoche-Shawano-ChalakaPowhatan-Metis, **with Margaret Peggy See (1)** of Young Walker/17647/16th Chalakatha-Mekoche-Shawano-Chalaka-Powhatan-Metis

GRANDSON

Cornstalk, Wolf aka **Cutenwha**-Kootenwha – 29/32nd ChalakathaMekoche-Shawano-Chalaka-Powhatan-Metis born 1732 PA-died after
1817 (likely OH) - 2nd son of **Cornstalk**/1710 & **Helizikinopo**/1715, Bear Clan, taught to cipher, read & speak some English by his father, Cornstalk War/1755-77, a **Chalakatha Chief** in OH by 1770, **an emissary for Cornstalk** 1774, **hostage of Virginians** 1775-76, Blue Jacket War/1777-88, husband 1750 OH of **Chalakatha Woman**/1735, children unknown but a son also called Cutenwha is thought

GRANDDAUGHTER

Cornstalk, Catherine (2) aka Katie-Katee-Kitty-Ketty Cornstalk - 29/32nd Chalakatha-Mekoche-Shawano-Chalaka-Powhatan-Metis born 1734 PA-died 1758 OH of smallpox - oldest daughter of **Cornstalk (6)**/1710 & **Helizikinopo**/1715, Bear Clan, a **Christian Chalakatha**, over 6' tall i.e. a **Grenadier Squaw**, taught to cipher, read & speak some English by her father, may have served as a translator-messenger for the whites, wife 1750 OH of adopted brother **Petella**/1730-adopted white, died in smallpox epidemic of 1758, children/1750-58 unknown but likely

GRANDSON

Cornstalk, Chenusaw – 29/32nd Chalakatha-Mekoche-ShawanoChalaka-Powhatan-Metis born 1736 PA-died after 1778 likely OH - 3rd son of **Cornstalk (6)**/1710 & **Helizikinopo**/1715, Bear Clan, a

Chalakatha warrior, taught to cipher, read & speak some English by his father, Cornstalk War/1755-77, **an emissary for Cornstalk** 1774, **hostage of Virginians** 1775-76, husband 1756 OH of **Chalakatha Woman**/1740, children unknown

GRANDSON

Cornstalk, Newa – 29/32nd Chalakatha-Mekoche-Shawano-Chalaka-Powhatan-Metis born 1738 PA-died after 1778 OH - 4th son of **Cornstalk (6)**/1710 & **Helizikinopo**/1715, Bear Clan, a Chalakatha warrior, taught to cipher, read & speak some English by his father, Cornstalk War/1758-76, **an emissary for Cornstalk** 1774, **hostage of Virginians** 1775-76, husband 1st 1757 OH of **Chalakatha Woman**/1742, 2nd 1763 OH of **Lois Sarah See**/1746-adopted-white, children/1757-87 **with Chalakatha** unknown, father **with See** of Son of Newa/17647/16th Chalakatha-Mekoche-Shawano-Chalaka-Powhatan-Metis (the son stayed with Newa when mother returned to whites 1765)

GRANDDAUGHTER

Cornstalk, Greenbrier – 29/32nd Chalakatha-Mekoche-ShawanoChalaka-Powhatan-Metis born 1740 PA-died after 1780 (WV-OH) - 3rd daughter of **Cornstalk (6)**/1710 & **Helizikinopo**/1715, Bear Clan, a **Christian Chalakatha**, about 6' tall i.e. a Grenadier Squaw & attractive, taught to cipher, read & speak some English by her father, likely a translator-messenger for the whites, associated in later years with a **McComas** family-(maybe in laws through marriage of a daughter?), wife by 1757 WV of **Reuben Kennison**/1737, widow in 1776, 8 children/1757-76 (including a Reuben Kennison Jr & a younger Greenbrier Kennison but dates unknown), often confused in white history with her sisters & aunts

GRANDDAUGHTER

Cornstalk, Aracoma aka Corn Flower-Aracoma Hokolesqua-Aracoma Baker – 29/32nd Chalakatha-Mekoche-Shawano-Chalaka-PowhatanMetis born 1742 OH-**killed** in battle 1780 **Logan Co. WV** - 2nd daughter of **Cornstalk (6)**/1710 & **Helizikinopo**/1715, Bear Clan, taught to cipher, read & speak some English by her father, established village near Logan WV 1760 with family & clan at current site of **Logan WV**, a **Chalakatha village Head Woman** before 1780, about 6' tall,

killed in battle defending the village, wife 1758 OH of **Boling Kikpelethee Baker**/1730-Shawano-Metis, mother of son Running Deer (Baker)/1764, son Laughing Water (Baker)/1766, daughter Snow Lily (Baker)/1768, daughter Raindrop (Baker)/1770, son Running Water (Baker)/1772 & son Blue Feather (Baker)/1774-all 7/16th ChalakathaMekoche-Shawano-Chalaka-Powhatan-Metis, 4 other children that died of disease

GRANDDAUGHTER

Cornstalk, Elizabeth (2) – 29/32nd Chalakatha-Mekoche-ShawanoChalaka-Powhatan-Metis born 1744 OH-died after 1777 likely OH - 5th daughter of **Cornstalk (6)**/1710 & **Helizikinopo**/1715, Bear Clan, about 6' tall i.e. a Grenadier Squaw, a **Christian Chalakatha**, taught to cipher, read & speak some English by her father, may have served as a translator-messenger for the whites, wife 1st 1760 OH of **John Swift**white, 2nd by 1770 OH of **Petella Cornstalk**/1730-adopted white, mother **with Swift** of four children/1760-62-64-66 names unknown but surname may have been Cornstalk, children/1770-77 **with Petella** unknown-all children 7/16th Chalakatha-Mekoche-Shawano-ChalakaPowhatan--Metis, often confused in white histories with her sisters or aunts

GRANDSON

Cornstalk, Young aka Cornstalk (7)-Strong Man Cornstalk (2)-Nenpemeshequa-Neenpeemeesheekwa-Wneypuechsika-Wynaypooeechseeka-Winaypooeachseeka – 29/32nd ChalakathaMekoche-Shawano-Chalaka-Powhatan-Metis born 1746 OH-died 1833
KS - 5th son of **Cornstalk (6)**/1710 & **Helizikinopo Mekoche**/1715, Bear Clan, about 6'6" tall & big built, taught to cipher, read & speak some English by his father & Elizabeth See, Cornstalk War/1755-77, **an emissary for Cornstalk** 1774, a **Chalakatha Chief** in OH 1774, Blue Jacket War/1777-94, Treaty 1814, 1817, a warrior at Wapakoneta 1817, moved to KS about 1828 **with William Perry**, **4th Chief in KS** 1833 under **John Perry**, husband 1st 1766 OH of **Chalakatha Woman**/1750, 2nd 1769 OH of **Elizabeth See**/1754-adopted-white, no record of children/1766-95 **with Chalakatha**, father **with Elizabeth See** of White

Wing Cornstalk/1770 & Son of Young Cornstalk/1772-both 7/16th Chalakatha-Mekoche-Shawano-Chalaka-Powhatan-Metis

GRANDSON

Cornstalk, Ellinipsico aka Helinipsiko-Heleeneepseeko-Native Warrior – 29/32nd Chalakatha-Mekoche-Shawano-Chalaka-Powhatan-Metis born 1748 OH-**murdered** 1777 Point Pleasant WV - youngest son of **Cornstalk (6)**/1710 & **Helizikinopo**/1715, over 6' tall, Bear Clan, taught to cipher, read & speak some English by his father & his white wife, Cornstalk War/1765-77, **an emissary for Cornstalk** 1774, a **Chalakatha Chief** in OH 1777, **murdered by whites** at Point Pleasant WV/Ft. Randolph 1777 with father **Cornstalk**, brother in law/adopted brother **Petella** & uncle **Red Hawk**, husband 1st 1763 OH of **Mary Catherine See**/1749-adopted white, 2nd 1765 OH of **Chalakatha Woman**/1750, 3rd 1772 OH of **Adopted White Woman**/1755, father with **See** of Margaret Peggy See (2)/1764-7/16th Chalakatha-Mekoche-Shawano-ChalakaPowhatan-Metis, children/1765-77 **with Chalakatha** & children/177277 **with White Woman** all unknown

GRANDDAUGHTER

Cornstalk, Mary (1) aka **Blue Sky** - 29/32nd Chalakatha-MekocheShawano-Chalaka-Powhatan-Metis born 1750 OH-died 1775 Ft. Pitt area PA/OH/WV - 4th daughter of **Cornstalk (6)**/1710 & **Helizikinopo**/1715, Bear Clan, about 6' tall i.e. a Grenadier Squaw & attractive, a Christian Chalakatha, taught to cipher, read & speak some English by her father, may have served as a translator-messenger for the whites, met while Adkins was in the Military in PA-abandoned by Adkins when he returned east, Adkins returned for children after her death, wife 1766 PA of **Parker V. Adkins**/1720, mother **with Adkins** of Littleberry Adkins/1766 & Charity Adkins/1768-both 23/32nd Chalakatha-Mekoche-Shawano-Chalaka-Powhatan-Metis, often confused in white history with her sisters & aunts

GRANDDAUGHTER

Cornstalk, Esther – 29/32nd Chalakatha-Mekoche-Shawano-ChalakaPowhatan-Metis born 1752 OH-died before 1836 PA - 6th

daughter of **Cornstalk (6)**/1710 & **Helizikinopo**/1715, Bear Clan, about 6' tall & attractive, a **Christian Chalakatha**, Shawnee name unknown, taught to cipher, read & speak some English by her father, may have served as a translator-messenger for the whites, about 6' tall i.e. a Grenadier
Squaw, wife 1768 OH/PA of **Thomas Sowards**/1746, mother of Griffin Sowards/1773, Thomas Sowards Jr/1775, Robert Sowards/1780, Esther Sowards/1781, Jacob Sowards/1783, John B. Sowards/1784, twins Rosannah & Diannah Sowards/1786, Rebecca Sowards/1790, George Sowards/1792-all 7/16th Chalakatha-Mekoche-Shawano-ChalakaPowhatan-Metis, often confused in white history with her sisters & aunts

GRANDDAUGHTER

Cornstalk, Oceana aka Ceanna-Cianna-Zeanna – 29/32nd ChalakathaMekoche-Shawano-Chalaka-Powhatan-Metis born 1754 OH- died 1770
WV - youngest daughter of **Cornstalk (6)**/1710 & **Helizikinopo**/1715, Bear Clan, about 6' tall & said to be very pretty, died after falling from a cliff on her way to visit her sister **Aracoma**, namesake of Oceana WV, apparently died single

BY CORNSTALK (6)/1710
WITH OUNACONOA MUSKRAT/1716

GRANDSON

Cornstalk, Black Beard (1) aka Wesekahnee-Weeseekahnee-Wissekapoway-Weeseekapoway-Black Beard Hokolesqua-**Black Beard (1)** - 29/32nd Chalakatha-Mekoche-Pekowi-Shawano-ChalakaPowhatan-Metis born 1730 PA/AL-died after 1808 MO - oldest son of **Cornstalk (6)** /1710 & **Ounaconoa Muskrat**/1716, Bear Clan, about 6' tall & burly, known for rare black beard like brother **Black Wolf**, taught to cipher, read & speak some English by his father, Cornstalk War/1755-77, a **Chalakatha Chief** in OH by 1768, Council March 1768, **an emissary for Cornstalk** 1774, Blue Jacket War/1777-94,

2nd **Chalakatha Chief** to **Black Hoof** 1779, Treaty Greenville 1795, Council
1795 Swan Creek OH with **Capt. Johnny, Bukangolas & George Ironside**, moved to MO 1796, Council 1797 with **Capt. Johnny, Borer, Buffalo & Capt. Mayne**-ENG, visited relatives in south 1808, husband 1755 Running Water TN of **Katee Killaqua**/1737, father of Daughter of Black Beard/1755, Young Black Beard Cornstalk/1760 & other children/1756-77 names unknown-all 15/32nd Chalakatha-MekocheShawano-Chalaka-Powhatan-Cherokee-Metis

GRANDSON

Cornstalk, Black Wolf (1) aka Benewiska-Beeneeweeska-**Black Wolf (2)** - 29/32nd Chalakatha-Mekoche-Pekowi-Shawano-Chalaka-PowhatanMetis born 1740 OH-died 1830 OH - 2nd son of **Cornstalk (6)**/1710 & **Ounaconoa Muskrat**/1716, Bear Clan, taught to cipher, read & speak some English by his father, Cornstalk War/1758-77, a **Chalakatha Chief** in OH by 1763, Grand Council 1763, Council 1765 Logstown, Council 1768 Stanwix, **an emissary for Cornstalk** 1774, Blue Jacket
War/1777-94, a **Chalakatha Chief** at Wapakoneta 1817, Treaty 1814, 1815, 1817, 1818, about 6' tall & burly, known for rare black beard like brother **Black Beard**, husband 1st 1758 Running Water TN of **Nikkee Killaqua**/1738, 2nd 1769 OH of **Pottawamee Woman**/1754, (possibly father of a child 1787 with **Jenny Sellards Wiley**/1760-adopted white), 3rd 1800 OH of **Daughter of William Jackson-Fish** aka **Miss Fish**/1781white, other wives possible, father **with Killaqua** of Young Black Wolf (1)/1760 & other children/61-85-all 15/32nd Chalakatha-MekocheShawano-Chalaka-Powhatan-Cherokee-Metis, **with Pottawamee** of Soldier Black Wolf/1770, Young Black Wolf (2)/1786 & other children/1771-1800-all 7/16th Chalakatha-Mekoche-Shawano-ChalakaPowhatan-Pottawamee-Metis, (name & gender of child **with Wiley** unknown but possibly a daughter born after Jenny's return to the whites), children **with Miss Fish** unknown

GRANDSON

Cornstalk, John (1) aka **Lawathtucheh**-Lawathtoochee-**John Wolf** – 29/32nd Chalakatha-Mekoche-Pekowi-Shawano-Chalaka-

PowhatanMetis born 1750 OH-died 1834 OH - 3rd son of **Cornstalk (6)**/1710 & **Ounaconoa Muskrat**/1716, Bear Clan, taught to cipher, read & speak some English by his father, Cornstalk War/1768-77, **an emissary for Cornstalk** 1774, Blue Jacket War/1777-94, a **Chalakatha Chief** in OH by 1787, apparently no part in War of 1812, Treaty 1817, husband 1780 OH of **Chalakatha Woman**/1765, father of daughter- Black Poddee Wolf/1775, sons Peter Temestehee Wolf/1770, Henry Nolesimo Clay/1780, Young John Wolf Cornstalk/1792 & Peter Wolf Cornstalk (3)/94-all 31/32nd Chalakatha-Mekoche-Pekowi-Shawano-Chalaka-Powhatan-Metis

GRANDSON

Cornstalk, Peter (1) aka Comes Flying-Peytehthator-**Pehathawtaw** – 29/32nd Chalakatha-Mekoche-Pekowi-Shawano-Chalaka-PowhatanMetis born 1755 AL/OH-**murdered** 1832 OH - youngest son of
Cornstalk (6)/1710 & **Ounaconoa Muskrat**/1716, Bear Clan, taught to cipher, read & speak some English by his father, about 6'6" tall, **an emissary for Cornstalk** 1774, Blue Jacket War/1777-94, no active part in War of 1812, a Chalakatha warrior at Wapaghonettat 1817, Treaty 1817, 1831, **murdered** by **Doc Bill**/1795-Chalakatha, **Capt. Bill**/1790 & **Sam Loon**/1800-both Mekoche, husband 1st 1775 OH of **Chalakatha Woman**/1760, 2nd by 1784 OH of **Mary Frances Avery**/1765-white, children/1775-83 **with Chalakatha** unknown, father **with Avery** of Peter Cornstalk (2)/1785, Mary Cornstalk/1796 & other children/87-1805-all 7/16th Chalakatha-Mekoche-Pekowi-Shawano-ChalakaPowhatan-Metis

GRANDDAUGHTER

Cornstalk, Susanna – 29/32nd Chalakatha-Mekoche-Pekowi-ShawanoChalaka-Powhatan-Metis born 1757 OH-died after 1820 Lynchburg VA
– daughter of **Cornstalk (6)**/1710 & **Ounacona Muskrat**/1716, Bear Clan, taught to cipher, read & speak some English by her father, wife 1774 Chota TN of **Thomas Jacob Maw**/1755, mother of John Maw/1799-23/64th Chalakatha-Mekoche-Pekowi-Shawano-Chalaka-

Powhatan-Cherokee-Metis

BY CORNSTALK/1710
WITH JULIA MULATTO/1720

GRANDSON

Cornstalk, Sun Fish aka Ionoca-Hionoca Cornstalk – 27/64th Chalakatha-Mekoche-Shawano-Chalaka-Powhatan-Black-Metis born 1742 PA-**killed** 1774 Point Pleasant WV - oldest son of **Cornstalk (6)/1710** & **Julia Mulatto**/1720, Bear Clan, over 6' tall, a Chalakatha warrior, taught to cipher, read & speak some English by his father & mother, Cornstalk War/1758-74, **an emissary to the Delaware for Cornstalk** 1774, husband 1760 OH of **Delaware Woman**/1745, father of six or seven children/1760-74-all 7/32nd Chalakatha-Mekoche-PekowiShawano-Chalaka-Powhatan-Delaware-Black-Metis names unknown

GRANDSON

Cornstalk, Elijah – 27/64th Chalakatha-Mekoche-Shawano-Chalaka-Powhatan-Black-Metis born 1744 OH-**killed** 1760 OH - 2nd son of **Cornstalk**/1710 & **Julia Mulatto**/1720, Bear Clan, a very young Chalakatha warrior, over 6' tall, **shot by whites** near Marietta OH while with his uncle **Silverheels**, died unmarried

GRANDSON

Ailstock, Abraham aka **Abraham Cornstalk**-Abraham Hokolesqua – 27/64th Chalakatha-Mekoche-Shawano-Chalaka-Powhatan-Black-Metis born 1750 OH-died after 1790 (VA-MD) - 4th son of **Cornstalk**/1710 & **Julia Mulatto**/1720, Bear Clan, a Chalakatha warrior, any Shawnee name unknown but may have only been Abraham, taught to cipher, read & speak some English by his father & mother, Cornstalk War/1766-74, Julia convinced Cornstalk to let their 3 younger sons return to the east after the death of the 2 older sons, abandoned his Chalakatha Wife & children when he returned to the whites, took surname from the family that allowed the 3 brothers to settle near them when they returned to the whites in 1775-(some family connection?), husband 1st 1770 OH of **Chalakatha Woman**/1755, 2nd by 1779 VA of **Elizabeth Going**/1760-(sister of Sally & Rebecca), 3rd 1784 VA of **Isabel Radcliff**/1765, father **with Chalakatha** of three children/1770-72-74, **with Going** of Rebecca Ailstock/1780 & Virginia Ailstock/1782-both 29/64th Chalakatha-Mekoche-Shawano-Chalaka-Powhatan-Black-Metis, any children **with Radcliff** unknown

GRANDSON

Ailstock, Absalom (1) aka **Absalom Cornstalk**-Absalom Hokolesqua – 27/64th Chalakatha-Mekoche-Shawano-Chalaka-Powhatan-Black-Metis born 1748 OH-died after 1814 (VA-MD) - 3rd son of **Cornstalk**/1710 & **Julia Mulatto**/1720, Bear Clan, any Shawnee name unknown but may have only been Absalom, taught to cipher, read & speak some English by his father & mother, a Chalakatha warrior, Cornstalk War/1768-74, Julia convinced Cornstalk to let their 3 younger sons return to the east after the death of the 2 older sons, took surname of family that allowed the 3 brothers to settle near them when they returned to whites 1775(some family connection?), abandoned Shawnee Wife & children 1775 when he returned to whites, Augusta Co-VA Militia-**with U.S. Army**Revolution, husband 1768 OH of **Chalakatha Woman**/1753, 2nd 1778
VA of **Sally Going**/1763 (sister of Rebecca & Elizabeth), father **with Chalakatha** of four children/68-70-72-74, **with Going** of John Ailstock/1779, Katy Ailstock/1782, Polly Ailstock/1786, Lawrence Ailstock/1788, Elizabeth Ailstock/1790, Andrew Ailstock/1792, David Ailstock/1794, James Ailstock/1796, Absalom Ailstock Jr/1798, William Ailstock/1800 & Thomas Ailstock/1802-all 13/64th ChalakathaMekoche-Shawano-Chalaiwa-Powhatan-Black-Metis

GRANDSON

Ailstock, Michael aka Michael Cornstalk – 27/64th ChalakathaMekoche-Shawano-Chalaka-Powhatan-Black-Metis born 1752 OH-died about 1791 VA - 5th son of **Cornstalk**/1710 & **Julia Mulatto**/1720, Bear Clan, Cornstalk War/1770-74, Shawnee name unknown/but may have just been Michael, taught to cipher, read & speak some English by his father & mother, Julia convinced Cornstalk to let their 3 younger sons return to the east after the death of the 2 older sons, took surname of family that allowed the 3 brothers to settle near them when they returned to whites 1775-(some family connection?), abandoned Chalakatha Wife & children 1775 when he returned to whites, husband 1st 1772 OH of **Chalakatha Woman**/1756, 2nd 1776 VA of **Rebecca Going**/1760- (sister of Sally & Elizabeth), father **with Chalakatha** of two children/1772 & 74, **with Going** of Mary Ailstock/1776, Joseph Ailstock/1778, Susanna Ailstock/1780, Michael Ailstock Jr/1782, Absalom Ailstock/1784 & Elizabeth Ailstock/1786-all 13/64th Chalakatha-Mekoche-Shawano-Chalaka-Powhatan-Black-Metis

BY CORNSTALK (6)/1710
WITH CATHERINE VANDERPOOLE SEE/1725

GRANDDAUGHTER

Cornstalk, Mary (2) aka **Mary See** – 27/64th Chalakatha-MekocheShawano-Chalaka-Powhatan-Metis born 1764 OH-died 1824 Warren
Co. OH - only child of **Cornstalk**/1710 & **Catherine Vanderpoole Sharpe See**/1725-adopted-white, returned to whites with mother-1765, Bear Clan, wife 1783 WV-OH of **Leonard Petro**/1750, mother of Margaret Petro/1788, Michael See Petro/1790 & John Petro/1792-all 7/32nd Chalakatha-Mekoche-Shawano-Chalaka-Powhatan-Metis

BY SAWELAHA-ELIZA/1712
WITH CHALAKATHA MAN/1710

GRANDSON

Cornstalk, Silverheels (2) aka **Aroas (1)**-Haroas-Silverheels Okowellos (2) – 59/64th Chalakatha-Mekoche-Shawano-Chalaka-Powhatan-Metis–(adopted Seneca) born 1732 OH/PA-**killed** 1770 IN/IL - son of **Sawelaha-Eliza Cornstalk**/1712 & **Chalakatha Man**/1710, clan of father unknown but not Bear, adopted son after 1745 of **Old Belt**/1700Seneca, taught to cipher, read & write English by his mother, scout-spy **for Colonial Army**-French-Indian War/1754-63-Ft.

Necessity/1754Braddock/1755 & Pontiac War/1762-66, translator-guide for **George Morgan**-white after Pontiac War, **killed about 1770 below Louisville KY**, husband 1752 OH of **Mekoche Woman**/1735, father of Daughter/1752, Young Aroas-Silverheels/1760-both 31/32nd Chalakatha-Mekoche-Shawano-Chalaka-Powhatan-Metis-(adopted Seneca)

GRANDSON

Cornstalk, Counasona aka Counasona Okowellos-Counasona Belt-Koonasona – 59/64th Chalakatha-Mekoche-Shawano-ChalakaPowhatan-Metis-(adopted Seneca-then Mohawk) born 1735 PA-died after 1778 (PA?) - son of **Sawelaha-Eliza**/1712 & **Chalakatha Man**/1710, clan of father unknown, taught to cipher, read & write English by his mother, adopted son (after 1745) of **Old Belt**/1700Seneca, Mohawk by marriage, scout-spy **with Colonial Army**-French-Indian War/1754-63-Braddock/1755-Pontiac War/1762-66-Dunmore War/1774-Point Pleasant/1774, Council Detroit 1778, nephew of **Cornstalk**/1710, husband about 1755 PA of **Mohawk Woman**/1740, children unknown

BY SEWELAHA-ELIZA/1712
WITH JAMES FRANCIS/1700

GRANDSON

Francis, David **Mumagechee** – 27/64th Chalakatha-Mekoche-ShawanoChalaka-Powhatan-Metis–(adopted-Creek) born 1740 PA/OH-died after 1805 AL - son of **Sawelaha-Eliza Cornstalk**/1712 & **James Francis**/1700-white British Officer, Bear Clan, taught to cipher, read & write English by his mother, nephew of **Cornstalk**/1710, adopted son of his uncle **Red Shoes Marchand**/1720-Creek-Metis, Treaty 1790, 1805, uncle (by marriage) of **Tecumseh**, husband 1759 of **Mary Rising Sun**/1744, father with **Mary** of John Francis/1760, Josiah Francis/1765, Joseph Francis/1770, Susan Francis/1775-all 29/64th ChalakathaKishpoko-Mekoche-Shawano-Chalaka-Powhatan-Creek-Metis

GRANDSON

Francis, John (1) – 27/64th Chalakatha-Mekoche-Shawano-ChalakaPowhatan-Metis born 1745 PA/OH-died after 1785 - son of **SawelahaEliza**/1712 & **James Francis**/1700-white British Officer, Bear Clan, nephew of **Cornstalk**/1710, taught to cipher, read & write English by his mother, husband 1765 of half-niece (granddaughter of his halfbrother) **Daughter of Silver Heels-Aroas**/1750, father of John Francis (3)/1780-45/64th Chalakatha-Mekoche-Shawano-Chalaka-PowhatanMetis–(adopted-Seneca)

BY CAWACHILE/1716
WITH COLD WATER-WEPENIPE/1710

GRANDSON

Cold Water, Son of - 59/64th Mekoche-Chalakatha-Shawano-ChalakaPowhatan-Metis born about 1732 PA-died of smallpox 1752 OH - son of **Cold Water-Wepenipe**/1710 & **Cawechile**/1716, a trusted ally of the French in the Ohio valley, wife & children unknown

GRANDSON

Cold Water, Young aka Cold Water (2)-Young Wepenipe – 59/64th Mekoche-Chalakatha-Shawano-Chalaka-Powhatan-Metis born 1740 OH-died after 1778 – son of **Cold Water-Wepenipe**/1710 & **Cawechile**/1716, taught to cipher, read & speak English by his mother, Cornstalk War/1758-74, husband 1760 OH of **Chalakatha Woman**/1745, father of Cold Water (3)/1760 & John Cold Water/1770 both 61/64th Mekoche-Chalakatha-Shawano-Chalaka-Powhatan-Metis

GRANDAUGHTER

Cold Water, Lacumtequa – 59/64th Mekoche-Chalakatha-Shawano-Chalaka-Powhatan-Metis born about 1744 OH-died after 1786 – daughter of **Cold Water-Wepenipe**/1710 & **Cawachile**/1716 – wife about 1760 OH of her uncle/2nd cousin (1st cousin of her mother-son of her grandmother's brother) **Moluntha/**1710, living in Moluntha village OH 1786, children unknown

BY NONHELEMA/1718
WITH WAHOOTASIKA-SAVANNAH KING/1710

GRANDAUGHTER

Wahootasika, Elder Daughter of - 59/64th Chalakatha-MekocheShawano-Chalaka-Powhatan-Metis born 1735 PA?-died about 1780 OH - daughter of **Nonhelema/**1718 & **Wahootasika-Savannah King/**1710, taught to cipher, read & speak English by her mother & husband, wife 1750 OH of **Chotschawanne Logan/**1725-adopted-white, several children/1760-80-all 29/64th Mekoche-Chalakatha-Shawano-Chalaka-Powhatan-Metis, may have had surname Logan

GRANDDAUGHTER

Wahootasika, Mellana – 59/64th Chalakatha-Mekoche-ShawanoChalaka-Powhatan-Metis born 1748 OH-**murdered** 1774 WV - daughter of **Nonhelema/**1718 & **Wahootasika-Savannah King/**1710, taught to cipher, read & speak English by her mother, wife 1765 OH of **Chief Logan Jr/**1745, **murdered** 1774 by Greathouse gang, children unknown

GRANDDAUGHTER

Wahootasika, Waheeta – 59/64th Chalakatha-Mekoche-ShawanoChalaka-Powhatan-Metis born about 1750 (OH?)-died after 1799 MO – twin daughter of **Nonhelema/**1718 & **Wahootasika-Savannah King/**1710, twin of Wynema Wahoot/50, taught to cipher, read & speak English by her mother, wife about 1775 OH of **Wahceetah/**1735, adopted mother 1775 of **Joab (Jacob) Barton/**1767, moved to Skaggs Creek KY 1797, moved to MO 1799 after persecution by whites, mother of Itahaha Wahcheeta/1780-29/64th Chalakatha-Mekoche-ShawanoChalaka-Powhatan-Metis

GRANDDAUGHTER

Wahootasika, Wynema aka Wynima-Wyneema-Pouter-She Pouts – 59/64th Chalakatha-Mekoche-Shawano-Chalaka-Powhatan-Metis born 1750 (OH?)-died after 1770 – twin daughter of **Wahootasika-Savannah King**/1710 & **Nonhelema**/1718, twin of Waheeta, very light complexioned & so thought to be mostly white, forced to return to whites by Bouquet Treaty 1764, returned quickly to Tribe 1765, taught to cipher, read & speak English by her mother, wife 1766 OH of **Chalakatha Man**/1746, children unknown

BY NONHELEMA/1718 WITH MOLUNTHA/1710

GRANDSON

Moluntha, Chieska - **Capt. Chieska**-Young King-Young Moluntha-**Capt. Tom**-Capt. Tommy-Cheachisika-Jakeshaw-Chakalakek-Cheacksca-Chiachisika-Capt. Shigsta – 59/64th Mekoche-ChalakathaShawano-Chalaka-Powhatan-Metis born 1755 OH-died of cholera 1833 KS - son of **Moluntha**/1710 & **Nonhelema**/1718, a Mekoche, over 6' tall, grandson of **Okowellos**, nephew of **Cornstalk**, Blue Jacket War/1777-94, scout-Capt. John Logan Co-Anthony Shane Co-William Wells Co-**with U.S. Army**-War of 1812, a **Chalakatha Chief** at
Wapaghonettat 1817, Treaty 1804, 1817, 1818, 1831, cousin of **Capt. John Logan-Big Horn**/1774, **Otter**/1770 & **Bright Horn**/1770, husband 1st 1779 OH of 1st cousin (daughter of mother's sister) **Polly Butler**/1765, 2nd 1780 OH of **Chalakatha Woman**/1765, father **with Butler** of Spy Buck Moluntha/1780-35/64th Mekoche-Chalakatha-Shawano-ChalakaPowhatan-Creek-Metis, children **with Chalakatha** unknown

GRANDDAUGHTER

Moluntha, Younger Daughter of – 59/64th Mekoche-ChalakathaShawano-Chalaka-Powhatan-Metis born 1757 OH-died about 1790 OH - daughter of **Nonhelema**/1718 & **Moluntha**/1710, a Mekoche, granddaughter of **Okowellos** & **Katee Mekoche**-(who was the aunt of Moluntha), niece of **Cornstalk**, wife 1st 1775 of **Mekoche**

Warrior/1755widow by 1785, 2nd 1785 of **William Wells**/1770-white-(adoptedMiami), children/1775-85 **with Mekoche** unknown, mother **with Wells** of William Wayne Wells/1786 & Mary Wells/1788-both 29/64th Mekoche-Chalakatha-Shawano-Chalaka-Powhatan-Metis - (adopted Miami)

GRANDSON

Moluntha, Capt. Johnny aka **Capt. Johnny (3)-Capt. John-Big John** – 59/64th Mekoche-Chalakatha-Shawano-Chalaka-Powhatan-Metis born 1759 OH-died after 1815 OH - son of **Nonhelema**/1718 & **Moluntha**/1710, grandson of **Okowellos**, nephew of **Cornstalk**, a Chalakatha warrior, attended Council 1785 with **Alexander McKee** & **Matthew Elliott**, Blue Jacket War/1777-94, scout-Capt. John Logan Co**with U.S. Army-**War of 1812, **killed Winnemak**-Pottawamee, nearly 7' tall, cousin of **Capt. John Logan-Big Horn**/1774, **Otter**/1770 & **Bright Horn**/1770, husband about 1785 OH of **Rachel Kizer**/1761-1/2 Chalakatha-Metis, father of two known children/1786-90

BY NONHELEMA/1718
WITH RICHARD BUTLER/1742

GRANDSON

Butler, Capt. aka **Tamenatha**-Little Corn-Little Cornstalk - 27/64th Chalakatha-Mekoche-Shawano-Chalaka-Powhatan-Metis born about 1763 OH-died about 1834 KS - son of **Nonhelema**/1718 & & **Richard Butler**/1742-white-(adopted-Seneca), Bear Clan, a Chalakatha warrior, nephew of **Cornstalk**, grandson of **Okowellos**, Blue Jacket War/178294, **refused Tecumseh**, scout-**with U.S. Army-**Prophet's Town/1811War 1812-Thames/1813, Treaty 1814, 1815, moved to KS about 1832, wife & children unknown

BY SIILVERHEELS (1)-HALOWAS/1724
WITH CHALAKATHA WOMAN/1730

GRANDSON

Cornstalk, Silverheels (4) aka **Young Halowas** – 59/64th ChalakathaMekoche-Shawano-Chalaka-Powhatan-Metis born 1760 OH-died after
1832 KS - son of **Halowas-Silver Heels (1)**/1724 & **Chalakatha Woman**/1730, grandson of **Okowellos**, a Chalakatha warrior, Bear Clan, Blue Jacket War /1777-94, scout-**with U.S. Army-**War 1812Thames/1813, an warrior at Lewistown OH 1817, Treaty 1817, moved to KS by 1832, nephew of **Cornstalk**, husband 1780 OH of **Chalakatha Woman**/1765, father of Moses Silverheels/1782, Halowas (3)Silverheels (5)/1782-both 61/64th Chalakatha-Mekoche-ShawanoChalaka-Powhatan-Metis

GRANDDAUGHTER

Cornstalk, Daughter of Halowas-Silverheels (1) – 59/64th ChalakathaMekoche-Shawano-Chalaka-Powhatan-Metis born 1770 OH-died after 1807 - daughter of **Silver Heels (1)Halowas**/1724 & **Chalakatha Woman**/1730, a Bear Clan Chalakatha, wife 1790 of 2nd cousin **John Cold Water**/1770, mother of Pamotee Cold Water/1800 & Stephen Cold Water/1807-both 61/64th ChalakathaMekoche-Shawano-Chalaka-Powhatan-Metis

GRANDDAUGHTER

Cornstalk, Sarah aka **Sarah Silverheels** - 59/64th Chalakatha-MekocheShawano-Chalaka-Powhatan-Metis born 1775 OH-died 1834 – youngest daughter of **Halowas-Silverheels (1)**/1724 & **Chalakatha Woman**/1730, a Bear Clan Chalakatha, granddaughter of **Okowellos**, niece of **Cornstalk**, wife 1790 OH of **John Featherstone**/1770, children unknown

BY ELIZABETH CORNSTALK/1726
WITH JOHN BUTLER/1720

GRANDDAUGHTER

Butler, Fanny – 11/64th Chalakatha-Shawano-Chalaka-Powhatan-Creek-Metis born about 1755-died after 1781 - daughter of **Elizabeth Cornstalk**/1726 & **John Butler (1)-Sugantah-Lodging Pole**/1730white-

(adopted-Seneca), Bear-Wind Clan, about 6' tall & called very attractive, adopted daughter of her aunt **Nonhelema**/1718, sadly listed as prostitute 1781, niece of **Cornstalk**, granddaughter of **Okowellos**, any husband & children unknown

GRANDSON

Butler, Tommy – 11/64th Chalakatha-Shawano-Chalaka-Powhatan-Creek-Metis born 1760 OH-died 1833 KS - son of **Elizabeth Cornstalk**/1726 & **John Butler-Lodging Pole**/1730-white-(adoptedSeneca), nephew of **Cornstalk**, grandson of Okowellos, Bear-Wind Clan, Blue Jacket War/1777-94, moved to KS 1832, husband about 1780 of **Daughter of Col. Alexander McKee**/1765-1/2 Pekowi-Metis, children unknown

BY CATHERINE CORNSTALK/1728 WITH WILLIAM BUTLER/1744

GRANDDAUGHTER

Butler, Polly – 11/64th Chalakatha-Shawano-Chalaka-Powhatan-CreekMetis born about 1765 OH-died about 1854 KS - daughter of **Catherine Cornstalk**/1728 & **William Butler (1)**/1744-white-(adopted-Seneca), about 6' tall, known for her blue eyes & beauty, niece of **Cornstalk**, granddaughter of **Okowellos**, Bear-Wind Clan, accused 1805 with her Daughter/1783 of being witches by followers of **Lalawethika-the
Prophet**, saved by Quaker Missionary, wife 1st 1779 OH of 1st cousin (son of mother's sister) **Chieska Moluntha**/1755, 2nd 1782 OH of **Joshua Renicks**/1746-adopted-white, mother **with Chieska** of Spy Buck Moluntha/1780-35/64th Chalakatha-Shawano-Chalaka-PowhatanCreek-Metis, **with Renicks** of Daughter of Renicks/1783-5/64th Chalakatha-Shawano-Chalaka-Powhatan-Creek-Metis

CHAPTER FIVE

Savannah Tom Carpenter/1680

Savannah Tom Carpenter/1680

Carpenter, Savannah Tom (1) aka Thomas Carpenter (4)-Corn Planter (4)-**Moytoy (3)** – 23/32nd Chalakatha-Shawano-Chalaka-PowhatanMetis born 1680 Chota TN-died 1710 Oconee SC - son of **Nancy Turkey Cornstalk/1664** & **Trader Tom Carpenter (2)-Moytoy (2)/1660**, from Chota & Running Water TN, associated with adopted brother (1st cousin) **Standing Turkey-Old Hop** & **Young Rainmaker**, taught to cipher, read & speak English by his father, husband 1st 1697 Upper Hiwassee VA of **Susan-Quatsey (2) Rainmaker/1682**-Cherokee, 2nd 1698 of her sister **Nancy Rainmaker/1683**-Cherokee, father **with Susan-Quatsey** of Savannah Tom Carpenter (2)-Corn Planter (5)/1698, **with Nancy** of Great Eagle Carpenter/1702, Elizabeth Tassel Carpenter/1704, Attakullakulla Carpenter/1706, Corn Tassel Carpenter/1708 & Susan Moytoy Carpenter/1710-all 23/64th Chalakatha-Shawano-Chalaka-Powhatan-Cherokee-Metis

SIBLINGS OF SAVANNAH TOM CARPENTER/1680

BROTHER

Carpenter, White Owl (1) aka White Owl Raven- White Owl (1)**Caulanna**-Collanah-**Moytoy (4)** – 23/32nd Chalakatha-ShawanoChalaka-Powhatan-Metis born 1678 Running Water TN-**killed 1741TN** in battle – son of **Trader Tom Carpenter (2)-Moytoy (2)/1660** & **Nancy Turkey Cornstalk/1664**, Long Hair Clan Cherokee, could cipher, read & speak some English, delegation to ENG 1730, leader of the 7 Cherokee Clans, killed in same battle as **Young Rainmaker**, husband 1st about 1698 (TN?) of **Unknown Woman**, 2nd 1711 TN of **Nancy Rainmaker**/1683-Cherokee, children/1698-1711 **with Unknown Woman** not known, father **with Nancy Rainmaker** of Killancea-Buck Carpenter/1712, Killaqua Carpenter/1714, Betsy-Eliza-Quatie Ooloocha Carpenter/1716, Tame Doe-Cati-Catherine Carpenter/1718, All Bones-Flying Squirrel Carpenter/1720, Oousta Carpenter/1722 & Bushy Head Carpenter/1724-all 11/32nd Chalakatha-ShawanoChalaka-Powhatan-Cherokee-Metis, **adopted father** 1710 with marriage to his brother's widow of Great Eagle Carpenter/1702, Elizabeth Tassel Carpenter/1704, Attakullakulla Carpenter/1706, (Old) Corn Tassel Carpenter/1708 & Susan Moytoy Carpenter/1710, adopted father 1715 of **Amoyah Pigeon Moytoy**/1715 (son of his sister **Pashmere Carpenter (2)**/1681)

SISTER

Carpenter, Pashmere (2) – 23/32nd Chalakatha-Shawano-ChalakaPowhatan-Metis born 1681 Chota TN-died 1715 Upper Hiwassee VA – daughter of **Trader Tom Carpenter (2)-Moytoy (2)**/1660 & **Nancy Turkey Cornstalk**/1664, could cipher, read & write some English, wife 1705 Upper Hiwassee VA of her adopted brother **Raven of Hiwassee Hop-Raven Moytoy**/1683, mother of Amoyah Pigeon Moytoy/1715-27/64th Chalakatha-Shawano-Chalaka-Powhatan-Metis

ADOPTED SIBLINGS OF SAVANNAH TOM CARPENTER/1680

ADOPTED BROTHER 1694

Turkey, Raven aka **Raven Moytoy**-Raven of Hiwassee-CollanahCorani-Corane-Raven Hop-Raven Cornstalk – 63/64th ChalakathaShawano-Chalaka-Powhatan born 1680 Upper Hiwassee VA-died 1756 Chewohe TN – son of **Big Turkey Cornstalk**/1660 & **Chalakatha Woman**/1664, parents killed 1694 VA by Catawba raiders, adopted son

1694 TN of **Trader Tom Carpenter (2)-Moytoy (2)**/1660 & his aunt **Nancy Turkey Cornstalk**/1664, took the surname Moytoy from his adopted father **Trader Tom aka Moytoy (2)**, could cipher, read & write some English, Treaty 1684 with SC, delegation to ENG 1730, husband 1st 1700 Upper Hiwassee TN of his adopted sister **Pashmere Carpenter (2)**/1681, 2nd 1718 of **Ahneewakee Muskrat**/1704, 3rd 1729 TN of **Cherokee Woman**/1714, father **with Pashmere** of Amoyah Pigeon Moytoy (1)/1715-27/64th Chalakatha-Shawano-Chalaka-PowhatanMetis, **with Ahneewakee** of Bushyhead Chiesatebe Moytoy/1718,
Savanooka Moytoy/1720, Goohsohly Moytoy/1722, Elizabeth-Raven's Sister Moytoy/1724, Nancy Augustus Moytoy/1726 & Amahetai Muskrat (3)-Moytoy (7)/1728-all 63/64th Chalakatha-Pekowi-ShawanoChalaka-Powhatan, children **with Cherokee** unknown

ADOPTED SISTER 1694

Turkey, Quatsis aka Quatsis Hop-Quatsis Aniwadi-Quatsis Cornstalk – 63/64th Chalakatha-Shawano-Chalaka-Powhatan born 1682 Great Tellico TN-died 1758 Tellico Plains TN – daughter of **Big Turkey Cornstalk**/1660 & **Chalakatha Woman**/1664, parents killed 1694 VA by Catawba raiders, adopted daughter 1694 TN of **Trader Tom Carpenter (2)-Moytoy (2)**/1660 & her aunt **Nancy Turkey**/1664, could cipher, read & speak some English, known as aunt of **Savanooka**/1720 & **Goohsohly**/1722-(sons of **Ahneewakee Muskrat**/1704 & her brother **Raven Moytoy**/1683), Red Paint Clan Cherokee, her sister **Oolootah** lived with her from 1699-1705, wife 1st 1697 Great Tellico TN of **John Beamer**/1676-ENG, 2nd 1705 Settico TN of **Tsula Fox-Smallpox Conjurer**/1670-Cherokee (husband 1741 of her sister **Aganunitsi**), 3rd 1709 Chota TN of **William Webber**/1680-ENG, mother **with Beamer** of Ooloosta Beamer/1698, John Beamer Jr/1700, Peggy Beamer/1702 & Nionee Beamer/1704-all 31.64th Chalakatha-Shawano-ChalakaPowhatan-Metis, **with Fox-Conjurer** of Rising Fawn (1)-Rising Fawn
Fox/1706 & Quatsis Fox/1708-both 31/64th Chalakatha-ShawanoChalaka-Powhatan-Cherokee, **with Webber** of Catherine Webber/1710
& William Webber (2)/1712-both 31/64th Chalakatha-Shawano-

Chalaka-Powhatan-Metis

ADOPTED SISTER 1694

Turkey, Swan aka Wapehti-Swan Hop – 63/64th Chalakatha-ShawanoChalaka-Powhatan born 1686 Upper Hiwassee TN-died 1754 Chota TN – daughter of **Big Turkey Cornstalk**/1660 & **Chalakatha Woman**/1664, parents killed 1694 VA by Catawba raiders, adopted daughter 1694 TN of **Trader Tom Carpenter (2)-Moytoy (2)**/1660 & her aunt **Nancy Turkey Cornstalk**/1664, could cipher, read & speak some English, wife 1703 Running Water TN of her adopted brother **Oshasqua-Muskrat (2)**/1686, mother of daughters Ahneewakee Muskrat/1704, children/1706-14, Ounacona Muskrat/1716, Tame Deer Muskrat/1720 & son Bad Water Muskrat-Moytoy (6)/1722-all 63/64th ChalakathaPekowi-Shawano-Chalaka-Powhatan, adopted mother 1708 TN-VA of
John Fork Tail Watts/1704-nephew of Oshasqua-Muskrat/1686-55/64th Chalakatha-Pekowi-Shawano-Chalaka-Powhatan-Metis

ADOPTED BROTHER 1694

Turkey, Standing (1) aka **Old Hop**-Kanagatoga-Standing Turkey Cornstalk-Uka-Fire King-Kanetekoka-Conarcorturer-Connecorte - 63/64th Chalakatha-Shawano-Chalaka-Powhatan born 1688 Chota TN (some records indicate Upper Hiwassee VA-where older siblings were born or further north-Ohio valley or further west in TN)-died 1761 Chota TN – son of **Big Turkey Cornstalk**/1660 & **Chalakatha Woman**/1664, parents killed 1694 VA by Catawba raiders, adopted son 1694 TN of **Trader Tom Carpenter (2)-Moytoy (2)**/1660 & his aunt **Nancy Turkey Cornstalk**/1664, commonly known as **Old Hop** from a limp due to an old injury, could cipher, read & speak some English, Wolf Clan Cherokee, removed British appointed (**Carpenter-Moytoy & Rainmaker**) leaders & united 4 (of 7) Cherokee clans at Chota 1751, leader of pro- French faction in French-Indian War/1754-61, sent warriors to support the Shawnee at Braddock/1755, **Principal Chief** of the Cherokee **1751-61**, passed actual power/authority to his nephews **Oconastota Rainmaker**/1702 & **Kitegista Rainmaker**/1710 upon his death in 1761 even though his son **Young Standing Turkey-Little**

Turkey/1709 succeeded him as titular Chief, husband by 1708 Chota TN of **Sugi Rainmaker**/1690-Wolf Clan Cherokee, known father of sons Young Standing Turkey-Little Turkey/1709, Young Turkey/1715 & daughter Grasshopper Turkey/1725-all 31/64th ChalakathaShawano-Chalaka-Powhatan -Cherokee, adopted father 1723 TN of his nephews **John French**/1710 & **Capt. French**/1712-both 31/64th Chalakatha-Shawano-Chalaka-Powhatan-Black-Metis-(sons of his sister Ghigoneli/1694)

ADOPTED SISTER 1694

Turkey, April-**Tkikami** aka Tkikami Hop-April Hop-Middle Sister of Old Hop-Middle Sister of Standing Turkey-Wife of Tsula Fox-Wife of Smallpox Conjurer-Wife of Richard Barnes - 63/64th ChalakathaShawano-Chalaka-Powhatan born 1690 Chota TN-died 1744 Upper
Hiwassee TN – daughter of **Big Turkey Cornstalk**/1660 & **Chalakatha Woman**/1664, parents killed 1694 VA by Catawba raiders, adopted daughter 1694 TN of **Trader Tom Carpenter (2)-Moytoy (2)**/1660 & her aunt **Nancy Turkey Cornstalk**/1664, could cipher, read & speak some English, wife 1st 1704 Chota TN of **Tsula Fox-Smallpox Conjurer**/1670, 2nd 1718 Chota TN of **Richard Barnes**/1695-white, children/1705-17 **with Fox-Conjurer** unknown, mother **with Barnes** of Mary Barnes/1720 & Charity Barnes/1726-both 31/64th ChalakathaShawano-Chalaka-Powhatan -Metis

ADOPTED BROTHER 1698

Muskrat (2) aka Oshasqua (2)-**Moytoy (5)**-Ossaghqua-OshkesquaHotthashkwa - 63/64th Pekowi-Chalakatha-Shawano-ChalakaPowhatan born 1686 Hiwassee TN-died 1754 Hiwassee TN – son of
Muskrat-Oshasqua (1)/1660 & **Sister Turkey-Daughter of Hokolesqua**/1666, parents killed 1698 VA-TN by Catawba, from the Straight Tail band, Turtle Clan, adopted son 1698 of **Trader Tom Carpenter (2)-Moytoy (2)**/1660 & aunt **Nancy Turkey Cornstalk**/1664, taught to read, speak & cipher in English by stepfather, husband 1704 of adopted sister **Swan-Wapehti Hop**/1686, father of daughters Ahneewakee Muskrat/1704, Ounacona Muskrat/1716, Tame Deer

Muskrat/1720, sons Oshasqua-Muskrat (3)/1718 & Bad Water Muskrat-Moytoy (6)/1722 & other unknown children/1705-31-all 63/64th Chalakatha-Pekowi-Shawano-Chalaka-Powhatan, adopted father 1708 of nephew **John Forked Tail Watts**/1704

WIVES OF SAVANNAH TOM CARPENTER/1680

1ST WIFE 1697 - VA

Rainmaker, Quatsey (2) aka **Susan Rainmaker** - Cherokee born 1682died after 1715 - daughter of **Rainmaker (1)**/1640 & **Quatsey (1)**/1650, Wolf Clan Cherokee through mother-Red Paint Clan by marriage, wife
1st 1697 TN of **Savannah Tom Carpenter (1)**/1680, 2nd 1698 TN of **Tsula Fox-Smallpox Conjurer-Jacob the Conjurer**/1670-Cherokee, 3rd 1704 TN of **John Bowles**/1688-white, mother **with Carpenter** of Savannah Tom Carpenter (2)/1698-23/64th Chalakatha-Shawano-ChalakaPowhatan-Cherokee-Metis, **with Fox** of daughter Ailsey Fox/1700, sons
Skalilosken Fox/1702, Rainmaker (3)-Rainmaker Fox/1704 & daughter Wurteh Tawsee Fox/1706-all Cherokee, **with Bowles** of Susan Bowles/1705-Cherokee-Metis (& associated somehow with Kitegista Rainmaker/1710)

2ND WIFE 1698 - VA-TN

Rainmaker, Nancy - Cherokee born about 1684 Great Tellico TN-died 1746 Great Tellico TN - daughter of **Rainmaker (1)**/1640 & **Quatsey (1)**/1650-both Cherokee, Wolf Clan Cherokee, wife 1st 1702 TN of **Savannah Tom Carpenter (1)**/1680, 2nd 1710 TN of his brother **White Owl Raven Carpenter**/1678, 3rd about 1726 TN of **Tauchee-Dutch Broom**/1680-Cherokee, mother **with Savannah Tom** of Great Eagle Carpenter/1702, Elizabeth Tassel-Euguioote-Elizabeth Carpenter/1704, Attakullakulla Carpenter/1706, Old Corn Tassel Carpenter/1708 & Susan Moytoy Carpenter/1710, **with White Owl** of Killancea Carpenter/1712, Killaqua Carpenter/1713, Betsy Carpenter/1714, Tame Doe Carpenter/1716, All Bones Carpenter/1718, Oousta Carpenter/1723, Bushyhead (2) -Chicsateehee Carpenter/1725-all

23/64th Chalakatha-Shawano-Chalaka-Powhatan-Cherokee-Metis, **with Dutch** of Young Broom/1727, Kaiyatahee Broom/1729 & Nancy Broom/1731-all Cherokee

CHILDREN OF SAVANNAH TOM CARPENTER/1680

BY SUSAN-QUATSEY RAINMAKER/1682

SON

Carpenter, Savannah Tom (2) aka Thomas Carpenter (5)-**Corn Planter (5)** – 23/64th Chalakatha-Shawano-Chalaka-Powhatan-Cherokee-Metis born 1698 Running Water TN-died after 1763 – son of **Savannah Tom Carpenter (1)-Corn Planter (4)-Moytoy (2)**/1680 & **Susan-Quatsey (2) Rainmaker**/1682, could cipher, read & speak English, associated **with Robert-Thigh-Cauquillehaneh McLemore, John French, Capt. French** & **John Lantaniak-**adopted French-Canadian in pro-French faction during the French-Indian War/1754-63, said to have had **Shawnee, Cherokee, Creek, black & white wives**, multiple unknown children

BY NANCY RAINMAKER/1683

SON

Carpenter, Great Eagle aka **Great Eagle**-Willenawah-WoolenawahTifftoy of Tenase-Tiftoa-Woolochuoah – 23/64th Chalakatha-Shawano-Chalaka-Powhatan-Cherokee-Metis born 1702 Great Tellico TN-died 1777 Great Tellico TN - son of **Savannah Tom Carpenter (1)-Moytoy (3)**/1680 & **Nancy Rainmaker**/1683, adopted son of his uncle **White Owl Carpenter-Moytoy (4)** upon death of his father 1710, could cipher, read & speak some English, from the Overhills, Tenase & Great Tellico, delegation to ENG 1730, Wolf Clan Cherokee through mother-Blind Savannah Clan through father, Cornstalk War/1755-74, Cherokee faction in Cherokee War/1775, protested but signed Treaty Sycamore Shoals 1775, adopted father of his half-sister **Oousta White Owl Carpenter**/1723, husband 1726 Tellico Plains TN of his 1st cousin (daughter of mother's sister Quatsey) **Wurteh Tawsee Fox**/1704Cherokee, father of Red Bird Carpenter-(Aaron Brock)/1727, Corn Tassel Carpenter/1730, Standing Turkey Carpenter/1738, Double Head Carpenter/1740, Pumpkin Boy Carpenter/1741, Nancy Great Eagle Carpenter/1745, Older Daughter/1749-(wife of **Cabin Smith**) & Younger Daughter/1752-(wife of **Leech**/1725)-all 11/64th ChalakathaShawano-Chalaka-Powhatan-Cherokee-Metis

DAUGHTER

Carpenter, Elizabeth Euguioote aka Elizabeth Carpenter (1)-Elizabeth Tassel (1) – 23/64th Chalakatha-Shawano-Chalaka-Powhatan-CherokeeMetis born 1704 Great Tellico TN-died 1755 Tellico Plains TN - daughter of **Nancy Rainmaker**/1683 & **Savannah Tom Carpenter (1)Moytoy (3)**/1680, step-daughter of her uncle **White Owl Carpenter**/1678, from the Overhills, Long Hair Clan Cherokee (?), could cipher, read & speak English, wife 1726 Great Tellico TN of **Ludovic Grant**/1698-white, mother of Mary Grant/1726 & Susannah Catherine Grant/1728-both 11/64th Chalakatha-Shawano-Chalaka-Powhatan-Cherokee-Metis

SON

Carpenter, Attakullakulla aka **Attakullakulla**-Leaning Wood-**Little Carpenter-Little Cornplanter**-Little Corn-Ookunaka-Thomas Carpenter (6)-Chugnonanto Tom-Chunconnunta-Chukenanta Warrior-TruconitaWhite Owl (2)-Attagulagula-Little Tom-Tommy of Tenase-OokanaskaUkwaneequa-Occounaco – 23/64th Chalakatha-Shawano-Chalaka-Powhatan-Cherokee-Metis born 1706 Great Tellico TN-died 1777 Nacheztown TN in battle – son of **Savannah Tom Carpenter (1)Moytoy (3)**/1680 & **Nancy Rainmaker**/1683, stepson of his uncle **White Owl Carpenter**/1678, Wolf Clan Cherokee, delegation to ENG 1730, captive of Ottawa or Chippewa in North 1738-45, (wrongly called a Chippewa or Ottawa due to his 8 years of captivity in the north which some thought to be at least partially voluntary), could cipher, read & speak some English, sent band raiding Ohio Valley/1758, sent warriors to Point Pleasant/1774, Cherokee faction in Cherokee

War/1775, Treaty Sycamore Shoals 1775, a **Principal Chief of Cherokee 1763-1775**, husband 1st 1734 TN of his 2nd cousin/niece (daughter of his 1st cousin) **Ollie Nionee Oconastota**/1720, father **with Ollie Nionee before captivity** of Dragging Canoe/1734, White Owl (3)/1736 & Tahchee Carpenter/1738-all 27/64th Chalakatha-Thawikila-ShawanoChalaka-Powhatan-Creek-Cherokee-Metis, (possibly 2nd 1738 in north of a northern Native during his captivity in the north & father of children/1738-45-see **Marie Lesperance**), father **with Ollie Nionee after captivity** of Shoe Boots/1750, Ollie Mollie/1754, Turtle At Home/1758 & Wurtegua Carpenter/1760-all 27/64th Chalakatha-Thawikila-Shawano-Chalaka-Powhatan-Creek-Cherokee-Metis, (adopted father after captivity of **Badger Hop**/1739, **Black Fox Hop**/1741, **Little Owl Hop**/1743 & **Sugi-Suki-Susannah Hop**/1745-all 31/64th Chalakatha-Thawikila-Shawano-Chalaka-Powhatan-CreekCherokee-(born during his captivity = children of **Young Hop**/1715 & Ollie Nionee Oconastota/1720), also adopted father & father in law of **Alexander Scotchee Cameron**/1730-white

SON

Carpenter, Corn Tassel (1) aka Corn Tassel (1)-**Old Corn Tassel**-Old Tassel-Utsidsata-Koateehee-First To Kill-**Onitositah**-Thistle Head-George Tassel – 23/64th Chalakatha-Shawano-Chalaka-Powhatan-Cherokee-Metis born 1708 Great Tellico TN-**murdered** 1788 Chuhowa TN - son of **Savannah Tom Carpenter (1)-Moytoy (3)**/1680 & **Nancy Rainmaker**/1683, stepson of his uncle **White Owl Carpenter**/1678, Wolf Clan Cherokee, could cipher, read & write some English, associated with **Cornstalk, John Forked Tail Watts, John Swift, Samuel Blackburn, Dragging Canoe, Doublehead & Nathaniel Gist**, Cornstalk War/1755-74, Cherokee faction in Cherokee War/1775, Treaty Sycamore Shoals 1775, Treaty Long Island 1777, Treaty 1785, from Chota, a **Principal Chief under Old Hop-Standing Turkey** 175161, a **Principal Chief & counselor under Oconastota** 1761-83 & also the **leading counselor under Kitegista** 1783-88, visited Philadelphia 1787met **Benjamin Franklin, murdered by John Kirk Jr & other whites** while under a flag of truce with 2nd wife Kaiyatahee (Hanging) Maw/1740, sons Double Tassel/1740, Young Tassel/1745 &

his wife's uncle **Old Abram-Ooskiah**/1721, husband 1st 1730 of **Tsigilili (Hanging) Maw**/1715-Cherokee, 2nd by 1779 of **Kaiyatahee (Hanging) Maw**/1740-Cherokee (both sisters of Hanging Maw), father **with Tsigilili** of Double Tassel-Corn Tassel (3)/1740, Young Tassel-Corn Tassel (4)/1745 & Susannah Corn Tassel/1749 & **with Kaiyatahee** of Elizabeth Corn Tassel/1780-all 11/64th Chalakatha-Shawano-ChalakaPowhatan-Cherokee-Metis

DAUGHTER

Carpenter, Susan Moytoy – 23/64th Chalakatha-Shawano-Chalaka-Powhatan-Cherokee-Metis born 1710 Tellico Plains TN-died 1764 Taluegue KY – daughter of **Savannah Tom Carpenter (1)-Moytoy (3)**/1680 & **Nancy Rainmaker**/1683, adopted daughter of her uncle **White Owl Carpenter**/1678, could cipher, read & speak some English, wife 1st 1730 TN of **Christian Gottleib Priber**/1697-GER, mother **with Priber** of Susanna Catherine Priber/1730, Grand Priber/1732 & Place Priber/1734-all 11/64th Chalakatha-Shawano-Chalaka-Powhatan-Cherokee-Metis

GRANDCHILDREN OF SAVANNAH TOM CARPENTER/1680

BY SAVANNAH TOM CARPENTER (2)/1698

UNKNOWN

BY GREAT EAGLE/1702 & WURTEH TAWSEE FOX/1705

GRANDSON

Carpenter, **Red Bird (1)** aka **Aaron Brock (1)**-Red Bird Great EagleTaleonteeskee-Cusawah-Tuchuwor-Tsisquaya-Totsuwha-DotsuwaTochuwar-Quagi – 11/64th Chalakatha-Shawano-Chalaka-PowhatanCherokee-Metis born 1727 Great Tellico TN-**murdered** 1796 Clay Co.

KY - son of **Great Eagle Carpenter**/1702 & **Wurteh Tawsee Fox**/1705, Red Paint Clan Cherokee, **Chief of Taluegue**-Red Bird village KY, could speak, read & write some English & cipher white style, Cornstalk War/1755-77, Chickamauga faction in Cherokee War/1775, Blue Jacket War/1777-78, a Chickamauga with **Dragging Canoe**/1775-78, Pigeon Co-Cherokee scouts-**with U.S. Army**-Revolution/1778-83, returned to support of **Dragging Canoe** & Chickamauga/1783-92, took whiteChristian name Aaron Brock for marriage to Susanna, returned to Native name Red Bird after death 1764 of Susanna, moved to Barrens TN 1778, moved back to KY 1789, **murdered by whites** with friend **Crippled Jack Cole**, husband 1748 Great Tellico TN of his half-niece **Susanna Caroline Priber**/1730, father of Red Bird Carpenter (2)-Aaron Brock Jr-**Tsisquaya**-Little Red Bird/1748, Mahala Susannah White Deer-Unegahiwiya Brock/1750, Jesse Hungry Fox-Gayasihatsula Brock/1752, George Brock/1754, Reuben Brock/1756, John Fire Raven-Atsilagolanu Brock/1758, Mary Polly Tame Dove-Ulunitagni Brock/1760, James Thunderstorm-Unalasgiunula Brock/1762 & Amon Brock/1764-all 11/64th Chalakatha-Shawano-Chalaka-Powhatan-Cherokee-Metis

GRANDSON

Carpenter, Corn Tassel (2) aka **Rayetaeh-**Corn Tassel (2)-Corn Tassel Great Eagle – 11/64th Chalakatha-Shawano-Chalaka-PowhatanCherokee-Metis born 1730 Great Tellico TN-died 1783 Great Tellico TN - son of **Great Eagle Carpenter**/1702 & **Wurteh Tawsee Fox**/1705, namesake of his uncle **Old Corn Tassel Onitositah Carpenter (1)**/1710(brother of his father), Cornstalk War/1755-74, Cherokee faction in Cherokee War/1775, Pigeon Co-Cherokee scouts-**with U.S. Army**Revolution/1778-83, Red Paint Clan Cherokee, could cipher, read & speak some English, husband 1750 Great Tellico TN of **Tali Cherokee**/1735, father of Elizabeth Tassel Carpenter (2)/1760, Corn Tassel Carpenter (5)/1765 & other children/1750-80-all 5/64th Chalakatha-Shawano-Chalaka-Powhatan-Cherokee-Metis

GRANDSON

Shawnee Heritage II

Carpenter, Standing Turkey (1) aka Standing Turkey Great Eagle**Standing Turkey (3)**-Gunakataga-**Kanagatoga**-Kanorcortuker-OcayulaOukah Ulah-Ruler To Be-Wahhatih- Boston – 11/64th ChalakathaShawano-Chalaka-Powhatan-Cherokee-Metis born 1738 Great Tellico TN-died 1794 Pendleton Co. SC - son of **Great Eagle Carpenter**/1702 & **Wurteh Tawsee Fox**/1705, Red Paint Clan Cherokee, from the Overhills-Chota, namesake of **Standing Turkey-Old Hop**, Cornstalk War/1758-74, Cherokee faction in Cherokee War/1775, could cipher, read & speak some English, Pigeon Co.-Cherokee scouts-**with U.S. Army**Revolution/1778-83, delegate to D.C. 1791, Treaty 1791, 1792, husband 1758 of **Polly Sutton**/1739, father of Standing Turkey (5)/1758, Robert Carpenter/1760, Mary Carpenter/1762, Thomas Carpenter/1764 & Nell Carpenter/1766-all 21/64th Chalakatha-PekowiShawano-Chalaka-Powhatan-Creek-Cherokee-Metis

GRANDSON

Carpenter, Doublehead (1) aka **Double Head (1)**-Taltsuska-TultsuskaChuquilatague-Two Heads-Autowee-Kill Baby-Ahtowhee-Walking Man-Dhuqualutauge-Dsugweladegi-Taliwuaskaskule – 11/64th Chalakatha-Shawano-Chalaka-Powhatan-Cherokee-Metis born about 1740 Great Tellico TN-**murdered** 1807 Hiawassee Ferry TN - son of **Great Eagle Carpenter**/1702 & **Wurteh Tawsee Fox**/1705-Cherokee, Red Paint Clan Cherokee, **associated with Dragging Canoe** & **Cornstalk in John Swift** silverming/1760-69, could cipher, read & speak some English, Cornstalk War/1768-77, Chickamauga faction in Cherokee War/1775, Blue Jacket War/1777-92, Ish Station & Cavett Station 1793, Chickamauga with **Dragging Canoe**, from the Overhills, Center Star & Muscle Shoals AL, delegate to D.C./1791, Treaty Sycamore Shoals 1775, 1791, 1792, 1794, 1805, 1806, Council Hanging Maw Town-survived attack by John Beard's renegade militia 1792, Conference at Henry's Station 1793, 3rd Treaty of Tellico 1806 with brother **Red Bird, murdered 1807** by **John Ridge** & nephews **Alexander Jeremiah Sanders** & **James Sanders** for signing 3rd Treaty of Tellico 1806 giving away Cherokee land or under blood vengeance for murdering his 4th wife Kateeyah Wilson, husband 1st 1757 of half-1st

cousin **Great Priber**/1739, 2nd 1787 of 3rd cousin/niece **Nancy-Nannie the Pain Drumgoole**/1767, 3rd 1795 of 5th cousin/niece **Margaret Peggy Scott**/1780, 4th 1797 of 4th cousin/niece **Kateeyah Wilson (2)**/1780, 5th 1800 of 5th cousin/niece **Sarah Scott**/1786-(sister of Margaret Peggy/83), 6th 1805 GA of **Jennie Foster**/1779, father **with Priber** of daughters Corn Blossom Doublehead/1758, Tuskiahoote Doublehead/1759, Soney Doublehead/1760, son Tuckahoe Doublehead/1761, daughters Seeleechie Doublehead/1763, Nigodigeyu Doublehead/1764, Gulustiyu Doulbehead/1766, Ishtonnarhay Doublehead/1768, son Tahlejewsco Doublehead/1770 & Daughter of Doublehead/1772-all 13/64th Chalakatha-Shawano-Chalaka-Powhatan-Cherokee-Metis, **with Drumgoole** of son Bird Doublehead aka Bird Tail/1790 & Nancy Doublehead/1792-both 9/64th Chalakatha-Pekowi-Shawano-Chalaka-Powhatan-Cherokee-Metis, **with Margaret Peggy Scott** of sons Two Heads Doublehead/1796 & Young Double Head (1)/1797-both 7/64th Chalakatha-Thawikila-Shawano-ChalakaPowhatan-Creek-Cherokee-Metis, **with Wilson** of son Tassel Doublehead/1797, daughters Alcy Doublehead/1798, Susannah Doublehead/1799 & Peggy Doublehead/1800-all 5/32nd Chalakatha-Thawikila-Kishpoko-Shawano-Chalaka-Powhatan-Black-CreekCherokee-Metis, **with Sarah Scott** of William Doublehead/1800 & Young Double Head (2)/1801-both 7/64th Chalakatha-ThawikilaShawano-Chalaka-Powhatan-Creek-Cherokee-Metis, **with Foster** of
Tom Doublehead/1806-37/64th Chalakatha-Thawikila-ShawanoChalaka-Powhatan-Cherokee-Metis

GRANDSON

Carpenter, Pumpkin Boy (1) aka Pumpkin Boy Great Eagle-**Pumpkin Boy**-Eyahchutlee-Iyahuwagiatsutsa-No Pumpkins – 11/64th Chalakatha-Shawano-Chalaka-Powhatan-Cherokee-Metis born 1741 Great Tellico TN-**killed** 1792 Ish Station TN in battle - son of **Great Eagle Carpenter**/1702 & **Wurteh Tawsee Fox**/1705, from the Overhills, Red Paint Clan Cherokee, Cornstalk War/1760-74, Chickamauga faction in Cherokee War/1775, Treaty Sycamore Shoals 1775, Blue Jacket War/1777-92, **killed in attack** on Ish's Station/1792, husband 1761 Great Tellico TN of **Chaueka Cherokee**/1745, father of children/1762-

67, Young Pumpkin Boy/1768, children/1766-81 & Catherine Pumpkin/1782-all 5/64th Chalakatha-Shawano-ChalakaPowhatan-Cherokee-Metis

GRANDDAUGHTER

Carpenter, Nancy aka Nanni-Nancy Great Eagle – 11/64th Chalakatha-Shawano-Chalaka-Powhatan-Cherokee-Metis born 1745 Great Tellico TN-died about 1816 Great Tellico TN - daughter of **Great Eagle Carpenter**/1702 & **Wurteh Tawsee Fox**/1704, Red Paint Clan Cherokee, wife 1759 TN of 1st cousin (son of father's brother) **Badger Hop-Ookuhmuh**/1738, mother of Young Badger-Ookuhmuh/1760, Nancy Ookuhmuh/1768, Jennie Ookuhmuh/1770, Johnson Ookuhmuh/1776 & John Welch Ookuhmuh/1782-all 21/64th Chalakatha-Thawikila-Shawano-Chalaka-Powhatan-Creek-Cherokee-Metis

GRANDDAUGHTER

Carpenter, Older Daughter of Great Eagle – 11/64th ChalakathaShawano-Chalaka-Powhatan-Cherokee-Metis born 1749-died after 1784
- daughter of **Great Eagle Carpenter**/1702 & **Wurteh Tawsee Fox**/1705, wife about 1765 NC of **Cabin Smith**-Cherokee, mother of children/1765-83, Archilla Smith/1784-all 5/64th Chalakatha-ShawanoChalaka-Powhatan-Cherokee-Metis

GRANDDAUGHTER

Carpenter, Younger Daughter of Great Eagle – 11/64th ChalakathaShawano-Chalaka-Powhatan-Cherokee-Metis born 1752-died after 1784
- daughter of **Great Eagle Carpenter**/1702 & **Wurteh Tawsee Fox**/1705, wife about 1767 NC of **Leech**/1725-Cherokee, children unknown

BY ELIZABETH TASSEL EUGUIOOTE CARPENTER/1704 & LUDOVIC GRANT/1698

GRANDAUGHTER

Grant, Mary – 11/64th Chalakatha-Shawano-Chalaka-PowhatanCherokee-Metis born 1726 Great Tellico TN-died 1766 Goose Creek SC
- daughter of **Elizabeth Tassel Euguioote Carpenter**/1704 & **Ludovic Grant**/1698-white, Long Hair Clan Cherokee (?), could speak, cipher, read & write English, wife 1744 Great Tellico TN of **William Emory**/1720-white, mother of William Emory Jr-Capt. Will/1744, Mary Emory/1746, Elizabeth Emory/1748, Susannah Emory (2)/1750, Nancy Emory/1752, Drury Emory/1754 & Abraham Emory/1756-all 5/64th Chalakatha-Shawano-Chalaka-Powhatan-Cherokee-Metis

GRANDDAUGHTER

Grant, Susannah Catherine – 11/64th Chalakatha-Shawano-ChalakaPowhatan-Cherokee-Metis born 1728 Great Tellico TN-died 1769 Goose
Creek SC – daughter of **Elizabeth Tassel Euguioote Carpenter**/1704 & **Ludovic Grant**/1698-white, could speak, cipher, read & write English, wife 1743 Great Tellico TN of **John Robert Emory**/1725-white, mother of Susannah Emory (1)/1744-5/64th Chalakatha-Shawano-ChalakaPowhatan-Cherokee-Metis

BY ATTAKULLAKULLA CARPENTER/1706 & OLLIE NIONEE OCONASTOTA/1720

GRANDSON

Carpenter, Dragging Canoe aka Tsiyigunsini-**Dragging Canoe (1)**Drags Canoe-Dragon-Dragging Canoe Attakullakulla-Chuconsene-Cheucunsee-Kunnesee – 27/64th Chalakatha-Thawikila-ShawanoChalaka-Powhatan-Creek-Cherokee-Metis – born 1734 Great Tellico TN-**died from wounds** 1792 Running Water TN – oldest son of **Attakullakulla Carpenter**/1706 & **Ollie Nionee Oconastota**/1720, Wolf Clan Cherokee, over 6' tall, broad-shouldered, muscular & poxmarked, from the Overhills & Running Water (Shawnee) village TN, could cipher, read & speak some English, **Headman** from Great Island TN, Cornstalk War/1758-74, associated with **Cornstalk** & **Doublehead** in

John Swift silverming/1760-69, raiding Ohio-New River valleys/75, attended but didn't sign Treaty Sycamore Shoals 1775, started Cherokee War/1775 **with Abraham-Ooskiah**/1721-Cherokee-Metis (half-brother of **Hanging Maw**),founder & leader of the Chickamauga faction, raiding VA-KY-OH-TN/1777-92 **with Cheeseekau & Chief Bob Benge**, adopted brother of **Alexander Cameron** aka **Scotchee**/1730-white (husband of his sister Ollie Mollie Carpenter/1754), with Shawnee at Crawford/1782, Harmar/1790, St. Clair/1791, died from wounds received at Buchanan Station/1792, **Principal Chief of the Chickamauga 1775-92**, succeeded as Chickamauga Chief by **John Young Tassel Watts Jr**/1748 & **Little Turkey Hop**/1715, husband 1749 TN of **Oogahloguh Leaf** /1735-Cherokee, father **with Leaf** of sons Little Owl Canoe/1750, Young Dragging Canoe/1752, daughters Sarah-Naky Canoe/1754, Eyoostee Canoe/1756, son Crying Snake Canoe/1758, daughter Giyosti Canoe/1770 & other children/1759-80-all 13/64th Chalakatha-Thawikila-Shawano-Chalaka-Powhatan-Creek-CherokeeMetis

GRANDSON

Carpenter, White Owl (3) aka White Owl (3)–**Ookoonaka** – 27/64th Chalakatha-Thawikila-Shawano-Chalaka-Powhatan-Creek-CherokeeMetis born 1735 Great Tellico TN-**killed** 1792 Buchanan Station TN - son of **Attakullakulla Carpenter**/1706 & **Ollie Nionee Oconastota**/1720, from the Overhills, Toqua & Natchey Creek TN, **namesake of step-grandfather White Owl Carpenter**/1678, could cipher, read & speak English, Cornstalk War/1758-74, Treaty Sycamore Shoals 1775, Chickamauga faction in Cherokee War/1775, raiding VA-KY-OH-TN/1777-92 **with Cheeseekau** & **Chief Bob Benge**, with Shawnee at Crawford/1782, Harmar/1790, St. Clair/1791, killed in attack on Buchanan Station/1792, called a **Creek Chief** (by marriage) of a mixed Shawnee-Creek-Cherokee village, husband 1756 TN of ½ **Kishpoko-Creek Woman**/1740, father of White Owl Carpenter (4)/1756 & other children/1757-85-all 29/64th Chalakatha-ThawikilaShawano-Chalaka-Powhatan-Creek-Cherokee-Metis

GRANDSON

Carpenter, Tahchee (1) aka **Tahchee (1)**-Datsi-Tatsi-Tahchee Attakullakulla – 27/64th Chalakatha-Thawikila-Shawano-

ChalakaPowhatan-Creek-Cherokee-Metis born 1736 Great Tellico TN-died before 1830 Audrain Co MO – son of **Attakullakulla Carpenter**/1706 &
Ollie Nionee Oconastota/1720, Wolf Clan Cherokee, Cornstalk War/1758-74, Chickamauga faction in Cherokee War/1775, could cipher, read & speak some English, Pigeon Co-Cherokee scouts-**with U.S. Army**-Revolution/1778-83, moved to MO about 1810, husband 1st 1755 Great Tellico TN of **Place Priber**/1738, 2nd 1756 Great Tellico TN of **Ailsey Red Paint**/1740-Cherokee, 3rd 1770 of **Susannah Catherine Red Horse**/1742-Cherokee, father **with Priber** of Nettle CarrierTalotiskee/1756-5/64th Chalakatha-Thawikila-Shawano-Chalaka-Powhatan-Creek-Cherokee-Metis, **with Ailsey** of Giyosta Tahchee/1756, Ooloosta Tahchee/1760 & Major Ridge/1771-all 13/64th Chalakatha-Thawikila-Shawano-Chalaka-Powhatan-Creek-CherokeeMetis, **with Susannah** of Sky Buck Ridge/1780, Young Tachchee/1785-
13/64th Chalakatha-Thawikila-Shawano-Chalaka-Powhatan-Creek-Cherokee-Metis

GRANDSON

Carpenter, Shoe Boots aka **Shoe Boots Attakullakulla**-Shoe Boots (1)-Dasigiyang-**Tuskorigo** – 27/64th Chalakatha-Thawikila-ShawanoChalaka-Powhatan-Creek-Cherokee-Metis born 1750 Great Tellico TNdied 1829 Thompson Ferry GA - son of **Attakullakulla Carpenter**/1706
& **Ollie Nionee Oconastota**/1720, Cornstalk War/1768-74, Chickamauga faction in Cherokee War/1775, Blue Jacket War/1777-94, wounded at St. Clair/1791, lived **with Shawnee** in OH 1780-1803, could cipher, read & speak some English, Capt.-**with U.S. Army**-Creek War/1813-Horseshoe Bend/1814, husband 1st 1770 Running Water TN of **Bird Clan Cherokee Woman**/1754, 2nd 1775 Shawnee Village OH of **Lecha**/1760-Chalakatha, 3rd 1794 Shawnee Village OH of **Clarinda Allington** (Arrington)/1780-adopted white, 4th 1805 Shawnee Village OH of **Dolly Black**/1790-former slave, children/1770-75 **with Bird Clan** unknown, father **with Lecha** of Young Shoe Boots-

Dasigiyagi/1775-45/64th Chalakatha-Thawikila-Shawano-ChalakaPowhatan-Creek-Cherokee-Metis, **with Clarinda** of John Allington
(Shoe Boots)/1794, Sally Allington (Shoe Boots)/1796, William Allington (Shoe Boots)/1798-all 13/64th Chalakatha-ThawikilaShawano-Chalaka-Powhatan-Creek-Cherokee-Metis, **with Dolly** of
Thomas Shoe Boots/1806, Ollie Shoe Boots/1810 & Napoleon Bonaparte (Shoe Boots)/1820 & other children- all 13/64th Chalakatha-Thawikila-Shawano-Chalaka-Powhatan-Creek-Cherokee-Black-Metis

GRANDDAUGHTER

Carpenter, Ollie Mollie aka Ollie Mollie Attakullakulla – 27/64th Chalakatha-Thawikila-Shawano-Chalaka-Powhatan-Creek-CherokeeMetis born 1754 Great Tellico TN-died after 1810 Cherokee Nation TN – daughter of **Attakullakulla Carpenter**/1706 & **Ollie Nionee Oconastota**/1720, Wolf Clan Cherokee, could cipher, read & speak some English, wife 1st 1769 Great Tellico TN of **Alexander Scotchee Cameron**/1730-adopted-white (he dies 1781 GA), 2nd 1780 Great Tellico
TN of **James Dougherty**/1742 (widowed 1791), 3rd 1795 Cherokee Nation TN of **Thomas Harrison**/1736-white, mother **with Cameron** of Susanne Cameron/1770, Archibald Cameron/1772 & David Cameron/1774-all 13/64th Chalakatha-Thawikila-Shawano-ChalakaPowhatan-Creek-Cherokee-Metis, **with Dougherty** of Annie Crying
Bear (Dougherty)/1780, James Dougherty Jr/1782, Susan Dougherty/1784, Elizabeth Dougherty/1786, Elsie Dougherty/1788, Rachel Dougherty/1790, Mary Dougherty/1792 (born after death of James)-all 31/64th Chalakatha-Thawikila-Pekowi-Shawano-ChalakaPowhatan-Creek-Cherokee-Metis, any children **with Harrison** unknown

GRANDSON

Carpenter, Turtle At Home aka Turtle At Home Attakullakulla-Sullicooahwolu-Fulaquokoko-Snapping Turtle - 27/64th Chalakatha-Thawikila-Shawano-Chalaka-Powhatan-Creek-Cherokee-Metis born

1758 Great Tellico TN-died after 1813 Running Water TN – son of **Attakullakulla Carpenter**/1706 & **Ollie Nionee Oconastota**/1720, Wolf Clan Cherokee, Cherokee faction in Cherokee War/1775, Pigeon Co-Cherokee scouts-**with U.S. Army**-Revolution/1778-83, **Headman** at Running Water (Shawnee) village 1792, could cipher, read & speak some English, operated ferry at Nickajack TN, Capt. in John Speers Co**with U.S. Army**-Creek War/1813, Treaty 1805, 1806, husband 1770 Nickajack TN of **Ahyague Cherokee**/1760, father of Tsinyahnehnaw (Turtle at Home) Carpenter/1777 & others-all 13/64th ChalakathaThawikila-Shawano-Chalaka-Powhatan-Creek-Cherokee-Metis

GRANDDAUGHTER

Carpenter, Wurtegua aka Wataga-Wautega-Wurtegua Attakullakulla – 27/64th Chalakatha-Thawikila-Shawano-Chalaka-Powhatan-CreekCherokee-Metis born 1752 Great Tellico TN-died after 1786 TN – daughter of **Attakullakulla Carpenter**/1706 & **Ollie Nionee Oconastota**/1720, Wolf Clan Cherokee, wife 1st 1768 Great Tellico TN of **Unknown Man**, 2nd 1779 Great Tellico TN of **John-Young Tassel Watts Jr**/1748, children/1768-78 **with Unknown** not known, mother **with Watts** of Mink Watts/1780, Capt. John Watts/1782, Soup Watts/1784 & Fish Tail Watts/1786-all 17/32nd Chalakatha-Pekowi-ThawikilaShawano-Chalaka-Powhatan-Creek-Cherokee-Metis

GRANDCHILDREN BY ADOPTION OF SAVANNAH TOM CARPENTER/1680

GRANDSON BY ADOPTION

Hop, Badger aka Badger Attakullakulla-**Ookuhmuh (1)**-Badger (1)Akumneh-Oguma-Badger Turkey – 31/64th Chalakatha-ThawikilaShawano-Chalaka-Powhatan-Creek-Cherokee - born 1738 Great Tellico TN-died after 1804 Great Tellico TN – son of **Young Hop**/1715 & **Ollie Nionee Oconastota**/1720, adopted son 1746 TN of **Attakullakulla Carpenter**/1706, from the Overhills, Wolf Clan or Red Paint Clan

Cherokee, Cornstalk War/1758-74, Chickamauga faction in Cherokee War/1775, Treaty Sycamore Shoals/1775, Pigeon Co-Cherokee scouts**with U.S. Army**-Revolution/1778-83, diplomatic missions to Detroit & Canada/1883-84, Council Eustinali 1788, Council Estinawa 1792, delegate to D.C./1791, Treaty 1791, Treaty 1792, husband 1759 Great Tellico TN of **Nancy Great Eagle Carpenter**/1745, father of Young Ookuhmuh-Young Badger/1760, Nancy Ookuhmuh/1768, Jennie Ookuhmuh/1770, Johnson Ookuhmuh/1776, John Welch Ookuhmuh/1782-all 5/16th Chalakatha-Thawikila-Shawano-ChalakaPowhatan-Creek-Cherokee-Metis

GRANDSON BY ADOPTION

Hop, Black Fox aka **Enoleha**-Black Fox (1)-Inali-Fox-Capt. Fox-Black Fox Attakullakulla-Black Fox Turkey – 31/64th Chalakatha-ThawikilaShawano-Chalaka-Powhatan-Creek-Cherokee born 1740 Great Tellico
TN-died 1811 KY – son of **Young Hop**/1715 & **Ollie Nionee Oconastota**/1720, adopted son 1746 of **Attakullakulla Carpenter**/1706, Wolf Clan Cherokee, Cornstalk War/1758-74, Chickamauga faction in Cherokee War/1775, Pigeon Co-Cherokee scouts-**with U.S. Army**Revolution/1778-83, **Chickamauga sub-Chief** under **Dragging Canoe**
1788-90, delegate to D.C./1791, Treaty 1791, 1805, 1806, 1807, **Principal Chief** 1802-06 upon death of **Little Turkey-Standing Turkey (2)**/1715, sided with **Double Head**/40 1806-10-deposed 1806-10-succeeded 180610 by **Path Killer**-reinstated 1810-11, husband 1759 Great Tellico TN of
Grand Priber/1737, father of Young Black Fox/1760, Nancy Black Fox-Nancy Fox/1762, Mary Ann Black Fox-Mary Ann Fox/1764-all 21/64th Chalakatha-Thawikila-Shawano-Chalaka-Powhatan-Creek-Cherokee-Metis

GRANDSON BY ADOPTION

Hop, Little Owl aka **Ookoosdi**-Little Owl (1)-Little Owl Attakullakulla**Nahoolah**-White Mankiller-Unegadihi-Unacata-IshettechiUnakateehee-Little Owl Turkey – 31/64th Chalakatha-

ThawikilaShawano-Chalaka-Powhatan-Creek-Cherokee born 1742 Great Tellico TN-**killed** 1792 Buchanan Station TN – son of **Young Hop**/1715 & **Ollie Nionee Oconastota**/1720, adopted son 1746 of **Attakullakulla Carpenter**/1706, from the Overhills, Wolf Clan Cherokee, Cornstalk War/1762-74, Chickamauga faction in Cherokee War/1775, Boonesboro/1778, a **seceding Headman** 1777, 1778 a **Chickamauga Chief**, raiding VA-KY-OH-TN/1777-92 **with Cheeseekau & Chief Bob Benge**, could cipher, read & speak some English, Dragging Canoe's **emissary to the British** in Detroit & CAN during Revolution, raiding Ohio River valley/1788, husband 1762 Great Tellico TN of **Bird Clan Kishpoko Woman**/1747, children/1762-92 unknown

GRANDDAUGHTER BY ADOPTION

Hop, Sugi aka Susannah-Suki Hop-Daughter of Attakullakulla-Sugi Turkey – 31/64th Chalakatha-Thawikila-Shawano-Chalaka-PowhatanCreek-Cherokee born 1744 Great Tellico TN-died after 1790 (TN?) – daughter of **Young Hop**/1715 & **Ollie Nionee Oconastota**/1720, adopted daughter 1746 of **Attakullakulla Carpenter**/1706, namesake of grandmother **Sugi Rainmaker**/1690, wife by 1763 TN of **Blue Sonicooie**/1730-Cherokee, mother of Susannah Sonicooie/1763, Young Sonicooie/1765 & Nancy Sonicooie/1768-all 15/64th ChalakathaThawikila-Shawano-Chalaka-Powhatan-Creek-Cherokee

BY CORN TASSEL CARPENTER/1708 & TSIGILILI (HANGING) MAW/1715

GRANDSON

Carpenter, **Double Tassel** aka Corn Tassel Carpenter (3)-**Corn Tassel (3)** – 11/64th Chalakatha-Shawano-Chalaka-Powhatan-Cherokee-Metis born 1740 Great Tellico TN-**murdered** 1788 Chuhowa TN - son of **Corn Tassel Carpenter (1)**/1709 & **Tsigilili (Hanging) Maw**/1715, Bird Clan Cherokee, Cornstalk War/1758-74, Cherokee faction in Cherokee War/1775, Pigeon Co-Cherokee scouts-**with U.S. Army-**Revolution/1778-83,, **murdered by John Kirk Jr & other whites** with his father, step-mother, brother & uncle while under a flag of truce, husband 1760 Great Tellico TN of a **Cherokee Woman**/1745, children unknown

GRANDSON

Carpenter, Young Corn Tassel aka Corn Tassel Carpenter (4)-Corn Tassel (4)-**Young Tassel**-Corn Tassel Jr-**Kunokeski** – 11/64th Chalakatha-Shawano-Chalaka-Powhatan-Cherokee-Metis born 1745 Great Tellico TN-**murdered** 1788 Chuhowa TN - son of **Corn Tassel Carpenter (1)**/1709 & **Tsigilili (Hanging) Maw**/1715, Bird Clan Cherokee, Cornstalk War/1758-74, Cherokee faction in Cherokee War/1775, Pigeon Co-Cherokee scouts-**with U.S. Army**-Revolution/1778-83,, **murdered by whites** with his father, step-mother, brother & uncle under a flag of truce, husband 1765 Great Tellico TN of a **Cherokee Woman**/1750, children unknown

GRANDDAUGHTER

Carpenter, Susannah aka **Susannah Corn Tassel**-Susannah Tassel-**Susannah Springfrog** – 11/64th Chalakatha-Shawano-Chalaka-Powhatan-Cherokee-Metis born 1749 Great Tellico TN-died 1851Cherokee Nation (OK?) - daughter of **Corn Tassel Carpenter (1)**/1709 & **Tsigilili (Hanging) Maw**/1715, Bird Clan Cherokee, wife 1772 Running Water TN of **Mitchell Sanders**/1750, mother of Alexander Jeremiah Sanders/1772, George Goguyelesgi Sanders/1774, James Sanders/1776, John Sanders/1778, twins-Jennie & Nancy Sanders/1782, Andrew Snake Sanders/1788, twins-Agnes & David Sanders/1790-all 21/64th Chalakatha-Mekoche-Shawano-ChalakaPowhatan-Cherokee-Metis

GRANDDAUGHTER

Carpenter, Elizabeth Corn Tassel aka Daughter of Old Tassel – 11/64th Chalakatha-Shawano-Chalaka-Powhatan-Cherokee-Metis born 1780 Great Tellico TN-died after 1808 (OK?) - daughter of **Corn Tassel Carpenter (1)**/1709 & **Kaiyatahee (Hanging) Maw**/1740, 1st wife by 1798 of **Ignatius Chisholm**/1777, mother of Jesse Chisholm/1800, John Chisholm/1806 & William Chisholm/1808-all 9/64th ChalakathaShawano-Chalaka-Powhatan-Cherokee-Metis

TN – daughter of **Susan Moytoy Carpenter**/1710 & **Christian Gottlieb Priber**/1697-German, wife 1st 1755 Great Tellico TN of **Tahchee Carpenter**/1736, 2nd 1759 Running Water TN of **Proud Boy**/1740-1/2 Kishpoko-Cherokee, mother **with Tahchee** of Talotiskee-Nettle Carrier/1756-5/64th Chalakatha-Thawikila-Shawano-ChalakaPowhatan-Creek-Cherokee-Metis, children/1760-83 **with Proud Boy** unknown

CHAPTER SIX

Standing Turkey-Old Hop/1688

Standing Turkey-Old Hop/1688

Turkey, Standing (1) aka **Old Hop**-Kanagatoga-Standing Turkey Cornstalk-Uka-Fire King-Kanetekoka-Conarcorturer-Connecorte - 63/64th Chalakatha-Shawano-Chalaka-Powhatan born 1688 Chota TN (some records indicate Upper Hiwassee VA-where older siblings were born or further north in the Ohio valley or further west in TN)-died 1761 Chota TN – son of **Big Turkey Cornstalk**/1660 & **Chalakatha Woman**/1664, parents killed 1694 VA by Catawba raiders, adopted son 1694 TN of **Trader Tom Carpenter (2)-Moytoy (2)**/1660 & his aunt **Nancy Turkey Cornstalk**/1664, commonly known as **Old Hop** or simply Hopper (perhaps a nickname that reflects back to the Norse term "hop" i.e. a small fortified place) , could cipher, read & speak some English, Wolf Clan Cherokee, in 1751 removed the British appointed (**Carpenter-Moytoy & Rainmaker**) leaders & united 4 (of 7) Cherokee clans at Chota, leader of pro- French faction in French-Indian War/1754-61, sent warriors to support the Shawnee at Braddock/1755, **Principal Chief** of the 4 Cherokee clans **1751-61**, passed actual

BY SUSAN MOYTOY CARPENTER/1710 & CHRISTIAN GOTTLIEB PRIBER/1697

GRANDDAUGHTER

Priber, Susanna Caroline aka Susanna Catherine Priber-Susanna Christian Priber-Susannah Davis – 11/64th Chalakatha-ShawanoChalaka-Powhatan-Cherokee-Metis born 1730 Great Tellico TN-died 1764 Taluegue KY – daughter of **Susan Moytoy Carpenter**/1710 &
Christian Gottlieb Priber/1697-German, wife 1748 Great Tellico TN of
Red Bird Carpenter (1)-Aaron Brock (1)/1727, mother of Red Bird Carpenter (2)-Aaron Brock Jr- **Tsisquaya**-Little Red Bird/1748, Mahala Susannah White Deer-Unegahiwiya Brock/1750, Jesse Hungry FoxGayasihatsula Brock/1752, George Brock/1754, Reuben Brock/1756,
John Fire Raven-Atsilagolanu Brock/1758, Mary Polly Tame Dove-Ulunitagni Brock/1760, James Thunderstorm-Unalasgiunula Brock/1762 & Amon Brock/1764-all 11/64th Chalakatha-ShawanoChalaka-Powhatan-Cherokee-Metis

GRANDDAUGHTER

Priber, Grand – 11/64th Chalakatha-Shawano-Chalaka-PowhatanCherokee-Metis born 1732 Great Tellico TN-died after 1810 Audrain Co. MO – daughter of **Susan Moytoy Carpenter**/1710 & **Christian Gottlieb Priber**/1697-GER, wife 1759 Great Tellico TN of **Black Fox Hop**/1740, mother of Young Black Fox/1760, Nancy Black Fox-Nancy Fox/1762,
Mary Ann Black Fox-Mary Ann Fox/1764-all 21/64th ChalakathaThawikila-Shawano-Chalaka-Powhatan-Creek-Cherokee-Metis

GRANDDAUGHTER

Priber, Place – 11/64th Chalakatha-Shawano-Chalaka-PowhatanCherokee-Metis born 1734 Great Tellico TN-died 1783 Running Water

power/authority to his nephews **Oconastota Rainmaker**/1702-(proBritish) & **Kitegista Rainmaker**/1710-(pro-French) upon his death in
1761 even though his son **Young Standing Turkey-Little Turkey**/1709(pro-French) succeeded him as titular Chief, husband by 1708 Chota TN of **Sugi Rainmaker**/1690-Wolf Clan Cherokee, known father of sons
Little Turkey-Young Standing Turkey/1709, Young Turkey-Young Hop/1715 & daughter Grasshopper Turkey/1725-all 31/64th Chalakatha-Shawano-Chalaka-Powhatan-Cherokee, adopted father 1723 TN of his nephews **John French**/1710 & **Capt. French**/1712-both 31/64th Chalakatha-Shawano-Chalaka-Powhatan-Black-Metis-(sons of his sister **Ghigoneli**/1694)

SIBLINGS OF STANDING TURKEY-OLD HOP/1688

BROTHER

Turkey, Raven aka **Raven Moytoy**-Raven of Hiwassee-CollanahCorani-Corane-Raven Hop-Raven Cornstalk – 63/64th ChalakathaShawano-Chalaka-Powhatan born 1680 Upper Hiwassee VA-died 1756 Chewohe TN – son of **Big Turkey Cornstalk**/1660 & **Chalakatha Woman**/1664, parents killed 1694 VA by Catawba raiders, adopted son 1694 TN of **Trader Tom Carpenter (2)-Moytoy (2)**/1660 & his aunt **Nancy Turkey Cornstalk**/1664, took the surname Moytoy from his adopted father **Trader Tom aka Moytoy (2)**, could cipher, read & speak some English, Treaty 1684 with SC, delegation to ENG 1730, husband 1st 1700 Upper Hiwassee TN of his adopted sister **Pashmere Carpenter (2)**/1682, 2nd 1718 of **Ahneewakee Muskrat**/1704, 3rd 1729 TN of **Cherokee Woman**/1714, father **with Pashmere** of Amoyah Pigeon Moytoy (1)/1715-27/64th Chalakatha-Shawano-Chalaka-PowhatanMetis, **with Ahneewakee** of Bushyhead Chiesatebe Moytoy/1718,
Savanooka-Raven Moytoy/1720, Goohsohly Moytoy/1722, Elizabeth Moytoy--Raven's Sister/1724, Nancy Augustus Moytoy/1726 & Amahetai Muskrat (3)-Moytoy (7)/1728-all 63/64th Chalakatha-Pekowi-Shawano-Chalaka-Powhatan, children **with Cherokee** unknown

SISTER

Turkey, Quatsis aka Quatsis Hop-Quatsis Aniwadi-Quatsis Cornstalk – 63/64th Chalakatha-Shawano-Chalaka-Powhatan born 1682 Great Tellico TN-died 1758 Tellico Plains TN – daughter of **Big Turkey Cornstalk**/1660 & **Chalakatha Woman**/1664, parents killed 1694 VA by Catawba raiders, adopted daughter 1694 TN of **Trader Tom Carpenter (2)-Moytoy (2)**/1660 & her aunt **Nancy Turkey**/1664, could cipher, read & speak some English, known as aunt of **Savanooka**/1720 & **Goohsohly**/1722-(sons of Ahneewakee Muskrat/1704 & her brother Raven Moytoy), Red Paint Clan Cherokee, her sister **Oolootah** lived with her from 1699-1705, wife 1st 1697 Great Tellico TN of **John Beamer**/1676-ENG, 2nd 1705 Settico TN of **Tsula Fox-Smallpox Conjurer**/1670-Cherokee (husband 1741 of her sister Aganunitsi), 3rd 1709 Chota TN of **William Webber**/1680-ENG, mother **with Beamer** of Ooloosta Beamer/1698, John Beamer Jr/1700, Peggy Beamer/1702 & Nionee Beamer/1704-all 31/64th Chalakatha-Shawano-ChalakaPowhatan-Metis, **with Fox-Conjurer** of Rising Fawn (1)-Rising Fawn Fox/1706 & Quatsis Fox/1708-both 31/64th Chalakatha-ShawanoChalaka-Powhatan-Cherokee, **with Webber** of Catherine Webber/1710 & William Webber (2)/1712-both 31/64th Chalakatha-Shawano-Chalaka-Powhatan-Metis

SISTER

Turkey, Aganunitsi aka **Wild Potato**-Aganunitsi Hop-Elder Sister of Old Hop-Elder Sister of Standing Turkey-Wife of **Young Rainmaker**-Anigatagewi Woman-Wife of **Smallpox Conjurer**-wife of Tsula FoxWild Potato Woman-Blind Savannah Woman - 63/64th ChalakathaShawano-Chalaka-Powhatan born 1684 Upper Hiwassee VA-died after 1741 TN - daughter of **Big Turkey**/1660 & **Chalakatha Woman**/1664, parents killed 1694 VA by Catawba raiders, adopted daughter 1694 TN of **Rainmaker (1)**/1640 & **Quatsey (1)**/1650-both Cherokee, Blind Savannah Clan Cherokee, wife 1st 1700 TN of her adopted brother
Young Rainmaker/1685-Cherokee, 2nd 1741 TN of **Tsula Fox-Smallpox Conjurer**/1670-Cherokee, mother **with Rainmaker** of son **Oconastota**/1702, child/1704, son Cloggoittah/1706, daughter

Ooloosta/1708, sons **Kitegista**/1710, Tathtowe/1712, Wallenaeoa-Gray Eagle/1714, Oukahoukah/1716, Kallannah/1718-all 31/64th Chalakatha-Shawano-Chalaka-Powhatan -Cherokee, children **with Smallpox Conjurer** unlikely due to her age

SISTER

Turkey, Swan aka Wapehti Turkey-Swan Hop- Wapehti Hop – 63/64th Chalakatha-Shawano-Chalaka-Powhatan born 1686 Upper Hiwassee TN-died 1754 Chota TN – daughter of **Big Turkey Cornstalk**/1660 & **Chalakatha Woman**/1664, parents killed 1694 VA by Catawba raiders, adopted daughter 1694 TN of **Trader Tom Carpenter (2)-Moytoy (2)**/1660 & her aunt **Nancy Turkey Cornstalk**/1664, could cipher, read & speak some English, wife 1703 Running Water TN of her adopted brother **Oshasqua-Muskrat (2)**/1686, mother of daughters Ahneewakee Muskrat/1704, children/1706-14, Ounacona Muskrat/1716, Tame Deer Muskrat/1720 & son Bad Water MuskratMoytoy (6)/1722-all 63/64th Chalakatha-Pekowi-Shawano-ChalakaPowhatan, adopted mother 1708 TN-VA of **John Fork Tail Watts**/1704(nephew of Oshasqua-Muskrat/1686)

SISTER

Turkey, April-**Tkikami** aka Tkikami Hop-April Hop-Middle Sister of Old Hop-Middle Sister of Standing Turkey-Wife of Tsula Fox-Wife of Smallpox Conjurer-Wife of Richard Barnes - 63/64th ChalakathaShawano-Chalaka-Powhatan born 1690 Chota TN-died 1744 Upper
Hiwassee TN – daughter of **Big Turkey Cornstalk**/1660 & **Chalakatha Woman**/1664, parents killed 1694 VA by Catawba raiders, adopted daughter 1694 TN of **Trader Tom Carpenter (2)-Moytoy (2)**/1660 & her aunt **Nancy Turkey Cornstalk**/1664, could cipher, read & speak some English, wife 1st 1704 Chota TN of **Tsula Fox-Smallpox Conjurer**/1670, 2nd 1718 Chota TN of **Richard Barnes**/1695-white, children/1705-17 **with Fox-Conjurer** unknown, mother **with Barnes** of Mary Barnes/1720 & Charity Barnes/1726-both 31/64th ChalakathaShawano-Chalaka-Powhatan -Metis

SISTER

Turkey, Oolootah aka Oolootah Hop-Ulutse-Oolootsee-Oolootah Rainmaker-Wife of John Bowles – 63/64th Chalakatha-ShawanoChalaka-Powhatan born 1692 Chota TN-died after 1756 TN - daughter of **Big Turkey**/1660 & **Chalakatha Woman**/1664, parents killed 1694
VA by Catawba raiders, adopted daughter 1694 TN of **Rainmaker (1)**/1640 & **Quatsey (1)**/1650-both Cherokee, Blue Holly Clan Cherokee, lived with sister **Quatsis Turkey-Beamer** from 1699-1705, wife 1st 1705 Chota TN of **Blue Holly Cherokee**/1685-(also husband 1707 of her sister Ghigoneli), 2nd by 1722 Settico TN of **John Bowles**/1688-Scot, children/1706-21 **with Blue Holly** unknown, mother **with Bowles** of Ghigoneli Bowles/1723-9/16th ChalakathaShawano-Chalaka-Powhatan-Metis

SISTER

Turkey, Ghigoneli aka Ghigoneli Hop-Younger Sister of Old Hop-Ghigoneli Rainmaker - 63/64th Chalakatha-Shawano-ChalakaPowhatan born 1694 Chota TN-died 1724 Chota TN – daughter of **Big Turkey**/1660 & **Chalakatha Woman**/1664, parents killed 1694 VA by Catawba raiders, adopted daughter 1694 TN of **Rainmaker (1)**/1640 & **Quatsey (1)**/1650-both Cherokee, Blue Holly Clan Cherokee, wife 1st 1707 TN of **Blue Holly Cherokee**/1685-(also husband 1705 of her sister Oolootha/1692), 2nd by 1710 TN of **French-Canadian Mulatto**/1690-(or a Melungeon?), 3rd 1720 TN of **May Apple**/1690-Kishpoko, any children/1707-10 **with Blue Holly** unknown, mother **with Mulatto** of John French (French John)/1710 & Capt. French (Cappee)/1712- both 31/64th Chalakatha-Shawano-Chalaka-Powhatan-Black-Metis, **with May Apple** of Ninihica Mayapple/1721 & Laskigitchi Mayapple/1723both 63/64th Chalakatha-Kishpoko-Shawano-Chalaka-Powhatan

COUSINS OF STANDING TURKEY-OLD HOP

COUSIN BY HIS UNCLE LITTLE TURKEY/1662

Turkey, Katie – 63/64th Chalakatha-Shawano-Chalaka-Powhatan born

1684 Nickajack TN-died 1738 Great Tellico TN – daughter of **Little Turkey Cornstalk**/1662 & **Chalakatha Woman**/1666, Turkey Clan, a niece of **Big Turkey**/1660 & **Nancy Turkey**/1664, wife 1698 Nickajack TN of **Thomas Caesar-Skiagunsta Greenwood**/1680, could read, speak & cipher some English, mother of Thomas Sutichettchee Greenwood/1698, John Cheesquatalone Greenwood/1700, children/1701-11, daughters Quatsis Atawaya Greenwood/1712, Sedano Greenwood/1715, son Big Turkey Greenwood/1718, daughter Nancy Greenwood/1720, children/1723-28 & daughter Ankee Greenwood/1729-all 51/64th Chalakatha-Thawikila-KishpokoShawano-Chalaka-Powhatan-Black-Metis

COUSINS BY HIS AUNT NANCY TURKEY/1664

Carpenter, Savannah Tom (1) aka Thomas Carpenter (4)-Corn Planter (4)-**Moytoy (3)** – 23/32nd Chalakatha-Shawano-Chalaka-PowhatanMetis born 1680 Chota TN-died 1710 Oconee SC - son of **Nancy Turkey Cornstalk**/1664 & **Trader Tom Carpenter (2)-Moytoy (2)**/1660, from Chota & Running Water TN, associated with adopted brother (1st cousin) **Standing Turkey-Old Hop** & **Young Rainmaker**, taught to inherited Moytoy title from his father but died young-passing the title to his brother White Owl, cipher, read & write English by his father, husband 1st 1697 Upper Hiwassee VA of **Susan-Quatsey (2) Rainmaker**/1682-Cherokee, 2nd 1698 of her sister **Nancy Rainmaker**/1683-Cherokee, father **with Susan-Quatsey** of Savannah Tom Carpenter (2)-Corn Planter (5)/1698, **with Nancy** of Great Eagle Carpenter/1702, Elizabeth Tassel Carpenter/1704, Attakullakulla Carpenter/1706, Corn Tassel Carpenter/1708 & Susan Moytoy Carpenter/1710-all 23/64th Chalakatha-Shawano-Chalaka-Powhatan-Cherokee-Metis

Carpenter, White Owl (1) aka White Owl Raven- White Owl (1)**Caulanna**-Collanah-**Moytoy (4)** – 23/32nd Chalakatha-ShawanoChalaka-Powhatan-Metis born 1678 Running Water TN-**killed 1741TN** in battle – son of **Trader Tom Carpenter (2)-Moytoy (2)**/1660 & **Nancy Turkey Cornstalk**/1664, Long Hair Clan Cherokee, could cipher, read & write some English, delegation to ENG 1730, fourth of the Moytoy dynasty 1710-1741, leader of all 7 Cherokee Clans, killed in same battle as **Young Rainmaker**, husband 1st about 1698 (TN?) of **Unknown Woman**, 2nd 1711 TN of **Nancy Rainmaker**/1683-Cherokee, children/1698-1711 **with Unknown Woman** not known, father **with Nancy Rainmaker** of Killancea-Buck Carpenter/1712, Killaqua Carpenter/1714, Betsy-Eliza-Quatie Ooloocha Carpenter/1716, Tame Doe-Cati-Catherine Carpenter/1718, All Bones-Flying Squirrel Carpenter/1720, Oousta Carpenter/1722 & Bushy Head Carpenter/1724-all 1/4th Chalakatha-Shawano-Chalaka-PowhatanCherokee-Metis, **adopted father** 1710 with marriage to his brother's widow of Great Eagle Carpenter/1702, Elizabeth Tassel Carpenter/1704, Attakullakulla Carpenter/1706, (Old) Corn Tassel Carpenter/1708 & Susan Moytoy Carpenter/1710, adopted father 1715 of **Amoyah Pigeon Moytoy**/1715 (son of his sister **Pashmere Carpenter (2)**/1681)

Carpenter, Pashmere (2) – 23/32nd Chalakatha-Shawano-ChalakaPowhatan-Metis born 1682 Chota TN-died 1715 Upper Hiwassee VA – daughter of **Trader Tom Carpenter (2)-Moytoy (2)**/1660 & **Nancy Turkey Cornstalk**/1664, could speak, cipher, read & write some
English, wife 1705 Upper Hiwassee VA of her adopted brother **Raven Turkey-Moytoy**/1683, mother of Amoyah Pigeon Moytoy/1715-27/64th Chalakatha-Shawano-Chalaka-Powhatan-Metis

COUSIN BY HIS AUNT SISTER TURKEY/1664

Muskrat (2) aka Oshasqua (2)-**Moytoy (5)**-Ossaghqua-OshkesquaHotthashkwa - 63/64th Pekowi-Chalakatha-Shawano-ChalakaPowhatan born 1686 Hiwassee TN-died 1754 Hiwassee TN – son of
Muskrat-Oshasqua (1)/1660 & **Sister Turkey**/1666, parents killed 1698 VA-TN by Catawba, from the Straight Tail band, Turtle Clan, adopted son 1698 of **Trader Tom Carpenter (2)-Moytoy (2)**/1660 & aunt **Nancy Turkey Cornstalk**/1664, taught to read, speak & cipher in English by stepfather, husband 1704 TN of his adopted sister **Swan-Wapehti Turkey**/1686, father of daughters Ahneewakee Muskrat/1704,

Ounacona Muskrat/1716, Tame Deer Muskrat/1720, sons OshasquaMuskrat (3)/1718 & Bad Water Muskrat-Moytoy (6)/1722 & other unknown children/1705-31-all 63/64th Chalakatha-Pekowi-Shawano-Chalaka-Powhatan, **adopted father** 1708 of his nephew **John Forked Tail Watts**/1704

WIFE OF STANDING TURKEY-OLD HOP
WIFE 1708 RUNNING WATER TN

Rainmaker, Sugi – Cherokee born about 1690 Chota TN-died 1743 Chota TN – daughter of **Rainmaker (1)**/1640 & **Quatsey Cherokee**/1650, Wolf Clan Cherokee, wife by 1708 TN of **Old HopStanding Turkey**/1688, mother of sons Little Turkey-Young Standing Turkey/1709, Young Turkey-Young Hop/1715 & daughter Grasshopper Turkey/1725-all 31/64th Chalakatha-Shawano-ChalakaPowhatan-Cherokee , adopted mother 1723 of nephews **John French**/1710 & **Capt. French**/1712-both 31/64th Chalakatha-Shawano-Chalaka-Powhatan-Black-Metis

CHILDREN OF STANDING TURKEY-OLD HOP/1688 & SUGI RAINMAKER/1690

SON

Turkey, Little Turkey (1) aka Standing Turkey (2)–Kanagatoga (2)Kanitta-Gundigaduhnyi-Little Turkey Hop - 31/64th ChalakathaShawano-Chalaka-Powhatan-Cherokee born 1709 Chota TN-died 1804
OH - son of **Standing Turkey (1)-Old Hop**/1688 & **Sugi Rainmaker**/1690-Cherokee, Wolf Clan Cherokee, could cipher, read & speak some English, succeeded his father as titular **Principal Chief 1761** but actual authority-power was held by his cousins **Oconastota**/1702 & **Kitegista**/1710, supported the Shawnee in Pontiac War/1762-66, living **with Shawnee in TN** (i.e. the Chickamauga) 1764-92, sent warriors to Point Pleasant/1774, sent warriors raiding KY-VA-WV-OH/1775-81,

lost power among Cherokee 1775 with Cherokee War, among founders of the Chickamauga 1775, sent warriors raiding Ohio River valley/1788-92, a **Chickamauga Principal Chief** 1792-1801, moved to northern KY 1792, Treaty 1798, moved family-band to OH 1800, husband 1st about 1729 Chota TN of **Cherokee Woman**/1715, 2nd about
1755 TN of **Chalakatha Woman**/1740, 3rd 1764 TN of **Unknown Woman**-(when Chalakatha returned to OH-KY), children **with Cherokee** unknown, father **with Chalakatha** of Young Little TurkeyStanding Turkey (4)/1760 & Auquotaque Turkey/1762-both 49/64th Chalakatha-Shawano-Chalaka-Powhatan-Cherokee, children **with Unknown Woman** unknown-(but she raised Young Little Turkey)

SON

Turkey, Young aka Young Hopper-Oukahulah-Young Hop-Young Standing Turkey - 31/64th Chalakatha-Shawano-Chalaka-Powhatan - Cherokee born about 1715 Chota TN-died 1764 Chota TN - son of **Standing Turkey-Old Hop**/1688 & **Sugi Rainmaker**/1690-Cherokee, Wolf Clan Cherokee, could cipher, read & speak some English, proFrench faction in French-Indian War/1754-63, husband 1st 1738 Chota TN of **Ollie Nionee Oconastota**/1720- (apparent widow of Attakullakulla), 2nd 1745 Running Water TN of **Chalakatha Woman**/1730, father **with Ollie Nionee** of Badger/1738, Black Fox/1740, Little Owl/1742 & Sugi-Suki-Susannah/1744-all 31/64th Chalakatha-Thawikila-Shawano-Chalaka-Powhatan-Creek-Cherokee & **all adopted 1746 by Attakullakulla**, children/1745-64 **with Chalakatha** unknown

DAUGHTER

Turkey, Grasshopper aka Grasshopper Standing Turkey-Grasshopper Hop-Granny Hopper - 31/64th Chalakatha-Shawano-ChalakaPowhatan-Cherokee born 1725 Chota TN-died 1785 Chota TN - daughter of **Standing Turkey-Old Hop**/1688 & **Sugi Rainmaker**/1690Cherokee, could cipher, read & speak some English, Wolf Clan Cherokee, called "small & pretty" in her youth, wife 1st 1740 Chota TN of **Unknown Man**/1720, 2nd 1752 Chota TN of **William David McDaniel**/1720-SCO-(McDaniel disappears 1785-apparently returned to whites family/relatives in Ashe Co NC where he bought property 1787), children/1740-51 **with Unknown Man** unknown, mother **with McDaniel** of Catherine McDaniel/1753, Alexander McDaniel /1754, Lewis McDaniel /1756, John McDaniel /1758, Mary McDaniel/1760, Nancy McDaniel /1762, Elizabeth McDaniel /1763, Susannah McDaniel /1764, Rachel McDaniel /1766, William McDaniel Jr/1768-all 15/64th Chalakatha-Shawano-Chalaka-Powhatan-Cherokee-Metis

ADOPTED CHILDREN OF STANDING TURKEYOLD HOP/1688

ADOPTED SON

French, John aka Jean French-French John Hop-Nephew of Old Hopadopted son of Old Hop – 31/64th Chalakatha-Shawano-ChalakaPowhatan-Black-Metis born 1710 Chota TN-died after 1775 - son of **Ghigoneli Turkey**/1694 & **French-Canadian Mulatto**/1690-(or a Melungeon-some sort of dark-skinned guy), adopted son 1720 TN of his uncle **Standing Turkey-Old Hop**, from the Overhills, could speak, cipher, read & write English & French, allied with **Savannah Tom Carpenter (2)**/1698, brother **Capt. French**/1712, **John Lantaniak**/1720, **Rainmaker (3)**/1706, **Muskrat (2)**/1718 & **Robert-Thigh-Cauquillehanah-McLemore**/1731 in pro-French faction during FrenchIndian War/1754-63, from the Overhills, a chief French agent at Ft. Toulouse AL & Chota TN in French-Indian War/1754-63, Cornstalk War/1755-74, Chickamauga faction in the Cherokee War/1775, halfbrother of **Ninihica Mayapple**/1721 & **Laskigitchi Mayapple**/1723, mistakenly identified as a slave by British of the time due to his dark skin, husband 1st 1730 Running Water TN of **Chalakatha Woman**/1715, 2nd 1759 Chota TN of **Cherokee Woman**/1744, children unknown

ADOPTED SON

French, Capt. aka Cappee French-Cappee Hop-Nephew of Old Hopadopted son of Old Hop – 31/64th Chalakatha-Shawano-

ChalakaPowhatan-Black-Metis born 1712 Chota TN-died after 1775 Tomatley NC – son of **Ghigoneli Turkey**/1694 & **French-Canadian Mulatto**/1690-(or Melungeon), brother of **John French**/1710, halfbrother of **Ninihica Mayapple**/1721 & **Laskigitchi Mayapple**/1723, adopted son 1720 TN of his uncle **Old Hop**/1688-Chalakatha & **Sugi Rainmaker**/1690-Cherokee, from Chota TN & Tomatley NC, allied with **Savannah Tom Carpenter (2)**/1698, **John Lantaniak**/1720, brother **John French**/1710, **Rainmaker (3)**/1706, **Muskrat (2)**/1718 & **Robert-Thigh-Cauquillehaneh McLemore**/1731 in pro-French faction during French-Indian War/1754-63, Cornstalk War/1755-74, could speak, cipher, read & write English & French, delegation to English **with Attakullakulla**, Cherokee faction in Cherokee War/1775, Treaty Sycamore Shoals 1775, mistakenly identified as a slave by British of the time due to his dark skin, husband 1st 1732 Running Water TN of **Chalakatha Woman**/1717, 2nd 1759 Chota TN of **Cherokee Woman**/1744, father **with Chalakatha** of Choosahete French/1737, Margaret Elizabeth French/1739-(wife 1755 of **Alexander Drumgoole (2)**/36), Black Skin French/1741, Catherine French/1748-(wife 1765 of **John Cherokee Vann**/1744), Susan-Sugi French/1755-(wife 1770 of **Capt. Will Emory**/1744)-all 49/64th Chalakatha-Shawano-Chalaka-Powhatan--Black-Metis, children **with Cherokee** unknown

NEPHEWS & NIECES OF STANDING TURKEY/1688

BY BROTHER RAVEN MOYTOY/1680 & PASHMERE CARPENTER/1681

NEPHEW

Moytoy, Amoyah Pigeon (1) aka **Amoyah Pigeon (1)**-Amoyah Moytoy (1)-Amoyah Turkey – 27/64th Chalakatha-Shawano-Chalaka-PowhatanMetis born 1715 Great Tellico TN-**killed** 1774 Point Pleasant WV in battle – son of **Raven Turkey-Moytoy**/1680 & **Pashmere Carpenter (2)**/1681, adopted son of **White Owl Carpenter**/1768 & **Nancy Rainmaker**/1683 upon death of his mother in childbirth, could cipher, read & speak some English, pro-French faction in French-Indian War/1754-63, Cornstalk War/1755-74, living in south OH after 1763, killed at Point Pleasant/1774, husband 1st 1735 TN of **Kishpoko Woman**/1720-Blind Savannah Cherokee, 2nd 1742 Nickajack TN of **Puki-Pequea Greenwood**/1724, father **with Kishpoko** of Amoyah Pigeon Moytoy (2)/1736-31/32nd Chalakatha-Kishpoko-ShawanoChalaka-Powhatan-Metis, **with Greenwood** of Katie-Naky Pigeon Moytoy/1745, Jane-Pugi Pigeon Moytoy/1748 & Jenny-Sula Pigeon Moytoy/1750-all 39/64th Chalakatha-Thawikila-Kishpoko-MekocheShawano-Chalaka-Powhatan-Black-Metis

BY BROTHER RAVEN MOYTOY/1680 & AHNEEWAKEE MUSKRAT/1704

NEPHEW

Moytoy, Bushyhead Chiesatebe aka **Bushy Head**-Bushyhead RavenBushyhead Hop-Bushyhead Greenwood-Bushyhead Turkey 63/64th Chalakatha-Pekowi-Shawano-Chalaiwa-Powhatan born 1718 Nickajack TN-died 1760 Nickajack TN - son of **Ahneewakee Muskrat**/1704 & **Raven Hop**/1680, adopted son of **John Cheesquatalone Greenwood**/1703, Blind Savannah Clan Cherokee, could cipher, read & speak English, husband 1st 1739 Great Tellico TN of **Oousta Carpenter**/1722, 2nd 1743 Great Tellico TN of **Nancy Greenwood**/1720, father **with Carpenter** of Tahnoyanteehee/1741 & Tahlonteeskee/1743both 21/32nd Chalakatha-Shawano-Chalaka-Powhatan-Cherokee-Metis , father **with Greenwood** of Posetha-Posie Greenwood/1749-31/32nd Chalakatha-Pekowi-Kishpoko-Black-Metis

NEPHEW

Moytoy, Savanooka (1) aka Savanooka Hop-Raven-Savanooka Raven-Shawnee-Raven of Chota-Little Raven-Young Raven-ColinnaSawanookee-Raven Colonah-Savanuka-Savanooka Turkey – 63/64th Chalakatha-Pekowi-Shawano-Chalaka-Powhatan born 1720 Chota TNdied after 1792 Great Tellico TN - son of **Ahneewakee Muskrat**/1704 & **Raven Moytoy**/1680, adopted son 1729 TN of **John Cheesquatalone Greenwood**/1703, Blind Savannah Clan Cherokee, reputed to have been the strongest man in the Cherokee territory &

unbeaten in wrestling, from the Overhills, Settico & Chota, a leader of the Great Tellico faction, nephew & advisor to **Oconastota Rainmaker**/1702, on the council of his cousin **Johnny Kitegista**/1735 of Tenase, pro-French faction in French-Indian War/1754-63, Cornstalk War/1755-74, Chickamauga faction at start of the Cherokee War/1775, Treaty Sycamore Shoals 1775, raiding whites in TN 1776 with **Dragging Canoe & Abram**, raiding Carter's valley-Hawkins Co TN 1776, sends **Nathaniel Gist** to plead for peace after the raids 1776, Lower Cherokee(i.e. those Natives from the Savannah River -Shawnee & Shawnee mixed bloods) flee over the mountains to join those in the Overhills, Head Man for the Overhills Cherokee-Oconastota, Attakullakulla, Ostenaca as advisors 1776, Treaty Long Island 1777, by 1778 **broke with Dragging Canoe** & Chickamauga & representing the Cherokee among the Overhills, Council with British 1779 with **Col. Alexander McKee**/1725-Irish, **William Caldwell**/1750Irish, **Matthew Elliott**/1730-Irish, **Simon Surphet**-Irish, **Simon Girty**/1741, **George Girty**/1746 & **James Girty**/1743, **Wryneck**/1725Pekowi, **Weed**/1750-Iroquois-Mingo & **River Bottom**/1750-Seneca-Mingo, raiding KY-VA-OH/1777-81, husband 1748 Chota TN of **Cheekee Greenwood**/1728, father with **Cheekee** of Savenooka Moytoy (2)/1750 & Skootekitehi-Fire Heart Moytoy/1752-both 59/64th Chalakatha-Pekowi-Thawikila-Kishpoko-Mekoche-Shawano-Chalaka-Powhatan-Black-Metis

NEPHEW

Moytoy, Gooshsohly aka Go Slowly-Gooshsohly Raven-Gooshsohly Moytoy-Golalu-Gooshsohly Turkey-Gooshsohly Hop – 63/64th Chalakatha-Pekowi-Shawano-Chalaka-Powhatan born 1722 Nickajack TN-**killed** 1755 Ft. Pitt PA - son of **Raven Moytoy**/1680 & **Ahneewakee Muskrat**/1704, adopted son 1729 TN of **John Cheesquatalone Greenwood**/1703, Blind Savannah Clan Cherokee, pro-French faction in French-Indian War/1754-55, captured by British near Ft. Pitt 1755 & executed, husband 1745 Nickajack TN of **Wolf Clan Woman**/1730Cherokee, children/1745-55 unknown

NIECE

Moytoy, Elizabeth aka Raven's Sister-Savanooka's Sister-Elizabeth Raven-Elizabeth Greenwood-Elizabeth Turkey-Elizabeth Hop – 63/64th Chalakatha-Pekowi-Shawano-Chalaka-Powhatan born 1724 Nickajack TN-died 1819 Nickajack TN - daughter of **Ahneewakee Muskrat**/1704 & **Raven Moytoy**/1680, adopted daughter 1729 TN of **John Cheesquatalone Greenwood**/1703, Blind Savannah Clan Cherokee, wife 1st 1739 Nickajack TN of **Bernard Hughes**/1719, 2nd 1744 Running Water TN of **John Trader Vann (2)**/1715, 3rd 1749 Nickajack TN of **David Rowe**/1720, mother **with Hughes** of James Hughes/1739, Charles Hughes/1741 & Sarah Hughes/1743-all 9/16th Chalakatha-Pekowi-Shawano-Chalaka-Powhatan-Metis, **with Vann** of John Cherokee Vann/1744, Polly–Wawli Vann/1746 & Elizabeth-Quedi Vann/1748-all 9/16th Chalakatha-Pekowi-Shawano-Chalaka-Powhatan-Cherokee-Metis, **with Rowe** of Richard Rowe (1)/1750, David Rowe Jr/1752 & Archibald Rowe (1)/1754-all 35/64th Chalakatha-PekowiShawano-Chalaka-Powhatan-Thawikila-Creek-Metis

NIECE

Moytoy, Nancy Augustus aka Nancy Augustus Hop-Kahtayah-Nancy Augustus Raven-Nancy Turkey – 63/64th Chalakatha-PekowiShawano-Chalaka-Powhatan born 1726 Nickajack TN-**killed** 1794 Lower Towns TN - daughter of **Raven Moytoy**/1680 & **Ahneewakee Muskrat**/1704, adopted daughter 1729 TN of **John Cheesquatalone Greenwood**/1703, Blind Savannah Clan Cherokee, killed in Major Orr's raids, wife 1st 1743 Great Tellico TN of **John Foreman (1)**/1720-white, 2nd by 1746 TN (of her uncle-son of her mother's aunt) **Bushyhead Chicsatihi Carpenter**/1724, 3rd 1757 Great Tellico TN of **Alexander Drumgoole (2)**/1736, 4th 1759 TN of **Richard "Texas Dick" Fields Sr**/1730-white, mother **with Foreman** of John Anthony Foreman (2)/1744 & Mary Foreman/1746-both 9/16th Chalakatha-Pekowi-Shawano-Chalaka-Powhatan-Metis, mother **with Bushyhead** of Bushyhead Chicsatihi Carpenter (2)/1750-21/32nd Chalakatha-PekowiShawano-Chalaka-Powhatan-Cherokee-Metis, **with Drumgoole** of
Chenelernkee Drumgoole/1758- 19/32nd Chalakatha-Pekowi-Shawano-Chalaka-Powhatan-Cherokee Metis, **with Fields** of Jack Fields

(1)/1760, Sarah Fields/1762, Thomas Fields/1764 & Susannah Fields/1766-all 9/16th Chalakatha-Pekowi-Shawano-ChalakaPowhatan-Metis (also raised **Fields'** Long Hair Clan children by **Susannah Emory**/1747)

NEPHEW

Moytoy, Amahetai aka Amahetai Raven-Amahetai Hop-Amahetai Greenwood-**Moytoy (7)** -**Muskrat (3)**-Raven of Hiawassee (2)-Mankiller of Hiawassee-Rain Conjurer-Colinna-King of the Valley-Amahetai Turkey – 63/64th Chalakatha-Pekowi-Shawano-Chalaka-Powhatan born 1728 Chota TN-died after 1775 Little Hiwassee TN - son of **Ahneewakee Muskrat**/1704 & **Raven Moytoy**/1680, adopted son 1729 TN of **John Cheesquatalone Greenwood**/1703, Blind Savannah Clan Cherokee, from the Overhills & Hiawassee, pro-French faction in French-Indian War/1754-63, raiding New-Jackson-Greenbrier River valleys/1763, Pontiac War/1762-66, Cherokee faction in Cherokee War/1775, Treaty Sycamore Shoals 1775, nephew of **Old Hop**/1688, 2nd cousin of **Attakullakulla Carpenter**/1706, husband 1748 Chota TN of **Wolf Clan Woman**/1735-Cherokee, children unknown

BY SISTER QUATSIS TURKEY/1682 & JOHN BEAMER/1676

NIECE

Beamer, Ooloosta – 31/64th Chalakatha-Shawano-Chalaka-PowhatanMetis born 1698 Chota TN-died 1728 Chota TN – daughter of **Quatsis Turkey**/1682 & **John Beamer**/1676-ENG, wife 1714 Chota TN of **John Bowles (1)**/1688-SCO, no clear record of children/1715-28

NEPHEW

Beamer, John (2) – 31/64th Chalakatha-Shawano-Chalaka-Powhatan-Metis born 1701 Chota TN-died 1734 Chota TN - son of **Quatsis Turkey**/1682 & **John Beamer**/1676-ENG, husband 1720 Chota TN of **Susan Bowles**/1705-Cherokee-Metis, children/1720-34 unknown

NIECE

Beamer, Peggy – 31/64th Chalakatha-Shawano-Chalaka-PowhatanMetis born 1702 Chota TN-died 1759 Chota TN – daughter of **Quatsis Turkey**/1682 & **John Beamer (1)**/1676-ENG, wife 1723 Chota TN of **John Holmes**/1700-SCO, mother of Martha Holmes/1750 & other children/1723-49-all 1/4th Chalakatha-Shawano-Chalaka-PowhatanMetis

NIECE

Beamer, Nionee – 31/64th Chalakatha-Shawano-Chalaka-PowhatanMetis born 1704 Chota TN-died 1728 Chota TN – daughter of **Quatsis Turkey**/1682 & **John Beamer**/1700-SCO, wife 1723 Chota TN of **John Drowning Bear Brown (1)**/1700-adopted white, mother of John Drowning Bear Brown (2)/1724 & Samuel Brown/1726-both 1/4th Chalakatha-Shawano-Chalaka-Powhatan-Metis

BY SISTER QUATSIS TURKEY/1682 & TSULA FOX-SMALLPOX CONJURER/1670

NEPHEW

Fox, Rising Fawn (1) aka **Rising Fawn (1)**-Rising Fawn Conjurer (1) – 31/64th Chalakatha-Shawano-Chalaka-Powhatan-Cherokee born 1706 Settico TN-died 1751 Settico TN – son of **Tsula Fox-Smallpox Conjurer**/1670-Cherokee & **Quatsis Turkey**/1682, a **Headman from Settico**, husband 1st 1726 of **Ooloosta Rainmaker**/1710, 2nd 1738 of **Ghigoneli Bowles**/1723, father **with Rainmaker** of Rising Fawn Fox (2)/1726 & others/1728-38-all 31/64th Chalakatha-Shawano-ChalakaPowhatan-Cherokee, father **with Bowles** of Rising Fawn Fox (3)/1740-
33/64th Chalakatha-Shawano-Chalaka-Powhatan-Cherokee-Metis

NIECE

Fox, Quatsis aka Quatsis Smallpox Conjurer-**Daughter of Quatsis Hop**Niece of Standing Turkey-Old Hop's Niece -31/64th

ChalakathaShawano-Chalaka-Powhatan-Cherokee born 1708 Settico TN-died after
1760 - daughter of **Quatsis Turkey**/1682 & **Tsula Fox-Smallpox Conjurer**/1670-Cherokee, wife 1st 1724 Settico TN of **John Fork Tail Watts**/1704 (left Watts 1735 when she remarried), 2nd (his 2nd of 3) 1735 Chota TN of 1st cousin **Oconastota Rainmaker**/1702 (left Oconastota 1738 when he married **Lucy Ward (1)**/1714-white) 3rd 1738 Running Water TN of **John Drowning Bear Brown (1)**/1700-adopted white, mother **with Watts** of Terrapin Watts/1726, Bark Watts/1728 & children/1729-34-all 47/64th Chalakatha-Pekowi-Shawano-ChalakaPowhatan-Cherokee-Metis, **with Oconastota** of Quatsis Oconastota/1736-31/64th Chalakatha-Shawano-Chalaka-PowhatanCherokee, **with Brown** of Alexander Brown/1738, children/1739-46,
Mary Brown/1747, Robert Brown/1749 & John Drowning Bear Brown (3)-Junaluska (1)/1751-all 15/64th Chalakatha-Shawano-Chalaka-Powhatan-Cherokee-Metis

BY SISTER QUATSIS HOP/1682 & WILLIAM WEBBER/1680

NIECE

Webber, Catherine – 31/64th Chalakatha-Shawano-Chalaka-Powhatan-Metis born 1710 Chota TN-died after 1760 Keowee TN – daughter of **Quatsis Turkey**/1684 & **William Webber (1)**/1680-ENG, wife 1725 Running Water TN of **May Apple**/1690-Kishpoko, **adopted mother** 1725 of **Ninihica Mayapple**/1721 & **Laskigitchi Mayapple**/1723-(sons of May Apple & Ghigoneli Hop) & **adopted mother** 1751 of nephew **William Webber (3)-Capt. Will**/1740

NEPHEW

Webber, William (2) – 31/64th Chalakatha-Shawano-ChalakaPowhatan-Metis born 1712 Chota TN-died 1751 Chota TN – son of **Quatsis Turkey**/1684-Chalakatha & **William Webber (1)**/1680-ENG, husband 1st 1732 of **Unknown Woman**/1727, 2nd 1738 of **Lucy Ward (3)**/1725-1/2 Kishpoko-Metis, children/1732-38 **with Unknown Woman** unknown, father **with Ward** of William Webber (3)-Capt. Will/1740-1/2 Chalakatha-Kishpoko-Shawano-Chalaka-PowhatanMetis

BY SISTER AGANUNITSI TURKEY/1684 & YOUNG RAINMAKER/1685

NEPHEW

Rainmaker, Oconastota aka **Oconastota**-Aganstata-Groundhog Sausage-Aganustata-Pounding Meat in a Mortar-Cunne Shoate - 31/64th Chalakatha-Shawano-Chalaka-Powhatan-Cherokee born 1702 Chota TN-died 1783 - son of **Aganunitsi Turkey**/1684 & **Young Rainmaker**/1685-Cherokee, named as a grandson of **Rainmaker (1)**/1640, Blind Savannah Clan Cherokee, delegation to ENG 1730, proBritish faction (against French & Shawnee) in French-Indian War/175463, **Principal Man of Chota** after death of uncle **Old Hop** in 1761, shared power/authority as **Cherokee Chief** 1761-75, with his brother **Kitegista** Rainmaker/1710, Pontiac War/1762-66, Cherokee faction in
Cherokee War/1775, Treaty Sycamore Shoals 1775, **Principle Chief** of Cherokee 1775-80, husband 1st 1718 Chota TN of **Ahneewakee (Anuwagi-Aniwadi) Red Paint**/1704-1/2 Thawikila-Creek, 2nd 1735 Chota TN of 1st cousin **Quatsis Fox**/1708, 3rd 1738 Chota TN of **Lucy Ward (1)**/1714-adopted-white, father **with Red Paint** of Ostenaca Oconastota/1718, Ollie Nionee Oconastota/1720, Shallelocke Oconastota/1722, Jennie Oconastota/1724 & Terrapin Oconastota (1)/1726-all 15/32nd Chalakatha-Shawano-Chalaka-Powhatan-CreekCherokee, **with Fox** of Quatsis Oconastota/1736-31/64th Chalakatha-Shawano-Chalaka-Powhatan-Cherokee, **adopted father of** her sons **Terrapin Watts-Terrapin (2)**/1726 & **Bark Watts**/1728-both 47/64th Chalakatha-Pekowi-Shawano-Chalaka-Powhatan-Cherokee-Metis, **with Ward** of Lucy Ward Oconastota/1742-15/32nd Chalakatha-Shawano-Chalaka-Powhatan-Cherokee

NEPHEW

Rainmaker, Cloggoittah - 31/64th Chalakatha-Shawano-ChalakaPowhatan-Cherokee born about 1706 Great Tellico TN-died after 1741 Tenase TN - son of **Young Rainmaker**/1680-Cherokee & **Aganunitsi**

Turkey/1684, delegation to ENG 1730, named as a grandson of **Rainmaker (1)**/1640, Blind Savannah Clan, from Tenase TN, wife & children unknown

NIECE

Rainmaker, **Ooloosta** aka Oolootah - 31/64th Chalakatha-ShawanoChalaka-Powhatan-Cherokee born 1708-died after 1739 - daughter of **Young Rainmaker**/1680-Cherokee & **Aganunitsi Turkey**/1684, namesake of aunt **Oolootah Turkey**/1692, named as a granddaughter of **Rainmaker (1)**/1640, Blind Savannah Clan Cherokee, wife 1st 1726 TN of **Rising Fawn Fox (1)**/1706, 2nd by 1738 TN of **Christian Priber**/1697-white, mother with **Rising Fawn (1)** of Rising Fawn Fox (2)/1726 & other children/1728-38-all 31/64th Chalakatha-ShawanoChalaka-Powhatan-Cherokee, mother **with Priber** of Great PriberDrags Blanket/1739-15/32nd Chalakatha-Shawano-Chalaka-Powhatan-Cherokee-Metis

NEPHEW

Rainmaker, **Kitegista** aka Kittegunsta-**Skalilosken**-Shallelocke-Prince of Chota-Speaker-Nephew of Old Hop - 31/64th Chalakatha-Shawano-ChalakaPowhatan-Cherokee born 1710 Chota TN-**killed** 1792 Buchanan Station TN - son of **Aganunitsi Turkey**/1684 & **Young Rainmaker**/1680-Cherokee, (mistakenly **rumored to be son of his aunt Quatsey Rainmaker (2)**/1682Cherokee & **John Beamer**/1676-white =1/2 Cherokee-Metis but is referred to as a **nephew of Old Hop**), named as a grandson of **Rainmaker (1)**/1640, from the Overhills-Middle towns & Chota, Blind Savannah Clan Cherokee, delegation to ENG 1730, shared power/authority with his brother **Oconastota** after death of **Old Hop** in 1761, Council with **Attakullakulla** & British, Chickamauga faction in Cherokee War/1775, a Chickamauga with **Dragging Canoe**/1775-92, delegation to Philadelphia 1791, Council Coyatee 1792, **killed at Buchanan Station 1792 with sons Young Kitegista** & **Kiachatalee**, husband 1st 1728 Chota TN of **Betty Turnbridge**/1710-(white?), 2nd 1735 Chota TN of **Cherokee Woman**/1720, father with **Turnbridge** of Kiachatalee

Kitegista-Rainmaker/1735-15/32nd Chalakatha-Shawano-Chalaiwa-PowhatanCherokee-Metis, **with Cherokee** of Johnny (of Tenase) Kitegista/1736, Young
Kitegista/1737, Betty Kitegista/1738-all 15/32nd Chalakatha-ShawanoChalaka-Powhatan-Cherokee

NEPHEW

Rainmaker, Tathtowe aka Tiftowee-Teptoa - 31/64th Chalakatha-Shawano-Chalaka-Powhatan-Cherokee born about 1712 TN-died after 1761 - son of **Aganunitsi Turkey**/1684 & **Young Rainmaker**/1680-Cherokee, from Hiwassee TN, named as a grandson of **Rainmaker (1)**/1640, Blind Savannah Clan Cherokee, delegation to ENG 1730, pro-French faction in the FrenchIndian War/1754-61, husband 1732 TN of **Cherokee Woman**/1716, father of
Skiarow Rainmaker/1733 & Georgera Rainmaker/1735-both 15/32nd Chalakatha-Shawano-Chalaka-Powhatan-Cherokee

NEPHEW

Rainmaker, Gray Eagle aka Wallenawoa - 31/64th Chalakatha-ShawanoChalaka-Powhatan-Cherokee born about 1714 TN-died after 1741 - son of **Young Rainmaker**/1680-Cherokee & **Aganunitsi Turkey**/1684, named as a grandson of **Rainmaker (1)**/1640, Blind Savannah Clan Cherokee, wife & children unknown

NEPHEW

Rainmaker, Oukahoukah aka **Rainmaker (4)** - 31/64th Chalakatha-ShawanoChalaka-Powhatan-Cherokee born 1722 TN-died after 1742 - son of **Aganunitsi Turkey**/1684 & **Young Rainmaker**/1680-Cherokee, named as a grandson of **Rainmaker (1)**/1640, Blind Savannah Clan Cherokee, wife & children unknown

NEPHEW

Rainmaker, Kallannah - 31/64th Chalakatha-Shawano-Chalaka-PowhatanCherokee born about 1718-died after 1745 - son of **Aganunitsi Turkey**/1684
& **Young Rainmaker**/1680-Cherokee, named as a grandson of **Rainmaker (1)**/1640, Blind Savannah Clan Cherokee, wife & children unknown

BY SISTER SWAN-WAPEHTI HOP/1686 & OSHASQUA MUSKRAT/1686

NIECE

Muskrat, Ahneewakee aka **Ahneewakee Moytoy**-Anuwagi – 63/64th Chalakatha-Pekowi-Shawano-Chalaka-Powhatan born 1704 Chota TNdied 1744 Chota TN - daughter of **Oshasqua (1)-Muskrat (1)-Moytoy (5)** & **Swan-Wapehti Turkey**/1686, Blind Savannah Clan Cherokee, read, spoke & ciphered in English, wife 1st 1718 Chota TN of her uncle **Raven Turkey**-Raven of Hiwassee-**Raven Moytoy**/1680, 2nd 1727 Chota TN of **John Cheesquatalone Greenwood**/1703, 3rd 1739 Chota TN of **Cornelius Dougherty**/1700, mother **with Raven Moytoy** of Bushyhead Chiesatebe Moytoy/1718, Savanooka Moytoy/1720, Goohsohly Moytoy/1722, Elizabeth-Raven's Sister Moytoy/1724, Nancy Augustus Moytoy/1726 & Amahetai Muskrat (3)-Moytoy (7)/1728-all 63/64th Chalakatha-Pekowi-Shawano-Chalaka-Powhatan, **with Greenwood** of John Sour Mush Greenwood/1730, Skienah-Hawk (GreenwoodMoytoy)/1732, Preachy (Greenwood-Moytoy/1734, Skiarow (Greenwood-Moytoy)/1736, Cheekee Greenwood (2)/1737 & Ground Squirrel-Skiuka (Greenwood-Moytoy)/1738-all 27/32nd ChalakathaPekowi-Thawikila-Kishpoko-Shawano-Chalaka-Powhatan-Black-Metis, adopted mother 1736 of **Amoyah Pigeon Hop**/1736, mother **with Dougherty** of Jennie Dougherty/1740, James Dougherty/1742, John Dougherty/1744-all 9/16th Chalakatha-Pekowi-Shawano-Chalaka-Powhatan-Cherokee-Metis

NIECE

Muskrat, Ounaconoa aka Ounacona Moytoy – 63/64th ChalakathaPekowi-Shawano-Chalaka-Powhatan born 1716 Chota TN-died after 1757 OH - daughter of **Swan-Wapehti Turkey**/1686 & **Oshasqua (1)Muskrat (1)-Moytoy (5)**/1686, could cipher, read & speak some English, Blind Savannah Clan Cherokee, wife 1734 Chota TN of **Keightughqua Cornstalk**/1710, mother of Black Beard/1735, Black

Wolf/1740, John Wolf/1750, Peter Cornstalk/1755, Susan Cornstalk/1757 & likely unknown daughters/1734-57-all 59/64th Chalakatha-Pekowi-Mekoche-Shawano-Chalaka-Powhatan-Metis

NIECE

Muskrat, Tame Deer aka Nanih-**Tame Deer Moytoy** - 63/64th Chalakatha-Pekowi-Shawano-Chalaka-Powhatan born 1720 Chota TN died after 1760 Cheowee NC - daughter of **Wapehti-Swan Turkey**/1686 & **Oshasqua-Muskrat-Moytoy (5)/1686**, Blind Savannah Clan Cherokee, could cipher, read & speak some English, Treaty Sycamore Shoals 1775, wife 1735 TN of **All Bones White Owl Carpenter**/1720, mother of All Bones Carpenter (2)/1750-39/64th Chalakatha-Pekowi-Shawano-Chalaka-Powhatan-Cherokee-Metis

NEPHEW

Moytoy, Bad Water aka **Moytoy (6)**-Bad Water Muskrat (1)**Amoscossite**-Dreadful Water-Young Emperor-Tacite of Euphasse-Emperor of Tellico-Mankiller of Hiwassee – 63/64th Chalakatha-Pekowi-Shawano-Chalaka-Powhatan born 1722 Chota TN-**killed** 1758 WV while raiding New River valley - son of **Swan-Wapehti Turkey**/1686 & **Muskrat (1)-Moytoy (5)**/1686, could cipher, read & speak some English, Blind Savannah Clan Cherokee, **appointed Emperor of the Cherokee 1741 by the British** but depended on the Council of his brothers, uncles & great-uncles, rejected the British & joined the pro-French faction in French-Indian War/1754-58, raiding New-Shenandoah River valleys/1755, raiding Ohio-New River valleys/1758, husband 1742 Chota TN of **Long Hair Woman**/1726, father of Bad Water Moytoy (2) -Amoscossite (2)/1748-9/16th Chalakatha-Pekowi-Shawano-Chalaka-Powhatan-Cherokee

ADOPTED NEPHEW

Watts, John Forked Tail aka John Watts (2)--John Watts Sr-Little Tassel-Old Forked Tongue – 55/64th Chalakatha-Pekowi-Shawano-Chalaka-Powhatan-Metis born 1704 VA-died 1779 Great Tellico TN – son of **Thomas Tassel Watts (2)/1682** & **Sister of Oshasqua-Muskrat (2)/1684**, adopted son 1708 TN-VA of **Swan-Wapehti Turkey**/1686 & his uncle **Oshasqua-Muskrat (2)-Moytoy (5)**/1686 when his family was killed by

Catawba, could speak, cipher, read & write English, Cornstalk War/1755-69, **associated with John Swift** silver-mining & counterfeiting/61-69, associated with **Cornstalk, Dragging Canoe, Doublehead, Nathaniel Gist, Sam Blackburn, Abram Flint, Herman Staley, Isaac Campbell, Shadrack Jefferson, Pierre St. Martin, Andrew Renound, Jeremiah Bates, Alexander Bartel, Henry Hazlitt & Moses Fletcher** on the frontier, husband 1st 1724 Settico TN of **Quatsis Fox**/1708, 2nd 1728 (officially in 1735) of **White Woman**/1712, 3rd 1743 Great Tellico TN of **Oousta Carpenter**/1722, 4th 1747 Running Water TN of **Ghigoneli Bowles**/1723, father with **Fox** of Son/1724, Terrapin Watts/1726, Bark Watts/1728 & other children/1724-35-all 47/64th Chalakatha-Pekowi-Shawano-Chalaka-Powhatan-Cherokee-Metis, father with **White Woman** of John Watts (3)-John Watt's Son-John Watson/1728 & other children/1729-43-all 27/64th Chalakatha-Pekowi-Shawano-Chalaka-Powhatan-Metis, father **with Carpenter** of Wurteh Watts/1744, John Watts Jr-Young Tassel-John Watts (3)/1746, Jacob Watts/1748, Elizabeth Watts/1750 & Unacata-White Mankiller Watts/1752-all 19/32nd Chalakatha-Pekowi-Shawano-ChalakaPowhatan-Cherokee-Metis, **with Bowles** of Nancy Watts/1748, Ghigoneli Watts-Ghigoneli Bowles (2)/1750 & John Watts (4)-John Bowles-Chief Bowl/1756-all 45/64th Chalakatha-Pekowi-ShawanoChalaka-Powhatan-Metis

BY SISTER APRIL-TKIKAMI TURKEY/1690 & RICHARD BARNES/1695

NIECE

Barnes, Mary – 9/16th Chalakatha-Shawano-Chalaka-Powhatan -Metis born 1720 Chota TN-died 1744 Davidson Co. NC (TN) - daughter of **April-Tkikami Turkey**/1690 & **Richard Barnes**/1695-white, wife 1738 (TN?) of **Edward Vann**/1720-1/2 Cherokee-Metis, mother of Joseph Vann/1738, Jennie Vann/1740, James Vann/1742 & Edward Ned Vann/1744-all 9/32nd Chalakatha-Shawano-Chalaka-PowhatanCherokee-Metis

NIECE

Barnes, Charity - 9/16th Chalakatha-Shawano-Chalaka-Powhatan Metis born 1726 Chota TN-died 1788 Cherokee Nation East - daughter of **April-Tkikami Turkey**/1690 & **Richard Barnes**/1695-white, 2nd wife 1744(TN?) of **Edward Vann**/1720-1/2 Cherokee-Metis, mother of Clement Vann/1744, Thomas Vann/1746, Avery Vann/1748, Edith Vann/1750, Susanna Vann/1752-all 9/32nd Chalakatha-Shawano-Chalaka-Powhatan-Cherokee-Metis

BY SISTER OOLOOTAH TURKEY/1692 & JOHN BOWLES/1688

NIECE

Bowles, Ghigoneli aka Chekawnahler-Forget Me Not - 9/16th Chalakatha-Shawano-Chalaka-Powhatan-Metis born 1723 Settico TNdied 1760 TN of smallpox - daughter of **Oolootah Turkey**/1692 & **John Bowles (1)**/1688-Scot, Blue Holly Clan Cherokee, niece of **Old Hop**/1688, namesake of mother's deceased younger sister, wife 1st 1738 Settico TN of **Rising Fawn Fox (1)**/1706, 2nd 1747 Running Water TN of **John Forked Tail Watts**/1704, mother **with Rising Fawn** of Rising Fawn (2)/1740-33/64th Chalakatha-Shawano-Chalaka-PowhatanCherokee-Metis, **with Watts** of Nancy Watts/1748, Ghigoneli Watts/1752 & John Watts (4)-**Chief Bowl**-John Bowles (2)/1756-all 45/64th Chalakatha-Pekowi-Shawano-Chalaka-Powhatan-Metis

BY SISTER GHIGONELI TURKEY/1694 & FRENCH-CANADIAN MULATTO/1690

NEPHEW

French, John aka Jean French-French John Hop-Nephew of Old Hopadopted son of Old Hop – 9/16th Chalakatha-Shawano-ChalakaPowhatan-Black-Metis born 1710 Chota TN-died after 1775 - son of **Ghigoneli Turkey**/1694 & **French-Canadian Mulatto**/1690-(or a Melungeon-some sort of dark-skinned, French-speaking guy), adopted son 1720 TN of his uncle **Old Hop**/1688, from the Overhills, could speak, read & write English & French, allied with **Savannah Tom Carpenter (2)/1698**, brother **Cappee Hop/1712, John Lantaniak/1720, Rainmaker (3)/1706, Muskrat (2)/1718 & Robert-Thigh-Cauquillehanah-McLemore/1731** in pro-French faction during FrenchIndian War/54-63, a chief French agent at Ft. Toulouse AL & Chota TN in French-Indian War/1754-63, Cornstalk War/1755-74, Chickamauga faction in Cherokee War/1775, half-brother of **Ninihica Mayapple/1721 & Laskigitchi Mayapple/1723**, mistakenly identified as a slave by British of the time, husband 1st 1730 Running Water TN of **Chalakatha Woman/1715**, 2nd 1759 Chota TN of **Cherokee Woman/1744**, children unknown

NEPHEW

French, Capt. aka Cappee French-Cappee Hop-Nephew of Old Hopadopted son of Old Hop – 9/16th Chalakatha-Shawano-ChalakaPowhatan-Black-Metis born 1712 Chota TN-died after 1775 Tomatley NC – son of **Ghigoneli Turkey/1694 & French-Canadian Mulatto/1690**-(or Melungeon-some sort of dark skinned, Frenchspeaking guy), brother of **John French/1710**, half-brother of **Ninihica Mayapple/1721 & Laskigitchi Mayapple/1723**, adopted son 1720 of uncle **Old Hop & Sugi Rainmaker**, allied with **Savannah Tom Carpenter (2)/1698, John Lantaniak/1720**, brother **John French/1710, Rainmaker (3)/1706, Muskrat (2)/1718 & Robert-Thigh-Cauquillehaneh McLemore/1731** in pro-French faction during French-Indian War/1754-63, Cornstalk War/1755-74, could cipher, read & write English & French, delegation to English **with Attakullakulla**, Cherokee faction in Cherokee War/1775, Treaty Sycamore Shoals 1775, from Chota TN & Tomatley NC, mistakenly identified as a slave by British of the time, husband 1st 1732 Running Water TN of **Chalakatha Woman/1717**, 2nd 1759 Chota TN of **Cherokee Woman/1744**, father with **Chalakatha** of Choosahete French/1737, Margaret Elizabeth French/1739-(wife 1755 of **Alexander Drumgoole** (2)/1736), Black Skin French/1741, Catherine French/1748-(wife 1765 of **John Cherokee Vann/1744**), Susan-Sugi French/1755-(wife 1770 of **Capt. Will Emory/1744**)-all 25/32nd Chalakatha-Shawano-Chalaka-PowhatanBlack-Metis, children after 1759 **with Cherokee** unknown

BY SISTER GHIGONELI TURKEY/1694 & MAY APPLE/1690

NEPHEW

Mayapple, Ninihica aka Ninihica Hop-Nephew (3) of Standing Turkey-Old Hop – 63/64th Chalakatha-Kishpoko-Shawano-Chalaka-Powhatan born 1721 Settico TN-**killed** 1776 PA - son of **May Apple**/1690-Kishpoko & **Ghigoneli Hop**/1694, half-brother of **John French**/1710 & **Capt. French**/1712, from Settico, Cornstalk War/1755-74, Chickamauga faction in Cherokee War/1775, captured by Americans near Ft. Pitt & executed while held prisoner, husband 1741 Running Water TN of **Blind Savannah Woman**/1728, children/1742-76 unknown

NEPHEW

Mayapple, Laskigitchi aka Laskigitchi Hop-Nephew (4) of Standing Turkey-Old Hop – 63/64th Chalakatha-Kishpoko-Shawano-Chalaka-Powhatan born 1723 Settico TN-**killed** 1776 Ft. Pitt PA - son of **May Apple**/1690-Kishpoko & **Ghigoneli Hop**/1694, from Settico, Cornstalk War/1755-74, Chickamauga faction in Cherokee War/1775, captured by Americans near Ft. Pitt & executed while held prisoner, half-brother of **John French**/1710 & **Capt. French**/1712, husband 1743 Running Water TN of **Blind Savannah Woman**/1730, children/1744-76 unknown

GRANDCHILDREN OF OLD HOP-STANDING TURKEY/1688

BY LITTLE TURKEY/1709 WITH CHALAKATHA WOMAN/1740

GRANDSON

Turkey, Young Little aka Standing Turkey (4)-Little Turkey (2)-Standing Turkey Jr-**Kannicuttocatoga**- 49/64th Chalakatha-Shawano-Chalaka-Powhatan-Cherokee born 1750 Chota TN-died after 1814 TN - son of

Little Turkey (1)-Standing Turkey (2)/1709 & Chalakatha Woman/1740, grandson of **Old Hop-Standing Turkey (1)**/1688, raised by Little Turkey's 3rd wife-Unknown Woman, Chickamauga faction in Cherokee War/1775, Capt. John Speers Co-**with U.S. Army**-Creek War/1813, wife & children unknown

GRANDSON

Turkey, Auquotaque aka **Auquotaque Little Turkey**-Auquotaque Standing Turkey-Little Turkey's Son-Auquotaque Turkey - 49/64th Chalakatha-Shawano-Chalaka-Powhatan-Cherokee born about 1762 Chota TN-died after 1798 OH - son of **Little Turkey-Standing Turkey (2)/1709 & Chalakatha Woman**/1740, returned north with mother 1764, living **with Shawnee** in OH-KY 1764-98, Blue Jacket War/1778-94, called a Chickamauga because allied with **Dragging Canoe** 1780-91, delegate to D.C. 1791, Treaty 1791, 1792, husband 1780 OH-KY of **Chalakatha Woman**/1765, children/1780-98 unknown

BY YOUNG TURKEY-YOUNG HOP/1715 WITH OLLIE NIONEE OCONASTOTA/1720

GRANDSON

Hop, Badger aka Badger Attakullakulla-**Ookuhmuh (1)**-Badger (1)Akumneh-Oguma-Badger Turkey – 31/64th Chalakatha-ThawikilaShawano-Chalaka-Powhatan-Creek-Cherokee - born 1738 Great Tellico
TN-died after 1804 Great Tellico TN – son of **Young Hop-Young Turkey/1715 & Ollie Nionee Oconastota**/1720, adopted son 1746 of **Attakullakulla Carpenter**/1706, from the Overhills, Wolf Clan or Red Paint Clan Cherokee, Cornstalk War/1755-74, Chickamauga faction in Cherokee War/1775, Treaty Sycamore Shoals/1775, Pigeon CoCherokee scouts-**with U.S. Army**-Revolution/1778-83, diplomatic missions to Detroit & Canada/1783-84, Council Eustinali 1788, Council Estinawa 1792, delegate to D.C. 1791, Treaty 1791, Treaty 1792, husband 1759 Great Tellico TN of **Nancy Great Eagle Carpenter**/1745, father of Young Ookuhmuh-Young Badger/1760, Nancy Ookuhmuh/1768, Jennie Ookuhmuh/1770, Johnson Ookuhmuh/1776, John Welch

Ookuhmuh/1782-all 21/64th Chalakatha-Thawikila-Shawano-Chalaka-Powhatan-Creek-Cherokee-Metis

GRANDSON

Hop, Black Fox aka **Enoleha**-Black Fox (1)-Inali-Fox-Capt. Fox-Black Fox Attakullakulla-Black Fox Turkey – 31/64th Chalakatha-Thawikila-Shawano-Chalaka-Powhatan-Creek-Cherokee born 1740 Great Tellico TN-died 1811 KY – son of **Young Hop-Young Turkey**/1715 & **Ollie Nionee Oconastota**/1720, adopted son 1746 of **Attakullakulla Carpenter**/1706, Wolf Clan Cherokee, Cornstalk War/1758-74, Chickamauga faction in Cherokee War/1775, Pigeon Co-Cherokee scouts-**with U.S. Army**-Revolution/1778-83, **Chickamauga sub-Chief** under **Dragging Canoe** 1784-90, delegate to D.C. 1791, Treaty 1791, 1805, 1806, 1807, a **Principal Chief** 1802-06 upon death of **Little TurkeyStanding Turkey (2)**/1715, 1806 sided with **Double Head**/1740, deposed 1806-10, succeeded 1806-10 by **Path Killer**, reinstated 1810-11, husband 1759 Great Tellico TN of **Grand Priber**/1737, father of Young Black Fox /1760, Nancy Black Fox-Nancy Fox/1762, Mary Ann Black Fox-Mary Ann Fox/1764-all 5/16th Chalakatha-Thawikila-ShawanoChalaka-Powhatan-Creek-Cherokee-Metis

GRANDSON

Hop, Little Owl aka **Ookoosdi**-Little Owl (1)-Little Owl Attakullakulla**Nahoolah**-White Mankiller-Unegadihi-Unacata-IshettechiUnakateehee-Little Owl Turkey – 31/64th Chalakatha-ThawikilaShawano-Chalaka-Powhatan-Creek-Cherokee born 1742 Great Tellico TN-**killed** 1792 Buchanan Station TN – son of **Young Hop-Young Turkey**/1715 & **Ollie Nionee Oconastota**/1720, adopted son 1746 of **Attakullakulla Carpenter**/1706, from the Overhills, Wolf Clan Cherokee, Cornstalk War/1762-74, Boonesboro/1778, a **seceding Headman** 1777, a **Chickamauga Chief**/1777-92, raiding KY-OH-VA/1777-81, Dragging Canoe's **emissary to the British** in Detroit & CAN, raiding Ohio River valley/1788, husband 1762 Great Tellico TN of **Bird Clan Thawikila Woman**/1747, children unknown

GRANDDAUGHTER

Hop, Sugi aka Susannah-Suki Hop-Daughter of Attakullakulla-Sugi Turkey – 31/64th Chalakatha-Thawikila-Shawano-Chalaka-PowhatanCreek-Cherokee born 1744 Great Tellico TN-died after 1790 (TN?) – daughter of **Young Hop-Young Turkey**/1715 & **Ollie Nionee Oconastota**/1720, adopted daughter 1746 of **Attakullakulla Carpenter**/1706, namesake of grandmother **Sugi Rainmaker**/1690, wife by 1763 TN of **Blue Sonicooie**/1730-Cherokee, mother of Susannah Sonicooie/1763, Young Sonicooie/1765 & Nancy Sonicooie/1768-all 15/64th Chalakatha-Thawikila-Shawano-ChalakaPowhatan-Creek-Cherokee

BY GRASSHOPPER HOP/1725
WITH WILLIAM DAVID MCDANIEL/1720

GRANDDAUGHTER

McDaniel, Catherine (1) - 15/64th Chalakatha-Shawano-ChalakaPowhatan-Cherokee-Metis born 1753 Chota TN-died about 1818 (TN?) - daughter of **Grasshopper Turkey**/1725 & **William D. McDaniel**/1720, Wolf Clan Cherokee, from Chota TN, 1st wife 1771 Chota TN of **John Jack Ward**/1750-1/2 Pekowi-Metis, mother of James Ward/1772, George Ugtiga Ward/1774, Samuel Ward/1776, Elizabeth Ward/1778, Susan Ward/1780, Bryan Ward/1782, Nancy Ward/1784, Charles Ward/1786, Lucy Ward/1788 & John S. Ward/1790-all 23/64th Chalakatha-Pekowi-Shawano-Chalaka-Powhatan-Cherokee-Metis

GRANDSON

McDaniel, Alexander (1) - 15/64th Chalakatha-Shawano-ChalakaPowhatan-Cherokee-Metis born 1754 Chota TN-died 1834 (Trail?) - son of **Grasshopper Turkey**/1725 & **William David McDaniel**/1720, Wolf Clan Cherokee, husband 1st 1774 Chota TN of **Native Woman**/1759, 2nd 1786 Chota TN of **Catherine Wilson**/1770, 3rd (simultaneously) 1787 Chota TN of her sister **Mary Wilson**/1772-both 31/64th ChalakathaKishpoko-Black-Metis, children/1774-86 **with Native** unknown, father **with Catherine Wilson** of James McDaniel/1790,

Catherine-Katy McDaniel/1796, Mary McDaniel/1798 & John B. McDaniel/1800, **with**
Mary Wilson of Lucy McDaniel/1788, Eleanor-Nell McDaniel/1790, Moses McDaniel/1792 & Susan-Sukey-Sugi McDaniel/1813-all 23/64th Chalakatha-Kishpoko-Shawano-Chalaka-Powhatan-Black-Cherokee-Metis

GRANDSON

McDaniel, Lewis - 15/64th Chalakatha-Shawano-Chalaka-Powhatan-Cherokee-Metis born 1756 Chota TN-died after 1785 - son of **Grasshopper Turkey**/1725 & **William D. McDaniel**/1720, Wolf Clan Cherokee, disappears the same time his father, wife & children unknown

GRANDSON

McDaniel, John - 15/64th Chalakatha-Shawano-Chalaiwa-Powhatan-Cherokee-Metis born 1758 Chota TN-died after 1785 - son of **Grasshopper Turkey**/1725 & **William D. McDaniel**/1720, Wolf Clan Cherokee, disappears the same time his father, wife & children unknown

GRANDDAUGHTER

McDaniel, Mary (1) - 15/64th Chalakatha-Shawano-Chalaka-PowhatanCherokee-Metis born 1760 Chota TN-died 1800 Ashe Co. NC - daughter of **Grasshopper Turkey**/1725 & **William D. McDaniel**/1720, Wolf Clan Cherokee, returned to whites with her father 1785, married
1777-1785 NC **William Weaver**/1750, mother of Joshua Weaver/1785-7/64th Chalakatha-Shawano-Chalaka-Powhatan-Cherokee-Metis

GRANDDAUGHTER

McDaniel, Nancy (1) aka Nannie - 15/64th Chalakatha-ShawanoChalaka-Powhatan-Cherokee-Metis born 1764 Chota TN-died after 1785 - daughter of **Grasshopper Turkey**/1725 & **William D. McDaniel**/1720, Wolf Clan Cherokee, disappears the same time as her father, husband & children unknown

GRANDAUGHTER

McDaniel, Elizabeth - 15/64th Chalakatha-Shawano-Chalaka-PowhatanCherokee-Metis born 1765 Chota TN-died after 1885 - daughter of **Grasshopper Turkey**/1725 & **William D. McDaniel**/1720, Wolf Clan Cherokee, disappears the same time as her father, husband & children unknown

GRANDDAUGHTER

McDaniel, Susannah - 15/64th Chalakatha-Shawano-Chalaka-Powhatan-Cherokee-Metis born 1766 Chota TN-died after 1785 - daughter of **Grasshopper Turkey**/1725 & **William D. McDaniel**/1720, Wolf Clan Cherokee, disappears the same time as her father, husband & children unknown

GRANDDAUGHTER

McDaniel, Rachel - 15/64th Chalakatha-Shawano-Chalaka-Powhatan-Cherokee-Metis born 1767 Chota TN-died after 1785 - daughter of **Grasshopper Turkey**/1725 & **William D. McDaniel**/1720, Wolf Clan Cherokee, disappears the same time as her father, husband & children unknown

GRANDSON

McDaniel, William David (2) aka William David McDaniel Jr - 15/64th Chalakatha-Shawano-Chalaka-Powhatan-Cherokee-Metis born 1768 Chota TN-died after 1842 - son of **Grasshopper Turkey**/1725 & **William D. McDaniel**/1720, Wolf Clan Cherokee, stayed with his mother in TN 1785, husband 1788 Chota TN of **Cherokee Woman**/1775, father of William D. McDaniel (3)/1802-7/64th Chalakatha-Shawano-Chalaka-Powhatan-CherokeeMetis

GRANDCHILDREN OF OLD HOP/1688 BY ADOPTION

BY CAPT. FRENCH/1712 WITH CHALAKATHA WOMAN/1717

GRANDSON BY ADOPTION

French, Choosahete – 49/64th Chalakatha-Shawano-Chalaka-Powhatan-Black-Metis born 1737 Running Water TN-died after 1757 TN – son of **Capt. French**/1712 & **Chalakatha Woman**/1717, later from Settico TN, associated with his father & uncle in pro-French faction in 1757, wife & children unknown (thought to have married a Cherokee)

GRANDDAUGHTER BY ADOPTION

French, Margaret Elizabeth aka Margaret Elizabeth Hop-Margaret Elizabeth Metis – 49/64th Chalakatha-Shawano-Chalaka-Powhatan--Black-Metis born 1739 Running Water TN-died 1759 Great Tellico TN – daughter of **Capt. French**/1712 & **Chalakatha Woman**/1717, 1st wife 1755 Running Water TN of **Alexander Drumgoole (2)**/1736, mother of James Drumgoole/1756-31/64th Chalakatha-Shawano-Chalaka-Powhatan--Black-Metis

GRANDSON BY ADOPTION

French, Black Skin aka LePeau Noire – 49/64th Chalakatha-ShawanoChalaka-Powhatan--Black-Metis born 1741 Running Water TN-died after 1790 (WI?) - son of **Chalakatha Woman**/1717 & **Capt. French**/1712, came north with raiders in 1758 & never returned to the south, Cornstalk War/1758-77, Blue Jacket War/1777-90, moved further north-west 1790 after Harmar/1790 taking a French name, husband about 1760 OH of **Kishpoko Woman**/1745, father of several children/1760-90

GRANDDAUGHTER BY ADOPTION

French, Catherine aka Catherine Hop-Catherine Metis – 49/64th ChalakathaShawano-Chalaka-Powhatan--Black-Metis born 1748 Running Water TN-died
1785 Running Water TN – daughter of **Capt. French**/1712 & **Chalakatha Woman**/1717, 2nd wife 1765 Running Water TN of **John Cherokee Vann**/1744, mother of John Oowayne Vann/1766, children/1767-73, Rebecca Vann/1774, Otiyu Vann/1776, Lucinda Vann/1780 & children/1781-84-all 21/32nd Chalakatha-Pekowi-Shawano-Chalaka-Powhatan-Black-CherokeeMetis

GRANDDAUGHTER BY ADOPTION

French, Susan-Sugi. aka Wife of Capt. Will Emory – 49/64th ChalakathaShawano-Chalaka-Powhatan--Black-Metis born 1755 Running

Water TN-died after 1780 OH – daughter of **Capt. French**/1712 & **Chalakatha Woman**/1717, abandoned in OH by Emory, wife 1770 (KY?) of **Capt. Will Emory**/1744, reported children/1755-78 unknown

CHAPTER SEVEN

Peter Chartier/1690

Loyparcoweh Straight Tail/1705

Peter Chartier/1690

Chartier, Peter aka **Wocunuckshenah-Pale Brother**-Wacanackshina - 1/2 Pekowi-Metis born about 1690 TN-died about 1759 on the Wabash IN (possibly in epidemic) - son of **Martin Chartier**/1655-adoptedFrench & **Sewatha Straight Tail**/1660, grandson of **Straight TailMeaurroway**, before 1697 moved with Opessa Band to Lancaster Co PA, 1707 living on Pequea Creek Lancaster Co PA, 1718 living in Dekanoagah Lancaster Co PA-obtained title to 300 acres on the Susquehanna River where his father had died, 1732 witnessed a letter from **Neucheconner** & other Shawnee Chiefs to the Governor of PA , 1732 attended Council Philadelphia with **Opakethwa, Opakeita** & **Kwassenung Pheasant,** 1734 founded Chartier's Town Alleghany Co PA, 1737 a **Pekowi Chief in PA**, 1738 signed **Petition to PA** with **Pride Opessa, Tecomteh Opessa** & **George Miranda**, 1744 left the British of PA with about 400 Pekowi & Kishpoko-including **Neucheconner** & **Tamenebuck,** to join the French of OH , (**Kakawatchekee** & **Kishacoquillas** refused to join them) moved southwest to the mouth of the Sciota River-Lower Shawnee Town with sons, 1745 moved on to near Winchester KY-(**Neucheconner** & **Tamenebuck** return to PA),

1746 moved to French Lick-Nashville TN, 1747 moved to the Coosa River AL, 1748 allegedly seen with some of his band in IL & Detroit when the French doubted his control of the band-(it was one of his sons **Francois Pale Croucher Chartier** or **Rene Pale Stalker Chartier** that was seen), 1749 met Col. **Celeron De Blainville** at the forks of the Ohio (Pittsburgh), 1750 a smallpox epidemic forces his band to flee to AL, 1753 present at a Council in Charleston SC with 9 other Shawnee headmen that were living among the Upper & Lower Creeks, 1754 returned to KY, active in opposition to the British on the frontier in the French-Indian War/1754-59, 1754 present with his Shawnee warriors at the murder of Capt. **Jumonville** & responsible for the French victory over **George Washington** at Ft. Necessity, 1758 in OH with band, last seen in a village on the Wabash, husband about 1710 PA of his 1st cousin **Snow White Opessa**/1695-Pekowi, father of Francois Pale Croucher Chartier/1712, children/1714-18, Rene Pale Stalker Chartier/1720, Anna Chartier/1730 & children/1732-36-all 3/4th Pekowi-Metis

WIFE

Opessa, Snow White aka **Blanceneige-Wapakonee**-Daughter of OpessaWife of Peter Chartier – Pekowi born about 1695 PA-died about 1737 PA - daughter of **Opessa**/1675 & **Pekowi Woman**/1680, granddaughter of **Straight-Tail-Meaurroway**/1630, wife 1710 PA of her first cousin **Peter Chartier**/1690, mother of Francois Pale Croucher Chartier/1712, children/1714-18, Rene Pale Stalker Chartier/1720, Anna Chartier/1730 & children/1732-36-all 3/4th Pekowi-Metis

CHILDREN OF PETER CHARTIER/1690 & SNOW WHITE/1695

SON

Chartier, Francois **Pale Croucher**-Chartier's Son - 3/4th Pekowi-Metis born about 1712 PA-died after 1763 - son of **Peter Chartier**/1690 & **Snow White Opessa**/1695-Pekowi, before 1744 worked as trader with father, 1744 left British of PA with his father to join the French in Lower Shawnee Town OH, 1745 moved on to Winchester KY, 1746 may have moved to French LickNashville TN, 1747 may have moved to the Coosa River AL, 1748 may have been the Chartier seen in IL & Detroit when the French doubted Peter Chartier's control over the band, 1752 returned to KY, 1758 in OH (Lower Shawnee Town?) with band, active in opposition to the British on the frontier in the French-Indian War/1754-63, husband about 1734 PA of **Younger Daughter of Poxinosa**/1721-Pekowi, father of Nancy Nadachine Chartier/1735 & others-all 7/8th Pekowi-Metis

SON

Chartier, Rene **Pale Stalker**-Chartier's Son - 3/4th Pekowi-Metis born about 1720 PA-died after 1777 OH-IN - son of **Peter Chartier**/1690 & **Snow White Opessa**/1695-Pekowi, a Pekowi warrior, 1744 left British of PA with his father to join the French in Lower Shawnee Town OH, 1745 moved on to Winchester KY, 1746 may have moved to French Lick-Nashville TN, 1747 may moved to the Coosa River AL, 1748 may have been the Chartier seen in IL & Detroit when the French doubted Peter Chartier's control over the band, 1752 returned to KY, 1758 in OH (Lower Shawnee Town?) with band, Cornstalk War/1755-77, traveled with **Corn Cob** to Detroit 1768, husband about 1740 PA of **Pekowi Woman**/1725, father of Elizabeth Chartier/1760, Mary Chartier/1770 & other children/1740-70-all 7/8th Pekowi-Metis

DAUGHTER

Chartier, Anna aka Anne Chartier - 3/4th Pekowi-Metis born about 1730 PA-died after 1779 (PA?) - daughter of **Peter Chartier**/1690 & **Snow White Opessa**/1695, namesake of **Anne LeTort**, remained in PA 1744 when father & brother's joined the French, wife about 1750 PA of **David Troxell**/1730, mother of Christian Troxell/1752, Solomon Troxell/1754, George Troxell/1756, **Jacob-Big Jake Troxell**/1758, John Troxell/1760, Fredrick Troxell/1762, twins Mary & Elizabeth Troxell/1764, **PeterLittle Jake Troxell**/1766, Abraham Troxell/1768, David Troxell Jr/1770
& Catherine Troxell/1772-all 3/8th Pekowi-Metis

GRANDCHILDREN OF PETER CHARTIER/1690

BY FRANCOIS PALE CROUCHER CHARTIER/1712 & YOUNG DAUGHTER OF POXINOSA/1720

GRANDDAUGHTER

Chartier, Nancy Nadachine - 7/8th Pekowi-Metis born about 1735 PA-died about 1787 NC - daughter of **Francois Chartier**/1712 & **Younger Daughter of Poxinosa**/1720-Pekowi, wife about 1750 PA of **John Three Rivers Yaunts**/1718-1/4th Pekowi-Delaware-Metis, mother of John Yaunts Jr/17519/16th Pekowi-Delaware-Metis

BY RENE-PALE STALKER CHARTIER/1720 & PEKOWI WOMAN/1725

GRANDDAUGHTER

Chartier, Elizabeth – 7/8th Pekowi-Metis born about 1760 OH-died 1806 – daughter of **Pale Stalker-Rene Chartier**/1720 & **Pekowi Woman**/1725, wife about 1776 PA of **George Troxell**/1756, children unknown

GRANDDAUGHTER

Chartier, Mary (2) aka Mary Chartteyr - 7/8th Pekowi-Metis born about 1770 OH-died after 1790 - daughter of **Pale Stalker-Rene Chartier**/1720 & **Pekowi Woman**/1725, a Pekowi, 1st wife about 1790 of **Francois Monjennier**/1770-French-Canadian-Metis, children unknown

BY ANNA CHARTIER/1730 & DAVID TROXELL/1730

GRANDSON

Troxell, Christian - 3/8th Pekowi-Metis born 1752 PA-died after 1779 (PA?) - son of **Anna Chartier**/1730 & **David Troxell**/1730, husband 1st about 1772 PA of **Pekowi-Metis Woman**/1752, 2nd after 1773 of **Catherine Doerr**, father **with Pekowi-Metis** of Peter Troxell/177311/16th Pekowi-Metis, children **with Doerr** unknown

GRANDSON

Troxell, Solomon – 3/8th Pekowi-Metis born 1754 MD/PA-died after 1779 – son of **Anna Chartier**/1730 & **David Troxell**/1730, wife & children unknown

GRANDSON

Troxell, George – 3/8th Pekowi-Metis born 1756 PA-died 1843 Dekalb Co AL – son of **Anna Chartier**/1730 & **David Troxell**/1730, PA Militia **with U.S. Army**-Revolution/1776-78, came south 1779 with **Big Jake**, apparently was wounded & fled Yahoo Falls 1810 to the AL village, husband 1st about 1776 PA of **Elizabeth Chartier**/1760, 2nd 1806 Washington Co MD of **Elizabeth Brewer**/1783, 3rd 1823 Wayne Co KY of **Elizabeth Blevins**/1796, father **with Chartier** of Peter Troxell/1781, Catherine Troxell/1784, Jane Marie Troxell/1800, Jacob William Troxell/1803 & other children/1777-98-all 5/8th Pekowi-Metis, children/1806-22 **with Brewer** unknown, **with Blevins** of Elizabeth Troxell/1824-43/64th Pekowi-Shawano-Chalaiwa-Nanticoke-Metis

GRANDSON

Troxell, Jacob (1) aka **Big Jake** – 3/8th Pekowi-Metis born 1758 MD/PA**killed** 1810 Yahoo Falls KY - son of **Anna Chartier**/1730 & **David Troxell**/1730, PA Militia-**with U.S. Army**-Revolution/1776-78, came to KY 1779 with older brother **George Troxell**, younger brothers **John Troxell, Fredrick Troxell, Peter Troxell** & sister **Elizabeth Troxell**-twin of Mary Troxell, Blue Jacket War/1780-94, husband 1779 KY of **Corn Blossom Doublehead**/1758, father of Jacob-Little Jake (2) Troxell Jr/1780, Catherine Troxell/1782, Peter Troxell/1784, Mary Polly Troxell/1786, Margaret Peggy Troxell/1788, child/90, child/92, child/94, Elizabeth Troxell/1796, Sarah Troxell/1798, William Troxell/1800-all 19/64th Chalakatha-Pekowi-Cherokee-Metis, (the **Jacob George Troxell** that died 1843 was apparently Jake's brother **George Troxell**/1756 who came south with Jake in 1779)

GRANDSON

Troxell, John - 3/8th Pekowi-Metis born 1760 MD-died 1830 Sullivan Co TN - son of **Anna Chartier**/1730 & **David Troxell**/1730, came south 1779 with **Big Jake**, husband about 1780 KY of **Eve Unknown** (likely Native)/1765, children unknown

GRANDSON

Troxell, Fredrick - 3/8th Pekowi-Metis born 1762 MD/PA-died 1824 Sullivan Co TN - son of **Anna Chartier**/1730 & **David Troxell**/1730, came south 1779 with **Big Jake**, husband by 1785 (KY-OH?) of **Anna Hess**/1765, children unknown

GRANDDAUGHTER

Troxell, Mary - 3/8th Pekowi-Metis born about 1764 MD/PA-died 1796 Scott Co TN - daughter of **Anna Chartier**/1730 & **David Troxell**/1730, twin of Elizabeth, wife by 1783 (PA?) of **Mr. Barr**/1760, children unknown

GRANDDAUGHTER

Troxell, Elizabeth (1) – 3/8th Pekowi-Metis born 1764 MD/PA-died 1851 McCreary Co KY – daughter of **Anna Chartier**/1730 & **David Troxell**/1730, twin of Mary, sent south 1779 with **Big Jake**, wife (1780?) KY of **Benjamin Burke**/1760, mother of Riley Burke/1781, James Burke/1783, Disa Burke/1785, Nancy Burke/1787, Sarah Burke/1788, Dicey Jane Burke/1790, Anna burke/1793, Benjamin Burke Jr/1795, Jonathan Burke/1797, Mary Polly Burke/1800, Allen Burke/1803, Hudson Burke/1805-all 7/16th Pekowi-Metis

GRANDSON

Troxell, Peter (1) aka **Little Jake** (1)-**Chief Peter** (1) - 3/8th PekowiMetis born 1766 Fredrick Co MD-**killed** 1810 Yahoo Falls KY - son of **Anna Chartier**/1730 & **David Troxell**/1730, moved to KY 1779 with **Big Jake**, Blue Jacket War/1780-94, husband 1st 1784 KY of **Rachel Chambers**/1768, 2nd 1786 KY of **Standing Fern**/1770-(a niece or cousin of Corn Blossom), no known children **with Chambers**, children/1786-1810 **with Fern** unknown but may have included a son Peter Troxell Chief Peter Troxell

GRANDSON

Troxell, Abraham - 3/8th Pekowi-Metis born 1768 VA/PA-died after 1794 - son of **Anna Chartier**/1730 & **David Troxell**/1730, husband 1794 of **Anna Elizabeth Holyman**/1774, children unknown

GRANDSON

Troxell, David Jr - 3/8th Pekowi-Metis born about 1770 VA/PA-died after 1790 - son of **Anna Chartier**/1730 & **David Troxell**/1730, wife & children unknown

GRANDDAUGHTER

Troxell, Catherine - 3/8th Pekowi-Metis born 1772 VA/PA-died after 1791 (VA?) - daughter of **Anna Chartier**/1730 & **David Troxell**/1730, wife 1791 Augusta Co VA (WV?) of **Michael Rodgers**/1770, children unknown

Loyparkoweh Straight Tail/1702

Straight Tail, Loyparkoweh aka **Loyparkoweh Opessa-LoapeckewayLawpakaway** – Pekowi born about 1702 PA-died after 1760 OH - son of
Opessa/1664 & **Pekowi Woman**/1670, grandson of **Straight TailMeaurroway**/1630, in west PA 1711-23 with father **Opessa**, returned to north MD/east PA area with **Opessa** 1723, living on the Alleghany River by 1727, a **Pekowi Chief** in PA by 1732, in 1732-1733-1734 signed letters to the Governor of PA as one of the Chiefs on the Alleghany complaining about the sale of rum to the natives, moved to AL 1734 with **Opessa**, left a wife & children in AL with relatives/clan members, returned to PA by 1738-sent letter to the Governor with **Neucheconner** & **Coycacolenne** protesting the sale of rum, then called a young Chief guided by vice regent **Neucheconner**, between 1738 & 1744 lived at Chartier's Town-Alleghany Co PA & Logstown-Alleghany Co PA, apparently moved to OH with **Peter Chartier** & **Neucheconner** in 174445 for he is living in Lower Shawnee Town OH in 1752 when he sent a letter with 3 other Shawnee Chiefs there to the Governor of PA reporting that they were still loyal to the British though most of their neighbors had gone over to the French, attended Council Philadelphia 1753 after **Opessa** moved to OH, apparently opposed the Shawnee participation in French-Indian War/1754-60, a minor **Pekowi Chief in OH** after death of **Opessa**, husband 1st 1720 MD of **Nancy Pekowi**/1706, 2nd 1738 PA of her sister **Elizabeth Pekowi**/1704, father with **Nancy** of child/1720, child/1722, Tecumsapah-Margaret/1724, Sewatha-Sarah/1726, child/1728, Watmeme-Polly/1730, child/1732,

Middle Daughter-Nancy/1734, Younger Daughter-Sarah/1736 & Metheotashe-Mary/1738-all Pekowi, children **with Elizabeth** unknown

WIVES OF LOYPARKAWEH

1ST WIFE 1725 MD

Nancy aka Mother of Metheotashe - Pekowi born about 1710 MD-died after 1752 AL – **parents unknown**, sister of **Elizabeth**/1705, moved to AL with **Opessa** 1735, didn't return to PA, remained with extended family in AL, her family in PA was among the Shawnee that moved to OH 1744 with **Peter Chartier & Neucheconner**, wife 1st about 1725 MD of **Loyparkoweh Opessa-Straight Tail**/1702, 2nd about 1739 AL of his brother **Wawwaythi**/1700-Pekowi, mother **with Loyparkoweh** of child/1720, child/1722, Tecumsapah-Margaret/1724, SewathaSarah/1726, child/1728, Watmeme-Polly/1730, child/1732, Middle Daughter-Nancy/1734, Younger Daughter-Sarah/1736 & Metheotashe-Mary/1738-all Pekowi, any children **with Wawwaythi** unknown

2ND WIFE 1738 PA

Elizabeth aka Aunt of Metheotashe - Pekowi born about 1704 MD-died after 1752 OH – **parents unknown**, sister of **Nancy**/1710, moved to AL with **Opessa** 1735, switched husbands (they were brothers) when her 1st husband stayed in AL 1738, remarried in PA to his brother, her family was among the Shawnee that moved to OH 1744 with **Peter Chartier & Neucheconner**, wife 1st about 1720 MD of **Wawwaythi Opessa-Straight Tail**/1700-Pekowi, 2nd 1738 PA of his brother **Loyparkoweh OpessaStraight Tail**/1702, children unknown

CHILDREN OF LOYPARCOWEH

DAUGHTER

Opessa, Tecumsapah aka Margaret – Pekowi born about 1724 PA-died after 1769 - daughter of **Loyparkoweh Opessa**/1702 & **Nancy Pekowi**/1706, namesake of grandmother **Margaret Opessa**/1670, aunt

of **Tecumseh**, moved to AL 1735 with grandfather **Opessa** & her father, returned to PA by 1738 with her father, remained in PA 1744 when **Peter Chartier** led Shawnee to OH to join the French, wife 1738 PA of **Thomas McKee**/1695-adopted-Irish, step-mother of **Thomas McKee**/1720-adopted by the Delaware & **Col. Alexander McKee**/1725adopted by the Shawnee, mother of Alexander "Trader" McKee/1738, Nancy McKee/1740, Hugh McKee/1742, Catherine McKee/1744,
Elizabeth McKee/1746, Thomas McKee/1750, John McKee/1753, James McKee/1755-all 1/2 Pekowi-Metis

DAUGHTER

Opessa, Sarah aka Older Daughter of Loyparkaweh-Mother of Tecumpolas-Older Sister of Metheotashe – Pekowi born 1726 MD-died after 1768 OH - daughter of **Loyparkoweh Opessa**/1705 & **Nancy Pekowi** /1710, namesake of her mother's mother **Sarah Pekowi**, aunt of **Tecumseh**, moved to AL 1735 with **Opessa** & her father, returned to PA by 1738 with her father, moved 1744 to OH with **Peter Chartier**, with Pekowi in the Ohio valley-west WV/east OH 1750, wife by 1742 PA of **Pekowi Man**/1722, mother of Tecumpolas-Margaret Opessa/1742, grandmother of Jane Collins/1768

DAUGHTER

Opessa, Watmeme aka Polly – Pekowi born 1730 PA-died 1797 MO – daughter of **Loyparkoweh Opessa**/1705 & **Nancy Pekowi/**1710, namesake of father's step-mother **Polly-Daughter of Sassoonan**/1695, moved to AL 1735 with **Opessa** & her father, returned to PA by 1738 with her father, moved 1744 to OH with **Peter Chartier**, moved to MO 1779 with adopted son **Stephen Ruddle**, Ruddle returned to whites 1797 upon her death, wife 1745 OH of **Black Fish**/1725, mother **with Black Fish** of sons Chinwa/1746, Young Black Fish (1)/1748, daughter Pimegeezhigoqua/1752, son Young Black Fish (2)/1754, daughters Chelatha/1756, Lamatashe/1758 & Parlie/1760-all ChalakathaMekoche-Pekowi, adopted mother 1760 & mother in law 1771 OH
Lewis Rogers/1750, adopted mother 1760 & mother in law 1775 OH
Henry Rogers/1755, adopted mother 1774 OH & grandmother in law

1789 OH of **William Jackson-Fish**/1770, adopted mother 1774 OH **Stephen Ruddle**/1768 & adopted mother & mother in law 1778 OH of **Capt. Joseph Dusquene**/1756

DAUGHTER

Opessa, Nancy aka Middle Daughter of Loyparkaweh-Wife of Daniel McQueen-Middle Sister of Metheotashe – Pekowi born 1734 AL-died after 1755 AL - daughter of **Loyparkoweh Opessa**/1705 & **Nancy Pekowi**/1710, namesake of her mother **Nancy**/1706, moved to AL 1735 with **Opessa** & her father, raised in AL by her mother & uncle/stepfather **Wawwaythi**, a Pekowi from Souvanogee (Shawnee) village AL, wife 1st (known) 1754 AL of **Daniel McQueen**/1736, mother of Elder Daughter-Margaret McQueen--**Mother of Seekaboo**/1755, Younger Daughter-Sarah McQueen/1758-(wife 2nd of her uncle **Robert McQueen**/1747) & son Joseph McQueen/1760-all 1/2 Pekowi-CreekMetis, grandmother of **Seekaboo**/1770-3/4th Kishpoko-Pekowi-CreekMetis

DAUGHTER

Opessa, Sarah aka Younger Daughter of Loyparkoweh-Wife of Isadore Chesne – Pekowi born about 1736 AL-died after 1756 (maybe in epidemics of 1758 in OH?) – daughter of **Loyparkoweh Opessa**/1702 & **Nancy Pekowi**/1706, namesake of father's sister **Sarah-Snow White Opessa**/1695 & father's aunt **Snow White Straight Tail-Sarah White**/1666, raised in AL by her mother & uncle/stepfather **Wawwaythi**, went north 1752 with members of the **Peter Chartier** band, wife 1754 OH of **Isadore Chesne**/1735-Wyandot-Metis, mother of Mary Shane/1754 & Capt. Joseph Dusquene/1756-both 1/2 PekowiWyandot-Metis

DAUGHTER

Opessa, Metheotashe aka Mary-Meetheeotashe-Methotasa-Turtle Laying Eggs – Pekowi born 1738 AL-died 1789 MO - daughter of **Loyparcoweh Opessa**/1702 & **Nancy Pekowi**/1706, namesake of her father's 1st cousin **Mary Chartier**/1688 who had just been murdered, a Pekowi from Souvanogee (Shawnee) village AL, raised in AL by her mother & uncle/stepfather **Wawwaythi**, 1st cousin of **Blue Jacket** & his siblings-(fathers were brothers), aunt of **Tecumoplas-Margaret Collins**/1742 & great-aunt of **Jane Collins**/1768, moved 1759 from AL to KY, moved 1760 from KY to OH, widowed 1774-lived with relatives in the **Black Fish** family/1774-79, moved 1779 to Apple Creek village MO with daughters **Menewaulakoose**/1764 & **Vocemassussia**/1771, wife 1st 1755 AL of **Puckenshinwa Rising Sun**/1735-1/2 KishpokoCreek-Metis-(widowed 1774), 2nd 1775 OH of **Young Hard StrikerPucksinwa Pheasant**/1738-Pekowi-(widowed the same year), mother with **Puckenshinwa** of son **Cheeseekau**/1756 AL, daughter **Tecumapease**/1758 AL, sons Sauwaseekou/1760 KY, (daughter Rising Star/1762 OH?), son Nahaaseema/1764 OH, daughter Menewaulakoose/1766 OH, sons **Tecumseh**/1768 OH, Kumshaka/1770 OH , daughter Vocemassussia/1772 OH & son **Lalawethika**-Shawnee Prophet/1774 OH -all 3/4th Kishpoko-PekowiCreek-Metis, adopted mother 1760 OH of **Joshua Renicks**/1746, 1768 OH of **John Sparks**/1760 & **Richard ShawunteSparks**/1765, 1772 OH of **Stephen Big Fish Ruddell**/1767 & **Abraham Black Hawk Ruddell**/1764, all adopted children went to other families in extended family upon death 1774 of Puckenshinwa, no known child **with Young Hard Striker**

GRANDCHILDREN OF LOYPARCOWAH
BY TECUMSAPAH-MARGARET OPESSA/1724 & THOMAS MCKEE/1695

GRANDSON

McKee, Alexander "Trader" - 1/2 Pekowi-Metis born about 1738 PAdied 1799 (?) - son of **Thomas McKee**/1695 & **Margaret Tecumsapah Opessa**/1724, half-brother of **Thomas-Pelewiechen McKee**/1720adopted-Delaware & **Col. Alexander-Wapimescheu McKee**/1725adopted-Shawnee, husband about 1758 (PA?) of **Pekowi Woman**/1740, father of Catherine McKee/1768-3/4th Pekowi-Metis

GRANDDAUGHTER

McKee, Nancy - 1/2 Pekowi-Metis born 1740 PA-died after 1765 - daughter of **Thomas McKee**/1695 & **Tecumsapah-Margaret Opessa**/1724, wife 1768 PA of **Patrick Dunn**, children unknown

GRANDSON

McKee, Hugh - 1/2 Pekowi-Metis born about 1742 PA-died after 1769 - son of **Thomas McKee**/1695-Irish & **Tecumsapah-Margaret Opessa**/1724, half-brother of **Col. Alexander Wapimescheu McKee**/1725-adopted Shawnee & **Thomas Pelewiechen McKee**/1720adopted Delaware, wife & children unknown

GRANDDAUGHTER

McKee, Catherine - 1/2 Pekowi-Metis born 1744 PA-died after 1765 - daughter of **Thomas McKee**/1695-Irish & **Tecumsapah-Margaret Opessa**/1724, namesake of grandmother **Catherine**-wife of **Alexander McKee**/1665, wife 1760 PA of **William Graydon**/1740, mother of Elizabeth Graydon/1761-1/4th Pekowi-Metis

GRANDAUGHTER

McKee, Elizabeth – ½ Pekowi-Metis born about 1746 PA-died after 1770 – daughter of **Thomas McKee**/1695 & **Margaret Tecumsapah Opessa**/1724, wife by 1764 (PA?) of **John Clark**, mother of John Clark/1764 & Thomas Alexander Clark-both 1/4th Pekowi-Metis

GRANDSON

McKee, Thomas - 1/2 Pekowi-Metis born 1750 PA-died after 1779 - son of **Thomas McKee**/1695 & **Tecumsapah-Margaret Opessa**/1724, husband by 1779 PA of **Martha Hoge**/1760, father of James McKee/1779-1/4th Pekowi-Metis

GRANDSON

McKee, John - 1/2 Pekowi-Metis born 1753 PA-died 1830 - son of **Thomas McKee**/1695 & **Tecumsapah-Margaret Opessa**/1724, husband 1778 PA of **Mary Hoge**/1762, father of Robert McKee/1780, Thomas McKee/1782, William McKee/1785, Mary McKee/1787, James McKee/1791, John McKee Jr/1793, Martha McKee/1795, David Logan McKee/1798 & Sarah McKee/1801-1/4th Pekowi-Metis

GRANDSON

McKee, James - 1/2 Pekowi-Metis born about 1756 PA-died 1834 - son of **Thomas McKee**/1695-Irish & **Tecumsapah-Margaret Opessa**/1724, husband 1774 PA of **Elizabeth Verner**/1759-white, father of Andrew McKee/1775, Maria McKee/1777, John McKee/1779, Thomas McKee/1781, Sarah McKee/1782, Alexander McKee/1784 & Jane McKee/1786-all 1/4th Pekowi-Metis

BY OLDER DAUGHTER-SARAH/1726 & PEKOWI MAN/1722

GRANDAUGHTER

Opessa, Tecumoplas aka Margaret (for lack of a better surname) – Pekowi born 1742 MD-died after 1791 (WV?) - daughter of **Sarah Opessa**-Older Daughter of Loyparkoweh/1726 & **Pekowi Man**/1722, a Pekowi in the North, 1st cousin of **Tecumseh**, wife 1767 (or maybe by 1757?) WV of **Rupert Collins**-white born about 1740-died after 1791, mother of Jane Collins/1768, Parker Collins/1780 & at least 6 other children/1769-82 (or 11 children/1758-82?) -all 1/2 Pekowi-Metis

BY WATMEME-POLLY OPESSA/1730 & BLACK FISH/1725

GRANDSON

Black Fish, Chinwa – Chalakatha-Mekoche-Pekowi born about 1746 OH-**killed** 1774 Point Pleasant WV - son of **Black Fish**/1725 & **Watmeme Opessa**/1730, Cornstalk War/1763-74, killed in battle at Point Pleasant/1774, called a relative of **Tecumseh**, husband about 1765 OH of **Chalakatha Woman**/1750, father of several children/1765-74(likely surnamed Blackfish)

GRANDSON

Black Fish, Young (1) aka **Black Fish (2)** – Chalakatha-Mekoche-Pekowi born about 1748 OH-**killed** 1788 KY - son of **Black Fish**/1725 & **Watmeme Opessa**/1730, Cornstalk War /1772-77, Blue Jacket

War/1777-88, **killed** in KY raid, with group that captured **John Taylor**/1781-white, called a relative of **Tecumseh**, husband about 1768 OH of **Chalakatha Woman**/1753, father of Young Black Fish (3)/1780 & Joseph Blackfish/1785-both Chalakatha-Mekoche-Pekowi

GRANDDAUGHTER

Black Fish, Pimegeezhigoqua – Chalakatha-Mekoche-Pekowi born about 1752 OH-died after 1826 - daughter of **Black Fish**/1725 & **Watmeme**/1730, Shawnee name unknown, went by Chippewa name after marriage to Dusquene, called a relative of Tecumseh, wife 1779 OH of **Capt. Joseph Dusquene**/1756, mother of Joseph Dusquene Jr/1780, Jean Baptiste Dusquene/1785, Isabella Dusquene/1790 & Susanne Dusquene/1795-all 1/2 Chalakatha-Mekoche-Pekowi-Wyandot-Metis

GRANDSON

Black Fish, Young (2) aka **Black Fish (3)** – Chalakatha-Mekoche-Pekowi born about 1754 OH-died after 1794 - son of **Black Fish**/1725 & **Watmeme Opessa**/1730, Cornstalk War/1766-77, called a relative of **Tecumseh**, husband 1774 OH of **Chalakatha Woman**/1759, father of Daughter-(wife of William Jackson)/1774 & Eli Blackfish/1790-both Chalakatha-Mekoche-Pekowi, adopted father of **George Ash**/1765adopted white

GRANDDAUGHTER

Black Fish, Parlie aka Polly – Chalakatha-Mekoche-Pekowi born about 1756 OH-died after 1799 MO - daughter of **Black Fish**/1725 & **Watmeme**/1730, called a relative of Tecumseh, wife about 1771 OH of **Lewis Rogers**/1750-adopted white, mother of Nancy Rogers/1772, Martha Rogers/1774, James Rogers/1778, Polly Rogers/1782, Lewis Rogers/1786-all 1/2 Chalakatha-Mekoche-Pekowi-Metis

GRANDDAUGHTER

Black Fish, Lamateshe aka Lematashe-Launatashe-Auqualanaux – Chalakatha-Mekoche-Pekowi born about 1758 OH-died after 1800 -

daughter of **Black Fish**/1725 & **Watmeme Opessa**/1730, called a relative of Tecumseh, wife 1st about 1778 OH of **Capt. Joseph Dusquene**/1756-1/2 Pekowi-Wyandot-Metis, 2nd about 1784 OH of his half-brother **Anthony Shane**/1763-1/4th Kishpoko-Creek-Wyandot-Metis, mother with **Dusquene** of David Deshane/1780-1/2 ChalakathaMekoche-Pekowi-Wyandot-Metis, **with Shane** of David Dushane/1785,
John Shane/1790, Charles Chesne/1795 & 2 daughters/1796-1800-all 5/8th Chalakatha-Kishpoko-Mekoche-Pekowi-Creek-Wyandot-Metis

GRANDDAUGHTER

Black Fish, Chelatha – Chalakatha-Mekoche-Pekowi born about 1760 OH-died after 1790 - daughter of **Black Fish**/1725 & **Watmeme Opessa**/1730, called a relative of **Tecumseh**, wife about 1775 OH of **Henry Rogers**/1755-adopted white, mother of Polly Rogers/1780 & William Rogers/1785-both 1/2 Chalakatha-Mekoche-Metis

BY MIDDLE DAUGHTER/1734 & DANIEL McQUEEN/1736

GRANDDAUGHTER

McQueen, Margaret aka Elder Daughter of Daniel-**Mother of Seekaboo**- Niece of Metheotashe - 1/2 Pekowi-Creek-Metis born about 1755 AL-died after 1775 - daughter of **Nancy Opessa**-Middle Daughter of Loyparkoweh/1734 & **Daniel McQueen**/1736, granddaughter on father's side of **James McQueen**/1700-white & **Katherine Fraser**/1705Creek, sister of **Joseph McQueen**/1760, 1st cousin of **Tecumseh,** wife about 1769 AL of **Father of Seekaboo**/1750-Kishpoko, mother of
Seekaboo/1770-3/4th Kishpoko-Pekowi-Creek-Metis

GRANDDAUGHTER

McQueen, Sarah aka Younger Daughter of Daniel – ½ Pekowi-CreekMetis-(Thawikila by 1st marriage) born about 1758 (AL?)-died after 1800

– daughter of **Daniel McQueen**/1736 & **Sarah Opessa**-Middle Daughter of Loyparkoweh/1734, wife 1st about 1775 AL of **Thawikila Man**/1755, 2nd about 1784 AL of her uncle **Robert McQueen**/1747-1/2 Creek-Metis-(son of **James McQueen**/1700 & **Katherine Fraser**/1705), children/1775-84 **with Thawikila** unknown, mother **with McQueen** of Nancy McQueen/1785 & William McQueen/1787-both 1/4th Pekowi-Creek-Metis

GRANDSON

McQueen, Joseph - 1/2 Pekowi-Creek-Metis born about 1760-died after 1830 - son of **Middle Daughter of Loyparkoweh Opessa** /1734 & **Daniel McQueen**/1736-1/2 Creek-Metis, brother of **Mother of Seekaboo**/1755, grandson (by mother) of **Loyparkoweh Opessa**/1700 & (by father) of **James McQueen**/1700-white & **Katherine Fraser**/1705-Creek, nephew of **Metheotashe Opessa**/1740, cousin of **Josiah Francis**/1765 & **Joseph Francis**/1770, uncle of **Seekaboo**/1770, **Tecumseh**/1768 & **Osceola**/1802, wife & children unknown

BY YOUNGER DAUGHTER-SARAH/1736 & ISADORE CHESNE/1735

GRANDDAUGHTER

Shane, Mary aka Mary Chesne – ½ Pekowi-Wyandot-Metis born about 1754 OH-died before 1840 Russell Co VA – daughter of **Isadore Chesne**/1735 & **Sarah Opessa**-Younger Daughter of Loyparkoweh/1736, namesake of **Mary Chartier**/1688, wife 1769 OH of **Jacob Castle Jr**/1748-1/2 Pekowi-Metis, mother of Margaret Castle/1770, Zedekiah Castle/1775, Joseph Jacob Castle/1780, Benjamin Castle/1785, Zachariah Castle/1787, Lydia Castle/1789, John Joshua Castle/1791, Elijah Castle/1793, James Castle/1795, William Castle/1797, Mary Polly Castle/1799 & Inman Castle/1801-all ½ Pekowi-Wyandot-Metis

GRANDSON

Dusquene, Capt. Joseph aka Joseph Chesne-Capt. Dusquene-Joseph

Duchene-Mushkedewin-Prairie Man – adopted-1/2 Pekowi-WyandotMetis-(adopted Chippewa) born about 1756 OH-died after 1835 - son of
Isadore Chesne/1735 & Sarah Opessa-Younger Daughter of Loyparkoweh/1736, raiding Ohio River valley/1774 **with Chief Logan**, Point Pleasant/1774, raiding OH-KY-VA/1775-81, Blue Jacket War/1777-94, Boonesboro/1778, raiding Ohio River valley/1781 **with Joseph Brant**, Crawford/1782, raiding Ohio River valley/1788-92, employed in fur trade 1795-1827, became U.S. citizen 1818, half-brother of **Anthony Shane**/1760 & **Joseph Shane**/1765, half-brother of **Mary Josette Chesne**/1775-Wyandot-Ottawa-Metis, adopted son 1778 & (double) son in law 1779-80 of **Black Fish**/1725, husband 1st 1779 OH of **Lamateshe Blackfish**/1758, 2nd 1780 OH of her sister **Pimegeezhigoqua Blackfish**/1752, father **with Lamateshe** of David Dusquene-Deshane/1780 & **with Pimegeezhigoqua** of Joseph Dusquene Jr/1781, Jean Baptiste Dusquene/1785, Isabella Dusquene/1790 & Susanne Dusquene/1795-all 1/2 Chalakatha-Mekoche-Pekowi-Wyandot-Metis

BY METHEOTASHE-MARY/1738 & PUCKENSHINWA RISING SUN/1735

GRANDSON

Puckenshinwa, Cheeseekau aka **Cheeseekau**-Chiksika-CheeseequaSting-a **Snake Biting**-Snakebite-Passquannakeek-Gunshot-Shawnee Warrior-Great Shawnee Warrior - 3/4th Kishpoko-Pekowi-Creek-Metis born 1756 AL-**killed** 1792 Buchanan Station TN - eldest son of **Puckenshinwa Rising Sun**/1735 & **Metheotashe Opessa**/1738, a **Kishpoko** War Chief, Point Pleasant/1774-75-78, Blue Jacket War/177792, raiding TN-KY-VA-OH/1777-81 **with Dragging Canoe** & **Chief Bob Benge**, Council Miami Jan. 1786, took sons by Kishpoko Woman with him to TN, an original Chickamauga/1777, living in Running Water (Shawnee) village 1789-92 **with Tecumseh**, killed leading Shawnee contingent **at Buchanan Station TN**, husband 1st 1776 OH of **Kishpoko Woman**/1760, 2nd 1780 TN of **Eyoostee Dragging Canoe**/1756, father **with Kishpoko** of Tecumqualuska-Graybeard/1777 & Great Shawnee Warrior (2)/1780-both 7/8th Kishpoko-Pekowi-Creek-Metis & likely another child or two, father **with Dragging Canoe** of

TeciekeapeaseGenevieve Marie/1790 & another child/1792-both 31/64th ChalakathaKishpoko-Thawikila-Pekowi-Creek-Cherokee-Metis, other children likely

GRANDDAUGHTER

Puckenshinwa, Tecumapease aka **Crossing The Water**-Tecumesa - 3/4th Kishpoko-Pekowi-Creek-Metis born 1758 AL-died 1815 Windsor CAN - oldest daughter of **Puckenshinwa Rising Sun**/1735 & **Metheotashe Opessa**/1738, moved to CAN 1815 with family & died there soon after, wife 1st 1773 OH of **Mink-Chaquiweshe**/1740-Mekoche, **widowed 1774**, 2nd 1775 OH of **Mathias Splitlog**/1758-Wyandot, 3rd 1779 OH **Stands Firm-Wasegobah**/1755-adopted-Chippewa, **widowed 2nd time 1813**, mother **with Mink** of Big Horn-Capt. Logan/1774-7/8th Kishpoko-Mekoche-Pekowi-Creek-Metis, no known children/1775-79 **with Splitlog**, mother **with Stands Firm** of LaNanette TecumapeaseNanette-Maryanne/1780 & other 3/8th Kishpoko-Chippewa-PekowiCreek-Metis children/1782-1805, (often confused with sisters & nieces by some white histories)

GRANDSON

Puckenshinwa, Sauwaseekou aka Sauwaseekou-**Panther Crouching for Prey** - 3/4th Kishpoko-Pekowi-Creek-Metis born 1760 KY-**killed** 1791 OH – 2nd son of **Puckenshinwa Rising Sun**/1735 & **Metheotashe Opessa**/1738, a Kishpoko warrior, born in KY during move from AL to OH, Blue Jacket War/1777-91, **killed 1791 at St. Clair**, husband by 1780 OH of **Unknown Woman**/1765-(Shawnee or white?), children/1780-91 unknown

(POSSIBLE GRANDDAUGHTER?)

Puckenshinwa, Rising Star - 3/4th Kishpoko-Pekowi-Creek-Metis born 1762 OH-died after 1778 – possible second daughter of **Puckenshinwa Rising Sun**/1735 & **Metheotashe Opessa**/1738, wife about 1776 OH of **Mathias Splitlog**/1758-Wyandot, children unknown

GRANDSON

Puckenshinwa, Nahaasema aka Nahaaseema - 3/4th Kishpoko-Pekowi-

Creek Metis born 1764 OH-**killed** 1788 KY - 3rd son of **Puckenshinwa**/1735 & **Metheotashe Opessa**/1738, Blue Jacket War/1782-88, **killed 1788 in KY raid**, husband about 1784 OH of **Unknown Woman**/1769-(Shawnee or white?), children/1785-88 unknown

GRANDDAUGHTER

Puckenshinwa, Menewaulakoose aka Menewaulakoose-Menewalakosi-**Lying Piled in a Hollow** - 3/4th Kishpoko-Pekowi-Creek-Metis born 1766 OH-died after 1819 MO – 2nd (known) daughter of **Puckenshinwa Rising Sun**/1735 & **Metheotashe Opessa**/1738, moved 1779 to Apple Creek village MO **with Metheotashe**, her marriage was opposed by brothers Cheeseekau & Tecumseh, wife 1782 MO of **Antoine Francois Maisonville**/1760-adopted-French/Canadian, mother of Francois Maisonville/1791-3/8th Kishpoko-Pekowi-Creek-Metis (often confused with her sisters by some white histories)

GRANDSON

Tecumseh aka Panther in the Sky-Panther Leaping at Prey-Tecumseh Puckenshinwa-Tecumshe-Tecumthe-Tecoomteh-Tecoomti -Tecomteh- 3/4th Kishpoko-Pekowi-Creek-Metis born 1768 Chillicothe OH-**killed** 1813 Thames River CAN - 4th son of **Puckenshimwa Rising Sun**/1735 & **Metheotashe Opessa**/1738, a Kishpoko War Chief, Blue Jacket War/1786-94, lived-raided 1790-92 **with Chickamaugua** & brother **Cheeseekua** in TN-KY-VA-NC-GA-AL, raiding OH-WV-VA-KY/1793- 99, called a brother in law of **Thomas Splitlog**/1756 & **Mathias Splitlog**/1758, reportedly a **British Colonel**-War 1812, Brownstown/1812- Monguagon/1812-1st Amherstburg/1812- Frenchtown/1813-Ft. Meigs/1813-2nd Amherstburg/1813, **killed at Thames**/1813, Council Miami 1786, Grand Council 1791, traveled much of 1795-1811 soliciting support for united Native force, Council Vincennes July & Aug. 1810, Council Amherstburg Mar. 1812, Council Massinawa May 1812, met with **Isadore Chesne** near Ft. Wayne June 1812, met with **Col. Brock** at Amherstburg July 1812, reportedly a member of the Masons in CAN, called the last great leader of Eastern Natives though never more than a War Chief, husband 1st 1788 OH of **Monetoshe Opessa**/1770-Pekowi, 2nd 1789 OH of **Mamate**

Baby/17741/2 Kishpoko-Metis, 3rd 1790 OH of **Adopted White Girl**/1777, 4th 1790 Running Water TN **Dark Star-Tahneh-Slow Head-Naomi**/1775Chickamauga, 5th 1793 OH of **White Wing-Big Nancy Cornstalk**/1770-15/32nd Chalakatha-Mekoche-Metis, 6th 1800 IN of **Wasigezeegoqua Poc**/1785-Pottawamee, 7th 1802 OH of **Wabelegunequa Half Moon**/1785-Chalakatha, 8th by 1805 IN **Winnipegoosqua Sturgeon**/1790-Chippewa, father **with Monetoshe** of Mahyawekawpawe/1788-7/8th Kishpoko-Pekowi-Creek-Metis, father **with Mamate** of Naythahwaynah/1790-5/8th Kishpoko-Pekowi-CreekMetis, father **with White Girl** of Michelana/1790-3/8th KishpokoPekowi-Creek-Metis, father **with Dark Star** of Lydia Tecumseh/1790, Tecumtequah/1792 & Chickamauga Daughter/1794-all 3/8th Kishpoko-Pekowi-Creek-Cherokee-Metis, father **with White Wing** of Paukeesaa/1794, Adjala/1796 & Serena/1798-all 39/64th Kishpoko-Chalakatha-Mekoche-Pekowi-Creek-Metis, father **with Wasigezeegoqua** of Pottawamee Son/1801, Elder Pottawamee Child/1803 & Younger Pottawamee Child/1805-all 3/8th Kishpoko-Pekowi-Creek-Pottawamee-Metis, no children/1802-07 **with Half Moon**, father **with Winnipegoosqua** of Child/1806, Child/1808, Child/1810, Child/1812-all 3/8th Kishpoko-Pekowi-Creek-Chippewa Metis, other unknown children with unknown women possible

GRANDSON

Puckenshinwa, Kumshaka aka Kumshaka-Kunshauskau-**Cat Flying In Air** - 3/4th Kishpoko-Pekowi-Creek-Metis born 1770 OH-died before 1824 CAN - 5th son of **Puckenshinwa Rising Sun**/1735 & **Metheotashe Opessa**/1738, a Kishpoko warrior, Blue Jacket War/1787-94, raiding OH-KY-VA-TN/1795-1810, Prophet's Town/1811, War 1812-Thames/1813 **with Tecumseh**, moved to CAN 1815, died before band returned to OH 1825, husband about 1790 OH of **Kishpoko Woman**/1774, children unknown

GRANDDAUGHTER

Puckenshinwa, Vocemassussia aka Isabella-Vokemassussia - 3/4th Kishpoko-Pekowi-Creek Metis born 1772 OH-died after 1815 - youngest daughter of **Puckenshinwa Rising Sun**/1735 & **Metheotashe Opessa**/1738, wife 1st 1786 OH of **Thomas Split Log**/1756-Wyandot, 2nd 1792 of **George Ironside Sr**/1760-adopted white-(Church married to Ironside 1810 at St. John's Parrish, Anglican Church), children/1786-91 **with Split Log** unknown, mother of **with Ironside** of Alexander Ironside/1793, George Ironside Jr/1806, 2 sons & 2 daughters/17941815-all 3/8th Kishpoko-Pekowi-Creek Metis, (often confused with sisters by some white histories)

GRANDSON

Puckenshinwa, Lalawethika aka Tenskawatawa-**Shawnee Prophet**-Open Door-Laulewashika-Lalawetheeka-Rattling Sound in Brush - 3/4th Kishpoko-Pekowi-Creek-Metis born 1774 OH-died 1837 KS - youngest son of **Puckenshinwa Rising Sun**/1735 & **Metheotashe Opessa**/1738, a Kishpoko, only one of triplet sons to survive infancy, youngest brother of **Tecumseh**, Fallen Timbers/1794, Council Greenville 1795, moved to IN 1798, defeated by **William Henry Harrison** at Prophet's Town aka Tippicanoe/1811, took little active (warrior) part in Tecumseh's campaign of 1795-1810 or War of 1812, moved 1815 to CAN with band of followers & family of Tecumseh, returned to OH 1825, moved to KS 1826 with nephew **Paukeesaa Tecumseh**, married 5 times, husband 1st about 1792 OH of **Kishpoko Woman**/1776, again by 1814 (IN-OH?) of **Pricilla Perkins**/1795adopted white, other 3 wives unknown for now, father **with Kishpoko** of John Prophet/1792, 1 other son & 3 daughters-all 7/8th KishpokoPekowi-Creek-Metis, **with Perkins** of Marcia Bates/1814-3/8th Kishpoko-Pekowi-Creek-Metis, children **with other wives** unknown

CHAPTER EIGHT

John Forked Tail Watts/1704

John Forked Tail Watts/1704

Watts, John Forked Tail aka John Watts (2)--John Watts Sr-**Little Tassel**-Old Forked Tongue – 55/64th Chalakatha-Pekowi-ShawanoChalaka-Powhatan-Metis born 1704 VA-died 1779 Great Tellico TN – son of **Thomas Tassel Watts (2)/1682 & Sister of Oshasqua-Muskrat (2)/1684**, adopted son 1708 TN-VA of **Swan-Wapehti Turkey (Cornstalk)/1686** & his uncle **Oshasqua-Muskrat (2)-Moytoy (5)/1686** when his family was killed by Catawba/Cherokee, could speak, cipher, read & write English, Cornstalk War/1755-69, **associated with John Swift** silver-mining & counterfeiting/1761-69, associated with **Cornstalk, Dragging Canoe, Doublehead, Nathaniel Gist, Sam Blackburn, Abram Flint, Herman Staley, Isaac Campbell, Shadrack Jefferson, Pierre St. Martin, Andrew Renound, Jeremiah Bates, Alexander Bartel, Henry Hazlitt & Moses Fletcher** on the frontier, husband 1st 1724 Settico TN of **Quatsis Fox/1708**, 2nd 1728 (officially in 1735) of **White Woman/1712**, 3rd 1743 Great Tellico TN of **Oousta Carpenter/1722**, 4th 1747 Running Water TN of **Ghigoneli Bowles/1723**, father with **Fox** of Son (John Watts?)/1724, Terrapin Watts/1726, Bark Watts/1728 & other children/1724-35-all 47/64th Chalakatha-Pekowi-Shawano-Chalaka-Powhatan-Cherokee-Metis, father with **White Woman** of John Watts (John Watt's Son-John Watson)/1728 & other children/1729-43-all 27/64th ChalakathaPekowi-Shawano-Chalaka-Powhatan-Metis, father **with Carpenter** of Wurteh Watts/1744, John Watts Jr-**Young Tassel**/1746, Jacob Watts/1748, Elizabeth Watts/1750 & **Unacata**-White Mankiller

Shawnee Heritage II

Watts/1752-all 19/32nd Chalakatha-Pekowi-Shawano-ChalakaPowhatan-Cherokee-Metis, **with Bowles** of Nancy Watts/1748, Ghigoneli Watts-Ghigoneli Bowles (2)/1750 & John Watts (John Bowles-Chief Bowl)/1756-all 45/64th Chalakatha-Pekowi-ShawanoChalaka-Powhatan-Metis

WIVES OF JOHN FORKED TAIL WATTS

1ST WIFE 1724 VA

Fox, Quatsis aka Quatsis Smallpox Conjurer-**Daughter of Quatsis Hop-Niece of Standing Turkey-Old Hop's Niece-John Watts' Wife** -31/64th Chalakatha-Shawano-Chalaka-Powhatan-Cherokee born 1708 Settico TN-died after 1760 - daughter of **Quatsis Turkey/1682** & **Tsula FoxSmallpox Conjurer/1670**-Cherokee, wife 1st 1724 Settico TN of **John Fork Tail Watts/1704** (left with her two younger sons Watts 1735 when he began living with a White Woman), 2nd (his 2nd of 3) 1735 Chota TN of 1st cousin **Oconastota Rainmaker/1702** (left Oconastota 1738 when he married **Lucy Ward (1)/1714**-white) 3rd 1738 Running Water TN of **John Drowning Bear Brown (1)/1700**-adopted white, mother **with Watts** of John Green Corn Top Watts/1724, Terrapin Watts/1726, Bark Watts/1728 & children/1729-34-all 47/64th Chalakatha-PekowiShawano-Chalaka-Powhatan-Cherokee-Metis, **with Oconastota** of
Quatsis Oconastota/1736-31/64th Chalakatha-Shawano-ChalakaPowhatan-Cherokee, **with Brown** of Alexander Brown/1738, children/1739-46, Mary Brown/1747, Robert Brown/1749 & John Drowning Bear Brown (3)-Junaluska (1)/1751-all 15/64th ChalakathaShawano-Chalaka-Powhatan-Cherokee-Metis

2ND WIFE 1728 VA

Watts, Wife of John Forked Tail aka John Watts' Wife – (apparently) white born about 1712 (VA?)-died after 1746, **parents unknown** but appear to have been from the settlements of southwestern VA, name unknown, living with him by 1728-by 1735 called the wife of **John Forked Tail Watts/1704**, mother of John Watts (3)-John Watson/1728 & other children/1729-46-all 27/64th Chalakatha-Pekowi-Shawano-

Chalaka-Powhatan-Metis

3ᴿᴰ WIFE 1743 GREAT TELLICO - TN

Carpenter, Oousta aka Oousta White Owl-Oousta Great Eagle-Kahtayah – 11/32nd Chalakatha-Shawano-Chalaka-Powhatan-Cherokee-Metis born 1722 Great Tellico TN-died 1768 Great Tellico TN - daughter of **Nancy Rainmaker**/1683 & **White Owl Carpenter**/1678, **adopted daughter** after 1726 of her half-brother **Great Eagle Carpenter**/1702 & **Wurteh Tawsee Fox**/1704-Cherokee, Red Paint Clan Cherokee (by adoption), could read & speak a little English, wife 1st 1736 Great Tellico TN of **Alexander Drumgoole (1)**/1710-white, 2nd 1737 Great Tellico TN of **John Anthony Foreman (1)**/1720-white, 3rd 1739 Great Tellico TN of **Bushyhead-Chiesatebe Hop**/1718, 4th 1743 Great Tellico TN of **John Forked Tail Watts**/1704, 5th 1752 Great Tellico TN of **Walker Cornstalk**/1730, mother **with Drumgoole** of Alexander Drumgoole (2)/1736-11/64th Chalakatha-Shawano-Chalaka-Powhatan-Cherokee-Metis, **with Foreman** of Thomas Foreman/1737 & Nancy Foreman/1739-both 11/64th Chalakatha-Shawano-Chalaka-PowhatanCherokee-Metis, **with Hop** of Tahnoyanteehee/1741 & Tahlonteeskee/1743-both 21/32nd Chalakatha-Shawano-ChalakaPowhatan-Cherokee-Metis, **with Watts** of Wurteh Watts/1744, John
Watts Jr-Young Tassel Watts/1746, Jacob Watts/1748, Elizabeth Watts/1750 & Unacata-White Mankiller Watts/1752-all 19/32nd Chalakatha-Pekowi-Shawano-Chalaka-Powhatan-Cherokee-Metis, **with Walker Cornstalk** of John Walker/1753-5/8th Chalakatha-Mekoche-Shawano-Chalaka-Powhatan-Cherokee-Metis

4ᵀᴴ WIFE 1747 RUNNING WATER TN

Bowles, Ghigoneli aka Chekawnahler-Forget Me Not - 9/16th Chalakatha-Shawano-Chalaka-Powhatan-Metis born 1723 Settico TNdied 1760 TN of smallpox - daughter of **Oolootah Turkey**/1692 & **John Bowles (1)**/1688-Scot, Blue Holly Clan Cherokee, niece of **Old Hop**/1688, namesake of her mother's deceased younger sister, wife 1st 1738 Settico TN of **Rising Fawn Fox (1)**/1706, 2nd 1747 Running Water TN of **John Forked Tail Watts**/1704, mother **with Rising Fawn** of Rising Fawn (2)/1740-33/64th Chalakatha-Shawano-Chalaka-

Powhatan-Cherokee-Metis, **with Watts** of Nancy Watts/1748, Ghigoneli Watts/1752 & John Watts (4)-**Chief Bowl**-John Bowles (2)/1756-all 45/64th Chalakatha-Pekowi-Shawano-Chalaka-PowhatanMetis

CHILDREN OF JOHN FORKED TAIL WATTS WITH QUATSIS FOX/1708

SON

Watts, **John Green Corn Top** aka John Watts (3)-John Green Corn Watts-John Trader Watts - 47/64th Chalakatha-Pekowi-ShawanoChalaka-Powhatan-Cherokee-Metis born 1724 Carolyn Co VA/Chota
TN-died 1775 – son of **John Forked Tail Watts**/1704 & **Quatsis Fox**/1708, husband 1751 (TN?) of **Giyostikoyohe Tarchee**/1736-Bird Clan, father of Malachi Watts/1752, Garrett Watts/1754, Henry Watts/1760, Benjamin Watts/1763-all 11/32nd Chalakatha-PekowiCherokee-Metis (still being researched)

SON

Watts, Terrapin aka **Terrapin Oconastota (2)**-Terrapin (2)-Tuckasee of Etowah-Tukasi – 47/64th Chalakatha-Pekowi-Shawano-ChalakaPowhatan-Cherokee-Metis born 1726 Chota TN-died after 1796 GA – son of **John Forked Tail Watts**/1704 & **Quatsis Fox**/1708, adopted son 1735 of **Oconastota**/1702, Red Paint Clan Cherokee, Pigeon CoCherokee scouts-**with U.S. Army**-Revolution/1778-83, Treaty Sycamore
Shoals 1775, Tellico 1794, husband 1st about 1746 TN of **Unknown Woman**/1730, 2nd 1757 Etowah TN of **Old Jennie**/1744-Cherokee, children/1746-56 **with 1st Wife** unknown, father **with Jennie** of Polly Terrapin (Watts)/1768 & Little Terrapin-Brother Terrapin (Watts)/1770both 13/64th Chalakatha-Pekowi-Shawano-ChalakaPowhatanCherokee-Metis

SON

Watts, Bark aka **Bark Oconastota-Bark of Chota** – 47/64th ChalakathaPekowi-Shawano-Chalaka-Powhatan-Cherokee-Metis born 1728 Chota TN-died 1754 TN of smallpox – son of **John Forked Tail Watts**/1704 &
Quatsis Fox/1708, adopted son 1735 of **Oconastota**/1702, Red Paint Cherokee, a medicine man, died 1754 of smallpox caught while doctoring the ill, husband 1748 Chota TN of his adopted sister **Jennie Oconastota**/1724, father **with Jennie** of Bark Watts (2)-Bark Oconastota (2)/1750-39/64th Chalakatha-Pekowi-Thawikila-Shawano-ChalakaPowhatan-Creek-Cherokee-Metis

WITH WHITE WIFE/1712

SON

Watson, John (1) aka John Watts' Son-John Watts (3) – 27/64th Chalakatha-Pekowi-Shawano-Chalaka-Powhatan-Metis born 1728 York Co PA (more likely in VA somewhere)-died 1802 Rutherford Co NC – son of **John Forked Tail Watts**/1704 & **White Woman**/1712, husband 1756 York Co PA of **Ann Anderson**/1740, father of John Watson Jr/1756, Jennie Watson/1762, Philadelphia Watson/1764, Sawncy Watson/1766, Obediah Watson/1768, Matthew Watson/1770, Joseph P. Watson/1772, William Watson/1774, David Watson/1776-all 13/64th Chalakatha-Pekowi-Shawano-Chalaiwa-Powhatan-Metis (still being researched)

WITH OOUSTA CARPENTER/1722

DAUGHTER

Watts, **Wurteh** aka Elizabeth Watts-Betsy Watts-Molly Running Wolf – 19/32nd Chalakatha-Pekowi-Shawano-Chalaka-Powhatan-Cherokee-Metis born 1744 Great Tellico TN-died 1779 NC - daughter of **John Forked Tail Watts**/1704 & **Oousta Carpenter**/1722, Red Paint Clan Cherokee (through mother)-later Bird Clan (by marriage?), known for her beauty, wife 1st 1757 Great Tellico TN of **Robert Due-Chief JollyJaulee**/1737, 2nd 1758 of **Nathaniel Gist**/1730, 3rd 1759 Great Tellico TN of **Bloody Fellow**/1740-Kishpoko, 4th 1760 of **John Trader Benge**/1730white, 5th by 1770 (VA?) of **Nathaniel Lawson**/1724-white, mother **with Due** of Chief John Jolly/1758-35/64th Chalakatha-Pekowi-ShawanoChalaka-Powhatan-Cherokee-Metis, **with Gist** of Sequoyah-George Gist/1759-19/64th Chalakatha-Pekowi-Shawano-Chalaka-Powhatan-Cherokee-Metis, **with Bloody Fellow** of Tahlonteeskee (2)Tahlonteeskee Bloody Fellow-Tahlonteeskee (Benge)/1760-51/64th Kishpoko-Chalakatha-Pekowi-Shawano-Chalaka-Powhatan-CherokeeMetis, **with Benge** of Martin-Utana-Tail Benge/1761, Robert-Chief Bench Benge/1762, Richard Benge/1763, Catherine Benge/1764, Tashliske-White Path Benge/1765 & Lucy Benge/1766-all 19/64th Chalakatha-Pekowi-Shawano-Chalaka-Powhatan-Cherokee-Metis, children **with Lawson** of Drury Lawson/1770-19/64th Chalakatha-Pekowi-Shawano-Chalaka-Powhatan-Cherokee-Metis

SON

Watts, John **Young Tassel** aka John Watts Jr-John Watts (4)-Kunoskeskie-Coatohee-Corn Tassel of Toquo-Green Corn Top – 19/32nd Chalakatha-Pekowi-Shawano-Chalaka-Powhatan-Cherokee-Metis born 1746 Wills Town AL-died 1808 Dekalb Co. AL - son of **Oousta Carpenter**/1722 & **John Forked Tail Watts**/1704, could cipher, read & speak some English, Red Paint Clan Cherokee, Treaty Sycamore Shoals 1775, Council Coyatee 1792, **succeeded Dragging Canoe as Chickamauga Chief** 1792 **with Little Turkey**-Standing Turkey (2)/1715-(son of **Old Hop-Standing Turkey**), raiding TN 1788 **with Major Ridge**, wounded 1792 while leading attack on Buchanan Station-with 310 mixed Native forces, Council Hanging Maw Town 1793-survived attack by **John Beard**'s renegade militia, 1794 joined **Chief Bowl** in attack on Muscle Shoals settlement, 1794 sued for peace following Major **James Orr's** invasion of the Chickamauga towns, 1796 met **George Washington** in Philadelphia, 1800 met the Moravian missionaries at Spring Place, signed the 1805 Treaty, husband 1st 1768 Great Tellico TN of **Mary Johnson**/1753-Deer Clan, 2nd 1778 Great Tellico TN of **Wurtegua Carpenter**/1760, 3rd 1780 Great Tellico TN of **Nancy Oousta Hanging Maw**/1750, 4th about 1799 (AL?) **Tsiyugi Cherokee**/1780-Cherokee, father **with Johnson** of John Watts Jr/1768, children/1769-78, Margaret Watts/1778-all 19/64th Chalakatha-

PekowiShawano-Chalaka-Powhatan-Cherokee-Metis, **with Carpenter** of Mink
Watts/1780, Capt. John Watts/1782, Soup-Chulusatah Watts/1784 & Fish Tail-Fork Tail Watts/1786-all ½ Chalakatha-Pekowi-Thawikila-Shawano-Chalaka-Powhatan-Creek-Cherokee-Metis, **with Maw** of Thomas Watts/1782, Two Wood-Double Tree Watts/1784, Peach Eater Watts/1786, Elizabeth Watts/1788 & Councilor John Watts/1792-all 15/64th Chalakatha-Pekowi-Shawano-Chalaka-Powhatan-CherokeeMetis, **with Tsiyugi** of Rachel Watts/1800, John Watts/1804, Mary
Polly Watts/1806-all 19/64th Chalakatha-Pekowi-Shawano-ChalakaPowhatan-Cherokee-Metis

SON

Watts, Jacob – 19/32nd Chalakatha-Pekowi-Shawano-ChalakaPowhatan-Cherokee-Metis born about 1745-died 1821 Anson NC – son of **John Forked Tail Watts**/1704 & **Oousta Carpenter**/1722, husband about 1765 NC-TN of **Cherokee Woman**/1750, father of Margaret Watts/1793-19/64th Chalakatha-Pekowi-Shawano-Chalaka-PowhatanCherokee-Metis

SON

Watts, Unacata aka White Mankiller-Unakateehee – 19/32nd Chalakatha-Pekowi-Shawano-Chalaka-Powhatan-Cherokee-Metis born 1748 Willstown AL-died after 1814 AL?)- son of **John Forked Tail Watts**/1704 & **Oousta Carpenter**/1722, Red Paint Clan Cherokee, Treaty Sycamore Shoals 1775, a Chickamaugua/1777-92, wounded 1792 at Buchanan Station, **with U.S. Army**-Creek War/1813-wounded 1814 at Horseshoe Bend, husband 1768 TN of **Cherokee Woman**/1755, father of Sally Watts/1771, Wat Watts/1776, Raven-Cawluhnah Watts/1778, Charles Watts/1780, Jennie Watts/1782, Betty Watts/1784 & Jackson Mankiller (Watts)/1786-all 19/64th Chalakatha-PekowiShawano-Chalaka-Powhatan-Cherokee-Metis

DAUGHTER

Watts, Elizabeth – 19/32nd Chalakatha-Pekowi-Shawano-ChalakaPowhatan-Cherokee-Metis born 1750 Willstown AL-died after

1790 - daughter of **Oousta Carpenter**/1722 & **John Forked Tail Watts**/1704, Red Paint Clan Cherokee, wife 1st 1765 (AL?) of **Unknown Man**, 2nd 1779 (AL?) of **William R. Campbell**/1760-white, 3rd 1789 AL of **Leckickee Natchez**/1750-Natchez, children/1765-79 **with Unknown Man** not known, mother **with Campbell** of William R. Campbell Jr/1780, Lucy Campbell/1782, Elizabeth Campbell/1786, Diana Campbell/1788-all 19/64th Chalakatha-Pekowi-Shawano-ChalakaPowhatan-Cherokee-Metis, **with Natchez** of Nancy Natchez/179019/64th Chalakatha-Pekowi-Shawano-Chalaka-Powhatan-NatchezCherokee-Metis

WITH GHIGONELI BOWLES/1723

DAUGHTER

Watts, Nancy aka Nannie-Nannte-Nionee-Ooloosta – 45/64th Chalakatha-Pekowi-Shawano-Chalaka-Powhatan-Metis born 1748 Great Tellico TN-died after 1786 - daughter of **Ghigoneli Bowles**/1723 & **John Forked Tail Watts**/1704, Blue Holly Clan Cherokee, wife 1767 Nickajack TN of **George Lowery (1)**/1740-white, mother of (Major) John Lowery/1768, (Major) George Lowery/1770, Elizabeth Lowery/1776, Sarah Lowery/1778, Jennie Lowery/1780, Aky Lowery/1782 & Nellie Lowery/1786-all 11/32nd Chalakatha-PekowiShawano-Chalaka-Powhatan-Metis

DAUGHTER

Watts, Ghigoneli aka Forget Me Not-Chekawnahler – 45/64th Chalakatha-Pekowi-Shawano-Chalaka-Powhatan-Metis born 1752 Running Water TN-died about 1804 TN - daughter of **Ghigoneli Bowles**/1723 & **John Forked Tail Watts**/1704, Red Paint Clan Cherokee (?), namesake of mother & great-aunt, wife 1st (his 2nd) 1769 Nickajack TN of **George Lowery (1)**/1740-white, 2nd 1772 Settico TN of her half-brother **Rising Fawn Fox (2)**/1730-1/2 Chalakatha-Cherokee, no children of record **with Lowery**, mother of **with Rising Fawn** of Rising Fawn (3)/1772, Catherine Rising Fawn/1774 & Polly Rising Fawn/1776-all 39/64th Chalakatha-Pekowi-Shawano-Chalaka-Powhatan-Cherokee-Metis

SON

Bowl, Chief aka **Chief John Bowles** (1)-John Watts (6)-Bold HunterToowayellah-Duwali – 45/64th Chalakatha-Pekowi-Shawano-ChalakaPowhatan-Metis - born 1756 Settico TN-**killed** in battle 1839 TX - son of **Ghigoneli Bowles**/1723 & **John Forked Tail Watts**/1704, **took white name of his grandfather John Bowles (1)**/1700-Scot upon his murder in 1769, as a big, strong 13 year old Bowl began hunting down the murders & eventually killed them all, Blue Holly Cherokee-Red Paint Clan (by marriage?), great-nephew of **Old Hop**, Treaty 1791, 1805, 1836,

1786 **Chief** of **Little Hiwassee Town** NC & 1790 **Chief** of **Running Water** TN, a Chickamaugua/1775-94, 1794 joined by his half-brother **John Young Tassel Watts** in attack on Muscle Shoals settlement, moved to mouth of St. Francis River AR-(LA Territory) 1795 joining the Chickamauga (mixed Shawnee-Cherokee) already there, **Chief of St. Francis AR village before 1800**, settlement destroyed by 1811 earthquake, moved to between Arkansas & White Rivers-continued as **Head Chief of AR Cherokee** 1800-1810, Capt. John MacIntosh Co-**with U.S. Army**-Creek War/1813, moved to TX when he was excluded from Treaty 1819, **Head Chief TX Chickamauga** 1827-39, founding member of Tahlequah OK Masonic Lodge, **killed 1839 in battle with Mexicans in TX**, most of family/band moved back to OK/1839, husband 1st 1776 Little Hiawassee TN of **Red Paint Woman**/1760-Cherokee, 2nd 1783 Running Water TN of **Ooloosta Tahchee**/1760, 3rd 1794 Running Water TN of **Jennie Due**/1764, 4th 1804 St. Francis AR of **Otiyu Vann**/1786, children/1776-83 **with Red Paint Woman** unknown, father **with Tahchee** of Lightning Bug-Lightning Bowles/1784, Tunooneski Bowles/1786, Standing Man Bowles/1788, Quatini Bowles/1790 & Tsagina Bowles/1792-all 11/32nd Chalakatha-Pekowi-ThawikilaShawano-Chalaka-Creek-Cherokee-Metis, **with Due** of John Bowles JrLittle Bowl/1796, French Bowles/1797, Nellie-Neli-Ghigoneli Bowles/1798, Standing Bowles/1799 & James Bowles/1800-all ½ Chalakatha-Pekowi-Shawano-Chalaka-Powhatan-Cherokee-Metis, **with Vann** of Samuel Bowles/1805, Rebecca Duga Bowles/1806, Standing In The Middle Bowles/1808, Nancy Bowles/1810, Catherine Bowles/1812 & Eliza Bowles/1814-all 43/64th Chalakatha-Pekowi-Shawano-ChalakaPowhatan-Black-Cherokee-Metis

GRANDCHILDREN OF JOHN FORKED TAIL WATTS
BY JOHN GREEN CORN TOP WATTS/1724 & GIYOSTIKOYOHE TARCHEE/1736

GRANDDAUGHTER

Watts, Bathsheba - 11/32nd Chalakatha-Pekowi-Cherokee-Metis born 1746 Edgecombe Co NC-died after 1804 – daughter of **John Green Corn Top Watts**/1724 & **Giyostikoyohe Tarchee**/1726, wife about 1770 Anson Co NC of **William Gulledge**/1740, mother of Britain Gulledge, Thomas Gulledge, Fredrick Gulledge, John Gulledge, Mary Gulledge, Stephen Malachi Gulledge, Alice Gulledge, Martha Gulledge, Elijah Gulledge, William Gulledge Jr & Virginia Rebecca Gulledge-all 11/64th Chalakatha-Pekowi-Cherokee-Metis (still being researched)

GRANDSON

Watts, Malachi - 11/32nd Chalakatha-Pekowi-Cherokee-Metis born 1752 NC/TN-died 1804 – son of **John Green Corn Top Watts**/1724 & **Giyostikoyohe Tarchee**/1726, husband about 1772 of **Annie Unknown**/1756, father of Elizabeth Watts, Frances Watts, Ann Watts, Polly Watts, Sarah Watts, Jemima Watts –all 11/64th ChalakathaPekowi-Cherokee-Metis (still being researched)

GRANDSON

Watts, Garrett aka Garrett Zachariah Watts - 11/32nd ChalakathaPekowi-Cherokee-Metis born 1756 Carolyn Co VA-died 1838 Perry Co
AL – son of **John Green Corn Top Watts**/1724 & **Giyostikoyohe Tarchee**/1726, husband 1781 VA (legally 1787 Anson Co NC) of **Anna Selph**/1766, father of Garrett Watts/1782 VA, John Zachariah Watts/1784 VA, William Jefferson Watts/1786 NC, Nancy Watts/1788, Malachi Watts/1790, Solomon Watts/1792, Spencer Watts/1794, Mary H. Watts/1800, Malinda Watts/1802, Vincent Watts/1804, Anna M. Watts/1806, Clinton Watts/1808, Jefferson J. Watts/1815-all at least

11/64th Chalakatha-Pekowi-Cherokee-Metis (still being researched)

GRANDSON

Watts, Henry - 11/32nd Chalakatha-Pekowi-Cherokee-Metis born 1760 Carolyn Co VA-died after 1792 – son of **John Green Corn Top Watts**/1724 & **Giyostikoyohe Tarchee**/1726, wife & children unknown

GRANDSON

Watts, Benjamin - 11/32nd Chalakatha-Pekowi-Cherokee-Metis born 1763 Carolyn Co VA-died after 1792 – son of **John Green Corn Top Watts**/1724 & **Giyostikoyohe Tarchee**/1726, wife & children unknown

BY TERRAPIN WATTS-OCONASTOTA/1726 & OLD JENNIE/1744

GRANDDAUGHTER

Terrapin, Polly aka Polly Watts – 13/64th Chalakatha-Pekowi-ShawanoChalaka-Powhatan-Cherokee-Metis born 1768 Etowah TN-died 1833 - daughter of **Terrapin Watts (Oconastota)**/1726 & **Old Jennie**/1744Cherokee, wife 1st about 1788 of **John Cherokee Vann**/1744, 2nd before
1807 of **Cherokee Man**/1760, mother **with Vann** of George Vann/1790 & John Boy Vann/1792-both 3/8th Chalakatha-Pekowi-Shawano-Chalaka-Powhatan-Cherokee-Metis, children **with Cherokee** unlikely

GRANDSON

Terrapin, Little Brother aka Little Brother Watts – 13/64th ChalakathaPekowi-Shawano-Chalaka-Powhatan-Cherokee-Metis born about 1770
Etowah TN-died after 1814 TN - son of **Terrapin Watts (Oconastota)**/1726 & **Old Jennie**/1744-Cherokee, wife & children unknown

BY BARK WATTS-OCONASTOTA/1728 & JENNIE OCONASTOTA/1724

GRANDSON

Watts, Bark (2) aka **Bark Oconastota (2)** – 39/64th Chalakatha-PekowiThawikila-Shawano-Chalaka-Powhatan-Creek-Cherokee-Metis born about 1750 Chota TN-died 1806 of smallpox - son of **Bark Watts**/1728 & **Jennie Oconastota**/1724, a medicine man, died 1806 of smallpox caught while doctoring the ill (as his father had done), Pigeon Co-Cherokee scouts-**with U.S. Army**-Revolution/1778-83, husband 1770 Chota TN of **Red Paint Cherokee**/1755, father of **with Red Paint** of Young Bark Watts/1780-1/8th Chalakatha-Pekowi-Thawikila-Shawano-Chalaka-Powhatan-Creek-Cherokee-Metis

BY JOHN WATSON/1728 & ANN ANDERSON/1740

GRANDSON

Watson, John (2) – 13/64th Chalakatha-Pekowi-Shawano-ChalakaPowhatan-Metis born 1756 York Co PA-died 1840 Etowah Co AL – son of **John Watson**/1728 & **Ann Anderson**/1740, husband (2nd?) about
1790 Rutherford Co NC of **Mahala Long**, father of Levi Edmond Watson/1792, Eli Watson/1795, John Watson (3)/1798, Joseph Watson/1800, William Watson/1805, Wimberley Fredrick Watson/1813, John Watson (4)/1816, Moses Watson/1818-all 3/32nd Chalakatha-Pekowi-Shawano-Chalaka-Powhatan-Metis

GRANDDAUGHTER

Watson, Jenny – 13/64th Chalakatha-Pekowi-Shawano-ChalakaPowhatan-Metis born 1762-died after 1778 – daughter of **John Watson**/1728 & **Ann Anderson**/1740, husband & children unknown

GRANDDAUGHTER

Watson, Philadelphia – 13/64th Chalakatha-Pekowi-Shawano-ChalakaPowhatan-Metis born 1764-died after 1780 – daughter of **John Watson**/1728 & **Ann Anderson**/1740, wife of **Mr. McCray**, children unknown

GRANDCHILD

Watson, Sawncy – 13/64th Chalakatha-Pekowi-Shawano-ChalakaPowhatan-Metis born 1766-died after 1782 – child of **John Watson**/1728 & **Ann Anderson**/1740, spouse & children unknown

GRANDSON

Watson, Obediah – 13/64th Chalakatha-Pekowi-Shawano-ChalakaPowhatan-Metis born 1768-died after 1788 – son of **John Watson**/1728 & **Ann Anderson**/1740, husband 1788 of **Sarah Unknown**/1771, children unknown

GRANDSON

Watson, Matthew – 13/64th Chalakatha-Pekowi-Shawano-ChalakaPowhatan-Metis born 1770-died after 1788 – son of **John Watson**/1728 & **Ann Anderson**/1740, wife & children unknown

GRANDSON

Watson, Joseph P. –13/64th Chalakatha-Pekowi-Shawano-ChalakaPowhatan-Metis born 1772-died after 1792 – son of **John Watson**/1728 & **Ann Anderson**/1740, husband about 1792 of **Cathan Harris**/1775, children unknown

GRANDSON

Watson, William (1) –13/64th Chalakatha-Pekowi-Shawano-ChalakaPowhatan-Metis born 1774-died 1846 Etowah Co AL – son of **John Watson**/1728 & **Ann Anderson**/1740, husband about 1794 of **Bethany Unknown**/1776, children unknown

GRANDSON

Watson, David –13/64th Chalakatha-Pekowi-Shawano-ChalakaPowhatan-Metis born 1776-died after 1794 – son of **John Watson**/1728 & **Ann Anderson**/1740, wife & children unknown

BY WURTEH WATTS/1744
& ROBERT DUE-JAULEE/1737

GRANDSON

Jolly, Chief John aka Kalanna-Akuludegee-Ooleteka-OoluntuskeeAnuludegi-Eulatakee-Throws Away The Drum-John Due-John Jaulee –
35/64th Chalakatha-Pekowi-Shawano-Chalaka-Powhatan-CherokeeMetis born 1758 Great Tellico TN-died 1838 Webber Falls OK - son of
Robert Due-Chief Jolly/1737 & **Wurteh Watts**/1744, Long Hair Clan Cherokee (but should have been Red Paint through his mother?), operated a trading post at juncture of Hiwassee & Tennessee Rivers TN, moved to AR about 1810, spoke English, French & several Native languages, succeeded half-brother **Tahlonteeskee Hop**/1743 as **Head Chief of AR Cherokee** 1819-38, half-brother through **Due** of **Tobacco Will**/1761, **Jennie Due**/1764, **Mary Due**/1770, **Betsy Houston (Due)**/1786 & **Jennie Houston (Due)**/1788, Treaty 1805, 1806, 1817, move to AR 1818, husband 1st 1779 TN of **Sarah Chickamauga**/1762, 2nd 1782 Great Tellico TN of **Elizabeth Emory**/1765, father **with Sarah** of Girt Jolly/1780, Rachel Jolly/1782, Price Jolly/1784, Elizabeth Jolly/1786, Sarah Jolly (2)/1788 & Golista Jolly/1790-all 17/32nd Chalakatha-Pekowi-Shawano-Chalaka-Powhatan-Cherokee-Metis, **with Emory** of William Jolly/1783 & John Jolly Jr/1785-both 35/64th Chalakatha-Pekowi-Shawano-Chalaka-Powhatan-Cherokee-Metis, adopted father of **Sam Houston**/1793-white-(some connection of Sam Houston/1793 to Betsy Houston-Due/1786 & Jennie Houston-Due/1788?)

BY WURTEH WATTS/1744
& NATHANIEL GIST/1720

GRANDSON

Gist, George (1) aka **Sequoyah**-George Guess-Sowgli-Sikwayi-Pig's

Foot-Horse – 19/64th Chalakatha-Pekowi-Shawano-Chalaka-Powhatan-Cherokee-Metis born 1758 Great Tellico TN-died 1843 MX - son of **Wurteh Watts**/1744 & **Nathaniel Gist**/1730, Red Paint Clan Cherokee, raised by step-grandfather **Red Horse-Sagwiligigagei**/1720-Cherokee, grandson of **Christopher Gist**/1705-white & (by Wurteh) of **Oousta White Owl Carpenter**/1725 & **John Forked Tail Watts**/1704, **created Cherokee alphabet & syllabary**, from Will's Town AL, John McLemore Co-**with U.S. Army**-Creek War/1813-Horseshoe Bend/1814, fingers cut off his right hand to 1st knuckle by Cherokee-American conspiracy to stop his writing, a blacksmith & silversmith by trade, moved to AR 1815, delegate to D.C. 1828, Treaty 1828, moved to OK 1829, died on trip to MX with son **Teesey Gist(1)**/1789, **Standing Bowles**/1799, **Standing Man Bowles**/1788 & with **Worm, John Elijah, Oowositi, Cahtata, Tallatoo & Coteska**-all (allegedly) Cherokee looking for the Shawnee-Cherokee in MX, step-brother of **Tobacco Will** (Red Horse)/1761, husband 1st 1779 of **Utiyu Ughui**/1765-Cherokee(divorced 1787), 2nd 1787 of **Sally Waters**/1770, 3rd about 1798 of
Wokteeyah Langley/1785-Creek-Metis, 4th 1802 of his half-1st cousin **Lucy Campbell**/1782, 5th 1806 **Tsiyosa Cherokee**/1790, 6th 1815 of his half-niece **Sally Benge**/1797, 7th 1817 AR **Ukatiya Tsoiyuka**/1796Cherokee, 8th 1826 AR of **Sally Agadiya Waters**/1790, father **with**
Utiyu of daughters Eyagu Sequoyah/1780, Ooloosta Sequoyah (1)/1782, Gooneki Sequoyah (1)/1784 & Atoyah Sequoyah (1)/1786-all 9/32nd Chalakatha-Pekowi-Shawano-Chalaka-Powhatan-Cherokee-Metis, **with Sally Waters** of Teeseey Gist (1)/1789, George Gist Jr (1)/1790, Polly Gist (1)/1792, Lightning Bug Gist-Richard Gist (1)/1794 & Tishali Gist (1)/1795-all 17/64th Chalakatha-Pekowi-ShawanoChalaka-Powhatan-Cherokee-Metis, **with Langley** of Oolootsa Gist
(2)/1799 & Gooneki Gist (2)/1800-both 9/32nd Chalakatha-PekowiShawano-Chalaka-Powhatan-Creek-Cherokee-Metis, **with Campbell** of
Richard Gist (2)/1802-19/64th Chalakatha-Pekowi-Shawano-ChalakaPowhatan-Cherokee-Metis, **with Tsiyosa** of George Wagonwheel/1806, Polly Gist (2)/1808 & Teesey Gist (2) Gist/1812-all 9/32nd

Chalakatha-Pekowi-Shawano-Chalaka-Powhatan-Cherokee-Metis, **with Benge** of Robert Gist/1816-19/64th Chalakatha-Pekowi-ShawanoChalaka-Powhatan-Cherokee-Metis, father **with Tsoiyuka** of Rachel Ayuqui Gist/1818, Andrew Gist/1820, Oolootsa Gist (3)/1822 & Patsy Gist/1824-all 9/32nd Chalakatha-Pekowi-Shawano-Chalaka-Powhatan-Cherokee-Metis, with **Sally Agadiya Waters** of Joseph Gist/1827, Lucinda Gist/1829, Susan Gist/1831, Elizabeth Gist/1833 & Mary Gist/1835-all 17/64th Chalakatha-Pekowi-Shawano-Chalaka-PowhatanCherokee-Metis

BY WURTEH WATTS/1744 & BLOODY FELLOW/1740

GRANDSON

Tahlonteeskee (2) aka Tahlonteeskee Bloody Fellow-**Tahlonteeskee Benge**-Tallotuskee-Tallunteeskee-Talluntusky-Tallotiskee-TalohuskeeTashiskee – 51/64th Kishpoko-Chalakatha-Pekowi-Shawano-ChalakaPowhatan-Cherokee-Metis born 1760 Great Tellico TN-died 1819 AR - son of **Wurteh Watts**/1744 & **Bloody Fellow**/1740-Kishpoko, adopted son of **John Trader Benge**, Red Paint Clan Cherokee, a Chickamauga/1777-92, Blue Jacket War/1782-94, operated a House of Entertainment 1801-1810, move to AR to join **Chief Bowl** 1810, Treaty 1806, **Principal Chief of AR Cherokee** 1810-19, succeeded by halfbrother Chief **John Jolly**/1757, Red Paint Clan Cherokee, husband 1st 1780 of **Elizabeth Tassel**/1760, 2nd 1795 of **Jennie Jane Lowery**/1780, children/1780-95 **with Tassel** unknown, father **with Lowery** of Tahlonteeskee (4)/1795-9/32nd Kishpoko-Chalakatha-Pekowi-Shawano-Chalaka-Powhatan-Black-Cherokee-Metis

BY WURTEH WATTS/1744 & JOHN BENGE/1730

GRANDSON

Benge, Martin Utana-Tail aka Martin Benge (1) – 19/64th ChalakathaPekowi-Shawano-Chalaka-Powhatan-Cherokee-Metis born 1761 Toqua TN-died 1838 (Trail?) - son of **Wurteh Watts**/1744 & **John Trader Benge**/1730-white, son in law of **Unacata Watts**-White Mankiller/1750, a Chickamauga/1777-99, Blue Jacket War/1778-94, from Will's Town AL (Shawnee-Cherokee village), husband 1st 1780 Running Water TN of **Daughter of Tahnoyanteehee Hop**/1765, 2nd 1788 of 1st cousin **Sally Watts**/1771, children/1780-88 **with Hop** unknown, father **with Watts** of Sally Benge/1797-19/64th Chalakatha-Pekowi-Shawano-Chalaka-Powhatan-Cherokee-Metis

GRANDSON

Benge, Robert aka **Chief Benge**-Bench-Robin Benge – 19/64th Chalakatha-Pekowi-Shawano-Chalaka-Powhatan-Cherokee-Metis born 1761 Toqua TN-**killed** 1794 Stone Mountain VA - son of **Wurteh Watts**/1744 & **John Trader Benge**/1730-white, Red Paint Clan Cherokee, known for his red hair, lived at Toquo village TN, Benge's Field AL & **with Shawnee in southern OH**, raiding 1777 **with Cheeseekau**-brother of Tecumseh, a Chickamauga/1778-94, Blue Jacket War/1778-94, from the Overhills, killed in VA after KY raid 1794, husband 1st 1781 (TN?) of **Dorcas Lightfoot**/1766, 2nd 1784 Running Water TN of **Tahneh-Dark Star-Slow Head Hop**/1769, 3rd 1786 Benge's Field GA of **Nancy Black Fox**/1762, father **with Lightfoot** of Edmund Benge-Edmund Duncan/1782 & Houston Benge/1784-41/64th Shawano-Thawikila-Chalakatha-Pekowi-Chalaka-Powhatan-CherokeeMetis, **with Tahneh-Slow Head** of Mary Polly (1)-Ooloosta Benge/1785 & Robert Benge Jr/1786-both 21/32nd Chalakatha-Pekowi-ShawanoChalaka-Powhatan-Cherokee-Metis is, **with Black Fox** of Richard Benge
(2)/1786, John Wagonmaster Benge/1788, Mary Polly Benge (2)/1790, Nancy Agnes Benge/1792-all 19/64th Chalakatha-Pekowi-ShawanoChalaka-Powhatan-Cherokee-Metis

GRANDSON

Benge, Richard (1) – 19/64th Chalakatha-Pekowi-Shawano-ChalakaPowhatan-Cherokee-Metis born 1763 Toqua TN-died after 1814

(AL?) - son of **Wurteh Watts**/1744 & **John Trader Benge**/1730-white, husband 1st 1782 Running Water TN of **Betsy Hop**/1767, 2nd 1802 (AL?) of **Wodiyohi Ugawalada**/1786-Cherokee, children/1782-1801 **with Betsy** unknown, father **with Wodiyohi** of Patsy Benge/1806, Tsawayuga Benge/1808, Nancy Benge/1810, Peggy Benge/1812 & Richard Benge Jr/1814-all 9/32nd Chalakatha-Pekowi-Shawano-Chalaka-PowhatanCherokee-Metis

GRANDDAUGHTER

Benge, Catherine Naquisi aka Naquese-Nakweesee – 19/64th Chalakatha-Pekowi-Shawano-Chalaka-Powhatan-Cherokee-Metis born 1764 Toqua TN-died after 1790 - daughter of **Wurteh Watts**/1744 & **John Trader Benge**/1730-white, husband & children unknown

GRANDSON

Benge, Tashliske aka White Path-Nunnahitsunega – 19/64th Chalakatha-Pekowi-Shawano-Chalaka-Powhatan-Cherokee-Metis born 1765 Toqua TN-**murdered** 1832 KY - son of **Wurteh Watts**/1744 & **John Trader Benge**/1730-white, leader of White Path (anti-Removal) Rebellion of 1820s-30s, **killed by whites 1832**, murdered in 1st group on Trail of Tears, husband 1st 1786 Running Water TN of **Daughter of Tahnoyanteehee Hop**/1771, 2nd 1814 (TN-KY?) of **Cherokee Woman**/1799, children/1786-1814 **with Hop** unknown, father **with Cherokee** of Matilda Benge/1815, Colejay Benge/1820, Ollie Benge/1822, Kalilahi Benge/1824, Sukey Benge/1826-all 9/32nd Chalakatha-Pekowi-Shawano-Chalaka-Powhatan-Cherokee-Metis

GRANDDAUGHTER

Benge, Lucy – 19/64th Chalakatha-Pekowi-Shawano-ChalakaPowhatan-Cherokee-Metis born 1766 Toqua TN-died 1847 OK - daughter of **Wurteh Watts**/1744 & **John Trader Benge**/1730-white, Red Paint Clan Cherokee, wife 1st 1783 of **Junaluska Drowning Bear (1)-John Drowning Bear Brown (3)**/1751, 2nd 1791 of **Major George Lowery Jr**/1768, mother **with Drowning Bear** of Junaluska Drowning Bear (3)/1784 & daughter Katolista Drowning Bear/1786-both 17/64th

Chalakatha-Pekowi-Shawano-Chalaka-Powhatan-Cherokee-Metis, **with Lowery** of James Lowery/1791, Susan Lowery/1793, George Lowery (3)/1799, Lydia Lowery/1803, Rachel Lowery/1805, John Lowery/1808, Anderson Pierce Lowery/1811-all 5/16th ChalakathaPekowi-Shawano-Chalaka-Powhatan-Metis

BY WURTEH WATTS/1744 & NATHANIEL LAWSON/1724

GRANDSON

Lawson, Drury - 19/64th Chalakatha-Pekowi-Shawano-ChalakaPowhatan-Cherokee-Metis born about 1770 Pittsylvania Co VA-died 1847 – son of **Wurteh Watts**/1744 & **Nathaniel Lawson**/1724, husband about 1788 (VA?) of **Hannah Potts**/1773, father of Stokely Lawson/1788, Nathaniel Lawson/1790, Thomas Lawson/1792, William Lawson/1796, Hannah Lawson/1798, Reuben Lawson/1802 & Amos Lawson/1804-all 9/32nd Chalakatha-Pekowi-Shawano-Chalaka-Powhatan-Cherokee-Metis

BY JOHN YOUNG TASSEL WATTS/1746 & MARY JOHNSON/1753

GRANDSON

Watts, John Jr - 19/64th Chalakatha-Pekowi-Shawano-ChalakaPowhatan-Cherokee-Metis born 1768 TN-died about 1840 (OK?) – son of **John Young Tassel Watts**/1746 & **Mary Johnson**/1753, Deer Clan Cherokee, John D. Brown-Lewis Hilderbrand Co-**with U.S. Army-**
Creek War/1838, husband about 1788 of **Daughter of Willico Maw**/1770, father of Daughter Watts/1790, John Watts Jr/1800-both 3/16th Chalakatha-Pekowi-Shawano-Chalaka-Powhatan-CherokeeMetis

GRANDDAUGHTER

Watts, Margaret – 19/64th Chalakatha-Pekowi-Shawano-Chalaka-PowhatanCherokee-Metis born 1778 Great Tellico TN-died 1798 in childbirth - daughter of **John-Young Tassel-Watts**/1746 & **Mary Johnson**/1753, Deer

Clan Cherokee, 1st wife 1794 of **Alexander Jeremiah Sanders**/1773, no children of record

BY JOHN WATTS JR-YOUNG TASSEL/1746

& WURTEGUA CARPENTER/1760

GRANDSON

Watts, Mink – ½ Chalakatha-Thawikila-Pekowi-Shawano-ChalakaPowhatan-Creek-Cherokee-Metis born 1780 Willstown AL-died before
1851 OK - son of **Wurtegua Carpenter**/1760 & **John-Young TasselWatts**/1746, Wolf Clan Cherokee, husband 1800 (AL?) of **Cherokee Woman**/1785, children unknown

GRANDSON

Watts, **Capt. John** - ½ Chalakatha-Thawikila-Pekowi-ShawanoChalaka-Powhatan-Creek-Cherokee-Metis born 1782 NC-died after
1850 Greene Co MO - son of **Wurtegua Carpenter**/1760 & **John-Young Tassel-Watts**/1746, Wolf Clan Cherokee, husband 1800 Willstown AL of **Mary Polly (1)-Ooloosta Benge**/1785-21/64th Chalakatha-Pekowi-Cherokee-Metis, father of Mary Chiouke Watts/1810, John Watts (10)/1815, Martha Watts/1818 & Cecilia Watts/1820-all 9/16th Kishpoko-Chalakatha-Pekowi-Thawikila-Shawano-Chalaka-Powhatan-Creek-Cherokee-Metis

GRANDSON

Watts, Soup Chulusatah – ½ Chalakatha-Thawikila-Pekowi-Shawano-Chalaka-Powhatan-Creek-Cherokee-Metis born 1784 NC-died after
1817 - son of **John-Young Tassel-Watts**/1746 & **Wurtegua Carpenter**/1760, Wolf Clan Cherokee, husband 1804 TN of **Cherokee Woman**/1788, children unknown

GRANDSON

Watts, Fishtail aka Fork-tail Watts – ½ Chalakatha-Thawikila-PekowiShawano-Chalaka-Powhatan-Creek-Cherokee-Metis born 1786

NC-died after 1835 OK - son of **Wurtegua Carpenter**/1760 & **John-Young Tassel-Watts**/1746, Wolf Clan Cherokee, husband 1806 TN of **Cherokee Woman**/1790, children unknown

BY JOHN YOUNG TASSEL WATTS/1746 & NANCY OOUSTA HANGING MAW/1750

GRANDSON

Watts, Thomas (3) – 15/64th Chalakatha-Pekowi-Shawano-Chalaka-Powhatan-Cherokee-Metis born 1781 AL-died before 1838 - son of **John-Young Tassel Watts**/1746 & **Nancy Oousta Hanging Maw**/1760, Wolf Clan Cherokee, husband 1st about 1800 of **Cherokee Woman**/1785, 2nd 1814 of his 1st cousin **Nellie Maw**/1797, children/1800-14 **with Cherokee** unknown, father **with Maw** of Polly Watts/1815, Doyuni Watts/1817 & Linda Watts/1819-all 1/8th Chalakatha-Pekowi-Shawano-Chalaka-Powhatan-Cherokee-Metis

GRANDSON

Watts, Two Woods aka **Atadiyoli-Double Tree** – 15/64th ChalakathaPekowi-Shawano-Chalaka-Powhatan-Cherokee-Metis born 1782 ALdied 1823 (AL?) - son of **John-Young Tassel Watts**/1746 & **Nancy Oousta Hanging Maw**/1760, Wolf Clan Cherokee, husband 1805 AL of
Tiyani-Dayeni Utlurtala/1790, father of Thomas Watts (4)/1819-7/32nd Chalakatha-Pekowi-Shawano-Chalaka-Powhatan-Cherokee-Metis

GRANDSON

Watts, Peach Eater aka Qunnuh-Peach-Granu – 15/64th ChalakathaPekowi-Shawano-Chalaka-Powhatan-Cherokee-Metis born 1784 ALdied after 1842 (OK?) - son of **John-Young Tassel Watts**/1746 & **Nancy Oousta Hanging Maw**/1760, Wolf Clan Cherokee, husband 1st 1804 AL of **Unknown Woman**/1789, 2nd 1824 AL of **Tiyani-Dayeni Utlurtala**/1790, 3rd 1838 of **Jennie Catateehee-Cahtahee-KatagiCahtagee**/1804, children/1804-24 **with Unknown Woman** unknown, father **with Utlurtala** of Jolly Watts/1824, Wat Watts/1826,

Charles Watts/1828 & Little Johnson Watts/1830-all 7/32nd Chalakatha-PekowiShawano-Chalaka-Powhatan-Cherokee-Metis, **with Catateehee** of Betty
Tuni-Toney Watts/1838, Raven-Cawluhnah Watts/1840 & Jennie Watts/1842-all 3/16th Chalakatha-Pekowi-Thawikila-ShawanoChalaka-Powhatan-Creek-Cherokee-Metis

GRANDDAUGHTER

Watts, Elizabeth – 15/64th Chalakatha-Pekowi-Shawano-ChalakaPowhatan-Cherokee-Metis born 1786 AL-died 1852 - daughter of **Nancy Oousta Hanging Maw**/1760 & **John-Young Tassel-Watts**/1746, Wolf Clan Cherokee, wife by 1810 of **Mr. Couch**/1786, mother of Isaac Couch/1820-7/32nd Chalakatha-Pekowi-Shawano-Chalaka-Powhatan-Cherokee-Metis

GRANDSON

Watts, **Councilor John** - 15/64th Chalakatha-Pekowi-ShawanoChalaka-Powhatan-Cherokee-Metis born 1792 AL-died after 1838 - son of **John-Young Tassel Watts**/1746 & **Nancy Oousta Hanging Maw**/1750, Wolf Clan Cherokee, husband by 1817 of **Cherokee Woman**/1800, father of Phillip Watts/1818-7/32nd Chalakatha-PekowiShawano-Chalaka-Powhatan-Cherokee-Metis

BY JOHN YOUNG TASSEL WATTS/1746 & TSIYUGI CHEROKEE/1780

GRANDDAUGHTER

Watts, Rachel – 19/64th Chalakatha-Pekowi-Shawano-ChalakaPowhatan-Cherokee-Metis born 1800 (AL?)-died after 1837 OK – daughter of **John Young Tassel Watts**/1746 & **Tsiyugi Cherokee**/1780, wife 1st about 1816 of **Mr. Thompson**/1790, 2nd about 1830 of **Isaac Vann**/1792, children unknown

GRANDSON

Watts, John Jr – 19/64th Chalakatha-Pekowi-Shawano-ChalakaPowhatan-Cherokee-Metis born 1804 (AL?)-died after 1840 OK – son of **John Young Tassel Watts**/1746 & **Tsiyugi Cherokee**/1780, husband about 1824 (AL?) of **Cherokee Woman**/1808, father of John Watts/1832, Thomas Watts/1834, James Watts/1836, Lucy Watts/1838, Yoksi Watts/1840-all 9/64th Chalakatha-Pekowi-ChalakaPowhatan-Cherokee-Metis

GRANDDAUGHTER

Watts, Mary Polly – 19/64th Chalakatha-Pekowi-ChalakaPowhatan-Cherokee-Metis born 1806 (AL?)-died 1836 in childbirth on
Trail – daughter of **John Young Tassel Watts**/1746 & **Tsiyugi Cherokee**/1780, wife 1st about 1829 of **Jack Chambers**/1806, 2nd about 1833 of **Edward Vann**/1802, mother **with Chambers** of Charles Chambers/1830 & Chiouke Chambers/1832-both 9/64th ChalakathaPekowi-Shawano-Chalaka-Powhatan-Cherokee-Metis, **with Vann** of
Catherine Vann/1834 & Martha Ann Ooloosta Vann/1836-both 31/64th Chalakatha-Kishpoko-Pekowi-Shawano-Chalaka-Powhatan-BlackCherokee-Metis

BY JACOB WATTS/1748
& CHEROKEE WOMAN/1750

GRANDDAUGHTER

Watts, Margaret – 19/64th Chalakatha-Pekowi-Shawano-ChalakaPowhatan-Cherokee-Metis born 1793 Haywood Co NC-died after 1813
– daughter of **Jacob Watts**/1748 & **Cherokee Woman**/1750, wife 1816 Haywood Co NC of **Asa Mullins**/1797, children unknown

BY ELIZABETH WATTS/1750
& WILLIAM R. CAMPBELL/1760

GRANDSON

Shawnee Heritage II

Campbell, William R. Jr. – 19/64th Chalakatha-Pekowi-ShawanoChalaka-Powhatan-Cherokee-Metis born 1780-died after 1818 - son of **Elizabeth Watts**/1750 & **William R. Campbell**/1755-white, Red Paint Clan Cherokee, husband 1st 1800 of **Blind Savannah Woman**/1785, 2nd by 1808 (her 5th) of his half-1st cousin **Sarah Lowery**/1774, 3rd (her 3rd) 1824 of **Mary Polly Scott**/1782, children/1800-07 **with Blind Savannah** unknown, father **with Lowery** of George William Campbell/1810 & Rope Campbell/1814-both 5/16th Chalakatha-Pekowi-Shawano-Chalaka-Powhatan-Cherokee-Metis, children **with Scott** unknown

GRANDDAUGHTER

Campbell, Lucy – 19/64th Chalakatha-Pekowi-Shawano-ChalakaPowhatan-Cherokee-Metis born about 1782 AL-died after 1810 - daughter of **Elizabeth Watts**/1752 & **William R. Campbell**/1755white, Red Paint Clan Cherokee, wife 1st 1801 of her half-1st cousin **Sequoyah-George Gist**/1758, 2nd 1803 of **James Orr**/1780-white, mother **with Sequoyah-George Gist** of Richard Gist/1802-19/64th Chalakatha-Pekowi-Shawano-Chalaka-Powhatan-Cherokee-Metis, **with Orr** of Nelson Orr/1805-9/64th Chalakatha-Pekowi-Shawano-ChalakaPowhatan-Cherokee-Metis

GRANDDAUGHTER

Campbell, Elizabeth – 19/64th Chalakatha-Pekowi-Shawano-Chalaka-Powhatan-Cherokee-Metis born 1786-died after 1812 - daughter of **Elizabeth Watts**/1750 & **William R. Campbell**/1755-white, Red Paint Clan Cherokee, wife 1806 TN of **Richard Riley (1)**/1788-(son of **Samuel Riley**/1747 & **Gulustiyu Doublehead**/1766), mother of Jeannie C. Riley/1807, Annie Claunch Riley/1809 & Elizabeth Riley (2)/1811-all 3/16th Chalakatha-Pekowi-Shawano-Chalaka-Powhatan-Cherokee-Metis

GRANDDAUGHTER

Campbell, Diana – 19/64th Chalakatha-Pekowi-Shawano-ChalakaPowhatan-Cherokee-Metis born 1788-died 1812 TN - daughter of **Elizabeth Watts**/1750 & **William R. Campbell**/1755-white, Red Paint

Clan Cherokee, 1st wife 1810 TN of **Richard Riley (2)**/1792-(son of Samuel Riley/1747 & Nigodigeyu Doublehead/1764), mother of Elizabeth Riley (3)/1812-3/16th Chalakatha-Pekowi-Shawano-ChalakaPowhatan-Cherokee-Metis

BY ELIZABETH WATTS/1750 & LECKICKEE NATCHEZ/1750

GRANDDAUGHTER

Natchez, Nancy – 19/64th Chalakatha-Pekowi-Shawano-ChalakaPowhatan-Natchez-Cherokee-Metis born 1790 AL-died 1843 (OK?) - daughter of **Leckickee Natchez**/1750 & **Elizabeth Watts**/1750, Red Paint Clan Cherokee, wife 1st 1804 of **Charles Wofford**/1784-white, 2nd
1807 of **Ebenezer Wilcox**/1784-white, mother **with Wofford** of James D. Wofford/1806-9/64th Chalakatha-Pekowi-Shawano-ChalakaPowhatan-Natchez-Cherokee-Metis, children/1807-30 **with Wilcox** unknown

BY UNACATA WATTS/1752 & CHEROKEE WOMAN/1755

GRANDDAUGHTER

Watts, Sally – 19/64th Chalakatha-Pekowi-Shawano-Chalaka-PowhatanCherokee-Metis born 1771 TN-died after 1846 - daughter of **Unacata
Watts**/1752 & **Cherokee Woman**/1755, 2nd wife about 1788 of 1st cousin **Martin Tail Benge**/1761, mother of Sally Benge/1797 & other childrenall 19/64th Chalakatha-Pekowi-Shawano-Chalaka-Powhatan-CherokeeMetis

GRANDSON

Watts, Wat (1) – 19/64th Chalakatha-Pekowi-Shawano-ChalakaPowhatan-Cherokee-Metis born 1776 TN-died after 1814 – son of
Unacata-White Mankiller Watts/1752 & **Cherokee Woman**/1755, wife

Shawnee Heritage II

& children unknown

GRANDSON

Watts, Raven (1) aka Cawluhnah Watts (1) – 19/64th ChalakathaPekowi-Shawano-Chalaka-Powhatan-Cherokee-Metis born 1778 TNdied after 1814 – son of **Unacata-White Mankiller Watts**/1752 & **Cherokee Woman**/1755, wife & children unknown

GRANDSON

Watts, Charles (1) – 19/64th Chalakatha-Pekowi-Shawano-Chalaka-Powhatan-Cherokee-Metis born 1780 TN-died after 1814 – son of **Unacata-White Mankiller Watts**/1752 & **Cherokee Woman**/1755, wife & children unknown

GRANDDAUGHTER

Watts, Jennie (1) – 19/64th Chalakatha-Pekowi-Shawano-Chalaka-Powhatan-Cherokee-Metis born 1782 TN-died after 1814 – daughter of **Unacata-White Mankiller Watts**/1752 & **Cherokee Woman**/1755, husband & children unknown

GRANDDAUGHTER

Watts, Betty – 19/64th Chalakatha-Pekowi-Shawano-ChalakaPowhatan-Cherokee-Metis born 1784 TN-died after 1814 – daughter of **Unacata-White Mankiller Watts**/1752 & **Cherokee Woman**/1755, husband & children unknown

GRANDSON

Watts, Jackson aka **Jackson Mankiller** – 19/64th Chalakatha-PekowiShawano-Chalaka-Powhatan-Cherokee-Metis born 1786 TN-died after 1837 (OK?) - son of **Unacata-White Mankiller Watts**/1752 & **Cherokee Woman**/1755, 2nd husband 1st 1806 of **Unknown Woman**/1790, 2nd 1837 of **Ollie Leslie**/1788, children unknown

BY NANCY WATTS/1748 & GEORGE LOWERY/1740

GRANDSON

Lowery, Major John aka John Lowery (1) – 11/32nd ChalakathaPekowi-Shawano-Chalaka-Powhatan-Metis born 1768 Nickajack TNdied 1817 TN - son of **Nancy Watts**/1748 & **George Lowery (1)**/1740white, Blue Holly Clan Cherokee, Major-**with U.S. Army**-Creek War/1813-Horseshoe Bend/1814, Treaty 1806, 1816, husband 1st 1790 of **Ganelugi Run After McLemore**/1775, 2nd 1794 of **Elizabeth Shorey**/1762, father **with McLemore** of John Lowery Jr/1790, Jennie Lowery/1795 & Eliza Lowery/1800-all 7/16th Chalakatha-PekowiKishpoko-Shawano-Chalaka-Powhatan-Black-Cherokee-Metis, **with**
Shorey of Elizabeth Lowery/1795-11/64th Chalakatha-PekowiShawano-Chalaka-Powhatan-Cherokee Metis

GRANDSON

Lowery, Major George Jr aka George Lowery Jr-Rising Fawn-Aginagili**Rising Man**-Agili-Ahgeehlim – 11/32nd Chalakatha-Pekowi-Shawano-Chalaka-Powhatan-Metis born 1768 AL-died 1852 OK - son of **Nancy Watts**/1748 & **George Lowery (1)**/1740-white, Blue Holly Clan Cherokee, nephew & stepson of **Ghigoneli Watts** (Rising Fawn)/1750, cousin of **Sequoyah**, delegate to **George Washington** on behalf of the Chickamauga 1791, 1st Cherokee National Convention 1814, Cherokee Constitutional Convention 1827 & 1839, Major-**with U.S. Army**-Creek War/1813-Horseshoe Bend/1814, Treaty 1816, 1817, 1819, from Tuskegee & Will's Town, **assistant Principal Chief** 1828-1843-1847, moved to AR 1839, husband 1st 1791 of **Lucy Benge**/1766, 2nd 1796 of **Elizabeth Shorey**/1762, 3rd about 1814 of **Cherokee Woman**/1780, 4th about 1820 of **Annie Fields**/1792, father **with Benge** of James Lowery/1791, Susan Lowery/1793, George Lowery (3)/1799, Lydia Lowery/1803, Rachel Lowery/1805, John Lowery/1808, Anderson Pierce Lowery/1811-all 21/64th Chalakatha-Pekowi-Shawano-Chalaka-Powhatan-Cherokee-Metis, **with Shorey** of Peggy Lowery/1796, Archibald Lowery (1)/1797, Washington Lowery (1)/1798, Charles Lowery (1)/1801-all 11/64th Chalakatha-Pekowi- Shawano-Chalaka-Powhatan-Cherokee-Metis, **with Cherokee** of John Lowery (3)/1814, Anderson Lowery/1816, Archibald Lowery (2)/1818-all 11/64th

Chalakatha-Pekowi-Shawano-Chalaka-Powhatan-Cherokee-Metis, **with Fields** of Washington Lowery (2)/1820, Charles Lowery (2)/1825-both 11/64th Chalakatha-Pekowi-Shawano-Chalaka-Powhatan-CherokeeMetis

GRANDDAUGHTER

Lowery, Elizabeth (1) – 11/32nd Chalakatha-Pekowi- Shawano-Chalaka-Powhatan-Metis born 1776 TN-died 1838 TN - daughter of **Nancy Watts**/1748 & **George Lowery (1)**/1740-white, Blue Holly Clan Cherokee, wife 1st 1794 Nickajack TN of **Joseph Sevier**/1763-white, 2nd 1799 TN of **John Walker (2)**/1770, mother **with Sevier** of Eliza Lowery Sevier/1795 & Mary Margaret Sevier/1797-both 11/64th ChalakathaPekowi-Shawano-Chalaka-Powhatan-Metis & **with Walker** of John Jack Walker/1800-23/64th Chalakatha-Pekowi-Mekoche-Shawano-ChalakaPowhatan-Cherokee-Metis

GRANDDAUGHTER

Lowery, Sarah – 11/32nd Chalakatha-Pekowi- Shawano-ChalakaPowhatan-Metis born 1774 Nickajack TN-died after 1816 - daughter of **Nancy Watts**/1748 & **George Lowery (1)**/1740-white, Blue Holly Clan Cherokee, wife 1st 1789 of **Cherokee Man**/1770, 2nd 1790 of **Bald Ridge**/1750-Cherokee, 3rd 1798 of **Stayed Rope**/1770-Cherokee, 4th 1799 of **Rattling Gourd Conrad**/1772, 5th by 1808 of **William R. Campbell Jr**/1780, 6th 1815 GA of **George Partridge McLemore**/1775, 7th after 1821 of **Jack Tesquatanosti Cersingle**/1775-Cherokee-Metis, mother **with Cherokee** of Switzler Lowery/1790-11/64th ChalakathaPekowi-Shawano-Chalaka-Powhatan-Cherokee-Metis, **with Bald Ridge** of Bluefoot Baldridge/1791, George Baldridge/1792, Garnae Baldridge/1793, Alsey Baldridge/1794, Oolusta Baldridge/1795, Garstochumlartoh Baldridge/1796, William Baldridge/1797 & Jennie Jane Baldridge/1798-all 11/64th Chalakatha-Pekowi-Shawano-Chalaka-Powhatan-Cherokee-Metis, **with Rope** of Tsagina Rope/99-11/64th Chalakatha-Pekowi-Shawano-Chalaka-Powhatan-Cherokee-Metis, **with Conrad** of Nona Lowery (Conrad)/1800 & Elizabeth Gourd

(Conrad)/1801-all 15/64th Chalakatha-Pekowi-Thawikila-ShawanoChalaka-Powhatan-Creek-Cherokee-Metis, **with Campbell** of George
William Campbell/1810 & Rope Campbell/1814-both 21/64th Chalakatha-Pekowi-Shawano-Chalaka-Powhatan-Cherokee-Metis, **with McLemore** of Robert Chugatooda McLemore/1821-17/64th Chalakatha-Pekowi-Kishpoko-Thawikila-Shawano-Chalaiwa-Powhatan-CreekBlack-Cherokee-Metis, children **with Cersingle** unknown

GRANDDAUGHTER

Lowery, Jennie Jane – 11/32nd Chalakatha-Pekowi-Shawano-ChalakaPowhatan-Metis born about 1780-died after 1824 - daughter of **Nancy Watts**/1748 & **George Lowery (1)**/1740-white, Blue Holly Clan Cherokee, wife 1st 1795 of **Tahlonteeskee (2)**/1760, 2nd before 1816 of **Robert Lovett**/1775-Creek-Metis, mother **with Tahlonteeskee** of Tahlonteeskee (3)/1795-37/64th Kishpoko-Chalakatha-Pekowi-Shawano-Chalaka-Powhatan-Cherokee Metis, **with Lovett** of Jesse Lovett/1816, George M. Lovett/1818, William Lovett/1820, Sarah Lovett/1822, Robert Lovett Jr/1824-all 11/64th Chalakatha-PekowiShawano-Chalaka-Powhatan-Creek-Metis

GRANDDAUGHTER

Lowery, Aky aka Akeye – 11/32nd Chalakatha-Pekowi-ShawanoChalaka-Powhatan-Metis born 1782 Nickajack TN-died after 1820 - daughter of **Nancy Watts**/1748 & **George Lowery (1)**/1740-white, Blue Holly Clan Cherokee, wife before 1800 of **Arthur Burns**/1780-white, mother of Mary Burns/1804 & Elizabeth Burns/1810-both 11/64th Chalakatha-Pekowi- Shawano-Chalaka-Powhatan-Metis

GRANDDAUGHTER

Lowery, Nellie – 11/32nd Chalakatha-Pekowi-Shawano-ChalakaPowhatan-Metis born 1786 Nickajack TN-died after 1824 - daughter of
Nancy Watts/1748 & **George Lowery (1)**/1740-white, Blue Holly Clan Cherokee, wife 1807 of **Edmond Fawling (2)**/1788, mother of Edmund

Fawling Jr/1808, Joseph Fawling/1810, Richard Rim Fawling/1812, Ellis Fawling/1814, Edward Fawling/1818, James Fawling/1820, Elizabeth Fawling/1822, Susan Fawling/1824-all 11/64th ChalakathaPekowi-Shawano-Chalaka-Powhatan-Cherokee-Metis

BY GHIGONELI WATTS/1752 & RISING FAWN FOX/1740

GRANDSON

Rising Fawn (4) aka Rising Fawn Fox (4) –39/64th Chalakatha-PekowiShawano-Chalaka-Powhatan-Cherokee-Metis born 1772 Settico TNdied 1814 during Creek War – son of **Ghigoneli Watts**/1752 & **Rising Fawn Fox (3)**/1740, Treaty 1785, 1791, 1792, 1798, delegate to D.C. 1790, **with U.S. Army**-Creek War/1813, husband 1792 Settico TN of **Cherokee Woman**/1777, children/1792-1814 unknown

GRANDDAUGHTER

Rising Fawn, Catherine aka Catherine Fox – 39/64th ChalakathaPekowi-Shawano-Chalaka-Powhatan-Cherokee-Metis born 1774 Settico TN- died 1835 AL - daughter of **Ghigoneli Watts**/1752 & **Rising Fawn Fox (3)**/1740, Red Paint Clan Cherokee, wife 1790 Settico TN-but moved quickly to AL of **John Gunter (2)**/1760-white, mother of Samuel Gunter/1796, Aky Gunter/1798, Martha Jane Gunter/1800, Edward Gunter/1803, Elizabeth Hunt Gunter/1804, John Gunter (3)/1806 & Catherine Gunter/1810-all 19/64th Chalakatha-Pekowi-ShawanoChalaka-Powhatan-Cherokee-Metis

GRANDDAUGHTER

Rising Fawn, Polly aka Polly Fox – 39/64th Chalakatha-PekowiShawano-Chalaka-Powhatan-Cherokee-Metis born 1776 Settico TNdied after 1817 (TN?) - daughter of **Ghigoneli Watts**/1752 & **Rising Fawn Fox (3)**/1740, Red Paint Clan Cherokee, wife 1st 1790 of **John Smith**/1770, 2nd 1810 of **Young Bald Ridge**/1770-Cherokee, mother **with Smith** of Jackson Smith/1791, Dorcas Smith/1793, Thomas Pig Smith/1795 & Walter Smith/1800 & **with Bald Ridge** of Elizabeth

Baldridge/1810 & Delia Baldridge/1815-all at least 19/64th
ChalakathaPekowi-Shawano-Chalaka-Powhatan-Cherokee-Metis

BY JOHN BOWLES-CHIEF BOWL/1756 & RED PAINT WOMAN/1760

UNKNOWN

BY JOHN BOWLES-CHIEF BOWL/1756 & OOLOOSTA TAHCHEE/1760

GRANDSON

Bowles, Lightning aka **Lightning Bug** –11/32nd Chalakatha-PekowiThawikila-Shawano-Chalaka-Creek-Cherokee-Metis born 1784 Running
Water TN-died after 1851 OK - son of **Chief Bowl**/1756 & **Ooloosta Tahchee**/1760, Red Paint Clan Cherokee, husband 1st 1804 AR of **Ayusu Cherokee**/1785, 2nd 1832 TX of **Ahquosa -Arquosah Cherokee**/1815, father **with Ayusu** of Joseph Bowles/1808, Caroline Bowles/1810, John Bowles/1812 & Jefferson Bowles/1814 & other children/1815-1832, **with Ahquosa** of Tekanusa Whiskey-Tecarnooser Whiskey Bowles/1836, Geyahi-Karyarhee Bowles/1838 & DekaquekaDaycarbecar Bowles/1840-all 7/32nd Chalakatha-Pekowi-ThawikilaShawano-Chalaka-Creek-Cherokee-Metis

GRANDSON

Bowles, Tunooneski aka Tununeksi – 11/32nd Chalakatha-PekowiThawikila-Shawano-Chalaka-Creek-Cherokee-Metis born 1786 Running
Water TN-**killed** 1839 TX - son of **Chief Bowl**/1756 & **Ooloosta Tahchee**/1760, Red Paint Clan Cherokee, killed in same battle with Mexicans as his father **Chief Bowl** & half-brother **John Bowles Jr**, husband 1806 AR of **Unknown Woman**/1790, children unknown but some mentioned as being captured by the Mexicans

GRANDSON

Bowles, Standing Man aka **Wagon**-Dugulilu-Duqulilu –11/32nd

Chalakatha-Pekowi-Thawikila-Shawano-Chalaka-Creek-Cherokee-Metis born 1788 Running Water TN-died after 1851 OK - son of **Chief Bowl**/1756 & **Ooloosta Tahchee**/1760, Red Paint Clan Cherokee, went to MX 1842 **with Sequoyah, Teesey Gist**/89-(ex-husband of half-sister **Rebecca Bowles**), half-brother **Standing Bowles**/99 & **Worm, John Elijah, Oowositi, Cahtata, Tallatoo** & **Coteska**-(all presumably Cherokee) looking for Cherokee in MX, husband 1st 1810 AR of **Catoosie-Katusi-Catoosee Cherokee**/1795, 2nd 1814 AR of **Fannie Davis**/1795-(sister of **John Porum Davis**-husband of **Eliza Bowles**), father **with Catoosie** of Johnson Bowles/1810 & Etta Kaniti-Carneetee Bowles/1812-both 7/32nd Chalakatha-Pekowi-Thawikila-ShawanoChalaka-Creek-Cherokee-Metis, **with Davis** of Elizabeth Bowles/1814
& Thomas Bowles/1816-both 15/32nd Chalakatha-Kishpoko-PekowiThawikila-Shawano-Chalaka-Creek-Cherokee-Metis

GRANDDAUGHTER

Bowles, Quatini –11/32nd Chalakatha-Pekowi-Thawikila-ShawanoChalaka-Creek-Cherokee-Metis born 1790 Running Water TN-died after 1839 OK - daughter of **Chief Bowl**/1756 & **Ooloosta Tahchee**/1760, Red Paint Clan Cherokee, wife about 1805 AR of **Unknown Man**/1785, children unknown

GRANDDAUGHTER

Bowles, Tsagina aka Chagina –11/32nd Chalakatha-Pekowi-Thawikila-Shawano-Chalaka-Creek-Cherokee-Metis born 1792 Running Water TN-died after 1839 OK - daughter of **Chief Bowl**/1756 & **Ooloosta Tahchee**/1760, Red Paint Clan Cherokee, 1st wife by 1810 of **Bird Tail Doublehead**/1790, mother of Gudegei Birdtail/1810, Ghigoneli Birdtail/1812 & Goyeni Birdtail (Doublehead)/1814-all 19/64th Chalakatha-Pekowi-Thawikila-Shawano-Chalaka-Creek-Cherokee-Metis

BY JOHN BOWLES-CHIEF BOWL/1756 & JENNIE DUE/1764

GRANDSON

Bowles, John (3) aka **John Bowles Jr**-Tewulle-Diwali-Bowl (2)-Little Bowl – ½ Chalakatha-Pekowi-Shawano-Chalaka-Powhatan-CherokeeMetis - born 1796 St. Francis AR-**killed** 1839 TX - son of **Chief Bowl**/1756 & **Jennie Due**/1766, Long Hair Clan Cherokee, **with U.S. Army**-Creek War/1813, Treaty TX 1836, killed in same battle with Mexicans as his half-brother **Tunooneski**/1786 & his father **Chief Bowl**/1756, husband 1816 AR of **Jennie Cherokee**/1800, no clear record of children/1816-39 but three were mentioned as being captured by the Mexicans 1839

GRANDSON

Bowles, French – ½ Chalakatha-Pekowi-Shawano-Chalaka-Powhatan-Cherokee-Metis born 1797 St. Francis AR-died after 1839 OK - son of **Chief Bowl**/1756 & **Jennie Due**/1766, Long Hair Clan Cherokee, husband 1817 AR of **Unknown Woman**/1800, children unknown

GRANDDAUGHTER

Bowles, Nellie aka Ghigoneli Bowles (2)-Neli Bowles – ½ ChalakathaPekowi-Shawano-Chalaka-Powhatan-Cherokee-Metis born 1798 St. Francis AR-died after 1839 OK - daughter of **Chief Bowl**/1756 &
Jennie Due/1766, Long Hair Clan Cherokee, namesake of grandmother **Ghigoneli Bowles**/1723, wife 1813 AR of **Unknown Man**/1793, children unknown

GRANDSON

Bowles, Standing – ½ Chalakatha-Pekowi-Shawano-Chalaka-Powhatan-Cherokee-Metis born 1799 St. Francis AR-died after 1850 MX - son of **Chief Bowl**/1756 & **Jennie Due**/1766, Long Hair Clan Cherokee, succeeded his father as **Principal Chief** of Texas Cherokee 1839, went to MX 1842 **with Sequoyah**, **Teesey Gist**/1789-(ex-husband of half-sister **Rebecca Bowles**), half-brother **Standing Man Bowles**/1788 & **Worm, John Elijah, Oowositi, Cahtata, Tallatoo** & **Coteska**-(all presumably Cherokee) looking for Cherokee in MX, husband 1st 1819 AR of **Unknown Woman**/1803, 2nd 1842 MX of a **Mexican Woman**/1826, children unknown

GRANDSON

Bowles, James – ½ Chalakatha-Pekowi-Shawano-Chalaka-PowhatanCherokee-Metis born 1800 St. Francis AR-died 1871OK - son of **Chief Bowl**/1756 & **Jennie Due**/1766, Long Hair Clan Cherokee, husband 1st 1820 TX of **Unknown Woman**/1805, 2nd by 1868 of **Elizabeth Choweyoukah Halfbreed**/1838, no record of children/1820-68 **with Unknown**, father **with Halfbreed** of Minnie Tuni Bowles/1869 & Richard H. Bowles/1870-both 5/16th Chalakatha-Pekowi-Shawano-Chalaka-Powhatan-Cherokee-Metis

BY JOHN BOWLES-CHIEF BOWL/1756 & OTIYU VANN/1786

GRANDSON

Bowles, Samuel – 43/64th Chalakatha-Pekowi-Shawano-ChalakaPowhatan-Black-Cherokee-Metis born 1805 St. Francis AR-died after 1845 OK - son of **Chief Bowl**/1756 & **Otiyu Vann**/1786, husband 1825 TX of **Idoosi Cherokee**/1810, father of George Bowles/1840-21/64th Chalakatha-Pekowi-Shawano-Chalaka-Powhatan-Cherokee-Metis

GRANDDAUGHTER

Bowles, Rebecca Duga – 43/64th Chalakatha-Pekowi-Shawano-Chalaka-Powhatan-Black-Cherokee-Metis born 1806 St. Francis AR-died 1866 OK - daughter of **Chief Bowl**/1756 & **Otiyu Vann**/1786, wife 1st by 1824 AR of **Teesey Gist (1)**/1788, 2nd 1841 OK of (his half-brother & namesake) **Teesey Gist (2)**/1812, mother **with Teesey (1)** of Sarah Gist/1824, Catherine Gist/1826, Ootayi Bowles/1834, Nancy Bowles/1836 & Kanita Bowles/1838-(no idea why the name switch on the last three children), **with Teesey (2)** of Sarah T. Gist/1842, Joseph Gist/1846 & Catherine Gist/1851-all 25/64th Chalakatha-PekowiShawano-Chalaka-Powhatan-Black-Cherokee-Metis

GRANDSON

Bowles, Stand In The Middle aka Stands In The Middle –43/64th

Chalakatha-Pekowi-Shawano-Chalaka-Powhatan-Black-CherokeeMetisborn 1808 St. Francis AR-died after 1851 OK - son of **Chief Bowl**/1756 & **Otiyu Vann**/1786, husband about 1830 of **Lucy** aka **Lusi-Loosee Cherokee**/1810, father of Thomas Bowles/1836 & Lucy Bowles/1838-both 21/64th Chalakatha-Pekowi-Shawano-Chalaka-Powhatan-Black-Cherokee-Metis

GRANDDAUGHTER

Bowles, Nancy aka Nannie - 43/64th Chalakatha-Pekowi-ShawanoChalaka-Powhatan-Black-Cherokee-Metis born 1810 St. Francis ARdied after 1845 OK - daughter of **Chief Bowl**/1756 & **Otiyu Vann**/1786, 2nd wife 1825 of **George Chisholm**/1798, children unknown

GRANDDAUGHTER

Bowles, Catherine - 43/64th Chalakatha-Pekowi-Shawano-ChalakaPowhatan-Black-Cherokee-Metis born 1812 White River village ARdied after 1839 OK - daughter of **Chief Bowl**/1756 & **Otiyu Vann**/1786, wife 1831 of **Arstorlartee Cherokee**/1810, mother of Asdolati aka Arstorlartee/1834-21/64th Chalakatha-Pekowi-ShawanoChalaka-Powhatan-Black-Cherokee-Metis

GRANDDAUGHTER

Bowles, Eliza - 43/64th Chalakatha-Pekowi-Shawano-ChalakaPowhatan-Black-Cherokee-Metis born 1814 White River AR-died after 1843 OK - daughter of **Chief Bowl**/1756 & **Otiyu Vann**/1786, wife 1st about 1830 of **Unknown Man**/1810, 2nd 1840 of **John Porum Davis**/1800- (brother of **Fanny Davis**-wife of her half-brother **Standing Man Bowles**), no record of children **with Unknown**, mother **with Davis** of John Davis/1843-35/64th Kishpoko-Chalakatha-PekowiShawano-Chalaka-Powhatan-Black-Cherokee-Metis

Shawnee Heritage II

CHAPTER NINE

Keightughqua-Cornstalk (6)/1710

Keightughqua-Cornstalk (6)/1710

Cornstalk, Keightughqua aka **Cornstalk (6)** -Strong Man CornstalkHokolesqua Cornstalk (3)-Okowellos Cornstalk (2)-Stalk of Corn-Stalk of Plant-Hokolesqua (3)-Hokoleshka (3)-Okowellos (2)-AkulusskaWneypuechsika-Waynaypooechseeka-Stout Man-SimaquanSeemakwan – 27/32nd Chalakatha-Mekoche-Shawano-ChalakaPowhatan-Metis born 1710 WV-**murdered** 1777 Ft. Randolph/Point Pleasant WV - son of **Okowellos Cornstalk**/1674 & **Katee Mekoche**/1680, taught to cipher, read & speak English by his father, went to AL with father by 1725, in PA by 1730-(married 1st 1730 PA), in TN by 1734-(married 2nd in Running Water TN 1734), a **Chalakatha Chief** in PA by 1740, raiding PA/1740, (married 3rd in PA 1741), moved to OH with **Peter Chartier** 1744, stayed in Lower Shawnee town when the Chartier group moved to KY & into the south, a **major Chalakatha Chief** in OH by 1749, Council near site of Ft. Pitt Nov. 1753, lead Chief & driving force in **Cornstalk War**/1755-77 (**Cornstalk War** = leading Shawnee Chief in French-Indian War/1754-63, leading Shawnee Chief at Braddock/1755, raiding New-Shenandoah valleys/1755-56, raiding

PA/1755-56, negotiated Treaty 1757 at mouth of Big Sandy River with **Thomas Lewis & William Preston**, led raiding Ohio-New River valleys/1758, Council Ft. Pitt June 1762, **Head Shawnee Chief** in Pontiac War/1762-66, led Shawnee at Bushy Run/1763, led raiding of New-Greenbrier-Jackson River valleys/1763, Council with **Col. Bouquet** Oct. 1764, hostage of Col. Bouquet winter 1764-65 with brothers **Wakeeampea, Ewikunwee, Naythakeina & Red Hawk**, negotiated Treaty Spring 1765 with **Col. Bouquet**, raiding Ohio-NewBig Sandy-Little Kanawha valleys/1772, traveled & sent emissaries 1774 to Shawnee & related Tribes in **VA-NC-SC-GA-AL-TN-KY-MO-IL-MI-WI-IN-OH-PA-MD-NY** enlisting support for upcoming Dunmore's War 1774, sought support of **nephew Dragging Canoe, Head Chief of Northern Confederacy** at Point Pleasant/1774, negotiated Treaty Camp Charlotte 1774 with **Lord Dunmore**, siege Ft. Blair/Point Pleasant/1775, Council Ft. Pitt 1775 with **Nimwha, Silver Heels, Wryneck & Blue Jacket**, Council Ft. Pitt-George Morgan 1776 with **Nimwha, Ellinipsico, sister Cawechile, Capt. Johnny, Blue Jacket & Black Caesar**, Council 1776 with **White Eyes-Delaware, John Montour-Seneca-Metis, Wyandot Half-King & William Wilson**, Council Ft. Pitt 1777**)**,living in AL 1754-55 (near the Chartier settlement), returned to OH in 1755, in AL for a while 1757-58(mentioned as **a Chief of the Shawnee among the Creeks**), returned to
OH in 1758 (upon the death of his father in epidemic), associated with **John Swift, Dragging Canoe, Double Head, Red Bird, John Forked Tail Watts & Nathaniel Gist** in silver-mines-counterfeiting 1755-69 furnishing silver to Shawnee & Northern Confederacy, **Head Chief of Chalakatha & All Shawnee** 1758-77, **Head Chief of 20 tribe Northern Confederacy** 1760-74-(most had been part of the pre-white, WesternShawnee confederacy), last home was at Cornstalk's village on Sippio Creek of Scioto River OH from early 1770's, **murdered** by whites at Ft. Randolph-Point Pleasant/1777 with brother **Red Hawk**, son **Ellinipsico** & son in law/adopted son **Petella**, taught most of his children to cipher, read & speak some English, husband 1st 1730 PA of **Helizikinopo Snake**/1715-Mekoche, 2nd 1734 Running Water TN of **Ounaconoa Muskrat**/1716, 3rd 1741 PA of **Julia Mulatto**/1720-adopted-Mulatto, (at least) 4th 1763 OH of **Catherine Vanderpoole See**/1725-adopted-white,

(other wives/1730-77 possible including a Creek or Shawnee-amongthe-Creek about 1757), **father with Helizikinopo** of WalkerPomeatha/1730, Wolf/1732, Catherine-Katee (Petella)/1734, Chenusaw/1736, Newa/1738, Greenbrier (Kennison)/1740, Aracoma (Baker)/1742, Elizabeth (Swift-Petella)/1744,Young Cornstalk/1746, Ellinipsico/1748, Blue Sky-Mary (Adkins)/1750, Esther (Soward)/1752, Oceana/1754-all 29/32nd Chalakatha-Mekoche-Shawano-Chalaka-Powhatan-Metis, **with Ounaconoa** of Black Beard/1736, Black Wolf/1740, John Wolf (Cornstalk)/1750, Peter Cornstalk/1755 & Susannah Cornstalk/1757-all 59/64th Chalakatha-Pekowi-MekocheShawano-Chalaka-Powhatan-Metis, **with Julia** of Sun Fish/1742, Elijah Cornstalk/1744, Abraham Cornstalk "Ailstock"/1748, Absalom Cornstalk "Ailstock"/1750 & Michael Cornstalk "Ailstock"/1752-all 27/64th Chalakatha-Mekoche-Shawano-Chalaka-Powhatan-Black-Metis, **with Catherine** of Mary (Cornstalk) See/1764-27/64th ChalakathaMekoche-Shawano-Chalaka-Powhatan-Metis, **adopted father** about 1740 PA of **Petella**/1730-white, 1763 OH of **Elizabeth See**/1754 & **John See**/1759-white, (unknown children with all wives likely & a Creek or southern Wife about 1758 & children also likely)

WIVES OF KEIGHTUGHQUA-CORNSTALK/1710

WIFE 1729 - PA

Snake, Helizikinopo - Mekoche born 1715 PA-died shortly after 1809 OH – **parents unknown** but father was a **Mekoche Chief** from the Snake Clan of high standing, sister of **Green Snake**/1717, **Big Snake**/1720 & **Great Snake**/1725, moved to OH with **Peter Chartier** 1744, stayed in Lower Shawnee town when the Chartier group moved to KY, signed Complaint to U.S. 1809 with brother **Big Snake**/1720, nephew **Capt. Snake**/1760, **Black Hoof**/1730, **Wahappi**-Delaware & **Beaver**-Delaware, 1st wife 1729 PA of **Keightughqua-Cornstalk (6)**/1710, mother of sons Walker/1730, Wolf/1732, daughter CatherineKatee/1734, sons Chenusaw/1736, Newa/1738, daughters Greenbrier/1740, Aracoma/1742, Elizabeth/1744, sons Young Cornstalk/1746, Ellinipsico/1748, daughters Mary-Blue Sky/1750,

Esther/1752 & Oceana/1754 & other unknown children/1730-60 (probably daughters)-all 29/32nd Chalakatha-Mekoche-ShawanoChalaka-Powhatan-Metis, **adopted mother** 1740 PA of **Petella**/1730white, 1763 OH of **John See**/1759 & **Elizabeth See**/1754-white, 1778
OH of **Martin Wetzel**/1762-white

WIFE 1734 - TN

Muskrat, Ounaconoa aka Ounacona Moytoy – 63/64th ChalakathaPekowi-Shawano-Chalaka-Powhatan born 1716 Chota TN- died after
1757 OH - daughter of **Swan-Wapehti Hop**/1686 & **Oshasqua (1)-Muskrat (1)-Moytoy (5)**/1686-Pekowi, could cipher, read & write English, Turtle Clan Shawnee but called Blind Savannah Clan Cherokee, brought north by Cornstalk & may have been at the hub of the community of "Northern Cherokee" i.e. Shawnee that came from the south to OH in the succeeding years, wife 1734 Chota TN of **Keightughqua-Cornstalk (6)**/1710, mother of Black Beard/1735, Black Wolf/1740, John Wolf (1)/1750, Peter Cornstalk (1)/1755 & Susannah Cornstalk/1757-all 59/64th Chalakatha-Mekoche-Pekowi-ShawanoChalaka-Powhatan-Metis, likely other unknown children/1736-60 (probably daughters)

WIFE 1741 PA

Mulatto, Julia - adopted-Mulatto born about 1720-died after 1775 OH – called a daughter of **Scot Pioneer** & **Black Slave Woman** (but there is some question whether or not she may have actually been a ShawneeBlack-Metis, especially considering her sons later easy acceptance by the Ailstock family), sister of **Negro Wife**/1725 & **Black Horse**/1730both adopted mulattoes taken in PA 1740, about 6' tall, light complexioned & said to be very pretty, captured & adopted 1740 PA by **Chief Hintoo-Intu** (some connection to Cornstalk family?), wife 1741 PA of **Cornstalk**/1710, stayed with tribe 1775 when 3 younger sons returned to whites, mother of Sun Fish Cornstalk/1742, Elijah Cornstalk/1744, Absalom "Ailstock"/1748, Abraham "Ailstock"/1750, Michael "Ailstock"/1752- all 27/64th Chalakatha-Mekoche-Shawano-Chalaka-Powhatan-Black-Metis, other unknown children/1741-65 (probably daughters) likely

(POSSIBLE) WIFE 1755 AL

An unknown **Creek Woman** from AL – likely mother of some unknown children/1755-77, all born in OH after 1755

WIFE 1763 OH

See, Catherine Vanderpool Sharpe - adopted-white born 1720 NY-died 1806 IN - daughter of **Adam Vanderpoole**, adopted 1763 **with all 7 of her children**, returned to whites 1765 **with all children except Elizabeth/1754 plus daughter Mary Cornstalk See/1764 & granddaughter Margaret Peggy (2) Cornstalk See/1764**, wife 1st by 1740 of **John Sharpe**/1710, 2nd 1744 of **Fredrick See**/1710, 3rd 1763 OH of **Keightughqua-Cornstalk (6)**/1710, 4th after 1765 (WV?) of **John Hardy**, mother **with Sharpe** of John Sharpe Jr/1740 & William Sharpe/1742, **with See** of Margaret Peggy See (1)/1744, Lois Sarah See/1746, Mary Catherine See/1748, Michael See/1750, Elizabeth See/1754, George See/1756 & John See/1758-all white, **with Cornstalk** of **Mary (Cornstalk) See**/1764-27/64th Chalakatha-Mekoche-ShawanoChalaka-Powhatan-Metis

CHILDREN OF CORNSTALK/1710 WITH HELIZIKINOPO SNAKE/1715

SON

Cornstalk, Walker aka **Pomeatha**-Passes By-Pomeseh-Mr. Walker – 29/32nd Chalakatha-Mekoche-Shawano-Chalaka-Powhatan-Metis born 1730 PA-died before 1825 OH – oldest son of **Cornstalk/1710 & Helizikinopo/1715**, over 6' tall, taught to cipher, read & speak English by his father, Cornstalk War/1755-77, a **Chalakatha Chief** in OH before 1774, **an emissary for Cornstalk** 1774, **hostage of Virginians** 1775-76, Blue Jacket War/1777-94, no part in War 1812, an **Elder Chalakatha Chief** at Wapakoneta 1817, Treaty 1814, 1817, 1818, husband 1st 1751 Great Tellico TN to **Oousta White Owl Carpenter**/1722, 2nd 1755 OH of **Chalakatha Woman**/1740, 3rd 1763 OH of **Margaret Peggy See**/1744-adopted-white, father **with Carpenter** of

John Walker/1752-5/8th Chalakatha-Mekoche-Shawano-ChalakaPowhatan-Cherokee-Metis, **with Chalakatha** of Capt. Walker/1760 & others/1755-85-all 23/32nd Chalakatha-Mekoche-Shawano-Chalaka-Powhatan-Metis, **with Margaret Peggy See (1)** of Young Walker/1764-29/64th Chalakatha-Mekoche-Shawano-Chalaka-Powhatan-Metis

SON

Cornstalk, Wolf aka **Cutenwha**-Kootenwha – 29/32nd ChalakathaMekoche-Shawano-Chalaka-Powhatan-Metis born 1732 PA-died after 1817 (likely OH) - 2nd son of **Cornstalk**/1710 & **Helizikinopo**/1715, taught to cipher, read & speak some English by his father, Cornstalk War/1755-77, a **Chalakatha Chief** in OH by 1770, **an emissary for Cornstalk** 1774, **hostage of Virginians** 1775-76, Blue Jacket War/177788, husband 1st 1752 OH of **Chalakatha Woman**/1736, father of Young Wolf-Young Cutenwha Cornstalk/1755-31/32nd Chalakatha-MekocheShawano-Chalaka-Powhatan-Metis

DAUGHTER

Cornstalk, Catherine (2) aka Katee - 29/32nd Chalakatha-MekocheShawano-Chalaiwa-Powhatan-Metis born 1734 PA-died 1758 OH of smallpox - oldest daughter of **Cornstalk**/1710 & **Helizikinopo**/1715, a **Christian Chalakatha**, over 6' tall i.e. a **Grenadier Squaw**, taught to cipher, read & speak some English by her father, may have served as a translator-messenger for the whites, wife 1750 OH of adopted brother **Petella**/1730-adopted white, died in the smallpox epidemic of 1758, children/1750-58 unknown but some likely

SON

Cornstalk, Chenusaw – 29/32nd Chalakatha-Mekoche-ShawanoChalaka-Powhatan-Metis born 1736 PA-died after 1778 likely OH - 3rd son of **Cornstalk**/1710 & **Helizikinopo**/1715, a Chalakatha warrior, taught to cipher, read & speak some English by his father, Cornstalk War/1755-77, **an emissary for Cornstalk** 1774, **hostage of Virginians** 1775-76, husband 1756 OH of **Chalakatha Woman**/1740, children unknown

SON

Cornstalk, Newa – 29/32nd Chalakatha-Mekoche-Shawano-Chalaka-Powhatan-Metis born 1738 PA-died after 1778 OH - 4th son of **Cornstalk**/1710 & **Helizikinopo**/1715, a Chalakatha warrior, taught to cipher, read & speak some English by his father, Cornstalk War/175876, **an emissary for Cornstalk** 1774, **hostage of Virginians** 1775-76, husband 1st 1757 OH of **Chalakatha Woman**/1742, 2nd 1763 OH of **Lois Sarah See**/1746-adopted-white, children/1757-78 **with Chalakatha** unknown, father **with See** of Young Newa/1764-29/64th Chalakatha-Mekoche-Shawano-Chalaka-Powhatan-Metis (the son stayed with Newa when mother returned to whites 1765)

DAUGHTER

Cornstalk, Greenbrier – 29/32nd Chalakatha-Mekoche-ShawanoChalaka-Powhatan-Metis born 1740 PA-died after 1780 (WV-OH?) - 3rd daughter of **Cornstalk**/1710 & **Helizikinopo**/1715, a **Christian Chalakatha**, about 6' tall i.e. a Grenadier Squaw & attractive, taught to cipher, read & speak some English by her father, likely a translatormessenger for the whites, associated in later years with a **McComas** family-(maybe in laws through marriage of a daughter?), wife by 1757 WV of **Reuben Kennison**/1737-white, widow in 1776, mother of about 8 children between 1757-76, surname Kennison including a Reuben Kennison Jr /BET 1757-76 & a younger Greenbrier Kennison/BET 1757-76--all 29/64th Chalakatha-Mekoche- Shawano-Chalaka-Powhatan-Metis, often confused in white history with her sisters & aunts

DAUGHTER

Cornstalk, Aracoma aka Corn Flower-Aracoma Hokolesqua-Aracoma Baker – 29/32nd Chalakatha-Mekoche-Shawano-Chalaka-PowhatanMetis born 1742 OH-**killed** in battle 1780 **Logan Co. WV** - 2nd daughter of **Cornstalk**/1710 & **Helizikinopo**/1715, taught to cipher, read & speak some English by her father, established village near Logan WV 1760 with family & clan at current site of **Logan WV**, a

Chalakatha village Head Woman before 1780, about 6' tall, **killed in battle** defending the village, wife 1758 OH of **Boling Kikpelethee Baker**/1730, mother of sons Running Deer (Baker)/1764, Laughing Water (Baker)/1766, daughters White Flower (Baker)/1768, Raindrop (Baker)/1770 & sons Running Water (Baker)/1772 & Blue Feather (Baker)/1774-all 11/16th Chalakatha-Mekoche- Shawano-Chalaka-Powhatan-Metis, 4 other children that may have died of disease

DAUGHTER

Cornstalk, Elizabeth (2) – 29/32nd Chalakatha-Mekoche-ShawanoChalaka-Powhatan-Metis born 1744 OH-died after 1777 likely OH - 5th daughter of **Cornstalk**/1710 & **Helizikinopo**/1715, about 6' tall i.e. a Grenadier Squaw, a **Christian Chalakatha**, taught to cipher, read & speak some English by her father, may have served as a translatormessenger for the whites, wife 1st 1760 OH of **John Swift**/1712, 2nd by 1770 OH of **Petella Cornstalk**/1730-adopted white, mother **with Swift** of four children/1760-62-64-66 names/gender unknown but may have been called Cornstalk's, any children/1770-77 **with Petella** unknown, often confused in white histories with her sisters or aunts

SON

Cornstalk, Young aka **Cornstalk (7)**-Stout Man-NenpemeshequaNeenpeemeesheekwa-Wneypuechsika-Wynaypooeechseeka-Winaypooeachseeka – 29/32nd Chalakatha-Mekoche-Shawano-Chalaka-Powhatan-Metis born 1746 OH-died 1833 KS - 5th son of **Cornstalk**/1710 & **Helizikinopo Mekoche**/1715, about 6'6" tall & big built, taught to cipher, read & speak some English by his father & Elizabeth See), Cornstalk War/1755-77, **an emissary for Cornstalk** 1774, a **Chalakatha Chief** in OH 1774, Blue Jacket War/1777-94, Treaty 1814, 1817, an elder at Wapakoneta 1817, moved to KS about 1828 **with William Perry**/1770, **4th Chief in KS** 1833 under **John Perry**/1775, husband 1st 1766 OH of **Chalakatha Woman**/1750, 2nd 1769 OH of **Elizabeth See**/1754-adopted-white, no record of children/1766-95 **with Chalakatha**, father **with Elizabeth See** of White Wing Cornstalk/1770

& Son of Young Cornstalk/1772-both 29/64th Chalakatha-MekocheShawano-Chalaka-Powhatan-Metis

SON

Cornstalk, Ellinipsico aka Helinipsiko-Heleeneepseeko-Native Warrior – 29/32nd Chalakatha-Mekoche-Shawano-Chalaka-Powhatan-Metis born 1748 OH-**murdered** 1777 Point Pleasant WV - youngest son of **Cornstalk**/1710 & **Helizikinopo**/1715, over 6' tall, taught to cipher, read & speak some English by his father & his white wife, Cornstalk War/1765-77, **an emissary for Cornstalk** 1774, a **Chalakatha Chief** in OH 1777, **murdered by whites** at Point Pleasant WV/Ft. Randolph 1777 with father **Cornstalk**, brother in law/adopted brother **Petella** & uncle **Red Hawk**, husband 1st 1763 OH of **Mary Catherine See**/1749-adopted white, 2nd 1765 OH of **Chalakatha Woman**/1750, 3rd 1772 OH of **Adopted White Woman**/1755, father with **Mary Catherine** of Margaret Peggy See (2)/1764-29/64th Chalakatha-Mekoche-Shawano-ChalakaPowhatan-Metis, children/1765-77 **with Chalakatha &** children/1772-
77 **with White Woman** unknown

DAUGHTER

Cornstalk, Mary (1) aka **Blue Sky** - 29/32nd Chalakatha-MekocheShawano-Chalaka-Powhatan-Metis born 1750 OH-died 1775 Ft. Pitt area PA/OH/WV - 4th daughter of **Cornstalk**/1710 & **Helizikinopo**/1715, about 6' tall i.e. a Grenadier Squaw & attractive, a **Christian Chalakatha**, taught to cipher, read & speak some English by her father, wife 1766 PA of **Parker V. Adkins**/1720, met while Adkins was with the Militia at Ft. Pitt-abandoned by Adkins when he returned east, Adkins returned for children after her death, mother **with Adkins** of Littleberry Adkins/1766 & Charity Adkins/1768-both 23/32nd Chalakatha-Mekoche-Shawano-Chalaka-Powhatan-Metis, often confused in white history with her sisters & aunts

DAUGHTER

Cornstalk, Esther – 29/32nd Chalakatha-Mekoche-Shawano-ChalakaPowhatan-Metis born 1751 OH-died before 1836 PA - 6th daughter of
Cornstalk/1710 & **Helizikinopo**/1715, about 6' tall & attractive, a

Christian Chalakatha, Shawnee name unknown, taught to cipher, read & speak some English by her father, may have served as a translatormessenger for the whites, about 6' tall i.e. a Grenadier Squaw, wife 1768 OH/PA of **Thomas Sowards**/1746, mother of Griffin Sowards/1773,
Thomas Sowards Jr/1775, Robert Sowards/1779, Esther Sowards/1781, Jacob Sowards/1783, John B. Sowards/1785, twins Rosannah & Diannah Sowards/1787, Rebecca Sowards/1790, George Sowards/1792-all 29/64th Chalakatha-Mekoche-Shawano-ChalakaPowhatan-Metis, often confused in white history with her sisters & aunts

DAUGHTER

Cornstalk, Oceana aka Ceanna-Cianna-Zeanna – 29/32nd ChalakathaMekoche-Shawano-Chalaka-Powhatan-Metis born 1752 OH-died 1770 WV - youngest daughter of **Cornstalk**/1710 & **Helizikinopo**/1715, about 6' tall & said to be very pretty, may have spoke some English, died after falling from a cliff on her way to visit her sister **Aracoma**, namesake of Oceana WV, died single

WITH OUNACONOA MUSKRAT/1716

SON

Cornstalk, Black Beard (1) aka Wesekahnee-Weeseekahnee-Wissekapoway-Weeseekapoway-Black Beard Hokolesqua-**Black Beard (1)** - 59/64th Chalakatha-Mekoche-Pekowi-Shawano-ChalakaPowhatan-Metis born 1730 PA/AL-died after 1808 MO - oldest son of **Cornstalk**/1710 & **Ounaconoa Muskrat**/1716, about 6' tall & burly, known for rare black beard like brother **Black Wolf**, read, spoke & ciphered in English, Cornstalk War/1755-77, a **Chalakatha Chief** in OH by 1768, Council March 1768, **an emissary for Cornstalk** 1774, Blue Jacket War/1777-94, **2nd Chalakatha Chief** to **Black Hoof** 1779, Treaty Greenville 1795, Council Swan Creek OH 1795 with **Capt. Johnny, Bukangolas & George Ironside**, moved to MO 1796, Council 1797 with **Capt. Johnny, Borer, Buffalo & Capt. Mayne**-ENG, visited relatives among the Cherokee in south 1808, husband 1755 Running Water TN of

Katee Killaqua/1737, father of Daughter of Black Beard/1755, Young Black Beard Cornstalk/1760 & other children/1755-77 names unknown- all 35/64th Chalakatha-Mekoche-Pekowi-Shawano-ChalakaPowhatan-Cherokee-Metis

SON

Cornstalk, Black Wolf (1) aka Benewiska-Beeneeweeska-**Black Wolf (2)** - 59/64th Chalakatha-Mekoche-Pekowi-Shawano-Chalaka-PowhatanMetis born 1740 OH-died 1830 OH - 2nd son of **Cornstalk/1710 &** **Ounaconoa Muskrat/1716**, read, spoke & ciphered in English, Cornstalk War/1758-77, Grand Council 1763, Council Logstown 1765, Council Stanwix Oct. 1768, a **Chalakatha Chief** in OH by 1773, **an emissary for Cornstalk** 1774, Blue Jacket War/1777-94, a **Chalakatha Chief** at Wapakoneta 1817, Treaty 1814, 1815, 1817, 1818, about 6' tall & burly, known for rare black beard like brother **Black Beard**, husband 1st 1758 Running Water TN of **Nikkee Killaqua**/1738, 2nd 1769 OH of **Pottawamee Woman**/1754, (possibly father of a child 1787 with **Jenny Sellards Wiley**/1760-adopted white), 3rd 1800 OH of **Daughter of William Jackson-Fish** aka **Miss Fish**/1781-white, other wives possible, father **with Killaqua** of Young Black Wolf (1)/1760 & other children/1761-85-all 35/64th Chalakatha-Mekoche-Pekowi-ShawanoChalaka-Powhatan-Metis, name & gender of child **with Wiley** unknown but born after Jenny's return to the whites, **with Pottawamee** of Soldier Black Wolf/1770, Young Black Wolf (2)/1786 & other children/1771-1800-all 27/64th Chalakatha-Mekoche-Pekowi-ShawanoChalaka-Powhatan-Pottawamee-Metis, name of child (possibly a daughter) **with Wiley** unknown but born after Jenny's return to the whites, any children **with Miss Fish** unknown

SON

Cornstalk, John (1) aka **Lawathtucheh**-Lawathtoochee-**John Wolf** – 59/64th Chalakatha-Mekoche-Pekowi-Shawano-Chalaka-Powhatan-Metis born 1750 OH-died 1834 OH - 3rd son of **Cornstalk/1710 &** **Ounaconoa Muskrat/1716**, spoke, read & ciphered in English, Cornstalk War/1768-77, **an emissary for Cornstalk** 1774, Blue Jacket War/1777-94, a **Chalakatha Chief** in OH by 1787, apparently little or no part in War of 1812, Treaty 1817, husband 1780 OH of **Chalakatha Woman**/1765, father of daughter-Black Poddee Wolf/1775, sons Peter Temestehee Wolf/1770, Henry Nolesimo Clay/1780, John Wolf Cornstalk (2)/1792 & Peter Cornstalk (3)/1794-all 31/32nd Chalakatha-Mekoche-Pekowi-Shawano-Chalaka-Powhatan-Metis

SON

Cornstalk, Peter (1) aka Comes Flying-Peytehthator-**Pehathawtaw** – 59/64th Chalakatha-Mekoche-Pekowi-Shawano-Chalaka-PowhatanMetis born 1755 AL/OH-**murdered** 1832 OH - youngest son of **Cornstalk**/1710 & **Ounaconoa Muskrat**/1716, about 6'6" tall, taught to cipher, read & speak some English by his father, Cornstalk War/177277, **an emissary for Cornstalk** 1774, Blue Jacket War/1777-94, no known active part in War of 1812, a **Chalakatha Elder** at Wapaghonettat 1817, Treaty 1817, 1831, **murdered** by **Doc Bill**/1795Chalakatha, **Capt. Bill**/1790 & **Sam Loon**/1800-both Mekoche, husband 1st 1775 OH of **Chalakatha Woman**/1760, 2nd by 1784 OH of **Mary Frances Avery**/1765-white, children/1775-83 **with Chalakatha** unknown, father **with Avery** of Peter Cornstalk (2)/1785, Mary Cornstalk/1796 & other children/1787-1805-all 27/64th ChalakathaMekoche-Pekowi-Shawano-Chalaka-Powhatan-Metis, possible child or two **with Avery** unknown

DAUGHTER

Cornstalk, Susanna – 59/64th Chalakatha-Mekoche-Pekowi-ShawanoChalaka-Powhatan-Metis born 1757 OH-died after 1820 Lynchburg VA – daughter of **Cornstalk**/1710 & **Ounacona Muskrat**/1716, spoke, read & ciphered in English, wife 1774 Chota TN of **Thomas Jacob Maw**/1755, mother of John Maw/1799-27/64th Chalakatha-MekochePekowi-Shawano-Chalaka-Powhatan-Cherokee-Metis

WITH JULIA MULATTO/1720

SON

Cornstalk, Sun Fish aka Ionoca-Hionoca Cornstalk – 27/64th

Chalakatha-Mekoche-Shawano-Chalaka-Powhatan-Black-Metis born 1742 PA-**killed** 1774 Point Pleasant WV - oldest son of **Cornstalk**/1710 & **Julia Mulatto**/1720, over 6' tall, a Chalakatha warrior, taught to cipher, read & speak some English by his father & mother, Cornstalk War/1758-74, **an emissary to the Delaware for Cornstalk** 1774, husband 1760 OH of **Delaware Woman**/1745, father of six children/1760-74 names & gender unknown

SON

Cornstalk, Elijah – 27/64th Chalakatha-Mekoche-Shawano-Chalaka-Powhatan-Black-Metis born 1744 OH-**killed** 1760 OH - 2nd son of **Cornstalk**/1710 & **Julia Mulatto**/1720, a very young Chalakatha warrior, over 6' tall, **shot by whites** near Marietta OH while with his uncle **Silverheels**/1724 while hunting, died unmarried

SON

Ailstock, Absalom (1) aka **Absalom Cornstalk** – 27/64th ChalakathaMekoche-Shawano-Chalaka-Powhatan-Black-Metis born 1748 OH-died after 1814 (VA-MD) - 3rd son of **Cornstalk**/1710 & **Julia Mulatto**/1720, any Shawnee name unknown but may have only been Absalom, a Chalakatha warrior, taught to cipher, read & speak English by his father & mother, Cornstalk War/1768-74, took white surname of family that allowed the 3 brothers to settle near them when they returned to whites 1775, abandoned Shawnee Wife & children 1775 when he returned to whites, Augusta Co-VA Militia-**with U.S. Army**Revolution, husband 1768 OH of **Chalakatha Woman**/1753, 2nd 1778 VA of **Sally Going**/1764, father **with Chalakatha** of four children/1768-70-72-74 names unknown, **with Sally Going** of John Ailstock/1779, Katy Ailstock/1782, Polly Ailstock/1784, Lawrence Ailstock/1786, Elizabeth Ailstock (2)/1788, Andrew Ailstock/1790, David Ailstock/1792, James Ailstock/1794, Absalom Ailstock Jr/1796, William Ailstock/1798 & Thomas Ailstock/1800-all 13/64th Chalakatha-Mekoche-Shawano-Chalaka-Powhatan-Black-Metis

SON

Ailstock, Abraham aka **Abraham Cornstalk** – 27/64th ChalakathaMekoche-Shawano-Chalaka-Powhatan-Black-Metis born

1750 OH-died after 1790 (VA-MD) - 4th son of **Cornstalk**/1710 & **Julia Mulatto**/1720, a Chalakatha warrior, any Shawnee name unknown but may have only been Abraham, taught to cipher, read & speak English by his father & mother, Cornstalk War/1766-74, abandoned Shawnee Wife & children when he returned to the whites, took white surname from the family that allowed the 3 brothers to settle near them when they returned to the whites in 1775, husband 1st 1770 OH of **Chalakatha Woman**/1755, 2nd by 1779 VA of **Elizabeth Going**/1762, 3rd 1784 VA of **Isabel Radcliff**/1765-white, father **with Chalakatha** of three children/1770-72
-74 names unknown, **with Going** of Rebecca Ailstock/1780 & Virginia Ailstock/1782-both 29/64th Chalakatha-Pekowi-Mekoche-Shawano-Chalaka-Powhatan-Black-Metis, any children **with Radcliff** unknown

SON

Ailstock, Michael aka Michael Cornstalk – 27/64th ChalakathaMekoche-Shawano-Chalaka-Powhatan-Black-Metis born 1752 OH-died about 1791 VA - 5th son of **Cornstalk**/1710 & **Julia Mulatto**/1720, taught to cipher, read & speak English by his father & mother, Cornstalk War/1770-74, Shawnee name unknown/but may have just been Michael-took white surname when returned to whites 1775, abandoned Chalakatha Wife & children 1775 when he returned to whites, husband 1st 1772 OH of **Chalakatha Woman**/1756, 2nd 1776 VA of **Rebecca Going**/1760, father **with Chalakatha** of two children/1772 & 74 names unknown, **with Going** of Mary Ailstock/1776, Joseph Ailstock/1778, Susanna Ailstock/1780, Michael Ailstock Jr/1782, Absalom Ailstock (2)/1784 & Elizabeth Ailstock (1)/1786-all 13/64th Chalakatha-Mekoche-Shawano-Chalaka-Powhatan-Black-Metis

WITH CATHERINE VANDERPOOLE SEE/1725

DAUGHTER

Cornstalk, Mary (2) aka **Mary See** – 27/64th Chalakatha-MekocheShawano-Chalaka-Powhatan-Metis born 1764 OH-died 1824 Warren
Co. OH - only daughter of **Cornstalk**/1710 & **Catherine Vanderpoole**

Sharpe See/1725, returned to whites with mother-1765, wife 1783 WVOH of **Leonard Petro**/1750, mother of Margaret Petro/1788, Michael
See Petro/1790 & John Petro/1792-all 13/64th Chalakatha-MekocheShawano-Chalaka-Powhatan-Black-Metis

ADOPTED CHILDREN OF CORNSTALK/1710

ADOPTED SON

Cornstalk, Petalla aka One Eye-Old Yie – adopted-white born 1730 (PA?)-**murdered** 1777 Point Pleasant WV - adopted son of **Cornstalk**/1710, white name unknown, taken 1740 in PA, never returned to whites (same series of raids that **Julia Mulatto**/1720 was taken), Cornstalk War/1755-77, a Chalakatha warrior, spoke, read & ciphered some English (from youth), **an emissary to the Shawnee for Cornstalk** 1774, blinded in one eye in battle with whites, **murdered** 1777 at Ft. Randolph/Point Pleasant WV with **Cornstalk**, adopted brother **Ellinipsico** & adopted uncle **Red Hawk, tortured & mutilated by whites** before his death, **the white son-in-law of Cornstalk mentioned in history of the murder**, likely source of the "Cornstalk's Curse" of Mason County/Point Pleasant WV since the other three died instantly from gunshot wounds, husband 1st 1750 OH of adopted sister **Catherine-Katee Cornstalk**/1734, 2nd 1770 OH of adopted sister **Elizabeth Cornstalk**/1744 (to raise her children by **John Swift**/1712), any children by either wife unknown but some likely

ADOPTED DAUGHTER

See, Elizabeth - adopted-white born 1754 Hampshire Co. WV-died 1807 Adams Co. OH - daughter of **Catherine Vanderpoole** (Sharpe)/1720 & **Fredrick See**/1710, adopted 1763, returned to whites about 1775, wife 1st 1769 OH of **Young Cornstalk**/1744, 2nd 1776 of **John Peter Shoemaker**/1750-white, mother **with Young Cornstalk** of White Wing/1770 & Young Cornstalk (2)/1772-both 29/64th ChalakathaMekoche-Shawano-Chalaka-Powhatan-Metis, **with Shoemaker** of several children/1776-91

ADOPTED SON

See, John - adopted-white born 1758 VA-died 1837 IN - son of **Catherine Vanderpoole** (Sharpe)/1725 & **Fredrick See**/1710, adopted 1763-returned to whites 1765-returned to tribe 1765-returned to whites after 1769, adopted into Cornstalk family with mother **Catherine** & sisters **Margaret Peggy (1)**/**1744, Lois Sarah**/1746, **Mary Catherine**/1748 & **Elizabeth**/1754, ransomed 1765 for $100 by his uncle **Michael See**, stationed at Ft. Randolph WV/1776-77-**witnessed murder of former adopted father Cornstalk**, scout-**with U.S. Army**-Revolution, lived on frontier, husband 1780 WV of **Margaret Elizabeth Jarrett** aka Garrett/1756-former adopted white, father of John See Jr/1800 & 12 more children/1781-1802

GRANDCHILDREN OF CORNSTALK/1710

BY WALKER-POMEATHA/1730
WITH OOUSTA CARPENTER/1722

GRANDSON

Walker, John (1) aka Major Walker – 5/8th Chalakatha-MekocheShawano-Chalaka-Powhatan-Cherokee-Metis born 1753 Great Tellico TN-died after 1819 - son of **Oousta Carpenter**/1722 & **Walker Cornstalk**/1730, Wolf Clan Cherokee, grandson of **White Owl**/1680 & of **Cornstalk**/1710, a Chickamaugua/1777-92 with **Dragging Canoe**, Buchanan Station 1792, Major-**with U.S. Army**-Creek War/1813, as a youth lived with his uncle **John Forked Tail Watts**/1704, ciphered, read & spoke English, Treaty 1818 **with Glass, Path Killer & Going Snake**, husband 1770 Chota TN of **Catherine Kingfisher**/1752, father of Jennie Walker/1772 & John Walker Jr/1775-both 23/64th ChalakathaMekoche-Shawano-Chalaka-Powhatan-Cherokee-Metis

BY WALKER-POMEATHA/1730
WITH CHALAKATHA WOMAN/1740

GRANDSON

Cornstalk, Capt. Walker – 23/32nd Chalakatha-Mekoche-ShawanoChalaka-Powhatan-Metis born about 1760 OH-died after 1792

– son of **Walker-Pometha Cornstalk**/1730 & **Chalakatha Woman**/1740, Blue
Jacket War/1777-92, raiding Ohio River valley/1781 **with Joseph Brant & George Girty**, wife & children unknown

BY WALKER-POMEATHA/1730
WITH MARGARET PEGGY SEE/1744

GRANDSON

Cornstalk, Young Walker aka Young Pomeatha – 29/64th ChalakathaMekoche-Shawano-Chalaka-Powhatan-Metis born 1764 OH-died after
1794 (OH?) – son of **Walker Cornstalk**/1730 & **Margaret Peggy See (1)**/1744-adopted-white, a Chalakatha warrior, Shawnee name unknown, stayed with Walker when mother returned to whites 1765, raised by Shawnee Wife of Walker, Blue Jacket War/1782-94, wife & children unknown

BY WOLF CORNSTALK/1732
WITH CHALAKATHA WOMAN/1735

SON

Cornstalk, Young Wolf aka **Young Cutenwha** - 31/32nd ChalakathaMekoche-Shawano-Chalaka-Powhatan-Metis born about 1755 OH-died after 1817 – son of **Wolf Cutenwha Cornstalk**/1732 & **Chalakatha Woman**/1736, husband 1st about 1775 OH of **Shawnee Woman**/1760, 2nd 1800 OH of **Daughter of Joseph Jackson**/1785-1/2 Mekoche-Metis, children unknown

BY CATHERINE-KATEE CORNSTALK/1734
WITH PETELLA/1730

UNKNOWN

BY CHENUSAW CORNSTALK/1736
WITH CHALAKATHA WOMAN/1740

UNKNOWN

BY NEWA CORNSTALK/1738
WITH CHALAKATHA WOMAN/1742

UNKNOWN

BY NEWA CORNSTALK/1738
WITH LOIS SARAH SEE/1746

GRANDSON

Cornstalk, Young Newa aka Newa (2) – 29/64th Chalakatha-Mekoche-Shawano-Chalaka-Powhatan-Metis born 1764 OH-died after 1794 (OH?) – son of **Newa Cornstalk**/1738 & **Lois Sarah See**/1746-adoptedwhite, a Chalakatha warrior, Shawnee name unknown, stayed with his father when his mother returned to whites 1765, raised by Shawnee Wife of Newa, Blue Jacket War/1782-94, wife & children unknown

BY GREENBRIER CORNSTALK/1740
WITH REUBEN KENNISON/1737

GRANDSON

Kennison, Reuben Jr – 29/64th Chalakatha-Mekoche-Shawano-ChalakaPowhatan-Metis born between 1757-1776-died after 1800 – son of **Greenbrier Cornstalk**/1740 & **Reuben Kennison**/1737, wife & children unknown

GRANDDAUGHTER

Kennison, Greenbrier – 29/64th Chalakatha-Mekoche-ShawanoChalaka-Powhatan-Metis born between 1757-76-died after 1800 – daughter of

Greenbrier Cornstalk/1740 & **Reuben Kennison**/1737, married a **McComas**, children unknown

BY ARACOMA CORNSTALK/1742
WITH BOLING KIKPELETHEE BAKER/1730

GRANDSON

Baker, Running Deer – 11/16th Chalakatha-Mekoche-Shawano-ChalakaPowhatan-Metis born 1764 Logan Co. WV-died after 1794 (OH?) – son of **Boling Kikpelethee Baker**/1730 & **Aracoma Cornstalk**/1742, raised by Cornstalk family after death of Aracoma in 1780, raised by Cornstalk family after death of Aracoma in 1780, Blue Jacket War/1782-94, wife & children unknown

GRANDSON

Baker, Laughing Water – 11/16th Chalakatha-Mekoche-ShawanoChalaka-Powhatan-Metis born 1766 Logan Co. WV-died after 1794
(OH?) – son of **Boling Kikpelethee Baker**/1730 & **Aracoma Cornstalk**/1742, raised by Cornstalk family after death of his mother 1780, Blue Jacket War/1784-94, wife & children unknown

GRANDDAUGHTER

Baker, White Flower aka Snow Lily-Snow Flower – 11/16th ChalakathaMekoche-Shawano-Chalaka-Powhatan-Metis born 1768 Logan Co. WVdied after 1810 (OH?) – daughter of **Boling Kikpelethee Baker**/1730 & **Aracoma Cornstalk**/1742, raised by Cornstalk family after death of
Aracoma in 1780, known for her light hair & complexion, lived until 1810 in Native-Metis-white community in Lawrence Co. OH, husband & children unknown

GRANDDAUGHTER

Baker, Raindrop aka Falling Rain – 11/16th Chalakatha-MekocheShawano-Chalaka-Powhatan-Metis born 1770 Logan Co. WV-died after 1810 (OH?) – daughter of **Boling Kikpelethee Baker**/1730 & **Aracoma Cornstalk**/1742, raised by Cornstalk family after death of Aracoma in 1780, husband & children unknown

GRANDSON

Baker, Running Water – 11/16th Chalakatha-Mekoche-ShawanoChalaka-Powhatan-Metis born 1772 Logan Co. WV-died after 1794 (OH?) – son of **Boling Kikpelethee Baker**/1730 & **Aracoma Cornstalk**/1742, Blue Jacket War/1790-94, wife & children unknown

GRANDSON

Baker, Blue Feather aka Blue Feather (2)-Young Blue Feather– 11/16th Chalakatha-Mekoche-Shawano-Chalaka-Powhatan-Metis born 1774 Logan Co. WV-died after 1794 (OH?) – son of **Boling Kikpelethee Baker**/1730 & **Aracoma Cornstalk**/1742, namesake of **Blue Feather (1)**Mekoche- cousin of Aracoma-a nephew of Helizikinopo that was killed at Point Pleasant 1774, raised by Cornstalk family after death of Aracoma in 1780, Blue Jacket War/1782-94, wife & children unknown

BY ELIZABETH CORNSTALK/1744

WITH JOHN SWIFT/1712

UNKNOWN

BY ELIZABETH CORNSTALK/1744

WITH PETELLA/1730

UNKNOWN

BY YOUNG CORNSTALK/1746

WITH CHALAKATHA WOMAN/1750

UNKNOWN

BY YOUNG CORNSTALK/1746 WITH ELIZABETH SEE/1754

GRANDDAUGHTER

Cornstalk, White Wing aka Nancy Adkins-**Big Nancy** – 29/64th Chalakatha-Mekoche-Shawano-Chalaka-Powhatan-Metis born 1770 OH-died before 1825 CAN - daughter of **Young Cornstalk**/1746 & **Elizabeth See**/1754-adopted white, about 6' tall, a Chalakatha, spoke & read some English-(learned from her father & 1st husband Adkins), later an occasional translator for **Tecumseh**, moved to CAN 1815 with Tecumseh followers & died before they returned in 1825, wife 1st 1784 Montgomery Co VA (=southern WV) of **Elijah Adkins**/1764, 2nd 1793 OH of **Tecumseh**/1768, abandoned Adkins & sons 1790 to become involved with Tecumseh, left daughter Little Nancy Adkins/1790 with Cornstalk family when she married Tecumseh, mother **with Adkins** of Lewis Adkins/1784, Elijah Adkins Jr/1786, Richard Adkins/1788 & Nancy Adkins aka Little Nancy/1790-all 19/32nd Chalakatha-Shawano-Mekoche-Chalaka-Powhatan-Metis, **with Tecumseh** of Paukeesaa Tecumseh/1794, Adjala Tecumseh/1796 & Serena Tecumseh/1798-all 19/32nd Chalakatha-Mekoche-Kishpoko-Pekowi- Shawano-Chalaka-Powhatan-Creek-Metis

GRANDSON

Cornstalk, Young (2) aka Son of Young Cornstalk – 29/64th Chalakatha-Mekoche-Shawano-Chalaka-Powhatan-Metis born 1772 OH-died after 1792 (OH?) - son of **Young Cornstalk**/1744 & **Elizabeth See**/1754-adopted-white, brother of **White Wing** Cornstalk/1770, a Chalakatha, wife & children unknown

BY ELLINIPSICO CORNSTALK/1748 WITH CHALAKATHA WOMAN/1750

UNKNOWN

BY ELLINIPSICO CORNSTALK/1748
With WHITE WOMAN/1755

UNKNOWN

BY ELLINIPSICO CORNSTALK/1748 WITH MARY CATHERINE SEE/1748

GRANDDAUGHTER

See, Margaret Peggy (2) aka Margaret Peggy Cornstalk-Margaret Peggy Ellinipsico – 29/64th Chalakatha-Mekoche-Shawano-Chalaka-Powhatan-Metis born 1764 OH-died after 1800 - only child of **Ellinipsico Cornstalk**/1746 & **Mary Catherine See**/1748-adopted white, returned to whites 1765 with mother, grandmother & family, husband & children unknown

BY BLUE SKY-MARY CORNSTALK/1750 WITH PARKER V. ADKINS/1720

GRANDSON

Adkins, Littleberry – 23/32nd Chalakatha-Mekoche-Shawano-ChalakaPowhatan-Metis born 1766 Ft. Pitt area PA-died 1848 Mercer Co. WV - son of **Mary Blue Sky Cornstalk**/1750 & **Parker V. Adkins**/1720, grandson of **Cornstalk**/1710, husband 1790 Franklin Co VA of 1st cousin **Nancy Adkins**/1767, father of Jesse Adkins/1791, Isom Adkins/1795, Hezekiah Adkins/1799, Littleberry Adkins Jr/1801, Christina Adkins/1805, Dicey Adkins/1807, Priscilla Adkins/1809 & Vicey Adkins/1811-all 27/64th Chalakatha-Mekoche-Shawano-ChalakaPowhatan-Metis

GRANDDAUGHTER

Adkins, Charity Adkins – 29/64th Chalakatha-Mekoche-ShawanoChalaka-Powhatan-Metis born 1768 PA-died 1820 Cabell Co

WV - daughter of **Mary Blue Sky Cornstalk**/1750 & **Parker V. Adkins**/1720, granddaughter of **Cornstalk**/1710, wife (2nd?) 1788 of 1st cousin **Randolph Adkins**/1759-(nephew of **Parker V. Adkins**/1720- son of his brother **William Adkins**/1721), mother of Parker Adkins/1789, Randolph Sprang Adkins/1791, Nancy Adkins/1794, William Adkins/1796, Jane Adkins/1803, Richard Adkins/1805, Rhoda Adkins/1810, Sylvester Adkins/1812, John T. Adkins/1814, Price Adkins/1816-all 27/64th Chalakatha-Mekoche-Shawano-Chalaka-Powhatan-Metis

BY ESTHER CORNSTALK/1751
WITH THOMAS SOWARDS/1746

GRANDSON

Sowards, Griffin aka Griffin Tipsword-Griffin Sword-Griffin Tipscord – 29/64th Chalakatha-Mekoche-Shawano-Chalaka-Powhatan-Metis born 1773-died 1845 IL - son of **Esther Cornstalk**/1751 & **Thomas Sowards**/1746, grandson of **Cornstalk**/1710, husband 1790 of **Ruth Abbott**/1774, father of Andrew Jackson Sowards/1797, Douglas Sowards/1799, Miliston Sowards/1801, John Adams Sowards/1803, Isaac Sowards/1805, Desha Sowards/1807, Rebecca Sowards/1809, Thomas Sowards/1813, Carlin Sowards/1815-all 15/32nd ChalakathaMekoche-Shawano-Chalaka-Powhatan-Metis

GRANDSON

Sowards, Thomas Jr – 29/64th Chalakatha-Mekoche-Shawano-Chalaka-Powhatan-Metis born 1775-died 1812 KY - son of **Esther Cornstalk**/1751 & **Thomas Sowards**/1746, grandson of **Cornstalk**/1710, husband 1793 of **Letitia Mills**/1772, father of Mahala Sowards/1794, Susanna Sowards/1800, Thomas G. Sowards/1804, Charles Sowards/1806-all 15/64th Chalakatha-Mekoche-Shawano-Chalaka-Powhatan-Metis

GRANDSON

Sowards, Robert – 29/64th Chalakatha-Mekoche-Shawano-Chalaka-

Powhatan-Metis born 1780-died after 1812 IN - son of **Esther Cornstalk**/1751 & **Thomas Sowards**/1746, grandson of **Cornstalk**/1710, wife & children unknown

GRANDDAUGHTER

Sowards, Esther – 29/64th Chalakatha-Mekoche-Shawano-Chalaka-Powhatan-Metis born 1781-died 1847 - daughter of **Esther Cornstalk**/1751 & **Thomas Sowards**/1746, granddaughter of **Cornstalk**/1710, wife 1st 1801 of **Robert Carlisle**/1776, 2nd 1830 of **Herman Hatfield**/1790, mother **with Carlisle** of Frances Carlisle/1805-15/64th Chalakatha-Mekoche-Shawano-Chalaka-Powhatan-Metis

GRANDSON

Sowards, Jacob – 29/64th Chalakatha-Mekoche-Shawano-ChalakaPowhatan-Metis born 1783-died after 1812 - son of **Esther Cornstalk**/1751 & **Thomas Sowards**/1746, grandson of **Cornstalk**/1710, wife & children unknown

GRANDSON

Sowards, John B. – 29/64th Chalakatha-Mekoche-Shawano-ChalakaPowhatan-Metis born 1784-died after 1812 - son of **Esther Cornstalk**/1751 & **Thomas Sowards**/1746, grandson of **Cornstalk**/1710, wife & children unknown

GRANDDAUGHTER

Sowards, Rosannah – 29/64th Chalakatha-Mekoche-Shawano-ChalakaPowhatan-Metis born 1786-died 1831 KY - daughter of **Esther Cornstalk**/1751 & **Thomas Sowards**/1746, twin of Diana, granddaughter of **Cornstalk**/1710, wife 1803 of **Thomas Doty**/1785white, children unknown

GRANDDAUGHTER

Sowards, Diana – 29/64th Chalakatha-Mekoche-Shawano-Chalaka-Powhatan-Metis born 1786-died after 1802 - daughter of **Esther Cornstalk**/1751 & **Thomas Sowards**/1746, twin of Rosannah, granddaughter of **Cornstalk**/1710, husband & children unknown

GRANDDAUGHTER

Sowards, Rebecca – 29/64th Chalakatha-Mekoche-Shawano-Chalaka-Powhatan-Metis born 1790-died about 1830 - daughter of **Esther Cornstalk**/1751 & **Thomas Sowards**/1746, granddaughter of **Cornstalk**/1710, wife 1st 1805 of **Garrett Harris**/1790, 2nd before 1830 of **Isaac Carson**/1790, mother **with Harris** of Garrett Harris Jr/1806 & Lucinda Harris/1809-both 15/64th Chalakatha-Mekoche-ShawanoChalaka-Powhatan-Metis

GRANDSON

Sowards, George Washington – 29/64th Chalakatha-Mekoche-ShawanoChalaka-Powhatan-Metis born 1792-died after 1812 - son of **Esther Cornstalk**/1751 & **Thomas Sowards**/1746, grandson of **Cornstalk**/1710, wife & children unknown

BY BLACK BEARD/1730
WITH KATEE KILLAQUA/1737

GRANDAUGHTER

Black Beard, Daughter of aka Daughter of Black Beard Cornstalk-Wife of Beauvais – 35/64th Chalakatha-Mekoche-Pekowi-Shawano-ChalakaPowhatan-Cherokee-Metis born 1755 OH-died after 1795 (MO?) - daughter of **Black Beard Cornstalk (1)**/1730 & **Katee Carpenter**/1737, a Chalakatha, granddaughter of **Cornstalk**/1710, wife 1770 (OH-IN?) of **Jean Baptiste St. Gem Beauvais**/1730, living in Apple Creek MO 1795, mother of Daughter of Beauvais/1770-17/64th Chalakatha-MekochePekowi-Shawano-Chalaka-Powhatan-Cherokee-Metis

GRANDSON

Cornstalk, Young Black Beard aka Black Beard Cornstalk (2)-Black Beard (3) – 35/64th Chalakatha-Mekoche-Pekowi-Shawano-ChalakaPowhatan-Cherokee-Metis born 1760 OH-died after 1812 - son of **Black Beard Cornstalk**/1730 & **Katee Killaqua**/1737, a Chalakatha warrior, grandson of **Cornstalk**/1710, Blue Jacket War/1777-94, **with U.S. Army**-Creek War/1813, husband about 1780 OH of **Mekoche Woman**/1765, children unknown

BY BLACK WOLF/1740

WITH NIKKEE KILLAQUA/1738

GRANDSON

Cornstalk, Young Black Wolf aka Black Wolf Cornstalk (2)-Black Wolf (3) – 35/64th Chalakatha-Mekoche-Pekowi-Shawano-ChalakaPowhatan-Cherokee-Metis born 1760 OH/IN-died after 1854 KS - son of **Black Wolf Cornstalk**/1740 & **Nikkee Killaqua**/1738, grandson of **Cornstalk**/1710, a Chalakatha warrior, Blue Jacket War/1777-94, raiding OH-KY-VA/1790-99, Prophet's Town/1811, War 1812-Thames/1813 **with Tecumseh**, remained in OH/IN 1815 when others moved to CAN, moved to KS 1826 **with Prophet & Paukeesaa Tecumseh**, husband 1780 OH/IN of **Pottawamee Woman**/1765, children unknown

BY BLACK WOLF/1740

WITH POTTAWAMEE WOMAN/1754

GRANDSON

Black Wolf, Soldier (1) aka **Maunahpeykaw**-Black Wolf's Son – 27/64th Chalakatha-Mekoche-Pekowi-Shawano-Chalaka-Powhatan-CherokeePottawamee-Metis born 1770 OH/IN-died after 1832 KS - son of **Black Wolf Cornstalk (1)**/1740 & **Pottawatamee Woman**/1754, grandson of **Cornstalk**/1710, Blue Jacket War/1788-94, scout-**with U.S. Army**-War 1812-Thames/1813-(against his sons), captured at Ft. Meigs/1813 & released by **Tecumseh**, Treaty 1832, moved to KS 1832, husband 1789 IN/OH of **Pottawatamee Woman**/1774, father of Young Soldier Black Wolf/1790-13/64th Chalakatha-Mekoche-Pekowi-Shawano-Chalaka-Powhatan-Cherokee-Pottawamee-Metis

GRANDSON

Black Wolf, Young – 27/64th Chalakatha-Mekoche-Pekowi-ShawanoChalaka-Powhatan-Cherokee-Pottawamee-Metis born 1786 OH-died after 1854 KS - son of **Black Wolf Cornstalk (1)/1740 & Pottawatamee Woman/1754**, grandson of **Cornstalk**/1710, Prophet's Town/1811, War
1812- Thames/1813 **with Tecumseh**-(against his father), remained with Pottawamee 1815 when Prophet & Paukeesaa moved to CAN, remained with Pottawamee when Prophet & Paukeesaa moved to KS
1826, Treaty 1854, moved to KS 1832, husband about 1806 (IN?) of **Pottawatamee Woman**/1790, children unknown

BY BLACK WOLF/1740
WITH JENNY WILEY/1760

POSSIBLE GRANDDAUGHTER

Thought to be a daughter-born 1787 after Jenny returned to the whites

BY JOHN WOLF CORNSTALK/1750
WITH CHALAKATHA WOMAN/1765

GRANDDAUGHTER

Wolf, Black Poddee aka Black Poddee Cornstalk – 31/32nd ChalakathaMekoche-Pekowi-Shawano-Chalaka-Powhatan-Metis born 1785 OHdied before 1846 KS - daughter of **John Wolf Cornstalk (1)/1750 & Chalakatha Woman**/1760, moved to KS by 1832, husband & children unknown

GRANDSON

Wolf, Peter Temestetee – 31/32nd Chalakatha-Mekoche-PekowiShawano-Chalaka-Powhatan-Metis born 1770 OH-died after 1815 - son of **John Wolf Cornstalk (1)/1750 & Chalakatha Woman**/1755, Blue Jacket War/1787-94, living in Apple Creek MO 1815, wife & children unknown

GRANDSON

Clay, Henry Nolesimo aka Nolesimo Wolf-Henry Clay Wolf – 31/32nd Chalakatha-Mekoche-Pekowi-Shawano-Chalaka-Powhatan-Metis born before 1781 OH-died 1846 KS - son of **John Wolf Cornstalk (1)**/1750 & **Chalakatha Woman**/1755, grandson of **Cornstalk**/1710, Treaty 1831, moved to KS 1832, a **sub-chief** 1835 KS under **John Perry**/1775 & **William Perry**/1770, husband 1st about 1801 OH of **Chalakatha Woman**/1785, 2nd 1820 OH of **Daughter of Jeremiah McClene**/1780, 3rd 1833 KS of **Ottawa Woman**/1815, children/1801-20 **with Chalakatha** unknown, father **with McLene** of William Clay/1822, Susan Clay/1832 & 2 sons/1823-31-all 15/32nd Chalakatha-Mekoche-Pekowi-Shawano-Chalaka-Powhatan-Metis, **with Ottawa** of Henry Clay Jr/1833-15/32nd Chalakatha-Mekoche-Pekowi-Shawano-ChalakaPowhatan-Ottawa-Metis

GRANDSON

Cornstalk, John (2) aka **John Wolf (2)** – 31/32nd Chalakatha-MekochePekowi-Shawano-Chalaka-Powhatan-Metis born 1792 OH-died after
1846 KS - son of **John Wolf Cornstalk**/1750 & **Chalakatha Woman**/1765, an alcoholic in later years, a Chalakatha warrior, Prophet's Town/1811, War 1812- Thames/1813 **with Tecumseh** & brother **Peter Cornstalk (3)**/1794, living in AR by 1825, moved to KS after 1837, wife & children unknown

GRANDSON

Cornstalk, Peter (3) aka Peter Wolf – 31/32nd Chalakatha-MekochePekowi-Shawano-Chalaka-Powhatan-Metis born 1794 OH-died after
1850 likely KS - son of **John Wolf Cornstalk (1)**/1750 & **Chalakatha Woman**/1755, Prophet's Town/1811, War 1812- Thames/1813 **with Tecumseh** & brother **John Cornstalk (2)**/1792, living in AR by 1825, a **village Chief** over mixed Shawnee-Cherokee **in AR**, went to CA 1848 to mine gold, moved to KS about 1850, husband 1st 1814 (OH-IN?) of **Kishpoko Woman**/1799, 2nd 1825 AR of **Mary Adams**/1808-white, children unknown

BY PETER CORNSTALK/1755
WITH CHALAKATHA WOMAN/1760
UNKNOWN
BY PETER CORNSTALK/1755
WITH MARY FRANCES AVERY/1765

GRANDSON

Cornstalk, Peter (2) aka **Wyamwiman**-Wiamweemaw-Peter Cornstalk Jr – 27/64th Chalakatha-Mekoche-Pekowi-Shawano-Chalaka-PowhatanMetis born 1785 OH-**murdered** 1841 KS - son of **Peter Cornstalk (1)**/1755 & **Mary Frances Avery**/1765-white, Treaty 1825, about 6'6" tall, , a **Chalakatha Chief** in OH by 1815, moved to MO about 1815 but living with Miami in 1825 (IN?), moved to KS by 1832, returned from MO/KS to OH 1832 & killed **Capt. Bill** & **Sam Loon**-both Mekoche in revenge for murdering his father but spared **Doc Bill**-a Chalakatha, **murdered** by **Peter A. Tyler**- former friend of the family, husband by 1805 OH of **Chalakatha Woman**/1790, father of Peter Cornstalk (4)/1805, Daughter/1810, John B. Cornstalk/1820 & other children/1805-20-all 47/64th Chalakatha-Mekoche-Pekowi-ShawanoChalaka-Powhatan-Metis

GRANDDAUGHTER

Cornstalk, Mary (3) – 27/64th Chalakatha-Mekoche-Pekowi-Shawano-Chalaka-Powhatan-Metis born 1796 OH-died after 1816 - daughter of **Peter Cornstalk (1)**/1755 & **Mary Frances Avery**/1765-white, wife 1816 OH of **William McNeel**/1795, children unknown

BY SUSANNA CORNSTALK/1757
WITH THOMAS JACOB MAW/1755

GRANDSON

Maw, John – 27/64th Chalakatha-Mekoche-Pekowi-Shawano-ChalakaPowhatan-Cherokee-Metis born 1799 TN-**murdered** before 1861 - son of **Thomas Jacob Maw**/1755 & **Susanna Cornstalk**/1757, **killed** on the Vann farm with a knife by **slave Uncle Joe** for whipping him, husband
1st 1815 of **Charity Vann**/1792, 2nd 1820 of her half-sister **Margaret Vann (3)**/1798, children unknown

BY SUNFISH CORNSTALK/1742
WITH DELEWARE WOMAN/1745

UNKNOWN

BY ABRAHAM AILSTOCK/1750
WITH CHALAKATHA WOMAN/1755

UNKNOWN

BY ABRAHAM AILSTOCK/1750 WITH ELIZABETH GOING/1762

GRANDDAUGHTER

Ailstock, Rebecca aka Becky Ailstock– 29/64th Chalakatha-PekowiMekoche-Shawano-Chalaka-Powhatan-Black-Metis born 1780 VA-died after 1799 - daughter of **Abraham Cornstalk-Ailstock**/1750 & **Elizabeth Going**/1762, raised by her uncles Absalom/1748 & Michael/1752, granddaughter of **Cornstalk**/1710 & **Julia Mulatto**/1720, wife 1799 VA of 1st cousin **James Going**/1779, children unknown

GRANDDAUGHTER

Ailstock, Virginia aka Jennie Ailstock – 29/64th Chalakatha-Pekowi-Mekoche-Shawano-Chalaka-Powhatan-Black-Metis born 1782 VA-died after 1799 - daughter of **Abraham Cornstalk Ailstock**/1750 & **Elizabeth Going**/1762, raised by uncles Absalom/1748 & Michael/1752, granddaughter of **Cornstalk**/1710 & **Julia Mulatto**/1720, wife 1799 of 1st cousin **Jesse**

Going/1780, children unknown

BY ABRAHAM AILSTOCK/1750
WITH ISABEL RADCLIFF/1768

UNKNOWN

BY ABSALOM AILSTOCK/1748

WITH CHALAKATHA WOMAN/1753
UNKNOWN

BY ABSALOM AILSTOCK/1748
WITH SALLY GOING/1764

GRANDSON

Ailstock, John – 13/64th Chalakatha-Mekoche-Shawano-ChalakaPowhatan-Black-Metis born 1779 VA-died after 1860 - 1st son of **Absalom Cornstalk Ailstock**/1748 & **Sally Going**/1764, grandson of **Cornstalk**/1710 & **Julia Mulatto**/1720, living **in Mason Co. WV** by 1840, husband 1st by 1800 VA of **Polly Jones**/1780, 2nd 1814 VA of her sister **Arsella Jones**/1783-both Mekoche-Black-Metis-(sisters of **Mary Jones**/1778 & **Sally Jones**/1785), father **with Polly** of Sally Ailstock/1802 & Mary Ailstock/1808, **with Arsella** of Rebecca Ailstock/1815, Mary Ailstock/1822, Susanna-Susan Ailstock/1825-all 23/64th Chalakatha-Mekoche-Shawano-Chalaka-Powhatan-Black-Metis, grandfather of Harriet Jane Moss/1854-11/64th Chalakatha-MekocheShawano-Chalaka-Powhatan-Black-Metis

GRANDDAUGHTER

Ailstock, Katy – 13/64th Chalakatha-Mekoche-Shawano-ChalakaPowhatan-Black-Metis born 1782 VA-died after 1830 - 1st daughter of **Absalom Cornstalk Ailstock**/1748 & **Sally Going**/1764, granddaughter of **Cornstalk**/1710 & **Julia Mulatto**/1720, unmarried in 1830, husband & children unknown

GRANDDAUGHTER

Ailstock, Polly – 13/64th Chalakatha-Mekoche-Shawano-ChalakaPowhatan-Black-Metis born 1784 VA-died after 1803 - 2nd daughter of **Absalom Cornstalk Ailstock**/1748 & **Sally Going**/1763, granddaughter of **Cornstalk**/1710 & **Julia Mulatto**/1720, unmarried in 1803

GRANDSON

Ailstock, Lawrence – 13/64th Chalakatha-Mekoche-Shawano-ChalakaPowhatan-Black-Metis born 1786 VA-died after 1823 VA - 2nd son of
Absalom Cornstalk Ailstock/1748 & **Sally Going**/1764, grandson of **Cornstalk**/1710 & **Julia Mulatto**/1720, wife & children unknown

GRANDDAUGHTER

Ailstock, Elizabeth – 13/64th Chalakatha-Mekoche-Shawano-ChalakaPowhatan-Black-Metis born 1788 VA-died after 1802 - 3rd daughter of **Absalom Cornstalk Ailstock**/1748 & **Sally Going**/1764, granddaughter of **Cornstalk**/1710 & **Julia Mulatto**/1720, unmarried in 1802

GRANDSON

Ailstock, Andrew – 13/64th Chalakatha-Mekoche-Shawano-ChalakaPowhatan-Black-Metis born 1790 VA-died 1862 VA - 3rd son of **Absalom Cornstalk Ailstock**/1748 & **Sally Going**/1764, grandson of **Cornstalk**/1710 & **Julia Mulatto**/1720, husband 1813 VA of **Phoebe Rickets**/1793, children unknown

GRANDSON

Ailstock, David – 13/64th Chalakatha-Mekoche-Shawano-ChalakaPowhatan-Black-Metis born 1792 VA-died after 1850 - 4th son of **Absalom Cornstalk Ailstock**/1748 & **Sally Going**/1764, grandson of **Cornstalk**/1710 & **Julia Mulatto**/1720, husband 1828 VA of **Patsy Craig**/1810, children unknown

GRANDSON

Ailstock, James – 13/64th Chalakatha-Mekoche-Shawano-ChalakaPowhatan-Black-Metis born 1794 VA-died after 1820 - 5th son of **Absalom Cornstalk Ailstock**/1748 & **Sally Going**/1764, grandson of **Cornstalk**/1710 & **Julia Mulatto**/1720, wife & children unknown

GRANDSON

Ailstock, Absalom Jr – 13/64th Chalakatha-Mekoche-Shawano-Chalaka-Powhatan-Black-Metis born 1796 VA-died about 1858 VA - 6th son of **Absalom Cornstalk Ailstock**/1748 & **Sally Going**/1764, grandson of **Cornstalk**/1710 & **Julia Mulatto**/1720, wife & children unknown

GRANDSON

Ailstock, William – 13/64th Chalakatha-Mekoche-Shawano-ChalakaPowhatan-Black-Metis born 1798 VA-died after 1820 - 7th son of **Absalom Cornstalk Ailstock**/1748 & **Sally Going**/1764, grandson of **Cornstalk**/1710 & **Julia Mulatto**/1720, wife & children unknown

GRANDSON

Ailstock, Thomas A. – 13/64th Chalakatha-Mekoche-Shawano-ChalakaPowhatan-Black-Metis born 1800 VA-died before 1840 - 8th son of
Absalom Cornstalk Ailstock/1748 & **Sally Going**/1764, grandson of **Cornstalk**/1710 & **Julia Mulatto**/1720, husband 1818 VA of his niece **Sally Ailstock**/1802, children unknown

BY MICHAEL AILSTOCK/1752
WITH CHALAKATHA WOMAN/1756

UNKNOWN

BY MICHAEL AILSTOCK/1752
WITH REBECCA GOING/1760

GRANDDAUGHTER

Ailstock, Mary aka Mary Two Pence – 13/64th Chalakatha-MekocheShawano-Chalaka-Powhatan-Black-Metis born 1776 VA-died after 1795 - 1st daughter of **Michael Cornstalk Ailstock**/1752 & **Rebecca Going**/1760, granddaughter of **Cornstalk**/1710 & **Julia Mulatto**/1720, wife 1790 VA of **Two Pence**/1770-Mekoche, widowed by 1795, mother of Rebecca Two Pence-Rebecca Ailstock/1790-31/64th ChalakathaMekoche-Shawano-Chalaka-Powhatan-Black-Metis

GRANDSON

Ailstock, Joseph – 13/64th Chalakatha-Mekoche-Shawano-ChalakaPowhatan-Black-Metis born 1778 VA-died after 1810 - 1st son of **Michael Cornstalk Ailstock**/1752 & **Rebecca Going**/1760, grandson of **Cornstalk**/1710 & **Julia Mulatto**/1720, husband 1792 VA of **Mary Jones**/1778-Mekoche-Black-Metis-(sister of **Polly**/1780, **Arsella**/1783 & **Sally**/1785), father of Sarah Ailstock/1792-23/64th ChalakathaMekoche-Shawano-Chalaka-Powhatan-Black-Metis

GRANDDAUGHTER

Ailstock, Susanna – 13/64th Chalakatha-Mekoche-Shawano-ChalakaPowhatan-Black-Metis born 1780 VA-died after 1803 - 2nd daughter of **Michael Cornstalk Ailstock**/1752 & **Rebecca Going**/1760, granddaughter of **Cornstalk**/1710 & **Julia Mulatto**/1720, mother with **White Ailstock Man** of William Ailstock/1794, Sarah Ailstock /1796, Ursella Ailstock/1797, Betsy Ailstock/1798, Lewis Ailstock/1799 & Kitty Ailstock/1801-all 3/16th Chalakatha-Mekoche-Shawano-Chalaka-Powhatan-Black-Metis

GRANDSON

Ailstock, Michael Jr – 13/64th Chalakatha-Mekoche-Shawano-ChalakaPowhatan-Black-Metis born 1782 VA-died after 1818 - 2nd son of **Michael Cornstalk Ailstock**/1752 & **Rebecca Going**/1760, grandson of **Cornstalk**/1710 & **Julia Mulatto**/1720, husband 1st 1799 VA of **Sally Jones**/1785-Mekoche-Black-Metis-(sister of **Mary**/1778, **Polly**/1780 & **Arsella**/1783) , 2nd 1818 VA of **Margaret Cosward**/1780-free widow of color, children unknown

GRANDSON

Ailstock, Absalom - 13/64th Chalakatha-Mekoche-Shawano-ChalakaPowhatan-Black-Metis born 1784-died after 1849 - 3rd son of **Michael Cornstalk Ailstock**/1752 & **Rebecca Going**/1760, grandson of **Cornstalk**/1710 & **Julia Mulatto**/1720, husband about 1804 VA of **Sally Jones**/1785-Mekoche-Black-Metis-(former wife of his brother **Michael Ailstock Jr**/1782), children unknown

GRANDDAUGHTER

Ailstock, Elizabeth aka Betsy – 13/64th Chalakatha-Mekoche-ShawanoChalaka-Powhatan-Black-Metis born about 1786-died after 1820 - 3rd daughter of **Michael Cornstalk Ailstock**/1752 & **Rebecca Going**/1760, granddaughter of **Cornstalk**/1710 & **Julia Mulatto**/1720, living **in Mason Co. WV** by 1820, wife 1800 VA of **Thomas Mason**/1770, children unknown

BY MARY CORNSTALK SEE/1764 WITH LEONARD PETRO/1750

GRANDDAUGHTER

Petro, Margaret – 13/64th Chalakatha-Mekoche-Shawano-ChalakaPowhatan-Metis born 1788 WV-died after 1860 IL - daughter of **Mary Cornstalk See**/1764 & **Leonard Petro (1)** /1750-former adopted-white, granddaughter of **Cornstalk**/1710, wife 1826 of **Moses Woodruff**/1787
NJ, mother of Esquire Woodruff/1827 & Martin Woodruff/1828- both 3/32nd Chalakatha-Mekoche-Shawano-Chalaka-Powhatan-Metis

GRANDSON

Petro, Michael See – 13/64th Chalakatha-Mekoche-Shawano-ChalakaPowhatan-Metis born 1790 WV-died 1869 IN - son of **Mary Cornstalk See**/1764 & **Leonard Petro**/1750, grandson of **Cornstalk**/1710, namesake of half-uncle **Michael See**/1750, husband 1811 of **Iva Sutton**/1792, father of Leonard Petro (2)/1812, David Sutton
Petro/1814, Jonathan Perry Petro/1815, Absalom Petro/1817, Mary See

Petro/1819, John Petro/1821, Anchor Sutton Petro/1823, Eliza Petro/1824, George Whitfield Petro/1825, Nancy Ward Petro/1826, David G. Petro/1827, Gabriel Sutton Petro/1829, Susanna Sutton Petro/1835 & Henry Jackson Petro/1837-all 3/32nd ChalakathaMekoche-Shawano-Chalaka-Powhatan-Metis

GRANDSON

Petro, John (1) – 13/64th Chalakatha-Mekoche-Shawano-ChalakaPowhatan-Metis born 1792 KY-died 1828 IN - son of **Mary Cornstalk See**/1764 & **Leonard Petro**/1750, grandson of **Cornstalk**/1710, husband 1812 of **Mary Sutton**/1794, father of Iva Petro/1813, Mary Catherine Petro/1814, James H. Petro/1816, Hannah Petro/1818, John Petro Jr/1819, Nancy Ann Petro/1820, David Sutton Petro/1822, Anchor Fox Petro/1823, Rebecca Petro/1825 & Michael Cornstalk Petro/1826-all 3/32nd Chalakatha-Mekoche-Shawano-ChalakaPowhatan-Metis

CHAPTER TEN

Nonhelema/1718 Sawelaha-Eliza/1712, Cawachile/1716, Elizabeth/1726,

Catherine-Kitty/1728,

Catherine-Katee/1734,

Greenbrier/1740,

Aracoma/1742,

Elizabeth/1744,

Mary Blue Sky/1750,

Esther/1752

THE MOST FAMOUS GRENADIER SQUAW

Nonhelema Cornstalk/1718

Cornstalk, Nonhelema aka Grenadier Squaw-Shawnee Warrior Woman-Nonhelema Okowellos-Nonhelema Hokolesqua - 27/32nd Chalakatha-Mekoche-Shawano-Chalaka-Powhatan-Metis born 1718 Greenbrier River WV-died after 1786 OH - daughter of **Okowellos**/1674 & **Katee Mekoche**/1680, about 6'6" tall, well built & attractive, often referred to as a giant, moved to AL by 1725 with Okowellos' band-returned to PA by 1730, moved to Lower Shawnee Town OH with **Peter Chartier** 1744, 1745 moved on to near Winchester KY-(**Neucheconner** & **Tamenebuck** return to PA), 1746 moved to French Lick-Nashville TN, 1747 moved to the Coosa River AL, returned north about 1754 (either with her 1st husband or just after his death), a **Chalakatha village Head woman** in OH by 1755, read & spoke some English, an occasional warrior in Cornstalk War /1755-74, Head Woman of Nonhelema's village on Sippio Creek of Sciota River OH before 1773, **an emissary to the Shawnee for Cornstalk** 1774, the **only woman warrior** Point Pleasant/1774, Grand Council 1782, Council Miami Jan. 1786, had the fingers cut off of her right hand to the 1st knuckle by whites following **murder of Moluntha** during Benjamin Logan's attack on Moluntha's village 1786, moved to Apple Creek MO area following death of Moluntha, returned to OH home to die after 1795, wife 1st 1734 PA of **Wahootasika-Savannah King**/1710Chalakatha-widowed 1754, 2nd 1754 OH of 1st cousin **Moluntha**/1708-Mekoche, unmarried partner (she never really left Moluntha) 3rd 1762 OH with **Richard Butler**/1742-white-(adopted Seneca), mother **with Wahootasika** of Elder Daughter/1735, daughter Mellana/1748, twin daughters Wynema & Waheeta/1750--all 59/64th Chalakatha-MekocheShawano-Chalaka-Powhatan-Metis, **with Moluntha** of Chieska/1755, Younger Daughter/1757 & Big Capt. Johnny/1759-all 59/64th MekocheChalakatha-Shawano-Chalaka-Powhatan-Metis, **with Richard Butler** of Capt. Butler-Tamenatha/1763-27/64th Chalakatha-Mekoche-ShawanoChalaka-Powhatan-Metis, adoptive mother of niece **Fanny Butler**/1755, often confused in white histories with her sisters & nieces

HUSBANDS OF NONHELEMA

HUSBAND 1734 - PA

Wahootasika aka **Savannah King** - Chalakatha born about 1710 VA**killed** 1754 (TN?) – **parents unknown**, in PA by 1734, moved to OH with **Peter Chartier** 1744, moved to Winchester KY with **Chartier** 1745, **Principal Chief by 1746** of the Shawnee-among-the-Cherokee i.e. **Chickamauga** in TN-KY, diplomat between Shawnee & Overhill Cherokee, killed at outbreak of the French-Indian War/1754, some relation of or connection to the **Hokolesqua-Okowellos-Cornstalk** family and/or the family of **Katee** & **Moluntha**, husband 1734 PA of **Nonhelema Cornstalk**/1718, father **with Nonhelema** of Elder Daughter/1735, daughter Mellana/1748, twin daughters Wynema &

Waheeta/1750--all 59/64th Chalakatha-Mekoche-Shawano-ChalakaPowhatan-Metis

HUSBAND 1754 OH

Moluntha aka Mequachake-Malunthy-Molunthy – Mekoche born about 1710 OH-**murdered** 1786 OH – **parents unknown** but he was a nephew of **Katee Mekoche**/1680-(sister of his father & wife of **Okowellos**/1674), a **Mekoche Chief** in OH before 1749, **Head Chief of Mekoche** by 1778, **split leadership of All Shawnee** with **Black Hoof**-Thawikila in 1779 after death of **Black Fish**, raiding PA-VA/1740, Cornstalk War /1755-77, sent warriors to Point Pleasant/1774, Grand Council June 1762, 1763, 1782, Council Logstown 1765, Council Miami Jan. 1786, Treaty 1786, brother of **Elk-Wabete**/1715, 1st cousin (his father & Cornstalk's mother were siblings) & brother in law (husband of Cornstalk's sister Nonhelema) of **Cornstalk**/1710, murdered by **Hugh McGeary** while holding Treaty of 1786, under U.S. flag, **succeeded as Head Chief** of his faction by **Capt. Johnny**/1726 (the brother of Black Hoof) but **Blue Jacket**/1735 led an opposing sub-faction within the group, (split = 3 groups-**Black Hoof** in OH, **Capt. Johnny** in MO & **Blue Jacket** in OH), husband 1st 1730 (AL?) of **Sister of Black Hoof**/1715-Thawikila, 2nd 1754 OH of 1st cousin **Nonhelema Cornstalk**/1718, 3rd 1760 OH of his niece/2nd cousin (daughter of his 1st cousin-granddaughter of his father's sister) **Lacumtequa Cold Water**/1744, 4th before 1786 of another **Younger Woman** aka **Lanatumque**-(possible white or Metis), father **with Sister of Black Hoof** of Older Daughter/1754-Mekoche-Thawikila & likely many younger children, with **Nonhelema** of Chieska Moluntha/1755, Younger Daughter/1757 & Big Capt. Johnny/1759-all 59/64th MekocheChalakatha-Shawano-Chalaka-Powhatan-Metis, **with Lacumtequa** of a child name/gender unknown, children with **Younger Woman-Lanatumque** unknown

HUSBAND 1762 OH

Butler, Richard - white-(adopted-Seneca) born 1742 IRE-**killed** 1791 OH – **parents unknown**, brother of **William Butler**/1744-(husband of **Catherine Cornstalk**/1728), a trader among the Shawnee in OH 1773 with his brother William Butler, Colonel **with Colonial Army** & General **with U.S. Army**-Revolution, **killed at St. Clair**/1791, unmarried husband 1762 OH of **Nonhelema Cornstalk**/1718, father of Capt. Butler-Tamenatha/1763-27/64th Chalakatha-Mekoche-ShawanoChalaka-Powhatan-Metis

CHILDREN OF NONHELEMA/1718

WITH WAHOOTASIKA-SAVANNAH KING/1710

DAUGHTER

Wahootasika, Elder Daughter of - 59/64th Chalakatha-MekocheShawano-Chalaka-Powhatan-Metis born 1735 PA?-died about 1780 OH - daughter of **Nonhelema**/1718 & **Savannah King-Wahootasika**/1710, wife 1750 OH of **Chotschawanne Logan**/1725-adopted-white, children/1750-80 may have had surname Logan

DAUGHTER

Wahootasika, Mellana – 59/64th Chalakatha-Mekoche-ShawanoChalaka-Powhatan-Metis born 1748 OH-**murdered** 1774 WV - daughter of **Nonhelema**/1718 & **Savannah King-Wahootasika**/1710, wife 1765 OH of **Chief Logan Jr**/1745, **murdered** 1774 WV by Greathouse gang, children unknown

TWIN DAUGHTER 1

Wahootasika, Waheeta – 59/64th Chalakatha-Mekoche-ShawanoChalaka-Powhatan-Metis born about 1750 OH?-died after 1799 MO – twin daughter of **Nonhelema**/1718 & **Savannah KingWahootasika**/1710, twin of **Wynema**, wife about 1775 of **Wahceetah**/1735, adopted mother 1775 of **Joab (Jacob) Barton**/1767, moved to Skaggs Creek KY 1797, moved to MO 1799 after persecution by whites, mother of Itahaha Wahcheeta/1780-29/64th ChalakathaMekoche-Shawano-Chalaka-Powhatan-Metis

TWIN DAUGHTER 2

Wahootasika, Wynema aka Wynima-Wyneema-Pouter-She Pouts – 59/64th Chalakatha-Mekoche-Shawano-Chalaka-Powhatan-Metis born 1750 OH?-died after 1770 – twin daughter of **Savannah KingWahootasika**/1710 & **Nonhelema**/1718, twin of **Waheeta**, very light complexion & so thought to be mostly white, forced to return to whites by Bouquet Treaty 1764, returned to Tribe 1765, wife 1766 OH of **Chalakatha Man**/1746, children unknown

WITH MOLUNTHA/1710

SON

Moluntha, Chieska - **Capt. Chieska**-Young King-Young Moluntha-**Capt. Tom**-Capt. Tommy-Cheachisika-Jakeshaw-ChakalakekCheacksca-Chiachisika-Capt. Shigsta –59/64th Mekoche-ChalakathaShawano-Chalaka-Powhatan-Metis born 1755 OH-died of cholera 1833 - son of **Moluntha**/1710-Mekoche & **Nonhelema** /1718, a Mekoche warrior, over 6' tall, Blue Jacket War/1777-94, scout-Capt. John Logan Co-Anthony Shane Co-William Wells Co-**with U.S. Army**-War of 1812, a **Chalakatha Chief** at Wapaghonettat 1817, Treaty 1804, 1817, 1818, 1831, husband 1st 1779 OH of 1st cousin (daughter of mother's sister) **Polly Butler**/1765, 2nd 1780 OH of **Chalakatha Woman**/1765, father **with Polly** of Spy Buck Moluntha/1780-35/64th Mekoche-ChalakathaShawano-Chalaka-Powhatan-Creek-Metis, children **with Chalakatha** unknown

DAUGHTER

Moluntha, Younger Daughter of – 59/64th Mekoche-ChalakathaShawano-Chalaka-Powhatan-Metis born 1757 OH-died about 1790 OH - daughter of **Nonhelema**/1718 & **Moluntha**/1710-Mekoche, a
Mekoche, granddaughter of **Okowellos**/1674 & **Katee Mekoche**/1680(who was also the aunt of her father), niece of **Cornstalk**/1710, wife 1st
1775 OH of **Shawnee Warrior**/1755-widow by 1785, 2nd 1785 of **William Wells**/1770-white-(adopted-Miami), children/1775-85 **with Shawnee** unknown, mother **with Wells** of William Wayne Wells/1786

& Mary Wells/1788-both 29/64th Mekoche-Chalakatha-ShawanoChalaka-Powhatan-Metis-(adopted Miami)

SON

Moluntha, Capt. Johnny aka **Capt. Johnny (3)-Capt. John-Big John** – 59/64th Mekoche-Chalakatha-Shawano-Chalaka-Powhatan-Metis born 1759 OH-died after 1815 OH - son of **Nonhelema**/1718 & **Moluntha**/1710, grandson of **Okowellos**/1680, nephew of **Cornstalk**/1710, a Chalakatha warrior, attended Council 1785 with **Alexander McKee** & **Matthew Elliott**, Blue Jacket War/1777-94, scoutCapt. John Logan Co-**with U.S. Army-**War of 1812, killed **Winnemak**Pottawamee, nearly 7' tall, cousin of **Capt. John Logan-Big Horn**/1774,
Otter/1770 & **Bright Horn**/1770, husband about 1785 OH of **Rachel Kizer**/1761, father of two known children/1786-90

WITH RICHARD BUTLER/1742

SON

Butler, Capt. aka **Tamenatha**-Little Corn-Little Cornstalk - 27/64th Chalakatha-Mekoche-Shawano-Chalaka-Powhatan-Metis born about 1763 OH-died about 1834 KS - son of **Nonhelema**/1718 & & **Richard Butler**/1742-white, a Chalakatha warrior, nephew of **Cornstalk**/1710, grandson of **Okowellos**/1674, Blue Jacket War/1781-94, **refused Tecumseh**, scout-**with U.S. Army-**Prophet's Town/1811-War 1812Thames/1813, Treaty 1814, 1815, moved to KS about 1832, wife & children unknown

ADOPTED DAUGHTER

Butler, Fanny – 11/64th Chalakatha-Shawano-Chalaka-PowhatanCreek-Metis born about 1755-died after 1781 - daughter of **Elizabeth Cornstalk**/1726 & **John Sugantah-Lodging Pole Butler**/1730-white, adopted daughter of her aunt **Nonhelema**/1718, listed as prostitute around Ft. Pitt 1781-(this could only indicate that she was no more than promiscuous), niece of **Cornstalk**/1710, granddaughter of **Okowellos**/1674, any husband & children unknown

GRANDCHILDREN OF NONHELEMA

BY WAHEETA WAHOOTASIKA/1750 & WAHCHEETA/1735

GRANDDAUGHTER

Wahcheeta, Itahaha aka Hitahaha-Eetahaha – 29/64th ChalakathaMekoche-Shawano-Chalaka-Powhatan-Metis born about 1780 OH?died about 1807 MO? – daughter of **Wahceeta**/1735 & **Waheeta Wahootasika**/1750, 1st wife about 1796 of **Joab Barton**/1767- adopted white, moved to Skaggs Creek KY 1797, moved to MO 1799 after persecution by whites, mother of Jenny Jane Barton/1798 & Marcy Barton/1800-both 7/32nd Chalakatha-Mekoche-Shawano-Chalaka-Powhatan-Metis

BY CHIESKA MOLUNTHA/1755 & POLLY BUTLER/1765

GRANDSON

Moluntha, **Spy Buck** aka Saukothkaw-Tahkaska-Spybuck Chieska – 35/64th Mekoche-Chalakatha-Shawano-Chalaka-Powhatan-Creek-Metis born about 1780 OH-died after 1831 - son of **Polly Butler**/1765 & **Chieska Moluntha**/1755, a Chalakatha warrior, grandson of **Moluntha**/1710, great-nephew of **Cornstalk**/1710, delegate to D.C. 1802 with **Wayweleapee, John Perry, Quaskee Black Hoof, Joseph Parks** & **Francois Duchoquet**, scout-**with U.S. Army-**War 1812Thames/1813, Treaty 1817, 1831, a warrior at Hog Creek & Wapaghonettat 1832, husband 1795 OH of **Daughter of Col. Barbee**/1780-white, father of George Spy Buck/1796, Daughter of Spy Buck/1798, John Spy Buck/1802 & Young Spy Buck/1806-all 17/32nd Mekoche-Chalakatha-Shawano-Chalaka-Powhatan-Creek-Metis

BY YOUNGER DAUGHTER/1757 & WILLIAM WELLS/1770

GRANDDAUGHTER

Wells, Mary - 29/64th Mekoche-Chalakatha-Shawano-ChalakaPowhatan-Metis-(adopted **Miami**) born about 1788-died after 1818 - daughter of **William Wells**/1770-adopted-white-Miami & **Younger Daughter of Moluntha**/1757, mentioned in Treaty 1818, raised by Wells' 2nd wife **Tukemung Sweet Breeze Little Turtle**/1775-Miami after the death of her mother, husband & children unknown

GRANDSON

Wells, William Wayne - 29/64th Mekoche-Chalakatha-ShawanoChalaka-Powhatan-Metis -(adopted **Miami**) born about 1786-died after 1818 - son of **William Wells**/1770-adopted white Miami & **Younger Daughter of Nonhelema**/1757, **with U.S. Army**-War 1812-Thames/1813, Treaty 1805, 1817, 1818, raised by Wells' 2nd wife **Tukemung Sweet Breeze Little Turtle**/1775-Miami after the death of his mother, husband about 1795 of **Jane S. Unknown**/1780-MiamiMetis, children unknown

CHILDREN OF CAPT. JOHNNY/1757 & RACHEL KIZER/1761

UNKNOWN

CHILDREN OF CAPT. BUTLER-TAMENATHA/1763

UNKNOWN

THE OTHER GRENADIER SQUAWS

It appears that nearly any of the native women that were considered tall, around six foot or so, were called "Grenadier' by the whites of their times, based on the fact that grenadiers were an especially tall group of soldiers. It may sound silly to us toda, but it was apparently rather common in the 1700's, as in numerous instances of men being called grenadier if they were considered to be large, as professional fighters or wrestlers or circus strongmen and giants. Oddly, I have only found this name applied to women from the extended Cornstalk family so far, his sisters and daughters especially, but it may have been applied to others as well. **Sawelaha-Eliza Cornstalk/1712**

Cornstalk, Sawelaha aka Sawelaha Okowellos-Eliza Cornstalk-Wife of James Francis-Wife of Old Belt-Grenadier Squaw –27/32nd Chalakatha-Mekoche-Shawano-Chalaka-Powhatan-Metis born 1712 PA-died after 1745 likely PA - daughter of **Okowellos**/1674 & **Katee Mekoche**/1680, she didn't move to OH 1744 with the **Peter Chartier** group, wife 1st 1730 PA of **Chalakatha Man**/1710, 2nd 1739 PA of **James Francis**/1700British Officer, wife 3rd about 1745 PA of **Old Belt**/1700-Seneca, mother **with Chalakatha** of Aroas-Silverheels (2)/1732 & Counasona/1735both 59/64th Chalakatha-Mekoche-Shawano-Chalaka-Powhatan-Metis - (later adopted Seneca), **with Francis** of David Francis/1740 & John Francis (1)/1742-both 27/64th Chalakatha-Mekoche-Shawano-ChalakaPowhatan-Metis, any children **with Belt** unknown

HUSBANDS OF SAWELAHA-ELIZA

HUSBAND 1730 PA

Chalakatha Man – born about 1710-died after 1744 – **parents unknown**, apparently separated from Sawelaha 1739 when she took up with Francis, moved to OH 1744 with **Peter Chartier**, husband about 1730 PA of **Sawelaha Eliza Cornstalk**/1712, father of AroasSilverheels/1732 & Counasona/1735-both 59/64th ChalakathaMekoche-Shawano-Chalaka-Powhatan-Metis -(both later adopted by **Old Belt**-Seneca)

HUSBAND 1739 PA

Francis, James - white born about 1700-died after 1745 – **parents unknown**, officer in Colonial Army in PA, unmarried partner 1739 PA of **Sawelaha Eliza Cornstalk**/1712, father of David Francis/1740 & John Francis (1)/1742-both 27/64th Chalakatha-Mekoche-ShawanoChalaka-Powhatan-Metis

HUSBAND ABOUT 1745 PA

Old Belt aka **Kaighswaghtaniant**-Old Belt of Wampum-White Thunder - Seneca born about 1700-died after 1762 – **parents unknown**, an important **Seneca Chief** in PA, 3rd husband about 1745 PA of **Sawelaha Eliza Cornstalk**/1712-(his last wife), adopted father of **SilverheelsAroas**/1730 & **Counasona**/1735, any children **with Sawelaha-Eliza** unknown

CHILDREN OF SAWELAHA-ELIZA WITH CHALAKATHA/1710

SON

Cornstalk, Silverheels (2) aka **Aroas (1)**-Haroas-Silverheels Okowellos (2) – 59/64th Chalakatha-Mekoche-Shawano-Chalaka-Powhatan-Metis-(adopted Seneca) born 1732 OH/PA-**killed** 1770 IN/IL - son of **Sawelaha-Eliza Cornstalk**/1712 & **Chalakatha Man**/1710, adopted son about 1745 PA of **Old Belt**/1700-Seneca, grandson of **Okowellos**/1674, called a nephew of **Cornstalk**/1710, scout-spy **with Colonial Army**French-Indian War/1754-63-Ft. Necessity/1754-Braddock/1755-Pontiac War/1762-66-Bushy Run/1763, translator-guide for **George Morgan**-white after Pontiac War, **killed about 1770 below Louisville KY**, husband 1752 PA of **Mekoche Woman**/1735, father of Daughter of Aroas/1752, Young Aroas-Silverheels (3)/1760, (possibly a daughterSarah wife of John Featherston-white)-both 61/64th Chalakatha-Mekoche-Shawano-Chalaka-Powhatan-Metis-adopted Seneca

SON

Cornstalk, Counasona aka Counasona Okowellos-Counasona Belt-Koonasona – 59/64th Chalakatha-Mekoche-Shawano-ChalakaPowhatan-Metis-(adopted Seneca then Mohawk) born 1735 PA-died after 1778 likely OH - son of **Sawelaha-Eliza Okowellos**/1712 & **Chalakatha Man**/1710, adopted son (after 1745) of **Old Belt**/1700Seneca, Mohawk by marriage, scout-spy **with Colonial Army**-FrenchIndian War/1754-63, Pontiac War/1762-66, Dunmore War/1774-Point Pleasant/1774, Council Detroit 1778, called a nephew of

Shawnee Heritage II

Cornstalk/1710, husband about 1755 PA of **Mohawk Woman**/1740, children unknown

WITH JAMES FRANCIS/1700

SON

Francis, David **Mumagechee** – 27/64th Chalakatha-Mekoche-ShawanoChalaka-Powhatan-Metis-(adopted-Creek) born 1740 PA/OH- died after 1805 AL - son of **Sawelaha-Eliza Okowellos**/1712 & **James Francis**/1700-British Officer, nephew of **Cornstalk**/1710, adopted son of **Red Shoes (1)**/1720-Creek-Metis (a connection of **Okowellos** & **Red Shoes** families through Okowellos' Creek wife-**Sister of Sehoy** & Red Shoes' mother-**Sehoy (1)**, Treaty 1790, 1805, uncle (by marriage) of **Tecumseh**/1768, husband 1759 of **Mary Rising Sun**/1744, father with **Rising Sun** of John Francis/1760, Josiah Francis/1765, Joseph Francis/1770, Susan Francis/1775-all 29/64th Chalakatha-Kishpoko-Mekoche-Shawano-Chalaka-Powhatan-Creek-Metis

SON

Francis, John (1) – 27/64th Chalakatha-Mekoche-Shawano-ChalakaPowhatan-Metis born 1742 PA/OH-died after 1785 - son of **SawelahaEliza Okowellos**/1712 & **James Francis**/1700-British Officer, nephew of **Cornstalk**/1710, husband 1765 of half-niece (granddaughter of halfbrother) **Daughter of Silver Heels (2)-Aroas**/1750, father of John Tapatacatha Francis/1780-11/16th Chalakatha-Mekoche-ShawanoChalaka-Powhatan-Metis

WITH OLD BELT/1700

CHILDREN UNKNOWN

GRANDCHILDREN OF SAWELAHA-ELIZA CORNSTALK/1712

BY SON SILVERHEELS-AROAS/1732 & MEKOCHE WOMAN/1735

GRANDDAUGHTER

Silverheels, Daughter of aka Daughter of Aroas - 61/64th Chalakatha-Mekoche-Shawano-Chalaka-Powhatan-Metis-(adopted Seneca) born 1752 OH-died after 1785 - daughter of **Aroas-Silverheels Cornstalk**/1732 & **Mekoche Woman**/1735, great-great-granddaughter of **Okowellos**, an adopted Seneca, wife 1767 OH of her half-uncle (halfbrother of her father) **John Francis**/1745 (a grandson of **Okowellos**), mother of John Tapatacatha Francis/1780-11/16th Chalakatha-MekocheShawano-Chalaka-Powhatan-Metis

GRANDSON

Silverheels, Young aka **Young Aroas** - Silverheels (3) - 61/64th Chalakatha-Mekoche-Shawano-Chalaka-Powhatan-Metis-(adopted Seneca) born 1760 OH-died after 1825 - son of **Aroas-Silverheels (2)**/1732 & **Mekoche Woman**/1735, an adopted Seneca, great-nephew of **Cornstalk**/1710, translator-guide for **George Morgan**-white after death of his father in 1770, scout-spy **with U.S. Army**-Blue Jacket War/1780-94, Treaty 1809, husband 1780 IN of **Miami Woman**/1765, children unknown

BY SON DAVID FRANCIS/1740 & MARY RISING SUN/1744

GRANDSON

Francis, John (2) – 29/64th Chalakatha-Kishpoko-Mekoche-ShawanoChalaka-Powhatan-Creek-Metis born 1760 AL-died after 1790 - son of **David Francis**/1740 & **Mary Rising Sun**/1744, delegate to D.C. for the Creeks 1790, Treaty 1790, brother of Creek prophets Josiah Francis/1765
& Joseph Francis/1770, great-nephew of **Cornstalk**/1710, 1st cousin of **Tecumseh**/1768 & 2nd cousin of **Osceola**/1802, wife & children unknown

GRANDSON

Francis, Josiah aka **Hillis Hadja** – 29/64th Chalakatha-KishpokoMekoche-Shawano-Chalaka-Powhatan-Creek-Metis born 1765 AL**hung** 1818 GA - son of **Mary Rising Sun**/1745 & **David**

Francis/1740, a Creek Prophet with brother **Joseph Francis**/1770, a Red Stick, **with Natives**-Creek War/1813-Burnt Corn-Ft. Mims, visited ENG 1816, brother in law of **Sam Moniac**/1778, 1st cousin of **Tecumseh**/1768 & 2nd cousin/uncle of **Osceola**/1802, great-nephew of **Cornstalk**/1710, **seized under flag of truce & hung by whites 1818**, husband 1799 of **Hannah Moniac**/1780, father of Millie Francis/1800 & Earle Francis-Jim Earley/1816 & at least another daughter-all 7/32nd Chalakatha-Kishpoko-Mekoche-Shawano-Chalaka-Powhatan-Black-Creek-Metis

GRANDSON

Francis, Joseph – 29/64th Chalakatha-Kishpoko-Mekoche-ShawanoChalaka-Powhatan-Creek-Metis born 1770 AL-**killed in battle 1813 Ft. Sinquefield AL** - son of **David Francis**/1740 & **Mary Rising Sun**/1744, a Creek Prophet with brother **Josiah Francis**/1765, great-nephew of **Cornstalk**/1710, 1st cousin of **Tecumseh**/1768 & 2nd cousin of **Osceola**/1802, a Red Stick, **with Natives**-Creek War/1813, **killed in attack on Ft. Sinquefield**, wife & children unknown

GRANDDAUGHTER

Francis, Susan – 29/64th Chalakatha-Kishpoko-Mekoche-ShawanoChalaka-Powhatan-Creek-Metis born 1775 AL-died after 1815 - daughter of **David Francis**/1740 & **Mary Rising Sun**/1744, 1st cousin of **Tecumseh**/1768, great-niece of **Cornstalk**/1710, wife 1800 (IN?) of **Thomas Spicer**/1783-1/2 Seneca-Metis, mother of Mary Ann Spicer/1801 & Elizabeth Walah Spicer/1805-both 7/32nd ChalakathaKishpoko-Mekoche-Shawano-Chalaka-Powhatan-Creek-Seneca-Metis

BY SON JOHN FRANCIS/1745 & DAUGHTER OF SILVERHEELS-AROAS/1750

GRANDSON

Francis, John **Tapatacatha** aka John Francis (3) – 11/16th ChalakathaMekoche-Shawano-Chalaka-Powhatan-Metis born 1780 OH-died 1848

KS - son of **John Francis (1)**/1745 & **Daughter of Silverheels (2)Aroas**/1750, **with U.S. Army**-War 1812-Thames/1813, **last traditional Chief of Shawnee** (which Shawnee?), double-great-grandson of **Okowellos**, great-nephew of **Cornstalk**/1710, 1st cousin of **Josiah Francis**/1765 & cousin of **Tecumseh**/1768, husband about 1800 (OH?) of **Wyandot Woman**/1782, father of Mary Ann Francis/1801, Nancy Francis/1825 & others-all 11/32nd Chalakatha-Mekoche-Shawano-Chalaka-Powhatan-Wyandot-Metis

Cawachile Cornstalk/1716

Cornstalk, Cawechile aka Cawachile Okowellos-Cawachile Hokolesqua-Wife of Cold Water – 27/32nd Chalakatha-MekocheShawano-Chalaka-Powhatan-Metis born 1716 PA-died after 1807 OH - daughter of **Okowellos**/1674 & **Katee Mekoche**/1680, a Chalakatha, moved to Lower Shawnee Town OH 1744 with **Peter Chartier** group, in later years the **Chief of the Women's Council**, speaker for the women & children, about 6' tall, Council Ft. Pitt 1776 with **Cornstalk, Nimwha, Ellinipsico, Blue Jacket, Capt. Johnny & Caesar** with George Morgan, Council Ft. Finney 1786 with **Moluntha, Capt. Johnny, Red Pole, Black Snake, Nianimissico (?), Wapachcawela (?), Nihipeewa & Nihinessiko**, wife 1st about 1731 PA of **Cold Water-Wepenipe**/1710-Chalakatha, 2nd 1753 OH 1st cousin of **Elk-Wabete**/1715-Mekoche, mother **with Cold Water** of Son/1732, Young Cold Water/1740, Lacumtequa Cold Water/1744 & other children-all 59/64th MekocheChalakatha-Shawano-Chalaka-Powhatan-Metis, any children **with ElkWabete** unknown

HUSBANDS OF CAWACHILE

1ST HUSBAND 1735 PA

Cold Water (1) aka **Wepenipe** – Chalakatha born about 1710 PA-died of smallpox 1752 OH – **parents unknown**, brother in law of

Cornstalk/1710, raiding PA/1740, moved to Lower Shawnee Town OH 1744 with **Peter Chartier**, called a trusted ally of the French in the Ohio valley at his death, husband about 1735 PA of **Cawechile Cornstalk**/1716, father of Son of Cold Water/1732, Young Cold Water/1740, Lacumtequa Cold Water/1744 & other children/1742-52 all 59/64th Mekoche-Chalakatha-Shawano-Chalaka-Powhatan-Metis

2ND HUSBAND 1753 OH

Elk aka Wabete (1) – Mekoche born about 1715 OH-**killed** 1786 OH - **parents unknown** but was a nephew of **Katee Mekoche**/1680-sister of his father & wife of **Okowellos**/1674), brother of **Moluntha/1710**, raiding PA/1740, Cornstalk War/1755-77, **killed in Col. Benjamin Logan's attack on Moluntha's village**, husband 1st 1735 OH of **Mekoche Woman**/1720, 2nd 1753 OH of **Cawechile Cornstalk** (Cold Water)/1716, father **with Mekoche** of Little Elk/1740, any children **with Cawechile** unknown

CHILDREN OF CAWECHILE/1716
WITH COLD WATER/1710

SON

Cold Water, Son of - 59/64th Mekoche-Chalakatha-Shawano-ChalakaPowhatan-Metis born about 1732 PA-died of smallpox 1752 OH - son of **Cold Water-Wepenipe**/1710 & **Cawechile**/1716, grandson of **Okowellos**/1674 & **Katee**/1680, a trusted ally of the French in the Ohio valley, died about the same time as his father, any wife & children unknown

SON

Cold Water, Young aka Cold Water (2)-Young Wepenipe – 59/64th Mekoche-Chalakatha-Shawano-Chalaka-Powhatan-Metis born 1740 OH-died after 1778 – son of **Cold Water-Wepenipe**/1710 & **Cawechile**/1716, grandson of **Okowellos**/1674 & **Katee**/1680, Cornstalk War/1758-77, Point Pleasant/1778, husband 1760 OH of **Chalakatha Woman**/1745, father of Cold Water (3)/1760 & John Cold Water/1770-both 61/64th Mekoche-Chalakatha-Shawano-Chalaka-Powhatan-Metis

DAUGHTER

Cold Water, Lacumtequa – 59/64th Mekoche-Chalakatha-ShawanoChalaka-Powhatan-Metis born about 1744 OH-died after 1786 – daughter of **Cold Water-Wepenipe**/1710 & **Cawachile**/1716, granddaughter of **Okowellos**/1674 & **Katee**/1680, living in Moluntha village OH 1786,wife about 1760 OH of her uncle/2nd cousin (1st cousin of her mother-son of her grandmother's brother) **Moluntha/**1710, children unknown

GRANDCHILDREN OF CAWACHILE/1716

BY SON YOUNG COLD WATER/1740

GRANDSON

Cold Water (3) – 61/64th Mekoche-Chalakatha-Shawano-ChalakaPowhatan-Metis born 1760 OH-died after 1832 KS - son of **Young Cold Water**/1740 & **Chalakatha Woman**/1745, a Chalakatha warrior, Blue Jacket War/1778-94, Capt. Shoe Boots Co-**with U.S. Army-**Creek War/1813, Treaty 1831, great-nephew of **Cornstalk**/1710, moved to KS about 1832, wife & children unknown

GRANDSON

Cold Water, John aka **John Coldwater** – 61/64th Mekoche-ChalakathaShawano-Chalaka-Powhatan-Metis born 1770 OH-died after 1832 KS – son of **Young Cold Water**/1740 & **Chalakatha Woman**/1745, a Chalakatha warrior, with John Lewis scouts-**with U.S. Army**-War 1812, with Joseph Parks Co-**with U.S. Army-**Seminole War 1832, greatnephew of **Cornstalk**/1710, husband 1795 OH of 2nd cousin **Daughter of Silver Heels (1)**/1780, father of Pamotee Coldwater/1800, Stephen Coldwater/1807-both 15/16th Mekoche-Chalakatha-Shawano-Chalaka-Powhatan-Metis

Cornstalk, Elizabeth aka Elizabeth Okowellos-Elizabeth Hokolesqua-

Sister of Cornstalk-Grenadier Squaw - 11/32nd Chalakatha-ShawanoChalaka-Powhatan-Creek-Metis born 1726 Shawnee village AL-died after 1817 OH - daughter of **Okowellos**/1674 & **Sister of Sehoy**/1709, in PA by 1730 with father, moved to OH with **Peter Chartier** 1744, appears to have not went with band to AL 1755-58, a Christian Chalakatha, about 6' tall i.e. a Grenadier Squaw & attractive, often a translator/messenger for the whites, wife 1st about 1744 PA of **Chalakatha Man**/1724, 2nd about 1754 OH of **John Lodging Pole Butler**/1730-white-(adopted Seneca), 3rd 1760 OH of **Unknown Man**/1720, children/1744-54 **with Chalakatha** unknown, mother **with Butler** of Fanny Butler/1755 & Tommy Butler/1760-both 11/64th Chalakatha-Shawano-Chalaka-Powhatan-Creek-Metis, children 1760-71 **with Unknown Man** unknown, often confused in white histories with her sisters & nieces

HUSBANDS OF ELIZABETH CORNSTALK/1726

HUSBAND 1744 PA
CHALAKATHA MAN/1724
CHILDREN/1744-53 UNKNOWN

HUSBAND 1754 OH

Butler, John (1) aka Sugantah-Lodging Pole-Capt. Butler - white(adopted-Seneca) born about 1730-died 1796 – **parents unknown**, adopted as youth & lived between Natives & whites, translator, messenger, Col. **with Colonial Army**, Council Ft. Stanwix Oct. 1768, husband by 1755 PA of **Elizabeth Cornstalk**/1726-sister of Cornstalk, father **with Elizabeth** of Fanny Butler/1755 & Tommy Butler/1760both 11/64th Chalakatha-Shawano-Chalaka-Powhatan-Creek-Metis

HUSBAND 1760 OH
UNKNOWN MAN/1720
CHILDREN/1761-70 UNKNOWN

CHILDREN OF ELIZABETH CORNSTALK/1726 WITH CHALAKATHA/1724

UNKNOWN

WITH JOHN LODGING POLE BUTLER/1730

DAUGHTER

Butler, Fanny – 11/64th Chalakatha-Shawano-Chalaka-PowhatanCreek-Metis born about 1755-died after 1781 - daughter of **Elizabeth Cornstalk**/1726 & **John Sugantah-Lodging Pole Butler**/1730-white(adopted-Seneca), adopted daughter of her aunt **Nonhelema**/1718, sadly listed as prostitute 1781 (but could have been no more than promiscuous), niece of **Cornstalk**/1710, granddaughter of **Okowellos**/1674, any husband & children unknown

SON

Butler, Tommy – 11/64th Chalakatha-Shawano-Chalaka-Powhatan-Creek-Metis born 1760 OH-died 1833 KS - son of **Elizabeth Cornstalk**/1726 & **John Lodging Pole Butler**/1730-white-(adoptedSeneca), nephew of **Cornstalk**/1710, Blue Jacket War/1777-94, moved to KS 1832, husband about 1780 of **Daughter of Col. Alexander McKee**/1765-1/2 Pekowi-Metis, children unknown

WITH UNKNOWN MAN/1720

UNKNOWN

Catherine-Kitty Cornstalk/1728

Cornstalk, Catherine aka Kitty-Catherine Okowellos-Kitty Okowellos-Kitty Cornstalk-Sister of Cornstalk-Grenadier Squaw – 11/32nd Chalakatha-Shawano-Chalaka-Powhatan-Creek-Metis born 1728 Shawnee village AL-died after 1797 likely OH - daughter of

Okowellos/1674 & **Sister of Sehoy**/1709-Creek, moved to OH with **Peter Chartier** 1744, a Christian Chalakatha, about 6' tall i.e. a Grenadier Squaw & attractive, often a translator/messenger for the whites, wife 1st 1745 OH of **Wrynek-Aquilsa**/1725-Pekowi, 2nd 1764 OH of **William Butler**/1744-white (adopted-Seneca), children/1745-65 **with Wrynek-Aquilsa** unknown, mother **with Butler** of Polly Butler/176511/64th Chalakatha-Shawano-Chalaka-Powhatan-Creek-Metis, often confused in white histories with her sisters & nieces

HUSBANDS OF CATHERINE-KITTY CORNSTALK

HUSBAND 1745 OH

Wrynek aka Aquilsa-Aquilisa-Ahkweeleesa-Hakweelsa-**Crooked Neck**Aquilsika-Akweelseeka-Hakwilsikia - Pekowi born about 1725 PAdied 1784 OH – **parents unknown**, moved to OH 1744 with **Peter Chartier**, may have moved on to KY 1746, then on to TN in 1747 & then AL in 1748, returned to OH by 1755, called "**Wrynek = "Irish term for wounded or scarred**" by the Irish pioneers (**McKee, Elliott** etc.) because of a large scar on his neck & head-received in battle that left his head marked or angled, Cornstalk War/1755-77, a village **Pekowi Chief** in OH by 1765, Blue Jacket War/1777-82, Council Ft. Pitt 1775 **with Corn Stalk, Silver Heels, Nimwha & Blue Jacket**, Council **with George Rogers Clark** 1778, Council with British 1779 with **Col. Alexander McKee**/1725-Irish, **William Caldwell**/1750-Irish, **Matthew Elliott**/1730-Irish, **Simon Surphet**-Irish, **Simon Girty**/1741, **George Girty**/1746 & **James Girty**/1743, **Savanooka Raven Moytoy**/172063/64th Chalakatha-Pekowi-Shawano-Chalaka-Powhatan-(Overhill Cherokee Chief), **Weed**/1750-Iroquois-Mingo & **River Bottom**/1750Seneca-Mingo, **Principal Chief of Pekowi** in OH 1779-84, husband about 1745 OH of **Catherine Cornstalk**/1728, children unknown

HUSBAND 1764 OH

Butler, William (1) - white-(adopted-Seneca) born 1744 ENG-died 1789 – **parents unknown**, brother of **Richard Butler**/1742, a trader among the Shawnee in OH with his brother William in 1773, Lt. Col.-4th PA Reg-**with U.S. Army**-Revolution, husband 1st 1764 OH of **Catherine**

Cornstalk/1728, 2nd about 1775 of **Jane Carmichael**/1751-white, father **with Catherine** of Polly Butler/1765-11/64th Chalakatha-ShawanoChalaiwa-Powhatan-Creek-Metis

CHILDREN OF CATHERINE-KITTY CORNSTALK/1728

WITH WRYNEK-AQUILSA/1725

UNKNOWN

WITH WILLIAM BUTLER/1744

DAUGHTER

Butler, Polly – 11/64th Chalakatha-Shawano-Chalaka-Powhatan-CreekMetis born about 1765 OH-died about 1854 KS – daughter of **Catherine Cornstalk**/1728 & **William Butler**/1744-white-(adopted-Seneca), about 6' tall, known for her blue eyes & beauty, half-niece of **Cornstalk**/1710, granddaughter of **Okowellos**/1674, accused 1805 with her Daughter/1783 of being witches by followers of **Lalawethika-the Prophet**, saved by a Quaker Missionary, wife 1st 1779 OH of 1st cousin (son of mother's sister) **Chieska Moluntha**/1755, 2nd 1782 OH of **Joshua Renicks**/1746-adopted-white, mother **with Chieska** of Spy Buck Moluntha/1780-35/64th Chalakatha-Mekoche-Shawano-ChalakaPowhatan-Creek-Metis, **with Renicks** of Peggy Renicks/1783-5/64th Chalakatha-Shawano-Chalaka-Powhatan-Creek-Metis

GRANDCHILDREN OF CATHERINE-KITTY CORNSTALK/1728

BY POLLY BUTLER/1765 & CHIESKA MOLUNTHA/1755

GRANDSON

Moluntha, Spy Buck aka Saukothkaw-Tahkaska-Spybuck Chieska – 35/64th Chalakatha-Mekoche-Shawano-Chalaka-Powhatan-Creek-Metis born about 1780 OH-died after 1831 – son of **Polly Butler**/1765 & **Chieska Moluntha**/1755, a Chalakatha warrior, grandson of **Moluntha**/1710, great-nephew of **Cornstalk**/1710, delegate to D.C. 1802 with **Wayweleapee, John Perry, Quaskee Black Hoof, Joseph Parks** & **Francois Duchoquet**, scout-with U.S. Army-War 1812Thames/1813, Treaty 1817, 1831, a warrior at Hog Creek & Wapaghonettat 1832, husband 1795 OH of **Daughter of Col. Barbee**/1780-white, father of George Spy Buck/1796, Daughter of Spy Buck/1798, John Spy Buck/1802 & Young Spy Buck/1806-all 17/64th Chalakatha-Mekoche-Shawano-Chalaka-Powhatan-Creek-Metis

BY POLLY BUTLER/1765
& JOSHUA RENICKS/1746
GRANDDAUGHTER

Renicks, Peggy – 5/64th Chalakatha-Shawano-Chalaka-PowhatanCreek-Metis born about 1783 OH-died after 1811 – daughter of **Joshua Renicks**/1746-adopted white & **Polly Butler**/1765, namesake of her grandmother **Peggy Renicks**/1728, accused about 1805 of being a witch with mother Polly Butler/1765 by followers of **Lalawethika**-the Shawnee Prophet, saved by Quaker Missionary, husband & children unknown

Daughters of Cornstalk/1710

Catherine-Katee Cornstalk/1734

Cornstalk, Catherine aka Katee Cornstalk-Catherine Hokolesqua-Katee Okowellos-Katee Hokolesqua-Grenadier Squaw – 29/32nd ChalakathaMekoche-Shawano-Chalaka-Powhatan-Metis born 1734 PA-died of smallpox 1758 OH – oldest daughter of **Cornstalk**/1710 & **Helizikinopo**/1715, a Christian Chalakatha, over 6' tall i.e. a **Grenadier**

Squaw, may have served as a translator-messenger for the whites, wife 1750 OH of adopted brother **Petella**/1730-adopted white, died with children in smallpox epidemic of 1758, children/1750-58 unknown

CHILDREN OF CATHERINE/1734 & PETELLA/1730

UNKNOWN

Greenbrier Cornstalk/1740

Cornstalk, Greenbrier – 29/32nd Chalakatha-Mekoche-ShawanoChalaka-Powhatan-Metis born 1740 PA-died after 1780 WV-OH? - 3rd daughter of **Cornstalk**/1710 & **Helizikinopo**/1715, a **Christian Chalakatha**, about 6' tall i.e. a Grenadier Squaw & attractive, likely a translator-messenger for the whites, associated in later years with a **McComas** family-(in laws through marriage of a daughter?), wife by
1757 WV of **Reuben Kennison**/1737, widow in 1776, mother **with Kennison** of about 8 children between 1757-76, surname Kennison including a Reuben Kennison Jr /BET 57-76 & a younger Greenbrier Kennison/BET 57-76--all 29/64th Chalakatha-Mekoche-ShawanoChalaka-Powhatan-Metis, often confused in white history with her sisters & aunts

CHILDREN OF GREENBRIER CORNSTALK/1740 & REUBEN KENNISON/1737

SON

Kennison, Reuben Jr – 29/64th Chalakatha-Mekoche-Shawano-ChalakaPowhatan-Metis born between 1757-1776-died after 1800 – son of **Greenbrier Cornstalk**/1740 & **Reuben Kennison**/1737, wife & children unknown

DAUGHTER

Shawnee Heritage II

Kennison, Greenbrier – 29/64th Chalakatha-Mekoche-ShawanoChalaka-Powhatan-Metis born between 1757-76-died after 1800 – daughter of **Greenbrier Cornstalk**/1740 & **Reuben Kennison**/1737, married a **McComas**, children unknown

Aracoma Cornstalk/1742

Cornstalk, Aracoma aka **Corn Flower**-Aracoma Hokolesqua-Aracoma Baker – 29/32nd Chalakatha-Mekoche-Shawano-Chalaka-PowhatanMetis born 1742 OH-**killed** in battle 1780 **Logan Co. WV** - 2nd daughter of **Cornstalk**/1710 & **Helizikinopo**/1715, established village near Logan WV 1760 with family & clan at current site of **Logan WV**, a **Chalakatha village Head Woman** before 1780, about 6' tall, **killed in battle** defending the village, wife 1758 OH of **Boling Baker Kikpelethee Baker**/1730, mother of son Running Deer (Baker)/1764, son Laughing Water (Baker)/1766, daughter Snow Lily-White Flower (Baker)/1768, daughter Raindrop-Falling Water (Baker)/1770, son Running Water (Baker)/1772 & son Blue Feather (Baker)/1774-all 11/16th Chalakatha-Mekoche-Shawano-Chalaka-Powhatan-Metis, 4 other children that may have died of disease (note the "water" names that may have actually been more like "stream", which might reflect some linkage of Aracoma &/or Boling Baker back to the very early families of 1400's & 1500's among the Chalaka & Shawano)

HUSBAND 1758 OH

Baker, Boling **Kikpelethee** - ½ Shawano-Metis born about 1735 on New River (Ashe Co) NC-died about 1810 Lawrence Co OH - son of **Andrew Baker**-white & **Shawano Wife**, captured-adopted 1755 at Point Pleasant after deserting whites at Braddock/1755, Cornstalk War/175877, Blue Jacket War/1777-88, left children to be raised by Cornstalk family after death of Aracoma in attack on their village in Logan Co. WV even though he remained among the tribe/clan, lived among Native & Metis community in Lawrence Co. OH across the Ohio River from the mouth of the Big Sandy River/Huntington WV, visited Aracoma's grave annually until his death, son in law of **Cornstalk**/1710, husband 1758 OH of **Aracoma Cornstalk**/1742, father of son Running Deer (Baker)/1764, son Laughing Water (Baker)/1766, daughter Snow Lily (Baker)/1768, daughter Raindrop-Rain Falling (Baker)/1770, son Running Water (Baker)/1772 & son Blue Feather (Baker)/1774-all 11/16th Chalakatha-Mekoche-Shawano-ChalakaPowhatan-Metis, 4 other children that may have died of disease (note the "water" names that may have actually been more like "stream", which might indicate some linkage of Aracoma &/or Boling Baker back to the very early families of 1400's & 1500's among the Chalaka)

CHILDREN OF ARACOMA CORNSTALK/1742 & BOLING KIKPELETHEE BAKER/1735

SON

Baker, Running Deer – 11/16th Chalakatha-Mekoche-Shawano-ChalakaPowhatan-Metis born 1764 Logan Co. WV-died after 1794 (OH?) – son of **Boling Kikpelethee Baker**/1735 & **Aracoma Cornstalk**/1742, raised by extended Cornstalk family after death of Aracoma in 1780, a Chalakatha warrior, lived until 1794 in Native/Metis community in Lawrence Co. OH, Blue Jacket War/1782-94, wife & children unknown

SON

Baker, Laughing Water aka Laughing Stream – 11/16th ChalakathaMekoche-Shawano-Chalaka-Powhatan-Metis born 1766 Logan Co. WVdied after 1794 (OH?) – son of **Boling Kikpelethee Baker**/1735 & **Aracoma Cornstalk**/1742, raised by Cornstalk family after death of his mother 1780, a Chalakatha warrior, Blue Jacket War/1784-94, lived until 1794 in Native/Metis community in Lawrence Co. OH, wife & children unknown

DAUGHTER

Baker, Snow Lily aka **Snow Flower**-White Flower – 11/16th ChalakathaMekoche-Shawano-Chalaka-Powhatan-Metis born 1768 Logan Co. WVdied after 1810 (OH?) – daughter of **Boling Kikpelethee Baker**/1735 & **Aracoma Cornstalk**/1742, raised by Cornstalk family after death of

Aracoma in 1780, lived until 1810 in Native/Metis community in Lawrence Co. OH, husband & children unknown but thought to have married a white

DAUGHTER

Baker, Raindrop aka Falling Rain – 11/16th Chalakatha-MekocheShawano-Chalaka-Powhatan-Metis born 1770 Logan Co. WV- died after
1810 (OH?) – daughter of **Boling Kikpelethee Baker**/1735 & **Aracoma Cornstalk**/1742, raised by Cornstalk family after death of Aracoma in 1780, lived until 1810 in Native/Metis community in Lawrence Co. OH, husband & children unknown

SON

Baker, Running Water aka Running Stream– 11/16th ChalakathaMekoche-Shawano-Chalaka-Powhatan-Metis born 1772 Logan Co. WVdied after 1794 (OH?) – son of **Boling Kikpelethee Baker**/1735 & **Aracoma Cornstalk**/1742, a Chalakatha warrior, Blue Jacket War/179094, lived until 1794 in Native/Metis community in Lawrence Co. OH, wife & children unknown

SON

Baker, Blue Feather – 11/16th Chalakatha-Mekoche-Shawano-ChalakaPowhatan-Metis born 1774 Logan Co. WV-died after 1794 (OH?) – son of **Boling Kikpelethee Baker**/1735 & **Aracoma Cornstalk**/1742, namesake of **Blue Feather (1)**-Mekoche-a nephew of Helizikinopo & cousin of Aracoma that was killed at Point Pleasant/1774, raised by Cornstalk family after death of Aracoma in 1780, a Chalakatha warrior, lived until 1794 in Native/Metis community in Lawrence Co. OH, Blue Jacket War/1792-94, wife & children unknown

Elizabeth Cornstalk/1744

Cornstalk, Elizabeth (2) –29/32nd Chalakatha-Mekoche-ShawanoChalaka-Powhatan-Metis born 1744 OH-died after 1777 likely OH - 5th daughter of **Cornstalk**/1710 & **Helizikinopo**/1715, about 6' tall i.e. a Grenadier Squaw, a Christian Chalakatha, may have served as a translator-messenger for the whites, wife 1st 1760 OH of **John**

Swift/1712, 2nd by 1770 OH of **Petella Cornstalk**/1730-adopted white, mother **with Swift** of four children/1760-62-64-66 names & gender unknown but may have been called Cornstalk's, any children/1770-77 **with Petella** unknown, often confused in white histories with her sisters or aunts

CHILDREN OF ELIZABETH CORNSTALK/1744 & JOHN SWIFT/1712

UNKNOWN

(but four are thought to have been born 1760-62-64-66)

CHILDREN OF ELIZABETH CORNSTALK/1744 & PETELLA/1730

UNKNOWN

Blue Sky-Mary Cornstalk/1750

Cornstalk, **Blue Sky** aka Mary Cornstalk (1) - 29/32nd Chalakatha-Mekoche-Shawano-Chalaka-Powhatan-Metis born 1750 OH-died 1775 Ft. Pitt area PA/OH/WV - 4th daughter of **Cornstalk**/1710 & **Helizikinopo**/1715, about 6' tall i.e. a Grenadier Squaw & attractive, a **Christian Chalakatha**, wife 1766 PA of **Parker V. Adkins**/1720, met while Adkins was serving with the **VA Militia-Colonial Army** at Ft. Pitt following the Pontiac War, abandoned by Adkins when he returned to VA, Adkins returned for children after her death, mother **with Adkins** of Littleberry Adkins/1766 & Charity Adkins/1768-both45/64th Chalakatha-Mekoche-Shawano-Chalaka-Hopia-Powhatan-Metis, often confused in white history with her sisters & aunts

HUSBAND 1766 - PA

Adkins, Parker V. – ½ Shawano-Metis born 1720 Henrico Co VA-died 1792 Giles Co VA – son of **William V. Adkins**/1690 & **Elizabeth**

Parker/1695, husband 1st (?) 1754 of **Mary Polly Jones**/1729-Hopia, 2nd 1766 Ft. Pitt PA of **Mary Blue Sky Cornstalk**/1750, father **with Jones** of Millington Adkins/1755, Isom Adkins/1757, Hezekiah Adkins/1759, Champ Adkins/1763, Elijah Adkins/1764, Sherrod Adkins/1765-all 3/4th Shawano-Hopia-Metis, **with Mary-Blue Sky** of Littleberry Adkins/1766 & Charity Adkins/1768-both 45/64th ChalakathaMekoche-Shawano-Chalaka-Hopia-Powhatan-Metis

CHILDREN OF BLUE SKY MARY CORNSTALK/1750 & PARKER V. ADKINS/1720

SON

Adkins, Littleberry – 45/64th Chalakatha-Mekoche-Shawano-ChalakaHopia-Powhatan-Metis born 1766 Ft. Pitt area PA-died 1848 Mercer Co. WV - son of **Blue Sky Mary Cornstalk**/1750 & **Parker V. Adkins**/1720, grandson of **Cornstalk**/1710, husband 1790 Franklin Co VA of 1st cousin **Nancy Adkins**/1767-(niece of **Parker V. Adkins**-daughter of his sister **Mary Adkins**/1735), father of Jesse Adkins/1791, Isom Adkins/1795, Hezekiah Adkins/1799, Littleberry Adkins Jr/1801, Christina Adkins/1805, Dicey Adkins/1807, Priscilla Adkins/1809 & Vicey Adkins/1811-all 15/32nd Chalakatha-Mekoche-Shawano-Chalaka-Hopia-Powhatan-Metis

DAUGHTER

Adkins, Charity Adkins – 45/64th Chalakatha-Mekoche-ShawanoChalaka-Hopia-Powhatan-Metis born 1768 PA-died 1820 Cabell Co WV - daughter of **Blue Sky-Mary Cornstalk**/1750 & **Parker V. Adkins**/1720, granddaughter of **Cornstalk**/1710, (2nd?) wife 1788 (VAWV?) of her 1st cousin **Randolph Adkins**/1759-(nephew of **Parker V. Adkins**-son of his brother **William Adkins**/1721), mother of Parker Adkins/1789, Randolph Sprang Adkins/1791, Nancy Adkins/1794, William Adkins/1796, Jane Adkins/1803, Richard Adkins/1805, Rhoda Adkins/1810, Sylvester Adkins/1812, Price Adkins/1814,-John T. Adkins/1816-all 15/32nd Chalakatha-Mekoche-Shawano-ChalakaHopia-Powhatan-Metis

GRANDCHILDREN OF BLUE SKY MARY/1750 BY LITTLEBERRY ADKINS/1766 & NANCY ADKINS/1767

GRANDSON

Adkins, Jesse – 15/32nd Chalakatha-Mekoche-Shawano-Chalaka-Hopia-Powhatan-Metis born 1791 Franklin Co VA-died after 1860 - son of **Littleberry Adkins**/1766 & **Nancy Adkins**/1767, great-grandson of **Cornstalk**/1710, husband 1813 Cabell Co WV of cousin **Nancy Ann Adkins**/1794, children unknown

GRANDSON

Adkins, Isom – 15/32nd Chalakatha-Mekoche-Shawano-Chalaka-Hopia-Powhatan-Metis born 1795 Giles Co VA-died after 1812 - son of **Littleberry Adkins**/1766 & **Nancy Adkins**/1767, great-grandson of **Cornstalk**/1710, wife & children unknown

GRANDSON

Adkins, Hezekiah –15/32nd Chalakatha-Mekoche-Shawano-ChalakaHopia-Powhatan-Metis born 1800 Wayne WV-died 1867 Wayne Co WV - son of **Littleberry Adkins**/1766 & **Nancy Adkins**/1767, greatgrandson of **Cornstalk**/1710, husband 1st 1819 Cabell Co WV of **Nancy Spears**/1800, 2nd 1834 of **Sarah Carter**/1814, 3rd 1847 of **Luvina Unknown**/1830, children unknown

GRANDSON

Adkins, Littleberry Jr – 15/32nd Chalakatha-Mekoche-ShawanoChalaka-Hopia-Powhatan-Metis born 1801 Wayne Co WV-died 1853 Cabell Co WV - son of **Littleberry Adkins**/1766 & **Nancy Adkins**/1767, great-grandson of **Cornstalk**/1710, husband 1822 Lawrence Co KY of likely cousin **Delphia Adkins**/1806, children unknown

GRANDDAUGHTER

Adkins, Christina –15/32nd Chalakatha-Mekoche-Shawano-ChalakaHopia-Powhatan-Metis born 1805 Wayne Co WV-died 1884 - daughter of **Littleberry Adkins**/1766 & **Nancy Adkins**/1767, great-granddaughter of **Cornstalk**/1710, wife 1820 Cabell Co WV of **David Fry**/1805-(possible Shawnee-Metis), children unknown

GRANDDAUGHTER

Adkins, Dicey –15/32nd Chalakatha-Mekoche-Shawano-Chalaka-HopiaPowhatan-Metis born 1807 Wayne Co. WV-died after 1860 - daughter of **Littleberry Adkins**/1766 & **Nancy Adkins**/1767, great-granddaughter of **Cornstalk**/1710, wife 1822 of cousin **Jacob Adkins**-born 1802 VAdied 1857, children unknown

GRANDDAUGHTER

Adkins, Priscilla –15/32nd Chalakatha-Mekoche-Shawano-ChalakaHopia-Powhatan-Metis born 1810 Cabell Co WV-died 1891 Wayne Co WV - daughter of **Littleberry Adkins**/1766 & **Nancy Adkins**/1767, great-granddaughter of **Cornstalk**/1710, wife 1826 of **James Fry**/1806(possibly Shawnee-Metis), children unknown

GRANDDAUGHTER

Adkins, Vicey – 15/32nd Chalakatha-Mekoche-Shawano-ChalakaHopia-Powhatan-Metis born 1811 Cabell Co WV-died 1895 Wayne Co WV - daughter of **Littleberry Adkins**/1766 & **Nancy Adkins**/1767 great-granddaughter of **Cornstalk**/1710, wife of **Moses Franklin Napier**-(possible Shawnee-Metis), children unknown

BY CHARITY ADKINS/1768
WITH RANDOLPH ADKINS/1759

GRANDSON

Adkins, Parker –15/32nd Chalakatha-Mekoche-Shawano-ChalakaHopia-Powhatan-Metis born 1789 Giles Co VA-died after 1819 - son of **Charity Adkins**/1768 & **Randolph Adkins**/1759, great-grandson of **Cornstalk**/1710, wife & children unknown

GRANDSON

Adkins, Randolph Sprang –15/32nd Chalakatha-Mekoche-ShawanoChalaka-Hopia-Powhatan-Metis born 1790 Giles Co VA-died after 1820 - son of **Charity Adkins**/1768 & **Randolph Adkins**/1759, greatgrandson of **Cornstalk**/1710, wife & children unknown

GRANDDAUGHTER

Adkins, Nancy (2) –15/32nd Chalakatha-Mekoche-Shawano-ChalakaHopia-Powhatan-Metis born 1794 Giles Co VA-died after 1815 - daughter of **Charity Adkins**/1768 & **Randolph Adkins**/1759, greatgranddaughter of **Cornstalk**/1710, wife 1815 of **Isaac McComas**/1787- (possible Native connection to the McComas family associated with her aunt **Greenbrier Cornstalk**?), mother of Surilda McComas/181513/64th Chalakatha-Mekoche-Shawano-Chalaka-Hopia-Powhatan-Metis

GRANDSON

Adkins, William –15/32nd Chalakatha-Mekoche-Shawano-Chalaka-Hopia-Powhatan-Metis born 1796 Giles Co VA-died after 1815 - son of **Charity Adkins**/1768 & **Randolph Adkins**/1759, great-grandson of **Cornstalk**/1710, wife & children unknown

GRANDDAUGHTER

Adkins, Jane –15/32nd Chalakatha-Mekoche-Shawano-Chalaka-Hopia-Powhatan-Metis born 1803 Giles Co VA-died after 1824 - daughter of **Charity Adkins**/1768 & **Randolph Adkins**/1759, great-granddaughter of **Cornstalk**/1710, husband & children unknown

GRANDSON

Adkins, Richard (2) –15/32nd Chalakatha-Mekoche-Shawano-ChalakaHopia-Powhatan-Metis born 1805 Giles Co VA-died after 1825 - son of
Charity Adkins/1768 & **Randolph Adkins**/1759, great-grandson of **Cornstalk**/1710, wife & children unknown

GRANDDAUGHTER

Adkins, Rhoda –15/32nd Chalakatha-Mekoche-Shawano-ChalakaHopia-Powhatan-Metis born 1810 WV-died after 1834 - daughter of **Charity Adkins**/1768 & **Randolph Adkins**/1759, great-granddaughter of **Cornstalk**/1710, wife 1834 of **Merritt Johnson**/1810-white, children unknown

GRANDSON

Adkins, Sylvester - 15/32nd Chalakatha-Mekoche-Shawano-ChalakaHopia-Powhatan-Metis born 1812 Cabell Co WV-died after 1839 - son of
Charity Adkins/1768 & **Randolph Adkins**/1759, great-grandson of **Cornstalk**/1710, wife & children unknown

GRANDSON

Adkins, Price – 15/32nd Chalakatha-Mekoche-Shawano-ChalakaHopia-Powhatan-Metis born 1814 Cabell Co. WV-died after 1835 - son of **Charity Adkins**/1769 & **Randolph Adkins**/1759, great-grandson of **Cornstalk**/1710, wife & children unknown

GRANDSON

Adkins, John T. – 15/32nd Chalakatha-Mekoche-Shawano-ChalakaHopia-Powhatan-Metis born 1816 Cabell Co. WV-died after 1836 - son of **Charity Adkins**/1768 & **Randolph Adkins**/1759, great-grandson of **Cornstalk**/1710, wife & children unknown

Esther Cornstalk/1752

Cornstalk, Esther – 29/32nd Chalakatha-Mekoche-Shawano-ChalakaPowhatan-Metis born 1752 OH-died before 1836 PA - 6th daughter of
Cornstalk/1710 & **Helizikinopo**/1715, about 6' tall & attractive, a **Christian Chalakatha**, Shawnee name unknown, may have served as a translator-messenger for the whites, about 6' tall i.e. a Grenadier Squaw, wife 1768 PA of **Thomas Sowards**/1746-white, mother of

children/1769-71, Griffin Sowards/1773, Thomas Sowards Jr/1775, Robert Sowards/1780, Esther Sowards/1781, Jacob Sowards/1783, John B. Sowards/1784, twins Rosannah & Diannah Sowards/1786, Rebecca Sowards/1790, George Sowards/1792-all 29/64th Chalakatha-MekocheShawano-Chalaka-Powhatan-Metis, often confused in white history with her sisters & aunts

CHILDREN OF ESTHER CORNSTALK/1752 & THOMAS SOWARDS/1746

SON

Sowards, Griffin aka Griffin Tipsword- Griffin Sword- Griffin Tipscord – 29/64th Chalakatha-Mekoche-Shawano-Chalaka-Powhatan-Metis born 1773 VA-died 1845 IL - son of **Esther Cornstalk**/1752 & **Thomas Sowards**/1746, grandson of **Cornstalk**/1710, husband 1792 (OH-IN) of **Ruth Abbott**/1774, father of Andrew Jackson Sowards-Tipsword/1797, Douglas Sowards-Tipsword/1799, Miliston Sowards-Tipsword/1801, John Adams Sowards-Tipsword/1803, Isaac Sowards-Tipsword/1805, Desha Sowards-Tipsword/1807, Rebecca Sowards-Tipsword/1809, Thomas Sowards-Tipsword/1814, Carlin Sowards-Tipsword/1815-all 31/64th Chalakatha-Mekoche-Shawano-Chalaka-Powhatan-Metis

SON

Sowards, Thomas Jr – 29/64th Chalakatha-Mekoche-Shawano-Chalaka-Powhatan-Metis born 1775-died 1812 KY - son of **Esther Cornstalk**/1752 & **Thomas Sowards**/1746, grandson of **Cornstalk**/1710, husband 1793 of **Letitia Mills**/1772, father of Mahala Sowards/1794, Susanna Sowards/1800, Thomas G. Sowards/1804, Charles Sowards/1806-all 7/32nd Chalakatha-Mekoche-Shawano-Chalaka-Powhatan-Metis

SON

Sowards, Robert – 29/64th Chalakatha-Mekoche-Shawano-Chalaka-Powhatan-Metis born 1780-died after 1812 IN - son of **Esther Cornstalk**/1752 & **Thomas Sowards**/1746, grandson of **Cornstalk**/1710, wife & children unknown

DAUGHTER

Sowards, Esther – 29/64th Chalakatha-Mekoche-Shawano-Chalaka-Powhatan-Metis born 1781-died 1847 - daughter of **Esther Cornstalk**/1752 & **Thomas Sowards**/1746, granddaughter of **Cornstalk**/1710, wife 1st 1801 of **Robert Carlisle**/1776, 2nd 1830 of **Herman Hatfield**/1790, mother **with Carlisle** of Frances Carlisle/1805-7/32nd Chalakatha-Mekoche-Shawano-Chalaka-Powhatan-Metis

SON

Sowards, Jacob – 29/64th Chalakatha-Mekoche-Shawano-ChalakaPowhatan-Metis born 1783-died after 1812 - son of **Esther Cornstalk**/1752 & **Thomas Sowards**/1746, grandson of **Cornstalk**/1710, wife & children unknown

SON

Sowards, John B. – 29/64th Chalakatha-Mekoche-Shawano-ChalakaPowhatan-Metis born 1784-died after 1812 - son of **Esther Cornstalk**/1752 & **Thomas Sowards**/1746, grandson of **Cornstalk**/1710, wife & children unknown

TWIN DAUGHTER 1

Sowards, Rosannah – 29/64th Chalakatha-Mekoche-Shawano-ChalakaPowhatan-Metis born 1786-died 1831 KY - daughter of **Esther Cornstalk**/1752 & **Thomas Sowards**/1746, twin of Diana, granddaughter of **Cornstalk**/1710, wife 1803 of **Thomas Doty**/1785, children unknown

TWIN DAUGHTER 2

Sowards, Diana – 29/64th Chalakatha-Mekoche-Shawano-Chalaka-Powhatan-Metis born 1786-died after 1802 - daughter of **Esther Cornstalk**/1752 & **Thomas Sowards**/1746, twin of Rosannah, granddaughter of **Cornstalk**/1710, husband & children unknown

DAUGHTER

Sowards, Rebecca – 29/64th Chalakatha-Mekoche-Shawano-Chalaka-

Powhatan-Metis born 1790-died about 1830 - daughter of **Esther Cornstalk**/1752 & **Thomas Sowards**/1746, granddaughter of **Cornstalk**/1710, wife 1st 1805 of **Garrett Harris**/1790, 2nd before 1830 of **Isaac Carson**/1790, mother **with Harris** of Garrett Harris Jr/1806 & Lucinda Harris/1809-both 7/32nd Chalakatha-Mekoche-Shawano-Chalaka-Powhatan-Metis

SON

Sowards, George Washington – 29/64th Chalakatha-Mekoche-ShawanoChalaka-Powhatan-Metis born 1792-died after 1812 - son of **Esther Cornstalk**/1752 & **Thomas Sowards**/1746, grandson of **Cornstalk**/1710, wife & children unknown

GRANDCHILDREN OF ESTHER CORNSTALK/1752 BY GRIFFIN SOWARDS-TIPSWORD/1773 WITH RUTH ABBOTT/1774

GRANDSON

Sowards, Andrew Jackson aka Andrew Jackson Tipsword – 31/64th Chalakatha-Mekoche-Shawano-Chalaka-Powhatan-Metis born 1799 OH-died after 1819 - son of **Griffin Sowards-Tipsword**/1773 & **Ruth Abbott**/1774, raised by Kickapoo neighbors of his father, greatgrandson of **Cornstalk**/1710, went hunting 1819 with some Kickapoo & never returned, husband 1818 of **Kickapoo Woman**/1803, children unknown

GRANDSON

Sowards, Douglas aka Douglas Tipsword – 31/64th ChalakathaMekoche-Shawano-Chalaka-Powhatan-Metis born 1800-**killed 1815** - son of **Griffin Sowards-Tipsword**/1773 & **Ruth Abbott**/1774, greatgrandson of **Cornstalk**/1710, **killed in battle** with the Kickapoo, Pottawamee & Winnebego, died single

GRANDDAUGHTER

Sowards, Miliston aka Miliston Tipsword – 31/64th ChalakathaMekoche-Shawano-Chalaka-Powhatan-Metis born 1801 OH-died 1840 - daughter of **Griffin Sowards**-Tipsword/1773 & **Ruth Abbott**/1774, great-granddaughter of **Cornstalk**/1710, wife 1817 of **John Myers**/1780, children unknown

GRANDSON

Sowards, John Adams aka John Adams Tipsword – 31/64th Chalakatha-Mekoche-Shawano-Chalaka-Powhatan-Metis born 1803 OH-died 1870 IL - son of **Griffin Sowards-Tipsword**/1773 & **Ruth Abbott**/1774, great-grandson of **Cornstalk**/1710, husband 1827 of 1st cousin **Frances Carlisle**/1805, children unknown

GRANDSON

Sowards, Isaac – 31/64th Chalakatha-Mekoche-Shawano-ChalakaPowhatan-Metis born 1805-died after 1826 - son of **Griffin Sowards-Tipsword**/1773 & **Ruth Abbott**/1774, great-grandson of **Cornstalk**/1710, husband 1826 of 2nd cousin **Lucinda Harris**/1809, children unknown

GRANDDAUGHTER

Sowards, Desha aka Desha Tipsword – 31/64th Chalakatha-MekocheShawano-Chalaka-Powhatan-Metis born 1807-died 1827 - daughter of **Griffin Sowards-Tipsword**/1773 & **Ruth Abbott**/1774, greatgranddaughter of **Cornstalk**/1710, wife 1826 of 2nd cousin **Garrett Harris Jr**/1806- (great-grandson of **Cornstalk**), children unknown

GRANDDAUGHTER

Sowards, Rebecca aka Rebecca Tipsword – 31/64th ChalakathaMekoche-Shawano-Chalaka-Powhatan-Metis born 1809-died 1830 - daughter of **Griffin Sowards-Tipsword**/1773 & **Ruth Abbott**/1774, great-granddaughter of **Cornstalk**/1710, husband & children unknown

GRANDSON

Sowards, Thomas aka Thomas Tipsword- 31/64th Chalakatha-Mekoche-Shawano-Chalaka-Powhatan-Metis born 1813-died after 1845 - son of **Griffin Sowards-Tipsword**/1773 & **Ruth Abbott**/1774, great-grandson of **Cornstalk**/1710, wife & children unknown

GRANDSON

Sowards, Carlin aka Carlin Tipsword- 31/64th Chalakatha-MekocheShawano-Chalaka-Powhatan-Metis born 1815-died after 1845 - son of **Griffin Sowards-Tipsword**/1773 & **Ruth Abbott**/1774, great-grandson of **Cornstalk**/1710, wife & children unknown

BY THOMAS SOWARDS JR/1775 WITH LETITIA MILLS/1772

GRANDDAUGHTER

Sowards, Mahala – 7/32nd Chalakatha-Mekoche-Shawano-Chalaka-Powhatan-Metis born 1794-died after 1820 - daughter of **Thomas Sowards Jr**/1775 & **Letitia Mills**/1772, great-granddaughter of **Cornstalk**/1710, husband & children unknown

GRANDDAUGHTER

Sowards, Susanna – 7/32nd Chalakatha-Mekoche-Shawano-Chalaka-Powhatan-Metis born 1800-died after 1820 - daughter of **Thomas Sowards Jr**/1775 & **Letitia Mills**/1772, great-granddaughter of **Cornstalk**/1710, husband & children unknown

GRANDSON

Sowards, Thomas G. – 7/32nd Chalakatha-Mekoche-Shawano-ChalakaPowhatan-Metis born 1804 KY-died 1860 - son of **Thomas Sowards Jr**/1775 & **Letitia Mills**/1772, great-grandson of **Cornstalk**/1710, wife & children unknown

GRANDSON

Sowards, Charles – 7/32nd Chalakatha-Mekoche-Shawano-ChalakaPowhatan-Metis born 1806-died after 1820 - son of **Thomas Sowards Jr**/1775 & **Letitia Mills**/1772, great-grandson of **Cornstalk**/1710, wife & children unknown

BY ESTHER SOWARDS/1781 WITH ROBERT CARLISLE/1776

GRANDAUGHTER

Carlisle, Frances – 7/32nd Chalakatha-Mekoche-Shawano-Chalaka-Powhatan-Metis born 1805-died 1860 - daughter of **Esther Sowards**/1780 & **Robert Carlisle**/1776, wife 1827 of 1st cousin **John Adams Sowards-Tipsword**/1803, children unknown

BY REBECCA SOWARDS/1790 WITH GARRET HARRIS/1790

GRANDSON

Harris, Garrett Jr – 7/32nd Chalakatha-Mekoche-Shawano-ChalakaPowhatan-Metis born 1806-died after 1827 - son of **Rebecca Sowards**/1790 & **Garrett Harris**/1790, great-grandson of **Cornstalk**/1710, husband 1826 of 2nd cousin **Desha Sowards**/1807- (a great-granddaughter of **Cornstalk**), children unknown

GRANDDAUGHTER

Harris, Lucinda – 7/32nd Chalakatha-Mekoche-Shawano-Chalaka-Powhatan-Metis born 1809-died after 1826 - daughter of **Rebecca Sowards**/1790 & **Garrett Harris**/1790, great-granddaughter of **Cornstalk**/1710, wife 1826 of 2nd cousin **Isaac Sowards**/1805-(a greatgrandson of **Cornstalk**), children unknown

CHAPTER ELEVEN

Black Fish/1725

Moluntha/1708

Blue Jacket/1735

Black Hoof/1730

Puckenshinwa Rising Sun/1735

Black Fish/1725

Black Fish aka **Chiungulla**-Cheeoongoola-Paheataheaseka-Makadaywahmayquah – Chalakatha-Mekoche born about 1725 PA **killed** 1779 KY - son of **Fish Clan Chief**/1705-Chalakatha & **Sister of Moluntha**/1710-Mekoche, raised by extended Chalakatha family after father's death 1739, moved to Lower Shawnee Town OH 1744 with Peter Chartier group, may have moved to Winchester KY 1745 with Chartier, returned to OH 1746, Cornstalk War/1755-77, a **Chalakatha Chief** in OH 1763, Grand Council 1763, **succeeded Cornstalk as Head Chief of Chalakatha & All Shawnee** in 1777, led 300+ warriors at Point Pleasant/1778 **with Dewentatee-Half King**/1730-Wyandot, **killed** in KY raid/1779, step-half-brother of **Blue Jacket**/1735 (through marriage of **his Mother**/1710 to **Pride Opessa**/1710 who was also married to **Sarah Rising Sun**/1715 the mother of Blue Jacket), was referred to as the uncle of **Tecumseh**/1768), brother in law of **Isadore Chesne**/1735-

Shawnee Heritage II 325

(they married sisters), husband 1745 OH (before move to KY) of **Watmeme Opessa**/1730-Pekowi, father **with Watmeme** of sons Chinwa/1746, Young Black Fish (1)/1748, daughter Pimegeezhigoqua/1752, son Young Black Fish (2)/1754, daughters Parlie/1756, Lamateshe/1758 & Cheletha/1760-all Chalakatha-Mekoche-Pekowi, adopted father 1760 of brothers **Lewis Rogers**/1750 & **Henry Rogers**/1755, adopted father about 1770 of **William Jackson-Fish**/1760-white, adopted father 1774 of **Stephen Ruddle-Big Fish**/1768, adopted father & father in law 1778 of **Capt. Joseph Duquesne**/1756-1/2 Pekowi-Wyandot-Metis

MOTHER OF BLACK FISH

Sister of Moluntha aka Mother of Black Fish-Mother of Red Pole – Mekoche born about 1710 (PA?)-died after 1760 OH – **parents unknown**, niece of **Katee Mekoche**/1680-(sister of her father & wife of Okowellos/1674), sister of **Moluntha**/1708 & **Elk-Wabete**/1715, wife 1st by 1725 PA of **Fish Clan Chief**/1705-Chalakatha, widowed 1st time by 1739, wife 2nd 1739 PA of **Pride Opessa**/1710-Pekowi, widowed 2nd time 1753, wife 3rd 1754 (OH?) of **Mekoche Chief**/1710, Mekoche Chief adopted her youngest son Red Pole upon their marriage & raised him Mekoche, mother **with Chalakatha** of Black Fish/1725, Kwatooka/1727, Nakanapaseka/1729 & likely others/1730-38-all Chalakatha-Mekoche, **with Pride** of Red Pole/1740-Pekowi-Mekoche, any children **with Mekoche** unlikely due to her age

WIFE OF BLACK FISH

WIFE 1745 OH

Opessa, Watmeme aka Polly – Pekowi born 1730 PA-died 1797 MO – daughter of **Loyparkoweh Opessa**/1705 & **Nancy Pekowi**/1710, namesake of father's step-mother **Polly-Daughter of Sassoonan**/1695, moved to AL 1735 with **Opessa** & her father, returned to PA by 1738 with her father, moved 1744 to OH with **Peter Chartier**, moved to MO 1779 with adopted son **Stephen Ruddle**, Ruddle returned to whites 1797 upon her death, wife 1745 OH of **Black Fish**/1725, mother **with Black Fish** of sons Chinwa/1746, Young Black Fish (1)/1748, daughter

Pimegeezhigoqua/1752, son Young Black Fish (2)/1754, daughters Chelatha/1756, Lamatashe/1758 & Parlie/1760-all ChalakathaMekoche-Pekowi, adopted mother 1760 & mother in law 1771 OH
Lewis Rogers/1750, adopted mother 1760 & mother in law 1775 OH
Henry Rogers/1755, adopted mother 1774 OH & grandmother in law 1789 OH of **William Jackson-Fish**/1770, adopted mother 1774 OH
Stephen Ruddle/1768 & adopted mother & mother in law 1778 OH of **Capt. Joseph Dusquene**/1756

CHILDREN OF BLACK FISH

SON

Blackfish, Chinwa – Chalakatha-Mekoche-Pekowi born about 1746 OH-**killed** 1774 Point Pleasant WV - son of **Black Fish**/1725 & **Watmeme Opessa**/1730, grandson of **Loyparkoweh Opessa**/1702, Cornstalk War/1763-74, **killed** in battle at Point Pleasant/74, called a relative of **Tecumseh**/1768, husband about 1765 OH of **Chalakatha Woman**/1750, father of several children/1765-74-(likely went by the surname Blackfish)

SON

Black Fish, Young (1) aka **Black Fish (2)** – Chalakatha-Mekoche-Pekowi born about 1748 OH-**killed** 1788 KY - son of **Black Fish**/1725 & **Watmeme Opessa**/1730, grandson of **Loyparkoweh Opessa**/1702, Cornstalk War /1772-77, Blue Jacket War/1777-88, **killed** in KY raid, with group that captured **John Taylor**/1781-white, called a relative of **Tecumseh**, husband about 1768 OH of **Chalakatha Woman**/1753, father of Young Black Fish (3)/1780 & Joseph Blackfish/1785-both Chalakatha-Mekoche-Pekowi

DAUGHTER

Blackfish, Pimegeezhigoqua – Chalakatha-Mekoche-Pekowi born about 1752 OH-died after 1826 - daughter of **Black Fish**/1725 & **Watmeme Opessa**/1730, granddaughter of **Loyparkoweh Opessa**/1702, Shawnee name unknown, went by Chippewa name after marriage to Dusquene, called a relative of **Tecumseh**/1768, 2nd wife 1780 OH of **Capt. Joseph Dusquene**/1756, mother of Joseph Dusquene Jr/1781, Jean Baptiste Dusquene/1785, Isabella Dusquene/1790 & Susanne Dusquene/1795all 1/2 Chalakatha-Mekoche-Pekowi-Wyandot-Metis

SON

Black Fish, Young (2) aka **Black Fish (3)** – Chalakatha-Mekoche-Pekowi born about 1754 OH-died after 1794 - son of **Black Fish**/1725 & **Watmeme Opessa**/1730, grandson of **Loyparkoweh Opessa**/1702, Cornstalk War/1766-77, called a relative of **Tecumseh**, husband 1774 OH of **Chalakatha Woman**/1755, father of Daughter-(wife of William Jackson)/1774 & Eli Blackfish/1790-both Chalakatha-Mekoche-Pekowi, adopted father of **George Ash**/1765-adopted white

DAUGHTER

Blackfish, Parlie aka Polly – Chalakatha-Mekoche-Pekowi born 1756 OH-died after 1799 (MO?) - daughter of **Black Fish**/1725 & **Watmeme Opessa**/1730, granddaughter of **Loyparkoweh Opessa**/1702, called a relative of **Tecumseh**/1768, wife about 1771 OH of **Lewis Rogers**/1750adopted white, mother of Nancy Rogers/1772, Martha Rogers/1774,
James Rogers/1778, Polly Rogers/1782, Lewis Rogers/1786-all 1/2 Chalakatha-Mekoche-Pekowi-Metis

DAUGHTER

Blackfish, Lamateshe aka Lematashe-Launatashe-Auqualanaux – Chalakatha-Mekoche born about 1758 OH-died after 1800 - daughter of **Black Fish**/1725 & **Watmeme Opessa**/1730, granddaughter of **Loyparkoweh Opessa**/1702, called a relative of **Tecumseh**/1768, wife 1st about 1779 OH of **Capt. Joseph Dusquene**/1756, 2nd about 1784 OH of his half-brother **Anthony Shane**/1763, mother with **Dusquene** of David Deshane/1780-1/2 Chalakatha-Mekoche-Pekowi-WyandotMetis, **with Shane** of David Dushane/1785, daughter/1787, John Shane/1790, Charles Chesne/1795, daughter/1797, daughter/1799-5/8th Chalakatha-Kishpoko-Mekoche-Pekowi-Creek-Wyandot-Metis

DAUGHTER

Blackfish, Chelatha – Chalakatha-Mekoche born about 1760 OH-died after 1790 - daughter of **Black Fish**/1725 & **Watmeme**/1730, granddaughter of **Loyparkoweh Opessa**/1700, called a relative of **Tecumseh**/1768, wife about 1775 OH of **Henry Rogers**/1755-adopted white, mother of Polly Rogers/1780 & William Rogers/1785-both 1/2 Chalakatha-Mekoche-Metis

ADOPTED CHILDREN OF BLACK FISH/1725

ADOPTED SON 1760 & SON IN LAW 1771

Rogers, Lewis (1) aka **Capt. Rogers** - adopted-white born about 1750 VA-died after 1819 MO – **parents unknown,** brother of **Henry Rogers**/1755, adopted son 1760 OH & then son in law 1771 OH of **Black Fish**/1725, Cornstalk War/1768-77, little activity in Blue Jacket War/1777-94, moved to MO about 1779 with Thawikila, **Chief of Black Fish-Rogers band in MO**, succeeded as **Chief** by his adopted brother **William Jackson-Fish**/1760, husband by 1771 OH of **Parlie Blackfish**/1756, father of Nancy Rogers/1772, Mary Rogers/1774, Lewis Rogers/1776, James Rogers/1778, William Rogers/1780, Martha Rogers/1782, Elizabeth Rogers/1784, Parlie Rogers/1786-all 1/2 Chalakatha-Mekoche-Pekowi-Metis

ADOPTED SON 1760 & SON IN LAW 1775

Rogers, Henry (1) aka **Chinwa Rogers** - adopted-white born about 1755 VA-died about 1803 MO – **parents unknown**, brother of **Lewis Rogers**/1750, adopted son 1760 OH & then son-in-law 1775 OH of **Black Fish**/1725, namesake of Black Fish's 1st son that was killed in 1774, Cornstalk War/1772-77, little activity in Blue Jacket War/1777-94, moved to MO about 1795, a **village Chief in MO** until his death, husband about 1775 OH of **Cheletha Blackfish**/1760, father of Polly Rogers/1780 & William Rogers/1785-both 1/2 Chalakatha-MekochePekowi-Metis

ADOPTED SON 1770

Jackson, William aka Fish-Capt Fish - adopted-white born about 1760died 1833 – **parents unknown**, adopted son about 1770 OH of **Black Fish**/1725, Blue Jacket War/1777-94, living in MO before 1819, succeeded adopted brother **Lewis Rogers**/1750 **as Chief of Band**, husband 1st about 1780 OH of **Elizabeth Bishop**/1765-adopted-white, 2nd about 1789 OH of **Daughter of Young Black Fish**/1774- (granddaughter of his adopted father Black Fish), 3rd 1797 OH of **Martha Rogers**/1782- (granddaughter of his adopted father Black Fish), father **with Bishop** of Daughter of Fish/1781, Joseph Jackson/1783, William Jackson Jr (1)/1785-all white-Shawnee, **with Black Fish** of Arch Fish/1790, Isaac Fish/1792, Andrew Fish/1794, Jesse Fish/1796, Betsy Jane Fish/1798-all 1/2 Chalakatha-Mekoche-Pekowi-Metis, **with Rogers** of Elizabeth Nakease Fish/1798, William Jackson Jr (2)/1800, Miss Fish/1802, Pascal Fish/1804, John Ficklin Fish/1806 & Charles Salahnewe Fish/1808-all 1/4th Chalakatha-Mekoche-Pekowi-Metis

ADOPTED SON 1774

Ruddle, Stephen aka Big Fish-Sinnanatha - adopted-white born 1768 VA-died 1845 IL - son of **Isaac Ruddle**, adopted son 1772 OH of **Puckenshimwa**/1735- (= adopted brother of **Tecumseh**), adopted son 1774 OH of **Black Fish**/1725-(after death of Puckenshinwa), moved to MO 1779 with Shawnee mother **Watmeme Opessa Blackfish**/1730, some activity in Blue Jacket War/1788-94, returned to whites 1795, translator for whites after 1795, abandoned Shawnee Wife & family when he returned to whites after death of Watmeme about 1795, husband 1st about 1788 OH of **Kishpoko Woman**/1773-Bird Clan, 2nd 1797 of **Catherine Kingery**/1780-white, 3rd 1809 of **Susanna Davis**/1782-1/2 Kishpoko-Cherokee-(sister of **Thomas Davis**/1778), 4th 1834 of **Rachel Wood**/1815-white, father **with Kishpoko** of four children/1788-95, children with **Kingery, Davis & Wood** unknown

ADOPTED SON 1778 & SON IN LAW 1779

Dusquene, Capt Joseph aka Joseph Chesne-Capt. Dusquene-Joseph Duchene-Mushkedewin-Prairie Man – adopted-1/2 Pekowi-WyandotMetis-(adopted Chippewa) born about 1756 OH-died after 1835 - son of
Isadore Chesne/1735 & **Sarah-Younger Daughter of Loyparkoweh Opessa**/1736, raiding Ohio River valley 1774 **with Chief Logan**, Point Pleasant/1774, Cornstalk War/1774-77, Blue Jacket War/1777-94, raiding Ohio River valley 1781 **with Joseph Brant**, employed in fur

trade 1795-1827, became U.S. citizen 1818, half-brother of **Anthony Shane**/1763 & **Joseph Shane**/1765, half-brother of **Mary Josette Chesne**/1775-Wyandot-Ottawa-Metis, adopted son 1778 & (double) son in law 1779-80 of **Black Fish**/1725, husband 1st 1779 OH of **Lamateshe Blackfish**/1758, 2nd 1780 OH of her sister **Pimegeezhigoqua Blackfish**/1752-both Chalakatha-Mekoche-Pekowi, father **with Lamateshe** of David Dusquene-Deshane/1780 & **with Pimegeezhigoqua** of Joseph Dusquene Jr/1781, Jean Baptiste Dusquene/1785, Isabella Dusquene/1790 & Susanne Dusquene/1795all 1/2 Chalakatha-Mekoche-Pekowi-Wyandot-Metis

GRANDCHILDREN OF BLACK FISH/1725
BY CHINWA BLACKFISH/1746
WITH CHALAKATHA WOMAN/1750
UNKNOWN CHILDREN/1765-74

BY YOUNG BLACK FISH (1)/1748
WITH CHALAKATHA WOMAN/1753

GRANDSON

Black Fish, Young (3) – Chalakatha-Mekoche-Pekowi born about 1780 OH-died after 1837 KS - son of **Young Black Fish (1)**/1748 & **Chalakatha Woman**/1753, moved to MO about 1800, moved to KS by 1833, Capt. John Brown Co-**with U.S. Army-**Creek War/1813 & Joseph Parks Co-**with U.S. Army-**Seminole War/1837, husband about 1800 MO of **Chalakatha Woman**/1785, father of Colatha Blackfish/1809Chalakatha-Mekoche-Pekowi

GRANDSON

Blackfish, Joseph – Chalakatha-Mekoche-Pekowi born about 1785 OHdied after 1837 KS - son of **Young Black Fish (1)**/1754 & **Chalakatha Woman**/1753, moved to KS by 1833, Joseph Parks Co-**with U.S.**

ArmySeminole War/1837, husband 1805 OH of **Chalakatha Woman**/1789, children unknown

BY PIMEGEEZHIGOQUA BLACKFISH/1752 WITH CAPT. JOSEPH DUSQUENE/1756

GRANDSON

Dusquene, Joseph (2) aka Joseph Jr-Joseph Duchene Jr-Joseph LaPrairie – 1/2 Chalakatha-Mekoche-Wyandot-Metis - born about 1781-died after 1845 (MN?) - son of **Capt. Joseph Dusquene**/1756 & **Pimegeezhigoqua Blackfish**/1752, grandson of **Black Fish**/1725 & of **Isadore Chesne**/1735, War of 1812-Thames/1813 **with Tecumseh & British**, Treaty 1826, husband 1800 of **Obimegeezhigoqua Chippewa**/1785, father of Pierre Dusquene/1801, Joseph Dusquene/1803 & Jean Baptiste Dusquene/1805-all 1/4th Chalakatha-Mekoche-Pekowi-WyandotChippewa-Metis

GRANDSON

Dusquene, Jean Baptiste (1) aka Jean Baptiste Duchene-Baptiste LaPrairie – 1/2 Chalakatha-Mekoche-Wyandot-Metis born about 1785died after 1850 (MN?) - son of **Pimegeezhigoqua Blackfish**/1752 & **Capt. Joseph Dusquene**/1756, grandson of **Black Fish**/1725 & of **Isadore Chesne**/1735, War of 1812-Thames/1813 **with Tecumseh & British**, moved to CAN 1815, Treaty 1826, husband about 1805 MI? of **Chippewa Woman**/1790, father of Jean Baptiste Dusquene/1817, Marcel Dusquene/1825-1/4th Chalakatha-Mekoche-Pekowi-WyandotChippewa-Metis

GRANDDAUGHTER

Dusquene, Isabella aka Isabella Duchene – 1/2 Chalakatha-MekochePekowi-Wyandot-Metis born about 1790-died after 1827 - daughter of **Pimegeezhigoqua Blackfish**/1752 & **Capt. Joseph Dusquene**/51756, granddaughter of **Black Fish**/1725 & of **Isadore Chesne**/1735, mentioned in Treaty 1826, wife 1st about 1805 MI? of **Joseph LaPorte**/1780-French/Canadian, 2nd by 1820 WI of **Daniel**

Dingley/1785-white, mother **with LaPorte** of Joseph LaPorte Jr/1805, **with Dingley** of Daniel Dingley Jr/1806, Sarah Dingley (1)/1820, William Dingley/1825 & Sarah Dingley (2)/1827-all 1/4th ChalakathaMekoche-Pekowi-Wyandot-Metis

GRANDDAUGHTER

Dusquene, Susanne aka **Susanne Duchene** – 1/2 Chalakatha-Mekoche-Wyandot-Metis - born about 1795-died after 1830 - daughter of **Pimegeezhigoqua Blackfish**/1752 & **Capt. Joseph Dusquene**/1756, granddaughter of **Black Fish**/1725 & of **Isadore Chesne**/1735, mentioned in Treaty 1826, wife by 1815 of **Thomas Conner**/1781-white, mother of Frances Conner/1824, Patrick Conner/1826, Peter Conner/1832 & Elizabeth Conner/1835-all 1/4th Chalakatha-MekochePekowi-Wyandot-Metis

BY YOUNG BLACK FISH (2)/1754
WITH CHALAKATHA WOMAN/1759

GRANDDAUGHTER

Black Fish, Daughter of Young (1) aka Wife of Fish-Wife of William Jackson – Chalakatha-Mekoche-Pekowi born about 1774 OH-died after 1798 – daughter of **Young Black Fish (2)**/1754 & **Chalakatha Woman**/1759, 2nd wife 1789 OH of **William Jackson Fish**/1760adopted white, mother of Arch Fish/1790, Isaac Fish/1792, Andrew Fish/1794, Jesse Fish/1796, Betsy Jane Fish/1798-all ½ Chalakatha-Mekoche-Pekowi-Metis

GRANDSON

Blackfish, Eli – Chalakatha-Mekoche-Pekowi born about 1790 OH-died after 1837 KS - son of **Young Black Fish (2)**/1754 & **Chalakatha Woman**/1759, no known part in War of 1812, moved to KS by 1833, husband about 1810 OH of **Chalakatha Woman**/1795, father of Thomas Blackfish/1830-Chalakatha-Mekoche-Pekowi

BY PARLIE BLACKFISH/1756 WITH LEWIS ROGERS/1750

GRANDDAUGHTER

Rogers, Nancy – ½ Chalakatha-Mekoche-Pekowi-Metis born about 1772 OH-died after 1832 KS – daughter of **Lewis Rogers**/1750 & **Parlie Blackfish**/1756, wife 1787 MO of **First White Man**-(called **Won't Hunt** by Lewis), 2nd by 1795 MO of **Second White Man**-(called **Won't Work** by Lewis), 3rd by 1810 of **John Cohun**/1770-Delaware, children/17871809 **with White Men** unknown, mother **with Cohun** of George Cohun/1825-1/4th Chalakatha-Mekoche-Pekowi-Delaware-Metis

GRANDDAUGHTER

Rogers, Mary (1) – ½ Chalakatha-Mekoche-Pekowi-Metis born 1774 OH-died about 1795 MO – daughter of **Lewis Rogers**/1750 & **Parlie Blackfish**/1756, wife 1790 MO of **Mackinaw Beauchemie**/1770adopted-Chippewa-Metis, children/1790-95 unknown

GRANDSON

Rogers, Lewis (2) aka **Indian Rogers**-Lewis Jr - 1/2 Chalakatha-Mekoche-Pekowi-Metis born about 1776 OH-died 1838 Howard Co MO - son of **Parlie Blackfish**/1756 & **Lewis Rogers**/1750, **with U.S. Army**War 1812, husband about 1793 MO of **Thawikila Woman**/1778, father of Henry Rogers/1794 & Lewis Rogers/1796-both 3/4th ThawikilaChalakatha-Mekoche-Pekowi-Metis

GRANDSON

Rogers, James **Onothe** aka James Rogers (1) - 1/2 Chalakatha-Mekoche-Pekowi-Metis born about 1778 OH-died after 1846 KS - son of **Parlie Blackfish**/1756 & **Lewis Rogers**/1750, moved to MO 1795 **with Black Bobb** band, **with U.S. Army**-War 1812, associated **with Shot Pouch**/1780, **Powder Horn**/1775 & **Little Captain**/1770-all 3/4th Thawikila-Metis (brothers), a **village Chief** on the Marmec River MO after 1800, established Rogers' village-Rogerstown MO, scout **with Fremont** 1841, scout **with Wharton** 1846, husband 1797 MO of **Thawikila Woman**/1780, father of Lewis Rogers/1798, George Washington Rogers/1800, Thomas Jefferson Rogers/1802, James Rogers/1804, Elder Daughter/1806, Middle Daughter/1808, Younger Daughter/1810, Andrew Jackson Rogers/1812-all 3/4th Chalakatha-Thawikila-Mekoche-Metis

GRANDSON

Rogers, William (1) - 1/2 Chalakatha-Mekoche-Pekowi-Metis born about 1780 MO -died 1829 KS - son of **Parlie Blackfish**/1756 & **Lewis Rogers**/1750-adopted white, husband 1st 1797 of **Kansa Woman**/1782, 2nd 1799 of 1825 KS of **Otoe Woman**/1784, 3rd 1806 of **Pawnee Woman**/1791, 4th 1808 KS of **Omaha Woman**/1795, father **with Kansa** of William David Rogers/1797 & Lewis Rogers/1799-both 1/4th Chalakatha-Mekoche-Pekowi-Kansa-Metis, **with Otoe** of Felicita Rogers/1800 & Elizabeth Rogers/1806-both 1/4th Chalakatha-Mekoche-Pekowi-Otoe-Metis, **with Pawnee** of William Rogers/1807- 1/4th Chalakatha-Mekoche-Pekowi-Pawnee-Metis, **with Omaha** of Mary Rogers/1808 & Margaret Rogers/1810-both 1/4th Chalakatha-MekochePekowi-Omaha-Metis

GRANDDAUGHTER

Rogers, Martha Rogers aka Polly Rogers-Parlie Rogers - 1/2 Chalakatha-Mekoche-Pekowi-Metis born about 1782 MO-died after 1800 - daughter of **Parlie Blackfish**/1756 & **Lewis Rogers**/1750adopted white, 3rd wife about 1797 MO of (her uncle by adoption) **William Jackson Fish**/1760-adopted white, mother of Elizabeth Nakease Fish/1798, William Jackson Jr/1800, Miss Fish/1802, Pascal Fish/1804, John Ficklin Fish/1806, Charles Salahnewe Fish/1808 -all 1/4th Chalakatha-Mekoche-Pekowi-Metis

GRANDDAUGHTER

Rogers, Elizabeth aka Betsy - 1/2 Chalakatha-Mekoche-Metis born about 1784 OH-died 1814 MO - daughter of **Parlie Blackfish**/1756 & **Lewis Rogers**/1750-adopted white, granddaughter of **Black Fish**/1725, wife by 1800 OH of **Mackinaw Beauchemie**/1770-adopted-ChippewaMetis, children/1800-1814 unknown

GRANDDAUGHTER

Rogers, Parlie aka Polly (2)-Mary Elizabeth-Betsy - 1/2 Chalakatha-Mekoche-Metis born about 1786 MO-died 1847 - daughter of **Lewis Rogers**/1750-adopted white & **Parlie Blackfish**/1756, wife 1st about 1802 of **Chalakatha Man**/1782, 2nd 1814 of **Mackinaw Beauchemie**/1770, children/1802-13 **with Chalakatha** unknown, mother **with Beauchemie** of Annie Beauchemie/1815, Alexander Beauchemie/1816, William Beauchemie/1817, Martha Beauchemie/1818, Louisa Beauchemie/1819, Julia Ann Beauchemie/1820 & John Beauchemie/1822-all 1/4th ChalakathaMekoche-Pekowi-Chippewa-Metis

BY LAMATASHE BLACKFISH/1758 WITH CAPT. JOSEPH DUSQUENE/1756

GRANDSON

Dusquene, David aka **David Deshane**-David Shane-David Duchene – 1/2 Chalakatha-Mekoche-Pekowi-Wyandot-Metis born about 1780 OHdied after 1854 - son of **Lamateshe Blackfish**/1758 & **Capt. Joseph Dusquene**/1756, raiding OH-KY-VA/1799-1810, Prophet's Town/1811, War of 1812-Thames/1813 with uncle/3rd cousin **Tecumseh**, Treaty 1854, stepson of (his uncle) **Anthony Shane**/1763, grandson of **Black Fish**/1725 & of **Isadore Chesne**/1735, husband about 1800 of **Chippewa Woman**/1785, children unknown

BY LAMATASHE BLACKFISH/1758 WITH ANTHONY SHANE/1763

GRANDSON

Dushane, David aka David Shane-David Dusquene-David Duchene – 5/8th Chalakatha-Kishpoko-Mekoche-Creek-Wyandot-Metis born about 1785-died after 1854 - son of **Anthony Shane**/1763 & **Lamateshe Blackfish**/1758, scout-Anthony Shane Co-**with U.S. Army-**War 1812,

Treaty 1854, grandson of **Black Fish**/1725 & of **Isadore Chesne**/1735, wife & children unknown

GRANDDAUGHTER

Shane, Elder Daughter of Anthony – 5/8th Chalakatha-KishpokoMekoche-Pekowi-Creek-Wyandot-Metis born about 1787-died after 1815 - daughter of **Anthony Shane**/1763 & **Lamateshe Blackfish**/1758, granddaughter of **Black Fish**/1725 & of **Isadore Chesne**/1735,, husband & children unknown

GRANDSON

Shane, John – 5/8th Chalakatha-Kishpoko-Mekoche-Pekowi-CreekWyandot-Metis-(adopted Ottawa) born about 1790-died after 1854 - son of **Anthony Shane**/1763 & **Lamateshe Blackfish**/1758, grandson (by Anthony) of **Isadore Chesne**/1735 & (by Lamateshe) of **Black Fish**/1725, no known part in War of 1812, husband about 1810 of **Ottawa Woman**/1794, children unknown

GRANDDAUGHTER

Shane, Younger Daughter of Anthony – 5/8th Chalakatha-KishpokoMekoche-Creek-Wyandot-Metis born about 1792-died after 1815 - daughter of **Anthony Shane**/1763 & **Lamateshe Blackfish**/1758, granddaughter of **Black Fish**/1725 & of **Isadore Chesne**/1735, husband & children unknown

GRANDSON

Chesne, Charles (2) aka Charles Shane-Charles Chene - 3/4th Chalakatha-Kishpoko-Wyandot-Metis born about 1795-died after 1833 - son of **Lamatashe Black Fish**/1758 & **Anthony Shane**/1763, grandson of **Black Fish**/1725 & of **Isadore Chesne**/1735, namesake of his greatgrandfather **Charles Chesne**/1690, in the **John Perry** band at Wapaghonettat, no known part in War of 1812, translator-Treaty 1833, husband about 1815 of **Chalakatha Woman**/1800, children unknown

BY CHELETHA BLACKFISH/1760 WITH HENRY ROGERS/1755

GRANDDAUGHTER

Rogers, Polly - 1/2 Chalakatha-Mekoche-Pekowi-Metis born about 1780 OH-died about 1803 MO - daughter of **Henry Rogers**/1755-adopted white & **Cheletha Blackfish**/1760, wife about 1795 MO of **Mackinaw Beauchemie**/1770-adopted-Chippewa-Metis, children/1795-1803 unknown

GRANDSON

Rogers, William (2) - 1/2 Chalakatha-Mekoche-Pekowi-Metis born about 1785 OH-died after 1860 KS - son of **Cheletha Blackfish**/1760 & **Henry Rogers**/1755-adopted-white, no known part in War of 1812, **Principal Chief 1860** of Fish-Jackson band **with Pascal Fish**, husband 1st about 1805 MO of **Shawnee Woman**/1790, children unknown

Moluntha/1708

Moluntha aka Mequachake-Malunthy-Molunthy – Mekoche born about 1710 OH-**murdered** 1786 OH – **parents unknown** but he was a nephew of **Katee Mekoche**/1680-(sister of his father & wife of **Okowellos**/1674), a **Mekoche Chief** in OH before 1749, **Head Chief of Mekoche** by 1774, **split leadership of All Shawnee** with **Black Hoof**-Thawikila in 1779 after death of **Black Fish**, raiding PA-VA/1740, Cornstalk War /1755-77, sent Mekoche warriors to Point Pleasant/1774, Grand Council June 1762, Grand Council 1763, Council Logstown 1765, Grand Council 1782, Council Miami Jan. 1786, Treaty 1786, brother of sister **Mother of Black Fish**/1710 & brother **Elk-Wabete**/1715, 1st cousin (his father & Cornstalk's mother were siblings), brother in law of **Fish Clan Chief**/1705-(husband of his **Sister**/1710 = parents of **Black Fish**) & brother in law (husband of Cornstalk's sister Nonhelema) of **Cornstalk**/1710, murdered by **Hugh McGeary** while holding Treaty of 1786, under U.S. flag, **succeeded as Head Chief** of his faction by **Capt. Johnny**/1726-(the brother of Black Hoof) but **Blue Jacket**/1735 led an opposing sub-faction within the group, (split = 3 groups-**Black Hoof** in OH, **Blue Jacket** in OH & **Capt. Johnny** in MO), husband 1st 1730 (AL?)

of **Sister of Black Hoof**/1715-Thawikila, 2nd 1754 OH of 1st cousin **Nonhelema Cornstalk**/1718-(daughter of his aunt Katee/1680), 3rd 1760 OH of his niece/2nd cousin (daughter of his 1st cousingranddaughter of his father's sister) **Lacumtequa Coldwater**/1744, 4th before 1786 of another **Younger Woman** aka **Lanatumque**-(white or Metis), father **with Sister of Black Hoof** of Older Daughter/1754Mekoche-Thawikila & likely many younger children, with **Nonhelema** of Chieska Moluntha/1755, Younger Daughter/1757 & Big Capt. Johnny/1759-all 59/64th Mekoche-Chalakatha-Shawano-ChalakaPowhatan-Metis, **with Lacumtequa** of a child name/gender unknown, any children with **Younger Woman-Lanatumque** unknown

SIBLINGS OF MOLUNTHA

SISTER

Sister of Moluntha aka Mother of Black Fish-Mother of Red Pole – Mekoche born about 1710 (PA?)-died after 1760 OH – **parents unknown**, niece of **Katee Mekoche**/1680-(sister of her father & wife of Okowellos/1674), wife 1st by 1725 PA of **Fish Clan Chief**/1705Chalakatha, widowed 1st time by 1739, wife 2nd 1739 PA of **Pride Opessa**/1710-Pekowi, widowed 2nd time 1753, wife 3rd 1754 OH of **Mekoche Chief**/1710, (Mekoche Chief adopted her youngest son Red Pole upon their marriage & raised him Mekoche), mother **with Chalakatha** of Black Fish/1725, Kwatooka/1727, Nakanapaseka/1729 & likely others/1730-38-all Chalakatha-Mekoche, **with Pride** of Red Pole/1740-Pekowi-Mekoche

BROTHER

Elk aka Wabete (1) – Mekoche born about 1715 OH-**killed** 1786 OH - - **parents unknown**, nephew of **Katee Mekoche**/1680-(sister of his father & wife of Okowellos/1674), brother of **Mother of Black Fish**/1710, Moluntha/1708, raiding PA/1740, Cornstalk War/1755-77, **killed in Col. Benjamin Logan's attack on Moluntha's village**, husband 1st 1735

OH of **Mekoche Woman**/1720, 2nd 1753 OH **of Cawechile Cornstalk** (Cold Water)/1716, father **with Mekoche** of Little Elk/1740, any children **with Cawechile** unknown

WIVES OF MOLUNTHA/1708

WIFE 1730 - KY-TN
SISTER OF BLACK HOOF/1715

Black Hoof, Sister of aka Wife of Moluntha – Thawikila born about 1715 AL-died about 1755 OH – daughter of **Wood Deer Hoof**/1682 & **Little Sugar**/1688-both Thawikila, moved to TN-KY about `1728, living near the Ohio River 1730, wife about 1730 OH-KY of **Moluntha**/1708Mekoche, mother of Daughter of Moluntha/1754 & many younger children

WIFE 1754 OH
NONHELEMA CORNSTALK/1718

Cornstalk, Nonhelema aka Grenadier Squaw-Shawnee Warrior Woman-Nonhelema Okowellos-Nonhelema Hokolesqua - 27/32nd Chalakatha-Mekoche-Shawano-Chalaka-Powhatan-Metis born 1718 Greenbrier River WV-died after 1786 OH - daughter of **Okowellos**/1674 & **Katee Mekoche**/1680, about 6'6" tall, well built & attractive, often referred to as a giant, moved to AL by 1725 with Okowellos' band-returned to PA by 1730, moved to Lower Shawnee Town OH with **Peter Chartier** 1744, 1745 moved on to near Winchester KY-(**Neucheconner** & **Tamenebuck** return to PA), 1746 moved to French Lick-Nashville TN, 1747 moved to the Coosa River AL, returned north about 1754 (either with her 1st husband or just after his death), a **Chalakatha village Head woman** in OH by 1755, read & spoke some English, possibly an occasional warrior in Cornstalk War /1755-74, Head Woman of Nonhelema's village on Sippio Creek of Sciota River OH before 1773, **an emissary to the Shawnee for Cornstalk** 1774, the **only woman warrior** Point Pleasant/1774, Grand Council 1782, Council Miami Jan. 1786, had the fingers cut off of her right hand to the 1st knuckle by whites following **murder of Moluntha** during Benjamin Logan's attack on Moluntha's village 1786, moved to

Apple Creek MO area following death of Moluntha, returned to OH home to die after 1795, wife 1st 1734 PA of **Wahootasika-Savannah King**/1710-Chalakatha-widowed 1754, 2nd 1754 OH of 1st cousin **Moluntha**/1708-Mekoche, unmarried partner (she never really left Moluntha) 3rd 1762 OH with **Richard Butler**/1742-white-(adopted Seneca), mother **with Wahootasika** of Elder Daughter/1735, daughter Mellana/1748, twin daughters Wynema & Waheeta/1750--all 59/64th Chalakatha-Mekoche-Shawano-Chalaka-Powhatan-Metis, **with Moluntha** of Chieska/1755, Younger Daughter/1757 & Big Capt. Johnny/1759-all 59/64th Mekoche-Chalakatha-Shawano-ChalakaPowhatan-Metis, **with Richard Butler** of Capt. Butler-Tamenatha/176327/64th Chalakatha-Mekoche-Shawano-Chalaka-Powhatan-Metis, adoptive mother of niece **Fanny Butler**/1755

WIFE 1760 OH
LACUMTEQUA COLDWATER/1744

Coldwater, Lacumtequa – 59/64th Mekoche-Chalakatha-ShawanoChalaka-Powhatan-Metis born about 1744 OH-died after 1786 – daughter of **Cold Water-Wepenipe**/1715 & **Cawachile Cornstalk**/1718, wife about 1760 OH of her uncle/2nd cousin (1st cousin of her mother-son of her grandmother's brother) **Moluntha**/1708, living in Moluntha village OH 1786, children unknown

WIFE BEFORE 1786 OH
LANATUMQUE/MUCH YOUNGER THAN HE WAS

Lanatumque – Metis or adopted white - born before 1770 (OH?)-died after 1786 – wife before 1786 of **Moluntha**/1708, any children unknown

CHILDREN OF MOLUNTHA/1708
WITH SISTER OF BLACK HOOF/1710

DAUGHTER

Moluntha, Older Daughter of – Mekoche-Thawikila born 1754 OH-died about 1770 - daughter of **Moluntha**/1708 & **Sister of Black Hoof**/1715, a Mekoche, wife by 1769 OH of **Brother of Mink**/1750-Chalakatha, mother of Otter/1770-Chalakatha-Mekoche-Thawikila

WITH NONHELEMA CORNSTALK/1718

SON

Moluntha, Chieska - **Capt Chieska**-Young King-Young Moluntha-**Capt Tom**-Capt Tommy-Cheachisika-Jakeshaw-Chakalakek-CheackscaChiachisika-Capt Shigsta – 59/64th Mekoche-Chalakatha-ShawanoChalaka-Powhatan-Metis born 1755 OH-died of cholera 1833 - son of **Moluntha**/1708-Mekoche & **Nonhelema Cornstalk**/1718, a Mekoche warrior, over 6' tall, Blue Jacket War/1777-94, scout-Capt. John Logan Co-Anthony Shane Co-William Wells Co-**with U.S. Army**-War of 1812, a **Chalakatha Chief** at Wapaghonettat 1817, Treaty 1804, 1817, 1818, 1831, husband 1st 1779 OH of 1st cousin (daughter of mother's sister) **Polly Butler**/1765, 2nd 1780 OH of **Chalakatha Woman**/1765, father **with Polly** of Spy Buck Moluntha/1780-35/64th Mekoche-ChalakathaShawano-Chalaka-Powhatan-Creek-Metis, children **with Chalakatha** unknown

DAUGHTER

Moluntha, Younger Daughter of – 59/64th Mekoche-ChalakathaShawano-Chalaka-Powhatan-Metis born 1757 OH-died about 1790 OH - daughter of **Nonhelema Cornstalk**/1718 & **Moluntha**/1708-Mekoche, a Mekoche, granddaughter of **Okowellos**/1674 & **Katee Mekoche**/1680-(who was the aunt of Moluntha), niece of **Cornstalk**/1710, wife 1st 1775 of **Shawnee Warrior**/1755-widow by 1785, 2nd 1785 of **William Wells**/1770-white-(adopted-Miami), children/1775-85 **with Shawnee** unknown, mother **with Wells** of William Wayne Wells/1786 & Mary Wells/1788-both 29/64th Mekoche-Chalakatha-Shawano-Chalaka-Powhatan-Metis-(adopted Miami)

SON

Moluntha, Capt. Johnny aka **Capt. Johnny (3)-Capt. John-Big John** – 59/64th Mekoche-Chalakatha-Shawano-Chalaka-Powhatan-Metis born 1759 OH-died after 1815 OH - son of **Nonhelema Cornstalk**/1718 & **Moluntha**/1708, grandson of **Okowellos**/1680, nephew of **Cornstalk**/1710, a Chalakatha warrior, attended Council 1785 with **Alexander McKee** & **Matthew Elliott**, Blue Jacket War/1777-94, scout-

Capt. John Logan Co-**with U.S. Army-**War of 1812, **killed Winnemak**Pottawamee, nearly 7' tall, cousin of **Capt. John Logan-Big Horn**/1774, **Otter**/1770 & **Bright Horn**/1770, husband about 1785 OH of **Rachel Kizer**/1761-1/2 Chalakatha-Metis, father of two known children/1786-90

WITH LACUMTEQUA COLDWATER 1744

UNKNOWN

WITH YOUNGER WOMAN-LANATUMQUE

UNKNOWN

GRANDCHILDREN OF MOLUNTHA/1708

BY OLDER DAUGHTER/1754
WITH BROTHER OF MINK/1750

GRANDSON

Otter – Chalakatha-Mekoche-Thawikila born about 1770 OH-died after 1815 MO/KS - son of **Brother of Mink**/1750 & **Daughter of Moluntha**/1754, a Mekoche warrior, Blue Jacket War/1788-94, scout**with U.S. Army-**War 1812-Thames/1813, half-brother through father of **Bright Horns**/1770, 1st cousin through his uncle **Mink**/1740 of **Big Horn-Capt. Logan**/1774 & cousin through **Tecumpease**/1758 of **Tecumseh**/1768 & cousin through mother of **Capt. Johnny**/1765, grandson of **Moluntha**/1708 & **Sister of Black Hoof**/1715, greatnephew of **Black Hoof**/1730, moved to MO after 1815 & on to KS by
1833, wife & children unknown

BY CHIESKA/1755
WITH POLLY BUTLER/1765

GRANDSON

Moluntha, Spy Buck aka Saukothkaw-Tahkaska-Spybuck Chieska –
35/64th Mekoche-Chalakatha-Shawano-Chalaka-Powhatan-Creek-Metis
born about 1780 OH-died after 1832 - son of **Polly Butler**/1765 &
Chieska Moluntha/1755, a Chalakatha warrior, grandson of
Moluntha/1708, great-nephew of **Cornstalk**/1710, delegate to D.C.
1802 with **Wayweleapee, John Perry, Quaskee Black Hoof, Joseph
Parks** & **Francois Duchoquet**, scout-with U.S. Army-War
1812Thames/1813, Treaty 1817, 1831, a warrior at Hog Creek &
Wapaghonettat 1832, husband 1795 OH of **Daughter of Col.
Barbee**/1780, father of George Spybuck/1796, Daughter of Spy
Buck/1798, John Spybuck/1802 & Young Spy Buck/1806-all 17/64th
Mekoche-Chalakatha-Shawano-Chalaka-Powhatan-Creek-Metis

BY YOUNGER DAUGHTER/1757 WITH WILLIAM WELLS/1770

GRANDSON

Wells, William Wayne - 29/64th Mekoche-Chalakatha-ShawanoChalaka-
Powhatan-Metis-(adopted Miami) born about 1786-died after
1818 - son of **William Wells**/1770-adopted white Miami & **Younger
Daughter of Moluntha**/1757, raised by **Tukemung Sweet Breeze Little
Turtle**/1775-Miami, with U.S. Army-War 1812-Thames/1813, Treaty
1805, 1817, 1818, husband about 1795 of **Jane S. Metis**/1780-
MiamiMetis, children unknown

GRANDDAUGHTER

Wells, Mary - both 29/64th Mekoche-Chalakatha-Shawano-
ChalakaPowhatan-Metis-(adopted Miami) born about 1788-died after
1818 - daughter of **William Wells**/1770-adopted-white-Miami &
**Younger
Daughter of Moluntha**/1757, raised by **Tukemung Sweet Breeze Little
Turtle**/1775-Miami, mentioned in Treaty 1818, husband & children
unknown

Whirlpool-Blue Jacket/1735

Blue Jacket aka Weyapiersenwha-**Whirlpool**-Sepettekenathe-(Big
Rabbit-child name) – Pekowi-Kishpoko born 1735 PA-died 1809 OH -

son of **Pride Opessa**/1710-Pekowi & **Sarah Rising Sun**/1715Kishpoko, grandson of **Opessa & Margaret Pekowi**, by 1755 trading with Ohio Fur Co. in PA **with brothers Lawagqua**/1733 & **WabeteElk**/1737, **Pekowi by birth** but reverted to mother's **Kishpoko** family with his mother upon death of Pride, Cornstalk War/1755-77, lead War Chief in **Blue Jacket War/**1777-94 (Blue Jacket War = allied **with** British-Revolution/1776-83, Vincennes/1778, Point Pleasant/1778, Boonesboro/1778, Martin & Ruddle Stations KY/1780, Lochery/1781, Blue Licks/1782, Crawford/1782, Ft. Finney/1786, raiding KYTN/1786, raiding Ohio River valley/1788-92, Harmer/1790, Dunlap Station/1791, St. Clair/1791, Ft. Recovery/1794, defeated by Anthony Wayne & American Army at Fallen Timbers 1794), a **Pekowi village Chief** in OH by 1772, by 1773 established Blue Jacket Town on Deer Creek of Sciota River OH, 1774 Treaty Camp Charlotte, 1775 Council Ft. Pitt **with Cornstalk, Silverheels, Nimwha** & **Wryneck**, 1776 Treaty Ft. Pitt, Grand Council 1782, **succeeded Black Snake as Head War Chief** 1785, Jan. 1786 Council Miami, 1786 attended Treaty Ft. Finney, 1786 leader of an opposing faction when **Capt. Johnny**/1726 succeeded **Moluntha**/1708 as Head of Chalakatha-Mekoche led faction (= 3 groups-**Black Hoof** in OH & **Blue Jacket** in OH, **Capt. Johnny** in MO), Grand Council 1791, Grand Council Sept. 1792, 1794 **succeeded Little Turtle**-Miami as **leader of United Tribes with Turkey Foot (1)**/1750adopted-Ottawa, 1794 stepped down as **Head War Chief** following defeat at Fallen Timbers but levered himself into recognition as a Civil Chief-(whether as a Pekowi his tribe by birth or as a Kishpoko the tribe he was raised in is unclear), 1795 Treaty Greenville, never openly opposed whites after 1795, Grand Council 1805, Treaty 1805, **refused Tecumseh** in early ventures but was supportive later, step-half-brother (by marriage 1739 of Pride Opessa/1710 to Mother of Black Fish/1710) of **Black Fish**/1725, 1st cousin of Metheotashe/1738-(fathers were brothers), **double-uncle of Tecumseh**/1768 (1st cousin of Metheotashe & brother-in-law of Puckenshinwa), husband 1st 1755 OH-KY of **Older Sister of Puckenshinwa**/1739-1/2 Kishpoko-Creek-Metis, 2nd 1762 OH of **Margaret Moore**/1746-adopted-white, 3rd 1765 OH of **Clear Water Baby**/1750-1/2 Pekowi-Metis, father **with Sister of Puckenshinwa** of

Young Whirlpool/1756, Spybeech/1758, Wayweleapee/1760 & George

Bluejacket (1)-Son of Blue Jacket/1762-all 3/4th Pekowi-KishpokoCreek-Metis, **with Moore** of Joseph Moore-Bluejacket/1763 & Nancy Moore/1765-(born after Margaret's return to the whites)-both 1/2 Pekowi-Kishpoko-Metis, **with Baby** of James Bluejacket/1766, Young Blue Jacket/1770, Marie Louise Bluejacket/1774, Sally Bluejacket/1776, Nancy Bluejacket/1778, George Bluejacket (2)/1780-all 3/4th PekowiKishpoko-Metis

FATHER'S FATHER

Straight Tail, Opessa aka Opethatha-Wapatha-Wopatha-Hopesha – Pekowi born 1664 OH-died latter 1760 OH - son of **Straight Tail-Meaurroway**/1630 & **Pekowi Woman**/1635, moved 1677 with band to IN, moved 1680 to IL, 1689 moved with band to TN-NC-KY-VA, by 1693 living in Cecil Co MD, about 1693 a **Pekowi Chief** under his father in Cecil Co MD, 1697 moved to Lancaster Co PA with band, 1697 succeeded **Straight Tail** as **Pekowi Chief** in Pequea PA, 1701 signed Treaty with **William Penn** with **Lemoytungh** & **Pemoyajagh**, 1706 Council Philadelphia, 1707 Conference at Pequea Lancaster Co PA with **Governor John Evans**, 1710 Conference at Conestoga PA with **John French & Henry Worley**, resigned 1711 to move to Sassoonan's Delaware village-Shamokin PA, succeeded 1711 as **Pekowi Chief** at Pequea PA by his brother **Cakundawanna**/1670, 1715 Conference Philadelphia with **Sassoonan**, 1722 moved to Old Town MD-upper Potomac & **Pekowi Chief** again by 1723, by 1732 moved to AL with band, by 1749 returned to western MD/southeast PA, Aug. 1749 Council Philadelphia, 1750 moved to OH, 1752 succeeded **PheasantKakawatchekee**/1680 as **Head Pekowi Chief** in OH, May 1756 Council
Tioga Point, Aug. 1760 Council Ft. Pitt, brother in law (through sister Snow White) of **Peter Chartier**/1690, connected with **Poxinosa**-Pekowi, **White Fish (1)**-Pekowi & **Okowellos Hokolesqua**-Chalakatha (Head Chiefs of bands), great-grandfather of **Tecumseh**/1768, husband by 1684 IN of **Margaret Pekowi**/1670, 2nd 1711 PA of **Polly-Daughter of Sassoonan**/1695-Delaware, father **with Margaret** of children/1685-94, Snow White/1695, Tecoomteh/1698, Waywayti/1700,

Loyparkoweh/1702 & Lawaquaqua-Pride Opessa/1710-all Pekowi, children **with Polly** unknown

MOTHER'S FATHER

Rising Sun, Chief – Kishpoko born about 1685 Tuckabatchee AL-died after 1744 (OH?) – moved with Band from AL to Lehigh valley of PA by 1705, lived near/among the **Kakawatchekee-Pheasant** Pekowi Band & the **Opessa** Pekowi Band & near/among the Mohawk community, a minor **Kishpoko Chief** in PA-MD by 1715, some of family including Young Rising Sun-Father of Puckenshinwa moved back to AL about 1730, among the Shawnee that went to OH 1744 with **Peter Chartier**, husband 1st about 1705 PA of **Kishpoko Woman**/1690, 2nd about 1730 PA of **Mohawk Woman**/1698-(sister of wife of **Cakundawanna Straight Tail**), father **with Kishpoko** of Young Rising Sun/1710-(father of Puckenshinwa), Sarah Rising Sun/1715-(mother of Blue Jacket)-both Kishpoko, children **with Mohawk** unknown

MOTHER

Rising Sun, Sarah – Kishpoko born 1715 PA-died after 1765 OH - daughter of **Rising Sun**/1685 & **Kishpoko Woman**/1690, lived in a mixed Kishpoko-Mohawk community in PA, wife 1st 1730 PA of **Pride Opessa**/1710-Pekowi, widowed 1753, wife 2nd 1753 OH of **Kishpoko Man**/1710-(from the mixed Kishpoko-Mohawk community that had moved to OH), widowed 1758, relative (by marriage to her uncle) of **Metheotashe Opessa**/1738, wife 3rd 1758 OH of **Mohawk Man**/1715-(from the mixed Kishpoko-Mohawk community that had moved to OH), widowed by 1765, mother **with Pride** of Lawagqua-Elder Son/1733, Blue Jacket-Whirlpool/1735, Wabete-Elk-Younger Son/1737 & Sarah Opessa/1739-all Pekowi-Kishpoko, **with Kishpoko** of No Worries-Mary Louise Sanschagrin/1754 & Yellow Britches-Edna Rising Sun/1756-Kishpoko, mother **with Mohawk** of Sarah Rising Sun/1759-1/2 Kishpoko-Mohawk, grandmother of **Bright Horn**/1772-3/4th Kishpoko-Mohawk & of **Billy Caldwell**/1776-1/4th Kishpoko-Mohawk-(adopted Chippewa)

FATHER

Opessa, Pride aka **Lawaquaqua**-Lawachkamekee-LawakakaItawachcomequi-Eetawachkomekee – born about 1710 MD-died 1753 SC - son of **Opessa**/1664 & **Margaret Pekowi**/1670, 1711 taken to Sassoonan's village with Opessa, 1722 returned to Opessa's Town MD with **Opessa**, 1732 remained in north when **Opessa** took band to AL, 1738 signed Petition to PA with **Peter Chartier**/1690, **George Miranda**/1700, brother **Tecoomteh**/1700 & 94 Natives to stop the sell of liquor to Natives, by 1738 a **Pekowi Chief** in west MD/central PA, raiding PA/1740, 1744 joined **Peter Chartier, Big Hominy** & others in moving to Lower Shawnee Town OH to support the French, 1748 Conference Logstown with **Conrad Weiser, Big Hominy & Kakawatchekee**, 1753 captured on trip to the south to locate Pekowi relatives on the Savannah River & died in SC prison, husband 1st 1730 east PA of **Sarah Rising Sun**/1715-Kishpoko, 2nd by 1739 east PA of
(widow) **Sister of Moluntha**/1710, father **with Rising Sun** of Lawagqua-Elder Brother of Blue Jacket/1733, Blue Jacket-Weyapiersenwha-Whirlpool /1735, Wabete-Elk-Younger Brother of Blue Jacket/1737 & Sarah Opessa-sister of Blue Jacket/1739-all Kishpoko-Pekowi, **with Sister of Moluntha** of Red Pole/1740Mekoche-Pekowi, step-father of **Black Fish**/1725, Kwatooka/1727, Nakanapaseka/1729-all Chalakatha-Mekoche

AUNT and UNCLES

SISTER OF FATHER

Opessa, Snow White aka **Blanceneige-Wapakonee**-Daughter of Opessa-Wife of Peter Chartier – Pekowi born about 1695 Cecil Co MDdied after 1744 OH-PA - daughter of **Opessa**/1664 & **Margaret Pekowi**/1670, namesake of her aunt **Snow White Straight Tail**/1665, wife 1710 PA of **Peter Chartier**/1690, mother of Francois Pale Croucher Chartier/1712, Rene Pale Stalker Chartier/1725, Anna Chartier/1730 & other children/1713-40-all 3/4th Pekowi-Metis

BROTHER OF FATHER

Opessa, Tecoomteh aka Tecomteh – Pekowi born about 1700 Lancaster Co PA-died after 1738 PA - son of **Opessa**/1664 & **Margaret Pekowi**/1670, 1738 called the 1st warrior of the band, 1738 signed Petition to PA to stop the sell of liquor to Natives with brother **Pride**/1710, brother in law **Peter Chartier**/1690, **George Miranda**/1700 & 94 other Natives, wife & children unknown

BROTHER OF FATHER

Opessa, Waywayti aka Wawwaythi-Waywaythee-Wauwaythee-Weyweyti-Wauweythi – Pekowi born about 1700 PA-died after 1750 (AL?) – son of **Opessa**/1664 & **Margaret Pekowi**/1670, grandson of **Meaurroway-Straight Tail**/1630, Turtle Clan, in west PA 1711-23 with father **Opessa**, returned to north MD/east PA area with **Opessa** 1723, living on the Alleghany River by 1727, moved to AL with **Opessa** 1735, husband 1st 1720 PA of **Elizabeth**-Aunt of Metheotashe/1705, 2nd 1739 AL of her sister **Nancy**-Mother of Metheotashe/1710, (he & his brother were married to sisters & switched wives in 1738) children/1720-38 **with Elizabeth** unknown but **stepfather** 1739 AL of Middle Daughter of Loyoarkoweh-**Nancy**/1734, Younger Daughter of Loyparkoweh-**Sarah**/1736 & **Metheotashe**-Mary/1738

BROTHER OF FATHER

Opessa, Loyparkaweh aka Loapeckeway-Lawakwakwa – Pekowi born about 1705 PA-died after 1760 OH - son of **Opessa**/1664 & **Pekowi Woman**/1670, grandson of **Straight Tail-Meaurroway**/1630, in west PA 1711-23 with father **Opessa**, returned to north MD/east PA area with **Opessa** 1723, living on the Alleghany River by 1727, a **Pekowi Chief** in PA by 1732, in 1732-1733-1734 signed letters to the Governor of PA as one of the Chiefs on the Alleghany complaining about the sale of rum to the natives, moved to AL with **Opessa** 1735-left a wife & children in AL with relatives/clan members, returned to PA by 1738sent letter to the Governor with **Neucheconner** & **Coycacolenne** protesting the sale of rum, then called a young Chief guided by vice regent **Neucheconner**, between 1738 & 1744 lived at Chartier's TownAlleghany Co PA & Logstown-Alleghany Co PA, apparently moved to

OH with **Peter Chartier** & **Neucheconner** in 1744-45 for he is living in

Lower Shawnee Town OH in 1752 when he sent a letter with 3 other Shawnee Chiefs there to the Governor of PA reporting that they were still loyal to the British though most of their neighbors had gone over to the French, attended Council Philadelphia 1753 after **Opessa** moved to OH, apparently opposed the Shawnee participation in French-Indian War/1754-60, a minor **Pekowi Chief in OH** after death of **Opessa**, husband 1st about 1725 MD of **Pekowi Woman**/1710, 2nd 1738 PA (having left his 1st wife in AL) of **Aunt of Metheotashe**/1705, (he & his brother were married to sisters & switched wives in 1738), father of Tecumsapah-Margaret/1725, Older Daughter-Sarah/1727, Watmeme-Polly/1730, Middle Daughter-Nancy/1734, Younger DaughterSarah/1736 & Metheotashe-Mary/1738-all Pekowi, any children with **Unknown 2nd Wife** are unknown

MOTHER'S BROTHER

Rising Sun, Young aka **Father of Puckenshinwa** – Kishpoko born about 1710 Lehigh valley PA-died after 1745 (OH?) – son of **Rising Sun**/1685 & **Kishpoko Woman**/1690, moved to Tallapoosa River AL about 1730 with Band/family, appears to have returned north (to OH?) about 1745, married about 1735 AL **Older Daughter of James McQueen**/1720, father of **Puckenshinwa**/1735, child/37, Older Sister of Puckenshinwa/1739-(1st Wife of Blue Jacket), Mary Rising Sun/1744(Wife of David Francis) -all 1/2 Kishpoko-Creek-Metis

SIBLINGS OF BLUE JACKET-WHIRLPOOL

By PRIDE OPESSA
& Sarah Rising Sun

BROTHER

Opessa, Lawagqua aka Lawoughqua-Lawagkwa-**Elder Brother of Blue Jacket** – Pekowi-Kishpoko born 1733 PA-died after 1774 (OH?) – son of **Pride Opessa**/1710-Pekowi & **Sarah Rising Sun**/1715-Kishpoko, trading with Ohio Fur Co. in PA **with Blue Jacket & Wabete** by early 1750's, Cornstalk War/1755-74, 1765 Council Logstown PA, 1765 a **Pekowi Chief** in OH, 1765 returned captives to Ft. Pitt, husband about 1753 OH of **Pekowi Woman**/1737, father of Resting Fish-Masemo/1760 & Resting Snake-Monetoshe/1770-both Pekowi-Kishpoko

BROTHER

Opessa, Wabete aka **Elk-Younger Son-Younger Brother of Blue Jacket** – Pekowi-Kishpoko born 1737 OH-died after 1774 OH - son of **Pride Opessa**/1710-Pekowi & **Sarah Rising Sun**/1715-Kishpoko, a PekowiKishpoko warrior, younger brother of **Blue Jacket**/1735, by 1755 trading with OH Fur Co. in PA in early with brothers Lawagqua & Blue Jacket, Cornstalk War/1755-74, father in law of **Blue Pocket Swearingen**/1763-adopted-white, husband 1757 OH of **Kishpoko Woman**/1742, 2nd 1766 OH of **Ms. Baby**/1752-1/2 Pekowi-Metis, children/1757-66 **with Kishpoko** unknown, father **with Baby** of SwanWapehti Opessa/1768-3/4th Pekowi-Metis - (some children may have been called Bluejacket's)

SISTER

Opessa, Sarah aka Sally Bluejacket-**Sister of Blue Jacket** – Pekowi-Kishpoko born 1739 OH-died after 1825 OH - daughter of **Pride Opessa**/1710-Pekowi & **Sarah Rising Sun**/1715-Kishpoko, namesake of father's sister **Sarah-Snow White Opessa**/1695 & father's aunt **Snow White Straight Tail-Sarah White**/1666, 1st cousin of **Metheotashe**(fathers were brothers), aunt of **Tecumseh**/1768, **Bright Horn**/1772, **Billy Caldwell**/1776, never known to have married

HALF-BROTHER
BY PRIDE OPESSA
& SISTER OF MOLUNTHA

Red Pole aka **Mesquakinoe**-Mesquakunigou-Meskwakeeno – PekowiMekoche (Thawikila by marriage) born about 1740 (PA?)-died 1797 PA
- son of **Pride Opessa**/1710-Pekowi & **Mother of Black Fish**/1710Mekoche, a **Pekowi** by birth but reverted to mother's division-
Mekoche with death of Pride 1753, then raised by mother's 3rd husband **Mekoche Chief**/1710, grandson of **Opessa**/1664, half-brother of **Blue Jacket**/1735 (through Pride/1710) & half brother of **Black Fish**/1725

(through Mother/1710), Cornstalk War/1758-77, a **Mekoche Chief** in OH by 1778, Blue Jacket War/1777-82, May 1782 Council Detroit, 1786 attended Treaty Ft. Finney, Sept. 1792 Council, Dec. 1792 Council, 1792 delegation to **Thomas McKee**, 1792-94 led delegation of **7 Shawnee & George Ash** to the Shawnee in TN-AL-GA, i.e. the Chickamauga (their leader **Cheeseekau**-brother of **Tecumseh** had just been killed near Nashville), then on to the Cherokee in NC & GA & Creek in AL & GA, Treaty Greenville 1795, a **Thawikila Chief** (by marriage) in OH before 1797, cousin of **Metheotashe**/1738-(through his uncle Loyparkoweh) & uncle of **Tecumseh**/1768, died returning from Council in Philadelphia 1797, husband about 1760 OH of **Thawikila Woman**/1745, children unknown

HALF-SISTER
BY SARAH RISING SUN/1715
& KISHPOKO MAN

Rising Sun, No Worries aka **Marie Louise Sanschagrin**-1st Half-sister of Blue Jacket-2nd wife of **Col. Matthew Elliott**-adopted white – Kishpoko born 1754 OH-died 1826 - daughter of **Sarah Rising Sun**/1715 & **Kishpoko Man**/1710, 2nd wife 1769 PA of **Col. Matthew Elliott**/1730adopted Irish, mother of Isabella Elliott/1770, Matthew Elliott Jr/1772, William Elliott/1775, Alexander Elliott/1780-all 1/2 Kishpoko-Metis, likely other unknown children

HALF-SISTER
BY SARAH RISING SUN
& KISHPOKO MAN

Rising Sun, Yellow Britches aka Edna-Daughter of Rising Sun-2nd Halfsister of Blue Jacket- 2nd wife of **Col. Alexander McKee**-adopted white – Kishpoko born 1756 OH-died after 1793 OH – daughter of **Sarah Rising Sun**/1715 & **Kishpoko Man**/1710, 2nd wife 1769 PA of **Col. Alexander McKee**/1725-adopted-Irish, mother of Thomas McKee/1770, Elizabeth McKee/1772, Alexander McKee/1775, Catherine McKee/1780 & at least 2 other children by 1780-all 1/2 Kishpoko-Metis

HALF-SISTER
BY SARAH RISING SUN
& MOHAWK MAN

Rising Sun, Sarah aka 3rd Half-sister of Blue Jacket-wife of Brother of Mink-wife of William Caldwell-Sarah Caldwell-wife of James Colwellwife of William Vance - 1/2 Kishpoko-Mohawk born 1759 OH-died after 1796 Gallia Co. OH - daughter of **Sarah Rising Sun**/1715Kishpoko & **Mohawk Man**/1710, wife 1st 1772 OH of **Brother of Mink**/1750-Mekoche,widowed 1774, 2nd 1776 OH of **William Caldwell Sr**/1750-white,seperated 1778, 3rd 1779 WV of **James Colwell**/1757, 4th 1789 WV of **William Vance**/1755-1/4th Pekowi-Metis, 1776 abandoned **Bright Horn** when she married **William Caldwell**/1755, 1779 abandoned **Billy Caldwell** & moved to WV, went by name of Sarah Caldwell in marriages to **Colwell** & **Vance**, mother **with Brother of Mink** of Bright Horn/1772-3/4th Mekoche-Kishpoko-Mohawk, **with Caldwell** of Billy Caldwell/1777-1/4th Kishpoko-Mohawk-Metis, **with Colwell** of James Colwell/1780, Jacob Colwell/1782, Sarah Colwell/1784 & Martha Patsy Colwell/1786 & **with Vance** of Thomas Vance/1790 & Christina Vance/1796-all 3/8th Kishpoko-PekowiMohawk-Metis

WIVES OF WHIRLPOOL-BLUE JACKET

1ST WIFE 1755 - OH

Rising Sun, Older Daughter of Young aka Older Sister of Puckenshinwa-Wife of Blue Jacket-Wife of Isadore Chesne-Wife of Big Swamp - 1/2 Kishpoko-Creek-Metis born 1739 AL-died about 1774 OH - daughter of **Young Rising Sun**/1710 & **Daughter of James McQueen**/1720-1/2 Creek-Metis, appears to have returned north (OH?) about 1745 with their father, 1st wife 1st 1755 OH of 1st cousin **Whirlpool-Blue Jacket**/1735, (left when Blue Jacket married Margaret Moore-white), 2nd 1762 OH of **Isadore Chesne**/1735-Wyandot-Metis, 3rd 1769 OH of **Big Swamp**/1730, mother **with Blue Jacket** of Young Blue Jacket-Young Whirlpool/1756, Spybeech/1758, Wayweleapee/1760 & George Bluejacket (1)/1762-all 3/4th Kishpoko-Pekowi-Creek-Metis, with **Chesne** of Anthony Shane-Chesne/1763 & Joseph ShaneChesne/1765-both 1/4th Kishpoko-Creek-Wyandot-Metis, **with Big Swamp** of Thick Water/1770-3/4th Kishpoko-Creek-Metis

2ND WIFE 1762 OH

Moore, Margaret – (aka Mary Moore?)- adopted-white born about 1746 VA-died after 1820 OH - adopted before 1761 with a sister (**Molly Moore**?), returned to whites 1765, 2nd wife 1762 OH of **Blue Jacket**/1735, mother of Joseph Moore-Joseph Bluejacket/1763 & Nancy Moore-Bluejacket/1765-both 1/2 Pekowi-Kishpoko-Metis

3RD WIFE 1765 - OH

Baby, Clear Water aka Clear Water Baubee - 1/2 Pekowi-Metis born about 1750 MI-died after 1832 KS - daughter of **Jacques Duperon Baby**/1733 & a **Pekowi Woman**, one of 11 illegitimate children of Baby by Native women, 3rd wife 1765 OH of **Blue Jacket**/1735, mother of James Bluejacket/1766, Young Blue Jacket (2)/1770, Marie Louise Bluejacket/1774, Sally Bluejacket/1776, Nancy Bluejacket/1778, George Bluejacket/1780-all 3/4th Pekowi-Kishpoko-Metis

CHILDREN OF BLUE JACKET/1735 WITH OLDER DAUGHTER OF YOUNG RISING SUN/1739

SON

Blue Jacket, Young aka **Young Whirlpool**-Blue Jacket (2) -Son of Blue Jacket - 3/4th Pekowi-Kishpoko-Creek-Metis born 1756 OH-**killed** 1792 OH - son of **Blue Jacket**/1735 & **Older Daughter of Young Rising Sun**/1739, grandson (through father) of **Pride Opessa**/1710 & **Sarah Rising Sun**/1715, great-grandson (through mother) of **James McQueen**/1700, half-brother (through mother) of **Thick Water**/1770, Cornstalk War/1774-77, Blue Jacket War/1777-92, **killed** in raid, not acknowledged after 1809 by the sons of Clear Water Baby for some reason, 2nd cousin of **Tecumseh**/1768, husband 1st about 1776 OH of **Pekowi Woman**/1760, partner 2nd 1780 OH of **Maria Knodler**

Hon/1750-adopted-white, children **with Pekowi**/1776-92 names unknown likely (may have been called Bluejacket's), father **with Hon** of Jim Bluejacket/1790-3/8th Pekowi-Kishpoko-Creek-Metis, other children/1780-92 **with Hon** likely (may have been called Bluejacket's)

SON

Bluejacket, Spy Beech aka **Spybeech**- 3/4th Pekowi-Kishpoko-CreekMetis born 1758 OH-died after 1817 - son of **Blue Jacket**/1735 & **Older Daughter of Young Rising Sun**/1739, grandson (through father) of **Pride Opessa**/1710 & **Sarah Rising Sun**/1715, great-grandson (through mother) of **James McQueen**/1700, half-brother (through mother) of **Thick Water**/1770, Blue Jacket War/1777-94, delegate to D.C. 1802 with brother **Wayweleapee, John Perry, Quaskee Black Hoof, Spy Buck, Joseph Parks & Francois Duchoquet**, Prophet's Town/1811, War of 1812- Thames/1813 with 2nd cousin **Tecumseh**, disowned after the death of Blue Jacket 1809 by the sons of Clear Water Baby for some reason, an elder at Wapaghonettat 1817, husband 1778 OH of **Chalakatha Woman**/1763, children unknown

SON

Bluejacket, Wayweleapee aka Waywalapee-Waywalaapee-Wayweleapee-Clearwater - 3/4th Pekowi-Kishpoko-Creek-Metis born 1760 OH-died 1843 KS - son of **Blue Jacket**/1735 & **Older Daughter of Young Rising Sun**/1739, grandson (through father) of **Pride Opessa**/1710 & **Sarah Rising Sun**/1715, great-grandson (through mother) of **James McQueen**/1700, half-brother (through mother) of **Thick Water**/1770, Blue Jacket War/1777-94, 2nd cousin of **Tecumseh**, scout-**with U.S. Army**-War 1812, delegate to D.C. 1802 with brother **Spy Beech, John Perry, Quaskee Black Hoof, Spy Buck, Joseph Parks & Francois Duchoquet**, an Elder at Wapaghonettat 1817, Treaty 1817, moved to KS by 1833, **3rd Chief** 1833 OH-KS under **John Perry**/1775, disowned by the sons of Clear Water Baby after Blue Jacket's death 1809 for some reason, husband 1780 OH of **Mekoche Woman**/1765, children unknown

SON

Shawnee Heritage II

Bluejacket, George (1) aka **Son of Blue Jacket**- 3/4th Pekowi-Kishpoko-Creek Metis born 1762 OH-**killed** 1813 Kingston CAN - son of **Blue Jacket**/1735 & **Older Daughter of Young Rising Sun**/1739, grandson (through father) of **Pride Opessa**/1710 & **Sarah Rising Sun**/1715, great-grandson (through mother) of **James McQueen**/1700, halfbrother (through mother) of **Thick Water**/1770, Blue Jacket War/178094, **with British Army**-War 1812, **killed** at Kingston CAN 1813, 2nd cousin of **Tecumseh**/1768, disowned by the sons of Clear Water Baby after the death of Blue Jacket 1809 for some reason, husband 1st about 1782 OH of **Catherine Hon**/1768-adopted white, 2nd 1795 OH of **Kishpoko Woman**/1780, father **with Hon** of five children/1782-94 names unknown-all 3/8th Pekowi-Kishpoko-Creek-Metis, **with Kishpoko** of eight children/1796-1812 (all may have been called Bluejacket's)

WITH MARGARET MOORE/1746

SON

Bluejacket, Joseph aka **Joseph Moore** - 1/2 Pekowi-Kishpoko-Metis born 1763 Scioto River OH-died before 1817 likely OH - son of **Blue Jacket**/1735 & **Margaret Moore**/1746-adopted white, grandson (through father) of **Pride Opessa**/1710 & **Sarah Rising Sun**/1715, raised by Blue Jacket after Margaret returned to the whites, Blue Jacket War/1780-94, War 1812-Thames/1813 with 2nd cousin **Tecumseh**, husband about 1783 OH of **Pekowi Woman**/1766, any wife & children unknown

DAUGHTER

Bluejacket, Nancy aka **Nancy Moore**-Nancy Stewert - 1/2 PekowiKishpoko-Metis born 1765 Hampshire Co WV-died 1840 Logan Co OH - daughter of **Blue Jacket**/1735 & **Margaret Moore**/1746-adopted white, granddaughter (through father) of **Pride Opessa**/1710 & **Sarah Rising Sun**/1715, born after Margaret returned to the whites, moved to OH about 1804, living at Lewistown OH 1817, 2nd cousin of **Tecumseh**, wife about 1785 WV of **James Stewert**/1765-white, mother of Elizabeth Stewert/1786, Henry Stewert/1788, Margaret Stewert/1790, John

Stewert/1792 & Sarah Ann Stewert/1794-all 1/4th Pekowi-KishpokoMetis

WITH CLEARWATER BABY/1750

SON

Bluejacket, James Teaskoota aka Thucusca-Teawascoota - 3/4th Pekowi-Kishpoko-Metis born 1766 Scioto River OH-died about 1845 KS - son of **Blue Jacket**/1735 & **Clear Water Baby**/1750, grandson (through father) of **Pride Opessa**/1710 & **Sarah Rising Sun**/1715, (through mother) of **Jacques Duperon Baby**/1733 & a **Pekowi Woman**, Blue Jacket War/1783-94, War 1812-Thames/1813 with 2nd cousin **Tecumseh**, Treaty 1814, 1817, moved to KS with Wyandot 1842, husband 1784 OH of **Wyandot Woman**/1770, father of James Patexie Bluejacket/1785 & Charles Bluejacket (1)/1790-3/8th Pekowi-Kishpoko-Wyandot-Metis

SON

Blue Jacket, Young (2) aka Son of Blue Jacket – 7/8th Kishpoko-PekowiMetis born about 1770 OH-**killed** 1792 OH – son of **Blue Jacket**/1735 &
Clear Water Baby/1750, grandson (through father) of **Pride Opessa**/1710 & **Sarah Rising Sun**/1715, (through mother) of **Jacques Duperon Baby**/1733 & a **Pekowi Woman**, **killed** in battle, called a large & muscular man, any wife & children unknown

DAUGHTER

Bluejacket, Marie Louise aka Mary Blue Jacket - 3/4th PekowiKishpoko-Metis born 1774 OH-died 1806 Detroit MI - daughter of **Blue Jacket**/1735 & **Clear Water Baby**/1750, granddaughter (through father) of **Pride Opessa**/1710 & **Sarah Rising Sun**/1715, (through mother) of **Jacques Duperon Baby**/1733 & a **Pekowi Woman**, 2nd cousin of
Tecumseh, wife 1790/church marriage 1801 Detroit MI of **JacquesCoco Lassalle**/1767-Metis, mother of Marie Antoinette Lassalle/1791, Jacques Lassalle Jr/1801, Susannah Lassalle/1804, Julia Lassalle/1806all 3/8th Pekowi-Kishpoko-Metis

DAUGHTER

Bluejacket, Sally - 3/4th Pekowi-Kishpoko-Metis born 1778 OH-died after 1823 MI - daughter of **Blue Jacket**/1735 & **Clear Water Baby**/1750, granddaughter (through father) of **Pride Opessa**/1710 & **Sarah Rising Sun**/1715, (through mother) of **Jacques Duperon Baby**/1733 & a **Pekowi Woman**, wife 1st 1794 of **William Short**/1774white, (abandoned by Short when he returned to ENG), 2nd 1799 **Charles Wilson**/1782, left Wilson when she joined followers of **Tecumseh** to go to CAN 1815, mother **with Short** of Thomas Short/1795-3/8th Pekowi-Kishpoko-Metis & **with Wilson** of Thomas Wilson (3)/1800-29/64th Chalakatha-Kishpoko-Thawikila-Black-Creek-Cherokee-Metis

DAUGHTER

Bluejacket, Nancy aka **Wanasee** - 3/4th Pekowi-Kishpoko-Metis born 1778 OH-died 1876 Wyandotte Co KS – daughter of **Blue Jacket**/1735 & **Clear Water Baby**/1750, granddaughter (through father) of **Pride Opessa**/1710 & **Sarah Rising Sun**/1715, (through mother) of **Jacques Duperon Baby**/1733 & a **Pekowi Woman**, 2nd cousin of **Tecumseh**, moved to KS 1832, not known to have married

SON

Bluejacket, George (2) - 3/4th Pekowi-Kishpoko-Metis born 1780 Mad River OH-died 1829 Piqua OH - son of **Blue Jacket**/1735 & **Clear Water Baby**/1750, grandson (through father) of **Pride Opessa**/1710 & **Sarah Rising Sun**/1715, (through mother) of **Jacques Duperon Baby**/1733 & a **Pekowi Woman**, Blue Jacket War/1786-94, translator-**with British Army**-War of 1812-Thames/1813 with 2nd cousin **Tecumseh**, husband about 1798 OH of **Kishpoko Woman**/1783, father of Henry Bluejacket/1799, George Bluejacket Jr/1802, Betsy Bluejacket/1806, Kate Bluejacket/1810, John Bluejacket/1814, Charles Bluejacket/1816all 7/8th Kishpoko-Pekowi-Metis, other children likely

GRANDCHILDREN OF BLUE JACKET/1735 BY YOUNG BLUE JACKET-YOUNG WHIRLPOOL/1756

WITH PEKOWI WOMAN/1760

UNKNOWN

BY YOUNG WHIRLPOOL-BLUE JACKET/1756
WITH MARIA KNODLER HON/1750

GRANDSON

Bluejacket, Jim aka Little Blue Jacket - 3/8th Pekowi-Kishpoko-CreekMetis born about 1790 OH-**killed** 1812 - son of **Young Whirlpool-Blue Jacket**/1756 & **Maria Knodler Hon**/1750-adopted white, Prophet's
Town/1811, allied with 3rd cousin/uncle **Tecumseh**, killed by **Beaver**Delaware while attempting to assassinate **William Henry Harrison**, any wife & children unknown

BY SPYBEECH/1758
WITH CHALAKATHA WOMAN/1763

UNKNOWN

BY WAYWELEAPEE/1760
WITH MEKOCHE WOMAN/1765

UNKNOWN

BY GEORGE-SON OF BLUEJACKET (1)/1762
WITH CATHERINE HON/1768

UNKNOWN

BY GEORGE-SON OF BLUEJACKET (1)/1762
WITH KISHPOKO/1780

UNKNOWN

BY JOSEPH MOORE/1763
WITH PEKOWI/1766

UNKNOWN

BY NANCY MOORE/1765
WITH JAMES STEWERT/1765

GRANDAUGHTER

Stewert, Elizabeth - 1/4th Pekowi-Kishpoko-Metis born about 1786 WV died after 1820 OH? - daughter of **Nancy Bluejacket Moore**/1765 & **James Stewert**/1765-white, granddaughter of **Blue Jacket**/1735 & **Margaret Moore**/1746, partner 1801 WV of **Unknown Man**, wife 1809 OH of **Thomas Miranda**/1781-3/8th Pekowi-Seneca-Metis, mother **with Unknown** of Anna Stewert/1802-1/8th Pekowi-Kishpoko-Metis, children **with Miranda** unknown

GRANDSON

Stewert, Henry - 1/4th Pekowi-Kishpoko-Metis born about 1788 WV died after 1820 OH? - son of **Nancy Moore-Bluejacket**/1765 & **James Stewert**/1765-white, grandson of **Blue Jacket**/1735 & **Margaret Moore**/1746, no wife or children of record

GRANDDAUGHTER

Stewert, Margaret - 1/4th Pekowi-Kishpoko-Metis born about 1790 WV died after 1820 OH? - daughter of **Nancy Moore-Bluejacket**/1765 & **James Stewert**/1765-white, granddaughter of **Blue Jacket**/1735 &

Margaret Moore/1746, no husband or children of record

GRANDSON

Stewert, John - 1/4th Pekowi-Kishpoko-Metis born about 1792 WV-died after 1820 OH? - son of **Nancy Moore Bluejacket**/1765 & **James Stewert**/1765-white, grandson of **Blue Jacket**/1735 & **Margaret Moore**/1746, no wife or children of record

GRANDDAUGHTER

Stewert, Sarah Ann - 1/4th Pekowi-Kishpoko-Metis born about 1794 WV-died after 1820 OH? - daughter of **Nancy Moore Bluejacket Moore**/1765 & **James Stewert**/1765-white, granddaughter of **Blue Jacket**/1735 & **Margaret Moore**/1746, wife 1812 OH of **Jonathan Miranda**/1784-3/8th Pekowi-Seneca-Metis, children unknown

BY JAMES TEASKOOTA BLUE JACKET/1766 WITH WYANDOT/1770

GRANDSON

Bluejacket, James **Patexie** aka James Bluejacket Jr - 3/8th Pekowi-Kishpoko-Wyandot-Metis born 1785 Maumee Rapids OH-died 1848 KS - son of **James Teaskoota Bluejacket**/1765 & **Wyandot Woman**/1770, grandson of **Blue Jacket**/1735 & **Clearwater Baby**/1750, War 1812Thames/1813 with 3rd cousin/uncle **Tecumseh**, moved to KS 1832, husband about 1805 of **Pekowi Woman**/1790, 2nd 1834 KS of **Mathahpease**/1790-1/2 Pekowi-Wyandot, father **with Pekowi** of David Bluejacket/1805-11/16th Pekowi-Kishpoko-Metis, **with Mathahpease** of Mary Wahpanasee Bluejacket/1835, Stephen Bluejacket/1840 & Rebecca Bluejacket/1848-all 7/16th PekowiKishpoko-Wyandot-Metis

BY YOUNG BLUE JACKET (2)/1770

UNKNOWN

BY MARIE LOUISE BLUEJACKET/1774 WITH JACQUES COCO LASSALLE/1767

GRANDDAUGHTER

Lassalle, Marie Antoinette aka Mary Anne-Nanette - 3/8th PekowiKishpoko-Metis born 1791 MI-died 1881 - daughter of **Marie Louise Bluejacket**/1774 & **Jacques Lassalle**/1767, granddaughter of **Blue Jacket**/1735 & **Clearwater Baby**/1750, wife 1817 Sandwich CAN of her half-uncle **Thomas Caldwell**/1788-1/8th Pekowi-Metis, mother of John Caldwell/1818, Charles Caldwell/1819, Mary Adeline Caldwell/1820, Francis Xavier Caldwell/1823, William Charles Caldwell/1826, Anthony Edward Caldwell/1827, Joseph Hubert Caldwell/1830, Teresa Caroline Caldwell/1832, Susanne Emily Caldwell/1838-all 1/4th Pekowi-Kishpoko-Metis

GRANDSON

Lassalle, Jacques Jr - 3/8th Pekowi-Kishpoko-Metis born 1802 MI-died 1827 MI - son of **Marie Louise Bluejacket**/1774 & **Jacques Lassalle**/1767-Metis, grandson of **Blue Jacket**/1735 & **Clearwater Baby**/1750, wife & children unknown

GRANDDAUGHTER

Lassalle, Julia - 3/8th Pekowi-Kishpoko-Metis born 1806 MI-died after 1840 - daughter of **Marie Louise Bluejacket**/1774 & **Jacques Lassalle**/1767-Metis, granddaughter of **Blue Jacket**/1735 & **Clearwater Baby**/1750, wife 1822 Detroit MI of **Lambert Leduc (dit Percy)**/1797, mother of James LeDuc/1823, Lambert LeDuc/1827, Angeline LeDuc/1829, Emily LeDuc/1830, Mary Adeline LeDuc/1832, Francis LeDuc/1836, Alexander Leduc/1840-all 3/16th Kishpoko-Pekowi-Metis

BY SALLY BLUEJACKET/1776 & WILLIAM SHORT/1774

GRANDSON

Short, Thomas - 3/8th Pekowi-Kishpoko-Metis born about 1795 Maumee River OH-died after 1833 MI? - son of **Sally Bluejacket**/1776 & **William Short**/1774-white, grandson of **Blue Jacket**/1735 & **Clearwater Baby**/1750, husband about 1820 OH of **Wyandot Woman**/1804, father of Joseph Short/1833-3/16th Pekowi-KishpokoWyandot-Metis

BY SALLY BLUEJACKET/1776 & CHARLES WILSON/1782

GRANDSON

Wilson, Thomas (3) – 29/64th Chalakatha-Kishpoko-Pekowi-ThawikilaBlack-Creek-Cherokee-Metis born about 1800-died after 1815 - son of **Sally Bluejacket** (Short)/1776 & **Charles Wilson**/1782, grandson of
Blue Jacket/1735 & **Clearwater Baby**/1750, taken by father when Sally left with followers of Tecumseh for CAN 1815, wife & children unknown

BY NANCY WANASEE BLUEJACKET/1778

NO KNOWN GRANDCHILDREN

BY GEORGE BLUEJACKET (2)/1780 & KISHPOKO/1784

GRANDSON

Bluejacket, Henry - 7/8th Kishpoko-Pekowi-Metis born 1799 Huron River MI-died 1855 Johnson Co KS - son of **George Bluejacket (2)**/1780 & **Kishpoko Woman**/1784, grandson of **Blue Jacket**/1735 & **Clearwater Baby**/1750, **with British Army**-War 1812-Thames/1813 with 3rd cousin/uncle **Tecumseh**, moved to KS 1832, husband 1st about 1820 OH of **Kishpoko Woman**/1805, 2nd by 1837 Johnson Co KS of **Eliza Chowapea**/1818-Pekowi, children/1820-38 **with Kishpoko** unknown, father **with Chowapea** of Stephen Bluejacket/1838, Thomas Bluejacket/1841, Sarah E. Bluejacket/1844, Silas Armstrong

Shawnee Heritage II

Bluejacket/1848, Isaac Bluejacket/1852, Emma Bluejacket/1854, Joseph Bluejacket/1856-all 15/16th Pekowi-Kishpoko-Wyandot-Metis, adopted father of Eliza's son **George Sarcoxie**/1836-1/2 Pekowi-Metis

GRANDSON

Bluejacket, George **Nawahtahth**a aka George Bluejacket Jr - 7/8th Kishpoko-Pekowi-Metis born 1802 Piqua OH-died 1867 Johnson Co KS - son of **George Bluejacket (2)**/1780 & **Kishpoko Woman**/1784, grandson of **Blue Jacket**/1735 & **Clearwater Baby**/1750, moved to KS 1832, Treaty 1854, husband about 1825 OH or by 1837 KS of **Mary Blackhoof**/1810-Thawikila-Mekoche, father of William George Bluejacket/1838, Charles Bluejacket/1846, Mary Bluejacket/1849, James Bluejacket/1851-all 15/16th Kishpoko-Pekowi-Thawikila-MekocheMetis

GRANDDAUGHTER

Bluejacket, Betsy – 7/8th Kishpoko-Pekowi-Metis born 1806 Huron River MI-died after 1847 KS – daughter of **George Bluejacket (2)**/1780 & **Kishpoko Woman**/1784, granddaughter of **Blue Jacket**/1735 & **Clearwater Baby**/1750, wife 1827 Shelby Co OH of **Joseph Barnett (3)**/1807, mother of Joseph Barnett/1834, Cassius Clay Barnett/1837, Louisa Esther Barnett/1844, Charles Graham Barnett/1846 & Mary E. Barnett/1847-all 9/16th Pekowi-Kishpoko-Wyandot-Metis

GRANDDAUGHTER

Bluejacket, Kate – 7/8th Kishpoko-Pekowi-Wyandot-Metis born 1810 (MI?)-died 1835 KS – daughter of **George Bluejacket (2)**/1780 & **Kishpoko Woman**/1784, granddaughter of **Blue Jacket**/1735 & **Clearwater Baby**/1750, wife by 1832 of **Charles Journeycake-Neshapanacumin**/1811-1/8th Thawikila-Delaware-Metis, children unknown

GRANDSON

Bluejacket, John **Ukalwe** – 7/8th Kishpoko-Pekowi-Metis born 1814 OHdied after 1832 KS – son of **George Bluejacket (2)**/1780 & **Kishpoko Woman**/1784, grandson of **Blue Jacket**/1735 & **Clearwater Baby**/1750, moved to KS 1832, husband by 1834 KS of **Mary Pekowi**/1816, father of

Sarah Bluejacket/1835 & Susan Bluejacket/1840-both 15/16th Pekowi-Kishpoko-Metis

GRANDSON

Bluejacket, Charles Kalue aka **Rev. Charles** Bluejacket - 7/8th KishpokoPekowi-Metis born 1816 Huron River MI-died 1897 Craig Co OK - son of **George Bluejacket (2)**/1780 & **Kishpoko Woman**/1784, grandson of
Blue Jacket/1735 & **Clearwater Baby**/1750, a minister, moved to KS 1832, a 32nd Degree Mason, husband 1st 1833 KS of **Pawasee Pekowi**/1815, 2nd 1843 KS of **Julia Ann Dougherty**/1815-1/2 PekowiSeneca, 3rd 1871 of **Louisa Captain**/1850-55/64th Mekoche-Chalakatha-
Metis, father **with Pawasee** of child/1834, Maciwapeasill/1836 & Robert Bluejacket/1840-all 15/16th Pekowi-Kishpoko-Metis, **with Dougherty** of Sarah Bluejacket/1844, David Likens Bluejacket/1846, Joseph Armstrong Bluejacket/1848, Angeline Bluejacket/1850, Price K. Bluejacket/1854, Willis G. Bluejacket/1856, Silas Daugherty Bluejacket/1858, Henry Clay Bluejacket/1860, Julia Ann Bluejacket/1863, Richard M. Bluejacket/1866 & 3 other children-all 11/16th Pekowi-Kishpoko-Seneca-Metis, **with Captain** of 6 daughters & 3 sons

Black Hoof/1730

Black Hoof aka **Catahekassa** – Thawikila born 1730 FL-AL-TN-KY?died 1831 OH – son of **Wood Deer Hoof**/1682 & **Little Sugar**/1684both Thawikila, may have been during a northern sojourn of his family (sister married in north 1730), could recall early childhood along the Gulf of Mexico, with Thawikila in AL-FL 1740, moved to TN-KY by 1750, moved to OH by 1754, Cornstalk War/1755-74, a **Thawikila Chief** in OH about 1763, moved to AL late in 1774, returned to OH about 1777, Blue Jacket War /1777-94, family/band stayed in OH when most of Thawikila moved to MO starting in 1779, **succeeded Black Fish as Head Chief of All Shawnee** 1779-when **leadership splits between Black Hoof**-(Head Chief of the Thawikila & Pekowi) & **Moluntha**(Head Chief of the Mekoche & Chalakatha), with some Kishpoko split among the groups), (split = 3 groups-**Black Hoof** in OH, **Capt. Johnny** in MO

& **Blue Jacket** in OH), Treaty Greenville 1795-never opposed the whites again, Delegation to Congress 1779, 1802, Grand Council 1763, 1782, 1791, 1805, 1815, signed Complaint to U.S. 1809 with **Helizikinopo Cornstalk**, her brother **Big Snake**, her nephew **Capt. Snake**-all Mekoche, **Wahappi**-Delaware & **Beaver**-Delaware, **refused Tecumseh, succeeded 1831 as Chief by John Perry**, one of the **Seven Brothers**, husband 1st 1750 OH of **Thawikila Woman**/1735, 2nd about 1790 OH of **Rabbit -Nenexsa**/1770-Rabbit Clan Mekoche, father **with Thawikila** of Quasakee/1759, Daughter/1761, Falling TreePeaitchtha/1763, Young Black Hoof/1770, Little Fox/1780-all Thawikila, **with Rabbit** of Thomas Blackhoof/1790, Mary Blackhoof/1810, Eli Blackhoof/1820-Thawikila-Mekoche, many other children by both wives very likely

PARENTS OF BLACK HOOF/1730

FATHER

Wood Deer Hoof – Thawikila born about 1682 Sciota River OH-died about 1758 OH – **parents unknown**, moved to AL by 1715, moved to TN-KY about `1728, living near the Ohio River 1730, moved to AL-FL by 1740, moved back to TN-KY by 1750, moved to OH 1754, may have died in epidemics of 1758, husband about 1702 OH of **Little Sugar**/1688, father of unknown childen/1703-14, **Wife of Moluntha**/1715, **Black Stump**/1720, **Kikusgowlawa**/1722, **Weasau**/1724, **Capt. Johnny-Kekewepelethee**/1726, **Yellow Hawk**/1728, **Black Hoof**/ 1730, **Kishkalwa-Tiger Tail**/1735-all Thawikila

MOTHER

Little Sugar – Thawikila born about 1688 Sciota River OH-died about 1758 OH – **parents unknown**, moved to AL by 1715, moved to TN-KY about `1728, living near the Ohio River 1730, moved to AL-FL by 1740, moved back to TN-KY by 1750, moved to OH 1754, may have died in epidemics of 1758, wife about 1702 OH of **Wood Deer Hoof**/1682, mother of unknown children/1703-14, **Wife of Moluntha**/1715, **Black Stump**/1720, **Kikusgowlawa**/1722, **Weasau**/1724, **Capt. Johnny-**

Kekewepelethee/1726, **Yellow Hawk**/1728, **Black Hoof**/ 1730, **Kishkalwa-Tiger Tail**/1735-all Thawikila

SIBLINGS OF BLACK HOOF/1730

SISTER

Black Hoof, Sister of aka Wife of Moluntha – Thawikila born about 1715 AL-died about 1755 OH – daughter of **Wood Deer Hoof**/1682 & **Little Sugar**/1688-both Thawikila, living moved to TN-KY about ˋ1728, near the Ohio River 1730, wife about 1730 OH-KY of **Moluntha**/1708Mekoche, mother of Daughter of Moluntha/1754 & many younger children

BROTHER

Black Stump aka **Ciuxa**-Seeookska –Thawikila born about 1720 ALdied after 1787 MO – son of **Wood Deer Hoof**/1682 & **Little Sugar**/1688-both Thawikila, living near the Ohio River 1730, with Thawikila in AL-FL 1740, moved to TN-KY by 1750, moved to OH by 1754, Cornstalk War/1755-74, Grand Council June 1762, a **Thawikila Chief** in OH before 1763, Treaty Camp Charlotte 1774, move south to AL late 1774, returned to OH 1777, moved to MO 1779 with (likely relatives) **Red Eagle & Red Snake**, brothers **Kikusgowlawa**, **Yellow Hawk** & 400 families, one of the **Seven Brothers**, wife & children unknown

BROTHER

Kikusgowlawa aka Keekoosgowlawa – Thawikila born 1722 AL-died after 1779 (MO?) - son of **Wood Deer Hoof**/1682 & **Little Sugar**/1688both Thawikila, living near the Ohio River 1730, with Thawikila in ALFL 1740, moved to TN-KY by 1750, moved to OH by 1754, Cornstalk War/1755-74, a **Thawikila Chief** in OH before 1763, moved to AL late 1774, returned to OH/1778, moved to MO/1779 with **Black Stump, Yellow Hawk, Red Eagle, Red Snake** & 400 families, one of the **Seven Brothers**, wife & children unknown

BROTHER

Weasau aka Wausawsa-Wayahsahoo – Thawikila born about 1724 ALdied after 1798 (AL?) - son of **Wood Deer Hoof**/1682 & **Little Sugar**/1688-both Thawikila, living near the Ohio River 1730, with Thawikila in AL-FL 1740, moved to TN-KY by 1750, moved to OH by 1754, Cornstalk War/1755-74, a **Thawikila Chief** in OH by 1763, moved to AL 1774-after Point Pleasant/74, may have returned to OH 1777, returned to AL about 1779, called **King of the Sawanogi (**Shawnee among the Creek) 1798, may have returned north after 1798, one of the **Seven Brothers**, husband 1st about 1744 AL-TN of **Thawikila Woman**/1729, 2nd about 1780 of **Creek (or Thawikila-Creek) Woman**/1764, father **with Thawikila** of Young Weasau/1760, children **with Creek-Thawikila-Creek** unknown

BROTHER

Capt. Johnny (1) aka **Kekewepelethee**-Kekewapiletee-Kakawipilathee-Tame Hawk-Aholdkawah-Scares Up Game-Kaykaywaypaylaythay – Thawikila born about 1726 AL-died shortly after 1810 likely MO – son of **Wood Deer Hoof**/1682 & **Little Sugar**/1688-both Thawikila, living near the Ohio River 1730, with Thawikila in AL-FL 1740, moved to TNKY by 1750, moved to OH by 1754, Cornstalk War/1755-77, a **Thawikila Chief** in OH by 1763, moved to AL with Thawikila band late 1774, returned to OH 1778, Blue Jacket War/1778-92, Council 1785 Wapakonetta with **Alexander McKee, Matthew Elliott & James Sherlock**, Council Miami Jan. 1786, Treaty Ft. Finney 1786, sided **with Moluntha over his brother Black Hoof** when Shawnee split in 1779, became **Head Chief of Moluntha faction** 1786 upon death of Moluntha (**Blue Jacket** was leader of an opposing faction within the group), Grand Council Nov. 1792, moved to MO 1st 1779 then permanently by 1792 & leadership of Shawnee splits (= 3 groups-Black Hoof in OH, Capt. Johnny in MO & Blue Jacket in OH), Council Swan Creek OH with **Black Beard, Bukangolas & George Ironside**, Council with **Black Beard, Borer, Buffalo & Capt. Mayne**-ENG, Council 1808 with **Black Oak & Buffalo**, Council Brownstown 1810, one of the **Seven Brothers,** husband 1st about 1745 AL-TN of **Thawikila Woman**/1730, 2nd 1755 OH of **Adopted White Woman**/1725, children/1745-50 **with Thawikila** unknown, children/1755-70 **with Adopted White** unknown

BROTHER

Yellow Hawk aka **Othawapeelethee**-Othahwahpaylaythay – Thawikila born about 1728 KY-died after 1817 MO – son of **Wood Deer Hoof**/1682 & **Little Sugar**/1688-both Thawikila, with Thawikila in ALFL 1740, moved to TN-KY by 1750, moved to OH by 1754, Cornstalk War/1755-74, **Thawikila Chief** in OH by 1768, moved to AL 1774 after Point Pleasant/1774, returned to OH 1778, moved to MO 1779 with **Black Stump, Kikusgowlawa, Red Eagle, Red Snake** & 400 families, possibly returned to OH by 1785, **succeeded Black Snake as a Civil Chief** of **Black Hoof**'s faction 1785, Treaty 1817, one of the **Seven Brothers**, husband by 1750 TN-KY of **Duck Laying Eggs**/1730-Thawikila, children unknown

BROTHER

Kishkalwa (1) aka **Tiger Tail**-Keeshkalwah – Thawikila born about 1735 KY-TN-died before 1832 MO – son of **Wood Deer Hoof**/1682 & **Little Sugar**/1688-both Thawikila, with Thawikila in AL-FL 1740, moved to TN-KY by 1750, moved to OH, by 1754, Cornstalk War/175574, a **Thawikila Chief** in OH before 1774, moved to AL 1774 after Point Pleasant/1774, returned to OH 1779, moved to MO about 1790, took no part in Blue Jacket War or War 1812, Delegation to D.C. 1825, succeeded by **Jim Squire-Paylawestha** as a **major Chief in MO**, youngest of the **Seven Brothers**, husband 1st by 1755 OH of **Thawikila Woman**/1740,
2nd about 1773 OH of **Gray Eyes**/1750-adopted white, father **with Thawikila** of Young-Kishkalwa/1760, Pamaloois/1770 & other children/1755-73, father **with Gray Eyes** of daughter Tohsi/1774, son Seleetha/1775 & 7 other sons-all 1/2 Thawikila-Metis

WIVES OF BLACK HOOF/1730

WIFE 1750 - OH

Thawikila Woman - born about 1735 (AL?)-died about 1790 – **name & parents unknown**, 1st wife 1750 KY-TN of **Black Hoof**/1730, mother of Quasakee/1759, Daughter/1761, Falling Tree-Peaitchtha/1763, Young Black Hoof/1770, Little Fox/1780-all Thawikila

WIFE 1790 - OH

Rabbit aka Nenexsa-**Neneksa**-Naynaykska – Mekoche born about 1770 OH-died after 1832 KS - **parents unknown**, Rabbit Clan, 2nd wife about 1790 OH of **Black Hoof**/1730, moved to KS 1832 after death of Black Hoof, mother of Thomas Blackhoof/1790, Mary Blackhoof/1810, Eli Blackhoof/1820, other children likely

CHILDREN OF BLACK HOOF/1730 BY THAWIKILA WOMAN/1735

SON

Blackhoof, **Quasakee** aka Kwasahkay– Thawikila born about 1759 OHdied 1853 KS - oldest son of **Black Hoof**/1730 & **Thawikila Woman**/1735, moved to AL 1774 with family, returned to OH 1777, Blue Jacket War /1778-94, never opposed whites after Treaty of Greenville 1795, delegate to D.C. 1802 with **Wayweleapee, John Perry, Spy Buck, Joseph Parks & Francois Duchoquet**, an elder at Wapaghonettat 1817, Treaty 1817, moved to KS 1832 after death of father, husband 1780 OH of **Rabbit (1)-Nenuxse**/1764-Rabbit Clan Thawikila, father of Thomas Blackhoof (1)-Young Quasakee/1785-Thawikila

DAUGHTER

Black Hoof, Daughter of aka Wife of Squirrel - Thawikila born about 1761 OH-died after 1832 KS - daughter of **Black Hoof**/1730 & **Thawikila Woman**/1735, moved to AL 1774, returned to OH 1777, wife about 1778 OH of **Squirrel**/1750-Thawikila, mother of James Squirrel/1800-Thawikila

SON

Blackhoof, Falling Tree aka **Peaitchtha**-Pht-Peethatha-Payaheetchthah – Thawikila born about 1764 OH-died 1832 OH - son of **Black Hoof**/1730 & **Thawikila Woman**/1735, moved to AL 1774 with family, returned to OH 1777, Blue Jacket War /1782-94, never opposed whites after 1795, a **Thawikila Head Chief** at Hog Creek 1817, Treaty 1817, 1831, husband

1784 OH of **Pony Racer-Montagnaia**/1768, father of Quintilla-Deborah Arvilla/1786-Thawikila

SON

Black Hoof, Young – Thawikila born about 1770 OH-died after 1854 KS - son of **Black Hoof**/1730 & **Thawikila Woman**/1735, moved to AL 1774 with family, returned to OH 1777, Blue Jacket War /1788-94, never opposed Americans after Fallen Timber/1794, a Thawikila warrior 1817, moved to KS before 1832, Treaty 1854, wife & children unknown

SON

Blackhoof, Little Fox aka **Naecimo**-Nahayseemo – Thawikila born about 1780 OH-died after 1835 KS - youngest son of **Black Hoof**/1730 & **Thawikila Woman**/1735, a Thawikila warrior at Hog Creek 1817, Treaty 1831, moved to KS 1832, **a Sub-chief** in KS 1835 under **John Perry** & **William Perry**, wife & children unknown

BY RABBIT-NENEXSA/1770

SON

Blackhoof, Thomas (2) – Thawikila-Mekoche born about 1790 OH-died after 1855 KS - son of **Black Hoof**/1730 & **Rabbit (2)-Nenexsa**/1770, moved to KS 1832, husband about 1810 OH of **Lenagess-Rabbit**/1793-Rabbit Clan, children unknown

DAUGHTER

Blackhoof, Mary – Thawikila-Mekoche born about 1810 OH-died after 1851 KS - daughter of **Black Hoof**/1730 & **Rabbit-Nenexsa**/1770, moved to KS 1832, wife 1825 OH or by 1837 KS of **George Bluejacket Jr**/1802, mother of William George Bluejacket/1838, Charles Bluejacket/1846, Mary Bluejacket/1849, James Bluejacket/1851 & other children-all 15/16th Pekowi-Kishpoko-Thawikila-Mekoche-Metis

SON

Blackhoof, Eli – Thawikila-Mekoche born about 1820 OH-died after 1856 KS - son of **Black Hoof**/1730 & **Rabbit-Nenexsa**/1770, moved to

KS 1832, John Perry Co-**with U.S. Army**-Seminole War/1837, husband 1st about 1840 KS of **Unknown Woman**, 3rd husband 1856 KS of **Eliza Chowapea** (Sarcoxie Blue Jacket) /1818, children unknown

GRANDCHILDREN OF BLACK HOOF/1730
BY QUASKEE/1759 & RABBIT-NENUXSE/1764

GRANDSON

Blackhoof, Thomas (1) aka Young Quasakee - Thawikila born about 1785 OH-died 1856 KS - son of **Quasakee Black Hoof**/1759 & **Rabbit (1)-Nenuxse**/1764, moved to KS before 1832, wife & children unknown

BY DAUGHTER/1762 & SQUIRREL-ANEQUEPI/1750

GRANDSON

Squirrel, James – Thawikila born about 1800 OH-died after 1832 KS - son of **Daughter of Black Hoof**/1761 & **Squirrel-Anequepi**/1750, wife & children unknown

BY FALLING TREE-PEAITCHTHA/1764 & PONY RACER-MONTAGNAIA

Blackhoof, Deborah Arvilla aka **Deborah Arvilla Gilbert** –Thawikila born 1786 OH-died after 1868 – daughter of **Falling Tree Black Hoof**/1764 & **Pony Racer-Montaignaia**/1768, adopted daughter 1790 of **Moses Gilbert** & **Lydia Mallory**, wife 1st of **Joseph G. Walton** (died 1840), 2nd 1843 of **Anthony Hall** (died 1868), mother **with Walton** of Rebecca M. Walton-(wife of Adam White), Olive G. Walton--died 1841- (wife of Samuel L. Watt), Arvilla Walton-died 1857- (wife of Abraham Hall), Harriet E. Walton-(wife of John Strickell), Lydia G.-Shining Star Walton/1813-1880- (wife 1st of Lodi Shawnee-died 1832, wife 2nd 1833 of William M. Hall-died 1881)-all ½ Thawikila-Metis

BY YOUNG BLACK HOOF/1770

UNKNOWN

BY LITTLE FOX-NAECIMO/1780

UNKNOWN

BY THOMAS BLACKHOOF/1790 & RABBIT-LENAGESS/1793

UNKNOWN

BY MARY BLACKHOOF/1810 & GEORGE BLUEJACKET JR/1802

GRANDSON

Bluejacket, William George aka Pahlahcha - 15/16th Pekowi-Thawikila-Metis born about 1838 KS-died 1861 (OK?) - son of **George Bluejacket Jr**/1802 & **Mary Blackhoof**/1810-Thawikila, husband about 1857 KS of **Jane Celequa Rogers**/1838, father of Moses Bluejacket/1858-25/32nd Pekowi-Thawikila-Chalakatha-Kishpoko-Mekoche-Metis

GRANDSON

Bluejacket, Charles (3) - 15/16th Pekowi-Thawikila-Metis born about 1846 KS-died after 1865 (OK?) - son of **George Bluejacket Jr**/1802 & **Mary Blackhoof**/1810-Thawikila, wife & children unknown

GRANDDAUGHTER

Bluejacket, Mary (2) - 15/16th Pekowi-Thawikila-Metis born about 1849 KS-died after 1865 (OK?) - daughter of **George Bluejacket Jr**/1802 & **Mary Blackhoof**/1810-Thawikila, husband & children unknown

GRANDSON

Bluejacket, James (3) - 15/16th Pekowi-Kishpoko-Thawikila-Metis born about 1851 KS-died 1874 - son of **George Bluejacket Jr**/1802 & **Mary Blackhoof**/1810, grandson of **Black Hoof**/1730, great-grandson of **Blue Jacket**/1735, wife & children unknown

BY ELI BLACKHOOF/1820
UNKNOWN WOMAN

UNKNOWN

BY ELI BLACKHOOF/1820
& ELIZA CHOWAPEA/1818

UNKNOWN

Puckenshinwa Rising Sun/1735

Rising Sun, Puckenshinwa aka Pookaynsheenwah-PukenshinwaPuckinshinoawa-Alights from Flying-Alight From Flying-Something
Coming Downward - 1/2 Kishpoko-Creek-Metis born 1735 Tuckabatchee AL-**killed** 1774 Point Pleasant WV - son of **Young Rising Sun**/1710 & **Older Daughter of James McQueen**/1720, grandson of **Rising Sun (1)**/1685 & of **James McQueen**/1700-white, nephew of **Sarah Rising Sun**/1715-mother of Blue Jacket, father returned to AL from the Lehigh valley PA about 1730, a Kishpoko from AL, moved to KY 1759-to OH 1760, French-Indian War in south/1754-58, Cornstalk War/1759-74, Grand Council June 1762, Sept. 1762, 1763, Council Bouquet Oct. 1764, **Head Chief of Kishpoko in OH** by 1770, **killed** in battle at Point Pleasant 1774, brother of **Older Sister**/1739-(1st wife of **Blue Jacket**) & **Younger Sister-Mary**/1745-(wife of **David Mumagechee Francis**), husband 1755 AL of **Metheotashe OpessaStraight Tail**/1738-Pekowi, father of son **Cheeseekau**/1756 AL, daughter **Tecumapease**/1758 AL, son Sauwaseekou/1760 KY,

(daughter Rising Star/1762 OH?), son Nahaaseema/1764 OH, daughter Menewaulakoose/1766 OH, sons **Tecumseh**/1768 OH, Kumshaka/1770 OH , daughter Vocemassussia/1772 OH & son **Lalawethika**-Tenskawatawa-Shawnee Prophet/1774 OH -all 3/4th Kishpoko-Pekowi-Creek-Metis, adopted father 1760 OH of **Joshua Renicks**/1746, 1768 OH of **John Sparks**/1760 & **Richard Sparks**/1757, 1772 OH of **Stephen Ruddell**/1767

WIFE 1755 - AL

Straight Tail, Metheotashe aka Mary Opessa-Metheotashe OpessaMeetheeotashe-Methotasa-Turtle Laying Eggs – Pekowi born 1738 ALdied 1789 MO - daughter of **Loyparcoweh Straight Tail**/1702 & **Nancy Pekowi**/1706, namesake of her father's 1st cousin **Mary Chartier/**1688 who had just been murdered, a Pekowi from Souvanogee (Shawnee) village AL, 1st cousin of **Blue Jacket** & his siblings-(fathers were brothers), aunt of **Tecumoplas-Margaret Collins**/1742 & great-aunt of **Jane Collins**/1768, moved 1759 from AL to KY, moved 1760 from KY to OH, widowed 1774-lived with relatives in the **Black Fish** family/1774, moved 1779 to Apple Creek village MO with daughters **Menewaulakoose**/1764 & **Vocemassussia**/1771, wife 1st 1755 AL of **Puckenshinwa Rising Sun**/1735-1/2 Kishpoko-Creek-Metis-(widowed 1774), 2nd 1775 OH of **Young Hard Striker-Pucksinwa Pheasant**/1738Pekowi-(widowed the same year), mother **with Puckenshinwa** of son **Cheeseekau**/1756 AL, daughter **Tecumapease**/1758 AL, son Sauwaseekou/1760 KY, (daughter Rising Star/1762 OH?), son Nahaaseema/1764 OH, daughter Menewaulakoose/1766 OH, sons **Tecumseh**/1768 OH, Kumshaka/1770 OH , daughter Vocemassussia/1772 OH & son **Lalawethika**-Shawnee Prophet/1774 OH -all 3/4th Kishpoko-Pekowi-Creek-Metis, adopted mother 1760 OH of **Joshua Renicks**/1746, 1768 OH of **John Sparks**/1760 & **Richard ShawunteSparks**/1765, 1772 OH of **Stephen Big Fish Ruddell**/1767 & **Abraham Black Hawk Ruddell**/1764, all adopted children went to other families in extended family upon death 1774 of Puckenshinwa, no known child **with Young Hard Striker**

CHILDREN

SON

Rising Sun, **Cheeseekau** aka Chiksika-Cheeseequa-Sting-A **Snake Biting**-Snakebite-Passquannakeek-Gunshot-Shawnee Warrior - 3/4th Kishpoko-Pekowi-Creek-Metis born 1756 AL-**killed** 1792 Buchanan Station TN - eldest son of **Puckenshinwa Rising Sun**/1735 & **Metheotashe Straight Tail**/1738, grandson of **Loyparkoweh**/1702, a **Kishpoko** War Chief, Point Pleasant/1774-75-78, Blue Jacket War/177792, raiding TN-KY-VA-OH/1777-81 **with Dragging Canoe** & **Chief Bob Benge**, Council Miami Jan. 1786, took sons by Kishpoko Woman with him to TN, an original Chickamauga/1777, living in Running Water (Shawnee) village 1789-92 **with Tecumseh**, killed leading Shawnee contingent **at Buchanan Station TN**, husband 1st 1776 OH of **Kishpoko Woman**/1760, 2nd 1780 TN of **Eyoostee Dragging Canoe**/1756, father **with Kishpoko** of Tecumqualuska-Graybeard/1777 & Great Shawnee Warrior/1780-both 7/8th Kishpoko-Pekowi-Creek-Metis & likely another child or two, father **with Dragging Canoe** of TeciekeapeaseGenevieve Marie/1790 & Daughter/1792-both 31/64th ChalakathaKishpoko-Thawikila-Pekowi-Creek-Cherokee-Metis, other children likely

DAUGHTER

Rising Sun, **Tecumapease** aka **Crossing The Water**-Tecumesa - 3/4th Kishpoko-Pekowi-Creek-Metis born 1758 AL-died 1815 Windsor CAN - oldest daughter of **Puckenshinwa Rising Sun**/1735 & **Metheotashe Straight Tail**/1738, granddaughter of **Loyparkoweh Opessa**/1702, moved to CAN 1815 with family & died there soon after, wife 1st 1773 OH of **Mink-Chaquiweshe**/1740-Mekoche, **widowed 1774**, 2nd 1775 OH of **Mathias Splitlog**/1758-Wyandot, 3rd 1779 OH **Stands FirmWasegobah**/1755-adopted-Chippewa, **widowed 2nd time 1813**, mother **with Mink** of Big Horn-Capt. Logan/1774-7/8th Kishpoko-MekochePekowi-Creek-Metis, no known children/1775-79 **with Mathias**, mother **with Stands Firm** of LaNanette Tecumapease-NanetteMaryanne/1780 & other 3/8th Kishpoko-Chippewa-Pekowi-CreekMetis children/1782-1805, (often confused with sisters & nieces by some white histories)

SON

Rising Sun, Sauwaseekou aka Sauwaseekou-**Panther Crouching for Prey** - 3/4th Kishpoko-Pekowi-Creek-Metis born 1760 KY-**killed** 1791 OH – 2nd son of **Puckenshinwa Rising Sun**/1735 & **Metheotashe Straight Tail**/1738, grandson of **Loyparkoweh**/1702, a Kishpoko warrior, born in KY during move from AL to OH, Blue Jacket War/1777-91, **killed 1791 at St. Clair**, husband by 1780 OH of **Unknown Woman**/1765-(Shawnee or white?), children/1780-91 unknown

(POSSIBLE DAUGHTER?)

Rising Sun, Rising Star - 3/4th Kishpoko-Pekowi-Creek-Metis born 1762 OH-died after 1778 – possible second daughter of **Puckenshinwa Rising Sun**/1735 & **Metheotashe Straight Tail**/1738, granddaughter of **Loyparkoweh**, husband & children unknown

SON

Rising Sun, Nahaasema aka Nahaaseema - 3/4th Kishpoko-PekowiCreek Metis born 1764 OH-**killed** 1788 KY - 3rd son of **Puckenshinwa**
Rising Sun/1735 & **Metheotashe Straight Tail**/1738, grandson of **Loyparkoweh**/1702, Blue Jacket War/1782-88, **killed 1788 in KY raid**, husband about 1784 OH of **Unknown Woman**/1769-(Shawnee or white?), children/1785-88 unknown

DAUGHTER

Rising Sun, Menewaulakoose aka Menewalakosi-**Lying Piled in a Hollow** - 3/4th Kishpoko-Pekowi-Creek-Metis born 1766 OH-died after 1819 MO – 2nd (known) daughter of **Puckenshinwa Rising Sun**/1735 & **Metheotashe Straight Tail**/1738, granddaughter of **Loyparkoweh**/1702, moved 1779 to Apple Creek village MO **with Metheotashe**, her marriage was opposed by brothers Cheeseekau & Tecumseh, wife 1782 MO of **Antoine Francois Maisonville**/1760adopted-French/Canadian, mother of Francois Maisonville/1791-3/8th Kishpoko-Pekowi-Creek-Metis (often confused with her sisters by some white histories)

SON

Rising Sun, Tecumseh aka Panther in the Sky-Panther Leaping at Prey-Tecumseh Puckenshinwa-Tecumshe-Tecumthe-Tecoomteh-Tecoomti Tecomteh- 3/4th Kishpoko-Pekowi-Creek-Metis born 1768 Chillicothe OH-**killed** 1813 Thames River CAN - 4th son of **Puckenshimwa Rising Sun**/1735 & **Metheotashe Opessa**/1738, grandson of **Loyparkoweh Opessa**/1702 & of **Young Rising Sun**/1710, great-grandson of **James McQueen**/1700, namesake of his great-uncle **Tecoomteh Opessa**/1698, a Kishpoko War Chief at times, Blue Jacket War/1786-94, lived-raided 1790-93 **with the Chickamaugua** & his brother **Cheeseekua** in TN, returned north after death of Cheeseekau, raiding OH-WV-VAKY/1793-99, absent from Prophet's Town/1811, reportedly a **Colonel with British Army**-War 1812 (War 1812 = Brownstown/1812-Monguagon/1812-1st Amherstburg/1812-Frenchtown/1813-Ft. Meigs/1813-2nd Amherstburg/1813-Thames/1813), **killed at Thames**/1813, Council Miami 1786, Grand Council 1791, traveled much of 1795-1811 soliciting support for united Native force, Council Vincennes July & Aug. 1810, Council Amherstburg Mar. 1812, Council Massinawa May 1812, met with **Isadore Chesne** near Ft. Wayne June 1812, met with **Gen. Isaac Brock** at Amherstburg 1812, reportedly a member of the Masons in CAN, called the last great leader of Eastern Natives though officially never more than a War Chief, nephew/2nd cousin of **Red Pole**-(mother's 1st cousin), 2nd cousin/uncle of **Seekaboo**(by mother's niece), cousin by marriage of **Anthony Shane**-(husband of 1st cousin **Lemateshe Blackfish**), step-2nd cousin of **Bright Horns**-(son of step-1st cousin **Sarah Rising Sun**), uncle of **Big Horns-Capt./John Logan**-(son of sister **Tecumapease** & **Mink**), uncle/2nd cousin of **Otter**(nephew of uncle **Mink**-husband of **Tecumapease**), uncle/2nd cousin of **David Deshane**-(son of 1st cousin **Lematashe Blackfish**), relative-same clan as **Elk in Water-Tekuntequa**, **Turkey Foot (2)**, **Turkey Foot (3)** & **Turtle**, husband 1st 1788 OH of **Monetoshe Opessa**/1770, 2nd 1789 OH of **Mamate Baby**/1774, 3rd 1790 OH of **Elizabeth Galloway**/1777adopted white, 4th 1790 Running Water TN **Dark Star-Tahneh-Slow Head-Naomi Hop**/1769, 5th 1793 OH of **White Wing-Big Nancy Cornstalk** (Adkins)/1770, 6th 1800 IN of **Wasigezeegoqua Poc**/1785Pottawamee, 7th 1802 OH of **Wabelegunequa Half Moon**/1785, 8th by 1805 IN **Winnipegoosqua Sturgeon**/1790-Chippewa, father **with**

Monetoshe of Mahyawekawpawe/1788-7/8th Kishpoko-Pekowi-CreekMetis, **with Mamate** of Naythahwaynah/1790-5/8th Kishpoko-Pekowi-Creek-Metis, **with Galloway** of Michelana/1790 & Rebecca Galloway/1792-both 3/8th Kishpoko-Pekowi-Creek-Metis, **with Dark Star** of Lydia Tecumseh/1790, Tecumtequah/1792 & Daughter/1794-all 43/64th Kishpoko-Pekowi-Shawano-Chalaka-Powhatan-CreekCherokee-Metis, **with White Wing** of Paukeesaa/1794, Adjala/1796 & Serena/1798-all 19/32nd Chalakatha-Mekoche-Kishpoko-Pekowi-Shawano-Chalaka-Powhatan-Creek-Metis, **with Wasigezeegoqua** of Pottawamee Son/1801, Elder Pottawamee Child/1803 & Younger Pottawamee Child/1805-all 3/8th Kishpoko-Pekowi-Creek-Pottawamee-Metis, no children/1802-07 **with Half Moon**, father **with Winnipegoosqua** of Child/1806, Child/1808, Child/1810, Child/1812all 3/8th Kishpoko-Pekowi-Creek-Chippewa Metis, other unknown children with unknown women possible

SON

Rising Sun, Kumshaka aka Kunshauskau-**Cat Flying In Air** - 3/4th Kishpoko-Pekowi-Creek-Metis born 1770 OH-died before 1824 CAN - 5th son of **Puckenshinwa Rising Sun**/1735 & **Metheotashe Straight Tail**/1738, grandson of **Loyparkoweh**/1705, a Kishpoko warrior, Blue Jacket War/1787-94, raiding OH-KY-VA-TN/1795-1810, Prophet's Town/1811, War 1812- Thames/1813 **with Tecumseh**, moved to CAN 1815, died before band returned to OH 1825, husband about 1790 OH of **Kishpoko Woman**/1774, children/1790-1815 unknown

DAUGHTER

Rising Sun, Vocemassussia aka Isabella-Vokemassussia - 3/4th Kishpoko-Pekowi-Creek Metis born 1772 OH-died after 1815 - youngest daughter of **Puckenshinwa Rising Sun**/1735 & **Metheotashe Straight Tail**/1738, granddaughter of **Loyparkoweh**/1705, wife 1st 1786 OH of **Thomas Split Log**/1756-Wyandot, 2nd 1792 of **George Ironside Sr**/1760-adopted white-(Church married to Ironside 1810 at St. John's Parrish, Anglican Church), children/1786-91 **with Split Log** unknown, mother of **with Ironside** of Alexander Ironside/1793, George Ironside Jr/1806, 2 sons & 2 daughters/1794-1815-all 3/8th Kishpoko-Pekowi-Creek Metis, (often confused with sisters by some white histories)

SON

Rising Sun, Lalawethika aka Tenskawatawa-**Shawnee Prophet**-Open Door-Laulewashika-Lalawetheeka-Rattling Sound in Brush - 3/4th Kishpoko-Pekowi-Creek-Metis born 1774 OH-died 1837 KS - youngest son of **Puckenshinwa Rising Sun**/1735 & **Metheotashe Straight Tail**/1738, grandson of **Loyparkoweh**/1705, a Kishpoko, only one of triplet sons to survive infancy, youngest brother of **Tecumseh**, Fallen Timbers/1794, Council Greenville 1795, moved to IN 1798, defeated by **William Henry Harrison** at Prophet's Town aka Tippicanoe/1811, took little active (warrior) part in Tecumseh's campaign of 1795-1810 or War of 1812, moved 1815 to CAN with band of followers & family of Tecumseh, returned to OH 1825, moved to KS 1826 with nephew **Paukeesaa Tecumseh**, married 5 times, husband 1st about 1792 OH of **Kishpoko Woman**/1776, again by 1814 (IN-OH?) of **Pricilla Perkins**/1795-adopted white, other 3 wives unknown for now, father **with Kishpoko** of John Prophet/1792, 1 other son & 3 daughters-all 7/8th Kishpoko-Pekowi-Creek-Metis, **with Perkins** of Marcia Bates/1814-3/8th Kishpoko-Pekowi-Creek-Metis, children **with other wives** unknown

GRANDCHILDREN

By CHEESEEKAU/1756 & KISHPOKO WOMAN/1760

GRANDSON

Cheeseekau, Tecumqualuska aka Graybeard - 7/8th Kishpoko-Pekowi-Creek-Metis born 1777 OH-died after 1848 OK - son of **Cheeseekau Rising Sun**/1756 & **Kishpoko Woman**/1760, came south 1789 with father & uncle Tecumseh, remained with step-mother **Eyoostee Dragging Canoe**/1756 & Chickamauga after death 1792 of **Cheeseekau**, from Running Water (Shawnee) village, moved west on Trail of Tears, husband about 1795 TN of **Chickamaugua**

Woman/1780, father of Johnson Graybeard/1821-7/16th Kishpoko-Pekowi-Creek-Cherokee-Metis

GRANDSON

Cheeseekau, Great Shawnee Warrior aka Great Shawnee Warrior (2)Young Shawnee Warrior – 7/8th Kishpoko-Pekowi-Creek-Metis born 1780 OH-**killed** 1810 Yahoo Falls KY - son of **Cheeseekau** Rising Sun/1756 & **Kishpoko Wife**/1760, raiding KY-VA-TN/1797-1810, **killed Yahoo Falls**/1810, nephew of **Tecumseh**/1768, husband 1798 of **Chickamauga Woman**/1782, father of Tommy Bright Star/1798-7/16th Kishpoko-Pekowi-Creek-Cherokee-Metis

By CHEESEEKAU/1756
& EYOOSTEE DRAGGING CANOE/1756

GRANDDAUGHTER

Cheeseekau, Teciekeapease aka Teseekeapease-Genevieve Marie – 31/64th Kishpoko-Pekowi-Chalakatha-Thawikila-Creek-Cherokee-Metis born about 1790-died 1838 - daughter of **Cheeseekau** Rising Sun/1756 & **Eyoostee Dragging Canoe**/1756, half-sister of Graybeard/1777 & Great Shawnee Warrior (2)/1780, living at Apple Creek village MO by 1807 with mother, wife 1808 of 1st cousin (son of her aunt Menewaulakoose/1765) **Francois Maisonville**/1791, mother of Francois Maisonville Jr/1811, Modest Maisonville/1819, Angelica Maisonville/1826 & 9 other children/1809-25-all 5/16th KishpokoPekowi-Chalakatha-Thawikila-Creek-Cherokee-Metis

GRANDDAUGHTER

Cheeseekau, Daughter of - 31/64th Kishpoko-Pekowi-ChalakathaThawikila-Creek-Cherokee-Metis born 1792 TN-died after 1807 - daughter of **Cheeseekau Puckenshinwa**/1756 & **Eyoostee Dragging Canoe**/1756, half-sister of **Graybeard**/1777 & **Great Shawnee Warrior (2)**/1780, living at Apple Creek village MO by 1807 with mother, husband & children unknown

By TECUMAPEASE/1758 & MINK-CHAQUIWESHE/1740

GRANDSON

Logan, Capt. John aka **Big Horn**-High Horn-Spencialawbe-**Capt. Logan** - born 1774 OH-**killed** 1812 OH - 7/8th Mekoche-Kishpoko-PekowiCreek-Metis - son of **Tecumapease** Rising Sun/1758 & **Mink Mekoche**/1740, a Mekoche warrior, captured at Moluntha's village 1786 during Benjamin Logan's raid, raised & given white name by **Col. Benjamin Logan**-white, translator, scout-**with U.S. Army**-Prophet's Town/1811 & War 1812, killed in battle with **Winnemak**-Pottawamee & British supporters, 1st cousin of **Tecumseh**/1768, **Big Capt. Johnny**/1765, **Bright Horn**/1770, **Otter**/1770, husband 1st 1789 OH of **Blue Bird**/1775-Mekoche, 2nd 1804 OH of **Spamaghlebee**/1790Mekoche, father **with Blue Bird** of Red Leaf Logan/1790, Cagashee Logan/1796, Aqueshka Logan/1795 & **with Spamaghlebee** of James Logan/1805-all 15/16th Mekoche-Kishpoko-Pekowi-Creek-Metis

By TECUMAPEASE/1758 & MATHIAS SPLITLOG/1756

UNKNOWN

BY TECUMAPEASE/1758 & STANDS FIRM-WASEGOBAH/1755

GRANDDAUGHTER

LaNanette aka Nanette-Maryanne - 3/8th Kishpoko-Pekowi-CreekChippewa-Metis born about 1780 OH-died after 1850 - daughter of **Tecumapease** Rising Sun/1758 & **Stands Firm-Wasegobah**/1755, granddaughter (by Stands Firm) of **White Sturgeon**/1730-Chippewa & (by Tecumapease) of **Puckenshinwa**/1735 & **Metheotashe**/1738, niece of **Tecumseh**/1768, **Yellow Cloud**/1760-adopted-Chippewa & **Mad**

Sturgeon/1765-Chippewa, 1st wife about 1796 of her uncle (cousin of her mother) **Billy Caldwell**/77, children unknown

By SAUWASEEKOU/1760 & UNKNOWN WOMAN
CHILDREN/1780-91 UNKNOWN

By RISING STAR/1762
UNKNOWN

By NAHAASEMA/1764 & UNKNOWN WOMAN
CHILDREN/1785-88 UNKNOWN

By MENEWAULAKOOSE/1766 & ANTOINE FRANCOIS MAISONVILLE/1760
GRANDSON

Maisonville, Francois aka Francois Maisonville Rivard dit LorangerLacullotte - 3/8th Kishpoko-Pekowi-Creek-Metis born about 1791 MOdied about 1756 - from Apple Creek village MO, son of **Menewaulakoose**/1766 & **Antoine Francois Maisonville**/1750adopted French-Canadian-Metis, nephew of **Tecumseh**/1768, nephew & son in law of **Cheeseekau**/1756, husband 1808 MO of 1st cousin **Genevieve Marie-Teciekeapease Cheeseekau**/1791-31/64th Kishpoko-Pekowi-Chalakatha-Thawikila-Creek-Cherokee-Metis, father of Francois Maisonville Jr/1811, Modest Maisonville/1819 & Angelica Maisonville/1826 & 9 other children/1808-25-all 5/16th KishpokoPekowi-Chalakatha-Thawikila-Creek-Cherokee-Metis

By TECUMSEH/1768 & MONETOSHE-RESTING SNAKE/1770

Shawnee Heritage II

GRANDSON

Tecumseh, Mahyawekawpawe aka **Young Tecumseh**-True Stepper**McLaughlin** - 7/8th Kishpoko-Pekowi-Creek-Metis born about 1788
OH-died 1868 KS - son of **Tecumseh**/1768 & **Monetoshe Opessa**/1770-Pekowi, a Kishpoko warrior, Prophet's Town/1811, War 1812-Thames/1813 **with his father Tecumseh**, Treaty 1817, didn't go to CAN 1815, moved to MO 1815, moved to KS **with Prophet** & **Paukeesaa** 1826, he or his children took white surname of **McLaughlin** or **Laughlin** in MO/KS, husband before 1826 (OH?) of **Tawpama**/1800-Mekoche, father of 5 children-at least one a daughter

By TECUMSEH/1768 & MAMATE BABY/1774

GRANDSON

Tecumseh, Naythahwaynah aka Panther Seizing Prey-**Young Tecumseh** - 5/8th Kishpoko-Pekowi-Creek-Metis born about 1790 OHdied about 1826 KS - son of **Tecumseh**/1768 & **Mamate Baby**/1774, a Kishpoko warrior, Prophet's Town/1811, War 1812-Thames/1813 **with his father Tecumseh**, moved to CAN 1815, returned to OH about 1825, moved to KS 1826 with **Prophet** & half-brother **Paukeesaa**, died shortly after arriving in KS, husband 1810 OH of **Sokomsee Kishpoko**/1795, father of twin daughters Maythahskse & Waylahse/1816, son Jim Fry/1818, daughters Nahswahpama/1820, Pahsequahmease/1822 & son Big Jim Tecumseh/1824-all 13/16th Kishpoko-Pekowi-Creek-Metis(become step-children of **Wapakwaha**/1795-Kishpoko)

By TECUMSEH/1768 & ELIZABETH GALLOWAY/1777

Grandson
Tecumseh, Michelana aka Machielaini-**Tecumseh's Son** - 3/8th Kishpoko-Pekowi-Creek-Metis born 1790 OH-**killed** 1839 (AR-OK?) - son of **Tecumseh**/1768 & **Elizabeth Galloway**/1777, stayed with the Shawnee when his mother returned to the whites, a Kishpoko

warrior/leader, Prophet's Town/1811, War 1812-Thames/1813 **with his father Tecumseh**, living in Apple Creek MO 1815, apparently didn't go to CAN 1815, moved to KS 1826 with Prophet & Paukeesaa, led group of mixed Natives from KS to AR 1839, group was **attacked & killed** by either Comanche's or whites in route to AR, wife & children unknown

GRANDDAUGHTER

Galloway, Rebecca - 3/8th Kishpoko-Pekowi-Creek-Metis born 1792 KYdied 1876 Greene Co OH – daughter of **Tecumseh**/1768 & **Elizabeth Galloway**/1777, born after her mother's return to the whites, adopted by her mother's uncle **James Galloway**/1750, taken to his home in OH & raised as his daughter, often visited by Tecumseh as she grew, giving rise to the silly fabrications that they were somehow lovers when it was just a father visiting a daughter he could never claim, wife 1812 Greene Co OH of a 2nd cousin **George Galloway**/1784, children unknown (but there was thought to be a daughter Rebecca)

By TECUMSEH/1768
& DARK STAR-NAOMI-TAHNEH-SLOW HEAD HOP/1769

GRANDDAUGHTER

Tecumseh, Lydia - 43/64th Kishpoko-Pekowi-Shawano-ChalakaPowhatan-Creek-Cherokee-Metis born about 1790 TN-died after 1824
AR - daughter of **Tecumseh**/1768 & **Dark Star-Tahneh-Naomi-Slow Head Hop (Benge)**/1769, sister of **Tecumtequah**/1792 & **Daughter of Tecumseh**/1794, moved to AR after 1814, wife 1808 TN of **Moses Downing**/1788, mother of daughter Dicey Downing/1808, sons James Downing/1810, Cash Downing/1812 & daughter Celia Downing/1814all 29/64th Kishpoko-Pekowi-Shawano-Chalaka-Powhatan-Creek-Cherokee-Metis

GRANDSON

Tecumseh, Tecumtequah aka Cross the Water-TakomtequaTaykoomteeqwa - 43/64th Kishpoko-Pekowi-Shawano-ChalakaPowhatan-Creek-Cherokee-Metis born 1792 NC-died after 1830 MT - son of **Tecumseh/1768** & **Dark Star-Tahneh-Naomi-Slow Head Hop (Benge)/1769**, moved to OH about 1810 to join his father, Prophet's Town/1811, War 1812-Thames/1813 **with father Tecumseh**, Treaty 1814, a Kishpoko warrior at Wapaghonettat 1817, Treaty 1817, traveled to Mississippi & Missouri valleys/1817-1826, moved to KS 1826 with uncle **Prophet** & half-brother **Paukeesaa**, moved north by 1830 to Dakotas or Montana to join his wife's people, husband 1st about 1810
OH of **Kishpoko Woman/1785**, 2nd about 1820 (SD-ND?) of **Seeshemeteh Flathead/1805**, children/1810-20 **with Kishpoko** unknown, father **with Seeshemeteh** of Angelica Josephete Cahkatshee Tecumtequah/1821-21/64th Kishpoko-Pekowi-Shawano-ChalakaPowhatan-Creek-Cherokee-Flathead-Metis, father in law of **Louis Tellier**-Metis

GRANDDAUGHTER

Tecumseh, Chickamauga Daughter of - 43/64th Kishpoko-PekowiShawano-Chalaka-Powhatan-Creek-Cherokee-Metis born about 1794 Running Water TN-died after 1812 (MO-TN?) - daughter of **Tecumseh/1768** & **Dark Star-Tahneh-Naomi-Slow Head Hop (Benge)/1769**, moved before 1812 to MO with mother, may have returned to TN after 1813, husband & children unknown

By TECUMSEH/1768 & WHITE WING-NANCY CORNSTALK/1770

GRANDSON

Tecumseh, Paukeesaa aka **Tecumseh Jr**-Pugeshashenwa-PahkeesaPahguesahah-Puchetha-Puggeesha-Panther Watching Prey – 19/32nd
Chalakatha-Mekoche-Kishpoko-Pekowi- Shawano-Chalaka-PowhatanCreek-Metis born 1794 OH-died 1843 KS - son of **Tecumseh/1768** &

White Wing Cornstalk/1770, Prophet's Town/1811, War 1812Thames/1813 **with father Tecumseh, Head Chief of Tecumseh followers in CAN** 1815 at 21 years old, succeeded 1816 by **Yealabaheah** as Head Chief in CAN, moved back to OH 1825, moved KS 1826 with his uncle **the Prophet-Lalawithika**/1774, a **Kishpoko Chief** in KS after 1826, husband 1815 CAN of **Kishpoko Woman**/1800, father of John Tecumseh/1820-51/64th Kishpoko- Chalakatha-Mekoche-Pekowi-Shawano-Chalaka-Powhatan-Creek-Metis

GRANDSON

Tecumseh, Adjala – 19/32nd Chalakatha-Mekoche-Kishpoko-Pekowi-Shawano-Chalaka-Powhatan-Creek-Metis born 1796 OH-died after 1826 (OH?) - son of **Tecumseh**/1768 & **White Wing Cornstalk**/1770, a Kishpoko warrior, Prophetstown/1811, War 1812- Thames/1813 **with father Tecumseh**, moved to CAN 1815 with band, returned to OH 1826, may have remained in OH 1826, husband 1816 CAN of **Kishpoko Woman**/1800, children unknown

GRANDDAUGHTER

Tecumseh, Serena aka Skwato – 19/32nd Chalakatha-MekocheKishpoko-Pekowi- Shawano-Chalaka-Powhatan-Creek-Metis born 1798 IN-died 1833 IN - daughter of **Tecumseh**/1768 & **White Wing Cornstalk**/1770, a Kishpoko, granddaughter-(by White Wing) of **Young Cornstalk**/1742 & **Elizabeth See**/1754-adopted white & (by Tecumseh) of **Metheotashe Opessa**/1740 & **Puckenshinwa Rising Sun**/1735, first a household servant of then 3rd wife 1808 (OH-IN?) of **William Rainey**/1776-Irish, mother of Matthew Rainey/1815-19/64th Chalakatha-Mekoche-Kishpoko-Pekowi- Shawano-Chalaka-PowhatanCreek-Metis

By TECUMSEH/1768 & WASIGEZEEGOQUA POC/1785

GRANDSON

Tecumseh, Pottawamee Son of - 3/8th Kishpoko-Pekowi-CreekPottawamee-Metis born about 1801 (IN?)-died after 1825 (WI?) - son of **Tecumseh**/1768 & **Wasigezeegoqua Poc** /1785, moved with family to WI after death/1813 of Tecumseh at Thames

GRANDCHILD

Tecumseh, Elder Pottawamee Child of - 3/8th Kishpoko-CreekPottawamee-Metis born about 1803 (IN?)-died after 1825 (WI?) - gender unknown, child of **Tecumseh**/1768 & **Wasigezeegoqua Poc** /1785, moved with family to WI after death/1813 of Tecumseh at Thames

GRANDCHILD

Tecumseh, Younger Pottawamee Child of - 3/8th Kishpoko-PekowiCreek-Pottawamee-Metis born about 1810 (IN?)-died after 1825 (WI?) - gender unknown, child of **Tecumseh**/1768 & **Wasigezeegoqua Poc** /1785, moved with family to WI after death/1813 of Tecumseh at Thames

By TECUMSEH/1768 & WINNIPEGOOSQUA STURGEON/1790

GRANDCHILD/1806

GRANDCHILD/1808

GRANDCHILD/1810

GRANDCHILD/1812

By KUMSHAKA/1770 & KISHPOKO WOMAN/1774

CHILDREN/1790-1815 UNKNOWN

By VOCEMASSUSSIA/1772 & THOMAS SPLITLOG/1756

CHILDREN/1786-91 UNKNOWN

By VOCEMASSUSSIA/1772 & GEORGE IRONSIDE/1760

GRANDSON

Ironside, Alexander - 3/8th Kishpoko-Pekowi-Creek Metis born about 1793-died after 1813 - son of **George Ironside**/1760-adopted-Irish & **Isabella-Vocemassussia Puckenshinwa**/1770 (sister of Tecumseh), **with British Army**-War 1812-Thames/1813 **with uncle Tecumseh**, wife & children unknown

GRANDSON

Ironside, George Jr - 3/8th Kishpoko-Pekowi-Creek-Metis born 1806 died 1863 - son of **George Ironside**/1760-adopted white & **IsabellaVocemassussia**/1770, Indian Agent after his father 1830-45, nephew of **Tecumseh**, husband by 1830 of **Annie Shawnee**/1810, children unknown

GRANDSON

Ironside, Son (1) of George - 3/8th Kishpoko-Pekowi-Creek Metis born between 1794-1815-died after 1832 – son of **George Ironside**/1760adopted-Irish & **Isabella-Vocemassussia Puckenshinwa**/1770 (sister of Tecumseh), wife & children unknown

GRANDSON

Ironside, Son (2) of George - 3/8th Kishpoko-Pekowi-Creek Metis born between 1794-1815-died after 1832 – son of **George Ironside**/1760adopted-Irish & **Isabella-Vocemassussia Puckenshinwa**/1770 (sister of Tecumseh), wife & children unknown

GRANDDAUGHTER

Ironside, Daughter (1) of George - 3/8th Kishpoko-Pekowi-Creek Metis born between 1794-1815-died after 1832 – daughter of **George Ironside**/1760-adopted-Irish & **Isabella-Vocemassussia Puckenshinwa**/1770 (sister of Tecumseh), husband & children unknown

GRANDDAUGHTER

Ironside, Daughter (2) of George - 3/8th Kishpoko-Pekowi-Creek Metis born between 1794-1815-died after 1832 – daughter of **George Ironside**/1760-adopted-Irish & **Isabella-Vocemassussia Puckenshinwa**/1770 (sister of Tecumseh), husband & children unknown

By LALAWETHIKA/1774 & KISHPOKO WOMAN/1776

GRANDSON

Prophet, John - 7/8th Kishpoko-Pekowi-Creek-Metis born about 1792**killed** before 1865 - son of **Kishpoko Woman**/1776 & **Shawnee Prophet-Lalawethika**/1774, Prophet's Town/1811, War 1812Thames/1813 **with his uncle Tecumseh, with Joseph Parks Co-U.S. Army-Seminole War/1837, killed during Civil War, husband 1812 (OH?) of Daughter of Spy Buck**/1798-9/16th Mekoche-ChalakathaCreek-Metis, father of John Prophet Jr/(1815?)-1/2 Kishpoko-PekowiMekoche-Chalakatha-Creek-Metis

By LALAWITHIKA/1774 & PRICILLA PERKINS/1795

GRANDDAUGHTER

Bates, Marcia - 3/8th Kishpoko-Pekowi-Creek-Metis born 1814 OH (or NY)-died 1876 MO – daughter of **Lalawethika-Shawnee Prophet**/1774 & **Pricilla Perkins**/1795, wife of **Orin B. Cummings**, children unknown

CHAPTER TWELVE

Tecumseh/1768

Lalawethika-the Prophet/1774

Tecumseh/1768 - OH

Tecumseh aka Panther in the Sky-Panther Leaping at Prey-Tecumseh Puckenshinwa-Tecumshe-Tecumthe-Tecoomteh-Tecoomti -Tecomteh-3/4th Kishpoko-Pekowi-Creek-Metis born 1768 Chillicothe OH-**killed 1813 Thames River CAN** - 4th son of **Puckenshimwa Rising Sun**/1735 & **Metheotashe Opessa**/1738, grandson of **Loyparkoweh Opessa**/1702 & of **Young Rising Sun**/1710, great-grandson of **James McQueen**/1700-(the white "governor" alluded to by the Prophet), namesake of his great-uncle **Tecoomteh Opessa**/1698, (despite what some fantasists have alleged his first real exposure to warfare apparently was during Col. Benjamin Logan's raid on the Shawnee towns in 1786), a Kishpoko War Chief at times, Blue Jacket War/178694, lived-raided 1790-92 **with the Chickamaugua** & his brother **Cheeseekua** in TN, returned north after death of Cheeseekau, (his real hatred for the Americans apparently began in 1792 with the death of Cheeseekau in TN), raiding OH-WV-VA-KY/1793-99, absent from Prophet's Town/1811, reportedly a **Colonel with British Army**-War 1812 (War 1812 = Brownstown/1812- Monguagon/1812-1st Amherstburg/1812-Frenchtown/1813-Ft. Meigs/1813-2nd Amherstburg/1813-Thames/1813), **killed at Thames**/1813, Council Miami 1786, Grand Council 1791, traveled much of 1795-1811 soliciting support for united Native force, Council Vincennes July & Aug. 1810, Council Amherstburg Mar. 1812, Council Massinawa May 1812, met with **Isadore Chesne** near Ft. Wayne June 1812, met with **Gen. Isaac Brock** at Amherstburg 1812, reportedly a member of the Masonic Lodge in CAN, called the last great leader of Eastern Natives though officially never more than a War Chief, nephew/2nd cousin of **Red Pole**-(mother's 1st cousin), 2nd cousin/uncle of **Seekaboo**-(by mother's niece), cousin by marriage of **Anthony Shane**-(husband of 1st cousin **Lemateshe Blackfish**), step-2nd cousin of **Bright Horns**-(son of step-1st cousin **Sarah Rising Sun**), uncle of **Big Horns-Capt./John Logan**-(son of sister **Tecumapease** & **Mink**), uncle/2nd cousin of **Otter**-(nephew of uncle **Mink**-the 1st husband of **Tecumapease**), uncle/2nd cousin of **David Deshane**-(son of 1st cousin **Lematashe Blackfish**), 1st cousin of **Thick Water**/1770-(son of his mother's sister, relative-same clan as **Elk in Water-Tekuntequa, Turkey Foot (2), Turkey Foot (3)** & **Turtle**, husband 1st 1788 OH of **Monetoshe Opessa**/1770, 2nd 1789 OH of **Mamate Baby**/1774, 3rd 1790 OH of **Elizabeth Galloway**/1777-(a niece of James Galloway/1750), 4th 1790 Running Water TN **Dark Star Tahneh-Slow Head-Naomi Hop** (Benge)/1769, 5th 1793 OH of **White Wing-Big Nancy Cornstalk** (Adkins)/1770, 6th 1800 IN of **Wasigezeegoqua Poc**/1785-Pottawamee, 7th 1802 OH of **Wabelegunequa Half Moon**/1785, 8th by 1805 IN **Winnipegoosqua Sturgeon**/1790-Chippewa, father **with Monetoshe** of Mahyawekawpawe/1788-7/8th Kishpoko-Pekowi-Creek-Metis, **with Mamate** of Naythahwaynah/1790-5/8th Kishpoko-Pekowi-Creek-Metis, **with Galloway** of Michelana/1790 & Rebecca Galloway/1792-(born after her mother's return to the whites & adopted by her mother's uncle James Galloway/1750)-3/8th Kishpoko-Pekowi-Creek-Metis (making Tecumseh's visits to the home of James Galloway that of a father visiting a daughter he could not claim), **with Dark Star** of Lydia Tecumseh/1790, Tecumtequah/1792 & Chickamauga Daughter/1794-all 43/64th Kishpoko-Pekowi-Shawano-Chalaka-Powhatan-CreekCherokee-Metis, **with White Wing** of Paukeesaa/1794, Adjala/1796 & Serena/1798-all 19/32nd Chalakatha-Mekoche-Kishpoko-Pekowi-Shawano-Chalaka-Powhatan-Creek-Metis, **with Wasigezeegoqua** of Pottawamee Son/1801, Elder Pottawamee Child/1803 & Younger Pottawamee Child/1805-all 3/8th Kishpoko-Pekowi-Creek-Pottawamee-Metis, no children/1802-07 **with Half Moon**, father **with Winnipegoosqua** of Child/1806, Child/1808, Child/1810, Child/1812all 3/8th Kishpoko-Pekowi-Creek-Chippewa Metis, other unknown children with unknown women possible

ANCESTORS OF TECUMSEH
(not listed elsewhere in this book)

FATHER'S GRANDFATHER

McQueen, James - white-(adopted-Creek) born about 1700-died 1811 AL – known to have lived among Creeks 1720-1811, the most influential non-government white man on the frontier in his time, husband 1st 1720 AL of **Katherine Fraser** (?)/1705-Wind Clan Creek, 2nd known before 1756 AL of **Niece of Katherine**/1740-Creek-(daughter of Brother of Katherine & Creek Woman), 3rd known by 1768 AL of **Creek-BlackMetis Woman**/1762-(daughter of Nephew of Katherine & Mulatto Woman), father **with Katherine** of Older Daughter/1720, daughters/1721-35, Daniel McQueen/1736, Nancy McQueen/1740, Mary McQueen/1745, Robert McQueen/1747 & Queen Ann-Nancy Ann McQueen/1750-all 1/2 Creek-Metis, **with Niece of Katherine** of Margaret McQueen/1757, Fulfunee McQueen/1760, John McQueen/1762, James McQueen/1770-all 1/2 Creek-Metis, **with Creek-Black-Metis** of Peter McQueen/1770, Daughter/1772, Daughter/1774, James McQueen/1776, Samuel McQueen/1778, Daughter/1780, John McQueen/1782, Rachel McQueen/1784, Donald McQueen/1788-all 1/4th Creek-Black-Metis, other children by these & other wives likely

FATHER'S MOTHER

McQueen, Older Daughter of James aka wife of Young Rising Sunmother of Puckenshinwa-wife of Red Shies Marchand - 1/2 CreekMetis born about 1720 AL-died 1748 AL - daughter of **James McQueen**/1700-white & **Katherine Fraser** (?)/1705-Wind Clan Creek, wife about 1735 AL of **Young Rising Sun**/1710, 2nd 1745 AL of **Red Shoes Marchand**/1720-1/2 Creek-Metis, mother **with Rising Sun** of Puckenshinwa/1735, child/1737, Older Daughter/1739-(1st wife of

Blue Jacket), child/1741, Younger Daughter-Mary Rising Sun/1744(wife of **David Francis**) -all 1/2 Kishpoko-Creek-Metis, **with Red Shoes** of Red Shoes (2)/1746-1/2 Creek-Metis, grandmother **through Puckenshinwa** of Cheeseekau/1756 AL, Tecumapease/1758 AL, Sauwaseekou/1760 KY, Nahaaseema/1764 OH, Menewaulakoose/1766
OH, Tecumseh/1768 OH, Kumshaka/1770 OH , Vocemassussia/1772 OH & Lalawethika-Tenskawatawa-Shawnee Prophet/1774 OH & **through Older Daughter** of Young Whirlpool/1756, Spybeech/1758, Wayweleapee/1760, George Bluejacket (1)/1760 & **through Younger Daughter-Mary of** John Francis/1760, Josiah Francis/1765, Joseph Francis/1770 & Susan Francis/1775

PARENTS OF TECUMSEH

FATHER

Rising Sun, Puckenshinwa aka Pookaynsheenwah-PukenshinwaPuckinshinoawa-Alights from Flying--Something Coming Downward -
1/2 Kishpoko-Creek-Metis born 1735 Tuckabatchee AL-**killed** 1774 Point Pleasant WV - son of **Young Rising Sun**/1710 & **Older Daughter of James McQueen**/1720, grandson of **Rising Sun (1)**/1685 & of **James McQueen**/1700-white, nephew of **Daughter of Rising Sun**/1715-(mother of Blue Jacket), father returned to AL from the Lehigh valley PA about 1730, a Kishpoko from AL, moved to KY 1759-to OH 1760, French-Indian War in south/1754-58, Cornstalk War/1759-74, Grand Council June 1762, Sept. 1762, 1763, Council Bouquet Oct. 1764, **Head Chief of Kishpoko in OH** by 1770, **killed** in battle at Point Pleasant 1774, brother of **Older Sister**/1739-(1st wife of **Blue Jacket**) & **Mary Rising Sun**/1744-(wife of **David Mumagechee Francis**), husband 1755 AL of **Metheotashe Opessa**/1738-Pekowi, father of son **Cheeseekau**/1756 AL, daughter **Tecumapease**/1758 AL, sons Sauwaseekou/1760 KY, (daughter-Rising Star/1762 OH), son Nahaaseema/1764 OH, daughter Menewaulakoose/1766 OH, sons **Tecumseh**/1768 OH, Kumshaka/1770 OH , daughter

Vocemassussia/1772 OH & son **Lalawethika**-Tenskawatawa-Shawnee Prophet/1774 OH -all 3/4th Kishpoko-Pekowi-Creek-Metis, adopted father 1760 OH of **Joshua Renicks**/1746, 1768 OH of **John Sparks**/1760 & **Richard Sparks**/1757, 1772 OH of **Stephen Ruddell**/1767, uncle of (by Sister/1745) John Francis/1760, **Josiah Francis**/1765 & Joseph Francis/1770

MOTHER

Opessa, Metheotashe aka Mary Opessa-Meetheeotashe-MethotasaTurtle Laying Eggs – Pekowi born 1738 AL-died 1789 MO - daughter of **Loyparcoweh Opessa**/1702 & **Nancy Pekowi**/1706, namesake of her father's 1st cousin **Mary Chartier/1688** who had just been murdered, a Pekowi from Souvanogee (Shawnee) village AL, 1st cousin of **Blue Jacket** & his siblings-(fathers were brothers), raised in AL by her mother's extended family, moved 1759 from AL to KY, moved 1760 from KY to OH, widowed 1774-lived with relatives in the **Black Fish** family/1774-79, moved 1779 to Apple Creek village MO with daughters **Menewaulakoose**/1764 & **Vocemassussia**/1771, wife 1st 1755 AL of **Puckenshinwa Rising Sun**/1735-1/2 Kishpoko-Creek-Metis, 2nd 1775 OH of **Young Hard Striker-Young Pucksinwa Pheasant**/1738-Pekowi-(widowed the same year), mother **with Puckenshinwa** of son **Cheeseekau**/1756 AL, daughter **Tecumapease**/1758 AL, sons Sauwaseekou/1760 KY, (daughter-Rising Star/1762 OH), son Nahaaseema/1764 OH, daughter Menewaulakoose/1766 OH, sons **Tecumseh**/1768 OH, Kumshaka/1770 OH, daughter Vocemassussia/1772 OH & son **Lalawethika**-Tenskawatawa-Shawnee Prophet/1774 OH -all 3/4th Kishpoko-Pekowi-Creek-Metis, adopted mother 1760 OH of **Joshua Renicks**/1746, 1768 OH of **John Sparks**/1760 & **Richard Sparks-Shawtunte**/1765, 1772 OH of **Stephen Ruddell-Big Fish**/1767 & **Abraham Ruddell-Black Hawk**/1764, all adopted children went to other families in extended family upon death 1774 of Puckenshinwa, no known child **with Young Hard Striker**

STEP-FATHER OF TECUMSEH
Young Hard Striker aka Young Pucksinwa-Young Hard Striker Pheasant– Pekowi born about 1738 OH-killed 1775 OH - son of **Pucksinwa-Hard Striker Pheasant**/1716 & **Pekowi Woman**/1720,

husband 1st 1758 OH of **Margaret Ice**/1741-adopted white, 2nd 1775 OH of **Metheotashe (Opessa) Rising Sun**/1738, children **with Ice** unknown, no children **with Metheotashe** but step-father for a few months of her children by Puckenshinwa

AUNTS OF TECUMSEH
SIBLINGS OF MOTHER

SISTER OF MOTHER
Wife of Thomas McKee

Opessa, Tecumsapah aka Margaret – Pekowi born about 1724 PA-died after 1769 - daughter of **Loyparkoweh Opessa**/1702 & **Nancy Pekowi**/1706, aunt of **Tecumseh**, remained in PA 1744 when **Peter Chartier** led Shawnee to OH to join the French, wife about 1738 PA of **Thomas McKee**/1695-adopted-Irish, step-mother of **Thomas McKee**/1720-adopted by the Delaware & **Col. Alexander McKee**/1725adopted by the Shawnee, mother of Alexander "Trader" McKee/1738, Nancy McKee/1740, Hugh McKee/1742, Catherine McKee/1744,
Elizabeth McKee/1746, Thomas McKee/1750, John McKee/1753, James McKee/1755-all 1/2 Pekowi-Metis

SISTER OF MOTHER
Wife of Pekowi Man

Opessa, Sarah aka Older Daughter of Loyparkaweh – Pekowi born 1727 MD-died after 1750 (OH?) - daughter of **Loyparkoweh Opessa**/1702 & **Nancy Pekowi**/1706, aunt of **Tecumseh**, moved to OH 1744 with **Peter Chartier**, may have moved to KY 1745 with Chartier, with Pekowi in the Ohio valley-west WV/east OH 1750, wife by 1742 PA of **Pekowi Man**/1722, mother of Tecumpolas-Margaret Opessa/1742, grandmother of Jane Collins/1768

SISTER OF MOTHER Watmeme
-wife of Black Fish

Opessa, Watmeme aka Polly – Pekowi born 1730 PA-died 1797 MO – daughter of **Loyparkoweh Opessa**/1702 & **Nancy Pekowi/**1706, moved to OH 1744 with **Peter Chartier**, wife 1745 OH of **Black Fish**/1725, moved to MO with adopted son Stephen Ruddle 1779, Ruddle returned to whites upon her death/1797, mother **with Black Fish** of sons Chinwa/1746, Young Black Fish (1)/1748, daughter Pimegeezhigoqua/1752, son Young Black Fish (2)/1754, daughters Chelatha/1756, Lamatashe/1758 & Parlie/1760-all ChalakathaMekoche-Pekowi, adopted mother & mother in law of **Capt. Joseph Dusquene**/1755, **Lewis Rogers**/1750 & **Henry Rogers**/1755, adopted mother 1774 of **William Jackson-Fish**/1770 & **Stephen Ruddle**/1768

SISTER OF MOTHER
Nancy-wife of Daniel McQueen

Opessa, Nancy aka Middle Daughter of Loyparkaweh – Pekowi born 1734 AL-died after 1755 (AL?) - daughter of **Loyparkoweh Opessa**/1702 & **Nancy Pekowi**/1706, a Pekowi from Souvanogee (Shawnee) village AL, wife 1st (known) by 1754 AL of **Daniel McQueen**-1/2 Creek-Metis born 1736 AL-died 1818, mother of Elder Daughter-Mother of **Seekaboo**-Niece of Metheotashe/1755, Younger Daughter/1758-(wife 1st of Thawikila Man/1755, 2nd of Robert McQueen/1747) & Joseph McQueen/1760-all 1/2 Pekowi-Creek-Metis, grandmother of **Seekaboo**/1770-3/4th Kishpoko-Pekowi-Creek-Metis

SISTER OF MOTHER Sarah-Wife
of Isadore Chesne

Opessa, Sarah aka Younger Daughter of Loyparkoweh – Pekowi born about 1736 AL-died about 1758 OH– daughter of **Loyparkoweh Opessa**/1702 & **Nancy Pekowi**/1706, wife 1754 OH of **Isadore Chesne**/1735-Wyandot-Metis, mother of Mary Shane/1754 & Capt. Joseph Dusquene/1756-1/2 Pekowi-Wyandot-Metis-(adopted-Chippewa)

OLDER SISTER OF FATHER
Wife 1st of Blue Jacket

Wife 2nd of Isadore Chesne
Wife 3rd of Big Swamp

Rising Sun, Older Daughter of Young aka Older Sister of Puckenshinwa-wife of Blue Jacket-wife of Isadore Chesne-wife of Big Swamp - 1/2 Kishpoko-Creek-Metis born 1739 AL-died about 1774 OH - daughter of **Young Rising Sun**/1710 & **Daughter of James McQueen**/1720-1/2 Creek-Metis, appears to have returned north (OH?) about 1745 with their father, 1st wife 1st 1755 OH of 1st cousin **Blue Jacket**/1735-Kishpoko-Pekowi, (remarried when Blue Jacket had a son by Margaret Moore-white), 2nd 1762 OH of **Isadore Chesne**/1735Wyandot-Metis, 3rd 1769 OH of **Big Swamp**/1730, mother **with Blue Jacket** of Young Blue Jacket-Young Whirlpool/1756, Spybeech/1758, Wayweleapee/1760 & George Bluejacket (1)/1762-all 3/4th KishpokoPekowi-Creek-Metis, **with Chesne** of Anthony Shane-Chesne/1763 & Joseph Shane-Chesne/1765-both 1/4th Kishpoko-Creek-Wyandot-Metis, **with Big Swamp** of Thick Water/1770-3/4th Kishpoko-Creek-Metis

SISTER OF FATHER

Mary-Wife of David Francis

Rising Sun, Mary aka Younger Daughter of Young Rising Sun-Younger Sister of Puckenshinwa-wife of David Francis - 1/2 Kishpoko-Creek-Metis born 1745 AL-died after 1805 - daughter of **Young Rising Sun**/1710 & **Older Daughter of James McQueen**/1720-1/2 Creek-Metis, remained in the south when their father returned to the north, aunt of **Tecumseh**, wife 1759 AL of **David Mumagechee Francis**/1740, mother of John Francis/1760, Josiah Francis/1765, Joseph Francis/1770 & Susan Francis/1775-all 29/64th Kishpoko-Chalakatha-MekocheShawano-Chalaka-Powhatan-Metis

UNCLES BY MARRIAGE OF TECUMSEH

HUSBAND 1738 PA OF TECUMSAPAH

McKee, Thomas - white born 1695 Antrim IRE-died 1772 Harrisburg PA - son of **Alexander McKee**-Irish born 1665-IRE-died 1740 Lancaster Co PA & **Catherine Unknown**/1670, moved to PA about 1735 with father **Alexander McKee**/1665, brother **Patrick McKee**/1690 & **2 other brothers** (an Alexander & James or John?) & sons **Thomas Pelewiechen McKee**/1720-adopted by the Delaware & **Col. Alexander Wapimescheu McKee**/1725-adopted by the Shawnee, 1st about 1715 IRE of **Elizabeth Gordon**/1700, 2nd 1738 PA of **Tecumsapah-Margaret Opessa**/1724-Pekowi, father **with Elizabeth Gordon** of Thomas McKee/1720 & Col. Alexander McKee/1725 & a daughter-wife of Mr. Surphlet, **with Tecumsapah-Margaret Opessa** of Alexander "Trader" McKee/1738, Nancy McKee/1740, Hugh McKee/1742, Catherine McKee/1744, Elizabeth McKee/1746, Thomas McKee/1750, John McKee/1753, James McKee/1755-all 1/2 Pekowi-Metis

HUSBAND 1742 MD OF SARAH OPESSA-OLDER DAUGHTER OF LOYPARKOWEH

Pekowi Man – born about 1722 PA-died after 1747 – among group that left PA 1744 with Peter Chartier, in Lower Shawnee Town 1745, moved to KY 1746, moved to AL 1747, husband 1742 MD of **Sarah Opessa-Older Daughter of Loyparkoweh**/1727, father of TecumpolasMargaret Opessa/1742, grandfather of Jane Collins/1768

HUSBAND 1745 OH OF WATMEME-POLLY

Black Fish aka **Chiungulla**-Cheeoongoola-Paheataheaseka-Makadaywahmayquah – Chalakatha-Mekoche born about 1725 PAkilled 1779 KY - son of **Fish Clan Chalakatha Chief**/1705 & **Sister of Moluntha**/1710-Mekoche, raised Chalakatha by father's family after father's death 1739, Cornstalk War/1755-77, Grand Council 1763, **succeeded Cornstalk as Head Chief of Chalakatha & All Shawnee** in 1777, led 300+ warriors at Point Pleasant/1778 **with Half King**Wyandot, **killed** in KY raid/1779, step-half-brother of **Blue Jacket** (through marriage of **his Mother**/1710 to **Pride Opessa**/1710 who was also married to **Sarah Rising Sun**/1715), was referred to as the uncle of **Tecumseh**, brother in law of **Isadore Chesne**/1735-(they married

Shawnee Heritage II

sisters), husband 1745 OH of **Watmeme Opessa**/1730-Pekowi, father with **Watmeme** of sons Chinwa/1746, Young Black Fish (1)/1748, daughter Pimegeezhigoqua/1752, son Young Black Fish (2)/1754, daughters Parlie/1756, Lamateshe/1758 & Cheletha/1760-all Chalakatha-Mekoche-Pekowi, adopted father 1760 of brothers **Lewis Rogers**/1750 & **Henry Rogers**/1755, adopted father about 1770 of **William Jackson-Fish**/1760-white, adopted father 1774 of **Stephen Ruddle-Big Fish**/1768, adopted father & father in law 1778 of **Capt. Joseph Duquesne**/1756-1/2 Pekowi-Wyandot-Metis

HUSBAND 1754 AL OF NANCY OPESSA-MIDDLE DAUGHTER OF LOYPARKOWEH

McQueen, Daniel - 1/2 Creek-Metis born about 1736-died 1818- son of **James McQueen**/1700 & **Katherine Fraser**/1705-Creek, husband 1st 1754 AL of **Nancy Opessa-Middle Daughter of Loyparkaweh**/1734, father of Elder Daughter-Margaret McQueen--mother of Seekaboo/1755, Younger Daughter –Sarah McQueen-wife of Robert McQueen/1758 & Joseph McQueen/1760-all 1/2 Pekowi-Creek-Metis, grandfather of **Seekaboo**/1770

HUSBAND 1754 OH OF SARAH OPESSA-YOUNGER DAUGHTER OF LOYPARKOWEH

Chesne, Isadore aka Shetoon-Hayanemadae - 1/2 Wyandot-Metis(adopted-Chippewa) - born about 1735-died 1828 - son of **Catherine Sauvage**/1695-Wyandot & **Charles Chesne (1)**/1690-French/Canadian-(adopted-Chippewa), some action in Cornstalk War/1755-77 including forays in French-Indian War/1754-63, Braddock/1755, Pontiac War/1762-66, Point Pleasant/1774, some role in Blue Jacket War/1777-94 including Boonesboro/1778, Crawford/1782,, Council Detroit 6-1778, 4-1781, 12-1781, 2-1782, 5-1782, 4-1783 & 5-1790, Council Sandusky 10-1791 & 9-1783, **met with Tecumseh** 6-1812 near Ft. Wayne, **Head Wyandot Chief of CAN**, succeeded by Solomon Warrow as Wyandot Chief, brother of **Antoine Chesne**/1730 & **Elleopelle-Mini Chesne**/1725, husband 1st about 1754 OH of **Sarah Opessa-Younger Daughter of Loyparkoweh**/1736Pekowi, 2nd by 1759 OH of **Older Daughter of Young Rising**

Sun/1739-1/2 Kishpoko-Creek-Metis, 3rd 1774 of **Therese Becquet**/1740-Ottawa-Metis, father **with Opessa** of Mary Shane/1754 & Capt. Joseph Dusquene/1756-1/2 Pekowi-Wyandot-Metis, **with Rising Sun** of Anthony Shane/1763 & Joseph Shane/1765-both 1/2 Kishpoko-Wyandot-Metis & **with Becquet** of Mary Josette Chesne/1775-Ottawa-Wyandot-Metis

HUSBANDS OF OLDER DAUGHTER OF YOUNG RISING SUN

1ST HUSBAND 1755 OH-KY (DOUBLE-UNCLE)

Blue Jacket aka Weyapiersenwha-**Whirlpool**-Sepettekenathe-Big Rabbit – Pekowi-Kishpoko born 1735 PA-died 1809 OH - son of **Pride Opessa**/1710-Pekowi & **Sarah Rising Sun**/1715-Kishpoko, grandson of **Opessa** & **Margaret Pekowi Woman, Pekowi by birth** but reverted to mother's **Kishpoko** family with his mother upon death of Pride, stephalf-brother of **Black Fish**-(by marriage 1739 of Pride Opessa/1710 to Mother of Black Fish/1710), 1st cousin of **Metheotashe**/1738-(fathers were brothers), double-uncle of **Tecumseh**-(1st cousin of **Metheotashe** & brother-in-law of **Puckenshinwa**), husband 1st 1755 OH-KY of 1st cousin **Older Sister of Puckenshinwa-Older Daughter of Young Rising Sun**/1739-1/2 Kishpoko-Creek-Metis, 2nd 1762 OH of **Margaret Moore**/1746-adopted-white, 3rd 1765 OH of **Clear Water Baby**/17501/2 Pekowi-Metis, father **with Sister of Puckenshinwa** of Young Whirlpool-Young Blue Jacket (1)/1756, Spybeech/1758, Wayweleapee/1760 & George Bluejacket (1)/1762-all 3/4th PekowiKishpoko-Creek-Metis, **with Moore** of Joseph Moore-Bluejacket/1763
& Nancy Moore/1765-(born after Margaret's return to the whites)-both 1/2 Pekowi-Kishpoko-Metis, **with Baby** of James Bluejacket/1766, Young Blue Jacket (2)/1770, Marie Louise Bluejacket/1774, Sally Bluejacket/1776, Nancy Bluejacket/1778, George Bluejacket/1780-all 3/4th Pekowi-Kishpoko-Metis

2ND HUSBAND 1762 OH (DOUBLE-UNCLE)

Chesne, Isadore aka Shetoon-Hayanemadae - 1/2 Wyandot-Metis(adopted-Chippewa) - born about 1735-died 1828 - son of **Catherine**

Sauvage/1695-Wyandot & **Charles Chesne (1)**/1690-French/Canadian-(adopted-Chippewa), some action in Cornstalk War/1755-77 including forays in French-Indian War/1754-63, Braddock/1755, Pontiac War/1762-66, Point Pleasant/1774, some role in Blue Jacket War/1777-94 including Boonesboro/1778, Crawford/1782,, Council Detroit 6-1778, 4-1781, 12-1781, 2-1782, 5-1782, 4-1783 & 5-1790, Council Sandusky 10-1791 & 9-1783, **met with Tecumseh** 6-1812 near Ft. Wayne, **Head Wyandot Chief of CAN**, succeeded by Solomon Warrow as Wyandot Chief, brother of **Antoine Chesne**/1730 & **Elleopelle-Mini Chesne**/1725, husband 1st about 1754 OH of **Sarah Opessa-Younger Daughter of Loyparkoweh**/1736Pekowi (aunt of Tecumseh), 2nd by 1759 OH of **Older Daughter of Young Rising Sun**/1739-(aunt of Tecumseh), 3rd 1774 of **Therese Becquet**/1740-Ottawa-Metis, father **with Opessa** of Mary Shane/1754 & Capt. Joseph Dusquene/1756-1/2 Pekowi-Wyandot-Metis, **with Rising Sun** of Anthony Shane/1763 & Joseph Shane/1765-both 1/2 Kishpoko-Wyandot-Metis & **with Becquet** of Mary Josette Chesne/1775-Ottawa-Wyandot-Metis

3RD HUSBAND 1769 OH

Big Swamp – Kishpoko born about 1730 (OH?)-**killed** 1774 Point Pleasant WV – **parents unknown**, Cornstalk War/1755-74, killed at Point Pleasant/1774 with brother-in-law **Puckenshinwa**/1735, husband 1st by 1750 OH of **Kishpoko Woman**/1735, 2nd 1769 OH of **Older Daughter of Young Rising Sun**/1739, father **with Kishpoko** of Young Swamp Water/1750, **with Rising Sun** of Thick Water/1770-3/4th Kishpoko-Creek-Metis

HUSBAND 1759 AL OF MARY RISING SUN

Francis, David **Mumagechee** – 27/64th Chalakatha-Mekoche-ShawanoChalaka-Powhatan-Metis -adopted-Creek born 1740 PA/OH-died after
1805 AL - son of **Sawelaha-Eliza Cornstalk**/1712 & **James Francis**/1700-white British Officer, nephew of **Cornstalk**/1710, adopted son of **Red Shoes Marchand**/1720-Creek-Metis, Treaty 1790, 1805, uncle (by marriage) of **Tecumseh**, husband 1759 AL of **Mary Rising**

Sun/1744, father with Mary of John Francis/1760, Josiah Francis/1765, Joseph Francis/1770, Susan Francis/1775-all 15/32nd Chalakatha-Mekoche-Kishpoko-Shawano-Chalaka-Powhatan-CreekMetis

SIBLINGS OF TECUMSEH

OLDEST BROTHER

Cheeseekau aka Chiksika-Cheeseequa-Sting-a **Snake Biting**-Snakebite-Passquannakeek-Gunshot-Shawnee Warrior - 3/4th Kishpoko-PekowiCreek-Metis born 1756 AL-**killed** 1792 Buchanan Station TN - eldest son of **Puckenshinwa Rising Sun**/1735 & **Metheotashe Opessa**/1738, grandson of **Loyparkoweh Opessa**/1702 & of **Young Rising Sun**/1710, great-grandson of **James McQueen**/1700-white, a **Kishpoko War Chief**, Cornstalk War/1774-77, Blue Jacket War/1777-92, raiding KY-VA-OH/1777-81 **with Dragging Canoe, Chief Bob Benge** & Chickamauga, Council Miami Jan. 1786, took sons by Kishpoko Woman with him to TN, a **Chickamauga War Chief**, living in Running Water (Shawnee) village 1789-92 **with Tecumseh, killed** leading Shawnee contingent **at Buchanan Station TN**, husband 1st 1776 OH of **Kishpoko Woman**/1760, 2nd 1780 TN of **Eyoostee Dragging Canoe**/1756-15/64th Chalakatha-Thawikila-Creek-Cherokee-Metis, father **with Kishpoko** of Tecumqualuska-Graybeard/1777 & Young Great Shawnee Warrior/1780-both 7/8th Kishpoko-Pekowi-Creek-Metis & likely another child or two, father **with Dragging Canoe** of TeciekeapeaseGenevieve Marie/1790 & another child/1792-both 31/64th ChalakathaKishpoko-Thawikila-Pekowi-Creek-Cherokee-Metis, other children likely

OLDEST SISTER

Tecumapease aka **Crossing The Water**-Tecumesa - 3/4th KishpokoPekowi-Creek-Metis born 1758 AL-died 1815 Windsor CAN - oldest daughter of **Puckenshinwa Rising Sun**/1735 & **Metheotashe Straight Tail**/1738, granddaughter of **Loyparkoweh Opessa**/1702,

moved to CAN 1815 with family & died there soon after, wife 1st 1773 OH of
Mink-Chaquiweshe/1740-Mekoche, **widowed 1774**, 2nd 1775 OH of
Mathias Splitlog/1758-Wyandot, 3rd 1779 OH **Stands Firm-Wasegobah**/1755-adopted-Chippewa, **widowed 2nd time 1813**, mother with Mink of Big Horn-Capt. Logan/1774-7/8th Kishpoko-MekochePekowi-Creek-Metis, no known children/1775-79 **with Mathias**, mother **with Stands Firm** of LaNanette Tecumapease-NanetteMaryanne/1780 & other 3/8th Kishpoko-Chippewa-Pekowi-CreekMetis children/1782-1805, (often confused with sisters & nieces by some white histories)

OLDER BROTHER

Sauwaseekou aka Sauwaseekou-**Panther Crouching for Prey** - 3/4th Kishpoko-Pekowi-Creek-Metis born 1760 KY-**killed** 1791 OH - 4th son of **Puckenshinwa Rising Sun**/1735 & **Metheotashe Opessa**/1738, grandson of **Loyparkoweh Opessa**/1702 & of **Young Rising Sun**/1710, great-grandson of **James McQueen**/1700-white, a Kishpoko warrior, born in KY during move from AL to OH, Blue Jacket War/1777-91, **killed 1791 at St. Clair**, husband by 1780 OH of **Unknown Woman**/1765, children unknown

OLDER SISTER?

Rising Sun, Rising Star - 3/4th Kishpoko-Pekowi-Creek-Metis born 1762 OH-died after 1778 – possible second daughter of **Puckenshinwa Rising Sun**/1735 & **Metheotashe Straight Tail**/1738, granddaughter of **Loyparkoweh**/1702, husband & children unknown

OLDER BROTHER

Nahaasema aka Nahaaseema - 3/4th Kishpoko-Pekowi-Creek Metis born 1764 OH-**killed** 1788 KY - 3rd son of **Puckenshinwa Rising Sun**/1735 & **Metheotashe Opessa**/1738, grandson of **Loyparkoweh Opessa**/1702 & of **Young Rising Sun**/1710, great-grandson of **James McQueen**/1700-white, a Kishpoko warrior, Blue Jacket War/1782-88, **killed 1788 in KY raid**, husband about 1784 OH of **Unknown Woman**/1769, possible children unknown

OLDER SISTER

Menewaulakoose aka Menewalakosi-**Lying Piled in a Hollow** - 3/4th Kishpoko-Pekowi-Creek-Metis born 1766 OH-died after 1819 MO - 2nd daughter of **Puckenshinwa Rising Sun**/1735 & **Metheotashe Opessa**/1738, granddaughter of **Loyparkoweh Opessa**/1702 & of **Young Rising Sun**/1710, great-granddaughter of **James McQueen**/1700-white, moved to Apple Creek village MO **with Metheotashe** 1779, marriage to a white opposed by brothers **Cheeseekau** & **Tecumseh**, wife 1782 MO of **Antoine Francois Maisonville**/1760-adopted-French/Canadian, mother of Francois Maisonville/1791-3/8th Kishpoko-Pekowi-Creek-Metis (confused with her sisters by some white histories)

YOUNGER BROTHER

Kumshaka aka Kunshauskau-**Cat Flying In Air** - 3/4th KishpokoPekowi-Creek-Metis born 1770 OH-died before 1824 CAN - 5th son of **Puckenshinwa Rising**/1735 & **Metheotashe Opessa**/1738, grandson of **Loyparkoweh Opessa**/1702 & of **Young Rising Sun**/1710, greatgrandson of **James McQueen**/1700-white, a Kishpoko warrior, Blue Jacket War/1787-94, raiding OH-KY-VA-TN/1795-1810, Prophet's Town/1811, War 1812-Thames/1813 **with Tecumseh**, moved to CAN 1815, died before band returned to OH 1825, husband about 1790 OH of **Kishpoko Woman**/1774, children unknown

YOUNGEST SISTER

Vocemassussia aka Isabella-Vokemassussia - 3/4th Kishpoko-PekowiCreek Metis born 1772 OH-died after 1815 - youngest daughter of **Puckenshinwa Rising Sun**/1735 & **Metheotashe Opessa**/1738, granddaughter of **Loyparkoweh Opessa**/1702 & of **Young Rising Sun**/1710, great-granddaughter of **James McQueen**/1700-white, wife 1st 1786 OH of **Split Log**/1756-Wyandot, 2nd 1792 of **George Ironside**/1760-adopted white-(Church married to Ironside 1810 at St. John's Parrish, Anglican Church), children **with Split Log** unknown, mother of **with Ironside** of Alexander Ironside/1793, George Ironside Jr/1806, 2 sons & 2 daughters/1794-1815-all 3/8th Kishpoko-

PekowiCreek Metis, (often confused with sisters by some white histories)

YOUNGEST BROTHER

Lalawethika aka Tenskawatawa-**Shawnee Prophet**-Open DoorLaulewashika-Lalawetheeka-Laloeshiga-Panther with Handsome TailRattling Sound in Brush - 3/4th Kishpoko-Pekowi-Creek-Metis born 1774 OH-died 1837 KS - youngest son of **Puckenshinwa Rising Sun**/1735 & **Metheotashe Opessa**/1738, grandson of **Loyparkoweh Opessa**/1702 & of **Young Rising Sun**/1710, great-grandson of **James McQueen**/1700-white, a Kishpoko, only one of triplet sons to survive infancy, Fallen Timbers/1794, Council Greenville 1795, moved to IN 1798, part in Tecumseh's campaign of 1795-1810,, defeated by **William Henry Harrison** at Prophet's Town aka Tippicanoe/1811, took little active (warrior) part in Tecumseh's campaign of War of 1812, attempted to assume leadership of his brother's confederacy after death of Tecumseh, moved to CAN with band of followers & family of Tecumseh 1815, returned to OH 1825, rejected by the Ohio Shawnee he led the group that moved to KS 1826 with nephew **Paukeesaa Tecumseh**, married 5 times, husband 1st about 1792 OH of **Kishpoko Woman**/1776, again by 1814 (IN-OH?) of **Pricilla Perkins**/1795adopted white, other 3 wives unknown for now, father **with Kishpoko** of John Prophet/1792, 1 other son & 3 daughters-all 7/8th KishpokoPekowi-Creek-Metis, **with Perkins** of Marcia Bates/1814-3/8th Kishpoko-Pekowi-Creek-Metis, children **with other wives** unknown

WIVES OF TECUMSEH

WIFE 1788 OH

Opessa, **Monetoshe** aka Resting Snake-Manetohse-Four Doves – Pekowi born about 1770 OH-died after 1815 – daughter of **Lawagqua Opessa**/1733 & **Pekowi Woman**/1737, from the Opessa Band, niece of **Watmeme Opessa**/1730-(wife of Black Fish), **Metheotashe Opessa**/1738-(Tecumseh's mother) & sister of **Resting FishMasemo**/1760, 1st wife 1788 OH of 1st cousin **Tecumseh**/1768, divorced after one year, mother of Young Tecumseh-

Mahyawekawpawe aka Young Tecumseh/1788-7/8th Kishpoko-Mekoche-Pekowi-Creek-Metis

WIFE 1789 OH

Baby, **Mamate** aka Mamate Baubee-French Metis Girl - 1/2 Kishpoko-Metis born 1774 OH/IN/MI-died 1790 OH - daughter of **Kishpoko Woman**/1755-(same clan/band as Tecumseh) & **Jacques Duperon Baby**/1733, one of 11 illegitimate children of Baby & Native women, 2nd wife 1789 OH of **Tecumseh**/1768, died shortly after birth of son, mother of Naythahwaynah-Panther Seizing Prey-Young Tecumseh/1790-5/8th Kishpoko-Pekowi-Creek-Metis

WIFE 1790 OH

Galloway, Elizabeth - adopted-white born 1775-77 KY?-died after 1792 - (parents uncertain but father was a brother of James Galloway/1750), captured 1788 KY-adopted 1788 OH, returned to whites in KY 1792, 3rd wife by 1790 OH of **Tecumseh**/1768, mother of Michelana Tecumseh/1790 & Rebecca Galloway/1792-(born after Elizabeth's return to the whites)-both 3/8th Kishpoko-Pekowi-Creek-Metis

WIFE 1790 RUNNING WATER TN

Hop, Tahneh aka **Dark Star** Hop-Naomi Hop-Slow Head Hop-Dark Star Bushyhead-Tahneh Bushyhead-Naomi Bushyhead-Slow Head Bushyhead - 19/32nd Chalakatha-Shawano-Chalaka-PowhatanCherokee-Metis born about 1769 TN-died after 1815 – daughter of
Tahnoyanteehee Hop/1741 & **Chickamauga Woman**/1746, children by Benge taken in by Benge's extended family upon their separation, remained in TN with children when Tecumseh returned to OH, moved to Apple Creek MO before 1812 with Daughter/1794, may have moved back to the Chickamauga villages after 1813, wife 1st 1784 Running Water TN of **Robert Benge**/1761, 2nd 1790 TN of **Tecumseh**/1768, mother of **with Benge** of Mary Polly-Ooloosta Benge/1784 & Robert Benge Jr/1786-both 21/32nd Chalakatha-Pekowi-Shawano-ChalakaPowhatan-Cherokee-Metis, **with Tecumseh** of Lydia Tecumseh/1790,

Tecumtequah/1792 & Daughter/1794-all 43/64th Kishpoko-PekowiShawano-Chalaka-Powhatan-Creek-Cherokee-Metis

WIFE 1793 OH

Cornstalk, White Wing aka Nancy Adkins-**Big Nancy** –29/64th Chalakatha-Mekoche-Shawano-Chalaka-Powhatan-Metis born 1770 OH-died before 1825 CAN - daughter of **Young Cornstalk**/1746 & **Elizabeth See**/1754-adopted white, about 6' tall, a Chalakatha, spoke & read a little English-(learned from her father & 1st husband Adkins), an occasional translator for **Tecumseh**, moved to CAN 1815 with Tecumseh followers and died before they returned in 1825, wife 1st 1784 Montgomery Co VA (=southern WV) of **Elijah Adkins**/1764, (abandoned Adkins & sons 1790 to become involved with Tecumseh, left daughter Nancy/1790 with Cornstalk family when she married Tecumseh), 2nd 1793 OH of **Tecumseh**/1768, mother **with Adkins** of Lewis Adkins/1784, Elijah Adkins Jr/1786, Richard Adkins/1788 & Nancy Adkins-Little Nancy/1790-all 19/32nd Chalakatha-ShawanoMekoche-Chalaka-Powhatan-Metis, **with Tecumseh** of Paukeesaa Tecumseh/1794, Adjala Tecumseh/1796 & Serena Tecumseh/1798-all 19/32nd Chalakatha-Mekoche-Kishpoko-Pekowi- Shawano-Chalaka-Powhatan-Creek-Metis

WIFE 1800 IN

Poc, Wasigezeegoqua aka Pottawamee Wife of - Pottawamee born about 1785 IN?-died after 1813 WI – a daughter of **Main Poc**/1750, 6th wife about 1800 (IN?) of **Tecumseh**/1768, moved with children to WI after death of Tecumseh at Thames/1813, mother of Pottawamee Son/1801, Elder Pottawamee Child/1803 & Younger Pottawamee Child/1805-all 3/8th Kishpoko-Pekowi-Creek-Pottawamee-Metis-(descendants among the Prairie Band Pottawatomie today)

WIFE 1802 OH

Wabelegunequa Half Moon – Chalakatha born about 1785 OH-died after 1807 – daughter of **Half Moon (3)**/1750 & **Chalakatha Woman**/1755, 7th wife 1802 OH-IN? of **Tecumseh**/1768, divorced 1807 due to infertility, no children

WIFE 1805 IN

Sturgeon, Winnipegoosqua aka Chippewa Wife of – Chippewa born about 1790 MI?-died after 1825 – daughter of **Mad Sturgeon**/1765 & **Chippewa Woman**/1770, 8th wife about 1805 IN-MI? of Tecumseh/1768, returned to the Chippewa (MI or beyond) 1813 after death 1813 of Tecumseh, mother of Child/1806, Child/1808, Child/1810, Child/1812-all 3/8th Kishpoko-Pekowi-Creek-Chippewa-Metis

CHILDREN OF TECUMSEH

WITH MONETOSHE-RESTING SNAKE/1770

SON

Tecumseh, Mahyawekawpawe aka **Young Tecumseh**-True Stepper**McLaughlin** - 7/8th Kishpoko-Pekowi-Creek-Metis born about 1788
OH-died 1868 KS - son of **Tecumseh**/1768 & **Monetoshe Opessa**/1770Pekowi, a Kishpoko warrior, Prophet's Town/1811, War 1812Thames/1813 **with father Tecumseh**, Treaty 1817, didn't go to CAN 1815, moved to MO 1815, moved to KS **with Prophet** & **Paukeesaa** 1826, he (or possibly his children) took white surname of **McLaughlin** or **Laughlin** in MO/KS, husband before 1826 (MO?) of **Tawpama**/1800Mekoche, father of 5 children-at least one a daughter

WITH MAMATE BABY/1774

SON

Tecumseh, Naythahwaynah aka Panther Seizing Prey-**Young Tecumseh** - 5/8th Kishpoko-Pekowi-Creek-Metis born about 1790 OHdied about 1826 KS - son of **Tecumseh**/1768 & **Mamate Baby**/1774, a Kishpoko warrior, Prophet's Town/1811, War 1812-Thames/1813 **with father Tecumseh**, moved to CAN 1815, returned to OH about 1825, moved to KS 1826 with **Prophet** & half-brother **Paukeesaa**, died shortly after arriving in KS, husband 1810 OH of **Sokomsee Kishpoko**/1795, father of twin daughters Maythahskse & Waylahse/1816, son Jim Fry/1818, daughters Nahswahpama/1820, Pahsequahmease/1822 & son Big Jim Tecumseh/1824-all 13/16th Kishpoko-Pekowi-Creek-Metis(become step-children 1826 of **Wapakwaha**/1795-Kishpoko)

WITH ELIZABETH GALLOWAY/1777

SON

Tecumseh, Michelana aka Machielaini-**Tecumseh's Son** - 3/8th Kishpoko-Pekowi-Creek-Metis born 1790 OH-died 1839 between KS & AR - son of **Tecumseh**/1768 & **Elizabeth Galloway**/1777, a Kishpoko warrior/leader, Prophet's Town/1811, War 1812-Thames/1813 **with father Tecumseh**, living in Apple Creek MO 1815, didn't go to CAN 1815, moved to KS 1826 with **Prophet & Paukeesaa**, left with a group of mixed Natives going from KS to AR 1839, attacked & killed by whites along the way, wife & children unknown

DAUGHTER

Galloway, Rebecca - 3/8th Kishpoko-Pekowi-Creek-Metis born 1792 KYdied 1876 Greene Co OH – daughter of **Tecumseh**/1768 & **Elizabeth Galloway**/1777, born after her mother's return to the whites, adopted by her mother's uncle **James Galloway**/1750, taken to his home in OH & raised as his daughter, often visited by Tecumseh as she grew, giving rise to the silly fabrications that they were somehow lovers when it was just a father visiting a daughter he could never claim, wife 1812 Greene Co OH of a 2nd cousin **George Galloway**/1784, children unknown (but a daughter Rebecca Galloway/1813 is thought)

WITH DARK STAR-NAOMI-TAHNEH-SLOW HEAD/1769

DAUGHTER

Tecumseh, Lydia - 43/64th Kishpoko-Pekowi-Shawano-ChalakaPowhatan-Creek-Cherokee-Metis born about 1790 TN-died after 1824
AR - daughter of **Tecumseh**/1768 & **Dark Star-Tahneh-Naomi-Slow Head Hop** (Benge)/1769, sister of **Tecumtequah**/1792 & **Daughter of**

Tecumseh/1794, moved to AR after 1814, wife 1808 TN of **Moses Downing**/1788, mother of daughter Dicey Downing/1808, sons James Downing/1810, Cash Downing/1812 & daughter Celia Downing/1814all 29/64th Kishpoko-Pekowi-Shawano-Chalaka-Powhatan-CreekCherokee-Metis

SON

Tecumseh, Tecumtequah aka Cross the Water-TakomtequaTaykoomteeqwa - 43/64th Kishpoko-Pekowi-Shawano-ChalakaPowhatan-Creek-Cherokee-Metis born 1792 NC-died after 1830 MT - son of **Tecumseh**/1768 & **Dark Star-Tahneh-Naomi-Slow Head Hop** (Benge)/1769, returned north 1811 with his father, War 1812-Thames/1813 **with father Tecumseh**, Treaty 1814, a **Kishpoko Chief** at Wapaghonettat 1817, Treaty 1817, traveled to Mississippi & Missouri valleys/1817-1826, moved to KS 1826 with uncle **Prophet** & halfbrother **Paukeesaa**, moved north by 1830 to Dakotas or Montana to join his wife's people, husband 1st about 1810 OH of **Kishpoko Woman**/1785, 2nd about 1820 SD-ND? of **Seeshemeteh Flathead**/1805, children/1810-20 **with Kishpoko** unknown, father **with Seeshemeteh** of Angelica Josephete Cahkatshee Tecumtequah/1821-21/64th Kishpoko-Pekowi-Shawano-Chalaka-Powhatan-Creek-CherokeeFlathead-Metis, father in law of **Louis Tellier**-Metis

DAUGHTER

Tecumseh, Chickamauga Daughter of aka Tecumseh's Daughter - 43/64th Kishpoko-Pekowi-Shawano-Chalaka-Powhatan-Creek-Cherokee-Metis born about 1794 Running Water TN-died after 1812 (MO-TN?) - daughter of **Tecumseh**/1768 & **Dark Star-Tahneh-NaomiSlow Head Hop** (Benge)/1769, moved before 1812 to MO with mother, may have returned to TN after 1813, husband & children unknown

WITH WHITE WING-NANCY CORNSTALK/1770

SON

Tecumseh, Paukeesaa aka **Tecumseh Jr**-Pugeshashenwa-PahkeesaPahguesahah-Puchetha-Puggeesha-Panther Watching Prey – 19/32nd Chalakatha-Mekoche-Kishpoko-Pekowi- Shawano-Chalaka-PowhatanCreek-Metis born 1794 OH-died 1843 KS - son of **Tecumseh**/1768 & **White Wing Cornstalk**/1770, Prophet's Town/1811, War 1812Thames/1813 **with father Tecumseh, Head Chief of Tecumseh followers in CAN** 1815 at 21 years old, succeeded 1816 by **Yealabaheah** as Head Chief in CAN, moved back to OH 1825, moved KS 1826 with his uncle **the Prophet-Lalawithika**/1774, a **Kishpoko Chief** in KS after 1826, husband 1815 CAN of **Kishpoko Woman**/1800, father of John Tecumseh/1820-51/64th Kishpoko- Chalakatha-Mekoche-Pekowi-Shawano-Chalaka-Powhatan-Creek-Metis

SON

Tecumseh, Adjala – 19/32nd Chalakatha-Mekoche-Kishpoko-Pekowi-Shawano-Chalaka-Powhatan-Creek-Metis born 1796 OH-died after 1826 OH? - son of **Tecumseh**/1768 & **White Wing Cornstalk**/1770, a Kishpoko warrior, Prophetstown/1811, War 1812- Thames/1813 **with father Tecumseh**, moved to CAN 1815 with band, returned to OH 1826, may have remained in OH 1826, husband 1816 CAN of **Kishpoko Woman**/1800, children unknown

DAUGHTER

Tecumseh, Serena aka Skwato – 19/32nd Chalakatha-MekocheKishpoko-Pekowi- Shawano-Chalaka-Powhatan-Creek-Metis born 1798 IN-died 1833 IN - daughter of **Tecumseh**/1768 & **White Wing Cornstalk**/1770, a Kishpoko, granddaughter-(by White Wing) of **Young Cornstalk**/1742 & **Elizabeth See**/1754-adopted white & (by Tecumseh) of **Metheotashe Opessa**/1738 & **Puckenshinwa Rising Sun**/1735, first a household servant of then 3rd wife 1808 (OH-IN?) of **William Rainey**/1776-Irish, mother of Matthew Rainey/1815-19/64th Chalakatha-Mekoche-Kishpoko-Pekowi- Shawano-Chalaka-Powhatan-Creek-Metis

WITH WASIGEZEEGOQUA POC/1785

SON

Tecumseh, Pottawamee Son of - 3/8th Kishpoko-Pekowi-CreekPottawamee-Metis born about 1801 IN?-died after 1825 (WI?) - son of **Tecumseh**/1768 & **Wasigezeegoqua Poc** /1785, moved with family to WI after death/1813 of Tecumseh at Thames

CHILD

Tecumseh, Elder Pottawamee Child of - 3/8th Kishpoko-Pekowi-CreekPottawamee-Metis born about 1803 IN?-died after 1825 (WI?) – gender unknown, child of **Tecumseh**/1768 & **Wasigezeegoqua Poc** /1785, moved with family to WI after death/1813 of Tecumseh at Thames

CHILD

Tecumseh, Younger Pottawamee Child of - 3/8th Kishpoko-PekowiCreek-Pottawamee-Metis born about 1810 IN?-died after 1825 (WI?) – gender unknown, child of **Tecumseh**/1768 & **Wasigezeegoqua Poc** /1785, moved with family to WI after death/1813 of Tecumseh at Thames

WITH WINNIPEGOOSQUA STURGEON/1790

CHIPPEWA CHILD/1806
CHIPPEWA CHILD/1808
CHIPPEWA CHILD/1810
CHIPPEWA CHILD/1812

GRANDCHILDREN OF TECUMSEH

BY MAHYAWEKAWPAWE-YOUNG TECUMSEH-MCLAUGHLIN/1788

& TAWPAMA MEKOCHE/1800

5 CHILDREN, AT LEAST ONE A DAUGHTER

BY NAYTHAHWAYNAH-YOUNG TECUMSEH/1790 & SOKOMSEE KISHPOKO/1795

WIFE OF NAYTHAHWAYNAH = **Sokomse Kishpoko** born about 1795 OH-died 1867 OK - daughter in law of **Tecumseh**, wife 1st 1810 OH of **Naythahwaynah Tecumseh**/1790, 2nd 1826 KS of **Wapakwaha**/1795-Kishpoko - after death 1826 KS of Naythahwaynah, mother **with Naythahwaynah** of Waylahskse & Maythahskse/1816, Jim Fry/1818, Nahwahpama/1820, Pahsaquawmease/1822 & Big Jim Tecumseh/1824-all 13/16th Kishpoko-Pekowi-Creek Metis – married widower **Wapakwaha**/1795 who became step-father 1826 of her children, he was then erroneously called the father of some of the younger children, she in turn was step-mother of his two children **Paneta**/1810 & **George Wildcat**/1815

TWIN GRANDDAUGHTER 1

Tecumseh, Waylahkse aka One Of Grace - 13/16th Kishpoko-Pekowi-Creek-Metis born about 1816 CAN-died 1869 KS - daughter of **Naythahwaynah Tecumseh**/1790 & **Sokomsee Kishpoko**/1795, granddaughter of **Mamate Baby**/1774 & **Tecumseh**/1768, twin to **Maythahskse**, wife about 1834 KS of her step-brother **George Wildcat "Alford"**/1815-1/2 Shawnee-Metis, mother of Nancy Ahlamawpama Alford (Hood)/1835, David Paymetahpeasekah Alford/1840, Nellie Nahwahtawpease Alford (Hood)/1845, Thomas Wildcat Ganwahpeasaka Alford/1860-all 13/16th Kishpoko-Pekowi-Creek-Metis

TWIN GRANDDAUGHTER 2

Tecumseh, Maythahskse - 13/16th Kishpoko-Pekowi-Creek-Metis born about 1816 CAN-died 1832 KS? - daughter of **Naythahwaynah Tecumseh**/1790 & **Sokomsee Kishpoko**/1795, twin to Waylahkse, granddaughter of **Tecumseh**/1768 & **Mamate Baby**/1774, killed by kicking horse when 16 years old, died unmarried

GRANDSON

Tecumseh, **Jim Fry** aka **Wakoskskaka** - 13/16th Kishpoko-Pekowi-Creek-Metis born about 1818 CAN-died 1865 KS?)- son of **Naythahwaynah Tecumseh**/1790 & **Sokomsee Kishpoko**/1795, grandson of **Tecumseh**/1768 & **Mamate Baby**/1774, husband 1st about 1835 KS of **Pahkepease Shawnee**/1815, 2nd about 1851 KS of **Chaneyqua Shawnee**/1827, children unknown but likely named **Fry**

GRANDDAUGHTER

Tecumseh, Nahswahpama - 13/16th Kishpoko-Pekowi-Creek-Metis born about 1820 CAN-died 1856 KS? - daughter of **Naythahwaynah Tecumseh**/1790 & **Sokomsee Kishpoko**/1795, a Kishpoko, granddaughter of **Mamate Baby**/1774 & **Tecumseh**/1768, wife about 1835 KS of **Nokskahway Shawnee**/1795, children unknown

GRANDDAUGHTER

Tecumseh, Pasequahmease - 13/16th Kishpoko-Pekowi-Creek-Metis born about 1820 CAN-died 1857 KS? - daughter of **Naythahwaynah Tecumseh**/1790 & **Sokomsee Kishpoko**/1795, a Kishpoko, granddaughter of **Tecumseh**/1768 & **Mamate Baby**/1774, wife 1st about 1835 KS of **Kyanthawtah Shawnee**/1790, 2nd about 1851 (KSOK?) of **Nahepamtha Shawnee**/1815, children unknown

GRANDSON

Tecumseh, Big Jim aka **Wahpahmeeto**-Gives Light As He Walks - 13/16th Kishpoko-Pekowi-Creek-Metis born 1824 CAN-died of smallpox 1900 MX - son of **Naythahwaynah Tecumseh**/1790 & **Sokomsee Kishpoko**/1795, (birth not registered until 1834 OK), a **Kishpoko Chief**, grandson of **Tecumseh**/1768 & **Mamate Baby**/1774, husband 1st about 1845 (KS-OK?) of **Mathotayse Shawnee**/1830, 2nd about 1877 of **Lahweppea Shawnee**/1855-(daughter of **Hahkooseka** "Clark" & **Tookwahnkea**), children with **Mathotayse** unknown, father with **Lahweppea** of Little Jim & Dapego/dates unknown

CHILDREN OF MICHELANA TECUMSEHTECUMSEH'S SON/1790

UNKNOWN

CHILDREN OF REBECCA GALLOWAY/1792 & GEORGE GALLOWAY/1784
UNKNOWN
(but possibly a granddaughter Galloway, Rebecca –born 1813)

BY LYDIA TECUMSEH/1790 & MOSES DOWNING/1788

GRANDDAUGHTER

Downing, Dicey aka Disi - 29/64th Kishpoko-Pekowi-ShawanoChalaka-Powhatan-Creek-Cherokee-Metis born about 1808-died after 1844 - daughter of **Lydia Tecumseh**/1790 & **Moses Downing**/1788, granddaughter of **Tecumseh**/1768 & **Tahneh-Naomi-Dark Star-Slow Head**/1769, 1st wife 1824 of **William Proctor**/1806-white, mother of Sarah Proctor/1824, Johnson Proctor/1828, Ezekial Proctor/1831, Elizabeth Proctor/1834-all 7/32nd Kishpoko-Pekowi-Shawano-ChalakaPowhatan-Creek-Cherokee-Metis

GRANDSON

Downing, James - 29/64th Kishpoko-Pekowi-Shawano-ChalakaPowhatan-Creek-Cherokee-Metis born 1810 TN-died after 1870 OH - son of **Moses Downing**/1788 & **Lydia Tecumseh**/1790, grandson of **Tecumseh**/1768 & **Dark Star -Tahneh-Naomi-Slow Head**/1769, husband 1st about 1830 of **Eliza Parris**/1810, 2nd about 1852 KY of **Jane Tucker (Baldwin)**/1818, children **with Parris** unknown, father **with Tucker (Baldwin)** of Nancy Downing/1853 & James Downing Jr/1857both 7/32nd Kishpoko-Pekowi-Shawano-Chalaka-Powhatan-Creek-
Cherokee-Metis

GRANDSON

Downing, Cash - 29/64th Kishpoko-Pekowi-Shawano-ChalakaPowhatan-Creek-Cherokee-Metis born about 1812-died after 1836 - son of **Moses Downing**/1788 & **Lydia Tecumseh**/1790, grandson of **Tecumseh**/1768 & **Dark Star -Tahneh-Naomi-Slow Head**/1769, husband about 1830 of **Elizabeth Gooden**/1810, children unknown

GRANDDAUGHTER

Downing, Celia (2) - 29/64th Kishpoko-Pekowi-Shawano-ChalakaPowhatan-Creek-Cherokee-Metis born about 1814-died about 1858 - daughter of **Lydia Tecumseh**/1790 & **Moses Downing**/1788, granddaughter of **Tecumseh**/1768 & **Tahneh-Naomi-Dark Star-Slow Head**/1769, 2nd wife about 1835 of **William Proctor**/1806-white, mother of Adam Proctor/1836, Archibald Proctor/1839, Rachel Proctor/1842 & Nancy Proctor/1844-all 7/32nd Kishpoko-Pekowi-Shawano-Chalaka-Powhatan-Creek-Cherokee-Metis

CHILDREN OF TECUMTEQUAH-SON OF TECUMSEH/1792 & KISHPOKO/1795

UNKNOWN

BY TECUMTEQUAH-SON OF TECUMSEH/1792 & SEESHEMETEH FLATHEAD/1805

GRANDDAUGHTER

Tecumtequah, Angelic Josephete aka Cahkatstshee - 21/64th KishpokoPekowi-Shawano-Chalaka-Powhatan-Creek-Cherokee-Flathead-Metis born 1823 CAN-died 1913 MN - daughter of **Tecoomteh-Tecumtequah Tecumseh**/1792 & **Seeshemeteh Flathead**/1805, granddaughter of **Tecumseh**/1768 & **Tahneh-Naomi-Dark Star-Slow Head**/1769Chickamauga, wife about 1840 of **Louis Tellier**-Metis, mother of

Nelson-Tecumseh Tellier/1841, Mary Tellier/1845, Cleofus-Clopis Tellier/1847, Narcissa Tellier/1849, Theodore Tellier/1851, Samuel Tellier/1853, Moses Tellier/1859, Isaac Tellier/1862, Adeline Tellier/1864-all 5/32nd Kishpoko-Pekowi-Shawano-Chalaka-PowhatanCreek-Cherokee-Flathead-Metis

BY CHICKAMAUGA DAUGHTER/1794

UNKNOWN

BY PAUKEESAA-TECUMSEH JR/1794 & KISHPOKO/1800

GRANDSON

Tecumseh, John - 51/64th Kishpoko- Chalakatha-Mekoche-Pekowi-Shawano-Chalaka-Powhatan-Creek-Metis born about 1820 CAN-died about 1866 (KS-OK?) - son of **Paukeesaa Tecumseh**/1796 & **Kishpoko Woman**/1800, grandson of **Tecumseh**/1768 & **White Wing Cornstalk**/1770, **with Black Bob** Band in 1862, husband before 1846 KS of **Wesalemah Thawikila**/1827, father of Kotawipto Tecumseh/1847 & Nowlawipto Tecumseh/1849-both 57/64th Thawikila-Kishpoko- Chalakatha-Mekoche-Pekowi- Shawano-ChalakaPowhatan-Creek-Metis

CHILDREN OF ADJALA TECUMSEH/1796 & KISHPOKO/1800

UNKNOWN

BY SERENA-SWATO TECUMSEH/1798 & WILLIAM RAINEY/1776

GRANDSON

Rainey, Matthew - 19/64th Chalakatha-Mekoche-Kishpoko-Pekowi-Shawano-Chalaka-Powhatan-Creek-Metis born about 1815 IN-died

1881 IN - son of **Serena Skwato Tecumseh**/1798 & **William Rainey**/1776-white, grandson of **Tecumseh**/1768 & **White Wing Cornstalk**/1770, husband 1836 of **Mary Polly Johnson**/1818, father of Nancy Rainey/1838, Eliza Jane Rainey/1840, Andrew Jackson Rainey/1841, Caroline Rainey/1842, Sarah Elizabeth Rainey/1843, Mary Elizabeth Rainey/1845, William H. Rainey/1848, Enoch Rainey/1849, Sylvester Rainey/1854, Martha Marie Rainey/1856, Florence Rainey/1859 & Mahala Rainey/1861-all 19/32nd Chalakatha-Mekoche-Kishpoko-Pekowi- Shawano-Chalaka-Powhatan-Creek-Metis

POTTAWAMEE GRANDCHILDREN

UNKNOWN

CHIPPEWA GRANDCHILDREN

UNKNOWN

1ST COUSINS OF TECUMSEH

BY AUNT TECUMSAPAH-MARGARET OPESSA/1725 & THOMAS MCKEE/1695-ADOPTED-IRISH

Alexander "Trader" McKee/1738,
Nancy McKee/1740,
Hugh McKee/1742,
Catherine McKee/1744,
Elizabeth McKee/1746,
Thomas McKee/1750,
John McKee/1753,
James McKee/1755
(All 1/2 pekowi-metis)

BY AUNT OLDER DAUGHTER OF LOYPARKOWEH-SARAH OPESSA/1727 & PEKOWI MAN/1722

Tecumpolas-Margaret Opessa/1742

BY AUNT WATMEME OPESSA/1730 & BLACK FISH/1725

Chinwa Blackfish/1746,
Young Black Fish (1)/1748,
Pimegeezhigoqua Blackfish/1752,
Young Black Fish 2)/1754, Parlie Blackfish/1756,
Lamateshe Blackfish/1758
Cheletha Blackfish/1760

BY AUNT NANCY OPESSA/1734 & DANIEL MCQUEEN/1736

Margaret McQueen (mother of Seekaboo)/1755
Sarah McQueen (McQueen)/1758
JOSEPH MCQUEEN/1760

BY AUNT SARAH OPESSA/1736 & ISADORE CHESNE/1735

Mary Shane/1754
Capt. Joseph Dusquene/1756

BY AUNT OLDER DAUGHTER OF YOUNG RISING SUN/1737 & BLUE JACKET/1735

Young Whirlpool-Young Blue Jacket/1756
Spybeech/1758

Wayweleapee/1760
George Bluejacket (1)/1762

BY AUNT OLDER DAUGHTER OF YOUNG RISING SUN/1737 & ISADORE CHESNE/1735

Anthony Shane-Chesne/1763
Joseph Shane-Chesne/1765

BY AUNT OLDER DAUGHTER OF YOUNG RISING SUN/1737 & BIG SWAMP/1730

Thick Water/1770

BY AUNT MARY RISING SUN/1739 & DAVID MUMAGECHEE FRANCIS/1740

John Francis/1760
Josiah Francis/1765
Joseph Francis/1770
Susan Francis/1775

IN LAWS OF TECUMSEH THROUGH HIS WIVES

BROTHER OF MONETOSHE

Resting Fish-Masemo Opessa/1760

HALF-SIBLINGS OF MAMATE BABY

Clear Water Baby-Clear Water Baubee/1750
Ms. Baby-Ms. Baubee/1752
Suzanne Baby-Suzanne Baubee/1760
James Baby-James Baubee/1763
Suzanne Baby/1766
Therese Baby/1767

Francois Baby-Francis Baby/1768
Jean Baptiste Baby-John Baptiste Baby/1770
Archangel Baby /1774
Pierre Baby-Peter Baby/1776
Monica Baby/1777
Baby, Daniel Baby/1778
Anthony Baby/1780 Louis Baby/1782

THROUGH ELIZABETH GALLOWAY/1777

UNKNOWN

THROUGH DARK STAR-TAHNEH-SLOW HEAD NAOMI

Oousta Hop (Benge)/1765
Elizabeth Hop (Benge)/1767
Wurteh Hop (Benge)/1771

BROTHER OF WHITE WING CORNSTALK

Son of Young Cornstalk/1772

THROUGH WASIGEZEEGOQUA POC

Unknown

THROUGH WABELEGUNEQUA HALF MOON

Unknown

THROUGH WINNIPEGOOSQUA STURGEON

Unknown

IN LAWS OF TECUMSEH THROUGH HIS SIBLINGS

BY HIS BROTHER CHEESEEKAU/1756

(1st marriage)
Kishpoko Woman/1760
(2nd marriage)
Eyoostee Dragging Canoe/1756

BY HIS SISTER TECUMAPEASE/1758

(1st marriage)
Mink-Chaquiweshe-Chakweeweshe/1740
(2nd marriage)
Mathias Splitlog/1756-Wyandot (3rd marriage)
Stands Firm-Wasegoboah/1755

BY BROTHER SAUWASEEKOU/1760

Kishpoko or Unknown Woman/1765

BY SISTER RISING STAR/1762

Unknown

BY BROTHER NAHAASEMA/1764

Kishpoko or Unknown Woman/1769

BY SISTER MENEWAULAKOOSE/1766

Antoine Francois Rivard Maisonville dit LorangerLaculotte/1750

BY BROTHER KUMSHAKA/1770

Kishpoko or Unknown Woman

BY SISTER VOCEMASSUSSIA/1772
(1st marriage)
Thomas Splitlog/1756
(2nd marriage)
George Ironside/1760

BY BROTHER LALAWETHIKA-THE PROPHET/1774
(1st marriage)
Kishpoko Woman/1776
(2nd marriage after 1794-simultaneous with first)
Unknown Woman
(3rd marriage after 1800-simultaneous with second)
Unknown Woman
(4th marriage before 1814-simultaneous with third)
Unknown Woman
(5th marriage 1814-simultaneous with fourth) Priscilla Perkins/1795

The Shawnee Prophet Lalawethika-Tenskawatawa/1774

Lalawethika aka Tenskawatawa-**Shawnee Prophet**-Open DoorLaulewashika-Lalawetheeka-Laloeshiga-Panther with Handsome TailRattling Sound in Brush - 3/4th Kishpoko-Pekowi-Creek-Metis born 1774 OH-died 1837 KS - youngest son of **Puckenshinwa Rising Sun**/1735 & **Metheotashe Opessa**/1738, grandson of **Loyparkoweh Opessa**/1702 & of **Young Rising Sun**/1710, a Kishpoko, only one of triplet sons to survive infancy, Fallen Timbers/1794, Council Greenville 1795, move to IN 1798, defeated by **William Henry Harrison** at

Prophet's Town aka Tippicanoe/1811, took little active (warrior) part in Tecumseh's campaign of 1795-1810 or War of 1812, moved to CAN with band of followers & family of Tecumseh 1815, returned to OH 1825, moved to KS 1826 with nephew **Paukeesaa Tecumseh**, married 5 times, husband 1st about 1792 OH of **Kishpoko Woman**/1776, 2nd (simultaneously with first) after 1794, 3rd (simultaneously with second) before 1814, 4th (simultaneously with third) by 1814 (IN-OH?) of **Pricilla Perkins**/1795-adopted white, 5th about 1815, father **with Kishpoko** of John Prophet/1792, 1 other son & 3 daughters-all 7/8th Kishpoko-Pekowi-Creek-Metis, **with Perkins** of Marcia Bates/18143/8th Kishpoko-Pekowi-Creek-Metis, children **with other wives** unknown

CHILDREN OF LALAWETHIKA-THE PROPHET/1774

BY KISHPOKO WOMAN/1776

SON

Prophet, John - 7/8th Kishpoko-Pekowi-Creek-Metis born about 1792**killed** before 1865 - son of **Kishpoko Woman**/1776 & **Shawnee Prophet-Lalawethika**/1774, Prophet's Town/1811, War 1812-Thames/1813 **with his uncle Tecumseh, with Joseph Parks** Co-U.S. Army-Seminole War/1837, killed during Civil War, husband 1812 of **Daughter of Spy Buck**/1798, father of John Prophet Jr-1/2 KishpokoPekowi-Mekoche-Chalakatha-Creek-Metis

SON

Prophet, Son of the - 7/8th Kishpoko-Pekowi-Creek-Metis born about 1794-died after 1826 KS? - son of **Kishpoko Woman**/1776 & **Shawnee Prophet-Lalawethika**/1774, moved to KS 1826 with his father & Paukeesaa Tecumseh, wife & children unknown

DAUGHTER

Prophet, Daughter of the - 7/8th Kishpoko-Pekowi-Creek-Metis born about 1796-died after 1826 KS? - daughter of **Kishpoko Woman**/1776 &

Shawnee Heritage II

Shawnee Prophet-Lalawethika/1774, moved to KS 1825 with her father & Paukeesaa Tecumseh, husband & children unknown

DAUGHTER

Prophet, Daughter of the - 7/8th Kishpoko-Pekowi-Creek-Metis born about 1798-died after 1826 KS - daughter of **Kishpoko Woman**/1776 & **Shawnee Prophet-Lalawethika**/1774, moved to KS 1825 with her father & Paukeesaa Tecumseh, husband & children unknown

DAUGHTER

Prophet, Daughter of the - 7/8th Kishpoko-Pekowi-Creek-Metis born about 1800-died after 1826 KS? - daughter of **Kishpoko Woman**/1776 & **Shawnee Prophet-Lalawethika**/1774, moved to KS 1825 with her father & Paukeesaa Tecumseh, husband & children unknown

BY PRICILLA PERKINS/1795

DAUGHTER

Bates, Marcia - 3/8th Kishpoko-Pekowi-Creek-Metis born 1814 OH-died after 1832 – daughter of **Lalawethika Puckenshinwa**/74 & **Pricilla Perkins**/1795, husband & children unknown

CHILDREN BY THREE OTHER WIVES

UNKNOWN

GRANDCHILDREN OF THE PROPHETLALAWETHIKA/1774

BY JOHN PROPHET/1792 & DAUGHTER OF SPY BUCK/1798

GRANDSON

Prophet, John Jr - 1/2 Kishpoko-Pekowi-Mekoche-Chalakatha-CreekMetis born after 1812-died after 1857 – son of **John Prophet**/1792 &
Daughter of Spy Buck/1798, husband before 1857 KS of **Nancy Daughtery**, father of William Prophet/1857

CHAPTER THIRTEEN

Flying Cloud/1735

Black Bob/1780

The Last Chief

Flying Cloud/1735

Flying Cloud aka **Paytakootha** –Thawikila born about 1735-died after 1779 MO – Cornstalk War/1755-77, moved to AL 1774, returned to OH 1778, moved to MO 1779, no known part in Blue Jacket War, husband 1755 OH of **Thawikila Woman**/1740, father of Young PayakoothaFlying Cloud (2)/1760

SON

Flying Cloud (2) aka **Paytakootha (2)-Young Paytakootha** – Thawikila born 1768 OH-died 1838 Montgomery Co IN – son of **Flying Cloud (1)Paytakootha**/1735 & **Thawikila Woman**/1740, went to AL with family
1774, returned to OH 1778, moved to MO 1779, no known part in Blue Jacket War or War of 1812, living in Apple Creek MO 1810, husband 1788 MO of **Little Vine**/1773-Thawikila, father of daughter Ulethi Kisathwa/1810

GRANDDAUGHTER

Flying Cloud, Ulethi Kisathwa – Thawikila born 1810 MO-died after

1832 – daughter of **Young Paytakootha**/1768 & **Little Vine**/1773, husband & children unknown

Flying Clouds (Payta-kootha) (Shawnee) He was an ambassador among tribes. As a Shawnee representative, he signed treaties beginning with the Treaty of Greenville in 1795 and ending with the Treaty with the Shawnee of 1825. In the latter treaty the Shawnee sold the last of their lands in Ohio and received lands in the State of Missouri.

Black Bob/1780

Black Bob aka William James Bobcat Wallen-**Wawahchepaehai**Dancing Water Bobcat-John Robert Wallen-John Bobb - ChalaiwaHopia-Shawano-Nanticoke-Metis born about 1780 OH-died 1864 OK - son of **Joseph Longtail Wallen**/1738 & **Millicent Jones**/1750, about 6'6" tall & called very intelligent by whites & Shawnee, moved to MO about 1795, a hereditary **Chalaiwa Chief**, a **Chalakatha Chief** in MO 1805, moved to AR 1826 to avoid arrival of Ohio Shawnee, moved to KS before 1845, a **Thawikila Chief** of Black Bobb's Band in KS by 1845, moved to OK 1864, husband 1st 1808 of **Chalkatha Woman**/1792, 2nd 1816 of **Mathanahse-Martha Scarlett**/1800-Thawikila, children/1808-15 **with Chalakatha** unknown, father **with Scarlett** of children/1816-26, Julia Bobb/1827, children/1828-39, Joseph Banks Longtail Wallen/1840-61/64th Chalaiwa-Thawikila-Hopia-Shawano-Nanticoke-Metis

WIVES OF BLACK BOB

1ST WIFE 1800 MO - Chalakatha Woman/1784

CHILDREN UNKNOWN

2ND Wife 1816 MO

Scarlett, Martha Mathanahse - Thawikila born about 1800 OH/MOdied after 1827 KS – 2nd wife about 1816 MO of **William James Bobcat Wallen-Black Bob-John Bobb**/1780, mother of children/1816-26, Julia Bobb-Julia Wallen/1827, children/1828-39, Joseph Banks Longtail

Wallen/1840-all 61/64th Chalaiwa-Thawikila-Hopia-ShawanoNanticoke-Metis

CHILDREN OF BLACK BOB

WITH CHALAKATHA WOMAN

UNKNOWN

WITH MARTHA SCARLETT

DAUGHTER

Bobb, Julia – 61/64th Chalaiwa-Thawikila-Hopia-Shawano-Nanticoke-Metis born 1827 AR-died after 1845 OK – daughter of **William James Bobcat Wallen-Black Bob**/1792 & **Martha Scarlett**/1800, husband & children unknown

SON

Wallen, Joseph Banks Longtail (2) aka **Longtail**-Chakalawa-Abraham Longtail-William Henry Wallen - 61/64th Chalaiwa-Thawikila-Hopia-Shawano-Nanticoke-Metis born 1840 KS-died 1912 OH – son of **William James Bobcat Wallen**/1780 & **Martha Scarlett**/1800, a hereditary **Chalaiwa Chief** in OK,43rd TN Mounted Infantry **C.S.A. Army** & Sergeant-Co L 8th Regiment TN Volunteer Calvary **U.S. Army**, later a Primitive Baptist preacher & member of Masonic Lodge, returned to OH 1865 after the Civil War, husband 1st about 1865 of **Susan Baker**/1844-Shawnee, 2nd 1869 OH of **Elizabeth Shafer/Eliza Tignor**/1850-Shawnee, father **with Baker** of Luther Wallen/1866 & Elizabeth Wallen/1868, **with Shafer/Tignor** of Sarah Jane Wallen/1870, twins Mary Edith Wallen & Martha Jane Wallen/1871, 2nd twins Cora Dell Wallen & Charles Chester Wallen/1873, Thomas Franklin Wallen/1874, **John Walter Pony Longtail Wallen**/1875, Melinda Wallen/1876, William Silas Wallen/1877, Leander Wallen/1878, Liza Jane Wallen/1881, Phoebe Tennessee Wallen/1882, Mae Elizabeth Wallen/1885, Viola Anna Wallen/1886, Joseph Lloyd Wallen/1887-all 61/64th Chalaiwa-Hopia-Shawano-Nanticoke-Metis

GRANDCHILDREN OF BLACK BOB

(still researching these grandchildren)
BY JULIA BOBB/1827

UNKNOWN

BY JOSEPH BANKS LONGTAIL WALLEN/1840 & SUSAN BAKER/1844

GRANDSON

Wallen, Luther - 61/64th Chalaiwa-Hopia-Shawano-Nanticoke-Metis born 1866 OH-died unknown – son of **Joseph Banks Longtail Wallen/1840 & Susan Baker/1844**, wife & children unknown

GRANDDAUGHTER

Wallen, Elizabeth - 61/64th Chalaiwa-Hopia-Shawano-Nanticoke-Metis born 1868 OH-died after 1889 – daughter of **Joseph Banks Longtail Wallen/1840 & Susan Baker/1844**, wife of **Mister Riffle**-Shawnee-Metis, children unknown

BY JOSEPH BANKS LONGTAIL WALLEN/1840 & ELIZA TIGNOR/1850

GRANDDAUGHTER

Wallen, Sarah Jane - 61/64th Chalaiwa-Hopia-Shawano-NanticokeMetis born 1870 OH-died 1913 – daughter of **Joseph Banks Longtail Wallen/1840 & Eliza Tignor/1850**, wife of **Richard Johnson**, children unknown

GRANDDAUGHTER

Wallen, Mary Edith - 61/64th Chalaiwa-Hopia-Shawano-NanticokeMetis born 1871 OH-died after 1887 – twin daughter of **Joseph Banks**

Longtail Wallen/1840 & Eliza Tignor/1850, wife of **Charles Frayer**, children unknown

GRANDDAUGHTER

Wallen, Martha Jane - 61/64th Chalaiwa-Hopia-Shawano-NanticokeMetis born 1871 OH-died 1901 – twin daughter of **Joseph Banks Longtail Wallen**/1840 & **Eliza Tignor**/1850, wife 1st of **Hampton Hurd**, 2nd of **Thomas Johnson**/1865, children unknown

GRANDDAUGHTER

Wallen, Cora Dell - 61/64th Chalaiwa-Hopia-Shawano-Nanticoke-Metis born 1873 OH-died 1904 – twin daughter of **Joseph Banks Longtail Wallen**/1840 & **Eliza Tignor**/1850, wife of **Frank Baker**, children unknown

GRANDSON

Wallen, Charles Chester - 61/64th Chalaiwa-Hopia-Shawano-Nanticoke-Metis born 1873 OH-died 1962 – twin son of **Joseph Banks Longtail Wallen**/1840 & **Eliza Tignor**/1850, husband 1900 of **Addie Yeary**, children unknown

GRANDSON

Wallen, Thomas Franklin - 61/64th Chalaiwa-Hopia-ShawanoNanticoke-Metis born 1874 OH-died 1898 – son of **Joseph Banks Longtail Wallen**/1840 & **Eliza Tignor**/1850, wife & children unknown

GRANDSON

Wallen, John Walter **Pony Longtail** - 61/64th Chalaiwa-Hopia-Shawano-Nanticoke-Metis born 1875 OH-died 1920 OH – son of **Joseph Banks Longtail Wallen**/1840 & **Eliza Tignor**/1850, husband of 1st 1898 OH of **Sarah Brotherton**, 2nd 1899 OH **Nina Pearl Foster-Kate Biggs-AohmxShe Is Wise**/1880, no children **with Brotherton**, father **with Foster** of

Isaac Leland Standing Turtle Longtail Wallen/1903-61/64th ChalaiwaHopia-Shawano-Nanticoke-Metis

GRANDDAUGHTER

Wallen, Malinda - 61/64th Chalaiwa-Hopia-Shawano-Nanticoke-Metis born 1876 OH-died 1936 – daughter of **Joseph Banks Longtail Wallen**/1840 & **Eliza Tignor**/1850, wife of **Burdine D. Fisher**, children unknown

GRANDSON

Wallen, William Silas - 61/64th Chalaiwa-Hopia-Shawano-Nanticoke-Metis born 1877 OH-died 1956 – son of **Joseph Banks Longtail Wallen**/1840 & **Eliza Tignor**/1850, husband 1902 of **Pearl Stafford**, children unknown

GRANDSON

Wallen, Leander - 61/64th Chalaiwa-Hopia-Shawano-Nanticoke-Metis born 1878 OH-died 1937 – son of **Joseph Banks Longtail Wallen**/1840 & **Eliza Tignor**/1850, husband 1906 of **Ida Waddle**, children unknown

GRANDDAUGHTER

Wallen, Liza Jane - 61/64th Chalaiwa-Hopia-Shawano-Nanticoke-Metis born 1881 OH-died after 1903 – daughter of **Joseph Banks Longtail Wallen**/1840 & **Eliza Tignor**/1850, wife 1903 of **Howard Miller**, children unknown

GRANDDAUGHTER

Wallen, Phoebe Tennessee - 61/64th Chalaiwa-Hopia-ShawanoNanticoke-Metis born 1882 OH-died 1974 – daughter of **Joseph Banks Longtail Wallen**/1840 & **Eliza Tignor**/1850, wife of **Lilburn J. Fisher**, children unknown

GRANDDAUGHTER

Wallen, Mae Elizabeth - 61/64th Chalaiwa-Hopia-Shawano-Nanticoke-

Metis born 1885 OH-died after 1904 – daughter of **Joseph Banks Longtail Wallen**/1840 & **Eliza Tignor**/1850, wife 1904 of **Carl Miller**, children unknown

GRANDDAUGHTER

Wallen, Viola Anna - 61/64th Chalaiwa-Hopia-Shawano-Nanticoke-Metis born 1886 OH-died after 1906 – daughter of **Joseph Banks Longtail Wallen**/1840 & **Eliza Tignor**/1850, wife of **Elmer Parker**, children unknown

GRANDDAUGHTER

Wallen, Joseph Lloyd - 61/64th Chalaiwa-Hopia-Shawano-Nanticoke-Metis born 1887 OH-died 1875– son of **Joseph Banks Longtail Wallen**/1840 & **Eliza Tignor**/1850, husband 1913 of **Ethel Bledsoe**, children unknown

APPENDIX 1
Guide to Pronouncing Shawnee

1. Consonants

The sounds [**p, t, ch** and **k**] sounds, though similar to English have some differences. Between vowels they may sometimes sound like b, d, dzh (as the "j" in **j**udge) in the speech of men. This is just a phonetic variation and not significant in Shawnee, though folks who wrote down names wrote sometimes one or the other ("b" for "p", for example). For non-native speakers it is best to ignore the slight differences and pronounce them like English is the best course:

"**p**" as in **p**ad, "**t**" as in **t**ad, ch as in **ch**urch and "**k**" as in **c**ool

Also regarding people who wrote down Shawnee names it may be noted that sometimes the sounds "t" and "k" were spoken so weakly they were missed.

The sounds [**th, sh**] dound pretty much like the English sounds in *th*ing and *sh*ip (though "sh" sometimes sounds a bit like "s" to English ears, especial before consonants (like"sk" and "sp" which I still write shk and shp as they are not quite like the English "s").

"**th**" as in **th**ing, "**sh**" as in **sh**ip

The sound [**h**] occurs at the beginning of words and is comparable to the sound in the English word *help*. Initial "h" is lightly pronounced and often missed by those writing down Shawnee names, so that it appeared they begin with a vowel.

The sound written with a raised comma, [**'**], does not occur in English as a regular sound, but can be heard in exclamations like "uh-oh" where it is written with a dash. It is a catch in the throat called a glottal stop and occurs in many languages. It occurs between vowels and before consonants. When it occurs before consonants, it has a rasping (frication) quality such that Gatschet wrote it as a combination of [**'**] and [h]:= 'h, but a quick catch is sufficient.

"**h**" as in **h**elp, "**'**" as in uh-oh

The sounds [m, n, l] are much like English, except m and l are pronounced more lightly. In addition, "m" at the beginning of words is often voiceless and those who wrote down names often missed it.

The semi-vowels [w, y] are pronounced much as in English with "y" as in *yes* and "w" as in *west*. Recorders of Shawnee names often missed the "y" and wrote a sequence of vowels instead.

2. Vowels

There are only four vowels, both short and long: [i, e, o, a]. Long vowels are written double [ii, ee, oo, aa], but the pronunciation of each can vary a great deal.

"**i**" as in *eat* [i] or *it* [ˆ] or *bait* [e] or *bet* ['']. A "i" as in *it* is best most of the time. Sometiems, as in Gatschet, it is written in broad phonetic transcription as "e". In many words, the sound "e" as in *bait* will often vary between "e" and "I".

"**e**" as in *mad*, but articulated a bit higher.

"**o**" as in *soup* or *soap*. Sometimes like "o" and sometimes like "u".

"**a**" as in *hot* or *father*.

If you have difficulty remembering the pronunciation, try rewriting a word with the same consonants as above except write a dash for the glottal stop: ' = -, but us a dash for the glottal stop and the following sounds for the vowels in a kind of phonics:: **i** = ee (meet), **e** = ae (man), **o** = oa (moat) and **a** = a (mot).

Example: Monetoshe 'Resting Snake'. *Maneto'shi* = "Manaetoa-shee".

APPENDIX 2 Timeline

THE TIMELINE:

- 5000 B.C. – Old Copper Culture rises among the natives in the Michigan-Ontario region of Lake Superior

- 3000 B.C. – Egyptian Pharaoh Manetho sends a fleet to explore the great continent west of the Atlantic, it returns 4 years later

- 3000 B.C. – Celts establish colonies from New England to the Carolina's, along the St. Lawrence & Great Lakes which become known, in time, as Mag-Mel, Hy-Breasail, Greater Ireland and to the Norse as Vitramannaland or White Man's Land

- 2500 B.C. – Minoan & Egyptian traders establish contact with the Old Copper Culture of MI and ONT

- 2500 B.C. – Minoan miners sinking mines on Isle Royale in Lake Superior, occupying full-time villages

- 2500-1000 B.C. – Egyptians & Minoans trading on a regular basis with natives from the St. Lawrence South to FL, west to the Mississippi River, up the Mississippi, Missouri and Ohio Rivers

- 2000 B.C to 150 A.D. – The Teuchitlan "circular pyramid building" culture flourishes in western MX

- 2150 B.C. – Egyptian Pharaoh Pepi II sends expeditions across the Atlantic to the inhabitants beyond the western horizon

- 1500 B.C. – Egyptian Queen Hatshepsut claims sovereignty over the Lands Beyond the Setting Sun, i.e., beyond the Atlantic horizon

- 1500 B.C. – Minoan traders/colonists present in Georgia

- 1700 B.C. – Norse King Woden-litha sends traders to Ontario to trade for copper with Old Copper Culture

- 1500 B.C. to 200 A.D. – The Adena "mound building" culture is centered in southern OH, spreading across most of the eastern U.S.

Shawnee Heritage II

- 1400 B.C. – Minoan culture destroyed by effects of the eruption of Mount Thera, survivors are overrun by the Greeks

- 1400 B.C. – Control of the Minoan-Egyptian trade network & colonies passes to the Phoenicians

- 1300 B.C. – Phoenicians maintain trading posts-colonies in the St. Lawrence, Susquehanna, Hudson, Potomac, James, Savannah, Mississippi, Ohio valleys as well as spots along the coasts of the Great Lakes, Atlantic & Gulf of Mexico

- 1200 B.C. – Phoenicians establish a literal monopoly on all crossAtlantic trade, bringing furs, lumber, gold & copper from their colonies & trade partners North & South America to Europe in exchange for wrought iron, glass items, textiles; North America is referred to as Asqua Samai or Great North Land & South America is called Colchis

- 1000 B.C. to 300 A.D. – The Adena culture overlaps-evolves into the Hopewell "mound -building" culture, centered in southern OH, spreading across most of the eastern U.S.

- 1000 B.C. – Hebrew colonists land in North America, penetrate as deeply as TN-KY-WV-OH

- 900 B.C. – Phoenicians establish Carthage in Tunisia, hence Carthaginians

- 900 B.C. – Celts proceed from Ireland & occupy Iceland

- 800 B.C. – Celts proceed from Iceland & occupy Greenland

- 800 B.C. – Phoenicians establish Cadiz & Tartesus in Spain, as main ports for transatlantic trade

- 600 B.C. – Celts proceed from Iceland and Greenland to the coast of
    North America and through the St. Lawrence to the Great Lakes and on to the Old Copper culture natives there

- 700 to 200 B.C. – Migration from & cultural contact with societies from Central America and Mexico

- 500 B.C.-500 A.D. – Teotihuacán MX serves as hub of commerce & culture in the Gulf of Mexico areas of North & South America

- 370 B.C. – Phoenicians sailing to their colony on the Susquehanna River

- 330 B.C. – Greek explorer Pytheas explores the Atlantic, perhaps reaching North America

- 200 B.C. – Central American flint corn is being cultivated by the Adena-Hopewell cultures in the Mississippi-Ohio valleys & along the Appalachians

- 200 B.C. – Crates of Mallos of Greece devises a globe of the earth showing the western hemisphere; Antipodea the northern continent & Peroikoi the southern continent

- 150 A.D. to 350 A.D. – The Teuchitlan "mound building" people begin to disappear from western Mexico

- 146 B.C. – Carthage falls to Rome, refugees flee across the Atlantic to their American colonies

- 50 B.C.-750 A.D. – Roman trade goods reach NC, SC, GA & AL to TN, KY, OH, AR & OK

  100 A.D. – Roman ships are sailing to the coast of New England

- 100 A.D. – Hebrews, escaping Roman persecution after their rebellion, flee to lands across the Atlantic, penetrate as deep as OH, KY & TN

- 135 A.D. – Hebrews flee Roman persecution to North America after a second rebellion, penetrating to TN, KY, OH, IN, IL & MO

- 200 A.D. – Greek geographer Pausania reports red-skinned inhabitants of the lands in the western Atlantic

- 200 A.D. – Celtic colonists/traders are present in NY, MA, VT, NC, OH & IL; i.e. in New England, the St. Lawrence valley, Susquehanna valley, the Ohio valley, the Missouri valley & down the eastern seaboard

- 200 A.D. – Phoenicians present in the Ohio valley, OH-PA-WV

- 200 A.D. to 800 A.D. – Some of the Adena-Hopewell culture evolve into the Allegiwi in the Mississippi & Ohio valley Aztalan in the western Great Lakes region Erie of the eastern Great lakes region Black Minquas in the upper Ohio valley Cahokia in the Mississippi valley Chalaka in the area north of Gulf region Chalaiwa in the middle Ohio valley Hopia in the middle Ohio valley Shawano east of the central Appalachians White Minquas of the Susquehanna valley Xuala east of the southern Appalachians

- 300 A.D. – Items from divergent origins found in mounds, burials & villages sites far distant from their point of origin reveal an extensive trading network that reached from the Gulf to the Lakes & from the Atlantic to the Mississippi fresh water pearls from the Great Lakes & Mississippi River pan pipes of apparent Central American design ear spools of apparent Central American design carved effigy pipes of apparent
    Central American design pottery of apparent Central American design sheets & figures cut from mica from NC ornamental items of copper from MI ornamental & everyday items of various flints from across the area sea shells from the Atlantic & Gulf grizzly teeth & claws from toward the Rockies shark teeth from the Atlantic & Gulf obsidian items from the southwest

- 300 to 700 – Migration from & cultural contact with Central American cultures continues

- 300 A.D. – Hebrew refugees/colonists penetrate as deeply as New Mexico

- 300 to 1300 A.D. – The Ancient Shawnee create earthen mounds, forts, villages from the Atlantic to the Mississippi & from the Lakes to the Gulf; Allegiwi are centered in the area of the junctions of the Ohio & Missouri with the Mississippi, including the 1,000 mile length of the Ohio. Aztalan are centered around the western Great Lakes, extend at least as far as KY Black Minquas are centered in northern OH, in the upper Ohio valley Erie are centered along the eastern Great Lakes Cahokia are centered near the junction of the Mississippi
    & Missouri Rivers, 6.Chalaka are centered between the Savannah & Coosa Rivers, from the Atlantic along the Gulf coast Chalaiwa are centered in southern OH Hopia are

-

centered in central OH, extend east of the Appalachians Shawano are centered between the James & Hudson Rivers, extend north & south White Minquas are centered in the Susquehanna valley Xuala are centered between the Savannah & the James Rivers, including the full length of the New River

- 500 A.D. – Christian monks fleeing the Vandals sail from Morocco to a huge wilderness in what they called the Great Northern Land" Asqua Samai, some return years later

- 535 A.D. – Krakatoa erupts in the Java sea, volcanic dust darkens the sky of the northern hemisphere for 18 months, turning the climate of Asia, Europe and North America colder

- 565-573 A.D. – St. Brendan & 17 Irish explorers/colonists land in North America & penetrate as deeply as the New River drainage of WV

    734 A.D. – Christian Spaniards fleeing the Moorish conquest sail to Antilla, with 6 Bishops, men and women

- 800 A.D. – Mississippian-Hopewell; i.e. the Ancient Shawnee, are cultivating eastern flint corn from Guatemala, beans from Central America squash from Central America

- 800 A.D. – Hebrew refugees fleeing Charlemagne's conquest travel as far as AZ, which they call Calalus

- 900 A.D. – Mayan culture collapses, some remnants flee north to parts unknown

- 900 A.D. – Pagan Norse occupy Iceland, Christian Celts flee to Greenland & their western colonies

- 984 A.D. – Pagan Norse occupy Greenland, as before, Christian Celts flee to their western colonies

- 1000 A.D. – Teotihuacán MX is virtually deserted due to changing climate, invasion, disease or a combination of these factors

- 1000 A.D. – Irish colonists are living in Greater Ireland, Vitramanland or White Man's Land, beyond the Appalachians & below the Great Lakes, i.e. OH & the Ohio valley

- 1000 A.D. – Welsh fleeing invasion sail to a land across the western seas called Avalon

- 1000-1350 A.D. – Leif Erikson & Norse explorers/colonists land in the future U.S. & penetrate, over the next 300 years, as far west as WI-MN & as far southwest as AR-OK

- 1003 A.D. – Leif Erikson names his campsite at Cape Cod MA Vinland for the wild grapes they find there

1005 A.D. - Thorvald Erikson, brother of Lief, has a fatal encounter with the Algonquian natives of MA, who the Norse call skraelings, savages or wretched ones

1007 A.D. - Thorfinn Karlsfeni, with his wife Gundrun, 7 ships loaded with supplies, tools and life-stock and 160 men and women, establishes a Norse colony, Norumbega, at Vinland, captures wo Irish children that tell of a great Irish colony further inland and trade with the Algonquians

1020 A.D. - Gudleif Gudlagsson & crew loose their way in a storm, land on the shore of Vitramannaland, are captured by the Celts but obtain their freedom by the intercession of fellow Norse Beorn of Broadwick, who had been captured many years before

1053 A.D. - Jon of Ireland becomes the first bishop of the Vinland diocese, which included a group of Danish Colonists that had fled Ireland

1121 A.D. - Eric Gnupssson becomes the second known bishop of the Vinland colony, leaving Ireland he is never heard from again

1154 A.D. - Persian traders are traveling to Great Ireland, beyond Iceland

1170 A.D. - Prince Madoc & Welsh colonists land in AL-west FL & penetrate as deeply as TN-KY-WV

1073 A.D. - Vinland is shown on maps made in Europe and continues to be shown for hundreds of years, with notes on colonies, resources etc.

1076 A.D. - North American nations are listed by the Norse as Vinland (Norse), Albania (Scottish) and Great Ireland (Danish-Norse from Ireland), the latter two being some part of

Vitramannaland (Irish), the Welsh colonies that may have been either too far south or too far inland to have been encountered aren't mentioned by the Norse

- 1200 A.D. – Welsh colonists had built stone structures in AL, GA, TN, KY, IN, IL & MO

  1200 A.D. – Mayapan MX is built under the direction of the whiteskinned god-king Kukulcan

- 1250 A.D. – Some Ancient Shawnee are located in the Savannah valley-SC-GA & reach into AL-TN-KY, likely some part of the Chalaka, Shawano & Allegiwi

- 1250 A.D. – Bjorn of Iceland meets horse-riding Celts in Great Ireland after his ship is driven to the great western land

- 1250 A.D. – Norse settlers leave Greenland to establish the colony of Norumbega in New England, south of Vinland, on the eastern & northern edges of Greater Ireland

- 1300 to 1650 A.D. – Fort Ancient culture is centered in the Ohio valley in KY-OH-IN-IL-WV-MD-PA, It extends into VA-NCSC-GA-AL-TN-DE-NJ-NY, physical evidence from mounds, burials & village sites identifies the Shawnee as those known as the Fort Ancient culture Fort Ancient earthworks at Cincinnati OH is identified as Shawnee Fort Ancient site at Starved Rock IL is identified as Shawnee

- 1300 A.D. – The Ancient Shawnee culture peaks across the eastern half of the continent thusly; Allegiwi in PA, MD, OH, WV, KY, IN, IL, MO, TN, IA, AR, MS, AL; Aztalan in OH, KY, WV, IN, MI, IL, WI, MN; Erie in OH, WV, PA, NY; Black Minquas in

OH, PA, WV, MD, VA; Cahokia in MO, IL, IN, MI, WI, MN, IA, KY, TN, AR, OK, MS; Chalaka in GA, FL, AL, SC, NC, TN, KY, VA, WV; Chalaiwa in OH, WV, KY, IN, PA; Hopia in OH, KY, WV, VA, MD, PA, MI, IN, IL; Shawano in VA, MD, DE, PA, NJ, NY, MA, CT, RI; White Minquas in PA, MD, VA, DE, NJ, NY; Xuala in NC, VA, WV, SC, GA, TN, AL, KY, FL

- 1300 A.D. – there are an estimated 3,000 to 6,000 Norse colonists in Norumbega and the New World, with 280 known farms, 17 Catholic churches and one cathedral, leaving records of paying taxes, tithes and travels

- 1346-51 A.D. – Bubonic plague sweeps the Norse colonies it Iceland, Greenland and North America

- 1347 A.D. – The last voyage of a Norse ship from North America to

Iceland carries a cargo of timber

- 1350 A.D. – The last Norse colonists in Greenland depart for the western colonies in an attempt to escape the plague, likely carrying it with them to North America

- 1355 A.D. – Norse King Magnus Eriksson sends Paul Knudson to lead an expedition to find the lost colonies and colonists.

- 1362 A.D. – a band of Norwegians & Swedes leave the Kensington Stone as a record of their fate in MN

- 1395-1404 A.D. – Scot Henry Sinclair reaches New England, explores in America for nine years before returning to Scotland

- 1400 A.D. – First record of Chippewa-Ottawa-Pottawamee on the east of Lake Huron, arriving from further north, along the Hudson Bay

- 1400 A.D. – Basque establish colonies on the coasts of VA and NC

- 1400 A.D. – Eskimos move eastward from Canada to Greenland

- 1415 A.D. – Rippling Stream-Chalaka born corner of VA-TN-KY

- 1419 A.D. – Portuguese Prince Henry the Navigator explores the Atlantic, reaching Satanazes-a northern land and Antilia-a southern land

- 1427 A.D. – Portuguese Prince Henry the Navigator explores the Atlantic, establish trading posts in Satanazes and Antilia

- 1450 A.D. – the copper-mining, metal-working & mound-building culture of the Ohio valley & the Great Lakes essentially disappears, likely victims of the worldwide bubonic plague epidemic

☉ 1474 A.D. – Dashing Stream-Chalaka-Shawano born on Lancer River of VA

☉ 1480 A.D. – Scent Flower Stream-Shawano born central VA

☉ 1497 A.D. – John Cabot reaches the mainland of North America for the British

☉ 1500 A.D. – Basque are fishing from camps on the coast of North America; from the St. Lawrence to the Potomac

☉ 1500 A.D. – The Ancient Shawnee can be identified from beyond the Mississippi to the Atlantic & from the Great lakes to the Gulf of Mexico with the Pre-Columbian versions of the nearly all "Algonquian" speaking tribes

☉ 1500 A.D. – 34 Ancient Shawnee Tribes or Clans as reported by Lalawethika-the Prophet: Snake, Turtle, Raccoon, Turkey, Hawk, Deer, Bear, Wolf, Panther, Elk, Buffalo, Fish, Rabbit, Skunk, Squirrel, Fox, Otter, Beaver, Swan, Eagle, Bald Eagle, Pigeon Hawk, Black Bird, Tree, Corn, Wind, Night, Cloud, Moon, Water, House, Stone, Dirt, Big Fire

☉ `1500 A.D. – 20 Algonquin speaking tribes & sub-tribes, known today as Abenaki-Penobscot-Maliseet-PassamaquoddieMicmac, Chippewa-Ottawa-Pottawamee, Coastal Algonquian of NC, Conoy–Kanawha-Piscataway, Cree- Menominee, SaukFox-Gros Ventre, Illinois-Peoria-Vermilion-Cahokia (not the ancient Shawnee)-Kaskaskia-Michigami-Tamora, KickapooMascouten, Leni Lenape-Munsee, Massachuset-NausetWampanoag, Mattabesic-Metoac-Wappinger , Miami-WeaPiankenshew-Eel, Mohegan-Pequot-Narragansett-NipmucNiantic-Montuak-Shinnecock, Mohican-Mahican-Pocumtuc,
Montagnais-Naskapi-Attikamek, Nanticoke, PowhatanPamukey-Chickahomney-Potomac, Shawnee-

ChalakathaThawikila-Pekowi-Mekoche-Kishpoko, Tuckabatchee, Arapaho- Blackfoot-Cheyenne

- 1500 A.D. – Of these Algonquin i.e. Shawnee-speaking tribes only 6
  tribes are known to have retained their identity as Shawnee, the others quickly adopted the names and identities given to them by the Europeans, their true past & origins become literally mythical

- 1500 A.D. – The Ancient Shawnee Tribes could be broken down thusly; as they begin to evolve into the Historic Shawnee Tribes: Allegiwi in the Ohio, Mississippi, Missouri, Kentucky, Illinois, lower Cumberland valleys, including PA, MD, OH, WV, KY, IN, IL, MO, TN, IA but some migrated south as far as MS & AL; Aztalan along & below the Great Lakes, to the upper Mississippi valley, including OH, KY, WV, IN, MI, IL, WI, MN; Erie along the eastern Great Lakes, including OH, PA, NY, WV, IN; Cahokia in the valleys of the lower Ohio, Tennessee, Cumberland, Kentucky, Mississippi, Missouri, including MO, IL, IN, MI, WI, MN, IA, KY, TN, AR, MS; Chalaka in the valleys of the Savannah, Suwannee, Coosa, Shawannoa, New, Yadkin, Chowan, Yadkin, Watauga, Hiawassee, Cumberland, Tallapoosa, Alabama, Chattahoochee, including GA, SC, FL, NC, TN, AL; Chalaiwa in the valleys of the mid-Ohio, Sciota, lower New, Muskingum, Monongahela, Alleghany, Big Sandy, including OH, KY, WV, VA, MD, PA, MI, IN, IL; Hopia in the valleys of the mid-Ohio to the Alleghany, including OH, KY, WV, VA, MD, PA, MI, IN, IL; Black Minquas in the upper Ohio valley, including OH, WV, PA; White Minquas in the Delaware, Susquehanna, upper Alleghany valleys, including MD, DE, PA, VA, WV; Shawano in the valleys of the Shenandoah, James, Potomac valleys, including VA, WV, MD, DE, PA, NJ, NY, MA; Xuala to the southeast, in the Savannah, Saluda, Catawba, Santee, Pee Dee, Yadkin, Suwannee, upper

New River valleys, including NC, VA, WV, SC, GA, TN, AL, KY, FL

- 1500 A.D. – The Ancient Tribes obviously overlap with one another in many areas &some later overlap/evolve into the Historic Tribes

- 1500 A.D. -The Ancient names hung on after the coming of the whites but largely disappeared during the 1600's or were misinterpreted by the whites, leaving the 5 Historic names in their place

- 1500 A.D. – an interesting dichotomy is noticed; the Algonquian-Shawnee natives are more culturally similar & have more shared words with the Celts of Pre-1300, while the Iroquoian natives are more similar to & have more shared words with the Norse of the same time period

- 1500 A.D. – Running Stream-Shawano-Chalaka born south-central VA

- 1500 A.D. – The Ancient Shawnee can be identified from beyond the Mississippi to the Atlantic with pre-Columbian versions of the nearly all Algonquian speaking tribes

- 1500 A.D. - The Ancient Shawnee Tribes & their succeeding Historic Shawnee Tribes are: ANCIENT – Allegewi; Aztalan; Erie; Black Minquas; Chalaka; Chalaiwa; Cahokia; Hopia; Shawano; White Minquas; Xuala. HISTORIC – Chalakatha; Kishpoko; Mekoche; Pekowi; Shawano; Thawikila. This widespread presence is misunderstood (incomprehensible to their small Europe-oriented minds) by the Europeans, causing the various "migration" theories to be created. Simply stated, the Shawnee Tribes were present from FL-GA-AL-MS to NY-MA-PA-OHMI-WI and all points between. Such a widespread culture would obviously have an extensive trade network, as found in the burials & sites of the Woodland-Mississippian-Ft. AncientShawnee, with the Shawnee Tribes likely having almost a monopoly on such trade. This trade network, in turn, would have an equally large communication system within it, as members of the Shawnee Tribes traveled from extreme to extreme or relayed information from point to point within it via the traders from the Shawnee Tribes of the various areas. This trade network would have required some sort of political system spanning the entire area, in order to conduct business with the localized Natives, including those speaking ShawneeAlgonquin dialects, Siouan, Iroquois & Muskogee languages, as well as maintain relations among the Shawnee Tribes. These 3 networks, trade, communication & political, would be the downfall of the Shawnee Tribes with the White Invasion

○ 1500-1600 A.D. – Almost instantly upon contact with the Europeans; Spanish, French, Dutch, Swedish & British explorers & colonists 3 Catastrophes befall the Shawnee Tribes; The First Catastrophe was the European diseases; measles, whooping cough, smallpox, chicken pox, typhoid fever & cholera – it is known that millions died in the first century after European contact, with the diseases reaching hundreds of miles inland from where any European set foot Understanding the 3 networks of the Shawnee Tribes, the huge territory that they were found in & the large population implied, it is likely that the majority of these would have been Shawnee, as the diseases spread along the 3 networks As literally whole communities were decimated by the white diseases, including the political leaders, religious leaders & the economic leadersthe traders, it is obvious that the whole social-cultural structure of the Shawnee Tribes was nearly destroyed. The Second Catastrophe was the whites giving firearms & steel weapons to the localized natives, the Algonquin/Shawneespeaking subtribes & those speaking the Siouan, Iroquois & Muskogee languages. As the localized-regionalized tribes of the Iroquois, the Delaware, Cherokee, the tribes of the Ohio River drainage, the tribes east of the

Appalachians, those along the Gulf Coast, those around the Great Lakes & other smaller former sub-tribes of the Shawnee were given weapons, they basically rebelled against the disease decimated Shawnee culture that had controlled their expansion or growth for centuries In combination with the die-off due to European diseases these rebellions killed thousands if not more of the Shawnee . With their society & their networks destroyed or damaged so badly by European diseases that they no longer functioned and their former localized sub-tribes now in possession of both white weapons & white trade goods, the scattered remnants of the Shawnee barely survived in pockets scattered across half the continent The Third Catastrophe was Europeans giving "names" to the localized sub-tribes, thinking them to be distinct tribes & most have henceforth regarded themselves as such, even to the point of the names they were given by the whites, like Delaware, Nanticoke, Miami, Kickapoo & such. The huge Shawnee systems were not mentioned by the rebelling local tribes in their conversations with the whites & no one from the Shawnee told any of the whites or if they did it was misunderstood or misinterpreted. As some of the localized tribes became more friendly, especially with the British which extended to become the Americans, their versions of pre-European history became accepted as fact & it almost entirely excluded any reference to the Shawnee systems & presence But the undeniable facts show that the Shawnee were the only Native culture-tribe found from the Atlantic to the Mississippi & from the Great Lakes to the Gulf of Mexico To try to see this huge Shawnee culture as merely wanderers or nomads is to go against prudent observation, for if seen in any context other than that of the Native Americans, anyone using sound judgment would say that the Shawnee were clearly the predominant culture of the area being seen In one of the greatest disgraces, the Iroquois, having adopted the governmental system of the great Shawnee realm, are credited with inventing this system and given credit as the forerunner of the system used by the United States

- 1500-1600 A.D. – one of earliest traditions of the Cherokee in TNNC-GA is of Groundhog's Mother a Shawano conjurer saving them by defeating the Great Horned Snake

- 1513 A.D. – Ponce De Leon lands in FL, claiming the continent for Spain

- 1515 A.D. – Morning Flower-Shawano born central VA

- 1516 A.D. – Ensenore-Powhatan born on the coast of VA

- 1519 A.D. – Bubonic plague sweeps through the Mayan Empire of MX & Central America

- 1521 A.D. - Allyon lands near Winyaw Bay SC, some Spanish taken as hostage likely introducing European blood, (Biscayan, Spanish-style axes are found among the Chalaka of SC-GA by Desoto in 1540)

- 1521 A.D. – Spanish conquer the Aztec of Mexico, possibly introducing European blood

- 1524 A.D. – Giovanni da Verrazano explores the east coast from FL to Newfoundland for France, reports tall, white-skinned natives in the Norumbega territory

- 1525 A.D. - Scent Flower Stream-Shawano-Chalaka born VA, later wife of Ensenore Powhatan, a Shawano Chief & Don Luis Velasco

- 1526 A.D. – Xuala-Shuala-Shawano living in New River valley – NCVA-WV (northern end called Kanawha valley)

- 1528 A.D. - Narvaez lands on west coast of FL, some Spanish taken hostage, likely introduces European blood

- 1532 A.D. – Inca of Peru call the invading Spanish Viracochas thinking they resemble the while-skinned people living at Lake Titicaca

- 1534 A.D. – Jacques Cartier's 1st voyage into the St. Lawrence, for France, likely introduces European blood

- 1535 A.D. – Jacques Cartier's 2nd voyage for France reaches site of Montreal, likely introduces European blood

- 1535 A.D. – Spanish explorer Francisco Pizzaro conquers the Inca of Peru, the Incan king & his family are described as whiter than the people of Spain

- 1537 A.D. - Cornstalk (1)-Chief Cornstalk (1)-Wind Clan Chalakatha born OH

- 1539 A.D. – In FL Desoto finds abandoned ruins that are attributed
    to a former Welsh colony which is known to Shawnee as late as the early 1800's & known to the Cherokee to have moved northward through TN, into NC then north into KY

- 1539 A.D. – Desoto in FL meets a survivor of the Narvaez expedition among the natives of FL, among them for 11 years, a likely introduction of European blood, Desoto proceeds north from FL Desoto moves north encounters Chalaqua-Chalaka beyond the Savannah River SC-GA. Desoto reaches the Cofitachequi
    people in SC, near Augusta GA on the Santee River (or is it Cofita-Chequi i.e. "land of the Chequi/Cheekee with Chequi=Chalaka who are not Cherokee or Creek). Desoto passes northward through Xuala-Shawano village at the base of the Blue Ridge in lower NC (not Cherokee). Desoto crosses the lower Blue Ridge Mountains & into the eastern edge of the Cherokee territory i.e. southwest NC in the mountains of

southwest NC Desoto passes through Guasili village (Cherokee Co NC), said to be Cherokee on the lower Hiawassee River of TN Desoto passes through Canasoga village, said to be Cherokee. Desoto then turns south into AL and Muskogee speaking people i.e. Creeks. Desoto's further exploration "discovers" territory as far west as the Mississippi (& perhaps to the Ohio) before dying in AR

- 1540 A.D. – Bear Clan Chief-Shawano born central VA

- 1541 A.D. – Jacques Cartier's 3rd voyage to North America for France, establishes Charlesbourg-Royal in Quebec, likely introduces European blood

- 1542 A.D. – Sieur DeRoberval, Governor of New France reports white-skinned natives in the Great lakes area

- 1545 A.D. – Chief Wahunsonacock Powhatan-Shawano-ChalakaPowhatan born James River of VA

- 1550 A.D. – Susquehannocks or Susquehanna i.e. the natives living on the Susquehanna River PA, the White Minquas, describe as literal giants

- 1550 A.D. – Of original known clans of the Creek in AL one is the "chil-o-kita, those of different speech" = Chalakatha-Chalaka

- 1555 A.D. – Opechan Stream-Shawano-Chalaka born New River of VA

- 1560 A.D. – French have "discovered" some part of all five Great Lakes, meeting the Shawnee at every point from NY to WI, likely introducing European blood

- 1562 A.D. – Nonoma Cornstalk-Chalakatha born central VA

- 1562 A.D. – Jean Ribault establishes a colony on the St. John's River FL for France, European blood likely introduced

- 1562 A.D. – Jean Ribault establishes a Huguenot colony for France at Parris Island SC, it fails by 1566, European blood possibly introduced

- 1565 A.D. - Spanish establish St. Elena near Beaufort SC, possibly introducing European blood & drive the French from FL

- 1566 A.D. - Pardo moves from St. Elena into the interior of SC-GA over 100+ miles into SC they reach the Cofitachequi. Moving northward they pass through Issa/Essaw in SC (later equals the Catawba) and further north (in NC) they reach XualaShawano in NC (later equals part of Chowan) from Xuala village in NC they can see the south end of the Blue Ridge Mountain range. Boyano is left at the Xuala villages in NC with detachment, possibly introducing European blood. Beyond Xuala Pardo travels southwest (into AL or GA?) & reach Quihanaqui (Keehanakee) and then Guatari (Huataree), the seat of power governed by two female chiefs (apparently Creek due to apparent matrilineal chiefs). Boyano & the Xuala
    Natives meet & attack their traditional enemies, the Cherokee. Boyano, his soldiers & the Xuala-Shawano travel west four days after the battle with the Cherokee (= 4 days march west of the southern end of the Blue Ridge in NC) into the mountains (of NC) & reach the first Cherokee town & destroy it. Beyond there (TN?) they reach villages of Cauchi & Tanasqui (= Cherokee towns?) They then move on to Chiaha a Creek town (in TN or AL?) previously visited by Desoto

- 1568 A.D. – NJ frontiersman John Hawkins encounters Welsh speaking natives among the Monacan

- 1568 A.D. - Amopotoiske Shawano-Chalaka born in central VA

- 1576 A.D. - Amopotuskee Bear Clan-Shawano born Shenandoah valley of VA

- 1577 A.D. - Cornstalk (2) -Cornstalk Wind Clan-Cornstalk Powhatan-Chalakatha-Shawano-Chalaka -Powhatan born VA

- 1584 A.D. – Roanoke Island colony established for British by Ralph Lane in NC, fails within three years i.e. by 1587, leaving cabins on Roanoke Island, European blood possibly introduced

- 1584 A.D. – Chawanock-Shawano village is found 120 miles inland from Raleigh's Roanoke NC colony

- 1587 A.D. – 2nd Roanoke colony of 110 settlers established for British by John White in NC, fails by 1590, leaving the mysterious message "Croatan" carved on a tree, likely introducing European blood

- 1587 A.D. – British drive Spanish out of the St. Elena colony at Charleston SC.

- 1587 A.D. – Some survivors of St. Elena (Spanish-PortugueseMediterranean) allegedly travel northwest to the corner of TNKY-VA to possibly become 200 years later through marriages with "Natives", i.e., the Shawnee & runaway blacks the Melungeons, obviously introducing European blood

- 1590 A.D. – Walking Panther-Chalaiwa born in Kanawha valley of WV-(his descendants are among the few that continue to refer to themselves as Chalaiwa in succeeding generations)

- 1598 A.D. - Cornstalk (3) -Cornstalk Wind Clan Powhatan (2)Chalakatha-Shawano-Chalaka-Powhatan born VA

- 1600 - Though their economic, political & cultural networks are either destroyed or crippled, the Shawnee Tribes remain a presence throughout the territory east of the Mississippi though known & referred to by a huge variety of names by the different Europeans & their contacts with the localized regionalized tribes. Ancient Tribes: Ancient Allegewi are apparently extinct; Ancient Aztalan are apparently extinct;

> Ancient Chalaka are apparently nearly extinct; Ancient Erie survive in decreasing numbers, in a reduced area; Ancient Black Minquas survive in decreasing numbers, in a reduced area; Ancient White Minquas survive in decreasing numbers, in a reduced area; Ancient Hopia survive in decreasing numbers, a sort of cultural elite that marry only other Shawnee; Ancient Chalaiwa survive in decreasing numbers; Ancient Shawano survive in decreasing numbers; Ancient Xuala are nearly extinct. Historic Tribes: Historic Chalakatha seem to be based in OH-WV-KY-PA; Historic Kishpoko seem to be based in AL-TN-KY-IN-IL-MO; Historic Mekoche seem to be based in OH-WV-KY-IN; Historic Pekowi seem to be based in OH-PA-MD-DE-NJ; Historic; hawikila seem to be based in GA-AL-TN

- 1600 – Jamestown colonist Capt. Peter Wynne encounters Welsh speaking natives near the falls of the James River VA, while others from Jamestown notice natives with iron & some with yellow hair & white skin.

- 1602 – Cleopatra "the Shawano" Powhatan-Shawano-ChalakaPowhatan born near Jamestown Colony VA

- 1603 – Shawano or Satanas living on the lakes of western NY, south of Lake Erie

- 1603 – Samuel Champlain fur trading/exploring on the St. Lawrence for France, encounters white skinned natives that he feels resemble the Norse

- 1607 – British establish Jamestown colony in VA, introducing European blood

- 1607 – John Smith reports Shawano on the Susquehanna River-east
    PA allied with the Mohican on Long Island NY at war with the Iroquois

- 1607 – Chawanock-Shawano referred to as living in VA by John Smith

- 1608 – Samuel Champlain establishes a post at the site of Quebec for France, likely introducing European blood

- 1610 – British, moving inland contact Shawano in central VA (after contacting the Powhatan-Pamokey-Chickahominey along the coast) begin taking wives, introducing European blood

- 1616 – Dutch & Swedes find "Sauwanew" i.e., Shawano on the east side of the Delaware River DE-NJ.

- 1616-1617 – Epidemics of measles, whooping cough, smallpox, chicken pox, typhoid fever & cholera kill tens of thousands from the Atlantic Coast inward, the majority likely from the Shawnee Tribes

- 1618 – Opechan-an adopted Shawano succeeds Powhatan as Chief of the Powhatan Confederacy of Algonquin speaking localregional tribes (little more than villages in most cases) in east VA

- 1620 – British colonists arrive at Plymouth MA, meet the "Algonquin" natives

- 1627 – Panther Paw-Thomas Wallen-Chalaiwa born Kanawha valley

WV

- 1628 – Hokolesqua Cornstalk-Shawano-Chalaka-Powhatan born southwest VA or the Shenandoah valley

- 1630 to 1730 – some bands from all 5 Historic Shawnee tribes remain in OH-west PA-west WV-the Ohio valley

- 1630 – Many Chalakatha & Kishpoko from OH-west PA-west WVOhio valley move to southwest VA-northwest NC-northeast TN-east KY–Cumberland valley above the territory of the Cherokee, called "northern Cherokee" by the British for political expediency

- 1630 to 1700 – Shawnee in the Cumberland valley are trading with the British from SC-GA-NC, introducing European blood

- 1632 – "Shaunetowa" i.e. Shawano on the Potomac River MD-VA

- 1632 – Jesuits seeking converts among the Shawnee of WI & territory to the west of Lake Superior

- 1633-35 – Smallpox epidemics ravage the native populations east of the Appalachians from GA to Canada

- 1634 – Jean Nicolet, exploring for France, reaches as far west as WI

- 1635 – Trader Tom Carpenter-Moytoy (1)-Chalakatha-ShawanoChalaka-Powhatan-Metis born Great Tellico TN

- 1637 – "Pequot", likely some of the Pekowi in a losing war with Massachusetts colonists MA, move southward (NY-NJ-DE-PA)

- 1637 – Pashmere Carpenter (1)-Chalakatha-Shawano-ChalakaPowhatan-Metis born Great Tellico TN

- 1638 – Swedes establish New Sweden colony DE, introducing European blood

- 1640 – Straight Tail-Meaurroway-Pekowi born OH-Ohio Valley

- 1640 – The father of Smallpox Conjurer-Tsula Fox is born, he remembers (but no mention of his son Tsula Fox remembering so between 1650 when he was 10 years old and about 1680 when Tsula would have been 10 years old or before 1670) when the "white Indians", i.e. Welsh left the Appalachians to move to the Missouri territory i.e. on the Missouri River, where the Mandan were later found

- 1641 – Thomas Skootekitehi-Fireheart Greenwood-ChalakathaShawano-Chalaka-Powhatan Metis born southwest VA

- 1643 – Villa Marie, later Montreal, established by the French, possibly introducing European blood

- 1643 – Locha Greenwood – Chalakatha-Shawano-ChalakaPowhatan-Metis born southwest VA

- 1644 – Mikona Carpenter - Chalakatha-Shawano-Chalaka-PowhatanMetis born southwest VA

- 1648 – Mekoche-Kishpoko-Pekowi-Chalakatha living in IL with the Mascouten

- 1650 – The first permanent white settlement in NC is established in the Albemarle area of northeast NC, introducing European blood

- 1650 to 1700 – Shawnee found in villages-IL-IN-OH-PA-DE-MD-VA-

WV-KY-NC-SC-TN-AL-GA

- 1654 – Chalakatha-Kishpoko-Shawano defeat British & Pamukey in VA

- 1654 – Wolf Straight Tail-Pekowi born OH

- 1655 – Dutch take over New Sweden colony PA, NJ, DE

- 1656 – Sauwanoos" i.e. Shawano between Schuylkill & Delaware Rivers east PA

- 1658 – Pierre Radisson "discovers" the head of the Mississippi in Minnesota & WI & meets Shawnee there

- 1656 – Nika-Wild Goose Straight Tail-Pekowi born OH

- 1660 – Trader Tom Carpenter (2)-Moytoy (2)-Chalakatha-ShawanoChalaka-Powhatan-Metis born Running Water TN

- 1660 – Big Turkey-Chalakatha-Shawano-Chalaka-Powhatan born northwest TN-southwest VA

- 1660 – Sewatha Straight Tail-Pekowi born OH

- 1660 - Joseph Gorhaleke-Winter Fever Greenwood-ChalakathaShawano-Chalaka-Powhatan Metis born Running Water TN

- 1661 – Mekoche-Chalakatha-Pekowi-Kishpoko living 1,000 miles west of the Iroquois on the Ohio River-OH-WV-KY-IN-IL

- 1662 – Longtail (1)-Thomas Wallen-Chalaiwa born Shawnee Town/Salem NJ

- 1662 – Cakundawanna Straight Tail-Pekowi born OH

- 1662 - Quaghcunnega Rainbow-Kishpoko-Black born Nickajack TN

- 1662 to 1674 – Shawnee from KY-TN-NC-SC-GA trading with the Spanish in FL

- 1663 – France sends 775 women to New France, the first French women to arrive (120 years after the first posts were established)

- 1664 – Opessa Straight Tail-Pekowi born OH

- 1665 – Shawnee have a major village on the Cumberland River at Nashville TN

- 1666 – Kishpoko-Mekoche-Pekowi-Chalakatha-Thawikila along the
  Mississippi River-south of the mouth of the Ohio River-KY-TN

- 1666 – Morgan Jones, captured by natives in NC, speaks Welsh to convince his captors to spare him, the same year another Welshman captured by natives of the NC coast is told by his captors that they were descended from ancient voyagers from across the sea

- 1666 – Snow White Straight Tail-Pekowi born OH

- 1669 – LaSalle's 1st expedition into the OH-IN-IL territory, he is warned about the ferocity of the Shawnee of the Ohio valleyOH-WV-KY-IN-IL, but undoubtedly finds them in his first exploration, he may have "discovered" the Falls of the Ohiosite of Louisville KY, European blood likely is introduced during his journey

- 1660 to 1670 – some Kishpoko-Mekoche from OH-IN-IL-Ohio valley move to east TN-east KY-west NC-southwest VA-

Shawnee Heritage II 463

Cumberland valley join the Chalakatha-Kishpoko, called "northern Cherokee" by the British

- 1669 - James Lederer explores VA back country & piedmont of the Appalachians

- 1670 - Hawk Sinnawa-Tlanuwa Greenwood- Chalakatha-ShawanoChalaka--Powhatan-Metis born Running Water TN

- 1670 - The Cumberland River TN called the "Riviere des Chaouannons"- the River of the Shawnee

- 1670 - Some Thawikila-Pekowi-Kishpoko from OH-Ohio valley move to GA-SC-Savannah valley join Chalaka, east of the Creeks & south of the Cherokee, called by British the "southern Cherokee"

- 1670 - Poxinosa-Pekowi born OH

- 1670 - Kakawatchekee-Pekowi born OH

- 1670 - Kishacoquillas-Pekowi born IL-IN

- 1670 - Neucheconner-Pekowi born OH

- 1670 - John White Straight Tail-Pekowi born OH

- 1670 - Tamenebuck Cornstalk-Chalakatha-Shawano-ChalakaPowhatan-Metis born in PA

- 1670-1720 - French establish trading posts, mills & mines on the tributaries of the Mississippi & Ohio, including the Beaver-PA, Kanawha-WV, Sciota-OH, Great Miami OH, Little Miami-OH, Wabash-IN, Cumberland-KY, Tennessee-KY, Tennessee-TN, Kentucky-KY, Big Sandy-KY-WV, Illinois-IL, Wisconsin-WI, Monongahela-PA, Fox-Kanakee-IN, St. Joseph-MI, Eel-IN,

Maumee-OH, Auglaize-OH. The French take wives from among the Shawnee they encounter, introducing European blood

- 1671 - Thomas Batts & Robert Fallon explore into VA back country & the Appalachians

- 1671 – Shawnee found gathering salt near site of Charleston on the Kanawha River in WV

- 1671 – The last of the Xuala-Shawano in Kanawha valley-WV killed by their ancient enemies the Cherokee, raiders from lower NC, who followed the New River

- 1672 – Shawano-Pekowi in PA allied with Andastes (Susquehanna) living south of the Seneca at war with the Iroquois

- 1673 – William Whitheford-Weatherford of Jamestown VA marries Susannah Shawano in central VA

- 1673 – Louis Joliet & Jacques Marquette travel down the Mississippi from WI to AR, finding Shawnee villages in every current State, return north via the Ohio & Illinois River, likely introducing European blood

- 1673 - James Needham & Gabriel Arthur explore across the Appalachian Mountains of VA

- 1674 – Cherokee follow New-Kanawha valley-NC-VA-WV, travel 3 days after crossing the Ohio River into OH to strike the Shawnee

- 1674 – Cornstalk (5)-Okowellos Cornstalk-Chalakatha-ShawanoChalaka-Powhatan-Metis born west PA

- 1674 – Marquette finds several Shawnee villages east of the mouth of the Ohio River-KY-IL-IN-OH

- 1674 – Randin locates Shawnee villages on the Mississippi Riversouth of the Ohio-KY-TN

- 1674 – Joliet locates Shawnee on the Cumberland River near the Ohio-TN-KY

- 1675 – Fortune Gilliam-Shawano-Metis born southwest VA

- 1675 – "Indians" i.e., Shawnee begin raids on VA frontier, resulting in Nathaniel Bacon's Rebellion

- 1676 – "Sauno"; i.e., Shawano at the mouth of the Schuylkill Rivereast PA

- 1676 – Sewatha Straight Tail-Pekowi marries Martin Chartier-French in IL

- 1677 – Some Pekowi-Kishpoko from OH-Ohio valley to northeast MD-southeast PA-Susquehanna valley, join the ShawanoPekowi already there, near the Delaware

- 1677 – Meaurroway-Straight Tail's Pekowi band from OH-Ohio valley to IN-IL-Miami & Illinois River valleys among Miami & Illinois

- 1677 – 70 Chalaka-Thawikila-Pekowi-Kishpoko families leave SC, headed for PA

- 1678 – White Owl Raven Carpenter-Moytoy (4)-Chalakatha-Shawano-Chalaka-Powhatan-Metis born Running Water TN

- 1678 – Madeleine Chartier-Pekowi-Metis born IL

- 1679 – French-Canadian deserters from LaSalle's group in IL leave message engraved on side of a boat – "Nous Somme Tous Savages"-We Are All Savages; i.e., living among the (mostly Shawnee) Natives

- 1680 – Major Shawnee locations thought by British to be the Cumberland valley-TN-KY & the Savannah valley-SC-GA

- 1680 – Some Shawnee near the Miami & Illinois in OH-IN-IL south of Lake Michigan

- 1680 – Shawnee establish village of Eskippakithiki or Big Licks in KY

- 1680 – Savannah Tom Carpenter (1)-Moytoy (3)- ChalakathaShawano-Chalaka-Powhatan-Metis born Chota TN

- 1680 – Raven Hop-Raven Moytoy-Raven of Hiawassee- ChalakathaShawano-Chalaka-Powhatan born southwest VA

- 1680 – Shawnee attacking the Westo, Winyaw, Appomattox, Chatot & Cherokee of SC-NC & GA & selling their captives to the British slave trade in Charleston SC, resulting in Native blood being introduced into the white & African lines (& Caribbean lines as some are shipped to the islands)

- 1680 – Shawnee are the dominant tribe in the Savannah valley of SCGA

- 1680 – Katee-Mekoche born OH

- 1680 – Thomas Caesar Skiagunsta Greenwood -Breed Slave-Catcher- Chalakatha-Thawikila Kishpoko-Shawano-Chalaka-PowhatanBlack-Metis born Nickajack TN

- 1681 – Pashmere Carpenter (2)-Chalakatha-Shawano-ChalakaPowhatan-Metis born Chota TN

- 1677 to 1683 – many Mekoche from OH-Ohio valley join Meaurroway-Straight Tail's Pekowi band in IN ILL-MiamiIllinois River valleys among Miami & Illinois

- 1682 – LaSalle's 2nd expedition descends the Ohio to the Mississippi and on to the mouth of the river, with Shawnee guides = brothers Nika-Wild Goose & Wolf

- 1682 – Kishpoko-Mekoche-Chalakatha-Pekowi are already present when LaSalle constructs Ft. St. Louis at Starved Rock IL, the Natives are called by LaSalle; Shawnee, Chaskepe, Ouabano & Cisca

- 1682 – Shawnee, likely Pekowi, are present in PA at Treaty with William Penn (they retained a copy of the treaty until the 1720's)

- 1682 - Quatsis Hop-Chalakatha-Shawano-Chalaka-Powhatan born southwest VA

- 1682 – LaSalle expedition escorted by Nika-Shawnee in the Ohio valley-OH-IN-KY-IL

- 1682 – Martin Chartier, adopted French in southern IL among the Pekowi

- 1682 – Some Thawikila-Mekoche from OH-Ohio valley join Pekowi in Susquehanna valley-southeast PA-Alleghany valleynortheast MD, near the Delaware & Mohawk

- 1682 - Wood Deer Hoof – Thawikila born on the Sciota River OH

- 1683 – Lesperance = Hope = Antoine Adhemer-a French-Canadian voyageur with Tonti leaves Montreal for the Illinois territory, others in the group include the Violet (le Violet), the Tulip (le Tulip) & the Pretty Heart

- 1683-85 – some Pekowi from Straight Tail's band join the Chalakatha-Mekoche-Kishpoko in east TN west NC-southwest VA-east KY-Cumberland valley

- 1684 – Shawnee defend their homeland against war parties of Iroquois in the Ohio valley-OH-WV-PA-MD

- 1684 – Aganunitsi-Wild Potato Hop-Chalakatha-Shawano-ChalakaPowhatan born southwest VA

- 1685 – Some Chalakatha from OH-Ohio valley join AL Thawikila-Kishpoko to establish a village on the Tuckabatchee River AL

- 1685 - Rising Sun Kishpoko born Tuckabatchee AL

- 1685 – Thawikila have a village on the Coosa in AL near the Creeks ⊙ 1686 – Swan Wapehti Hop Chalakatha-Shawano-Chalaka-Powhatan born southwest VA

- 1686 – Muskrat (1)–Oshasqua (1)-Moytoy (5) Pekowi-ChalakathaShawano-Chalaka-Powhatan born Hiwassee TN

- 1687 – Martin Chartier-adopted-French with Pekowi in IL-IN-on lower Ohio valley

- 1688 – Mary Chartier Pekowi-Metis born IL-IN

- 1688 – Standing Turkey-Old Hop Chalakatha-Shawano-ChalakaPowhatan born southwest VA

- 1688 – French colony Ft. St. Louis near Victoria TX is overrun, 5 children are taken captive

- 1688 - Little Sugar – Thawikila born about 1688 on the Sciota River OH

- 1689 – Some Mekoche from IN-IL-Illinois-Miami valleys-lower Ohio valley join Chalakatha, Mekoche, Kishpoko in east TN-west NC-southwest VA-east KY-Cumberland valley above Cherokee

- 1689 – One Mekoche band from IL-IN-Illinois valley to northeast PALehigh valley near Delaware, Mohican & Mohawk

- 1689 – King William's War – Algonquian-Shawnee-speaking Natives
    aid both French & English colonists in skirmishes in CAN, NY & New England colonies

- 1683-89 – some of Meaurroway-Straight Tail's Pekowi band from ILIN joins Chalakatha-Mekoche and Kishpoko in east TN-west NC-east KY-southwest VA-Cumberland valley near Cherokee

- 1690 – Peter Chartier-Pekowi-Metis born TN (not MD-PA)

- 1690 – Some Mekoche-Pekowi from OH-Ohio valley join Chalakatha-Mekoche-Kishpoko in east TN west NC-east KYsouthwest VA-Cumberland valley near Cherokee

- 1690 – Some of Meaurroway-Straight Tail's Pekowi band including
    Opessa move on from TN Cumberland valley to join Shawano-Pekowi in Cecil Co MD

- 1690 – April Tkikami Hop-Chalakatha-Shawano-Chalaka-Powhatan born southwest VA

- 1690 – An emissary from the "Delaware-Leni Lenape-River Men" on the Susquehanna River-PA travels to IL to ask the Pekowi there to come assist them is resisting the whites

- 1690 – Tonti comes down the Mississippi River passing Lake St. Joseph & the Red River

- 1690 – Traders, mostly British, from Charleston SC, traveling into the Appalachian mountains

- 1692 – Oolootah Hop-Chalakatha-Shawano-Chalaka-Powhatan born southwest VA

- 1693 – "Shallnarooners" i.e. Shawano-Pekowi from Cecil Co MD living in Chester Co PA

- 1693 – 20 Cherokee Chiefs complain to the Governor of SC about the Shawnee making slave raids on them, those sold as slaves introduce Native blood into the white & African lines

- 1694 – Kakawatchekee-Pheasant's Pekowi band from Ohio valley joins Mekoche in northeast PA-Lehigh River valley among Delaware, Mohican & Mohawk

- 1694 – Ghigoneli Hop-Chalakatha-Shawano-Chalaka-Powhatan born southwest VA, parents killed the same year

- 1694 – Big Turkey & wife, parents of Old Hop/1688 killed by Catawba hired by whites to raid, in southwest VA

- 1694 – Standing Turkey-Old Hop/1688, brother Raven/1680, sisters Quatsis/1682, Swan/1686 & April/1690 are adopted in Running Water TN by Trader Tom Carpenter (2)-Moytoy (2)/1660 & their aunt Nancy Turkey/1664, their sisters Aganunitsi-Wild Potato /1684, Oolootah/1692 & Ghigoneli/1694 are adopted by Rainmaker (1)-Cherokee in east TN

- 1695 – Snow White Opessa-Blanceneige-Wapakonee- Snow in the Face– Pekowi born Cecil CoMD

- 1695 to 1712 – Shawnee living on the Saluda River of central SC, eventually move to the Susquehanna River of PA

- 1695 – Polly Sassoonan-Delaware born PA, later wife of Opessa

- 1697 – Opessa a Pekowi Chief from Cecil Co MD moves with 70 families to Lancaster Co PA

- 1698 – Muskrat (1) adopted by Trader Tom Carpenter (2)-Moytoy (2)/1660 & Nancy Turkey/1664 after death of his parents

- 1698 – Tecoomteh Opessa-Pekowi born in Lancaster Co PA

- 1698 – Shawnee living in AL accompanied by a Frenchman from the LaSalle expedition

- 1698 - trader Thomas Welch travels & explores from Charleston SC to the Arkansas River AR passing mainly through TN

- 1698 – French Jesuit Pierre Charlevoix reports seeing blonde, bearded natives

- 1698 – Savannah Tom Carpenter (2)-Chalakatha-Shawano-ChalakaPowhatan-Cherokee-Metis born Running Water TN

- 1699 – Shawnee villages are found: on the Ohio River PA-OH-WVKY-IN-ILlon the Cumberland River TN-KY;on the Tennessee Rivers-TN
  1699 – Shawnee from the Cumberland valley-TN alleged by whites to attack "Cahokia" Indians on the Mississippi just below the mouth of the Illinois

- 1699 – The colony of Louisiana is established by France

- 1700 – Shawnee villages are found at & onL Hardy Co WV, Shenandoah Co VA; Alleghany Co MD; Winchester VA; Shenandoah River VA; Greenbrier River WV; Tennessee River TN; Kentucky River KY; Mason Co WV; Gallia Co OH; Sciota Co OH; Logan Co OH; Wood Co WV; Monongahela Co WV;
  Washington Co OH; Sciota River OH[Harrison Co WV; Berkeley Co WV; Big Sandy River WV-KY

- 1700 to 1765 – Shawnee are found: East PA on the Susquehanna River; South of the St. Lawrence in NY-PA; Along the south & west shores of the Great Lakes in NY-PA-OH-IN-IL-MI-WI; East & west of the Appalachians in PA-MD-VA-WV-KY-TNNC-SC-GA-AL; In Ohio valley in PA-OH-WV-KY-IN-IL-MO;
  On the Mississippi-above & below the mouth of the Ohio in ILMO-KY-TN; On the Pee Dee River of SC; On the Tennessee River of TN; On the Yadkin & New Rivers of NC; On the Alleghany River in PA & MD; On the Catawba River SC; On the Santee River SC

- 1700 – Most of Pekowi band remaining in NC-TN-VA-KY in northeast MD-southeast PA-Susquehanna valley among Delaware

- 1700 – Some Kishpoko-Mekoche from OH-Ohio valley join Mekoche & Kakawatchekee-Pheasant's Pekowi band in northeast PALehigh River valley among Delaware, Mohican & Mohawk

Shawnee Heritage II

- 1700 – Waywayti Opessa-Pekowi born PA

- 1700 - Henry Lawson among the Natives of the Carolinas, mentions the Shawannoa = Shawano = Chowan

- 1700 – John White Jr-Pekowi born PA
  1700 – John Drowning Bear Brown born IRE, immigrated to VA about 1720

- 1701 – Shawnee are represented by Opessa, Lemoytungh & Pemoyajagh at Treaty in Philadelphia PA with William Penn

- 1701 – Some Shawnee from SC arrive on the Susquehanna River PA

- 1701 – Shawnee living on the south end of the Ashley River NC

- 1702 - Queen Anne's War – Algonquian-Shawnee speaking Natives aid French & English colonists in skirmishes in CAN, FL & New England colonies

- 1702 – Loyparkoweh Opessa-Pekowi born PA

- 1702 – Great Eagle Carpenter-Chalakatha-Shawano-ChalakaPowhatan-Cherokee-Metis born Great Tellico TN

- 1703 - John Cheesquatalone-Yellow Bird Greenwood-ChalakathaThawikila-Kishpoko-Black Metis born Nickajack TN

- 1704 – Wakuta Cornstalk-Chalakatha-Mekoche-Shawano-ChalakaPowhatan-Metis born Running Water TN

- 1704 - Sehoy (1)-Sehoy Coushatta-Sehoy Marchand – Wind Clan Creek-born on Coosa River AL

- 1704 - Elizabeth Euguioote Carpenter-Elizabeth Tassel (1)-Chalakatha-Shawano-Chalaka Powhatan-Cherokee-Metis born Great Tellico TN

- 1706 – Some Thawikila-Pekowi-Kishpoko from SC-Savannah valley join Mekoche-Pekowi in northeast PA-Lehigh River valley among Mohawk, Mohican & Delaware

- 1706 – Some Thawikila-Pekowi-Kishpoko from GA-SC-Savannah valley to AL-Chattahoochee & Tallapoosa River valleys among Creeks

- 1706 – Some Thawikila-Pekowi-Kishpoko from SC-Savannah valley join Chalakatha-Mekoche Kishpoko in east TN-west NCsouthwest VA-east KY-Cumberland valley near Cherokee

- 1706 – Attakullakulla Carpenter-Chalakatha-Shawano-ChalakaPowhatan-Cherokee-Metis born Great Tellico TN

- 1707 – Okowellos Cornstalk & his mostly Chalakatha band in OHwest PA-Ohio valley

- 1707 – Thawikila found in village of Eskippeck on the Apalachicola River in northern FL

- 1708 – Long Knife Longtail-Elisha Wallen-Chalaiwa-Nanticoke-Metis born NJ

- 1708 – Lawson reports Shawnee, likely some remnants of Chalaka & Pekowi, are living on Savannah River SC-GA

- 1708 – Gallatin reports Shawnee, likely some remnants of Chalaka & Shawano, are living on the Catawba, Santee & Yadkin Rivers in NC

- 1708 - Corn Tassel Carpenter-Corn Tassel (1)-Old Corn Tassel-Chalakatha-Shawano-Chalaka -Powhatan-Cherokee-Metis born Great Tellico TN

- 1709 - Sister of Sehoy-Wind Clan Creek born about on Coosa River AL

- 1710 – Keightughqua-Cornstalk (6)-Chalakatha-Mekoche-ShawanoChalaka-Powhatan-Metis born PA

- 1710 – Moluntha-Mekoche born OH

  1710 – Wahootasika-Savannah King-Chalakatha born western VA/WV

  1710 – Young Rising Sun-Kishpoko born Lehigh valley PA

- 1710 - Susan Moytoy Carpenter-Chalakatha-Shawano-ChalakaPowhatan-Cherokee-Metis born Tellico Plains TN

- 1710 - Some Thawikila, Pekowi, Kishpoko move from Ohio valley to the Chattahoochee River in AL

- 1710 - Some Pekowi, Kishpoko move from Ohio valley to Lancaster Co PA

- 1710 - Some Pekowi, Thawikila, Kishpoko move from Ohio valley to north AL

- 1710 - Pride Opessa-Pekowi born MD

- 1710 – Corn Cob Cornstalk-Chalakatha-Pekowi-Shawano-ChalakaPowhatan-Metis born PA

- 1711 – Opessa's Pekowi band move from northeast MD-southeast PA-Susquehanna valley among Delaware to the Potomac River-western MD

- 1711 – Natchez tribe of MS-LA destroyed by the French, one band of survivors settles near the Shawnee town of Tuckabatchee in AL

- 1711-1713 – Tuscarora War – Iroquoian & Algonquian (i.e. ShawanoChalaka) speaking Natives of NC defeated by English colonists
  & Native supporters

- 1712 – Sawelaha Eliza Cornstalk-Chalakatha-Mekoche-ShawanoChalaka-Powhatan-Metis born WV

- 1712 – Daniel Blevins-Chalaiwa-Nanticoke-Metis born NJ

- 1715 – Sarah Rising Sun (later to be the mother of Blue Jacket)Kispoko born Lehigh River valley PA among Mohawk, Mahican & Delaware

  1715 – Chalakatha-Kishpoko-Thawikila-Mekoche-Pekowi in east TN-west NC-east KY-southwest VA Cumberland valley make peace with Cherokee following dispute

- 1715 – Some Chalakatha-Kishpoko-Thawikila-Mekoche-Pekowi from east TN-west NC-east KY southwest VA-Cumberland valley move to OH-west WV-north KY-west PA-Ohio valley

- 1715 – "Indians living along the Savannah River SC-GA"=ThawikilaPekowi-Kishpoko-Chalaka & "those Indians living in the (NC) piedmont"=Chalakatha-Kishpoko-Shawano join the Yamasee in the Yamasee War

- 1715 – some Chalakatha-Kishpoko-Thawikila-Mekoche-Pekowi from east TN-west NC-east KY southwest VA-Cumberland valley join Thawikila-Kishpoko in AL among Creeks in
  Tuckabatchee, Wetumpka, Sawanugi, Talladega, Sylacauga, Tallapoosa, Marbury & Kyamulga villages

- 1715 – Wife of Moluntha-Sister of Black Hoof-Thawikila born AL

- 1715-17 - Yamasee War included Creeks, Choctaws, some Cherokee and "the Indians living along the Savannah River and northward into the piedmont" i.e. the earlier locations of the Chalaka and Xuala

- 1715-17 - During the Yamasee War most Cherokee joined with the whites & killed other Native emissaries

- 1716 – Cawachile Cornstalk-Chalakatha-Mekoche-ShawanoChalaka-Powhatan-Metis born WV

- 1716 – Alexander Spotswood "discovers" the Shenandoah River-VA

- 1717 – After the Yamasee War, Creeks in AL receive many "nonMuskogee speakers" some =Shawnee

    1717 – One band of Thawikila settles on the Chattahoochee River between GA-AL

    1717 – Some Thawikila living in village of Ikanhatki on the Tallapoosa River AL

- 1717 - French build Ft. Toulouse on the Alabama River

- 1718 – Martin Chartier dies in PA among Pekowi band

- 1718 – New Orleans is founded by French

- 1718 – Nonhelema Cornstalk-Chalakatha-Mekoche-ShawanoChalaka-Powhatan-Metis born Greenbrier River WV

- 1720 – Aqueloma, Chief of Thawikila band in west PA-northeast OH-west WV-Ohio valley

- 1720 – Big Tree-Thawikila born PA

- 1720 – Big Snake-Shemeneto-Mekoche born PA

- 1720 – Black Stump-Thawikila born AL

- 1720 – Anna-Nanye-Pekowi born SC

- 1720 – Tall Oak-Chalakatha born PA

- 1720 - Eagle Wings-Tuckabatchee Chief-Thawikila born Tuckabatchee AL

- 1720 – Parker V. Adkins-Shawano-Metis born Henrico Co VA

- 1720 – Nimwha Cornstalk-Chalakatha-Mekoche-Shawano-ChalakaPowhatan-Metis born WV

- 1720 – Bukangelos Cornstalk-Chalakatha-Shawano-ChalakaPowhatan-Delaware-Metis born PA

- 1721 – Edward Ned Sizemore-Shawano-Metis born VA

- 1722 – Kikusgowlawa-Thawikila born AL

  1722 – Sowege-Gliding Swan-Pekowi born Lancaster Co PA

1722 - Sehoy (2)-Sehoy Hatali-Sehoy Marchand-Creek-Metis born Ft. Toulouse Elmore Co AL

1722 – Red Hawk Cornstalk-Chalakatha-Mekoche-ShawanoChalaka-Powhatan-Metis born WV

1723 – Okowellos' Chalakatha band in PA

1723 – Opessa's Pekowi band in northwest MD-northern VA

1723 – Squirrel King's Savannah Band Chickasaw living with Shawnee at Old Savannah Town near Augusta GA

1724 – Weasau-Thawikila born AL

1724 – Silverheels Cornstalk-Chalakatha-Mekoche-ShawanoChalaka-Powhatan-Metis born PA

1725 – Okowellos' Chalakatha band from PA is in AL among Creeks

1725 – Shawnee establish a village later called Logstown PA

1725 – Black Fish-Chalakatha-Mekoche born in PA

1725 – Black Oak-Chalakatha born PA

1725 – Some Thawikila living on the Savannah River GA-SC

1725 - Wryneck-Aquilsa-Pekowi born in PA

- 1726 – Kekewepelethee-Capt. Johnny-Thawikila born AL

- 1726 – Elizabeth Cornstalk Chalakatha-Shawano-Chalaka-PowhatanCreek-Metis born AL

   1727 – "Kings of the Five Nations" i.e. the Chiefs of the 5 Shawnee Tribes living in Washington Co MD eastern panhandle of WVupper Potomac valley

- 1728 – Yellow Hawk-Thawikila born AL

- 1728 – Catherine Kitty Cornstalk Chalakatha-Shawano-ChalakaPowhatan-Creek-Metis born AL

- 1728 – Robert Brown-Big Bear-Chalakatha-Shawano-ChalakaPowhatan-Metis born Chota TN

- 1729 – some Chalakatha-Kishpoko-Thawikila-Pekowi-Mekoche from AL-Chattahoochee-Tallapoosa River valleys among Creeks return to north TN-north/central KY-southern OH-west WVOhio valley

- 1730-79 – most of 5 Tribes are in OH-west PA-west WV-Ohio valley except as noted are living in the Ohio River drainage

- 1730 – Black Hoof-Thawikila born TN (or KY or FL)

- 1730 – Most Chalakatha-Kishpoko-Thawikila-Mekoche from southeast PA-north MD-Susquehanna valley to west PA-east OH-west WV-north KY-Ohio valley

- 1730 – Some Chalakatha-Kishpoko-Thawikila-Mekoche from AL-SCNC-TN to west PA-east OH west WV-north KY-Ohio valley

- 1730 – Most Pekowi-Thawikila-Mekoche from north MD-southeast PA-Susquehanna valley among Delaware to west PA-east OHwest WV-Ohio valley

- 1730 – Some Shawnee, likely Thawikila, living on Suwannee River AL

- 1730 – Most Mekoche-Thawikila-Kishpoko from northeast PALehigh valley among Delaware, Mohican & Mohawk to west PA-east OH-west WV-Ohio valley

- 1730 – Big Hominy-Big Hanoana-Missemediqueety a Pekowi Chief in west PA

  1730 – Moose-Big Deer-Big Elk-Chalakatha born PA
  1730 – Edmond Atkin among the Natives of the southeast

- 1730 – John Sour Mush-Ookoseta-Ogosata Greenwood-ChalakathaPekowi-Thawikila-Kishpoko Black-Metis born Chota TN

- 1730 – Anna Chartier-Pekowi-Metis born PA

- 1731 – Okowellos' Chalakatha band is in west PA-east OH-west WVOhio valley

- 1733 – Some Shawnee living at Winchester VA – sold land to Abraham Hollingsworth

- 1733 – Thawikila from Chattahoochee River GA-AL moved to Tallapoosa River AL accompanied by some "Yuchi "

- 1734 – Young Rising Sun (Father of Puckenshinwa) with PekowiKishpoko band living in AL among Creeks

- 1734 – Opessa's Pekowi band in AL among Creeks

- 1734 – Nancy-Middle Daughter of Loyparkoweh-Pekowi born AL among Creeks

- 1735 – Some Pekowi-Thawikila-Kishpoko-Mekoche from AL-TNNC-VA-KY to west PA-east OH west WV-Ohio valley

- 1735 – Some Pekowi-Thawikila-Kishpoko-Mekoche from east PAnorth MD to west PA-east OH-west WV-north KY-Ohio valley

- 1735 – Whirlpool-(Blue Jacket)-Pekowi-Kishpoko born west PA-east OH-Ohio valley

- 1735 – Black Snake-Kishpoko born OH

- 1735 – Kishkalwa-Thawikila born OH

- 1735 - James Adair among the natives of GA-AL

- 1735 – Puckenshinwa Rising Sun-Kishpoko-Creek-Metis born Tuckabatchee AL

- 1735 – Samuel Sanders born ENG, adopted 1760 VA by Shawnee

- 1736 – Some Thawikila from east OH-west WV-north KY-Ohio valley to SC-AL among Creeks

- 1737 – Peter Chartier a Pekowi Chief in west PA-Allegheny valley

- 1738 – Metheotashe Opessa-Pekowi born AL among Creeks

- 1738 – French explorer Pierre Gauthier de Varennes encounters a tribe of fair-skinned, Welsh speaking Mandan near Bismarck

ND

- 1738 – Longtail (2)-Joseph Wallen-Chalaiwa-Shawano-NanticokeMetis born in MD

- 1739 – Some Shawnee are living at the old Savannah Town-Aiken Co GA with mixed Shawnee Chickasaw band-allied with the British of SC-GA

- 1739-1742 – War of Jenkin's Ear – some Shawnee aid English in skirmishes with Spanish in GA-FL-AL

- 1739 - Older Daughter of Young Rising Sun-Kishpoko-Creek-Metis born Tuckabatchee AL, later wife of Blue Jacket, wife of Isadore Chesne & wife of Big Swamp

- 1740 – John Howard & James Salling-British explorers are captured on the Great Kanawha-WV by a band of Shawnee, French & blacks & taken to New Orleans returning to VA in 1643

- 1740 – Black Hoof with family in AL-SC among Creeks-later on to FL

- 1740 – Opessa's Pekowi band from AL among Creeks to north MDsoutheast PA

    1740 – Bloody Fellow-Kishpoko born Running Water TN
    1740 - Gardner Green-Red Wolf-Gigageiwaya – ChalakathaShawano born VA

- 1742 – Shawnee, at least Pekowi & Chalakatha, living in Wyoming valley of PA

- 1743 – Kakawatchekee-Pheasant's Pekowi band from southeast PA-north MD move to Logstown-west PA-east OH-Ohio valley

- 1743 – Paxinosa succeeds Pheasant-Kakawatchekee as Head Pekowi
    Chief in north MD-southeast PA, when Pheasant moves to east OH-west PA-Ohio valley

- 1744 – Some Thawikila-Pekowi-Chalakatha from north MD-southeast PA to AL among Creeks

- 1744 – Peter Chartier moved to Sciota River OH with band

- 1744 – Shawnee permit John Findley to become the first British to live in KY

- 1744 – French build a grist mill on the Cumberland River, abandoned after the French-Indian War

- 1744-1748 – King George's War – Algonquian-Shawnee speaking Natives take different sides to aid French & English colonists in CAN & New England colonies against one another

- 1745 – Some Pekowi-Thawikila-Mekoche from north MD-southeast PA-Susquehanna valley to east TN west NC-east KY-southwest VA-Cumberland valley then on to south IN-IL-Ohio River valley

- 1745 – Peter Chartier's band moved to Winchester KY

- 1745 – Mary Rising Sun-Kishpoko-Creek-Metis born Tuckabatchee AL, later wife of David Mumagechee Francis

- 1745 – George All Chief Sizemore-Shawano-Metis born VA

- 1746 – Some Pekowi-Thawikila-Mekoche remain in east TN-west NC-east KY-southwest VA Cumberland valley

- 1746 – Peter Chartier moves some of his band on to French LickNashville TN

- 1747 – Many Pekowi-Thawikila-Mekoche from south IN-IL-lower Ohio valley to west PA-east OH-west WV-Ohio valley

- 1747 – Peter Chartier & band moved to upper Coosa River AL

- 1747 – Samuel Riley-Pekowi-Metis born MD

- 1748 – Big Hominy, a Pekowi Chief in OH associated with Peter Chartier

- 1748 – Peter Chartier with band reported in south IL-lower Ohio valley (more likely a brother or son)

- 1748 – Chartier band with some Chalakatha-Thawikila from east OH-west PA establish Chalakagay Sylacauga village in AL among Creeks

- 1750 – Big Turtle-Shekaghkela-Chalakatha later from the Black Fish band born OH

- 1749 – Cornstalk is a major Chalakatha Chief in east OH-west PAnorthwest VA

- 1749 – Celeron de Blainville spends 5 days in the Shawnee village at site of Portsmouth OH

- 1750 – Opessa's Pekowi band in OH-Ohio valley

- 1750 – Shawnee living on Cumberland River in KY

- 1750 to 1794 – some Pekowi-Thawikila-Mekoche remain in scattered pockets in north MD-northeast VA east PA
  1750 – Red Giant-Chalakatha born (IN-IL-MI) along Great Lakes

- 1750 – Mixed Shawnee-Seneca from western PA move to Keowee SC, a "lower Cherokee" town

- 1750 – Christopher Gist, Nathaniel Gist & company exploring in the Ohio valley

- 1750 – George Croghan operating a trading post at the mouth of the Muskingum River OH

- 1750 – Lewis Rogers born VA, adopted son 1760 OH of Black Fish

- 1752 – Opessa succeeds Pheasant-Kakawatchekee as Head Pekowi Chief in OH

- 1752 – Welshman named (Fredrick/Freydeck) Owens said to be only white within 50 miles, said to be living on the forks of the Yadkin River at the mulberry fields but Christopher Gist-a white was living at the mulberry fields on the forks of the Yadkin also that year so Owens was likely on the forks of the New River locale known as mulberry fields (now Ashe Co NC) which would be about 50 miles from Gist. This camp or small village was called Freydeck or Freydeck's

- 1752 – smallpox erupts in the villages friendly to the French in the Ohio valley; Cold Foot & his son,-two of the most trusted Natives are among the dead

- 1752 – Charles Langlade leads a party of 250 Shawnee, Chippewa & Ottawa to destroy Pickawilly & kill Old Britain-Miami

- 1753 – Pride Opessa dies in SC prison, his family-clan attack the whites in retribution

- 1754 – Capt. John Reed (1) & George Bennett-both Shawano from Gates Co NC living at the old Savannah Town-Aiken Co GA with mixed Shawnee-Chickasaw band-allied with the British of SC-GA

- 1754-1763 – French-Indian War - most Natives west of the Appalachians, headed by the Ohio valley Shawnee, join the French against the British & the non-Shawnee Natives from east of the Appalachians

- 1754-63 – "Indians" of northeast TN-east KY-northwest NCsouthwest VA i.e. Shawnee attack whites fleeing Ohio valley

- 1754-63 – Cornstalk is foremost leader of Shawnee aligned with the French in French-Indian War

- 1754-63 – Cherokee of southeast TN-southwest NC align with British to fight "other Indians" from northeast TN-northwest NCsouthwest VA-east KY-Shawnee aligned with French

- 1755 – A delegation from west PA-Ohio valley goes to Philadelphia PA to sue for peace & are hung by the British

- 1755 – Some of Opessa's Pekowi band in AL among Creeks

- 1755 – Peter Chartier returns to OH but some of his Pekowi band remains in AL among Creeks

- 1755 – Okowellos' & Cornstalk's Chalakatha band in AL among Creeks

- 1755 – Shawnee crush the Catawba in SC & kill Chief Haiglar, ending any pretense of Catawba as a solely Native power forever

- 1755 – Black Hoof & family Thawikila from AL to OH with Cornstalk's Chalakatha band

- 1755 – Black Horse-Chalakatha born AL among the Creeks

- 1755-59 – Shawnee war parties raiding central & west PA-west WVwest MD-southwest VA-east KY-east TN-northwest NC-Ohio Valley & Appalachian frontiers, kill 2,500+ whites, capture & adopt hundreds
  1755 – Black Fish a War Chief in OH-west PA-Ohio Valley

- 1755-69 – Cornstalk is associated with John Swift-white in silver-mining in northeast KY-southwest VA southwest WV-Big Sandy valley, producing counterfeit money for 5 United Shawnee Tribes & eventual 20 Tribe Northern Confederacy

- 1756 – Paxinosa's Pekowi band from west PA-Ohio valley to northeast PA-Lehigh valley among Delaware, Mohican & Mohawk

- 1756 – Some Pekowi-Thawikila-Mekoche from east TN-west NCsouthwest VA-east KY-Cumberland valley to east OH-west WV-Ohio valley

- 1756 – Most Chalakatha-Kishpoko-Thawikila-Mekoche from north KY-west WV to east OH-Ohio valley

- 1756 – Chief Bowl-John Bowles-John Watts-Chalakatha-Pekowi-Shawano-Chalaka-Powhatan -Metis born Little Hiwassee TN

- 1756 – Shawnee living in a village near Nashville TN

- 1757 – Paxinosa's Pekowi from northeast PA to northwest NY with Christian Delaware

- 1758 – Okowellos & Cornstalk's Chalakatha bands in east OH-Ohio valley

- 1758 – Paxinosa's Pekowi band from northwest NY to east OH-west PA-west WV-Ohio valley

- 1758 – Most Shawnee are in west PA-east OH-west WV between Allegheny & Scotia Rivers except some Thawikila-Chalakatha-Kishpoko-Mekoche in AL among Creeks & some in TN-west
  NC-west VA-east KY-Cumberland valley & some PekowiThawikila-Mekoche-Kishpoko in southeast PA north MD

- 1757-58 – Smallpox Epidemic kills thousands of Shawnee in OH-PA-
  WV-VA-KY-TN-NC-SC-AL, including over six dozen Chiefs

& Headmen in the Ohio valley alone, including Okowellos & 2nd Husband of the Sarah Rising Sun

1758 – Cornstalk's Chalakatha band in AL with Creeks for a short time, fleeing epidemic, returns to OH upon death of Okowellos

1758 – Cornstalk succeeds Okowellos as Chief of the Chalakatha

1758 – Rising Sun-Kishpoko in northeast PA-Lehigh valley with Paxinosa's Pekowi band

1758 – Sequoyah-George Gist –Chalakatha-Pekowi-Shawano-Chalaka-Powhatan-Cherokee-Metis born Great Tellico TN

1758 – First child of Anglo-Saxon parents to be born in TN is born at Ft. Louden in what is now Nashville

1759 – Puckenshinwa moves with wife & children from AL to KY

1759 – Peter Chartier in east OH-Ohio valley with band

1759 - Sehoy (3)-Sehoy Tuckabatchee-Sehoy Eagle Wings-ThawikilaCreek-Metis born Ft. Toulouse AL

1759 – Bloody Fellow-Kishpoko living among Cherokee & Chickamauga-(mixed Shawnee & Cherokee) east TNnorthwest NC-southwest VA-east KY

1760 – Paxinosa's Pekowi band in east OH-upper Ohio valley

1760 – Puckenshinwa moves from KY to central OH-Ohio valley

1760 – Anthony Shane- Kishpoko-Creek-Wyandot-Metis born OH

- 1760 - Henry Timberlake among the natives of northeast TN

- 1760 – William Jackson-Fish born VA, adopted son 1770 OH of Black Fish

  1760 – Elisha Long Knife Wallen in the Clinch & Powell valleys of TN

  1761 - Robert Benge-Chief Benge-Robin Benge-Chalakatha-Pekowi-
  Shawano-Chalaka Powhatan-Cherokee-Metis born Toqua TN

- 1763 – Cornstalk unites the 5 Shawnee Tribes, based in OH

- 1763-1766 – Pontiac War – "Great Lakes Indians", including Shawnee lead by Cornstalk, battle British across the frontier

- 1763-66 – Cornstalk's 5 United Shawnee Tribes are Pontiac's most ardent & successful supporters

- 1764 – Maurice Griffith stays among the white Welsh-speaking Mandan, about the same time a James Girty completes a "Welsh-Indian Vocabulary of Welsh words and terms used by the Mandan

- 1765 – At conclusion of Pontiac War, Col. Bouquet attempts to force the return of all adopted whites & blacks, of 650+ known captives adopted by the Shawnee only about 300 actually return, of that over 200 return to the tribe or the frontier

- 1768 – Tecumseh-Kishpoko-Pekowi-Creek-Metis born OH

- 1769 – Col Alexander McKee & Col. Matthew Elliott-adopted-Irish living among Shawnee in OH-Ohio valley, with their Shawnee wives & Metis children

- 1770 – Red Giant moves from the Great Lakes area moves to east OH-Ohio valley

- 1771 – Longtail Cat-James Carr Wallen-Chalaiwa-Hopia-ShawanoNanticoke-Metis born VA

- 1772 – Sarah Rising Sun (2) living in OH-Ohio valley

- 1772 – Big Bear-Robert Brown, the major Chief of the Natives in northwest NC, i.e. the Shawnee & the great enemy of the Cherokee, guides the (soon to be) Americans to the Cherokee in northwest GA

- 1773 – Cornstalk issues orders that any Virginian found on Shawnee land be killed, any Pennsylvanian found on Shawnee land be robbed & whipped, this applied in KY-southwest VA-all of WV-west MD-west PA-all of OH

- 1774 – Dunmore's War - Cornstalk's 5 United Shawnee Tribes are the core of his 20 Tribe Native Confederacy in the Battle of Point Pleasant

- 1774 – Immediately following the Battle of Point Pleasant, Black Hoof & brothers Weasau, Black Stump, Kikusgowlawa, Capt. Johnny-Tame Hawk, Yellow Hawk & Kishkalwa-Tiger Tail move from OH to AL villages among Creeks in an attempt to distance themselves from white reprisals in the north

- 1774 – Black Snake succeeds Puckenshinwa as Head Kishpoko Chief in OH

- 1775 – A great French partisan deputy from the Shawnee, i.e. Red Hawk, speaks to the Chickamauga in TN against the Americans

- 1775 - John Bear Hunter-Green-Chalakatha-Pekowi-Shawano-Metis born southwest VA

- 1777 – Black Hoof & all brothers except Weasau, move from AL to OH-Ohio valley

- 1777 – Some Thawikila from OH-Ohio valley to MO-St. Louis area

- 1777-79 – Black Fish becomes Chief of Chalakatha & All Shawnee, at least in OH-Ohio valley, following the murder of Cornstalk, Red Hawk, Ellinipsico & Petella

- 1778 – Capt. Joseph Dusquene- Pekowi-Wyandot-Metis adopted by Black Fish in OH
  1779-84 – Wryneck-Aquilsa – Chief of Pekowi band in OH-Ohio valley

  1779 – Leadership of All Shawnee (formed under Cornstalk) splits between most of the Thawikila, Pekowi & some Kishpoko under Black Hoof-a Thawikila and most of the Chalakatha &
  Mekoche with some Pekowi & Kishpoko under Moluntha-a Mekoche

- 1779 – most Thawikila-Pekowi & Kishpoko from OH-Ohio valley (including Black Stump, Kikusgowlawa, Yellow Hawk, Red Eagle, Red Snake) move to MO-St. Louis area

- 1779 – Most Chalakatha-Mekoche with some Pekowi & Kishpoko & Black Hoof Thawikila family remain in east OH-Ohio valley

- 1779 – Sarah Rising Sun (2) in west WV-Ohio valley

- 1779 – Metheotashe (Opessa) Puckenshinwa & Watmeme (Opessa) Black Fish-both widows move to MO-St. Louis area with their families

- 1779 - Jonathan Jont Blevins-Shawano-Chalaiwa-Nanticoke-Metis born VA 1780 – Cheeseekau with Chickamauga in Running Water TN

- 1780 – Bobcat-Black Bob-William James Wallen-Chalaiwa-HopiaShawano-Nanticoke-Metis born OH

- 1785 – Old Chelelagathe in Running Water TN village among Cherokee

- 1785 – Black Snake steps down as Head Kishpoko Chief under Black
    Hoof's faction, is succeeded by Blue Jacket as War Chief & Yellow Hawk as Civil Chief of faction in OH

- 1786 – Moluntha murdered by whites, faction splits again with Blue
    Jacket as leader of the Pekowi-Kishpoko group with some Chalakatha & Mekoche in OH & Capt. Johnny Kekewepelethee as leader of a Thawikila-Pekowi with some

Chalakatha & Mekoche group in OH

- 1787 – Most remaining Pekowi & Kishpoko from OH-Ohio valley move to MO-St. Louis area

- 1788 – Longtail (3)Joseph Banks Wallen-Chalaiwa-Hopia-ShawanoNanticoke-Metis born in TN

- 1790 – Chief Bowl – Chief of Little Hiwassee village TN

- 1790 – Tecumseh joins Cheeseekau in Running Water TN with Chickamauga

- 1790 – Tecumseh marries Tahneh Hop-Dark Star-Naomi-Slow Head in TN in another "political" marriage

- 1790 – Most of Thawikila-Pekowi & Kishpoko living at Cape Girardeau-MO

- 1793 – Tahneh Hop-Dark Star-Naomi-Slow Head moves to a Shawnee village in MO with Daughter of Tecumseh, when Tecumseh returns to the north

- 1794 – Chief Bowl Chief of Running Water TN village

- 1795 – Some Chalakatha-Mekoche-Thawikila-Kishpoko-Pekowi in Lewistown, Hog Creek & Wapakonetta villages stay in east OH-Ohio valley

- 1795 – Some Chalakatha-Mekoche & most of the remaining Thawikila-Pekowi-Kishpoko from OH Ohio valley to MO-St. Louis area

- 1795 – Some Thawikila-Pekowi-Kishpoko-Chalakatha from AL villages among Creeks to MO-St. Louis area

- 1795-1812 – Tecumseh travels to various parts of the nation, trying to unite the natives

- 1795-1819 – Chief Bowl, Chief of AR mixed Shawnee-Cherokee

- 1796 – Sarah Rising Sun (2) living in Gallia County OH

- 1798 – Some Chalakatha-Mekoche-Kishpoko from OH move to White River IN

- 1798 – Weasau-Thawikila - King of the Sawanogi-Shawnee among the Creeks in AL

- 1811 – Most followers of Tecumseh gathered in north IN & are defeated at Prophet's Town

- 1811 – Some followers of Tecumseh move to MO-St. Louis area following Prophet's Town

- 1812 – Most Thawikila-Mekoche-Chalakatha-Pekowi-Kishpoko from AL to MO-St. Louis area

- 1813 – Most followers of Tecumseh scatter from IN to OH-Ohio valley & MO-AR-Mississippi valley

- 1815 – A band of followers of Tecumseh led by his brother Prophet, his sister Tecumapease & his son Paukeesaa move to CAN

- 1815 – Some followers of Tecumseh move to MO-St. Louis area

- 1815 – Some followers of Tecumseh move to AR, joining the mixed Shawnee-Cherokee there

- 1819 – Chief Bowl moved to TX with Cherokee-Shawnee band

- 1822 – Some Shawnee in MO (some from all 5 Tribes) move to TX with Chief Bowl

- 1825 – Most followers of Tecumseh return from CAN to OH with the Prophet & Paukeesaa

- 1826 – Some followers of Tecumseh move from OH to KS, with the Prophet & Paukeesaa

- 1830 – "The 5 Civilized Tribes (in the eyes of the Americans) of the southeast; Cherokee, Creek, Choctaw, Chickasaw & Seminole stand in stark contrast (in white estimation) to the "wild Indians" further north", i.e. the Shawnee

- 1831 – Black Hoof dies in OH, his family are the last Thawikila in OH

- 1832 – Lewistown Chalakatha band, including the mixed MohawkCayuga-Seneca band, move from OH to OK

- 1832 - Wapakonetta Mekoche band from OH to KS

- 1832 – Most of other Shawnee & mixed-ancestry Shawnee move from MO to KS

- 1839 – Some followers of Tecumseh in KS, led by Michelana-the Son
    of Tecumseh, leave for AR, they are attacked & killed enroute by either Comanche or whites

- 1839 – Chief Bowl killed in TX, band removes to OK

APPENDIX 3
Names for Ancient & Historic Shawnee Tribes

1. Adena – a name given to the mound-building Shawnee of 1500 B.C. to 200 A.D., centered in the mid-Ohio valley, extending for hundreds of miles, often giants in stature
2. Akochakanen – an Iroquois name for Shawnee
3. Allegewi – a name for an Ancient Shawnee Tribe, the ancient rulers of the eastern half of the continent, centered in the mid-Mississippi valley, often giants in stature
4. Allegans – a name for the ancient giant rulers of the eastern half of the continent, often giants in stature
5. Alleghans – a name for the ancient rulers of the eastern half of the continent, often giants in stature
6. Ancient Ones – a name for the ancient rulers of the eastern half of the continent, often giants in stature
7. Ani-Kutani – a Cherokee name for the ancient rulers of the eastern half of the continent, often giants in stature
8. Ani-Sawanugi – a Cherokee name for Shawnee, Mooney 1900
9. Ani-Suwall – a Cherokee name for Cheraw-Xuala-Shawnee
10. Assiwikala – a name for Thawikila
11. Asswikales – a name for the Thawikila
12. Aztalans – one of the Ancient Shawnee Tribes & ancient rulers of the eastern U.S., centered in WI & upper Mississippi valley, but their remains were said to litter the ground in KY, often giants in stature
13. Aztlans – a name for the Aztalans
14. Bear River Indians – those found on the Pamlico River NC in colonial times
15. Bicowetha – a name for the Pekowi
16. Cacahouanous – Joutel 1687
17. Cahokia – one of the Ancient Shawnee Tribes, the Shawnee culture of 300 A.D. to 1300 A.D., centered near St. Louis IL-MO in the

midMississippi valley, extending for hundreds of miles, often giants in stature, later an Illinois Tribe of the 1700's
18. Canoise - a name for the Kanawha
19. Cawala – a Sioux name for Shawnee, also the name of a Teton division descended from an adopted Shawnee, Dorsey 1886
20. Cawana – an Omaha, Ponca, Osage name for Shawnee, Dorsey 1878
21. Chaganons – Tonti 1680
22. Chaguanos – a Spanish name for Shawnee, Alegre 1841
23. Chalaakaatha – a name for the Chalakatha
24. Chalahgawtha – a name for the Chalakatha
25. Chalaka – one of the Ancient Shawnee Tribes, centered in the Savannah valley, extending for hundreds of miles, encountered by Desoto in the 1540's
26. Chalakagee – Chalakatha in AL by 1748
27. Chalakatha – "First Man or first born", the 1st or oldest Tribe of the Historic Shawnee, according to some the Head Chief of all Shawnee, when there is one, must be a Chalakatha or Thawikila
28. Chalaqua – encountered by Desoto 1540 on the Savannah River
29. Chalaiwa – a name for an Ancient Shawnee Tribe, centered in the midOhio valley, extending for hundreds of miles
30. Chanousanons – letter in N.Y. 1756
31. Chaoianon – Gravier 1670
32. Chaonanons – Celeron 1749
33. Chaonanons – Domenech 1860
34. Chaoni – Vater 1816
35. Chaouannons – 1756 Montreal conference
36. Chaouanon – Charlevoix 1868
37. Chaouanon – Nicholson 1698
38. Chaouanong – Jesuit Relations 1672
39. Chaouanos – LaTour 1782
40. Chaouans – Hind 1863
41. Chaouanua – Gravier 1700
42. Chaouennons – Lambertville 1684
43. Chaouenon – Hennepin 1698, Senex 1710
44. Chaouens – Hennepin 1698
45. Chaouesnons – LaSalle 1681
46. Chaounons – Montcalm 1757
47. Chaouoinons – Vauderuil 1760

48. Chaowanons – d'Abbadie 1765
49. Charanons – Shea 1861
50. Chaskepe – Franquelin 1684, a name for Kishpoko
51. Chateanons – Denonville 1688
52. Chattahoochee – Shawnee in AL 1715
53. Chauanons – French 1668
54. Chauenese – Colden 1764
55. Chauenous – Chauvignerie 1736
56. Chaunis – Vater 1816
57. Chaunous – McIntosh 1853
58. Chaunys – De la Foi 1841
59. Chavanons – Alcedo 1787
60. Chavanons – Crepy 1755
61. Chavouanons – Sheldon 1856
62. Chawanock – Smith 1607
63. Chawanoes – Cox 1741
64. Chawanons – 1759 NY
65. Chawenons – Vauderuil 1758
66. Cheraw – a name for the Xuala-Shawnee 1670
67. Cheremons – Lambertville 1686
68. Chillicothe – a name for the Chalakatha
69. Chillicotheans – a name for Chalakatha
70. Chillokee – a Creek name for Shawnee
71. Chilokila – a Creek name for Shawnee
72. Chiouanons – Galinee 1669
73. Chiouonons – De L'Isle 1700
74. Chonque – Tonti 1690
75. Chouanongs – Boudinot 1816
76. Chouanons – Iberville 1702
77. Chouanous – Vaugondy 1778
78. Chouenons – map in NY 1706
79. Chouesnons – LaSalle 1681
80. Chowan – an Anglofied version of a French name for Shawnee or a shortening of Shawano
81. Chowanock – Dane 1584, a name for the Shawano in northeast NC, inland from the Roanoke colony
82. Chuanoes – Marquette 1673
83. Cisca – Franquelin 1684

84. Cofitachequi – encountered by Desoto 1540 on the Santee River SCGA
85. Congaree – in the Santee valley SC-NC 1701
86. Conhoy - a name for the Kanawha
87. Conoy – a name for the Kanawha
88. Coranine – a name for Coree
89. Coree – on the Neuse River of NC
90. Cwarenoc – Lane 1585, an early name for Coree
91. Eskippeck – Shawnee in FL before 1707
92. Fort Ancient – a name given to the last of the pre-European Shawnee cultures 1300 A.D. to 1650 A.D. centered in the mid-Ohio valley, extending for hundreds of miles
93. Ganawese – a name for the Kanawha
94. Hathagilgi – a Creek name for Shawnee
95. Hathawekela – a name for the Thawikila
96. Hathawikila – a name for the Thawikila
97. Hikanagi – a name for the Mahican
98. Hopia – one of the Ancient Shawnee Tribes, centered in the mid-Ohio valley, extending for hundreds of miles, the last full-blood died in the very early 1800's
99. Hopewell – a name for the mound-building Shawnee 1000 B.C. to 300

    A.D. centered in the Ohio valley, extending for hundreds of miles
100. Ispokogi – a name for the Kishpoko
101. Kanawha – an Ancient Tribe of Shawnee, centered in the lower New River valley, extending for hundreds of miles, often giants in stature
102. Kanhaways – a name for the Kanawha
103. Kishpoko – the 5th Tribe of the Historic Shawnee, but also called the third oldest brother after the Chalakatha & Pekowi, though aligned more closely with the Thawikila & Pekowi, all three having ancient & strong connections in the south
104. Kispokotha – a name for the Kishpoko
105. Keyauwee – 1701
106. Kiscopocoke – a name for the Kishpoko
107. Kiskapoke – a name for Kishpoko
108. Kiskapooke – a name for Kishpoko
109. Kispocotha – a name for Kishpoko
110. Kispogogi – a name for Kishpoko
111. Kispokotha – a name for Kishpoko

112. Kispugo – a name for Kishpoko
113. Kispugoki – a name for Kishpoko
114. Loupes – a French name for some Shawnee
115. Machachach – a name for Mekoche
116. Mackachak – a name for Mekoche
117. Macochee – a name for Mekoche
118. Macqueechaick - a name for Mekoche
119. Macqueechek – a name for Mekoche
120. Maguck – a name for Mekoche
121. Makochee – a name for Mekoche
122. Makujay – name for Mekoche
123. Maquck – a name for Mekoche
124. Massawomekes – Smith 1608
125. Maykujay – a name for Mekoche
126. Maykujayki – a name for Mekoche
127. Meguck – a name for Mekoche
128. Mekoce – a name for the Mekoche
129. Mekoche – "a perfect man", 2nd Tribe of the Historic Shawnee, also called the second oldest brother of the five Tribes, most often aligned closely with the Chalakatha, both having ancient connections in the north
130. Mequachake – a name for Mekoche
131. Mequache – a name for Mekoche
132. Mequck – a name for Mekoche
133. Mequatchaiki – Franquelin 1684, a name for Mekoche
134. Minquas, Black – an Ancient Shawnee Tribe in the upper Ohio valley 1500-1650, rulers of the upper regions of the 2nd great river drainage if going from east to west, Gulf drainage-connections, often giants in stature
135. Minqua, White – pre-1600 to 1700 Shawnee in the Susquehanna valley 1500-1700's, rulers of the 1st great river drainage if going from east to west, Atlantic drainage-connections, of giants in stature
136. Mississippian – a name for the ancient mound-building culture of 300 A.D. to 1300 A.D., also called the Cahokia culture
137. Moneton - 1673
138. Mosopelean – Franquelin 1684
139. Nanticoke – an Ancient Tribe of the Shawnee, in PA-DE-NJ-MD
140. Nhikana – a name for the Mahicahn

141. **Nicotoni** – a Cherokee name for the ancient rulers of the eastern half of the continent, often giants in stature
142. Oawikila – a name for the Thawikila
143. Ofo/Ofogoula – Iberville 1699
144. Ontwaganha – an Iroquois name for Shawnee
145. Orunges – Chauvignerie 1736
146. Oshawanoag – an Ottawa name for Shawnee
147. Ouabano – LaSalle 1682
148. Ouchaouanag – Jesuit Relations 1648
149. Ouchawanag – Smith 1866
150. Ouispe – Iberville 1699
151. Pechoquealin – a name for Pekowi
152. Peckuwetha – a name for Pekowi
153. Pecquealin – a name for Pekowi
154. **Pee Dee** – on the Pee Dee River of NC
155. Pekuwe – a name for the Pekowi
156. Pekowi – "risen from ashes", the 4th Historic Shawnee Tribe, but also called the second brothers of Shawnee after the Chalakatha, most often aligned with the Thawikila & Kishpoko, all three having ancient & strong connections in the south
157. Pekowitha – a name for the Pekowi
158. Pequa – a name for the Pekowi
159. Pequea – a name for the Pekowi
160. Pequot – a name for Pekowi in MA
161. Pickaway – a name for Pekowi
162. Pickawillany – a name for Pekowi
163. Piqua – a name for Pekowi
164. **Piscataway** – an ancient division of Shawnee
165. River Indians – Shawnee on Delaware River 1500's
166. **Ronnongwetowanea** – an Iroquois name for the ancient rulers of the eastern half of the continent, often giants in stature
167. Sabanas – Five Nations 1747
168. Sabanoes – TX 1835
169. Saguanos – TX 1832
170. Sahwaunoo – Macauley 1829
171. Salt Indians – Fallows 1671
172. Saludas – Shawnee in SC-NC on the Saluda River 1750
173. Santanas – Drake 1852

174. Santee – Shawnee in the Santee valley SC-NC
175. Sarannahs – Archdale 1707
176. Sarannas – Archdale 1708
177. Saraw – a name for Xuala
178. Satanas – Smith 1603, Colden 1727
179. Satans – Ruttenber, Tribes of Hudson River
180. Sauno – Roggeveen 1676
181. Sauouans – Macauley 1829
182. Sauounons – Macauley 1829
183. Saura – a name for Xuala-Shawnee
184. Sauvanogee – Hawkins 1799
185. Sauwanew – map 1614
186. Sauwanogee – Hawkins 1799, a Shawnee village among the Creeks
187. Sauwanoos – Vandernock 1656
188. Sauwanous – Shawnee among the Creeks 1788
189. Savanahs – Homan Heirs map of Carolinas 1730
190. Savanas – Lawson 1709, in NC
191. Savanaus – Johnson 1708, in SC
192. Savannahs – Shawnee in GA-SC
193. Savannas – Lattre map 1784 as the Shawnee among the Creeks, Swan 1791
194. Savannechers – Hywood, TN 1823
195. Savannerhers – Haywood TN 1823
196. Savannucas – Bartram 1792, a Creek name for Shawnee
197. Savanoes – Drake 1852
198. Savanoos – Ruttenber, Tribes of the Hudson
199. Savanore – Randolph 1689, a Shawnee town on the Savannah River
200. Savanos – Barnwell 1715, the Shawnee on the Savannah River
201. Savanos – Ruttenber, Tribes of the Hudson
202. Sawakola – a name for Thawikila
203. Sawala – Riggs-Dorsey Dakota dictionary
204. Sawanan – Lattre 1784, Shawnee village on the upper Potomac MDVA
205. Sawanee – Drake 1848
206. Sawanees – Putnam, Middle TN 1859
207. Sawano – Gastchet 1884, a Tonkawa name for Shawnee
208. Sawanogi – Gatschet 1884, a Creek name for Shawnee
209. Sawanoono – Morgan 1851, a Seneca name for Shawnee

210. Sawanoos – DeLaet 1633, on the Delaware River
211. Sawanos – Barton 1798
212. Sawanuhaka – Barton 1885, Tuscarora name for Shawnee
213. Sawanuka – Ten Kate 1884, a Cherokee name for Shawnee
214. Sawanwa – Smith 1854, plural = Sawanwaki
215. Sawanwakee – Morgan 1871
216. Sawekela – McKenny & Hall
217. Sawakola – a name for Thawikila
218. Sawakoli – a name for Thawikila in AL
219. Sawoncas – Creek Talk 1793
220. Sawunoki – Grayson, Creek vocabulary
221. Sawwanew – map 1614, on the Delaware River
222. Sawwannoo – Barton 1798
223. Sawwanoo – Vater 1816
224. Scahantoarrhonouns – Jesuit Relations 1735
225. Schaouanos – DeMofras 1844
226. Schavanna – Albany Conference 1737
227. Schaveno – Albany Conference 1737
228. Schawanese – Gussefeld 1784
229. Schawanno – Heckwelder 1798
230. Schawanooes – Clinton 1750
231. Schawans – Schuyler 1694
232. Schawenoes – Albany Conference 1737
233. Schawenons – deFoi 1828
234. Schawnoah – LeTour map 1779
235. Serannas – Hewatt quoted 1836
236. Sewanne – Putnam Middle TN 1859
237. Sewickley – a name for the Thawikila
238. Shamanese – LaTour 1782, opposite Wyoming PA
239. Shanaws – Homan Heirs map 1756
240. Shannoahs – Washingotn 1753
241. Shanoas – Washington 1753
242. Shaonois – Evans 1707
243. Shaononons – Boudinot 1816
244. Shapatha – a name for Mekoche
245. Shauanos – Smith 1877
246. Shaunas – Croghan 1760
247. Shaunetowa – Fleet 1632

248. Shauwaunoes – Brainerd 1746
249. Shavanos – Post 1758, Vater 1816,
250. Shawahahs – Livingston 1717
251. Shawala – a Sioux name for Shawnee, also the name of a Teton division descended from an adopted Shawnee
252. Shawana – Lewney 1760, an Omaha, Ponca, Osage, Kansas, Quapaw name for Shawnee
253. Shawanahaac – document of 1788
254. Shawanahs – Lindsey 1751
255. Shawanapi – Squier 1877
256. Shawana – an Omaha, Ponca, Osage name for Shawnee
257. Shawanaws – Dalton 1783
258. Shawane – Croghan 1754
259. Shawanees – PA Records 1731 260. Shawanese – PA Records 1701
261. Shawanesse – Proud, PA 1798 & Drake 1852
262. Shawanies – Campbell 1761
263. Shawaniese – Johnson 1757
264. Shawanna – Penn's Treaty 1701
265. Shawannoa – a name for Shawnee in the southern States
266. Shawannohs – Smith quoted 1866
267. Shawannos – Vater 1816
268. Shawano – one of the Ancient Shawnee Tribes, centered in the Shenandoah valley, extending hundreds of miles north & south east of the Appalachian mountains, said to be the largest & greatest but died off due to disease & warfare, mentioned by Gatschet 1884, later a generic term for all Shawnee
269. Shawanoeese – Brown 1817
270. Shawanoes – document from 1692
271. Shawanoh – Adair 1775
272. Shawanois – PA Records 1707
273. Shawanoki – Rafinesque 1836, Delaware name for Shawnee
274. Shawanons – DeSmet 1843
275. Shawanooki – a name for the Shawnee of AL
276. Shawanos – Ft. Johnson Conference 1756
277. Shawanos – Gatschet, settlements among the Creeks
278. Shawanose – Loskiel 1794
279. Shawanous – McKinney & Hall 1854
280. Shawanowi – Walam Olam 1833

281. Shawans – Schuyler 1693
282. Shawanu – Rafinesque 1836 & Delaware name for Shawnee
283. Shawanuwak – Rafinesque 1836 & Delaware name for Shawnee
284. Shawanwa – a name for the Shawnee, individual or as a group
285. Shawanwaki – a plural name for the Shawnee as a whole
286. Shawenoes – Albany Conference 1737
287. Shaweygila – a name for the Thawikila, Trowbridge 1824
288. Shawnees – Stuart 1775
289. Shawneese – Campbell 1761
290. Shawnese – Croghan 1750
291. Shawnessee – Croghan 1765
292. Shawneys – Crowley 1775
293. Shawno – Mandrillon map 1785
294. Shawnoah – Morse map 1798
295. Shawnoes – Esnauts-Rapilly map 1777
296. Shawonese – Thomas 1745
297. Shawonoes – Pike 1811
298. Shawunoag – Warren 1852
299. Shawunogi – a Fox & Sauk name for Shawnee
300. Shevanoo – Tillman 1697
301. Shipotha – a name for the Mekoche
302. Shoccoree – reference in 1677
303. Showammers – NY Conference 1753
304. Showanhoes – Livingston 1711
305. Showannees – Clarkson 1694
306. Showannoes – Clarkson 1693
307. Showanoes – Schuyler 1694
308. Showonese – Weiser 1748
309. Showonoes – Livingston 1700
310. Shpito – a name for the Mekoche
311. Shpitotha – "Big Toad", a name for Mekoche
312. Shuala – a name for the Xuala, Desoto 1540
313. Shualla – a name for the Xuala, Desoto 1540
314. Shwanoes – Castor Hill Treaty 1832
315. Sipotha – a name for the Kishpoko
316. Sirinueses – Barcia 1723
317. Sissipahaw -
318. Skipachi – a name for Kishpoko

319. Skipaki – 1684 Franquelin, a name for Kishpoko
320. Sowanakas – Woodward 1859
321. Sowanokas – Woodward 1859
322. Sowanokees – Woodward 1859
323. Sowonno – Whipple 1856
324. Spitotha – a name for the Kishpoko
325. Stabbernowles – in MD with Martin Chartier, said to be from IN
326. Suali – a name for Xuala
327. Susquehanna – pre-1600's Shawnee on the Susquehanna River, often giants in stature
328. Suwali - a name for Xuala-Shawnee
329. Suwannee – Shawnee in GA & FL 1500-1600's
330. Suwanoes – DeLaet 1633
331. Swickly – a name for Thawikila
332. Talligeu – a name for the Allegiwi, ancient rulers of the eastern half of the continent, often giants in stature
333. Talligewi – a name for the Allegiwi, ancient rulers of the eastern half of the continent, often giants in stature
334. Taogria – Gravier 1699
335. Tcilokogalgi – a Creek name for Shawnee
336. Thawegila – a name for the Thawikila
337. Thawikila – possibly "the Eagle people", 3rd Tribe of the Historic Shawnee, but also called the elder brother of the five, according to some the Head Chief of all the Shawnee, when there is one, must be a Chalakatha or Thawikila, most closely aligned with the Pekowi & Kishpoko, all three having ancient and strong connections in the south
338. Tihotitachse – Cammeroff 1750
339. Toagenha – Galinee 1669, a Seneca name for Shawnee
340. Tshilikauthee – a name for Chalakatha
341. Tuckabatchee – Kishpoko in AL before 1685
342. Woketamosi - a name for a lost Shawnee Tribe
343. Xuala – one of the Ancient Shawnee Tribes, met by Pardo 1565, near the lower Blue Ridge in NC
344. Yadkin – on the Yadkin River 1673
345. Yosta – a Yuchi name for Shawnee

Appendix 4

CLANS OF THE SHAWNEE

(* indicates a Clan on more than one list; **Bold** = shows up in all 8 listings)

I. Shawnee Clans

   A. Trowbridge 1824

      1. Snake*
      1. **Turtle***
      2. Raccoon*
      3. **Turkey***
      4. Hawk*
      5. Deer*
      6. **Bear***
      7. **Wolf***
      8. Panther*
      9. Elk*
      10. Buffalo*
      11. Fish*
      12. Rabbit*
      13. Eagle*
      14. Fox*
      15. Otter*
      16. Beaver*
      17. Swan*
      18. Skunk*
      19. Squirrel
      20. Tree
      21. Corn
      22. Wind
      23. Night
      24. Cloud
      25. Moon
      26. Water
      27. House
      28. Stone
      29. Dirt
      30. Big Fire
      31. Bald Eagle
      32. Pigeon Hawk

33. Blackbird

B. Morgan 1877
1. **Wolf****
2. Loon*
3. **Bear****
4. Buzzard*
5. Panther**
6. Owl*
7. **Turkey****
8. Deer**
9. Raccoon*
   *
10. **Turtle****
11. Snake**
12. Horse*
13. Rabbit**

C. Gatschet 1878
1. Snake****
2. **Turtle******
3. Fish**
4. Raccoon****
5. **Turkey******
6. Deer****
7. **Bear******
8. **Wolf******
9. Panther****

D. Spencer 1908
1. Rabbit***
2. Raccoon***
3. Panther***
4. **Turtle*****
5. **Wolf*****
6. Deer***
7. **Turkey*****
8. Snake***
9. **Bear*****

10. Wildcat
11. Eagle**
12. Owl**

E. Michelson 1927

1. **Turtle*****
2. Raccoon*****
3. **Turkey*****
4. **Bear*****
5. **Wolf*****
6. Panther*****

F. Speck

1. Snake*****
2. **Turtle******
3. **Turkey******
4. **Bear******
5. **Wolf******

G. Voegelin 1935

1. Bird * or Fowl (by extrapolation to include)

a. **Turkey*******
b. Eagle***
c. Owl***
d. Buzzard**
e. Hawk**

2. Aquatic (by extrapolation to include)

a. Reptiles –
    i. **Turtle****
    ii. Snake******
b. Fish*** - all fish
c. Aquatic Birds –
    iii. Swan** iv. Loon**
    v. Goose

          vi. Duck
          vii. Heron

d. Aquatic Animals – viii. Beaver**
    ix. Otter**

3. Round Foot (carnivores)

a. **Wolf*******
b. Panther******
c. Wildcat**
d. Fox**

4. Hoofed

a. Deer*****
b. Buffalo**
c. Elk**
d. Horse**

5. Long Foot or Scratching Foot (omnivores)

a. **Bear*******
b. Raccoon******
c. Skunk**

6. Gentle Natured

a. **Rabbit****

H. Howard 1981

    1. **Wolf********
a. Dog
    2. **Bear********
    3. Horse***
    4. Rabbit******
    5. **Turkey*****
a. Bird**
b. Chicken
    6. **Turtle*********

7. Raccoon*******
8. Deer******

I. **All Clans** (more or less) **are found in all 5 historic Shawnee Tribes.**

    a. Each of the 5 modern Tribes has all 8 modern Clans within it or all 6 Name Groups with sub-clans within them, i.e. a Chalakatha Wolf and a Pekowi Wolf, or Kishpoko Rabbit and a Thawikila Rabbit.

    b. Thus marriage of a Chalakatha Wolf and a Kishpoko Wolf **were not of the same clan but the clan of another tribe** and thus did not violate the "clan incest" law.

J. **Clans of neighboring Tribes** for comparison (**Bold** indicates a corresponding Clan among the Shawnee

    1. Cherokee Clans

        a. **Wolf**-Aniwaya - red color-warriors & chiefs-war clan
        b. **Panther**-Holly-Blue Holly-Anishoni - blue color-herbalists & medicine-peace clan
        c. **Wind**-Long Hair-Anigilahi-(I don't know an animal) - yellow color-Chiefs & warriors-war clan
        d. **Bird-Hawk-Eagle-Owl-Turkey**- Anisisqua - purple colormessengers-peace clan
        e. **Deer-Buffalo**-Anikawi - brown color-hunters-peace clan
        f. Red Paint-Aniwadi-(I don't know an animal) - white colorconjurers & medicine-war clan
        g. **Bear-Raccoon**-Blind Savannah-Wild Potato-Anigatagewi - green color-farmers-peace clan

    2. Creek Clans

        a. **Wind** = a white or peace clan - Hathagilgi
        b. **Beaver** = a white or peace clan
        c. **Bear** = a white or peace clan
        d. **Bird** = a white or peace clan - Hathagilgi
        e. **Chilokila**- Tcilokogalgi-Those of Different Speech = all other clans within the Creek confederation or red clan

3. Delaware or Lenape Clans (note extremely limited original range)
   a. **Wolf** or Munsee – mountain people, between Blue-Kittatinny Mountains & sources of the Susquehanna & Delaware Rivers-PANY-NJ, they have been considered a separate tribe in that they differ greatly from the other two & speak a different dialect
   b. **Turtle** or Unami – down river people, on both sides of Delaware River, DE-PA, the principal chief of the Turkey clan was considered the "King" of the combined clans
   c. **Turkey** or Unalachtigo – people by the sea, on lower Delaware River & Delaware Bay, DE-PA-MD-NJ
   d. A note pertaining to the Delaware being called the "grandfathers of the Shawnee. Since Shawnee called all male relatives for at least four generations back "Grandfather" could it not be possible that the whites misinterpreted the term as it was being used, to think that the three Delaware Clans i.e. the Delaware Tribe (which the whites thought were a separate & distinct people) as being an older Tribe when in fact the Shawnee were referring to actual blood kinship i.e. the people then called Delaware were blood relations of the people known then as Shawnee but from an ancient group, long separated (anywhere from one generation to four or more generations) from the main body?

4. Chickasaw Clans

   a. **Panther**-Koi Phratry or Family

      i. **Wildcat**-Koinchnsh-Kointchuch
      ii. **Bird**-Ilatakfushi-Fushi
      iii. **Fish**-Nunni-Nanni
      • **Deer**-Issi

   b. Spanish-Ishpanee Phratry or Family
      i. **Raccoon**-Shauee-Shawi ii. Spanish-Ishppanee-Ishpani iii. Royal-Mingko-Mingo iv. **Skunk**-Hushkoni-Huskoni v. **Squirrel**-Tunni vi. Alligator-Hochouchabba-Hotchontehapa vii. **Wolf**-Nashola-Nashoba viii. **Blackbird**-Chuhhla-Tchuhla

K. Comparison of Algonquin & Ancient Shawnee Tribes

Algonquin Tribes	Ancient Shawnee Tribes
Abnaki	Snake
Amalecite-Maliseet	Turtle
Arapaho-Blackfoot-Cheyenne	Fish
Chippewa-Ottawa-	Pottawamee Raccoon
Conoy-Kanawha-Piscataway	Bear
Cree,	Skunk
Croatan	Turkey
Delaware-Leni Lanape,	Hawk
Fox-Sauk-Gros Ventre	Eagle
Kickapoo,	Bald Eagle
Massachuset	Pigeon Hawk
Menominee,	Deer
Miami-Wea-Piankenshew	Buffalo
Mohegan-Chickahominey,	Elk
Shawnee,	Wolf
Wampanoag	Fox
Mohican Montagnais	Panther
Montauketts	Squirrel
Munsee	Rabbit
Nanticoke	Otter
Narragansett	Beaver
Naskapi	Swan
Nipmuc	Tree
Penobscot,	Corn
Pequot	Wind
Powhatan-Pamukey	Night Cloud
	Moon
	Water
	House
	Stone
	Dirt
	Big Fire

Appendix 5
SHAWNEE VILLAGES

(including villages of other Tribes in which the Shawnee lived along with other tribes)

ALABAMA

1. Alabama River (on the) –
2. Chalakagee – Talladega Co
3. Chattahoochee River (on the) –
4. Coosa River (on the) –
5. Ikanhatki – 6. Long Island Town –
7. Okfuskee (on the Tallapoosa River) -
8. Sauvanogee (on the Tallapoosa River -
9. Sawanogi – Macon Co
10. Sylacauga – Talladega Co
11. Tallapoosa River (several villages on the) – 12. Tallassee (on the Coosa River) - 13. Tuckabatchee –
14. Will's Town –

CANADA

15. Bois Blanc (in Detroit River) – Ontario
16. Ft. Malden – 17. Grosse Ile – Ontario
18. Tonihata/Grenadier Island (in St. Lawrence River – Leeds Co Ontario
19. Walpole Island – Ontario

CONNECTICUT

1. Housatonic River (on the) –

DELAWARE

1. Chikihoki – junction of Christianna River with Delaware River
2. Delaware River (on the west side of) –
3. Hopokohacking – site of Wilmington
4. Memankitonna – site of Claymont

FLORIDA

1. Eskippeck -
2. Cedar Key (site of) -

GEORGIA

1. Chalaqua (site of Augusta) -
2. Etowah -
3. Ft. Gaines (site of) - 4.   Lookout Mountain –
5. Shawnee Town -
6. Suwannee River (on the) – Ware Co

ILLINOIS

1. Cahokia –
2. Chaskepe –
3. Cisca –
4. Illinois River (on the) – 5. Kaskaskia – LaSalle Co
6. Lake Michigan (along) – 7. Mascouten Town (Mascouten) –
8. Ohio River (mouth of) -
9. Ouabano –
10. Saline River (on the) –
11. Sawmehnaug (Pottawamee) – (on Fox River)
12. Shabeni's Town (Pottawamee) - (on Fox River)
13. Shawnee Town – Gallatin Co
14. St. Louis (site of) –
15. Starved Rock – LaSalle Co
16. Wabash River (on the) –

INDIANA

1. Big Shawnee Creek – Fountain Co
2. Black Snake's Town - (near Ft. Wayne)

3. Black Hawk's village – Shelby Co
4. Blue Jacket's Town - (near Ft. Wayne)
5. Bukangelos' Town - (near Ft. Wayne)
6. Chillicothe - (on the Maumee River)
7. Chillicothe - (on Great Miami River)
8. Chillicothe - (on Wabash River) 9. Kekionga (Miami) – Allen Co
10. Kickapoo Town – Tippicanoe Co
11. Kowasika/Thorntown – Boone Co
12. Lake Michigan - (along)
13. Miami Town (Miami) - (near Ft. Wayne)
14. Old Shawnee Town – Posey Co
15. Pekowi (on Great Miami River) –
16. Pekowi (on Wabash River) – 17. Prophet's Town – Tippicanoe Co
18. Rum's Town (Pottawamee) – St. Joseph Co
19. Shawnee Town - (on Maumee River)
20. Shawnee Town - (on Maumee River)
21. Shawnee Town - (on Maumee River)
22. Sonnioto – Tippecanoe Co
23. St. Joseph's River (on the) –
24. Vincennes – Knox Co
25. White River (on the) – 26. Whitewater River (on the) -
27. Wild Cat Creek (on) –
28. Winnebago Town – Tippicanoe Co
29. Winamac's Town (Pottawamee) – Pulaski Co

KANSAS

1. Long Tail's Town – Johnson Co
2. Prophet's Town – Wyandotte Co

KENTUCKY

1. Big Bone Lick (near Cincinnati OH) -
2. Big Lick - 3.   Big Sandy River (on the) -
4. Blue Licks -
5. Boone Lick –
6. Clay Co (in)
–
7. Cumberland River (several villages on) -
8. Eskippakithiki – Clark Co

Shawnee Heritage II

9. Knox Co (in) – 10. Lexington (site of) – 11. Louisa (site of) -
12. Louisville (site of) – Jefferson Co
13. Mud Lick – Johnson Co
14. Ohio River (south of the mouth of) - 15. Rock Castle (site of) – Trigg Co
16. Rockcastle Co (in) - 17. Shelby Co (in) –
18. Taogria - (on the Ohio River) -
19. Upper Blue Licks –

MARYLAND
1. Caluctecue – Alleghany Co
2. Cumberland (site of) –
3. Hancock (site of)
4. Northeast (site of) – Cecil Co
5. Old Town – Allegheny Co
6. Opessa's Town – Alleghany Co
7. Shawnee Town –
8. Will's Town – Alleghany Co
9. Youghiogheny –

MASSACHUSETTS

1. Great Barrington (near) –

MICHIGAN

1. Blue Jacket's Town (near Brownstown MI) –
2. Detroit - (site of)
3. St. Joseph's River (on the) –

MINNESOTA

1. Minnesota River (on the) (Sioux) –

MISSOURI

2. Apple Creek (on) – Perry Co
1. Apple Creek (on) – Perry Co
2. Cape Girardeau – Perry Co
3. Chillicothe – Perry Co
4. James Roger's Town –

5. Jimmy Rogers Town – 6. Merrimack River (on the) -
7. New Madrid –
8. Shawnee Town
9. St. Louis (site of) –

NEW JERSEY

1. Chilihoki – Burlington Co
2. Depue Island (on) – 3. Edgpiiliik – (western NJ)
4. Eriwonee – Gloucester Co
5. Mageckqueshou – Trenton
6. Minisink – Sussex Co
7. Peckwes – site of Hackensack
8. Salem (site of) – Gloucester Co
9. Shawnee Island (on) –
10. Warren Co (in) –

NEW YORK

1. Achsinning (Munsee) – Tioga Co
2. Cahunghage – (south side of Onieda Lake)
3. Chautauqua Co (in) – 4. Chemung (Seneca) - (site of)
5. Columbia Co (in) – 6. Delaware River (on) – Orange Co
7. Dutchess Co (in) - 8. Hudson River (on the)
9. Kanestio – Steuben Co
10. Lake Champlain (along) –
11. Long Island (on) – 12. Mamekoting – Ulster Co
13. Manckatawagum – Tioga Co
14. Manhattan Island (on) - 15. Onnahee (Seneca) – Ontario Co
16. Osquake (Mohawk) – Montgomery Co
17. Owego – Tioga Co
18. Pakadasank (Munsee) – Orange Co
19. Papagonk (Munsee) – Ulster Co

Shawnee Heritage II 522

20. Pepacton – Delaware Co
21. Satanas Town - (south of Lake Erie)
22. Schaunactada (Mohawk) – (near Albany)
23. Shawangunk Creek – Ulster Co
24. Staten Island (on) -
25. Tonawanda (Seneca) – Niagara Co
26. Vestal (site of) -

NORTH CAROLINA

1. Ashe Co (in) –
2. Bear River – on the Pamlico River
3. Bennett's Creek (Chowan) – 4. Coranine (Coree) – Carteret Co
5. Catoking (Chowan) – Gates co
6. Chawanock – Hertford Co
7. Cheraw – Henderson, Polk & Rutherford Co
8. Chowan Co (in) – 9. Chowan River (on the) – 10. Core Creek (Coree) – Craven Co
11. Dan River (on the) -
12. Freydeck – Ashe Co
13. Gates Co (village) –
14. Lower Saura Town (Xuala) – map 1760
15. Maraton (Chowan) – Chowan Co
16. Mattsmuskeet Lake (Coree-Machapunga) – Hyde Co
17. Meherrin – Hertford Co
18. Narhantes (Chowan-Tuscarora) - (near Newbern)
19. Neuse River (Chowan) – Carteret-Craven Co
20. New River (on the) – Ashe Co
21. Nottoway (Chowan-Nanticoke) – Hertford Co
22. Ohanoak (Chowan) – Hertford Co
23. Old Fields – Ashe Co
24. Old Town – Hertford Co
25. Pee Dee River (Chowan) – NC-SC line
26. Person Co (in) –
27. Ramushonok (Chowan) – Hertford Co
28. Raruta (Coree) – Carteret Co
29. Raudauquaquark (Bear River) -
30. Saluda (Xuala) – NC-SC line
31. Santee River (Chowan on the)
32. Suwali Gap (Xuala) -
33. Swannanoa – Buncombe Co
34. Upper Saura Town (Xuala) – Stokes Co

35. Uwaharrie River (Xuala on the) - 36. Wilkes Co (village) – 37. Yadkin River (on the) –

OHIO

1. Auglaize River (on the) –
2. Black Beard's Town (on Swan Creek) – Logan Co
3. Black Bird's Town- (on the Maumee River
4. Black Fish's Town (Chalakatha) - 5. Black Hoof's Town - (St. John's) - Auglaize Co
6. Black Snake's Town – Logan Co
7. Black Snake's Town (on the Maumee River) –
8. Black Stump's Town - 9. Blanchard River (on the) – 10. Blue Jacket's Town – Logan Co
11. Blue Jacket's Town (on Mad River) – Logan Co
12. Blue Jacket's Town - (on Maumee River)
13. Bridgeport (site of) – Belmont Co
14. Buck Creek (on) – Clark Co
15. Buffalo's Town (on Swan Creek) – Logan Co
16. Bukangelos' Town (Delaware) – Logan Co
17. Caesar's Creek – Warren Co
18. Capt. Johnny's Town – Logan Co
19. Chesapeake (site of) – Lawrence Co
20. Chilihoki – (on Miami River)
21. Chillicothe - Adams Co
22. Chillicothe/Chalahgawtha – Ross Co
23. Chillicothe/Chalahgawtha – Greene Co
24. Chillicothe – Miami Co
25. Chiuxa' s Town -
26. Cincinnati (site of) – Hamilton Co
27. Cornstalk's Town - Pickaway Co
28. Coshocton (Delaware) –
29. Crane Town (Wyandot) – Fairfield Co
30. Crane Town (Wyandot) – Crawford Co
31. Crooked Neck/Nose's Town – Logan Co
32. Cross Creek – Belmont Co (?)
33. Crow's Town – 34. Darke Co (in) -
35. Deer Creek (on) – Madison Co
36. Deer Creek - (on the Sciota River)
37. Fallen Timber - (on the upper Auglaize River not battle site)
38. Girty's Town - (St. Mary's) - Auglaize Co
39. Gray Eye's Town - (on upper Auglaize)

40. Greene Co (in) - 41. Greenville -
42. Grenadier Squaw's Town – Pickaway Co
43. Hog Creek - Allen Co
44. Kakinathucca's Town (on Swan Creek) – Logan Co
45. Kekeko –
46. Kikusglowlowa's Town - 47. Kishkeminetas – Gallia Co
48. Kishpoko Town – Pickaway Co
49. Kishpoko Town - (on Great Miami River)
50. Kishpoko Town - (on Great Miami River)
51. Kishpoko Town – Logan Co
52. Letart Falls – Meigs Co
53. Lewis' Town - Logan Co
54. Lick Town – (near Circleville)
55. Little Auglaize River (on the) – Auglaize Co
56. Little Turtle's Town (Miami) – Logan Co
57. Logan's Sciota Camp – Hardin Co
58. Logan's Yellow Creek Camp (Mingo) – Jefferson Co
59. Lorimier's Trading Post -
60. Lower Shawnee Town/Chillicothe – on the Scioto
61. Mackachak (on the Mad River) – Logan Co
62. Mackachak - (on Great Miami River)
63. Maguck – Pickaway Co
64. Mamocomink -
65. Marietta (site of) – Washington Co
66. Maumee Rapids (near Perrysburg) - 67. Maumee River (on the) -
68. McKee's Town – Logan Co
69. Mequachake – Logan Co
70. Mequachake – Pickaway Co
71. Mercer Co (in) – 72. Meshepeshe's Town – 73. Meshkemau (Ottawa) – Lucas Co
74. Miami Town (Miami) (on the Maumee River) - 75. Mingo Bottom (Mingo) – Jefferson Co
76. Mingo Town (Mingo) – Logan Co
77. Moluntha's Town – Logan Co
78. Old Shawnee Town – Gallia Co
79. Old Town - Greene Co
80. Oquanoxa (Ottawa) – Paulding Co
81. Ottawa River (on the) – 82. Owl's Town – Coshocton Co
83. Paint Creek - Ross Co
84. Pecowick – Pickaway Co
85. Pickawillany (Miami) – Miami Co
86. Pigeon's Town – Logan Co

87. Pipe's Town (Wyandot) – Wyandot Co
88. Piqua (site of Springfield) – Clark Co
89. Piqua - Miami Co
90. Piqua, Lower – Miami Co
91. Piqua, Upper – Miami Co
92. Pluggy' s Town (Mingo) – (site of Delaware)
93. Powhatan Point (site of) – Belmont Co
94. Puckshanoses – 95. Reed's Town – Logan Co
96. Ripley (site of) – Brown Co
97. Roundhead's Town (Wyandot) – Hardin Co
98. Roche de Boeuf (Ottawa) – Lucas Co
99. Salt Lick – Warren Co
100. Scoutash's Town – Logan Co
101. Sciota River (on the) - 102. Sciota River (on the) –
103. Sciota River (on the) –
104. Sciota River (on the) – 105. Sciota River (on the) -
106. Seekonk (site of Columbus) – Franklin Co
107. Seneca Town (Seneca) – Seneca Co
108. Shabawywyagun (Ottawa) – (near Toledo)
109. Solomon's (Solomon Warrow) Town (Wyandot) -
110. Sonnioto (site of Portsmouth) – Sciota Co
111. Standing Stone -
112. Swan Creek - (site of Toledo)
113. Tecumseh's Town - Champaign-Madison Co
114. Tom's Town – Ross Co
115. Tullihas – (on Muskingum River)
116. Waccachalla (on the Sciota) -
117. Wakatomica (on the Muskingum River) – Muskingum Co
118. Wakatomica (on the Mad River) – Logan Co
119. Wapakoneta - Auglaize Co
120. Warren Co (in) – 121. Waugau (Ottawa) – Lucas Co
122. White Feather's Town - Auglaize Co
123. Will's Town – Muskingum Co
124. Wolf's Town - (on the Maumee River)
125. Xenia (site of) – Greene Co
126. Yellow Hawk's Town - (Paint Creek enters Sciota)
127. Yellow Springs – Greene Co

PENNSYLVNIA

1. Alamingo - (on Susquehanna)

2. Algonquin Junction – Luzerne Co
3. Allegheny Junction – Butler Co
4. Allegheny Landing – Berks Co
5. Allegheny Mines – Butler Co
6. Allegheny River (on the) –
7. Aughwick – Huntingdon Co
8. Aughwick Mills – Huntingdon Co
9. Bedford Co (in) –
10. Big Island – Clinton Co
11. Black Hawk – Beaver Co
12. Black Legs' Town – Indiana Co
13. Black Leg's village – Armstrong Co
14. Black Log – Huntingdon Co
15. Blue Rock – Lancaster Co
16. Brandt's Town (Mohawk) – Susquehanna Co
17. Bridgeville (near site of) – Alleghany Co
18. Buckaloon (Seneca) – Warren Co
19. Callapatscink – Cumberland Co
20. Canadohta – Crawford Co
21. Canaserage – Lycoming Co
22. Canowsa (Munsee) – Lackawanna-Wyoming line
23. Capt. John's Town (Munsee) – Northampton Co
24. Catawissa – Columbiana Co
25. Catawissa Bridge – Columbiana Co
26. Catawissa Junction – Columbiana Co
27. Catfish's Camp – Washington Co.
28. Chambersburg (site of) – Franklin Co
29. Chartier's Town – Alleghany Co
30. Chenastry – Northumberland Co
31. Cherryville (near site of) – Northampton Co
32. Chester Co (in) -
33. Chillisquaque – Northumberland Co
34. Chugnut – Susquehanna Co
35. Coaquannock – Philadelphia
36. Codorus – York Co
37. Cohocksink - Philadelphia
38. Conedogwint – Cumberland Co
39. Conejohela – Lancaster Co
40. Conemaugh – Cambria Co
41. Conemaugh River (on the) –
42. Conestoga – Chester co
43. Conestoga – Lancaster Co
44. Conestoga Station – Lancaster Co

45. Connewango (Seneca) – Warren Co
46. Connewango (Seneca) – (site of Tionesta)
47. Conococheague – Franklin Co
48. Conoloway – Fulton Co
49. Cononodaw – McKean Co
50. Conoquenessing – Beaver-Lawrence Co
51. Conoy Town – Northumberland Co
52. Copeechan – Lehigh Co
53. Cussewago (Munsee) – Crawford Co
54. Cussewago (Seneca) – Erie Co
55. Custaloga (Munsee) – Mercer Co
56. Dekanoagh - Lancaster Co
57. Delaware River (on the) - 58. Delaware River (Forks of) – 59. Delaware Water Gap – Monroe Co
60. Fishing Creek – Columbiana Co
61. Ganagarahhare – Venango Co
62. Glasswanoge – Montour Co
63. Goschgoschunk (Munsee) – Forest Co
64. Harrisburg (site of) -
65. Hickory Town (Munsee) – Forest Co
66. Irvineton (near site of) – Warren Co
67. Jedakne (Delaware) – Northumberland Co
68. Juniata River (on the) – Bedford Co
69. Kaghoughsage – (in western PA)
70. Keckenepaulin's Town – Westmoreland Co
71. Keckenepaulin's Cabin – Somerset Co
72. Kishacoquillas – Mifflin Co
73. Kishacoquillas – Crawford Co
74. Kishacoquillas Junction – Mifflin Co
75. Kishkeminetas – Armstrong Co
76. Kiskomonnetta – Westmoreland Co
77. Kittanning – Armstrong Co
78. Kushequa – McKean Co
79. Kushusdatening – Warren Co
80. Kuskuski (Delaware) – Lawrence Co
81. Lancaster Co (several villages in) –
82. Lawunkhannek (Delaware) – Venango Co
83. Lehigh River (on the) – Monroe Co
84. Lehigh Valley – Lehigh Co
85. LeTort's Spring – Lancaster Co
86. LeTort's Town –Indiana Co
87. Logan's Town (Mingo) – Beaver Co

88. Logan's Spring (Mingo) – Mifflin Co
89. Logstown – Alleghany Co
90. Lower Coplay – Lehigh Co
91. Maghingquechahocking (Munsee) – Crawford Co
92. Mahantango – Dauphin Co
93. Mahantango – Juniata Co
94. Mahontango – Northumberland Co
95. Mahusquechikoken (Munsee) – Venango Co
96. Malson – Wyoming Co
97. Manatawny – Berks Co
98. Manorville (near site of) – Armstrong Co
99. McConnelsburg (near site of) – Fulton Co
100. McKee's Cabin – Northumberland Co
101. McKee's Rocks – Alleghany Co
102. Meshawmin – Wyoming Co
103. Millsborough (near site of) – Greene Co
104. Mingo (Mingo) – Lackawanna Co
105. Mingoville (Mingo) – Centre Co
106. Minisink (Munsee) – Pike Co
107. Minqua – Lancaster Co
108. Mohawk (Mohawk) – Crawford Co
109. Monongahela – Washington Co
110. Monongahela River (mouth of) - Allegheny Co
111. Muncy (Munsee) – Lycoming Co
112. Muncy Valley (Munsee) – Sullivan Co
113. Nanticoke – Luzerne Co
114. Nescopeck – Luzerne Co
115. Neshamminy – Bucks Co 116. Neshannock – Mercer Co
117. New Castle (site of) – Lawrence Co
118. New Cumberland (site of) – Cumberland Co
119. Nittabaconk – Philadelphia
120. Nuagola – Luzerne Co
121. Ohesson – Mifflin Co
122. Opasiskunk – Lancaster Co
123. Oskohary – Columbia Co
124. Ostonwakin – Lycoming Co
125. Ostuacky – Lycoming Co
126. Ottawa – Montour Co
127. Paxinosa – Northumberland Co
128. Paxtang – Dauphin Co
129. Paxtang River (on the) - 130. Pechaquealin – Monroe Co
131. Pechoquealin – Sussex Co

132. Peixan - Dauphin Co
133. Pematuning – near Shenango
134. Pequea – Lancaster Co
135. Picture Rocks – Chester Co
136. Pigeon Creek – Washington Co
137. Pine Creek – Tioga-Potter Co
138. Playwickey – Bucks Co
139. Plymouth (site of) – Luzerne Co
140. Pochapuchkug (Munsee) – Lehigh Co
141. Queenasahwakee – (on the Susquehanna)
142. Quessinawonink - Philadelphia
143. Quialutimack – Lackawanna Co
144. Ray's Town – Bedford Co
145. Redstone – Fayette Co
146. Sakhauwotung – Northampton Co
147. Santee – Northampton Co
148. Saucon – Lehigh Co
149. Sauconk – Beaver Co
150. Seconchan – Luzerne Co
151. Schuylkill River (mouth of) –
152. Sciota – Centre Co
153. Seven Houses – Beaver Co
154. Sewickley – Westmoreland Co
155. Sewickley – Alleghany Co
156. Sewickley – Beaver Co
157. Shamokin (Delaware) – Northumberland Co
158. Shannopin's Town (Delaware & Seneca) – Beaver Co
159. Shawanese – Luzerne Co
160. Shawnee – Cambria Co
161. Shawnee – Montour Co
162. Shawnee – Lancaster Co
163. Shawnee – Luzerne Co
164. Shawnee on Delaware – Monroe Co
165. Shawnee Cabins – Bedford Co
166. Shawnee Flats – Luzerne Co
167. Shawnee Run – Monroe Co
168. Shawmut – Clearfield Co
169. Shenango (Seneca) – Beaver Co
170. Shenango (Seneca) – Lawrence Co
171. Shenango – (junction Connewango & Allegheny Rivers)
172. Sheshequin – Bradford Co
173. Shingas' Town – Alleghany Co

174. Shingiss – Washington Co
175. Siamocon – Wyoming Co
176. Siousca – Clinton Co
177. Skehandowana – Luzerne Co
178. Skippack – Montgomery Co
179. Smith's Ferry (site of) – Beaver Co
180. Snake Town – Cumberland Co
181. Snake Town – Dauphin Co
182. Snake Town – Perry Co
183. Standing Stone – Bradford Co
184. Standing Stone – Huntingdon Co
185. Starrucca – Susquehanna Co
186. Starrucca – Wayne Co
187. Susquehanna – Lancaster Co
188. Susquehanna – Susquehanna Co
189. Susquehanna Junction – Clearfield Co
190. Susquehanna River (several villages on the) –
191. Swatara – Schuylkill Co
192. Swatara Gap – Lebanon Co
193. Swatara Station – Dauphin Co
194. Swatara River (on the) -
195. Tawandaemenk (Munsee) – Bradford Co
196. Thompson Station (near site of) – Alleghany Co
197. Tinicum – Bucks Co
198. Tinicum – Delaware Co
199. Tioga (Munsee) – Bradford Co
200. Tiquamingy Town – Clinton Co
201. Tohogueses Cabins – Indiana Co
202. Turkey Foot – Fayette-Somerset Co
203. Turtle Creek – Alleghany Co
204. Two Lick Creek – Indiana Co
205. Umbelicamence – Montgomery Co
206. Venango – Crawford Co
207. Venango – Venango Co
208. Wapasening – Bradford Co
209. Warrior Run – Luzerne Co
210. Warrior Run – Northumberland Co
211. Warrior Ridge – Huntingdon Co
212. Waukesha – Clearfield Co
213. Wechquetank – Monroe Co
214. Wesauking – Bradford Co
215. West Chester (near site of) – Chester Co

216. Wilkes-Barre (near site of) – Luzerne Co
217. Willawanna (Munsee) – Bradford Co
218. Will's Creek – Bedford-Somerset Co
219. Written Rock – Alleghany Co
220. Wyalusing (Munsee) – Bradford Co
221. Wyoming – Luzerne Co
222. Yellow Breeches Creek – Cumberland Co
223. Youghiogheny – Alleghany Co
224. Youghiogheny River (on the) – Fayette Co
225. Youghiogheny River (on the) – Westmoreland Co

SOUTH CAROLINA

1. Augusta (site of) – 2. Cheraw – Chesterfield Co
3. Keowee -
4. Saluda River (on the) – Pickens & Oconee Co
5. Savannah River (on the) –
6. Savannah Town -

TENNESSEE

1. Black Fox's Town (site of Murfreesboro) –
2. Chattanooga (site of -
3. Cumberland River (several villages on the) –
4. Memphis (site of) - 5. Nashville (site of) - 6. Nickajack – Marion Co
7. Running Water – Marion Co
8. Shawnee Town –
9. Taogria (on the Cumberland River) - 10. Tennessee River (several villages on the) –
11. Will's Town –

VIRGINIA

1. Chawanock –
2. Dan River (on the) - 3. James River (on the) - 4. King George Co (village)
   -
5. Petersburg (site of) -
6. Richmond (site of) -

7. Shawnee Springs - 8. Shenandoah River (on the) -
9. Stafford Co (village) -
10. Winchester (site of) – Franklin Co

WEST VIRGINIA

1. Apple Grove (site of) – Mason Co
2. Blennerhassett Island (village on) – Wood Co
3. Buffalo (site of) – Putnam Co
4. Buffalo (site of) – Wayne Co
5. Bull's Town – Wood Co
6. Campbell's Creek – Kanawha Co
7. Cedar Grove (site of) – Kanawha Co
8. Conedogwinit-Upper Shawnee Town – Mason Co
9. Cross Creek – Ohio Co
10. Elk River (on the) – Kanawha Co
11. Gallipolis Ferry (site of) – Mason Co
12. Greenbrier (on the) -
13. Hardy Co (village) - 14. Kanouoara – Ohio Co
15. Kanawha River (on the) – Mason-Putnam-Kanawha Co
16. Kishkeminetas – Mason Co
17. Letart (site of) – Mason Co
18. Little Kanawha River (on the) - 19. Logan (site of) – Logan Co
20. Old Town – Mason Co
21. Parkersburg (site of) – Wood Co
22. Pocatalico (site of) – Putnam Co
23. Point Pleasant (site of) - Mason Co
24. Roane Co (village) -
25. Ten Mile Creek – Mason Co
26. Tyler Co (village) - 27. Wayne Co (village -
28. Wheeling (site of) – Ohio Co

WISCONSIN

1. Caraymaunee's Town (Winnebago) (Green Lake) -
2. Lake Koshkonong (Pottawamee) – 3. Grand Rapids of Fox River (Pottawamee) – 4. Green Bay – (near)

Appendix 6 SOURCES

This is a list of some of the authors, editors and sources used in this research. The various works have been read, compared and used as reference material only. Anyone reading my work will know that I reach my own conclusions. I try to take into account the jingoism, biases and prejudices of the various Nations, Tribes and writers and allow for the discrepancies and falsehoods that have echoed for decades before reaching a decision as to who was whom in this work.

1. Abenaki, Histories of the
2. Adair, Histories of John
3. AL, County Histories of
4. AL, Histories of
5. Alabama, Histories of the
6. Albright, Edward
7. Alden, John Richard
8. Alder, Histories of Jonathan
9. Alexander, Henry
10. Alford, Thomas Wildcat
11. Algonquians of NC, Histories of the
12. Allen, Robert S.
13. Alvord, Clarence W.
14. American Indian Quarterly
15. American State Papers – Indian Affairs
16. Anderson, Fred
17. Andrews, Edward D.
18. Anderson, W.R.
19. Anson, Bert
20. Apalachicola, Histories of the
21. AR, County Histories of
22. AR, Histories of
23. Armstrong, John
24. Aron, Stephen
25. Ashe, Geoffrey
26. Askin, John
27. Atwater, Caleb
28. Bacon, Edward
29. Bailey, Francis

30. **Bamberg, Glenn Michael – special thanks**
31. Bancroft, Hubert H.
32. Barker, Felix
33. Bear River Indians, Histories of the
34. Beckwith, Hiram
35. Belue, Ted Franklin
36. Bennett, John
37. **Bishop, Debra – special thanks**
38. Black Elk
39. Black Minquas, Histories of the
40. Black, Glenn- Collections
41. Blackfoot, Histories of the 42. Blanchard, Rufus
43. Bliss, Eugene F.
44. Blue Jacket, Histories of
45. Boone, Histories of Daniel 46. Boorstien, Daniel
47. Bowe, John P.
48. Bradley, Michael
49. British Colonial Office Papers
50. British War Office Papers
51. Brown, Dee 52. Brown, John P.
53. Brunson, Alfred
54. Burks, Samuel
55. Burnet, Jacob
56. Butler, Mann 57. Butler, Papers of Richard
58. Butterfield, Consul W.
59. Caddo, Histories of the
60. Cahokia, Histories of
61. Callender, Charles 62. Calloway, Colin G.
63. CAN, Public Archives of
64. CAN, Indian Affairs Papers of 65. CAN, Military Papers of
66. Chapman, Paul H.
67. Carter, Clarence E.
68. Cass, Lewis
69. Catawba, Histories of the
70. Catlin, George 71. Cave, Alfred A.
72. Cayuga, Histories of the
73. Chalkey, Lyman
74. **Chartier, Vernon – special thanks**
75. Cheraw, Histories of the
76. Cherokee, Histories of the
77. Chestnut, Don

78. Chiaha, Histories of the
79. Chicago, Historical Society of
80. Chickahominey, Histories of the
81. Chickamauga, Histories of the
82. Chickasaw, Histories of the
83. Chippewa, Histories of the
84. Choctaw, Histories of the
85. Chowan, Histories of the
86. Chowanock, Histories of the
87. Christian, Shirley
88. Cincinnati, Historical Society of 89. Clark, Histories of George Rogers
90. Clark, Jerry E.
91. Clark, Peter Dooyentate
92. Clark, Thomas D.
93. Clark, Histories of William
94. Collins, Lewis
95. Comstock, Jim
96. Congaree, Histories of the
97. Conoy, Histories of the
98. Coosa, Histories of the
99. Coree, Histories of the 100. **Cornsilk, David – special thanks** 101. Cotterill, R.S.
102. **Crawford, Madeleine Chartier – special thanks**
103. Creek, Histories of the
104. Croatan, Histories of the
105. Croghan, Histories of George
106. Cumberland Valley, Histories of the
107. Cummings, Pamela
108. Curnoe, Greg
109. Cusabo, Histories of the 110. Cushman, H.B.
111. Dakota, Histories of the 112.
Dally, Flory – special thanks 113. Danzinger, Edward L.
114. Darlington, W.M.
115. Davies, Kenneth G.
116. **Davis, Dean – special thanks** 117. Davis, W.B.
118. Day, Sherman
119. DE, County Histories of
120. DE, Histories of
121. Delaware Valley, Histories of the
122. DeHass, Wills
123. Delaware, Histories of the
124. DeMarce, Virginia

125. Denissen, Christian
126. Dixon, David
127. Dockstader, Frederick J.
128. **Domer, Jean Amos – special thanks** 129. **Domer, Jessica Alyss – special thanks** 130. Donehoo, George P.
131. Dowd, Gregory E.
132. Downes, Randolph C. 133. **Downing, Gregg – special thanks**
134. Drake, Benjamin
135. Drake, Richard B.
136. Drake, Samuel G.
137. Draper, Lyman C.
138. **East, Don – special thanks**
139. Eckert, Allen
140. Edmunds, R. David
141. Encyclopedia Britannica 142. Encyclopedia, Columbia
143. Encyclopedia, Funk & Wagner
144. Encyclopedia, World Book
145. Eno, Histories of the
146. Erie, Histories of the
147. Everts & Peck
148. **Ewing, Tom – special thanks**
149. Fell, Barry
150. Fester, Robert
151. Filson Club Quarterly
152. Filson, John 153. Finley, James B.
154. FL, County Histories of
155. FL, Histories of
156. Flick, Alexander
157. **Fowler, Bob – special thanks**
158. Fox, Histories of the
159. GA, County Histories of
160. GA, Historical Society of
161. GA, Histories of 162. Galloway, William A.
163. Ganawese, Histories of the
164. **Garen, Stephen – special thanks**
165. Gayarre, Charles 166. Gibson, Arnell M.
167. Gilbert, Bill
168. Goss, Dwight
169. Great Lakes-Ohio Valley Ethno-history Archives 170. Green, Michael D.
171. **Greene, Don – files of**
172. **Greene, Keegan Von – special thanks**

173. **Greene, Patricia Riley – extra special thanks** 174. Hagen, William T.
175. Hahn, C.F.
176. Hall, James
177. Hall, Tony
178. Hancks, David
179. **Hancock, Virginia – special thanks** 180. Hardesty, H.H.
181. Harmar, Histories of Josiah
182. Harrison, Mary Roberts
183. Harrison, William Henry
184. Harvard Historical Studies
185. Harvey, Henry
186. Hatteras, Histories of the
187. Haywood, John
188. Hearn, Histories of Samuel
189. Heckwelder, Histories John
190. Heyerdahl, Thor 191. Hildreth, S.P.
192. Hinshaw, Carlyle
193. Hitchiti, Histories of the
    194. Hoberg, Walter R.
195. Hodge, Fredrick W.
196. **Holland, Dave & Samantha – special thanks**
197. Holt, Reinhart
198. Honniasont, Histories of the
199. Horowitz, David
200. Horsfield, Timothy
201. Horsman, Reginald
202. Houck, Louis 203. Howard, James H.
204. Howe, Henry
205. **Hunt, Chief Gary – special thanks**
    206. Hunter, William A.
207. Huron, Histories of the
208. Hurt, R. Douglas
209. IA, County Histories of
210. IA, Histories of
211. IL, County Histories of
212. IL, Historical Society of
213. IL, Histories of
214. Illinois, Histories of the
215. IN, Academy of Science of
216. IN, County Histories of
217. IN, Historical Collections of
218. IN, Historical Society of
219. IN, Magazine of History of

220. IN, Histories of
221. Indian Claims Commission
222. Indians of Person Co NC, History of
223. Ironside, Histories of George
224. Iroquois, Histories of the
225. Jablow, Joseph
226. Jacob, Axel 227. Jacobs, Wilbur R.
228. James, James Alton
229. **Jaynes, Reba – special thanks**
230. Johnson, Louise Franklin
231. Johnson, Histories of Sir William
232. Johnston, Charles 233. Johnston, David A.
234. Johnston, Histories of John
235. Johnston, Michael
236. Jones, Histories of Rev. David 237. Josephy, Alan M. 238. Kanawha, Histories of the 239. Kappler, Charles J. 240. Kaskinampo, Histories of the 241. Kellogg, Louise P.
242. Kelsey, Isabel
243. Kenney, James
244. Kenton, Dena
245. Kenton, Histories of Simon
246. Kercheval, Samuel
247. **Kerns, Terri – special thanks**
248. Keyauwee, Histories of the
249. Kickapoo, Histories of the 250. Kingston, John T.
251. Kinietz, Vernon
252. Kinnaird, Lawrence
253. Klinck, Carl F.
254. Klopfenstien, Carl G.
255. Knight, Kevin
256. Koasati, Histories of the
257. KS, County Histories of
258. KS, Histories of
259. KY, County Histories of
260. KY, Filson Club of
261. KY, State Papers of
262. KY, Histories of
263. Lamb, Annette
264. **Langley, Cheryl – special thanks**
265. Lassalle Papers
266. Leach, Douglas E.
267. **Lee, Carrie – special thanks**
268. **Lehmann, Barbara – special thanks**

269. Leni Lenape, Histories of the
270. Lewis, Histories of Andrew
271. **Lewis, Chief Eagle – special thanks**
272. Lewis, Histories of Meriwether
273. Lewis, Virgil
274. Logan, Histories of Chief
275. **Longtail, Chief Gray Cloud – special thanks** 276. Lossing, Benson J. 277. Louden, Archibald 278. Lucier, Armand F.
279. Lumbee, Histories of the 280. MA, County Histories of
281. MA, Historical Society
282. MA, Histories of
283. MA, Provincial Councils of
284. Machapunga, Histories of the
285. MacIntosh, Histories of Lachlan
286. Mahican, Histories of the
287. Mallery, Arlington
288. Manahoac, Histories of the
289. Marks, Paula Mitchell
290. Marshall University, Library of
291. Martin, Ken
292. Martini, Don
293. Mascouten, Histories of the
294. Massachuset, Histories of the
295. Mastin, Betty Lee
296. Matson, Nehemiah 297. McAfee, Robert B. 298. **McClure, Jerry – special thanks** 299. McConnell, Michael N. 300. McCoy, Histories of Isaac 301. McDowell, J.L.
302. McGee, Malcolm
303. McKee, Histories of Alexander
304. McKee, Histories of Thomas 305. McKenny, Thomas L. 306. **McQuinn, Starfire – special thanks**
307. Meherrin, Histories of the
308. Menominee, Histories of the
309. Metis, Histories of the
310. MD, County Histories of
311. MD, Histories of
312. MI, County Histories of
313. MI, Historical Collections of
314. MI, Pioneer & Historical Society of
315. MI, Histories of
316. Miami, Histories of the
317. Middleton, Carol

318. Middleton, Richard
319. Mingo, Histories of the
320. Mississippi Valley, Histories of the
321. Mississippi Valley Historical Review
322. Missouri Historical Review
323. Missouri, Histories of the
324. MO, County Histories of
325. MO, Histories of
326. Mobile, Histories of the
327. Mohawk, Histories of the   328. Mohegan, Histories of the   329. Mohr, Walter H.
330. Monacan, Histories of the
331. Moneton, Histories of the
332. Montagnais, Histories of the   333. Moore, John H.
334. Moore, S.M.
335. Moorehead, Warren K.
336. Moratok, Histories of the
337. Morgan, Histories of George
338. Mosopelean, Histories of the
339. Muklasa, Histories of the
340. Munsee, Histories of the
341. Muskogee, Histories of the
342. Nanticoke, Histories of the
343. Natchez, Histories of the   344. National Archives of the U. S.
345. NC, Colonial Records of
346. NC, County Histories of
347. NC, State Records of
348. NC, Histories of   349. Nelson, Larry L.
350. Neusiok, Histories of the
351. Neutrals, Histories of the
352. NJ, County Histories of
353. NJ, Histories of   354. Noe, Randolph
355. Northwest Ohio Quarterly
356. Northwest Territory Collection
357. Nottoway, Histories of the
358. NY, County Histories of
359. NY, Library of
360. NY, Histories of
361. Occaneechi, Histories of the   362. O'Callaghan, Edmund B.
363. O'Donnell, James H.
364. OH, Archeological & Historical Society of
365. OH, County Histories of

366. OH, Historical Collections of
367. OH, Historical Society of
368. OH, Historical & Philosophical Society of
369. OH, Histories of
370. Ohio Valley, Histories of the 371. Olmsted, Earl P.
372. Oneida, Histories of the
373. Onondaga, Histories of the
374. Osage, Histories of the
375. Ottawa, Histories of the
376. PA, County Histories of
377. PA, Historical Collections of
378. PA, Historical Magazine of Western
379. PA, Historical Society of
380. PA, Provincial Councils of
381. PA, State Archives
382. PA, Histories of
383. **Paine, Myron – special thanks**
384. Pamlico, Histories of the
385. Pamukey, Histories of the 386. **Pangburn, Richard – special thanks** 387. Parker, Arthur C. 388. Parkman, Francis 389. Peckham, Howard H.
390. Pedee, Histories of the
391. Pequot, Histories of the
392. Perdue, Theda 393. Perkins, Elizabeth A. 394. Perrin du Lac, F.M.
395. Pickett, Albert James
396. Piscataway, Histories of the
397. Pittsburgh, Carnegie Library of
398. **Pope, Chief Hawk – special thanks**
399. Porter, Frank W. III
400. Pottawatomie, Histories of the
401. Powhatan, Histories of the 402. Quaife, Milo M.
403. Rappahannock, Histories of the
404. Reynolds, John
405. Rice, Otis K.
406. Ridout, Histories of Thomas
407. Roanoke, Histories of the
408. **Roush, Reba Dell Justice Greene – special thanks** 409. Royce, Charles C.
410. Saluda, Histories of the
411. Sandersson, Ivor
412. Santee, Histories of the
413. Saponi, Histories of the
414. Sauk, Histories of the 415. Saunders, William L.

416. Savannah Valley, Histories of the
417. Sawakoli, Histories of the
418. Sayre, Gordon M.
419. SC, County Histories of
420. SC, Histories of
421. Schoolcraft, Henry Rowe
422. **Scoggins, Peggy – special thanks**
423. SCOT, National Archives of
424. **Schutz, Noel – files of**
425. Seaver, James C.
426. Secotin, Histories of the
427. Seelye, Elizabeth
428. Seneca, Histories of the
429. Shakori, Histories of the
430. Shawnee, Histories of the Absentee
431. Shawnee, Histories of the Eastern
432. Shawnee, Histories of the Loyal
433. Shenandoah Valley, Histories of the
434. **Sherman, Hal – special thanks**
435. Shoemaker, Nancy
436. **Shoults, Kelly – special thanks**
437. Siberell, Lloyd E.
438. Sioux, Histories of the
439. Sipe, C. Hale
440. Sissipahaw, Histories of the
441. Smith, Dwight
442. Smith, Histories of John
443. Smith, William
444. Smith, Z.F.
445. Sosin, Jack M.
446. Spencer, Joab
447. Spencer, Histories of Oliver M.
448. St. Clair, Histories of Arthur
449. Staab, Rodney
450. Starr, Emmett
451. Steele, Ian
452. Stevens, Paul L.
453. Stiggens, George
454. Stockbridge, Histories of the
455. Stone, William L.
456. Stotz, Charles M.
457. Stuart, Charles A.
458. Stuart, Histories of John
459. Sturtevant, William C.
460. Sugaree, Histories of the
461. **Sugden, John – special thanks**
462. Sultzman, Lee

463. Susquehanna, Histories of the 464. Susquehanna Valley, Histories of the 465. Swain, George T. 466. Swanton, John R.
467. Sword, Wiley
468. Tankersley, Kenneth
469. Tanner, Helen Hornbeck
470. Tecumseh, Histories of
471. Tennessee Valley, Histories of the 472. Thatcher, B.B.
473. **Thomas, Debra – special thanks**
474. Thom, James A. & Claudia
475. Thompson, Charles
476. Thompson, Gunnar
477. Thorne, V. Keith 478. Thrapp, Dan L.
479. TN, County Histories of
480. TN, Histories of
481. **Todd, Maya Sue – special thanks** 482. Trowbridge, Charles C.
483. Troxell, Dan
484. **Truman, Tim – special thanks**
485. Tuckabatchee, Histories of the 486. Turner, Fredrick J.
487. Tuscarora, Histories of the
488. Tuskegee, Histories of the
489. Tutelo, Histories of the 490. Thwaites, Reuben G.
491. U.S. History Manuscripts
492. U.S., Annals of 1st thru 15th Congresses of
493. U.S., Congressional Documents – Indian Land Cessions 1784-1894
494. U.S., Congressional Documents 1784-1873
495. U.S., National Archives of the
496. VA, County Histories of
497. VA, Historical Register of
498. VA, Journal of Executive Council 1776-78
499. VA, Library of
500. VA, Magazine of History & Biography of
501. VA, University of
502. VA, Histories of
503. **Vann, Ironhead – special thanks** 504. **Veronese, Debrah – special thanks** 505. Voeglin, Charles F.
506. Voeglin, Ermine W.
507. Waccamaw, Histories of the
508. Wainwright, Nicholas 509. Wallace, Paul A.
510. Wampanoag, Histories of the
511. War of 1812 Manuscripts
   512. Ward, Matthew c.
513. Warren, Stephen
514. Wateree, Histories of the

515. **Watters, Chief Tula – special thanks**
516. Waxhaw, Histories of the
517. Wayne, Histories of Anthony
518. Weapemeoc, Histories of the
519. Weld, Isaac
520. Wells, Histories of William 521. Weslager, C.A.
522. White Minquas, Histories of the
523. White, Richard
524. WI, County Histories of
525. WI, Historical Collections of
526. WI, Magazine of History of
527. WI, Histories of 528. Wilcox, Frank N.
529. Williams, Samuel Cole
530. Winnebago, Histories of the
531. Winyaw, Histories of the
532. Withers, Alexander Scott
533. Witthoft, John
534. **Wood, Mary Jane – special thanks**
535. Wright, J. Leitch Jr
536. **Wright, Melissa – special thanks**
537. WV, County Histories of
538. WV, State Archives of
539. WV, University of
540. WV, Histories of
541. Wyandot, Histories of the 542. Xuala, Histories of the
543. Yamasee, Histories of the
544. **Yates, Jennifer – special thanks**
545. Yuchi, Histories of the
546. Zeisberger, Diaries of David

About The Author

I am Don Greene and I am often described as blessed, intelligent, strong and softhearted. I want to thank my departed mother and my wonderful elementary teachers for instilling in me the love of reading and in the old-style 3 R's education that has served me so well. My education began in a one-room school and continued until I had attended two State Colleges and two Universities. I've been everything from hick to a jock and a hippy to a redneck and more. I've been called tough, radical, weird and too smart. I've tried to help my fellow man by being an activist in labor, social, educational and environmental issues and in politics. While working and raising a family I still found time to study everything from literature to law and from anthropology and philosophy. In my younger years I did some wrestling, boxing and weightlifting with a fair amount of success. Treading where wise men seldom go, I've found myself in too many brawls and was fortunate to have come out of them battered but not beaten too badly. My zeal for life seems to be working its' vengeance on me now in the form of myriad physical complaints.

I've had a few poems, stories and articles published in various publications, from poetry anthologies, labor publications and ancient history magazines and a long series of letters to some West Virginia newspapers. I've written over five hundred columns for the "Communicator" from Clay County West Virginia and continue the bi-weekly column, addressing everything from national politics to Shawnee history. Please visit the column under "Don Greene-the WV Radical" at www.claywestvirgina.com to see some of my rambling thoughts. When I can find the time I enjoy doing landscapes in my humble self-taught style and have works in several homes in West Virginia.

I am blessed with a daughter Kelly and a son Keegan. My first son Cody Von was killed in a tragic car accident in 1978. Kelly and her husband Mike have in turn blessed us with two beautiful girls; Kady and Kennedy, while Keegan and his wife Kristal have blessed us with another granddaughter Kelsie and a grandson Keegan Jr. Through my second marriage to the lovely and gentlehearted Patty Lynn, I am blessed with two beautiful daughters, Annie and Sarah. They have blessed us seven grandchildren. Annie's four are Taylor,

Isabella, James and Jacob. Sarah has gifted Patty and me with our two great joys, Emily and Gabriella that have lived with us their entire lives and another grandson Elijah who lives with his father.

Always concerned with preserving our past, I relocated and registered with the State of West Virginia three small, badly ravaged Adena mounds in Mason County West Virginia, now humbly named the Greene Mounds 1, 2 and 3.

After health problems ended my career in public work, I recovered to expand my research in earnest, realizing that my true passion was for the Shawnee and their erroneously recorded history. I've expanded my research to include everyone ever that had any Shawnee blood. With Noel Schutz I've helped maintain a website containing some of my work at www.shawneetraditions.com/Names and encourage anyone that might have some Shawnee ancestry to visit there. As I've pieced together the trails of many of the families with Shawnee blood, I've gained a deeper understanding of the role the Shawnee played in the true history of the United States from before 1500 until the removal to the west. I'm honored that my work is being used widely by many groups and families.

You can now find me high in the mountains of the extreme northwest North Carolina, near the continental divide, enjoying the tranquility of the highlands with my dear Patty, continuing my Great Work daily, playing with and teaching Emy and Gabby, puttering around our modest abode, conversing and exchanging information on the Shawnee with friends far and wide via the Internet, phone and mail, volunteering a little of my time, especially to the Ola Belle Reed Mountain Music Festival. Please visit www.olabellefest.com to find out about the well received and rapidly growing festival in her honor in Lansing, North Carolina.

I am a member of and we attend church at Pleasant Chapel Baptist church next door, where I sing an occasional solo when the Spirit moves me.

A revelation of sorts from my Great Work has been the discovery of Shawnee blood in many of my own family lines. So I have gone from merely being "part-Indian" to being what I call in my work "Shawnee-Metis", a descendant of Shawnee and white ancestors.

For the last few years I have humbly served as Chief of the Shawnee Appalachian Tribe, a proud collection of those of Shawnee descent from many locales coast to coast.

The photo at the top of the bio was taken by my sweetheart Emily at age three and a half and it may be the best one taken of me in many years. I give kudos to my Golden Sun Child, Emily's Shawnee name.

SOURCES

This is a list of some of the authors, editors and sources used in this research. The various works have been read, compared and used as reference material only. Anyone reading my work will know that I reach my own conclusions. I try to take into account the jingoism, biases and prejudices of the various Nations, Tribes and writers and allow for the discrepancies and falsehoods that have echoed for decades before reaching a decision as to who was whom in this work.

1. Abenaki, Histories of the
2. Adair, Histories of John
3. Alabama, County Histories of
4. Alabama, Histories of the
5. Albright, Edward
6. Alden, John Richard
7. Alder, Histories of Jonathan

8. Alexander, Henry

9. Alford, Thomas Wildcat

10. Algonquians of North Carolina, Histories of the

11. Allen, Robert S.

12. Alvord, Clarence W.

13. American Indian Quarterly

14. American State Papers – Indian Affairs

15. Anderson, Fred

16. Andrews, Edward D.

17. Anderson, W.R.

18. Anson, Bert

19. Apalachicola, Histories of the

20. Arkansas, County Histories of

21. Arkansas, Histories of

22. Armstrong, John

23. Aron, Stephen

24. Ashe, Geoffrey

25. Askin, John

26. Atwater, Caleb

27. Bacon, Edward

28. Bailey, Francis

29. **Bamberg, Glenn Michael – special thanks**

30. Bancroft, Hubert H.

31. Barker, Felix

32. Bear River Indians, Histories of the

33. Beckwith, Hiram

34. Belue, Ted Franklin

35. Bennett, John

36. **Bishop, Debra – special thanks**

37. Black Elk

38. Black Minquas, Histories of the

39. Black, Glenn- Collections

40. Blackfoot, Histories of the

41. Blanchard, Rufus

42. Bliss, Eugene F.

43. Blue Jacket, Histories of

44. Boone, Histories of Daniel

45. Boorstien, Daniel

46. Bowe, John P.

47. Bradley, Michael

48. British Colonial Office Papers

49. British War Office Papers

50. Brown, Dee

51. Brown, John P.

52. Brunson, Alfred

53. Burks, Samuel

54. Burnet, Jacob

55. Butler, Mann

56. Butler, Papers of Richard

57. Butterfield, Consul W.

58. Caddo, Histories of the

59. Cahokia, Histories of

60. Callender, Charles

61. Calloway, Colin G.

62. Canada, Public Archives of

63. Canda, Indian Affairs Papers of

64. Canada, Military Papers of

65. Chapman, Paul H.

66. Carter, Clarence E.

67. Cass, Lewis

68. Catawba, Histories of the

69. Catlin, George

70. Cave, Alfred A.

71. Cayuga, Histories of the

72. Chalkey, Lyman

73. **Chartier, Vernon – special thanks**

74. Cheraw, Histories of the

75. Cherokee, Histories of the

76. Chestnut, Don

77. Chiaha, Histories of the

78. Chicago, Historical Society of

79. Chickahominey, Histories of the

80. Chickamauga, Histories of the

81. Chickasaw, Histories of the

82. Chippewa, Histories of the

83. Choctaw, Histories of the

84. Chowan, Histories of the

85. Chowanock, Histories of the

86. Christian, Shirley

87. Cincinnati, Historical Society of

88. Clark, Histories of George Rogers

89. Clark, Jerry E.

90. Clark, Peter Dooyentate

91. Clark, Thomas D.

92. Clark, Histories of William

93. Collins, Lewis

94. Comstock, Jim

95. Congaree, Histories of the

96. Conoy, Histories of the

97. Coosa, Histories of the

98. Coree, Histories of the

99. **Cornsilk, David – special thanks**

100. Cotterill, R.S.

101. **Crawford, Madeleine Chartier – special thanks**

102. Creek, Histories of the

103. Croatan, Histories of the

104. Croghan, Histories of George

105. Cumberland Valley, Histories of the

106. Cummings, Pamela

107. Curnoe, Greg

108. Cusabo, Histories of the

109. Cushman, H.B.

110. Dakota, Histories of the

111. **Dally, Flory – special thanks**

112. Danzinger, Edward L.

113. Darlington, W.M.

114. Davies, Kenneth G.

115. **Davis, Dean – special thanks**

116. Davis, W.B.

117. Day, Sherman

118. Delaware, County Histories of

119. Delaware, Histories of

120. Delaware Valley, Histories of the

121. DeHass, Wills

122. Delaware, Histories of the

123. DeMarce, Virginia

124. Denissen, Christian

125. Dixon, David

126. Dockstader, Frederick J.

127. **Domer, Jean Amos – special thanks**

128. **Domer, Jessica Alyss – special thanks**

129. Donehoo, George P.

130. Dowd, Gregory E.

131. Downes, Randolph C.

132. **Downing, Gregg – special thanks**

133. Drake, Benjamin
134. Drake, Richard B.
135. Drake, Samuel G.
136. Draper, Lyman C.
137. **East, Don – special thanks**
138. Eckert, Allen
139. Edmunds, R. David
140. Encyclopedia Britannica
141. Encyclopedia, Columbia
142. Encyclopedia, Funk & Wagner
143. Encyclopedia, World Book
144. Eno, Histories of the
145. Erie, Histories of the
146. Everts & Peck
147. **Ewing, Tom – special thanks**
148. Fell, Barry
149. Fester, Robert
150. Filson Club Quarterly

151. Filson, John

152. Finley, James B.

153. FL, County Histories of

154. FL, Histories of

155. Flick, Alexander

156. **Fowler, Bob – special thanks**

157. Fox, Histories of the

158. Georgia, County Histories of

159. Georgia, Historical Society of

160. Georgia, Histories of

161. Galloway, William A.

162. Ganawese, Histories of the

163. **Garen, Stephen – special thanks**

164. Gayarre, Charles

165. Gibson, Arnell M.

166. Gilbert, Bill

167. Goss, Dwight

168. Great Lakes-Ohio Valley Ethno-history Archives

169. Green, Michael D.

170. **Greene, Chief Don – files of**

171. **Greene, Keegan Von – special thanks**

172. **Greene, Patricia Riley – extra special thanks**

173. Hagen, William T.

174. Hahn, C.F.

175. Hall, James

176. Hall, Tony

177. Hancks, David

178. **Hancock, Virginia – special thanks**

179. Hardesty, H.H.

180. Harmar, Histories of Josiah

181. Harrison, Mary Roberts

182. Harrison, William Henry

183. Harvard Historical Studies

184. Harvey, Henry

185. Hatteras, Histories of the

186. Haywood, John

187. Hearn, Histories of Samuel

188. Heckwelder, Histories John

189. Heyerdahl, Thor

190. Hildreth, S.P.

191. Hinshaw, Carlyle

192. Hitchiti, Histories of the

193. Hoberg, Walter R.

194. Hodge, Fredrick W.

195. **Holland, Dave & Samantha – special thanks**

196. Holt, Reinhart

197. Honniasont, Histories of the

198. Horowitz, David

199. Horsfield, Timothy

200. Horsman, Reginald

201. Houck, Louis

202. Howard, James H.

203. Howe, Henry

204. **Hunt, Chief Gary – special thanks**

205. Hunter, William A.

206. Huron, Histories of the

207. Hurt, R. Douglas

208. Iowa, County Histories of

209. Iowa, Histories of

210. Illinois, County Histories of

211. Illinois, Historical Society of

212. Illinois, Histories of

213. Illinois, Histories of the

214. Indiana, Academy of Science of

215. Indiana, County Histories of

216. Indiana, Historical Collections of

217. Indiana, Historical Society of

218. Indiana, Magazine of History of

219. Indiana, Histories of

220. Indian Claims Commission

221. Indians of Person Co NC, History of

222. Ironside, Histories of George

223. Iroquois, Histories of the

224. Jablow, Joseph

225. Jacob, Axel

226. Jacobs, Wilbur R.

227. James, James Alton

228. **Jaynes, Reba – special thanks**

229. Johnson, Louise Franklin

230. Johnson, Histories of Sir William

231. Johnston, Charles

232. Johnston, David A.

233. Johnston, Histories of John

234. Johnston, Michael

235. Jones, Histories of Rev. David

236. Josephy, Alan M.

237. Kanawha, Histories of the

238. Kappler, Charles J.

239. Kaskinampo, Histories of the

240. Kellogg, Louise P.

241. Kelsey, Isabel

242. Kenney, James

243. Kenton, Dena

244. Kenton, Histories of Simon

245. Kercheval, Samuel

246. **Kerns, Terri – special thanks**

247. Keyauwee, Histories of the

248. Kickapoo, Histories of the

249. Kingston, John T.

250. Kinietz, Vernon

251. Kinnaird, Lawrence

252. Klinck, Carl F.

253. Klopfenstien, Carl G.

254. Knight, Kevin

255. Koasati, Histories of the

256. Kansas, County Histories of

257. Kansas, Histories of

258. Kentucky, County Histories of

259. Kentucky, Filson Club of

260. Kentucky, State Papers of

261. Kentucky, Histories of

262. Lamb, Annette

263. **Langley, Cheryl – special thanks**

264. Lassalle Papers

265. Leach, Douglas E.

266. **Lee, Carrie – special thanks**

267. **Lehmann, Barbara – special thanks**

268. Leni Lenape, Histories of the

269. Lewis, Histories of Andrew

270. **Lewis, Chief Eagle – special thanks**

271. Lewis, Histories of Meriwether

272. Lewis, Virgil

273. Logan, Histories of Chief

274. **Longtail, Chief Gray Cloud – special thanks**

275. Lossing, Benson J.

276. Louden, Archibald

277. Lucier, Armand F.

278. Lumbee, Histories of the

279. MA, County Histories of

280. MA, Historical Society

281. MA, Histories of

282. MA, Provincial Councils of

283. Machapunga, Histories of the

284. MacIntosh, Histories of Lachlan

285. Mahican, Histories of the

286. Mallery, Arlington

287. Manahoac, Histories of the

288. Marks, Paula Mitchell

289. Marshall University, Library of

290. Martin, Ken

291. Martini, Don

292. Mascouten, Histories of the

293. Massachuset, Histories of the

294. Mastin, Betty Lee

295. Matson, Nehemiah

296. McAfee, Robert B.

297. **McClure, Jerry – special thanks**

298. McConnell, Michael N.

299. McCoy, Histories of Isaac

300. McDowell, J.L.

301. McGee, Malcolm

302. McKee, Histories of Alexander

303. McKee, Histories of Thomas

304. McKenny, Thomas L.

305. **McQuinn, Starfire – special thanks**

306. Meherrin, Histories of the

307. Menominee, Histories of the

308. Metis, Histories of the
309. MD, County Histories of
310. MD, Histories of
311. MI, County Histories of
312. MI, Historical Collections of
313. MI, Pioneer & Historical Society of
314. MI, Histories of
315. Miami, Histories of the
316. Middleton, Carol
317. Middleton, Richard
318. Mingo, Histories of the
319. Mississippi Valley, Histories of the
320. Mississippi Valley Historical Review
321. Missouri Historical Review
322. Missouri, Histories of the
323. MO, County Histories of
324. MO, Histories of
325. Mobile, Histories of the

326. Mohawk, Histories of the

327. Mohegan, Histories of the

328. Mohr, Walter H.

329. Monacan, Histories of the

330. Moneton, Histories of the

331. Montagnais, Histories of the

332. Moore, John H.

333. Moore, S.M.

334. Moorehead, Warren K.

335. Moratok, Histories of the

336. Morgan, Histories of George

337. Mosopelean, Histories of the

338. Muklasa, Histories of the

339. Munsee, Histories of the

340. Muskogee, Histories of the

341. Nanticoke, Histories of the

342. Natchez, Histories of the

343. National Archives of the U. S.

344. NC, Colonial Records of

345. NC, County Histories of

346. NC, State Records of

347. NC, Histories of

348. Nelson, Larry L.

349. Neusiok, Histories of the

350. Neutrals, Histories of the

351. NJ, County Histories of

352. NJ, Histories of

353. Noe, Randolph

354. Northwest Ohio Quarterly

355. Northwest Territory Collection

356. Nottoway, Histories of the

357. NY, County Histories of

358. NY, Library of

359. NY, Histories of

360. Occaneechi, Histories of the

361. O'Callaghan, Edmund B.

362. O'Donnell, James H.

363. OH, Archeological & Historical Society of

364. OH, County Histories of

365. OH, Historical Collections of

366. OH, Historical Society of

367. OH, Historical & Philosophical Society of

368. OH, Histories of

369. Ohio Valley, Histories of the

370. Olmsted, Earl P.

371. Oneida, Histories of the

372. Onondaga, Histories of the

373. Osage, Histories of the

374. Ottawa, Histories of the

375. PA, County Histories of

376. PA, Historical Collections of

377. PA, Historical Magazine of Western

378. PA, Historical Society of

379. PA, Provincial Councils of

380. PA, State Archives

381. PA, Histories of

382. **Paine, Myron – special thanks**

383. Pamlico, Histories of the

384. Pamukey, Histories of the

385. **Pangburn, Richard – special thanks**

386. Parker, Arthur C.

387. Parkman, Francis

388. Peckham, Howard H.

389. Pedee, Histories of the

390. Pequot, Histories of the

391. Perdue, Theda

392. Perkins, Elizabeth A.

393. Perrin du Lac, F.M.

394. Pickett, Albert James

395. Piscataway, Histories of the

396. Pittsburgh, Carnegie Library of

397. **Pope, Chief Hawk – special thanks**

398. Porter, Frank W. III

399. Pottawatomie, Histories of the

400. Powhatan, Histories of the

401. Quaife, Milo M.

402. Rappahannock, Histories of the

403. Reynolds, John

404. Rice, Otis K.

405. Ridout, Histories of Thomas

406. Roanoke, Histories of the

407. **Roush, Reba Dell Justice Greene – special thanks**

408. Royce, Charles C.

409. Saluda, Histories of the

410. Sandersson, Ivor

411. Santee, Histories of the

412. Saponi, Histories of the

413. Sauk, Histories of the

414. Saunders, William L.

415. Savannah Valley, Histories of the

416. Sawakoli, Histories of the

417. Sayre, Gordon M.

418. SC, County Histories of

419. SC, Histories of

420. Schoolcraft, Henry Rowe

421. **Scoggins, Peggy – special thanks**

422. SCOT, National Archives of

423. **Schutz, Noel – files of**

424. Seaver, James C.

425. Secotin, Histories of the

426. Seelye, Elizabeth

427. Seneca, Histories of the

428. Shakori, Histories of the

429. Shawnee, Histories of the Absentee

430. Shawnee, Histories of the Eastern

431. Shawnee, Histories of the Loyal

432. Shenandoah Valley, Histories of the

433. **Sherman, Hal – special thanks**

434. Shoemaker, Nancy

435. **Shoults, Kelly – special thanks**

436. Siberell, Lloyd E.

437. Sioux, Histories of the

438. Sipe, C. Hale

439. Sissipahaw, Histories of the

440. Smith, Dwight

441. Smith, Histories of John

442. Smith, William

443. Smith, Z.F.

444. Sosin, Jack M.

445. Spencer, Joab

446. Spencer, Histories of Oliver M.

447. St. Clair, Histories of Arthur

448. Staab, Rodney

449. Starr, Emmett

450. Steele, Ian

451. Stevens, Paul L.

452. Stiggens, George

453. Stockbridge, Histories of the

454. Stone, William L.

455. Stotz, Charles M.

456. Stuart, Charles A.

457. Stuart, Histories of John

458. Sturtevant, William C.

459. Sugaree, Histories of the

460. **Sugden, John – special thanks**

461. Sultzman, Lee

462. Susquehanna, Histories of the

463. Susquehanna Valley, Histories of the

464. Swain, George T.

465. Swanton, John R.

466. Sword, Wiley

467. Tankersley, Kenneth

468. Tanner, Helen Hornbeck

469. Tecumseh, Histories of
470. Tennessee Valley, Histories of the
471. Thatcher, B.B.
472. **Thomas, Debra – special thanks**
473. Thom, James A. & Claudia
474. Thompson, Charles
475. Thompson, Gunnar
476. Thorne, V. Keith
477. Thrapp, Dan L.
478. TN, County Histories of
479. TN, Histories of
480. **Todd, Maya Sue – special thanks**
481. Trowbridge, Charles C.
482. Troxell, Dan
483. **Truman, Tim – special thanks**
484. Tuckabatchee, Histories of the
485. Turner, Fredrick J.
486. Tuscarora, Histories of the

487. Tuskegee, Histories of the

488. Tutelo, Histories of the

489. Thwaites, Reuben G.

490. U.S. History Manuscripts

491. U.S., Annals of 1st thru 15th Congresses of

492. U.S., Congressional Documents – Indian Land Cessions 1784-1894

493. U.S., Congressional Documents 1784-1873

494. U.S., National Archives of the

495. VA, County Histories of

496. VA, Historical Register of

497. VA, Journal of Executive Council 1776-78

498. VA, Library of

499. VA, Magazine of History & Biography of

500. VA, University of

501. VA, Histories of

502. **Vann, Ironhead – special thanks**

503. **Veronese, Debrah – special thanks**

504. Voeglin, Charles F.

505. Voeglin, Ermine W.

506. Waccamaw, Histories of the

507. Wainwright, Nicholas

508. Wallace, Paul A.

509. Wampanoag, Histories of the

510. War of 1812 Manuscripts

511. Ward, Matthew c.

512. Warren, Stephen

513. Wateree, Histories of the

514. **Watters, Chief Tula – special thanks**

515. Waxhaw, Histories of the

516. Wayne, Histories of Anthony

517. Weapemeoc, Histories of the

518. Weld, Isaac

519. Wells, Histories of William

520. Weslager, C.A.

521. White Minquas, Histories of the

522. White, Richard

523. WI, County Histories of

524. WI, Historical Collections of

525. WI, Magazine of History of

526. WI, Histories of

527. Wilcox, Frank N.

528. Williams, Samuel Cole

529. Winnebago, Histories of the

530. Winyaw, Histories of the

531. Withers, Alexander Scott

532. Witthoft, John

533. **Wood, Mary Jane – special thanks**

534. Wright, J. Leitch Jr

535. **Wright, Melissa – special thanks**

536. WV, County Histories of

537. WV, State Archives of

538. WV, University of

539. WV, Histories of

540. Wyandot, Histories of the

541. Xuala, Histories of the

542. Yamasee, Histories of the

543. **Yates, Jennifer – special thanks**

544. Yuchi, Histories of the

545. Zeisberger, Diaries of David

Made in the USA
Las Vegas, NV
23 October 2021